**Business Management of
Local School Systems**

EXPLORATION SERIES IN EDUCATION
Under the Advisory Editorship
of
John Guy Fowlkes

BUSINESS MANAGEMENT OF LOCAL SCHOOL SYSTEMS

By

Stephen J. Knezevich
STATE UNIVERSITY OF IOWA

and

John Guy Fowlkes
UNIVERSITY OF WISCONSIN

 HARPER & BROTHERS, PUBLISHERS, NEW YORK

Contents

Preface

School business management is a significant phase of educational administration. Sooner or later the fiscal and material resources necessary in the educational process must be determined, procured, and cared for. As important as fiscal management may be, however, it is regarded in this book as a means to an end. The system of management that is designed must be evaluated in terms of how well it contributes to the realization of the objectives of education in an American democracy. School business procedures should be kept in an educational perspective.

Public education in America is a multibillion dollar enterprise. Prudent management of the financial and material resources of public education has, therefore, become more important than ever before. One goal of business administration is to help the schools obtain the greatest educational services possible from each tax or aid dollar collected and spent. The determination of whether the school money is to be spent for particular educational programs should not be limited to financial considerations alone. Philosophical questions related to the purposes of education in America must be considered before cost implications of starting, continuing, or stopping educational offerings. The decision as to whether the educational benefits are worth the cost should be made after all affected by the decision have been consulted. Once the decision is reached, it becomes a particular obligation of school business officials to design and implement business services to minimize losses and waste in the utilization of financial and material resources in any educational program. This book is dedicated to these purposes.

This is not to imply that school business officials are to be segregated from the mainstream of educational activities. Far from it! The school business official should be recognized as an important member of the administrative team who has a significant contribution to make in the decision-making process as well as in executing business functions. For this reason he must be well grounded in educational matters as well as in business management. Teaching experience is highly desirable for a person in such an administrative position. His program of professional preparation should include experiences and understandings in educational philosophy, educational psychology, problems of classroom instruction, and an overall view of educational administration. With a background in teaching and professional preparation rooted in public education in general and business management in particular, the school business official is in a position to participate under the superintendent's leadership in making educational decisions as well as in doing an efficient job in "hanging price tags on educational proposals."

It is postulated herein that many procedures employed by private and industrial concerns can be used in school business affairs. There are, however, fundamental differences in the objectives of schools and private concerns and these will of necessity be reflected in school business practices. The similarities and differences in certain business practices used in schools and private concerns are highlighted throughout this book.

This publication attempts to bridge the gap that exists between public school and governmental accounting and auditing. Public school accounting and auditing is regarded as a special phase of governmental accounting and auditing. The terminology and procedures recommended by the National Committee on Governmental Accounting are given special recognition in Chapters 3 and 8. Books devoted to governmental accounting are frequent sources of reference in Chapter 3 in particular and in other chapters as well.

The need for a new and comprehensive treatise on school business affairs was precipitated by the many significant changes in school accounting and other aspects of school business operations during the past few years. Important developments in school business management were the direct result of research and publications of the U.S. Office of Education working in coöperation with many educational organizations such as the Association of School Business Officials, American Association of School Administrators, Council of Chief State School Officers, National School Boards Association, and National Education Association. This book draws heavily on the significant USOE State Educational Records and Reports Series. The 1957 USOE financial accounting manual for local and state school systems (Handbook no. 2) forms the backbone of Chapters 4 and 7. Some publications of the U.S. Office of Education were still in the process of development when this book went to press but many of their concepts and recommendations were incorporated herein nonetheless. Chapter 11 is based in part on the first preliminary draft of the USOE publication on accounting for student body activity funds. Much of the substance of the chapter on property accounting (Chapter 14) is drawn from the third preliminary draft of the USOE property accounting manual. It is one purpose of this book to help promote uniformity in school accounting, and the utilization of the recommendations in the USOE publications was prompted by this need for uniformity in keeping financial records.

This book was designed with the twofold purpose of serving as a text for college classes devoted to school business procedures and as a source book for superintendents and school business officials. It is based on a practical approach to business problems with many illustrations drawn from actual school situations. Frequent references are made to the writings of school business officials actively engaged in the affairs of public school districts. The materials in Chapters 4, 7, 11, 14, and the Appendix help the book to serve as a manual as well as a text. On the other hand, the theoretical framework for the design of an accounting system was developed in Chapter 3. The last portion of Chapter 3 was written for the college student who may be unacquainted with even the simplest accounting terminology. Both authors have taught courses in the business management of schools and have also served as consultants in this field to local and county school systems and state departments of education.

The authors are indebted to Dr. Russell T. Gregg of the University of Wisconsin, Dr. H. C. DeKock of the State University of Iowa, and Wilbur N. McDaniels of the Madison Public Schools for their helpful suggestions in the writing of the manuscript. The services of O. Eugene Albright, Dr. Fred F. Beach, I. N. Seibert, and Franklin Stone in supplying various materials for this publication are also recognized. Grateful acknowledgment is also given to Hubert Wheeler, Commissioner of Education, and Bernard H. Voges, Director of School Finances and Statistics of the Missouri State Department of Education, for permission to use Forms 1–10 and 29 shown in this book. Special acknowledgment is awarded to Mrs. Mona Burns and Mrs. Janet Jess for their help in preparing the manuscript for printing.

STEPHEN J. KNEZEVICH
JOHN GUY FOWLKES

CHAPTER 1

Financial Management— A Means to an End

THE FUNCTIONS OF EDUCATION IN AMERICA ARE many and varied. Education promotes the development and extension of our democratic beliefs, contributes to the realization of individual potentialities, and prepares the way for future progress and change. It transmits and perpetuates the cultural achievements of each generation as well as advancing the economic well-being of the nation. These are only a few of the many reasons why schools are organized.

Ample evidence exists to indicate that the American public continues to maintain confidence in the most comprehensive common school system the world has known. Tax revenue for public school support is measured in billions of dollars. Total expenditures, including capital outlay, interest, debt retirement, and current operation, were almost $12.9 billion in 1957–1958.[1] Each year since the end of World War II, it is reported that more public school classrooms were constructed, higher teacher salaries were paid, and greater lay participation in public education was apparent than ever before. An eminent historian has stated: "No other people ever demanded so much of education as have the Americans. None other was ever served so well by its schools and educators."[2] Never before in history have so many been educated so well. Public education, a bulwark for democracy, has helped the nation prosper and gain prominence in the world.

The purposes of education, however well defined and inspiring, are not self-executing. Means must be devised to attain the ends of education. Those activities necessary for the realization of purposes in a democratic framework can be classified as (1) legislative or political, (2) administrative or managerial, and (3) judicial. It is obvious that these activities include all of government, and the whole of governmental organization influences in various degrees the realization of the ends of education. The contents of this book will be limited to administrative or managerial activities and their unique contributions to the effectiveness of schools.

The function of school administration is to facilitate progress toward the goals of education. School administration grows out of the need for planning, organizing, directing, coördinating, and controlling the human efforts and material resources necessary to promote education. Thus, a curriculum must be planned, developed, and put into practice; personnel needed in the operation of the school program must be employed and their efforts must be coördinated; financial resources must be procured; school plants must be planned, financed, and erected; and school equipment and supplies must be budgeted, purchased, and accounted for. These are some of the activities and problems of administration. Administration is the same in principle in a small school system as in a large one; the same duties are performed in a rural community as in a metropolitan area.[3]

The terms "administration" and "management" are, for the purposes of this volume, synonymous. The two terms are used interchangeably even though some writers, particularly those in the field of industrial or private firm management, have attempted to draw a definite distinction between administration and management. Thus Spriegel and Lansburgh[4] distinguish

[1] National Education Association, Research Division, *Research Bulletin*, Washington, D.C.: February, 1958, *36*:9.

[2] Henry Steele Commager, "Our Schools Have Kept Us Free," *Life*, October 16, 1950, pp. 46–47.

[3] American Association of School Administrators, *The American School Superintendency*, Washington, D.C.: the Association, 1952, p. 66.

[4] William B. Spriegel and Richard H. Lansburgh, *Industrial Management*, New York: John Wiley & Sons, Inc., 4th ed., 1947, pp. 11–12.

between the two on the grounds that administration determines the policies and establishes the major program whereas management executes the broad plans laid down by administration and follows through the details to their ultimate conclusion. Administration is looked upon as largely determinative whereas management is essentially executive. At the top level of industrial management, such as president of a large concern, it is possible to have the two functions of policy formulation and policy execution combined, in various degrees, in the same person. The checks and balances in governmental organization, however, tend to separate fairly sharply the functions of formulating major policy decisions and executing such decisions. In fields of public or governmental administration, such as school administration, bodies concerned primarily with major policy formulation are called legislative or political bodies. Bodies concerned primarily with the execution of policy are called executive or administrative bodies. In many respects the management of schools is similar to the management of private businesses. There are, however, certain fundamental differences in the purposes of schools and of private concerns, and consequently different administrative practices as well as terminology will prevail. Educational administration is a distinctive field of administration and must be developed and studied with full cognizance of its purposes and the special conditions under which it operates.

The terms "financial management," "business management," or "business administration" have meanings in public school administration that are quite different from their accepted and rather broad definitions in private, commercial, or industrial management circles. Business management of schools is but a part of the total educational administrative activities. As a part it is subordinate to the function of educational institutions as well as to school administration in general. Business management can be defined as *that phase of educational administration that is primarily concerned with procuring, expending, accounting for, protecting, organizing, and maintaining fiscal and material resources in an efficient manner so that human resources and efforts are aided in achieving educational goals.* According to this definition business management would include such activities as budget making, procuring and handling funds, purchasing or the expending of funds, inventorying, accounting, auditing, financial reporting, cost analysis, maintaining property, insurance programming, operating cafeterias, operating transportation systems, etc. The purpose of such activities must at all times be kept clearly in mind lest the activity become an end in itself.

There is a close and vital relationship between school business administration and other aspects of public school programs and operation. As J. C. Wright, State Superintendent of Public Instruction of Iowa, declared:

The passing years have brought forth an evolution of curriculum and instructional methods. These changes, in turn, have demanded new types of school facilities, new concepts of school district adequacy, new techniques of school administration, and more efficient practices of financing and budgeting.

Schools exist to educate children. The entire area of school administration and business management is, therefore, a means to an end rather than an end in itself. It is easy, however, for today's school official to become burdened by a minutiae of administrative details which sometimes seem to interfere with, rather than promote, a sound educational program. The modern educational system needs more than a teacher, a boy, and a log, but the "bonds, buildings, budgets, and buses" should always support the best possible classroom activities.[5]

The very nature of business management is such that it pervades all of the educational activities. Sooner or later the business aspects of any activity must receive consideration. It is not just a mechanical chore involving only material things and systems. Like all phases of management the "human equation" is present and there must be coördinated human activity to attain objectives. As in other phases of management, the human, personal, and organic aspects of business administration should receive due consideration lest they be lost in what appear to be necessary but mechanical, impersonal, and routine tasks.

THE IMPORTANCE OF BUSINESS ADMINISTRATION

The fundamental task of school administration is to provide leadership. In America the expressions and processes of leadership operate in a democratic culture. The leadership role of the executive is influenced by the changing social and economic structure of the nation. School administrators who seek to be democratic leaders, rather than just "titular leaders," must evolve programs with the help of other school personnel rather than dictate programs. For the democratic leader is one who can release energy in other men, that is, he is literally an agent who can cause others to change by calling forth initiative and

[5] Quoted in A. B. Grimes and I. N. Seibert, *School Business—A Manual for School Officials,* Des Moines: The Iowa State Department of Public Instruction, 1958, Foreword.

creative talents. As an educational leader the school administrator must know how to "tap" the creative abilities of the school personnel. As a community leader the school administrator is a "catalyst" working toward community improvement and the resultant school improvement.

Leaders are made; they are not born fully fledged. There are certain competencies or professional skills and understandings that a superintendent must have at his command if he is to be a leader. Five major areas of competence that present-day administrators should possess when they complete their professional preparation were identified by the American Association of School Administrators as:

1. Competence in community leadership as it concerns the development of basic educational policy and program.
2. Competence as a leader in developing the content, experience, and methods which compose the needed instructional program of the schools and other educational agencies of the community.
3. Competence in selecting, organizing, and leading the school staff of the community.
4. Competence in making the case for the necessary facilities of education.
5. Competence in the philosophy and procedures of democratic leadership.[6]

To realize competence in the third item above would require knowledge of the various areas of specialization in educational administration such as personnel administration, business management, and school plant administration.[7]

Some writers, in an attempt to spotlight the importance of the educational and community leadership aspects of school administration, have intimated that little or no emphasis should be placed upon the "mechanical" or "technical" aspects of administration such as business management. Emphasis on leadership, however, should not have to be gained at the expense of a thorough command of the principles of business management or any other area of specialization in school administration. In this day and age of complex educational institutions which expend billions of dollars annually, administrators must be fully acquainted with the principles of sound business administration. It is important that educational administrators know business management so thoroughly that they can spend a minimum amount of time on such problems and be free to spend a maximum amount of time on other problems of educational and community leadership.

[6] American Association of School Administrators, *op. cit.,* pp. 389–391.
[7] *Ibid.,* p. 390.

Considerable and valid criticism can be made of the superintendent of schools who is predominantly a business manager of a static educational program—the "boss" at the central office—and is blissful in his ignorance of instructional, personnel, and community problems. Of what value is it for a man to know bonds and the bond market so well that he can gauge the most opportune time to market bonds at a favorable rate of interest plus a premium if the bond issue is defeated at a community election? There is no question but that the "office manager" type of administrator who has complete command of the technical aspects of administration and little else is less likely to succeed in today's schools than ever before. On the other hand, the administrator who fails to take the financial pulse of the school district and understand its implications, using as his excuse the fact that he must spend his time "out in the community" or "in educational circles," soon earns the same community reputation as the mother who neglects her children because she spends all her time lecturing to women's clubs on "Child Care." The stereotyped "office manager" type of administrator who neglects educational and community leadership is to be criticized along with the "politician" type who wields influence and has community backing but lacks the technical knowledge and skills to realize fully the fruits of his accomplishments. It is tragic, indeed, to have a bond issue pass at a carefully planned election only to have much of the money squandered because of poor business management. In either of the extreme cases, schools fail to realize fundamental purposes. Clearly, then, it is not a question of whether there shall be leadership or competence in a technical phase of school administration such as business management. The administrator of present-day school systems needs information and skill in all aspects of educational administration.

A superintendent remarked to one of the writers that he delegated the function of business administration to his assistant superintendent in charge of business services and, therefore, had little need to know, and cared less, about this particular phase of administration. The implication is clear—delegation of authority for business administration relieves the chief executive officer of responsibility and technical knowledge in this area. It is certainly true that for most efficient operation of private business or governmental operations, particularly in large institutions, the chief executive must delegate to assistants the authority that is commensurate with responsibility for performance of the task assigned. Delegation is necessary to perform the duties and details of the job. The superintendent delegates some of his duties to his principal assistants who form the administrative team, and they in turn subdivide responsibilities among others. But delegation of authority does not in any way justify ignorance of the principles of the functions and duties delegated. The chief administrator does not get rid of his responsibilities by this action, for the chief executive is held accountable for the acts of assistants. Top management has the further responsibility to consult with and review the progress and efforts of assistants. It is important for the chief executive to have a basic knowledge of all functions delegated or he would scarcely be in a position to evaluate the functioning and reporting of assistants. One of the most difficult tasks confronting the general superintendent of schools is how to maintain the "feel" or the "pulse" of the school system in face of the need to delegate authority for and performance of the details of administration. When there is a thorough understanding of that which is delegated, the feel or pulse can be maintained by rapid review of the reports of operations. It can be concluded that the principles of sound business management must be known by the large-system superintendent who must delegate functions as well as by the small-system superintendent upon whom falls the burden of performing many of the details of business management.

The school building principal should also have an understanding of business administration. The large sums of money deposited in and expended from "extracurricular" or "internal" accounts make it imperative that principals understand the principles of financial accounting, purchasing, and auditing. Principals have lost their positions because of "innocent" mismanagement of school activity funds. As custodian of the building, the principal can no more excuse his ignorance of building maintenance on the argument that the central business office knows what is best than he can claim ignorance of instructional procedures and methods on grounds that the central office subject matter supervisors know what is best for instruction. It is emphasized that the primary function of a school administrator, be he superintendent or principal, is one of leadership, but this in no way decreases the importance of knowing the principles of sound business management.

Good schools demand adequate financial support. The tremendous increase in current expenditures for education by governmental units during the past half-century can be noted by comparing the $282 million spent in 1902 with $9.5 billion expended for education in the 1957–1958 school year. This increase of over $9.33 billion annually can be attributed to such factors as changing economic conditions, greater professional-

ization of teachers, expansion of educational programs, longer school terms, and the decreased value of the dollar. An additional $3.4 billion was expended for public school capital outlay, interest, and debt retirement in the school year 1957–1958, making the total expenditures almost $12.9 billion for that year.

In spite of tremendously expanded enrollments, the percent of national wealth (gross national product) expended for education declined from 3 percent in 1939 to 2.4 percent in 1954. One source predicted that by 1965 the cost of educating elementary and secondary school-age children will be $5 to $10 billion higher than in 1953.[8] Those persons who have attempted to predict the size of future school expenditures appear in agreement that the present large, but nonetheless inadequate, multi-billion dollar expenditures must be increased as the school-age population continues to grow and the character of American public education becomes more complex.

The fact that education is a multibillion dollar business should be sufficient to point to the need for sound business management of educational enterprises to promote wise utilization of financial and material resources and to prevent waste or loss of such funds. The trend in reduction of the number of local school districts through reorganization into larger administrative units is gaining momentum. Thus, there were approximately 188,000 local school districts in the United States in 1920, 100,000 in 1948, and about 48,000 in 1958. Dawson and Ellena estimated that only 10,200 basic school administrative units and 2500 intermediate units were needed for efficient operation of public schools in the United States.[9] Clearly, then, multibillion expenditures are managed in fewer districts than ever before, making each remaining individual educational unit a more complex institution from a business standpoint.

The demands for the many governmental services other than education and the cost of such services is still increasing. Although more money was spent for public education in 1957–1958 than ever before, tax money and bond issues were harder to obtain. The competition for the tax dollar among the various governmental agencies plus taxpayer resistance to tax increases indicates that the battle for the tax dollar is going to become even more serious than at present. As the amount of funds needed to support a desirable program of educational opportunities increases, and

[8] National Citizens Commission for the Public Schools, *Financing Public Education in the Decade Ahead,* Public Education Finance Committee Report, New York: the Commission, December, 1954, pp. 16–21.

[9] Howard H. Dawson and William J. Ellena, "School District Reorganization," *The School Executive,* July, 1954, p. 42.

the tug of war for tax resources grows, wise business management becomes more necessary than ever. Prudent business management can make a substantial contribution toward insuring the maximum of educational services from each locally collected tax dollar and from each state or federal aid dollar received by the district.

RELATIONSHIPS AND ORGANIZATION IN BUSINESS MANAGEMENT

Business management does not operate in a vacuum. In its relationships to other educational functions, it influences and is in turn influenced by public education in general. Public school systems, likewise, are only a part of the total governmental framework in America. The relationships among local school districts, other local governmental agencies, and state governmental agencies have a bearing upon the operation of school business management. An understanding of these relationships is imperative for designing, organizing, or evaluating the business management of schools.

To organize, according to Webster's *New International Dictionary,* means to put in working order. In organization the related parts are arranged to work together. Whether an organization is good or bad can be judged only in relation to the purposes or functions for which it is organized. Clearly, then, purposes precede and justify organization. Or, organizational structure follows or is determined by institutional functions. The term "functional organization" simply means that the organization was designed with a purpose, namely that of serving as a vehicle in executing the functions of an institution. Organization has no validity in itself nor can any particular structure insure complete success without regard to human elements and unique local conditions and mores. Human personalities can contribute to or diminish the success of even functional organization. Notwithstanding these facts some types of organization are more likely to contribute to the ends of education than others. The problem, then, is to discover the organizational fabrics for business administration that will promote the ends of education.

THE STATE AND LOCAL SCHOOL DISTRICTS

The relationship between the state and the local school district has important implications for the design of the structure for business administration. The existing relationship between the local school district and the state is one of a subordinate unit to the plenary authority that created it. The school district is a civil subdivision of the state, organized and empowered by the state to carry out the function of education in the name of the state and of the people. The local school district is a creature of the state, operating under delegated authority and responsible for executing the will of the state. Most states, however, have wisely provided for a marked degree of local participation and control of education. This policy of keeping the schools close to the people while at the same time using the state's power to minimize the danger of local initiative degenerating into local inertia has done much to strengthen educational institutions.

The school district is, in a legal sense, a quasi-municipal corporation. A quasi-municipal corporation is a municipal corporation designed to perform rather specific functions, that is, it is a limited municipal corporation. As a municipal corporation, even though limited in scope of authority, the school district performs a governmental function as do general municipal corporations. The various definitions of municipal corporations given by such authorities as Dillon,[10] and McQuillan[11] indicate that a municipal corporation is a public corporation granted power through a state charter and having broad and general powers of government over primarily *local* affairs. These broad and general municipal corporations *primarily* regulate *local* functions and secondarily act as arms of the state government. In contrast, school districts are quasi-municipal corporations and, from a legal point of view, are *primarily* arms of the *state* government. A quasi-municipal corporation has all the powers of a municipal corporation except that its acts must be limited to those needed to execute its limited functions.

As a quasi-municipal corporation, a school district has no inherent authority to act in government. The powers of a school district are delegated to it by the state. In other words, a school district has only those powers that are specifically granted, those that can be clearly implied from other grants, or those that are vitally necessary in the execution of its functions. When doubt exists as to whether or not the school district has a power, the doubt is resolved against the district having such power.

Constitutional provisions, statutory enactments, and state department of education regulations provide the matrix in which the business management of schools must operate. What the superior authority demands of

[10] John G. Dillon, *Commentaries on the Law of Municipal Corporations,* Boston: Little, Brown & Co., 5th ed., 1911, vol. 1, sec. 31.

[11] Eugene McQuillan, *The Law of Municipal Corporations,* Chicago: Callaghan & Company, rev. ed., 1940, vol. 1, sec. 362, p. 994.

school districts in business administration, the local district must perform without regard to local feelings or principles of sound management. America is a nation of 50 state school systems. This makes it difficult to describe with any degree of accuracy business procedures demanded of school systems throughout the nation. Thus state constitutional mandates, statutory prescriptions, and department of education requirements outline procedures in budgeting, purchasing, managing indebtedness, and a whole host of other details of business management. Where such state requirements are based on unsound business practices, improvement in business operations often has to wait upon changes in state statutes or state board of education regulations.

LOCAL SCHOOL DISTRICTS AND OTHER GOVERNMENTAL UNITS

The state creates school districts and determines what shall be the relationship between school districts and other local governmental units. This relationship also has a significant impact on the organization of school business administration. More frequently this problem is discussed under a single phase of relationship, namely, fiscal dependence or independence of school districts from general municipal corporations. In the absence of clear evidence to the contrary, the courts have held that a school district is a separate and distinct legal entity from a municipal corporation even though the boundaries of the two are coterminous. This general rule of independence of school districts from the control of cities, villages, townships, or counties in which they are located may be altered by the state through statutory enactments or special charters granted to certain municipalities. Chattanooga stands out as an illustration of the exception to the general rule since education in this city is organized as a municipal department of education, that is, as primarily an arm of city government rather than state government.

The crux of the argument concerned with determining desirable relationships between local school districts and local governmental units is control over fiscal affairs. If the legally elected or appointed school district authorities have complete and final authority to levy local property taxes and expend funds for education, the school district is said to be fiscally independent of other local governmental units. In fiscally independent school districts, boards of education, or the electors in annual meeting, have complete and final control over fiscal affairs within the framework of state

law and do not need to obtain approval of other municipalities on such financial matters as the local tax levy for schools or the size of the education budget. When the school district lacks complete authority and, therefore, cannot levy local property taxes for school support nor expend money budgeted for educational purposes without prior approval from some other local governmental agency, it is said to be fiscally dependent. Local nongovernmental agencies often have other forms of fiscal control over school districts such as custody and disbursement of school funds or keeping school financial records. The critical issues for school operation and particularly for business management remain the final control over budget determination and the final decision concerning the school tax rate. The control that some primarily local governmental agencies have over local school districts often includes such matters as selecting school personnel (particularly noncertificated personnel such as janitors), purchasing supplies and equipment, and holding title to school property. These control aspects are not as significant as those concerned with power to revise educational budgets or to fix school tax rates on local property.

STATUS OF FISCAL RELATIONSHIPS

There are various degrees and types of fiscal relationships between school boards and local governmental agencies. As with respect to most other problems it is usually not a case of pure black and pure white. It is not possible to classify all school districts as either completely independent or completely dependent fiscally, for there are different degrees of fiscal dependence. Thus in one city the school district may have the final authority to determine the budget but the municipality may have the final word on the amount of the school tax levy. In other situations the reverse may be true. In determining the fiscal status of school districts in relation to municipalities, the budgetary aspects of the problem will be examined separately from the tax levy aspects.

The most recent extensive study of fiscal relationships between city school boards and municipalities was reported in 1950.[12] Fifty percent of the 3795 cities with a population of 2500 or more (based on 1940 census) provided data reported in the study. This study revealed that in almost all city school districts the board of education prepared its annual budget independently

[12] National Education Association, Research Division, "Fiscal Authority of City School Boards," *Research Bulletin,* Washington, D.C.: NEA, April, 1950, *28:*46–79.

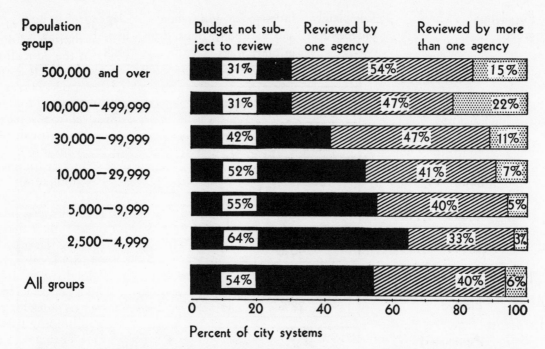

Population group	Budget not subject to review	Reviewed by one agency	Reviewed by more than one agency
500,000 and over	31%	54%	15%
100,000—499,999	31%	47%	22%
30,000—99,999	42%	47%	11%
10,000—29,999	52%	41%	7%
5,000—9,999	55%	40%	5%
2,500—4,999	64%	33%	3%
All groups	54%	40%	6%

Percent of city systems

FIGURE 1. Percent of City School Districts in Which School Budgets Are Subject to Review
SOURCE: National Education Association, Research Division, "Fiscal Authority of City School Boards," *Research Bulletin*, Washington, D.C.: NEA, April, 1950, 28:54.

but when once prepared the budget was subject to review by some outside agency in 46 percent of these districts. Fifty-four percent of the city school districts reported that the budget was *not* subject to review; 40 percent indicated that the budget was reviewed by one agency.

It is apparent from Figure 1 that the larger the city in which a school district is located, the more likely it is that the budget will be reviewed by some outside agency. Thus, in only 31 percent of the cities with a population of 100,000 or more (1940 census) is the school budget *not* subject to review.

The powers of control exercised by the various reviewing agencies over the school budget vary greatly. In 18 percent of the city systems in the study mentioned, the school budget had to be approved by the reviewing agency as submitted by the board of education. At the other extreme, in 6 percent of the city school systems the reviewing agency had the power to change specific budget items. In the remainder of the districts the reviewing authority could disapprove the budget as a whole and return it to the school board with or without recommendations for needed changes. In summary it can be stated that 72 percent of the city school systems are relatively independent in deciding the amount of the school budget. The figure of 72 percent includes the 54 percent which are not required to

submit the school budget for review and the 18 percent which require that the school budget be approved by the reviewing agency as submitted by the board of education.

It can be noted in Table 1 that in 83 percent of city school districts with *appointive* boards of education, the school district budget is subjected to review by some outside agency. In contrast to this, only 40 percent of city school districts with *elective* boards are required to submit budgets to some local governmental agency for review.

Fiscal dependence or independence in finally determining local tax revenues for education is complicated by the twofold problem of levying and collecting taxes. Only 10 percent of the city school boards both levy and collect local property taxes for school purposes. The most significant aspect of this problem is the power to determine finally the amount of the levy for school purposes. Collection is the administrative or mechanical chore based on the levy decision. Approximately 18 percent of the city school districts in the 1950 study previously mentioned finally decided the official school tax levy even though they did not collect the levy. In an additional 35 percent of the city school systems, the school tax rate recommended by the school board had to be approved by the nonschool reviewing agency without modification. Thus it can be concluded

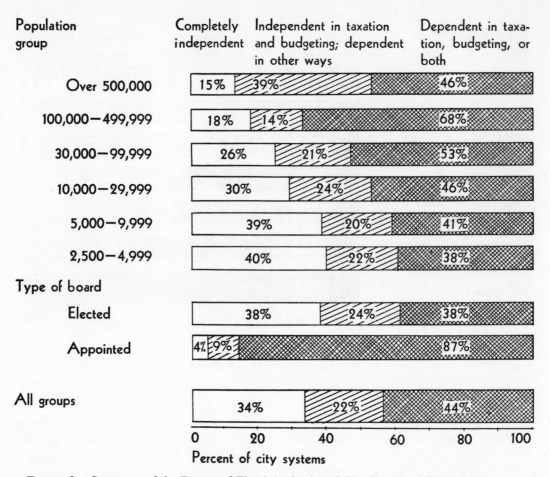

Population group	Completely independent	Independent in taxation and budgeting; dependent in other ways	Dependent in taxation, budgeting, or both
Over 500,000	15%	39%	46%
100,000—499,999	18%	14%	68%
30,000—99,999	26%	21%	53%
10,000—29,999	30%	24%	46%
5,000—9,999	39%	20%	41%
2,500—4,999	40%	22%	38%
Type of board			
Elected	38%	24%	38%
Appointed	4%	9%	87%
All groups	34%	22%	44%

Percent of city systems

FIGURE 2.   Summary of the Degree of Fiscal Authority of City Boards of Education
SOURCE: National Education Association, Research Division, "Fiscal Authority of City School Boards," *Research Bulletin*, Washington, D.C.: NEA, April, 1950, *28*:56.

that 63 percent of the city school districts were essentially free to establish the local tax levy without interference from nonschool agencies.

In some city school districts the school tax rates are controlled by referring the matter to a vote of the residents of the district. Only 12 percent of the city school systems reporting in 1950 indicated that all school tax rates had to be approved by a vote of the people. The larger the city, the less likely it is that the school tax rate is referred to a vote of the people when school board members are appointed to office rather than elected.

Sixty-four percent of the city school districts studied in 1950 had custody of the school funds, that is, the districts received, deposited, and disbursed funds without any outside help. The smaller the city, the more likely it was that custody of school funds were controlled solely by boards of education. Where the school district did not have custody of funds, custody was given to the city or county treasurer. Three-fourths of the city school systems had exclusive control over the official school financial records. In only 6 percent of the city school systems were the school financial records maintained entirely by a nonschool agency.

To summarize, 56 percent of the city school systems are for all practical purposes fiscally independent of local governmental control of the type that could materially influence educational policy formulation. It is significant that only 13 percent of the cities having appointive boards of education are essentially fiscally independent whereas 62 percent of the cities having elective boards of education are essentially fiscally independent. Mort and Reusser reported that there has been a recent trend toward a slight increase in the fiscal dependence of city school boards.[13] Increased frequency of property tax limitations and the activity of

[13] Paul R. Mort and Walter C. Reusser, *Public School Finance*, New York: McGraw-Hill Book Company, rev. ed., 1951, p. 57.

TABLE 1. Number and Percent of City School Systems in Which the Annual School Budget Must Be Submitted for Review to Some Agency of Local Government

| | | Districts with Budgets Subject to Outside Review | | Percent in Which the Review Is by | |
Group	Number of City School Systems	Number	Percent	One Agency	More Than One Agency
1	2	3	4	5	6
Population					
500,000 and over	13	9	69	54	15
100,000–499,999	71	49	69	47	22
30,000–99,999	222	129	58	47	11
10,000–29,999	562	272	48	41	7
5,000–9,999	481	216	45	40	5
2,500–4,999	543	195	36	33	3
Type of Board					
Elected	1,642	663	40	35	5
Appointed	250	207	83	66	17
Location of District					
Within one city	883	509	58	47	11
In two or more jurisdictions	1,009	361	36	33	3
All Groups	1,892	870	46	40	6

SOURCE: National Education Association, Research Division, "Fiscal Authority of City School Boards," *Research Bulletin*, Washington, D.C.: NEA, April, 1950, *28*:56.

TABLE 2. Powers of the Electorate over the Local Tax Rate for Schools in City Systems

| | Percent of City-School Systems in Which the Voters | | | | | |
Group	Number Reporting This Item	Approve All Proposed Tax Rates	Approve Rates Beyond a Specified Maximum	Vote When City and School Authorities Disagree	Have Miscellaneous Powers[a]	Have No Direct Authority
1	2	3	4	5	6	7
Population						
500,000 and over	12	0	33	0	0	67
100,000–499,999	67	10	27	0	2	61
30,000–99,999	206	3	41	1	4	51
10,000–29,999	538	10	34	*	5	51
5,000–9,999	444	14	33	1	4	48
2,500–4,999	500	16	39	1	3	41
Type of Board						
Elected	1,540	13	39	[b]	4	44
Appointed	227	5	16	3	5	71
All Groups	1,767	12	35	1	4	48

[a] For example, "The voters set a maximum tax rate. The board of education may levy that amount or a smaller amount as needed."

[b] Less than one-half of 1 percent

SOURCE: National Education Association, Research Division, "Fiscal Authority of City School Boards," *Research Bulletin*, Washington, D.C.: NEA, April, 1950, *28:61*.

groups interested in achieving what is considered by these groups to be "simplicity" in governmental organization have probably influenced the slight trend toward fiscal dependence.

There were approximately 83,000 school districts in the United States in 1950. School districts located in cities of 2500 or more amount to less than 5 percent of the total number of local educational units. Clearly, then, the 1950 status study of fiscal relationships has been concerned with a relatively small number of school districts of a special type—namely, city school districts. No single study to date has reported the fiscal relationships between local districts and other local governmental agencies for the nation as a whole and for all types of school districts. In 1950 Fuller declared that more than 85 percent of the local school boards in the nation were fiscally independent from municipalities, most of the remaining 15 percent that were fiscally dependent being located in the older parts of the country.[14] It appears reasonable to assume that the percent of school districts in the nation as a whole that are fiscally independent is considerably greater than the percent reported for city school systems. It should be recalled that the smaller the community, the more likely that the school district is fiscally independent. The fiscal affairs of thousands of common school districts are finally determined by the vote of the people at the annual school meeting.

ARGUMENTS FOR AND AGAINST FISCAL INDEPENDENCE

Arguments concerning fiscal independence of school districts from other local governmental agencies have been raging since at least the early 1920's without any apparent letup. The arguments are concerned with a small minority of the total number of local school districts in the nation, but nonetheless they constitute a very important minority when the total number of children involved is considered. Educators are in almost solid agreement in favoring fiscal independence of school districts whereas most political scientists favor fiscal dependence and the integration of education with other affairs of municipal government.

There has been some research on fiscal relationships of school districts. In 1922 Frasier reported that a comparison between fiscally independent and dependent city school systems indicated that the more dependent a school district was, the less efficient it was as measured by Frasier's "efficiency index."[15] Some have questioned the validity of his index of efficiency. Frasier summarized the case for fiscal independence by declaring that it was right in principle; it was not a violation of tax principles; it worked better in practice; it made for continuity of educational policy; it provided adequate financial safeguards for the community; and it tended to keep politics out of the schools. Two years after Frasier's study, McGaughy discovered that certain financial and educational factors were significantly larger, on the average, in fiscally independent city school districts but other financial and education factors were significantly higher, on the average, in fiscally dependent city systems.[16] There were a greater number of desirable financial and education factors in fiscally independent school systems than in fiscally dependent school systems, according to McGaughy. In 1947 Woodward conducted a study covering much the same ground as the McGaughy study and concluded that there were no significant changes in the status of the cities studied in the quarter of a century since McGaughy's study.[17] Woodward also reported that in the 85 cities with a population of 100,000 to 1,000,000 the mean per pupil expenditure was 4 percent more in 1929–1930 in the fiscally dependent systems than in the fiscally independent systems. The mean per pupil expenditures were nearly 12 percent more in the fiscally dependent districts in 1943–1944 than in the fiscally independent districts of this same class.[18]

Henry and Kerwin completed a study of cities with a population of 50,000 or more in 1938. They found that there was no marked difference in coöperation on community problems and that political interference might be present or absent in fiscally independent as well as in fiscally dependent school systems.[19] Henry and Kerwin concluded that the results of their nonstatistical study tended to favor, or at least did not oppose, fiscal dependence. In spite of some excellent contributions, research to date has not supplied the final answer as to whether fiscal independence is related to effective functioning of local school systems. Until more conclusive evidence is produced, the argument must be resolved on a different basis.

[14] From a paper on *Education in the Reorganization of the Federal Government* by Edgar Fuller, Executive Secretary, National Council of Chief State School Officers, January 7, 1950. Also quoted in Mort and Reusser, *op. cit.,* p. 60.

[15] G. W. Frasier, *The Control of City School Finances,* Milwaukee: The Bruce Publishing Company, 1922.

[16] J. R. McGaughy, *The Fiscal Administration of City School Systems,* New York: The Macmillan Company, 1924.

[17] Henry B. Woodward, *The Effect of Fiscal Control on Current School Expenditures,* Doctoral Dissertation, New York: Teachers College, Columbia University, 1948.

[18] *Ibid.,* p. 14.

[19] Nelson B. Henry and Jerome G. Kerwin, *Schools and City Government,* Chicago: University of Chicago Press, 1938.

Educators argue in favor of fiscal independence and emphasize that education is a state function with state financial resources being utilized to equalize educational opportunities in the local school districts. Education is better compared with the judicial system of the state (which is likewise independent of municipalities even though located within municipal boundaries) than with the many *ad hoc* local governmental districts such as sewage, drainage, paving, and irrigation districts. Burke[20] and Eberle[21] pointed out that fiscal dependence can destroy the responsibility-authority principle of public administration. Fiscal controls can make a mockery out of previously allocated governmental responsibility. "Control of the purse strings" leads to virtual control of policy making in education. As Burke so eloquently stated, "where school boards are fiscally dependent upon some other agency of local government having power to reduce or alter the school budget, the school board becomes a redundant appendage of local government."[22] The agency having fiscal control and authority finally determines educational policies even though the original intent may have been only to simplify governmental structure.

Political scientists, on the other hand, generally favor fiscal dependence of school systems. Certain political scientists, such as Anderson, have gone so far as to recommend:

First, there would be no separate school districts in the county whatsoever. Under state control and supervision the several counties, cities, larger towns, and larger villages would administer the local schools within their limits. Advisory or even administrative school boards might exist in many places, but not separate corporate school districts.

It is recognized that this is an advanced proposal, but it follows from the principle of having only one local government in each area. The existing separation between school government and other local government, however much it may have been justified in the past, now stands in the way of adequate local governmental operation. To separate the functions of education from other functions of government, to give school authorities and teachers a feeling of irresponsibility for the rest of government, to permit school budgets to be made, school taxes to be levied, and school bonds to be issued without reference to other governmental needs is in the long run unwholesome for the educational system itself and for other political institutions of the country.[23]

[20] Arvid J. Burke, *Financing Public Schools in the United States,* New York: Harper & Brothers, rev. ed., 1957, pp. 221–227.

[21] August W. Eberle, "Fiscal Independence—An Answer to Political Scientists," *American School Board Journal,* December, 1953, p. 24.

[22] Burke, *op. cit.,* pp. 224–225.

[23] William Anderson, *The Units of Government in the United States,* Public Administration Service, Washington, D.C.: U. S. Government Printing Office, 1949, p. 17.

No scientific research or other objective evidence is offered by Anderson to support the sweeping statements made by him. Under the organization proposed by political scientists the education function would be transferred to a departmental status under city mayors or managers. The superintendent of schools would then become the head of a city department of education. The penchant for "simplicity" in local government through unification of school and city administration and the desire for administrative efficiency and fiscal economy resulting from such unification are influential factors in the reasoning of political scientists. It is questionable just how much simpler municipal administration would be through the addition of budgets almost double that of existing municipal government, for school budgets are often equal to or greater than the budgets of municipalities in which the districts lie. It is also significant that most of the texts devoted to municipal government and administration devote relatively little space, if any, to the topic of school administration. In such texts, school administration is briefly mentioned along with such other relatively "minor" administrative problems as library administration or recreation.

The Research Division of the National Education Association has summarized the pro and con arguments concerning fiscal independence as follows:

Those who favor fiscal independence for boards of education maintain that:

1. Any intermediary authority standing between the school board and the state makes it difficult if not impossible for the board to be *in fact* responsible to the people and to the state.
2. Fiscal control often leads to de facto control of educational policies such as whether or not kindergartens may be established, home economics be taught, or classes be provided for handicapped children.
3. Fiscal dependence may result in coercion with respect to technical and professional matters. The controlling board may let it be known that either the school board will adopt certain policies or its budget will be cut.
4. Fiscal independence is the only sure way to avoid the diversion of school funds to nonschool purposes.
5. Fiscally dependent boards are sometimes told where purchases are to be made, the firms to which contracts are to be awarded, and the persons who are to be employed.
6. Fiscal dependence results in greater competition for the tax dollar and to strained relations between municipal and school governing boards.
7. All school boards cannot be dependent since many of them are not coterminous with any unit of local government. If the state regards this as sound policy for such districts, why is it not equally sound for all school districts?
8. Fiscal independence leads to greater stability and conti-

nuity in educational planning—school authorities know what they can count on.

9. School financial accounting is so different from other municipal accounting that there are few advantages in combining them.

10. Fiscally dependent boards must waste much time and energy presenting and justifying their budgets to the controlling agencies.

11. Public education is complex enough and important enough to have its policies and its budget determined by a board which gives exclusive attention to that function.

12. Although neither independence nor dependence can guarantee economy, the evidence so far available indicates that, by and large, greater economy has been practiced by fiscally independent boards.

Those who believe in fiscal dependence for boards of education reply upon arguments such as these:

1. Determination of expenditures for all purposes, in proper relationship to one another, requires a single local legislative authority.

2. School superintendents and boards often are unaware of and unconcerned about the needs and fiscal problems of the general government.

3. Intergovernmental relations are made more complex by independent agencies which in some matters operate in the same areas such as records, reports, and taxation.

4. Divided control and responsibility lead to overlapping functions and duplication of effort.

5. The tax *collecting* agency should make the levy and fix the budget. If school boards fix the rate and make their budgets, they should be required to collect their own taxes.

6. Fiscal independence brings no positive assurance of freedom from politics.

7. With overlapping units of government the tendency is to increase the total load of bonded debt and the limits on tax rates above those that would exist if a single unit of government were wholly responsible for them.

8. The recent trend has been toward abolition of special boards and taxing units such as library, sanitation, park, fire protection, police, and highway.[24]

It is the point of view of the authors that education has a unique function in our American democracy. If education is to be compared with some other governmental agency it should be compared with the judicial system of the state. Efficient business management of the educational enterprise is more likely to occur under an organization characterized by fiscal independence. School business management should serve the ends of education rather than "simplified" municipal operations. Unnecessary, undesirable, and time-consuming "red tape" should not be allowed to ensnarl business management in public school systems. The significant points that lead to acceptance of fiscal independence of school systems are as follows:

[24] National Education Association, Research Division, *op. cit.,* p. 67.

1. Efficiency and simplicity are best measured in terms of realization of the education function.

2. The ends of education are important to the welfare of our democracy and can best be realized by those who devote considerable effort and time to their realization.

3. School boards become useless appendages unless they are able to control the fiscal implications of educational planning.

4. Public education in many cities is already a large and complex organization operating under efficient and professional administrative management.

5. The boundaries of many cities are not coterminous with school district boundaries.

6. Education is a state function and a local board of education represents the people of the state as well as the people living in the local district.

INTERNAL ORGANIZATION OF SCHOOL DISTRICTS

The duly elected or appointed school board of the school district is the legal agent empowered by law to control the conduct of educational affairs in the district. In the absence of specific state legislation to the contrary, the local board has the legal authority to determine policies which influence the organization for school business administration. It is most important that school boards carefully and clearly state policies that set the framework of the organizational fabric for the business management of schools.

Although board policies determine business organization, the actual execution or operation of school business affairs should be delegated to those persons professionally competent to perform such work. School board members are laymen usually engaged in a full-time occupation and are not in a position to execute the details of school business management. To whom and under what conditions executory responsibility for school business management is delegated by the board of education is most important for efficient operation of schools.

The board may choose to delegate responsibility for the execution of the entire educational program (instructional and business) to a single executive officer, usually called the superintendent of schools. This plan of operation is known as the unit type of organization for school administration. One individual, the superintendent, is charged with the responsibility of administering all aspects of the school system. Under such an arrangement the superintendent is the only professional employee who regularly reports to and deals directly with the board of education. In other words, the superintendent is the chief executive officer of the school board. All other employees in the school system, professional or nonprofessional, are subordinate to the superintendent and generally report to the board through the superintendent.

On the other hand, the board may choose to delegate responsibility for the execution of the various facets of the educational program to more than one executive officer. This is the multiple type of organization for school administration. In this type of organization two or more persons report directly to the board of education and report independently of any and all others. Certain functions in education, such as the instructional and business functions, would be separated and administered by a coördinate executive. These several executives are coördinate officers of the board of education. A few boards have gone so far as to divide the responsibilities of the school system into instruction, business, finance, buildings, and auditing and assign an executive to each of them. Under such a plan each of the five executives is coördinate in power and each may operate independently from the others. The superintendent of instruction would have to have a strong or dominant personality to assume a position of importance in this type of organization of executive activity. The dual type is the most common type of multiple organization. In the dual type of organization there is usually a director of business affairs who reports directly and independently to the board of education and is considered coördinate with the superintendent of schools.

There is presently ample research and other evidence available to indicate the superiority of the unit type of administrative organization over any form of multiple executive organization. Reeder, in summarizing the research on administrative relationships in school business affairs, stated: "These studies show in the main that multiple-headed school systems spend more annually per pupil than the unit headed ones. They also reveal that business functions require a larger percentage of the budget under multiple organizations than under unit organizations. All the studies cite instances of a lack of an educational point of view on the part of business officials in multiple organizations; all give examples of friction in such organizations; and all argue finally for centralized control which one head only can provide."[25] Earlier in this chapter it was emphasized that business administration should be subordinated to the purposes of the

educational institution and to general school administration of which it is but a part. With a business manager coördinate with the superintendent of schools there is a real and grave danger that the very reason for the existence of public education may be submerged in favor of perfectionism in business details. Heer, writing in 1926, cited several "suggested causes for separation of business and educational departments." Some of these causes were:

1. In many cities business affairs were administered by the board of education or a business manager was appointed several years before a superintendent of instruction.
2. When "Formal Discipline" was the aim of education, there was very little to connect educational and business departments.
3. The general opinion held at that time that superintendents of schools understood educational problems, but they had no business ability.[26]

A 1947 study of business administration in certain city school systems indicated that in only 25 percent of the cities studied was the business manager directly responsible to the superintendent of schools.[27] It appeared that the smaller the city, the less likely it was that the business manager was directly responsible to the general superintendent of schools. The multiple executive organization is found chiefly in the East in the states of New Jersey, New York, and Pennsylvania although examples of this type of organization can be found in certain cities in other states as well. There is clearly a need for a change in the internal organization of city school districts where more than one executive officer of the board of education exists. In all cases the individual in charge of business affairs should be clearly responsible to the superintendent of schools who should be the chief executive officer of the board of education.

ORGANIZATION OF THE DEPARTMENT OF BUSINESS SERVICES

It is established that the unit type of executive organization is more efficient than others. A further and more detailed examination of an organization for business management within the unit type of framework is necessary to ascertain working relationships.

[25] Ward G. Reeder, "Business Administration of Schools" in Walter D. Monroe (ed.), *Encyclopedia of Educational Research*, New York: The Macmillan Company, 1950, p. 103.

[26] Amos L. Heer, *The Present Status of Business Executives in the Public Schools of the United States in Cities of 25,000 and More Inhabitants*, Doctoral Dissertation, Columbus: Ohio State University, 1926, pp. 32–34.

[27] W. E. Rosenstengel and Willard S. Swiers, "Business Administration in City Schools-I," *American School Board Journal*, March, 1947, p. 26.

Who shall be given executive responsibilities for a department of business services? What functions shall be found within this department? How shall such a department of business affairs be organized? What should be the status of this department in the line and staff organization of the school?

Authority in school business affairs was one of the last responsibilities to be entrusted to professional school administrators. The various boards of education or committees of citizens held on to direct control of business functions as long as they could in the face of the ever increasing complexity of educational institutions. The vestigial remains of board execution of business affairs and the reluctant delegation of authority in this area are still apparent in many school systems. One vestige of such board executive activity is the secretary or treasurer to the board of education. The secretary or treasurer to the board enjoys special status and his position often makes him coördinate with the general superintendent. The functions performed by such individuals include such activities as operation of business affairs, preparation of board agendas, and recording and keeping the minutes of board meetings. Rosenstengel and Swiers[28] reported that in 60.5 percent of the city systems studied the business manager served as secretary to the board of education. In one-third of the same cities the business manager served as treasurer to the school board. If the superintendent of schools is the *chief* executive officer of the school system is there a need for an independent board of education secretary or treasurer? The answer is *no*. It is assumed that members of the board of education are laymen who definitely need the services of a professionally educated chief executive officer to carry out the policies adopted by the board. The board of education and the chief executive are members of the same team and should not be construed as competing agencies. With centralization of responsibility in the superintendent of schools there should be a centralization of authority. Under this arrangement the functions of the board's secretary or treasurer would be assumed by a department of the chief executive's line and staff organization. The board does not lose any control for it always controls the chief executive and directs his activities along policies approved by the board. Control by the board would merely be channeled through the superintendent rather than around him. In effect, the chief executive should be regarded as the executive secretary of the board of education.

The general executive responsibility for all business affairs should be that of the superintendent of schools.

[28] "Business Administration in City Schools-II," *American School Board Journal*, May, 1947, p. 19.

In very small school systems this function is not only lodged in one person, but it is also executed by one person, namely, the superintendent of schools. As the size of the school system increases, so do the business problems, and this necessitates the delegation of business management responsibilities to an assistant superintendent in charge of business affairs. The function has not changed but more people are required to carry out the function. The difference between small and large school systems is not in function but in organization and number of people necessary to realize the function.

The functions of the assistant superintendent in charge of business affairs can be subdivided into four main divisions:

1. *School Budget Division.* This division can be subdivided further into bureaus of treasury, accounts and records, and comptroller and audit.
2. *Purchasing and Supplies Division.* This division can be subdivided further into bureaus of requisitions and purchasing, inventory and supplies control, and distribution.
3. *School Building and Sites Division.* This division can be subdivided further into the bureaus of schoolhouse construction and schoolhouse maintenance.
4. *Auxiliary Services Division.* This division can be subdivided further into the bureaus of cafeteria and foods management, pupil transportation, etc.

The organization to achieve these functions of business management can be diagrammed as on page 15.

Since the accompanying chart shows the functions or duties that are performed in the execution of business operations, it can be applied to both small and large school systems. For small schools the chart should be useful in pointing out the various tasks in business administration that confront the single school administrator found in such school systems. As the size and complexity of the educational institution increase, more personnel are required to execute the business management functions and their attendant details. As the small school system increases in size, some point is reached where a business manager is needed to relieve the overburdened superintendent of schools. For a time a single person is all that may be required to discharge the business functions. Further growth may necessitate the employment of two or more individuals to care for divisional functions under an assistant superintendent in charge of business affairs. In very large systems specially trained individuals with clerical assistants may be needed to execute the functions of a bureau within a division of the business department.

The functions and duties in the execution of busi-

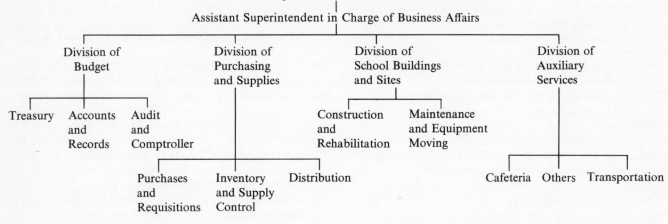

People

Board of Education

Other Functions—Superintendent of Schools—Other Functions

Assistant Superintendent in Charge of Business Affairs

Division of Budget | Division of Purchasing and Supplies | Division of School Buildings and Sites | Division of Auxiliary Services

Treasury   Accounts and Records   Audit and Comptroller

Construction and Rehabilitation   Maintenance and Equipment Moving

Purchases and Requisitions   Inventory and Supply Control   Distribution

Cafeteria   Others   Transportation

ness affairs, partially enumerated in the diagram, will be analyzed in further detail in subsequent chapters. The purpose of this chapter has been to "set the stage" to provide the framework in which school business administration operates.

SUMMARY

School administration is a means to an end. Financial management is a part of educational administration concerned with the various aspects of administering the fiscal and material resources needed to achieve the goals of education. Sooner or later the business aspects of any educational activity reveal themselves and call for attention. The principles of sound business management must be known by the large-system superintendent who delegates the performance of business management to others as well as by the small-system superintendent who personally executes many of the details of financial management. Prudent financial management can help to achieve the goal of a maximum of educational services from each local, state, or federal tax dollar received by the district.

The relationships between the state or local governmental agencies and the local school districts are often determined by law or regulations. The school district is a quasi-municipal corporation. Legal enactments provide the matrix in which school financial management must operate. America is a nation of 50 state school systems and the laws regulating school business affairs vary among the states. If statutory or other legal requirements are unsound from a business management viewpoint, they must be followed nevertheless.

Improvement in financial administration must often wait upon statutory or constitutional changes. Leaders in school business affairs must work to make state mandates consistent with sound business practices.

The crux of the argument concerned with desirable relationships between local school and local governmental units is control over fiscal affairs. Fiscally independent school districts have complete and final authority to levy local property taxes and budget school funds whereas fiscally dependent districts must look to some other local unit to obtain final approval for taxes or budgets. Most school districts are fiscally independent but the larger the city school district, the more likely it is to be fiscally dependent to some degree. Research has not as yet supplied the answer as to whether a school district should or should not be fiscally dependent. Most educators are of the opinion that fiscal independence is most desirable.

In the absence of specific legislation to the contrary, the local board has the legal authority to determine policies which influence the organization for school business administration. There is ample evidence to support the contention that the unit type of administrative organization is superior to any type of multiple-headed organizations. Authority over the execution of school business affairs was one of the last responsibilities to be delegated by lay school boards to professional school administrators. The general executive responsibility for all business affairs should rest with the general superintendent of schools. As the size of the system increases, the need for a special assistant superintendent in charge of business affairs subordinate to the general superintendent will become more apparent.

QUESTIONS

1. What are the basic responsibilities or functions of school financial management?
2. Is it more desirable for the superintendent to become proficient in school business affairs or in school personnel administration? Justify your position.
3. How much should a large-city superintendent know about business administration? A large-city building principal? A . small-school district superintendent?
4. Arrange a debate on the following proposition:
Resolved: All public school districts should be fiscally independent.
5. When is a school fiscally dependent?
6. What are the advantages and the disadvantages of the multiple type of administrative organizations?

SELECTED REFERENCES

American Association of School Administrators, *The American School Superintendency,* Washington, D.C.: the Association, 1952, chaps. III, IV, and VII.

Burke, Arvid J., *Financing Public Schools in the United States,* New York: Harper & Brothers, rev. ed., 1957, chaps. II, IV, and V.

Dawson, Howard A., and Ellena, William J., "School District Reorganization," *The School Executive,* July, 1954.

Eberle, August W., "Fiscal Independence—An Answer to Political Scientists," *American School Board Journal,* December, 1953.

Henry, Nelson B., and Kerwin, Jerome G., *Schools and City Government,* Chicago: University of Chicago Press, 1938.

National Citizens Commission for the Public Schools, *Financing Education in the Decade Ahead,* Public Education Finance Committee Report, New York: the Commission, December, 1954.

National Education Association, Research Division, "Fiscal Authority of City School Boards," *Research Bulletin,* Washington, D.C.: NEA, April, 1950, *28:*46–79.

National Education Association, Research Division, *Research Bulletin,* Washington, D.C.: NEA, February, 1958, *36:*9.

Rosenstengel, W. E., and Swiers, Willard S., "Business Administration in City Schools-I," *American School Board Journal,* March, 1947.

CHAPTER 2

The Educational Budget—
The Heart of Fiscal
Management

BUDGET IS A SIMPLE WORD WITH PROFOUND implications for educational administration. The more one probes into its potentialities, the more varied and complex its meanings become. At the federal level of government the budget can serve as an instrument of fiscal policy—that is, it can influence the development and stabilization of the national economy. At all levels of government—local, state, or national—it is one of the important instruments of fiscal management along with the accounts, payroll procedures, purchasing practices, the audit, financial reports, and other safeguards. The budget, however, deserves recognition as the very heart of fiscal management.

The budget can be defined in many ways such as:

1. A plan for financial operation which includes an estimate of proposed expenditures for a given period of time and a proposed means of financing expenditures.

2. A systematic plan for the efficient utilization of man power, material, or other resources.

3. A financial plan which serves as a pattern for and control over future operations of an institution.

There are other ways of saying the same thing, but it takes more than a memorization of a definition to truly comprehend the use and significance of budgets. It was Prime Minister Gladstone of Britain who profoundly observed that: "Budgets are not merely matters of arithmetic, but in a thousand ways go to the root of prosperity of individuals, and relation of classes, and the strength of kingdoms."

In public education, budgets are likewise more than "merely matters of arithmetic," i.e., adding up the proposed expenditures and the anticipated receipts for a given period. The budget must be regarded as the fiscal translation of the educational program. Sooner or later everything we desire to do in public education must be translated into its dollars and cents equivalent. Reducing proposed expenditures or refusing to raise necessary receipts has more than mere monetary significance. It touches upon the quality and quantity of educational services to be made available in a district. It was during Gladstone's days that the maxim of "expenditure depends upon policy" won acceptance. It applies today in public education, for the expenditures planned within the budget document should be based on educational policies that are to be realized. The budget is another way of expressing the educational hopes and aspirations of the people of the school district.

A SHORT HISTORY OF BUDGETING

Budgets came into being when and where there existed a need for economy and efficiency in financial operations. They accompanied the growth of representative government and the financial complexity of governmental operations. Burkhead described the interesting derivation of the word "budget": "The word 'budget' originally meant the money bag or the public purse, which served as a receptacle for the revenue and expenditure of a state. In Britain the term was used to describe the leather bag in which the Chancellor of the Exchequer carried to Parliament the statement of the Government's needs and resources. Eventually the term came to mean the documents which were contained in the bag—plans for government finances submitted for the approval of the legislature."[1]

The practice of budgeting was developing in England more than two centuries prior to its inception in the United States government. It can be construed as part of a movement toward representative or popular control over the sovereign. Parliament was first concerned with the taxes imposed upon the people and only later with the supervision of the King's personal outlays or expenditures. One might infer that the Magna Charta (1215) was the rudimentary beginning of one aspect of budgeting, namely, popular control over taxes to be levied. The Revolution of 1688 in Britain precipitated the right of Parliament to authorize all expenditures made by the Crown and hence rounded out the other aspect of budgeting, namely, the planning of expenditures. But it was not until 1822 that full-fledged budgeting began in the British government.[2] At that time the formal governmental budget was prepared by the Chancellor of the Exchequer and presented to Parliament. In British practice, money spent upon public service is spent by the Crown, but all money is granted by Parliament. Furthermore, Parliament will not grant any money unless requested by a minister representing the Crown and for a purpose clearly specified in the minister's request. This represents the beginning of the practice whereby the executive prepares and submits the budget, the legislative branch of government approves the budget, and the executive branch administers the approved budget. This remains a desired method of procedure in public education in America today.

The emergence of representative governments on the European continent was likewise related to governmental budgeting. It occurred in these countries at a subsequent period and in a somewhat modified form from British practice.

A full-fledged national budget in the United States was not realized until about 100 years following its adoption in Britain. Our founding fathers were wrestling with the problem of national organization at a time when England did not yet have a fully developed budget system. Furthermore, the wealth of America was great and the concern for the discipline of a budget during times of rather large treasury surpluses was not consistent with a robust, wealthy, youthful nation. Deficits were noted in the last decade of the nineteenth century. The need for economy and efficiency in national financial operations became even more apparent during Taft's administration (1908–1912) as deficits replaced surpluses and public antipathy toward graft and corruption reached new heights. In 1909 the Senate appointed a committee to investigate deficits, and later that year President Taft called for a commission "to inquire into the methods of transacting the public business." The commission reported in 1912 and revealed detailed information on the character of governmental expenditures and recommended the adoption of a national budget. The commission viewed the budget as "a document for congressional action, an instrument of control and management by the Chief Executive, and a basis for the administration of departments and agencies."[3] A peculiar set of political circumstances deferred the establishment of a national budget system until the successful passage of the Budget and Accounting Act of 1921. President Harding said of this act in his first budget message that it was ". . . the greatest reformation in governmental practices since the beginning of the Republic." Governmental budgeting became one of the major processes by which the use of public resources was planned and controlled.

Budgeting in municipal and state governments actually preceded that in national affairs. The influences which contributed to the development of the federal budget were similar to those which brought about city and state budgets at an earlier date. The National Municipal League drafted a model municipal corporation in 1899, and one feature of this model was a municipal budget system. The establishment of the New York Bureau of Municipal Research in 1906 gave even greater impetus to the development of city budgeting. The bureau's proposal for budgeting for New York City's health activities met with favor and was soon extended to other city functions.[4] The development of city budgeting was part of the reform movement to instill responsibility in government operations and to fight "boss rule," graft, and corruption. As city expenditures grew, businessmen became more concerned with governmental affairs and added their influence to promote better business procedures. It is estimated that by the mid-1920's most major American cities went through a reform in municipal finance practices and established some sort of a budget system.[5]

State governments did not face any serious financial pressure until the start of the twentieth century. The typical state was a comparatively small tax-collecting and tax-expending unit of government until the turn of the century. The forces operating on cities and the

[1] Jesse Burkhead, *Government Budgeting*, New York: John Wiley & Sons, Inc., 1956, p. 2.

[2] *Ibid.*, pp. 2–6.

[3] *Ibid.*, pp. 9–12.

[4] *Ibid.*, p. 13.

[5] *Ibid.*

federal government had their effect on the state level as well and began to become more intense after 1910. Ohio, in 1910, was the first state to have a state budget law, followed by Wisconsin and California in 1911. Only six states enacted budgetary laws by 1913, but the movement gained strength so that by 1920, 44 states had adopted some kind of improvement in budgeting.[6]

It is clear that the budgeting in United States governmental affairs is an early twentieth century phenomenon even though its use was evident in the nation's private business and industry prior to that time. It was inevitable that interest in more careful financial planning through the development of budgeting was to spread to public school districts of America as well. Local school districts were among the last of the various governmental units to develop and use the budget. Perhaps part of this delay can be attributed to the relative simplicity of operation and small sums for school expenditures prior to 1920. Another factor was the inadequate executive powers possessed by most school superintendents during the early decades of the twentieth century. Control of finances was jealously guarded by most school boards and the superintendent had little authority to develop financial planning to the degree necessary. What Burkhead declared about the development of budgeting in cities could apply to school districts: "The growth of the budget system in American cities was hampered by the relatively inadequate executive powers possessed by most mayors. In the cities, financial authority was typically concentrated in the city councils; the mayor did not possess more than authority to sit with or to be represented in the finance committee of the council. Therefore, the adoption of the budget system necessitated a reorganization of city government and a redistribution of authority. Budget reform and governmental reorganization usually went hand in hand in efforts to improve the financial practises of the cities."[7]

Twente[8] made the first comprehensive study of city school budgetary practices in 1922. His sample of 263 cities disclosed a variety of budgetary requirements, procedures, and practices followed by local school boards. It can be concluded that budgetary practices in local school systems prior to 1920 were relatively undeveloped and nonstandardized. Improvements followed, although quite slowly. There was evidence of greater uniformity in state budgetary requirements and practices in city school systems during the 1930's, but even then public school budgetary practices in most school districts left much to be desired. The earliest bibliography on budgeting, compiled by Clark[9] in 1926, listed 481 references and indicated a growing wave of interest among educators. Many others have been prepared by other writers since then. It can be said that nowhere in school administration has the literature been more voluminous, more helpful, and more rapidly growing than in budgeting. At the same time, the recommendations found in the research and literature have been applied and practiced in a very limited way. Many of the earlier studies on school budgeting were of the survey type and were concerned with the status quo in city school districts. State-wide studies are of more recent vintage, starting in New Mexico in 1937 and including such states as Illinois, Pennsylvania, Colorado, Nebraska, and Missouri.

PRESENT STATUS OF SCHOOL BUDGETING

The fiscal year for the school budget has not changed much during the twentieth century. In 1953–1954, 35 states (including Alaska) had a fiscal year which started on July 1 and ended on June 30 the year following.[10] Thirty-nine states (including Alaska) prescribed a budget form to be used by school districts. Thirty-six states (including Alaska) required that the local school district file a copy of their budget with the state education agency. In most cases, this was for informational purposes only. In very few states did the state have authority to revise or change any item of the budget. In 21 states, no county or local nonschool agency was empowered to act upon the school budget. In general, it can be said that state educational departments or nonschool agencies were entitled to a copy of the budget for information purposes and could do little about it.

FISCO-EDUCATIONAL PLANNING

Planning in public education must of necessity be of the long-range variety with continuing modifications to compensate for the sudden and dramatic shifts in our dynamic culture. Realizing the goals of public

[6] *Ibid.,* p. 23.
[7] *Ibid.,* p. 14.
[8] John W. Twente, *Budgetary Procedure for Local School Systems,* Montpelier, Vt.: Capitol Press, 1922.

[9] Harold F. Clark, *A Cross Indexed Bibliography on School Budgets,* Bloomington: Indiana University, 1926, Bulletin no. 5, vol. 2.
[10] Clayton D. Hutchins and Albert R. Munse, *Public School Finance Programs of the United States,* U.S. Office of Education, Miscellaneous no. 22, Washington, D.C.: U.S. Government Printing Office, 1955, pp. 50–52.

education requires many years. Although the plans and benefits of social services such as public education are not as easily described or as readily apparent as a red fire truck or a concrete roadway, they remain matters of primary importance nonetheless. If long-range educational plans are to be something more than idle daydreams, they must be translated into human, material, and fiscal resources needed to make them blossom into reality. Educational and financial planning for any period of time, long or short, go hand in hand. Planning for financial resources has meager significance without an accompanying statement of educational goals. Likewise educational plans have little practical significance without consideration of their financial impact.

The term *fisco-educational planning* is introduced to denote the type of planning which involves educational and financial considerations in a continuous fashion for an indeterminate period of time. Simpson and Lake[11] described what they called the "budgetary process" as "an administrative process devoted to weighing the relative merits of financial outlays as they relate to an educational plan." Others refer to the same idea using the term "long-term budgeting." The term fisco-educational planning implies much the same and is recommended to reduce the double meanings which some of these existing terms have acquired. Thus "budgetary process" is used by Burke[12] to denote the continuous process of (1) presentation and adoption, (2) administration, and (3) appraisal of the budget. In this volume, budgetary process shall mean the process of developing a budget for a definite period of time such as a fiscal year. Fisco-educational planning refers to the continuous process covering an indeterminate period of time during which educational programs and financial resources are related to each other to aid administrators in charting a desired course of action for the educational institution.

THE BUDGET DOCUMENT

The budget is the general financial and educational plan for a stated period of time. It evolves from the continuously developing, never ceasing, fisco-educational planning. It represents, in effect, the merger of educational and financial plans for a given time span. In other words, it is the fiscal interpretation of the edu-

cational program envisioned for a particular fiscal year.

The budget document is a precise statement of the budget for the period. The popular conception of a budget is the budget document. The introduction of the term fisco-educational planning makes it unnecessary to differentiate between the two terms on any other grounds than that the budget is the more general and the budget document the more specific term. The budget document is the instrument used to present to an authorizing body a comprehensive financial plan based on a known educational program for a given period of time. At the time of its presentation to the school board by the superintendent, it is looked upon as a plan of attack. When adopted by the board of education and supported by the appropriations necessary to activate it, the budget document becomes the ruler of financial acts that follow. At this point it becomes an instrument of financial control over the future expenditure acts necessary to fulfill the educational objectives. Actually, the budget system has little value in school administration without budgetary control over future fiscal operations. The budget document can be regarded as the means and budgetary control as the end.

The budget document for the period in question will contain a balanced statement of estimated revenues (or receipts) and estimated expenditures (or disbursements), the justification of the expenditures anticipated based on the desired educational program, and the exhibits reporting in some detail the current financial condition of various funds at the start of the fiscal period. How the budget document comes into being is the matter of next concern.

THE BUDGETARY PROCESS

The budgetary process or budget cycle represents the process of evolution of a budget from its conception to its execution and also its inevitable appraisal. The specific phases of budget development are somewhat cyclical in character. These phases are given different names and organized in particular ways by the various writers on budgeting. In this volume the budgetary process or budget cycle shall consist of the following phases:

1. *Preparation.* An executive function.
2. *Presentation.* An executive function.
3. *Adoption and authorization.* A legislative function.
4. *Administration or execution.* An executive function.
5. *Appraisal.* A combined executive-legislative function.

---

[11] Alfred D. Simpson and Ernest G. Lake, "The Budgetary Process," in R. L. Johns and E. L. Morphet (eds.), *Problems and Issues in Public School Finance,* New York: Teachers College, Columbia University, 1952, p. 327.

[12] Arvid J. Burke, *Financing Public Schools in the United States,* New York: Harper & Brothers, rev. ed., 1957, p. 438.

PREPARATION OF THE BUDGET DOCUMENT

Responsibility for budget preparation should rest with the superintendent of schools. A wealth of information on the program desired and resources needed must be available. In larger systems, the assistant superintendent in charge of business services is delegated responsibility for accumulation of all the facts pertinent to the development of the budget document for the fiscal period. Planning the education and financial program for a given fiscal year is greatly facilitated in systems where long-range or fisco-educational planning is in evidence.

The three main factors to be considered in budget preparation are (1) the educational program for the period in question; (2) the estimate of expenditures (or disbursements) necessary to realize the educational program; and (3) the estimate of revenues (or receipts) anticipated from local, state, or federal sources which are needed to support the anticipated expenditures (or disbursements). These factors are often referred to as the educational plan, the expenditure (or disbursement) plan, and the revenue (or receipts) plan.

Strange as it may seem, the educational plan appears to be the most difficult to express in the budget document. There is substantial agreement that this factor is perhaps the most important part of budget preparation, but very few superintendents include a statement of the educational program to be realized with the budget developed. It is difficult to defend professionally a budget request without justification based on educational goals envisioned. If the board finds it necessary to reduce the total amount of the budget, it begs the question of which educational service shall be curtailed or eliminated. Intelligent evaluation of the budget or reduction in size of the budget to fit the community pocketbook is impaired seriously if the educational plan is not included in the budget. A statement of general objectives of education is only the beginning. Sweeping generalizations must be broken down into specific implications for action before they have meaning in budget preparation and justification. Thus, it can be said that one purpose of the educational plan is "to have students think and communicate clearly." This is a worthy goal but precisely what does it mean in terms of regular teachers to be employed, remedial teaching staff needed, equipment and supplies to be purchased, etc.? Thus, one of the more specific purposes arising out of this general objective would be to provide the remedial services necessary to help secondary school youth whose records show difficulties in oral communication. This can be translated into the number of speech therapists, special rooms, and special equipment needed to achieve the specific purpose. The educational plan is much too big to be spelled out with the degree of precision necessary by the superintendent alone or the business manager alone. It points to the need for involving the entire teaching force of the system in working with and through the administrative and supervisory personnel in the preparation of the educational plan for the fiscal year. The time needed to achieve this will be discussed in a subsequent paragraph concerned with the budget calendar.

Preparing the educational plan is only the first step. The program of educational action must be translated into reasonably accurate expenditure estimates. The expenditure plan is just another way of expressing the educational plan. It is difficult to translate the quantitative and qualitative aspects of a school program into precise expenditure requirements. The material resources in particular—such as books, supplies, and equipment to be used to realize the educational plan —present problems in precise estimation for the fiscal period in question. When prices can be expected to remain stable and up-to-date catalogues are available, cost estimates can be made with a fairly high degree of precision. In times of considerable flux, the accuracy of cost estimates is materially impaired. Many districts without a clear-cut educational plan base anticipated expenditures on what was spent the last year or the year previous. A fuzzy estimated increase or the same amount as expended in the previous year is put down for the ensuing year. Comparisons have value, but they should not be the sole determiner of what is justifiable for the next year.

This is not to infer that the educational plan must be accepted without modification or that needed funds must be made available for every bit of the school program envisioned. There is the inevitable paring down of requests to fit the community pocketbook. The growth of the educational program must be gradual as well as justifiable.

In view of the difficulty in making a precise expenditure plan, some argue for the inclusion of "emergency" or "contingency" funds within the budget. Others point out that a large contingency fund defeats the very purpose of budgeting. It leads to what is known as "padding" and if "padding" is suspected, boards may well lose confidence in the reliability as well as the validity of executive-prepared school budgets. Some states prohibit the provision for contingency funds. Simpson and Lake[13] indicate that the amount of the "emergency" or contingency fund should be limited to 1 or 2 percent of the total school budget and

[13] Simpson and Lake, *op. cit.,* pp. 334, 335.

that utilization of such funds shall be made only with the approval of the school board. Where the expenditures must be made from the "emergency" or contingency fund, approval should be sought before any obligation is incurred. Clearly, the difficulty in precisely determining the expenditure plan points to the need for some money for emergencies or contingencies which are more likely to be experienced during inflationary periods. The argument revolves around the size of the amount budgeted for such purposes. The practice of annually listing very large sums of money under the "emergency" or similar titles and spending them without regard to emergency needs cannot be condoned. Sloppy budget practices are sure to result where large contingency or emergency funds are set aside. Careful inventory practices and preventative maintenance programs, as well as extended and well-developed budgetary procedures, can hold emergencies to a minimum.

It should not be construed that no consideration is given to the revenue plan until expenditures are known. The three phases of budget preparation go on at the same time. You cannot ignore one while preparing the other. In determining the revenues to be available for the fiscal year, an estimation must be made of anticipated state aids and other nontax revenues. Nontax revenues includes fees, fines, rentals, etc. The sum of these items subtracted from the accepted expenditure estimates results in the estimated local tax burden. How large a local tax burden the community will bear is dependent upon the value that is attached to public education. Willingness of consumers to spend more of their incomes on public education through increased school taxes will determine the top school tax limits since most state laws do not do so. Consumer willingness is related to the economic life of the community and the nation as well as to the value system. The demands of other governmental services purchased through tax funds likewise cannot be ignored in arriving at what the local school tax burden shall be. At any rate, in the absence of specific statutory enactments to the contrary, the maximum size of the school tax must be regarded as a subjective matter, based on the value system, the economic condition of the culture, and the demands for other governmental services. It follows that expenditures must be pared down where necessary to fit the revenue plan.

Burke pointed out that "perfect budgetary balance is impossible because both the expenditure and the revenue plans involve judgment and prediction, and because certain variables, such as prices, continue to operate after the budget has been adopted. The best that can be expected is relative balance with receipts and expenditures almost equalling each other."[14] In this sense, a "balanced" budget is a relative term indicating that there is a close approximation between the expenditure and the revenue plans. In schools, a balanced budget usually means one which has a slight excess of revenue over expenditures at the end of the budgetary period.

Legal requirements on dates for budget preparation are concerned usually with budget approval or publication dates. Statutes do not prescribe the period of time required for budget preparation. Budgets should be submitted for approval by no later than the start of the fiscal year to be covered by budgetary control. Budget documents prepared a week or two prior to the start of the fiscal year cannot hope to reach the full potential of the budget system.

The length of period necessary to prepare the budget document carefully will vary with the complexity of the system and the personnel available for the task. In one sense, planning a new budget document for the ensuing fiscal year starts the moment the budget for the present fiscal year takes effect. In this sense, budget preparation is a continuous process and approaches what has been called fisco-educational planning. The *formal* preparation period for a new budget document should start at least six months prior to the start of the fiscal year it will cover. It usually begins with a call to various school building principals or central office department heads to prepare estimates for educational plans and expenditures for the next school year. It ends with the budget adoption. The suggested calendar shown at the top of page 23 might prevail.

A comparable budget preparation and submission calendar for the United States budget was described by Burkhead as shown on page 23.

The format of the prepared budget varies among the school districts in the various states. It is often dictated by state requirements. At times state budget requirements are based on outmoded forms which no longer fit the needs of existing school districts. Where this occurs, a more functional format must be prepared by the district, even though the required budgetary forms will be used as the mode of reporting to state officials. The budget document should be based on the functional character classifications used in accounting, auditing, and other financial reports.

It is recommended that the revenue and nonrevenue receipts accounting classifications adopted by the state or recommended by such national agencies as the U.S. Office of Education be used. It is hoped that eventually all school districts will use the following Expenditure Accounts: Administration, Instruction, Attendance

[14] Burke, *op. cit.,* p. 438.

CALENDAR FOR THE PREPARATION OF THE BUDGET FOR FISCAL YEAR JULY 1,
1960 TO JUNE 30, 1961

Date	Activity
January 1, 1960 (or thereabouts)	Call for estimates from building principals or others for educational and expenditure plans for fiscal year 1960–1961.
February 1, 1960	Due date for estimates from building principals and others.
March 1, 1960	Building principals and others meet with budget preparation officers to reconcile differences.
April 1, 1960	Formal consolidated budget document presented to superintendent and central office staff.
May 1, 1960	Budget document presented to board of education for discussion.
June 1–30, 1960	Period of publication, hearing, and formal adoption.

PREPARATION AND SUBMISSION OF THE U.S. BUDGET
(FOR FISCAL 1957)[15]

Date	Activity
Prior to April 1955	Bureau (unit) planning for fiscal 1957.
April 1955	Budget call from departmental budget offices.
May 1955	Consolidation of department's field budget with over-all budget for department.
June 1955	Over-all budget policy development; clearance from President; revenue estimates from Treasury.
	Bureau of the Budget; Director's policy letter; call for estimates; announcement of ceilings.
July–August 1955	Departmental review, hearings and adjustments.
September 30, 1955	Departments submit appropriation requests.
September 30–November 15, 1955	Bureau of the Budget examiners' review.
October 10–November 20, 1955	Hearings in the Bureau of the Budget.
October–November 1955	Review by the Director of the Bureau of the Budget.
November–December 1955	Presidential review. Preparation of the budget message. Preparation of the budget document.
January 1956	Submission of the budget to Congress.

and Health Services, Pupil Transportation Services, Operation of Plant, Maintenance of Plant, Fixed Charges, Food Services and Student Body Activities, Community Services, Capital Outlay, Debt Services, and Outgoing Transfer Accounts. These classifications are described more completely in Chapters 4 and 7. The expenditures recommended by the superintendent in what is often referred to as the "executive budget" for the forthcoming fiscal year as well as those actually

15 Burkhead, *op. cit.*, p. 89.

made in the present and in previous years should be placed side by side for each line item of the budget. A blank column should follow these entries for each expenditure classification or line item of the budget. The blank space is needed to enter the precise amount approved or appropriated for each line item of the budget by the board of education.

A statement of the procedures used in preparing the Des Moines public school budget for 1958–1959 follows:

FINANCIAL REQUIREMENTS OF THE DES MOINES
PUBLIC SCHOOLS FOR THE FISCAL YEAR 1958–1959[16]

A. HOW SCHOOL BUDGET ESTIMATES ARE PREPARED

There are three basic steps involved in the preparation of any budget. These three steps are as follows:

1. The program must be decided upon; this requires the making of a comprehensive list of the various things which we would like to have or do and then determining which of these things are most important.
2. Estimates must be made as accurately as possible to determine the cost of carrying out this program; this will often require the weighing of one proposed item against another.
3. The sources of revenue must be studied to determine whether funds will be available to support the program which has been decided upon.

The preparation of the budget for the Des Moines Public Schools is a cooperative undertaking in which a great many people participate. Actually the work of budget making is carried on throughout the entire school year whenever any person connected with the school system becomes conscious of the greater needs and possibilities of the educational program. Basically every member in the community has a voice in the preparation of a public budget when he makes known to those responsible for the program any specific need or requirement. It follows that the detailed responsibility for budget organization must be delegated to certain designated individuals.

There are many staff members who are responsible for various phases of budget preparation. During April and May each of these staff members compiles and submits to the Assistant Superintendent in Charge of Finance and Statistic a detailed estimate of requirements for the following year for each of the budget accounts for which he is responsible. This list must show a detailed breakdown of expenditures for the current school year and the staff member must explain and justify any significant changes proposed in the policies now in force. Staff members must include in their budget report suggestions concerning certain items which might be eliminated from their askings, together with a statement showing the probable results if such elimination should be found necessary. Suggested changes in existing budgetary appropria-

[16] John H. Harris, Superintendent, *Annual Budget Report and Budget Estimates for the Fiscal Year 1958–1959,* Des Moines Public Schools, Des Moines, Iowa, July, 1958, pp. 1–2.

tions which would improve the educational program through the expenditure of additional funds are also proposed by these staff members.

The reports submitted by these staff members are prepared in considerable detail. Collectively they consist of more than 1,000 sheets of typed materials which fill seven large binders on file in the office of the Assistant Superintendent. The financial needs for the school system are represented by these reports since every proposed expenditure is defined in terms of its contribution to the proposed educational program. It must be recognized that the budget is more than a compilation of statistics and facts; its true purpose is to provide a background of educational outcomes which should be available to those who attend school in Des Moines, showing the financial support which is required to carry out the proposed program.

ANYONE WHO WISHES TO EVALUATE THE EDUCATIONAL PROGRAM AND ANALYZE THE BUDGETARY NEEDS PRESENTED IN THIS REPORT IS INVITED TO EXAMINE THE ORIGINAL DATA UPON WHICH THIS SUMMARY IS BASED. CERTAINLY NO BLANKET REDUCTIONS OR PROPOSED REVISIONS CAN BE CONSIDERED VALID WITHOUT THOROUGH STUDY OF ALL THE FACTS CONTAINED IN THESE REPORTS.

The facts submitted in these reports are studied carefully by the Assistant Superintendent who analyzes in detail all of the materials presented, making comparisons with expenditures for several prior years and critically examining each request for appropriations for the ensuing year. Every proposed increase is checked carefully against the salary schedules or policies which have been approved by the Board of Education and other proposed changes are subject to close scrutiny. The Superintendent of Schools and the Assistant Superintendent then hold detailed conferences with each of the administrative officers concerned. In these conferences the educational program of the department, together with its financial requirements, is discussed in considerable detail. Possible eliminations from the educational offerings are analyzed together with essential additions thereto. As an outgrowth of these conferences, a summary is prepared showing the proposed appropriation for each of the 241 operating budget accounts as presented in this report. This compilation shows the total estimated financial requirement of the school district for the ensuing fiscal year except for payments for the building program which are made from schoolhouse funds.

It is unfortunate that the sum of the estimates presented by staff members is always more than it seems possible to provide and the long slow process of elimination begins. It is frequently necessary to disregard what is best for boys and girls in order to reduce the preliminary budget, solely for the sake of economy. A reading of the detailed budget estimates as submitted by administrative heads of departments shows the types of activities which have been eliminated. Some of the reductions which have been made have been discussed in the comments which are shown in Section III of this report; however, the full significance of these cuts can be understood only from an examination of the detailed budget data as submitted by department heads and from conferences with these supervisors and with principals and teachers.

The next step is to provide members of the Board of Education with a preliminary report of budget needs for study and discussion. This group of citizens, representing the school district as a whole, must adopt a budget which provides for essential educational needs of the school system in the best manner possible which is consistent with their judgment of the willingness and ability of the community to support such a program. Members of the Board of Education feel this obligation keenly and are reluctant to handicap the educational program of the schools. The budget which is presented here represents a compromise on the part of the members of the Board of Education between educational needs and financial ability.

PRESENTATION

Presentation or submission of the budget document is also an executive activity. A part of this phase of the budgetary process is often regulated by state laws or state departments of education rules and regulations. One authority to which the budget must be presented is, of course, the board of education.

The executive budget, or the budget as prepared by the superintendent, is the basis upon which the board makes its final decisions. The superintendent's presentation to the board must be carefully prepared by him or a staff member such as the school business official. It implies that there will be the necessary explanatory material to justify each item within the budget.

A letter of transmittal is usually included. Within the letter the superintendent states matters pertinent to understanding the budget document to follow. Excerpts from a letter of transmittal to the Des Moines, Iowa, Board of Education follow:

DES MOINES PUBLIC SCHOOLS[17]
Office of the Superintendent
July 15, 1958

TO: Members of the Board of Education
FROM: John H. Harris, Superintendent of Schools
SUBJECT: Annual budget report for fiscal year 1958–1959

The following pages will present the budget proposals for the school year 1958–1959. This procedure is in accordance with the School Code of the State of Iowa adopted in 1954 and set forth in Chapter 24, Section 24.9. The school code governs the operations of the various school districts of the State of Iowa.

The preparation of this proposed school budget has extended over a long period of time and deliberate effort has been exercised to keep appropriations within a safe minimum. Mounting instructional costs, together with those of maintenance, operation, and conservative expansion, present difficult problems and challenges to budget makers. Careful study of

[17] *Ibid.*, pp. i, ii, iii.

this proposed budget will reveal the magnitude of responsibility and insight displayed by those directors, staff members, and many others who assisted in the compilation of the detail. It has been well done, and Mr. W. C. Findley, Assistant Superintendent in Charge of Finance and Statistics, is to be commended for his contribution.

[Paragraph omitted.]

As a growing organization it is essential that appropriate increases be allowed in various budget accounts. Some items of expenditure have been reclassified and a few new ones added.

This budget reflects some increases in the number of personnel and the size of our ever-growing plant. When school opens in September, sixty-nine additional personnel will be employed and we will occupy, for the first time, several new buildings and additions. They are Cowles Elementary School with ten classrooms, Garton Elementary School with eighteen classrooms, Mitchell Elementary School with fourteen classrooms, Tech High School, one of the largest schools in the state, and the ten-room addition at Rice Elementary School, five-room addition at Howe Elementary School, and eighteen additional rooms at Franklin Junior High School. These new facilities continue to increase the problems of administration, management, and maintenance.

A school budget expresses the philosophy of education designed by a Board of Education and its administrators. This budget reflects a broad and comprehensive philosophy. It provides educational service for all the children of the community at minimum costs. This budget is not ultra-conservative, nor is it cloaked with extravagance in any section.

This year our costs per pupil were:

Elementary, $282.00   Junior High, $365.00
Senior High, $432.00

We estimate the increase for 1958–1959 to be approximately 6½% or an average of $21.00 per child.

Education, like progress, does not move in reverse. It goes forward. We must keep ourselves abreast of the times and put into practice the best and most economical methods of operation. Educational costs continue to spiral upward and efficiency should become our by-word, but not to the neglect of our major purpose, namely, to provide adequate educational opportunity for every child in the community.

Salary adjustments account for the largest single increased expenditure in this budget. It is a parallel to all business and industry. The business of education is fast becoming one of our most important and largest community enterprises. It is allied with our survival. During the past decade we have made desirable progress in the salary lag for professional personnel and in the years ahead we'll be expected to do considerably more. We as citizens of a city, state, and nation must put forth great effort to help build a strong teaching profession and to increase the supply of qualified teachers for our youth and the preservation of our Republic. Teaching, as a profession, must be made secure and attractive.

[Paragraph omitted.]

Our program of building libraries will have an impetus this year. A Director of Libraries will be in charge of this important task and her major responsibility will be to assist teachers with the improvement of instruction. Our Library Development Program will be a major item in the budgets for the next decade if we are to provide central libraries in keeping with the demands of the day.

[Paragraph omitted.]

Food Service Management has now become a responsibility of the Board of Education and the administrative costs hereafter will be reflected in the budget. However, food costs, operations, and sales income will be accounted for in an auxiliary budget and will not be considered as a part of tax appropriations and expenditures. This phase of school administration has become one of major importance and during the coming school year will involve expenditures estimated to be in excess of one million dollars. Our goal in food service is to provide wholesome meals and to be self-sustaining, making no profit and sustaining no loss.

Educational television is quickly becoming a reality in our community. During this year our station will be occupying its place on the air waves. The results will be well worth the expenditures. A new kind of classroom will emerge and an enriched program will be offered in our schools and the schools of Greater Des Moines. TV Channel 11 will be an open circuit available to all who wish to tune in. Eventually the adults of our community will be numbered among our most interested students and they will have first-hand information about the teaching procedures and instruction going on in our schools. Patients in sick rooms and hospitals and others unable to attend regular classes will find educational television a great source of learning and inspiration. We anticipate that educational television will increase our effectiveness as an educational institution.

Transportation costs within this budget reveal substantial increases. New rates were given to us in March of this year and every sign points upward for the future. The transportation problem and cost is one of major importance for Board study.

[Three paragraphs omitted.]

As a member of the Board of Education you can be proud of your role in guiding the educational program of our community. The citizens of the school district have charged you with a great responsibility and look to you for leadership.

The budget proposal is submitted for your consideration, study, suggestions, and modifications as you direct, and for public review. Your final adoption of the budget will set the pattern of operation for the coming year.

Mort and Reusser indicated that there were at least four other types of agencies to which presentation is a matter of law in some states. These are:

1. Presentation of the budget to some person or board for the purpose of making clerical corrections only.
2. Presentation to local, county, or state board or officials who have authority to increase or decrease the budgetary allotments.
3. Presentation of the budget or estimates to the electors of the district for their approval and for purposes of levying the necessary local tax.
4. Presentation to some county or state official or board for purposes of making necessary levy after the budget has been approved by the local board of education.[18]

A fifth type of presentation would be to the public through newspaper ads or public hearings or both. These are also prescribed by law in most states. Studies of these matters indicate that school budget notices carry too little information to promote public understanding of the school budget. Public hearings on the school budget are poorly attended. Some states define a "protest period" during which time taxpayers may file a legal protest against the inclusion of certain budgetary items. Such laws need not impede financial operation if the protest period is of short duration or no longer than one month after the start of the fiscal year and if the decisions are rendered promptly.

ADOPTION OF THE BUDGET

The adoption or authorization of the budget rests with the legislative body or the board of education. It was pointed out in Chapter 1 that the annual school budget was subject to the review of a nonschool agency in 46 percent of the cities. The larger the city the more likely it was that the budget would be subject to review. In 18 percent of the city systems the school budget had to be approved by the reviewing agency as submitted and approved by the board. Bowler[19] concluded that there was little difference in the quality of the budget or the budgetary process in the New England schools that were fiscally independent as opposed to those who were fiscally dependent. There is, likewise, little evidence to vindicate state review and approval of budgets as a means of expenditure control. Most authorities are in agreement that individuals unfamiliar with local school needs and removed from the influence of local public opinion are seldom capable of exercising sound discretionary judgment on school budgets.

All this adds up to the declaration that the approval or adoption of the school budget should rest with the local board of education. The board's decision on the budget should be made known to others for informational rather than for outside control purposes. In most cases, state review and approval of local school district budgets are for informational purposes only. However,

[18] Paul R. Mort and Walter C. Reusser, *Public School Finance,* New York: McGraw-Hill Book Company, 1951, pp. 157, 158.

[19] John Francis Bowler, *School-Municipal Fiscal Relations and Their Effect on the Budget and Budgetary Procedures,* Doctoral Dissertation, Cambridge: Graduate School of Education, Harvard University, 1950.

in some states, such as Alabama, the local school budget must be approved by the state superintendent of public instruction. In Louisiana the Department of Education can change any item in the budget. In New Mexico the Tax Commission can change any amount in the budget. In most other cases little is done by the state or local nonschool agencies to change the school budget.

Board of education action on the budget should indicate appropriations approved for each line item of the budget and approval of the revenue plan which will set the school tax rate as well. It is desirable that these actions be made with the clarity necessary to avoid confusion and subsequent legal entanglements.

ADMINISTRATION OF THE SCHOOL BUDGET

The budget is sometimes confused with appropriation and control of expenditures. The budget is not, in a precise sense, the ruler of operations. It is the plan upon which the appropriation may be founded. After the estimated expenditures and receipts have been presented, the board approves (and appropriates by such actions amounts of money for) various items of the budget. It is the appropriation act which makes the budget document a controlling instrument in financial management.

Following the approval of the budget and the appropriation act, the various budget allotments are transferred to the accounts of the school district. These entries call attention to the original appropriation or authorization for each item of budget operation. As expenditures are made they are accounted for at given periods of time, with the amount of the unencumbered balance remaining.

The administration of the budget is an executive act. It should not be necessary for the administrator to seek formal approval from the board of education for each pencil or pad of paper purchased by the school district. The authorization to expend the amounts appropriated and as stated in the budget document should be delegated to the chief executive officer of the board of education. So long as he expends funds within budgetary allotments, there should be no need for board approval prior to purchase. However, where there are extra-budgetary purchases, prior board approval should be mandatory.

The failure of many small school districts to plan carefully and adopt a school budget results in unnecessarily stringent purchasing controls over the chief executive officer. Budgets can be effective means for controlling the activities of an enterprise when the amounts budgeted are given sufficient appropriation by the authorized body. The budget represents the means, and the budget control is the end result. A budget without budgetary control has little, if any, value in school administration. Likewise, budgetary control without a budget is meaningless.

APPRAISAL OF THE BUDGET

The appraisal of the budget document for the fiscal period in question is a combined board of education and superintendent function. Primary responsibility rests with the legislative body, however. At this stage the board can determine to what extent the financial resources allocated for the given period of time have been utilized to realize the educational plan. A well-made budget, under favorable circumstances, will show a balance at the end of the period at least equal to that at the beginning of the fiscal period. The board can judge and demand explanation for amounts expended over and above that actually appropriated. If some portions of the educational program have not been realized due to meager budgetary appropriations, this too should be noted and remedied in the next fiscal period.

A SAMPLE BUDGET DOCUMENT

A budget must show the educational, expenditure, and revenue plans. For purposes of illustration a summary of the amounts allocated for the various expenditure classifications only along with the anticipated revenues will be shown. The figure used will be rounded off whereas actual amounts to the dollar will be shown in the budget. Examples of more detailed parts of the budget with justifications will follow. Illustrations of what should be included in an educational plan and also the letter of transmittal were given in other parts of this chapter. Note that the district on page 28 does not include or provide Community Services within its budget.

| I. Expenditure Plan | 1957–1958 | | 1958–1959 | |
	Amount Budget Appropriated	Actual Expenditure	Amount Recommended for Appropriation	Approved and Appropriated by Board Action
A. ADMINISTRATION	$ 325,000	$ 320,000	$ 355,000	_____
B. INSTRUCTION	9,100,000	9,105,000	9,850,000	_____
C. ATTENDANCE AND HEALTH SERVICES	372,000	370,000	400,000	_____
D. PUPIL TRANSPORTATION SERVICES	500,000	490,000	550,000	_____
E. OPERATION OF PLANT	1,495,000	1,505,000	1,610,000	_____
F. MAINTENANCE OF PLANT	540,000	530,000	535,000	_____
G. FIXED CHARGES	80,000	82,000	79,000	_____
H. CAPITAL OUTLAY	425,000	440,000	415,000	_____
I. DEBT SERVICE	2,300,000	2,275,000	2,200,000	_____
Total All Expenditures	$15,137,000	$15,117,000	$15,994,000	_____

II. Revenue Plan	Actual Revenue 1956–1957	Actual Revenue 1957–1958	Estimated Revenue 1958–1959
A. Revenue Receipts			
1. Local District Tax Levy	$12,338,000	$12,950,000	$13,780,000
2. Tuition	102,000	119,000	100,000
3. County Aid	125,000	126,000	125,000
4. State Aids:			
Flat Grants	1,008,000	1,013,000	1,010,000
Equalization	none	340,000	340,000
Special Education	111,000	114,000	115,000
Transportation	340,000	342,000	410,000
5. Federal Aids	65,000	88,000	84,000
B. Nonrevenue Receipts			
Miscellaneous	30,000	29,000	30,000
Total	$14,119,000	$15,121,000	$15,994,000

This summary statement leads to a detailed breakdown of each major accounting classification for expenditures. Thus, INSTRUCTION can be detailed as per the following *partial* outline:

B. INSTRUCTION—200 SERIES

	Expenditures 1957–1958	Amount Sought 1958–1959
210—*Salaries*		
211—Principals	$ 422,000	$ 446,900
212—Consultants or Supervisors	105,000	140,000
213—Teachers	7,500,000	8,250,000
220—*Textbooks*	78,000	124,000
230—*School Libraries and Audio-Visual Materials*	11,000	65,000
240—*Teaching Supplies*	60,000	90,000

A specific budget entry for salaries paid to principals would be as follows:

Account 211—Salaries, Principals

	1957–1958		1958–1959	
Appropriation	$420,000	Amount Recommended for Appropriation	$446,900
Expenditures	422,000	Number of Personnel	55
Number of Personnel	52		

The principal is in daily contact with parents and pupils. He directs the work of the instructional staff in the buildings. A full-time principal is assigned to each of the 14 junior and senior high schools. Twenty-one of the larger elementary schools have a full-time principal and other elementary schools are assigned so that no principal has more than two buildings. For this year three additional elementary school principals have been added because three additional elementary schools are to be opened.

Another illustration would be:

Account 213—Salaries, Teachers

	1957–1958		1958–1959	
Appropriation	$7,600,000	Appropriation Sought	$8,250,000
Expenditures	7,500,000	Personnel	1410
Personnel	1365		

It is estimated that the enrollment in September will be approximately 1000 greater than a year ago. It is obvious that additional teachers must be provided. Counselors in junior and senior high schools equivalent to one for every seven teachers are also provided for.

In March the Board of Education amended the salary schedule for classroom teachers by granting adjustments which it was estimated would increase the average salary paid classroom teachers, as compared with last year, by 7.5 per cent. The average salary paid classroom teachers for the year just closed was $5400; it is estimated that the average for the current year will be $5800.

It must be understood that the teachers now being employed are better qualified than ever before; no new teacher has been employed this year with less than a bachelor's degree or the equivalent. This is to be desired but means higher paid teachers. Presently employed teachers are acquiring more professional preparation and experience. Salaries should be adjusted for this purpose as well.

In common with other school systems in the country, we are faced every year with the problem of supply and demand. There are not enough qualified teachers to staff all schools in the nation. If we are to secure the necessary number of teachers to staff every classroom in our district, it is necessary to offer a salary which is sufficient to induce prospective teachers to come to our schools. The certainty of increasing enrollments will demand additional teachers every year. It makes inevitable advances in the salary schedule year after year in order to obtain the required number of teachers.

Teachers are allowed a number of days off without loss of pay for illness or for other reasons specified in rules of the Board of Education. For the current year expenditures for this purpose are being set up as a separate budget account. It is estimated that for the current year, the number of days of such pay will amount to 9500, a little less than an average of seven days per teacher; since the rate of pay for substitute teachers is $16 per day the appropriation for this purpose is based upon this estimate. Of necessity this budget account varies from year to year, depending upon the prevalence of epidemics and other circumstances requiring the absence of teachers.

SUMMARY

The budget is the very heart of fiscal management. It is more than the arithmetical presentation of anticipated expenditures and revenues for a given fiscal period. It is the fiscal interpretation of the educational program.

Budgets came into being when and where there existed a need for economy and efficiency in complex governmental affairs. They developed first in the government of England and then a hundred years later were adopted in American governmental operations. The school districts were among the last governmental units to employ budgets as an instrument of planning and control of resources.

Fisco-educational planning is a continuous process of relating educational programs to available financial resources. It is an aid in plotting the desired course of action for an educational institution. The budget document describes the financial and educational plans of a stated period. It evolves from fisco-educational planning.

The budgetary process includes preparation, presentation, adoption, administration, and appraisal. The executive is primarily responsible for preparation, presentation, and administration whereas the legislative body is primarily responsible for adoption and appraisal. "Balanced budget" is a relative term which usually means a slight excess in revenues over expenditures during the fiscal year. The budget is a means of controlling future fiscal operations of an institution. Although the educational plan is considered of prime importance in preparing a school budget, it receives much less attention than the expenditure or revenue plans.

QUESTIONS

1. What are the functions of an educational budget?
2. By use of a sample budget and/or timetable, illustrate the budgetary process. Include preparation, presentation, adoption and authorization, administration and execution, and appraisal.
3. Differentiate between the planning and control functions of an educational budget.
4. What conditions may have retarded the adoption of sound budgetary processes by school districts?

SELECTED REFERENCES

Burke, Arvid J., *Financing Public Schools in the United States,* New York: Harper & Brothers, rev. ed., 1957, chap. XVI.

Burkhead, Jesse, *Government Budgeting,* New York: John Wiley & Sons, Inc., 1956, chap. 1.

Mort, Paul R., and Reusser, Walter C., *Public School Finance,* New York: McGraw-Hill Book Company, 1951, chap. 9.

Simpson, Alfred D., and Lake, Ernest G., "The Budgetary Process," in R. L. Johns and E. L. Morphet (eds.), *Problems and Issues in Public School Finance,* New York: Teachers College, Columbia University, 1952, pp. 324–358.

CHAPTER 3

Factors Influencing the Construction and Design of School Accounting Systems

FINANCIAL ACCOUNTING IS ONE OF THE PROCesses necessary for the prudent financial management of schools. The instruments essential for effective financial administration are the budget, the accounts, the audit, and the financial reports. The budget is the fiscal interpretation of the educational program for a specific period of time. When formally adopted and supported by the necessary revenue and appropriation acts, it becomes the controlling instrument over all financial transactions and operations. In the previous chapter the budget was described as the heart of financial management.

The accounts, or systems of accounting, are based on a system of records of various financial transactions. They help to reveal a picture of the educational program as it develops and as contained in the school budget, and they also indicate changes in the financial status of the district. It is the purpose of this chapter to indicate some of the factors which have a significant impact upon the development of a system of accounting for schools. Subsequent chapters will be concerned with auditing and financial reporting which complete the cycle of instruments essential to prudent financial administration.

Accounting has been defined by the Committee on Terminology of the American Institute of Accountants as "the art of recording, classifying, and summarizing in a significant manner and in terms of money, transactions and events which are, in part at least, of a financial character, and interpreting the results thereof."[1] The central aspects of accounting are the maintenance of essential records in which are summarized the financial transactions of the institution plus the reporting and interpretation of such data.

The precise nature of the records to be kept and the manner in which financial information is to be classified and summarized is dependent upon the following factors:

1. The purposes of the institution in which the accounting system is to operate.
2. The financial information required for prudent administration of the institution.
3. The principles and practices of accounting which are considered sound and valid by recognized authorities.

There is no one set of records or one inflexible bookkeeping procedure which can be employed satisfactorily in all types of institutions—private or public, large or small. Many accounting principles and standards apply to both commercial and public school accounting. Illustrations of these accounting similarities will be presented in a later section of this chapter. There are also fundamental differences between commercial or industrial concerns and governmental units, such as school districts, which are reflected in accounting design.

PUBLIC SCHOOL ACCOUNTING CONTRASTED WITH COMMERCIAL ACCOUNTING

It should be recalled that a school district is a civil subdivision of the governmental unit called the state. A school district is a type of public or govern-

[1] See Eric L. Kohler, *A Dictionary for Accountants*, Englewood Cliffs, N.J.: Prentice-Hall, Inc., 1952, p. 9.

mental corporation known as a quasi-municipal corporation. School accounting should be regarded, therefore, as a special type of governmental accounting. The purposes and unique characteristics of governmental corporations, such as school districts, must of necessity result in the design of an accounting system that is different, in certain respects, from the design of an accounting system for a private corporation or commercial accounting.

The public school district exists to provide educational services to the people residing therein. In contrast, a private corporation has as its primary purpose to earn a profit for those who have invested therein. The major uses of financial accounts in commercial corporations which aid in the attainment of corporate purposes were identified by May as follows:

1. A report of stewardship.
2. A basis for fiscal policy.
3. A determination of the legality of dividends.
4. A guide to wise dividend action.
5. A basis for granting credit.
6. Information for prospective investors in an enterprise.
7. A guide to the value of investments already made.
8. An aid to government supervision.
9. A basis for price or rate regulation.
10. A basis for taxation.[2]

It should be obvious from an examination of the list of major functions of financial accounts in commercial corporations that many would have little or no significance in the financial administration of public schools. Some of the major functions of financial record keeping for school districts, in contrast, would be: (1) ascertaining what revenues were collected and those remaining to be collected, (2) ascertaining if expenditures were made in accordance with budgetary allotments, (3) determining if the legal mandates for school financial management were met, etc.

In addition to difference in purposes there are unique characteristics of governmental corporations which contrast rather sharply with private business concerns.[3, 4] Governmental units find that legal mandates governing financial transactions are more specific, more restrictive, and exert considerably more influence upon the design of governmental accounting procedures than upon private concerns. Public laws do

regulate the financial activities of private corporations to some extent, but such laws are fewer in numbers, much broader in scope, and less concerned with the specific details of financial administration. Very often school revenues and expenditures are segregated into special funds to insure their use in accordance with legal pronouncements. This introduces a degree of inflexibility in fund accounting for governmental units that is not found in commercial fund accounting. Another illustration of the impact of legal restrictions on governmental units is found in budgeting. The preparation and execution of school district budgets and related accounting procedures are often carefully regulated by legal provisions. Seldom do state legal provisions concern themselves with the specifics of budgetary and accounting procedures for commercial corporations.

Furthermore, private corporations may borrow as much as lenders are willing to provide. State or federal laws do not specifically define the purposes of commercial borrowing. It is necessary that commercial accounting records show net assets and also the present and prospective earning power of the corporation. These items form the basis of the ability of the private corporation to borrow. Loans made to private concerns are secured by the assets of the corporation. If a private corporation defaults upon a loan, its assets may be sold to meet the creditors' demands. A school district lacks authority to borrow unless given specific authorization to do so. Its borrowing authority by law is limited in amount and in purpose. The amount of money which a district can borrow is related to taxable property valuation within the district. The precise purpose of school district borrowing is limited by law which often permits borrowing to finance construction of new buildings, purchase of equipment, procurement of sites, and purchase of school buses but little else. Furthermore, governmental property cannot be used to liquidate liabilities nor is the value of "income producing" property actually owned by the district employed as the basis of borrowing. A school district as a governmental corporation has the authority to borrow (when so granted by the legislature or constitution) without reference to assets and earning power.

Still another unique characteristic of governmental corporations is the authority to levy taxes. State laws or constitutional provisions enable school districts to levy taxes for school purposes, with statutory limitations of such taxation often defined and means of enforcement of taxes clearly stipulated. The taxes so levied must be properly accounted for. The private

[2] George O. May, *Financial Accounting: a Distillation of Experience*, New York: The Macmillan Company, 1943, pp. 3–4.

[3] Lloyd Morey and Robert P. Hackett, *Fundamentals of Governmental Accounting*, New York: John Wiley & Sons, Inc., 1951, pp. 1–19.

[4] Irving Tenner, *Municipal and Governmental Accounting*, Englewood Cliffs, N.J.: Prentice-Hall, Inc., 3rd ed., 1955, pp. 1–4.

corporation has no authority to enforce purchase of goods or services from which revenues are derived much less the right to levy taxes.

To recapitulate, the purposes and unique characteristics of governmental corporations, such as school districts, are such as to necessitate accounting systems that differ in several important respects from those generally found in commercial enterprises. Some of the specific points of variation in accounting are summarized in the following paragraphs.[5]

1. Profit and loss accounting is not required in school or most other governmental units. In accounting for governmental financial activity emphasis is placed on accounting for revenues and expenditures during each fiscal period. It is important to know what revenues are available for incurring obligations and whether there is an excess or deficiency of revenues over expenditures.

2. There is no one figure of "net worth" for school districts. This implies that accounts that express ownership interest, such as individual or partner's capital or of capital stock, are not required. As stated by Morey and Hackett: "Accounts expressing proprietorship of a governmental body consist simply of various surplus accounts or their equivalent. These accounts constitute the excess of certain assets (and in some cases other resources) over liabilities and reserves and represent chiefly the accumulated excess of revenues over expenditures."[6] As will be more carefully developed in a later portion of this chapter, the nature of fund accounting in school districts is such that there is no *one* surplus account. Each fund is a separate and distinct fiscal entity in governmental accounting. A school endowment fund or an investment in fixed assets is an illustration of equity or "proprietorship" for public corporations.

3. Budgetary accounts play an important role and are often required in governmental corporations. Budgetary accounts are required in school district accounting to control financial management and indicate the progress and status of the budget. Accounts for (1) estimated and realized revenues, (2) appropriations for obligations, (3) expenditures made, and (4) unencumbered balance of authorizations should be included within the system of records. Budget accounts constitute a basis for enforcement of limitations imposed by the board of education or higher authorities with power to review and set limits to school budgets. Comparisons between estimates prepared and actual revenues received or expenditures made are readily

available through budgetary accounts. Budgets employed in private industry do not cover the entire range of financial operations but are limited to certain areas and programs. Because budgets are both comprehensive and binding in governmental corporations it is appropriate to incorporate them in the general books of account and reflect them in financial statements. The budgetary accounts "may be said to represent a further extension of the accrual principle in accounting, by recording anticipated operations, which have been formalized by the action of legislative or other bodies having power to authorize and set limits on such operations."[7]

4. Fund accounting is required and is more comprehensive and binding upon governmental corporations than upon private concerns. The income and property received by school districts are often subject to special restrictions. To be sure that such income is used in the manner intended by law, separate funds are established for each restricted item. Earmarked resources can be held inviolate to satisfy specific purposes by keeping each fund a complete accounting entity. It follows that as a consequence of such strict fund accounting the governmental balance sheet is in fact a group of balance sheets rather than the single statement so characteristic of commercial accounting. Special course funds, transportation funds, general funds, schoolhouse funds, etc., are illustrations of the extent of fund accounting in schools.

PURPOSES OF PUBLIC SCHOOL ACCOUNTING

An accounting system for public schools must be compatible with its purposes and geared to satisfy the demands of its unique characteristics. The more specific functions of an accounting system for public schools are:

1. To safeguard school district funds from loss, theft, waste, or misuse.
2. To promote budgetary control.
3. To provide information to management that is necessary in policy formulation.
4. To provide information necessary to the public and the school board to appraise the management of the local school system.
5. To provide necessary data for required state reports.
6. To show that legal mandates have been complied with.

[5] Morey and Hackett, *op. cit.,* pp. 21–24.

[6] *Ibid.,* p. 22.

[7] *Ibid.,* p. 23.

In summary, accounting must indicate the financial condition and operations of the district.

BASIC PRINCIPLES OF SCHOOL ACCOUNTING

In addition to the purposes and unique characteristics of governmental corporations, there are ascertainable principles of accounting which should play a significant role in the design of accounting systems. The National Committee on Governmental Accounting[8] has developed a number of basic principles and standard procedures for governmental accounting which, for the most part, are applicable to all governmental bodies. These authoritative and comprehensive accounting principles can and should be applied to school accounting design. They are presented herewith with special comments and adaptations to show their relationship to school accounting systems.

1. *Compatibility with Legal Requirements Principle.* In addition to reflecting the financial condition and operations, a school accounting system must show that the legal requirements established by statute or mandate of the state department of public instruction have been complied with. Where conflicts exist between legal and sound accounting provisions, legal requirements must take precedence. It is the professional responsibility of school administrators, particularly school accounting officers, to assume leadership necessary to make legal requirements compatible with sound accounting principles.

2. *The General Ledger Principle.* "The general accounting system should be on a double-entry basis with a general ledger in which all financial transactions are recorded in detail or in summary. Additional subsidiary records should be kept where necessary."[9]

Every account in the school accounting system is controlled by the General Ledger and every financial transaction is recorded in summary or in detail therein. Leading to the General Ledger are the General Journal and other supporting registers. Supplementing the General Ledger and controlled by it are the various subsidiary, distribution, or detailed ledgers. The larger the school district, the greater the need for such a ledger, but no school district is too small to do without this fundamental record. Fowlkes[10] pointed out that

the General Ledger could be used "as a running summary, a controlling instrument, and a closing device as well as an opening device." The precise procedures employed in keeping the school's General Ledger are explained in the following chapter.

3. *The Uniform Terminology Principle.* A uniform terminology and standardized classification should be used consistently throughout the budget, accounts, and financial reporting. This principle is too obvious and generally accepted to necessitate further elaboration upon its meaning.

Considerable effort has been expended by state and national educational agencies to bring about uniformity of terminology and classification in school accounting. As far back as 1912 the U.S. Bureau of Education, in coöperation with other educational agencies, published a report which brought substantial agreement on the definition and appropriate use of many terms in school accounting. When Hutchinson[11] studied school costs in certain cities he discovered wide variations in accounting forms, procedures, and methods of reporting. He designed a system of school accounting which he hoped might achieve the desired goal of uniformity in school financial record keeping. Other writers such as Peel,[12] Engelhardt and Von Borgersrode,[13] and Engelhardt and Engelhardt[14] during the 1920's and Fowlkes[15] during the 1930's devised systems of financial accounting for schools which differed from each other in various degrees but which also based many of their accounting classifications on those recommended by the U.S. Bureau of Education. The well-known Circular 204 of the U.S. Office of Education, which was first published in 1940 and was revised in 1948, contributed much to the establishment of uniformity in accounting terminology, forms, practices, and procedures.[16] More recently another publication of the U.S. Office of Education entitled *Financial Accounting for Local and State School Systems*[17] was de-

[8] National Committee on Governmental Accounting, *Municipal Accounting and Auditing*, Chicago: the Committee, 1951, pp. 1–3.

[9] *Ibid.,* p. 1.

[10] John Guy Fowlkes, *Principles and Practices of Financial Accounting for Schools*, Eau Claire, Wis.: E. M. Hale and Company, 1934, p. 100.

[11] J. Howard Hutchinson, *School Costs and School Accounting*, Contributions to Education no. 62, New York: Teachers College, Columbia University, 1914, p. 98.

[12] Arthur J. Peel, *Simplified School Accounting*, Milwaukee: The Bruce Publishing Company, 1925.

[13] Fred Engelhardt and Fred Von Borgersrode, *Accounting Procedures for School Systems,* New York: Teachers College, Columbia University, 1927.

[14] N. L. Engelhardt and Fred Engelhardt, *Public School Business Administration,* New York: Teachers College, Columbia University, 1927.

[15] Fowlkes, *op. cit.*

[16] Emery M. Foster and Harold E. Akerly, *Financial Accounting for Public Schools,* Circular 204, rev. ed., 1948, U.S. Office of Education, Washington, D.C.: U.S. Government Printing Office.

[17] Paul L. Reason and Alpheus L. White, *Financial Accounting for Local and State School Systems, Standard Receipt and Expenditure Accounts,* Bulletin 1957, no. 4, U.S. Office of Education, Washington, D.C.: U.S. Government Printing Office, 1957.

signed as a manual to foster standard receipt and expenditure accounts for schools. This 1957 USOE manual is the basis of standard receipts and expenditure accounts described in Chapters 4 and 7 of this book. That much remains to be done to achieve uniformity in school accounting was implied by Fowlkes and Hansen[18] when their report based on a review of the significant research revealed a considerable lack of uniformity in present-day accounting classifications and practices. Morphet[19] substantially agreed with Fowlkes and Hansen and remarked that in school accounting "we have much more uniformity in theory than we do in practice." More specific information on school accounting terminology and classifications is presented in Chapters 4 and 7.

4. *The Segregation of Funds Principle.* Every school district must establish such funds as are necessary to comply with legal requirements or sound financial administration. Since a large number of funds needlessly complicates a financial system and introduces an element of inflexibility, there should be as few funds as possible within the framework of financial operating requirements. Specific funds are required to insure that revenues and other receipts accruing are used or handled in the manner prescribed by a given authority. The National Committee on Governmental Accounting has defined a fund in governmental accounting "as a sum of money or resources segregated for the purpose of carrying on specific activities or attaining certain objectives in accordance with special regulations, restrictions, or limitations and constituting an independent fiscal and accounting entity."[20] It should be recognized that each fund has financial resources from which revenues are derived, but that these resources have "strings" attached to them. Since there are "strings" attached each fund must be handled as an independent fiscal and accounting entity. Accounting procedures must guarantee for each fund the identity of its resources, obligations, receipts, and disbursements so that its revenues and expenditures are continually maintained and easily observed. There should be a complete self-balancing set of accounts for each fund showing its assets, liabilities, reserve, surpluses, revenues, and expenditures. It is not essential, however, to have a separate bank account for the cash of each fund unless, of course, legal requirements make this mandatory. In contrast to the stringent requirements and regulation of governmental fund accounting, a fund in commercial accounting is simply an earmarked sum of money or other resources which does not require a complete self-balancing group of accounts.

A fund may be created by constitutional mandates, statutory enactments, ordinance resolutions, or even administrative orders. Funds set aside for the purchase of school sites and construction of school buildings are usually created by statutes. The resources available for the schoolhouse fund would include such items as (1) the authority of a school district to call for a bond election, (2) the authority to sell bonds in an amount approved by the electorate, (3) the authority to levy taxes for the amortization of bonds, (4) the power to expend the receipts gained from the sale of bonds for school building construction, and (5) the authority to accept gifts and donations for school building construction or site acquisition. The fact that the law in many states specifies that money in the schoolhouse fund can be used only to construct new buildings and cannot be employed to rehabilitate existing structures is an illustration of the nature of some of the more stringent requirements attached to the establishment of funds.

A fund should not be confused with an appropriation for a specific purpose. An appropriation is usually a part of a fund. To illustrate, one often hears of expending money from the "textbook fund" or "library fund" or "the building custodian's supply fund." In this sense the term "fund" is synonymous with "appropriation" and to some degree with the term "money." This is an erroneous use of the term "fund" in business management. It is more accurate to say that there are appropriations of given amounts within the so-called "general fund" for the purchase of textbooks or library materials or custodial supplies. The creation of a fund does not result also in authority to expend money from that fund. Expenditures from funds require appropriations. The appropriation act is a separate action from the fund creation act. The appropriation act is related to action on the budget during the course of which a responsible and legally constituted body authorizes the expenditure in a certain manner and amount of all or part of the resources of a given fund. Appropriations are then accounted for within the related fund.

Keep in mind that a fund is characterized and usually established as follows:

1. An authorization of specific financial resources which are to constitute the fund. This authority is usually granted by some legislative body which

[18] John Guy Fowlkes and Abner Hansen, "Business Management—Accounting, Auditing, and Reporting" in R. L. Johns and E. L. Morphet (eds.), *Problems and Issues in Public School Finance,* New York: Teachers College, Columbia University, 1952, pp. 464–481.

[19] Edgar Morphet, "Differences in State School Accounting," *Proceedings of the Association of School Business Officials,* 1953, p. 206.

[20] National Committee on Governmental Accounting, *op. cit.,* pp. 3–4.

grants some inferior unit the right to levy taxes, sell bonds, accept gifts, receive fees, etc., for a specific purpose.

2. Authority is vested in the school district to collect the financial resources granted. This function is performed by some administrative body. The municipal taxing agency often specifically performs the collection function on behalf of the school district.

3. Authorization to make expenditures from the duly constituted funds is usually made through budgetary appropriations approved by the local board of education. Actual expenditures are executed by the administrative official in accordance with the approved budget.

The term "general fund" is used to a great extent in school accounting. The general fund is simply the fund which contains all revenues, and the activities financed by such revenues, which are not accounted for in some other or special fund. All other funds in school accounting are given specific names such as bond funds, sinking funds, special courses fund, etc. Most of the ongoing or "regular" educational activities are supported by the revenues from the "general fund." Transfer of resources from one fund to another is not permissible without special authorization of a superior governing body. Board of education action is usually all that is required to change appropriations allocated to various education activities financed by the same fund.

5. *Segregation of Fixed Items Principle.* "A clear segregation should be made between accounts relating to current assets and liabilities and those relating to fixed assets and liabilities."[21] A fixed asset is defined as "a tangible asset held for the services it yields in the production of other goods and services; any item of plant."[22] Fixed assets are relatively long-lasting assets and fixed liabilities are relatively long-term liabilities. Fixed assets are not available to meet current expenses. Fixed or long-term liabilities are payable out of revenues to be raised in the future and, except for those maturing at an early date, are not a charge against current assets. The school building, site, equipment, etc., are illustrations of fixed assets whereas cash on hand, taxes or tuition receivable, etc., are illustrations of current assets. A school bond is fixed or long-term liability. Bond principal and interest payments are accounted for in the debt service funds rather than within the general fund. The very contrasting nature of fixed and current assets or liabilities necessitates a segregation of these items into separate self-balancing groups of accounts.

[21] *Ibid.,* p. 2.
[22] Kohler, *op. cit.,* p. 179.

The fixed asset accounts of the school district should be maintained on the basis of estimated or actual original costs. Depreciation is not necessary to compute unless cash for replacements of fixed assets can be legally set aside. This serves as another interesting contrast between governmental and commercial accounting. Computation of depreciation of governmental property is not considered desirable because property values in government are not used as a basis for credit. The chief interest and importance in connection with permanent property is its cost to taxpayers. Public bodies would experience difficulty in carrying depreciation balances forward into the next fiscal period. In commercial accounting computation of depreciation is a must or else a true picture of profit and loss, borrowing ability, etc., would not be available.

6. *The Budgetary Control Principle.* An accounting system for schools should include budgetary control accounts for both revenues and expenditures. Financial statements should reflect, among other things, whether financial operations are carried out in accordance with estimates and limits indicated in the budget. Merely preparing and adopting a budget does not guarantee against financial difficulty. The financial records must be so formulated that control accounts for budget authorizations are maintained.

Accounts for each of the school funds can be classified as either budgetary accounts or proprietary accounts. Accounts which indicate the status of the budget and course of budgetary operations are called budgetary accounts. Their purpose is budgetary control over financial operations. The accounts needed to reflect budget operation and condition at all times are estimated revenues account, revenues account, estimated appropriation accounts, and appropriation accounts. The revenue accounts and appropriation accounts can be combined in one set of records. In addition there should be a system of encumbrance accounting so that obligations of funds are represented by outstanding orders or contracts for which payment is expected and for which financial provisions must be made. Another system of budgetary control accounts is accomplished through the General Ledger supported by its subsidiary ledgers.

Accounts which actually show financial operation and condition reflecting the assets and liabilities, and displaying the results of operations in terms of revenue, expense, surplus, or deficit, are called proprietary accounts. The term "proprietary" should not be confused with "proprietorship." There are no proprietorship accounts as such in governmental accounting. Proprietary accounts are distinguished from budgetary accounts and are exemplified by such accounts as cash, taxes receivable, vouchers payable, bonds payable, etc.

Proprietary accounts can be further classified into real accounts and nominal accounts. "A real account is one which represents an asset, a liability, or capital."[23] The assets represent real things owned such as cash, tuition receivable, taxes receivable, sites, equipment, inventories, etc. Debts, which include outstanding bonds and bills payable, are liabilities. The balances for real accounts are not closed out at the end of the accounting period but are brought forward to the next period.

Nominal accounts are accounts which reflect or explain any changes in real accounts. They are subsidiary records of receipts and payments (when accounting is done on a cash basis) or revenue and expenses (when accounting is done on the accrual basis). Nominal accounts are but temporary accounts and are closed out completely at the end of each fiscal year. The school revenue account is an illustration of a nominal account which gives a picture of revenue transactions during a fiscal period. At the end of the fiscal period the revenue account is closed out to the cash account which is one of the real accounts making up the proprietary accounts.

7. *The Accrual Basis of Accounting Principle.* "The use of the accrual basis in accounting for revenues and expenditures is recommended to the extent applicable. Revenues, partially offset by provisions for estimated losses, should be taken into consideration when earned, even though not received in cash. Expenditures should be recorded as soon as liabilities are incurred."[24] One of the problems encountered in accounting is to find the most desirable basis for establishing accounting procedures. There are two bases for accounting with several modifications possible from each. One of these bases is called cash accounting and the other is called accrual accounting. The element of time plays a significant role in differentiating between these designated bases. A time must be established to determine when revenues are considered earned and when expenditures are considered completed.

Cash accounting is the simplest basis of accounting and provides much data of value in other types of accounting. Within this system is recorded how much cash was taken in during the fiscal period, how much was disbursed, and the remaining cash balance. Under the cash basis of accounting, a receipt is considered earned when it is actually received by the treasurer of the school district regardless of the date the receipt was due the district. Assume that high school tuition

[23] Stanley B. Tunick and Emanuel Saxe, *Fundamental Accounting,* Englewood Cliffs, N. J.: Prentice-Hall, Inc., 1950, p. 119.

[24] National Committee on Governmental Accounting, *op. cit.,* p. 2.

bills were mailed and marked payment due July 1, 1959, but that payment was not received until January 1, 1960. The tuition money would not be counted as a recipt in the cash accounting system until actually received on January 1, 1960. Likewise expenditures are not considered as executed until actual cash disbursement from the school treasury becomes a fact, i.e., when the liability is liquidated. Assume that $500 worth of textbooks were ordered August 1, delivered and invoice marked due on September 1, but not actually paid for until December 1, 1959. In the cash system of accounting the expenditure for texts would be considered as incurred on December 1, 1959, the date money was actually disbursed from the treasury without regard to the fact that payment of the invoice for the texts was due September 1. It should be obvious that cash accounting merely shows how much has actually been received and how much was actually spent and, therefore, cannot reveal the true financial condition of the district. Some of the items not properly accounted for under this system are tax collections in arrears, money refunded, tuition due from other school districts, temporary loans, withholding of payment on bills due because of lack of cash, revolving funds, state aid receivable.

It does not follow, however, that under the cash basis all receipts are revenues and all disbursements are expenditures. There are nonrevenue receipts resulting from the sale of notes (which creates a liability) or sale of school property. Likewise the payment of notes is not an expenditure because it results in the reduction of a liability.

Under a complete accrual basis of accounting all revenues would be recorded as earned when payment is due even though the actual money was not received into the treasury. By the same token an expenditure is incurred when materials are received or services rendered even though actual money payment occurs at some later date or even during another fiscal period. Using the illustration in a previous paragraph, the high school tuition bills due on July 1, 1959, would be recorded as a revenue accruing to the district on July 1, 1959, even though monies were not received into the treasury until January 1, 1960. Similarly, in the textbook illustration used previously, the receipt of the textbooks and the invoice marked due on September 1, 1959, would constitute an expenditure incurred on September 1, 1959, under accrual accounting even though the treasury did not disburse money for payment of the bill until December 1, 1959. Sometimes it happens that revenues earned during one period are not received until the following fiscal period or expenditures incurred are not paid for until a subsequent fiscal period. Expenditures should be considered incurred, under accrual accounting, in the year in which the benefit is received and not when actual disbursement or payment from the treasury is made.

Slight modification of accrual accounting may be necessary for such items as locker fees, textbook rentals, and laboratory fees which are not usually billed prior to payment. In such cases, items of revenue are not recorded as earned until they are actually received in cash. Such small items do not significantly violate the basic structure of an accrual accounting system. The accrual basis is recommended because it permits a more accurate comparison of expenditures and revenues than is provided with any other basis. It also enables a more accurate computation of unit costs.

Between the complete accrual basis and complete cash basis is the system known as the modified cash basis of accounting. The modified cash basis could also be called the modified accrual basis but tradition has favored the former term. It represents a somewhat inconsistent compromise between the complete cash or accrual basis. It is a conservative approach to the problem, for revenues are not considered earned until actually collected in cash, but expenditures are considered realized as soon as the liability is incurred. The National Committee on Governmental Accounting has recommended the use of the accrual basis, or some slight modification thereof, to the extent it is applicable. There are occasions when legislative mandates require operation on a cash or modified cash basis. When this is the case additional accounts should be set up to accumulate information that would show receivables and payables. The modified cash basis is preferred to the cash basis, but the accrual basis is the most desirable of the three.

STANDARD PROCEDURES IN SCHOOL ACCOUNTING

Principles are concerned with design of the accounting system and standard procedures with operational problems and, hence, influence the actual practices. The following procedures for accounting were recommended by the National Committee on Governmental Accounting and can be adapted to use in public school accounting.

1. *Centralization of Accounts.* "The accounts should be centralized under the direction of one officer. He should be responsible for keeping and supervising all accounts and for preparing and issuing financial reports."[25] In the small school systems the accounting officer is the superintendent of schools. In other systems he may be the secretary to the board of education or an assistant superintendent or business manager working under the direction of the general superintendent of schools.

2. *Budget Preparation.* As indicated previously, a budget is a must in governmental corporations. A budget should be prepared by every school district—no matter how small or large—even though it is not required by law. A budget is most essential to financial procedures for without it prudent management of financial affairs would be made most difficult.

3. *Encumbrance Recording.* "As soon as purchase orders or contracts are signed, the resulting obligations should be recorded as encumbrances of the funds and appropriations affected."[26] It is important that a distinction be drawn between expenditures and encumbrances. No matter what the basis of accounting employed (cash, modified cash, or accrual) it is desirable to establish an encumbrance system under which appropriations are earmarked pending the recording of the expenditure. Encumbering an appropriation is not the same as recording an expenditure from an appropriation. Encumbrance merely insures that the amount of money encumbered cannot be used for anything else until the actual expenditure has been determined or realized and charged against the appropriation. Keep in mind that an expenditure is not incurred until materials are received or services rendered to the school district, thereby creating a liability on part of the district's funds. Under no circumstances should an encumbrance be thought of as an expenditure because a benefit cannot be considered to have accrued to the school district until it receives the materials or services. An encumbrance is, in effect, a commitment. Let us consider the illustration of the $500 worth of textbooks ordered on August 1, delivered and invoice marked due on September 1, and payment finally rendered on December 1. The textbook appropriation should be encumbered to the amount of $500 on August 1, the date the materials were ordered. This means that $500 is set aside for textbook purchases made on August 1 and the same $500 cannot be used for any other purpose. The total appropriation balance on August 1 less $500 is called the unencumbered balance. The expenditure of $500 for textbooks is recorded on September 1 or December 1, depending upon whether the school system is on the accrual basis or cash basis.

There is a difference in meaning between "expendi-

25 *Ibid.,* p. 3.
26 *Ibid.,* p. 3.

tures" and "expenses" in governmental accounting. The term "expenditure" has the broader meaning and refers to amounts paid or incurred for all purposes, including amounts for capital outlay and debt retirement as well as expenses for current operations. The term "expenses" is more narrowly construed and is confined to costs of current operations such as teacher's salaries, textbook purchases, central administrative office costs, maintenance. It can be said in school accounting that all expenses are expenditures but not all expenditures are for expenses. The word "current" often modifies the term "expenses" in school business discussions.

4. *Inventory of Property.* Inventories of consumable and physical properties of the school district should be taken at least once a year and kept in subsidiary records controlled by accounts in the general accounting system.

5. *Financial Reporting.* "Financial reports should be prepared monthly or oftener, to show current condition of the budgetary accounts and other information necessary to control operations. At least once each year a general financial report should be prepared and published."[27] As uniformity in accounting classifications is desirable for all school districts in the United States, so should there be general uniformity in financial reporting.

6. *Periodic Audits.* There should be periodic audits of school district accounts by independent and certified public accountants. The various types and periods of auditing are elaborated upon in a separate chapter.

CHART OF ACCOUNTS

Accounts are means to an end through which financial data are collected and classified and then interpreted in financial statements. The many and different accounts needed for prudent financial management can prove most confusing and difficult to comprehend. A chart of accounts can be prepared to show the organization of accounting for various school funds. Accounting work can be greatly facilitated by classification of accounts within each school fund. This chart, or master list, of accounts is based on classification of accounts according to funds with further reclassification within each fund. The purpose here is to present the total picture of school accounts. Detailed analysis and operating procedures will be provided in the following chapter.

Accounts in each fund can be classified into budgetary and proprietary accounts. It was previously

pointed out that budgetary accounts were employed to show budgetary operations and conditions. Proprietary accounts were those showing actual financial operations and conditions. Proprietary accounts could be further subdivided into real and nominal accounts. The National Committee on Governmental Accounting has recommended that "budgetary and proprietary operations be reflected in a single group of accounts."[28] This procedure simplifies accounting by avoiding much duplication.

For the purposes of preparing the financial balance sheet, fund accounts may be classified into those reflecting (1) assets and other debits, (2) liabilities and other credits, and (3) surplus. A chart of balance sheet accounts for the school general fund is presented below. It should be noted that no differentiation is made between budgetary or proprietary accounts.

CHART OF ACCOUNTS FOR THE GENERAL FUND OF THE
SCHOOL DISTRICT
(BALANCE SHEET ACCOUNTS ONLY)

100. *Assets and Other Debits Accounts*
    Assets—Other Than Fixed
      Cash
           Cash in Treasury
           Petty Cash
      Taxes Receivable
           Current Taxes Receivable
           Delinquent Taxes Receivable
      Estimated Uncollectable Taxes (Credit)
           Current Taxes Uncollectable
           Delinquent Taxes Uncollectable
      Accounts Receivable
           Elementary School Tuition from Other Districts or Persons
           Secondary School Tuition from Other Districts or Persons
      Federal Aid Receivable
      State Aid Receivable
      County Aid Receivable
      Investments
      Due from Other Funds
      Inventory of Materials and Supplies
    Other Debits
      Estimated Revenues
      Revenues (Credit)

200. *Liabilities and Other Credits*
    Liabilities—Other Than Long Term
      Vouchers Payable
      Unaudited Accounts Payable
      Judgments Payable
      Due to Other School Funds

[27] *Ibid.,* p. 3.

[28] *Ibid.,* p. 12.

Due to Other School Districts or Other Governmental
Units
Short-Term Loans or Bonds Payable
Short-Term Loans or Bonds Interest Payable
Other Credits
Appropriations
Appropriation Expenditures (Debit)
Encumbrances (Debit)
Reserve for Encumbrances

300. *Surplus*
Unappropriated Surplus
Reserve for Inventories

A chart of accounts for other school funds could be prepared in much the same manner.

Operating statement accounts reflect the changes in financial condition of a fund and, therefore, are differentiated from the balance sheet accounts. The operating accounts are broken down into two main classifications which are (1) Revenue Accounts and (2) Expenditure Accounts. The revenue and the expenditure accounts can be further reclassified according to character, function, object, etc. The reclassification of revenue and expenditure accounts for schools is described in considerable detail in the following chapter.

THE MECHANICS OF ACCOUNTING PROCEDURES

Thus far emphasis has been placed on the purposes and unique characteristics of governmental corporations such as school districts insofar as they influence design and procedures in accounting. It was indicated that there are reasonable explanations for differences between governmental and commercial accounting system design and operations. Accounting serves best when it communicates an accurate picture of the financial nature of the unique organization wherein it is found. As various cultural pressures necessitate fundamental changes in institutional organization and operation, there must be corresponding changes in accounting system design and practice. This implies that school accounting systems should be flexible so that shifts in design and operation can be made as educational programs change in character and scope. Superfluous records should be eliminated. Inefficiency can result from having too many as well as too few records. "Red tape" is just another way of saying that needless financial records are maintained, that is, records are kept that have no real function to fulfill in school financial administration. Vigilance must be exercised to prevent the degeneration of fi-

nancial accounting into just so much "red tape." Accounting should be judged by the results it produces. It is not a matter of slavishly following unchanging rules. Good accounting is determined by the best practices in financial management.

Principles as well as broad statements of operating procedure must be reduced to the necessary detail work and document record forms before the purposes of an accounting system can be realized. Likewise, a mastery of the terminology of accounting is necessary before proceeding with actual practice exercises in school accounting. A summary of the mechanics of accounting will be presented herein. The student should refer to anyone of the elementary and standard texts of accounting if a more detailed discussion of the concepts is desired.

ACCOUNTING AND BOOKKEEPING COMPARED

According to *A Dictionary for Accountants*[29] accounting is a broad concept involving the recording and reporting of financial transactions and bookkeeping is but one phase of accounting. Accounting is concerned with: (1) the design of a financial control and recording system, (2) bookkeeping or maintaining the records of financial transactions, (3) auditing or continually testing at various periods the effectiveness of controls and the accuracy and propriety of records, and (4) reporting or revealing and interpreting the financial information. It should be noted that accounting involves the analyzing and interpreting of transactions of a financial nature as well as recording, classifying, and summarizing such information in a significant manner. A bookkeeper may also be an accountant if, in addition to maintaining transaction records, he prepares or supervises the preparation of financial statements, designs the accounting system employed, or supervises the recording of transactions.[30]

When the various and ofttimes complicated financial transactions are summarized under headings or classifications, they become known as accounts. An account is simply a systematic statement of a financial fact dealing with a particular operation. The precise information which can be derived from an account is dependent upon the design and construction of records within the system. It is necessary that each account be appropriately named to reveal clearly its nature and content. The various classifications of ac-

[29] Kohler, *op. cit.,* pp. 8–9.
[30] *Ibid.,* p. 61.

counts employed in the financial management of public schools are described in the following chapter.

BOOKS OF ORIGINAL ENTRY

Many business transactions may take place in different buildings or departments of a school system during a single day. Thus, within a single day purchase orders may be placed with vendors, invoices on previous orders may be received, and payments by check may be disbursed for goods or services received on still another occasion. These papers, notations, or memoranda of business activity are called original documents or vouchers. They are filed as permanent evidence of the transaction. The financial information contained in the vouchers or original documents is usually recorded in a special book called a journal before its formal entry into account records. The journal is a bookkeeping record of importance as it contains a complete explanation of transactions. The transactions are entered in chronological order. A journal is in effect a diary showing the financial transaction in its entirety and analyzing it into debit and credit elements. The journal (or journals) is referred to as a book of original entry simply because of giving first expression to transactions. In other words, the entry of a financial transaction into the school accounting system is made through the journal. The process of recording financial facts in the journal is called journalizing.

The simplest type of journal is a single book wherein all financial transactions are recorded. In more complex business enterprises special journals may be employed particularly for frequently recurring transactions. The many purchases executed can be recorded in a purchase order journal which serves as the diary of school purchases. The invoices received for goods or services rendered can be recorded in the accounts payable journal where accrual accounting is observed.

A ledger is a book in which various school accounts are kept. A ledger may be kept in several different forms, each with certain advantages and limitations. Thus a ledger may be kept in a permanently bound form or a looseleaf form or simply as a file of cards. A looseleaf ledger is more flexible than one permanently bound, but it may prove undesirable if pages are removed and then lost. There are problems in keeping records in a permanently bound ledger for when one page is filled space limitations on the following pages may necessitate a continuation of the account on many pages far removed from the original. The looseleaf ledger appears to be the best type for school accounting. Ledger forms for use with accounting machines must of necessity be of the looseleaf type. Ledger forms for machine accounting are of a narrower but longer size than those used in the manual or pen-and-ink methods.

Information on financial transactions recorded in a single journal or in a special journal (book of original entry) is classified and summarized and then transferred to various accounts. In one sense a crude form of an accounts payable or encumbrance journal would be bills or invoices filed in chronological order. Entry to the various accounts is made from the file of bills or invoices. Similarly, check stubs serve as a crude type of journal of financial transactions. One difficulty with recording transactions directly from vouchers or original documents to ledger accounts is that is is not possible to know what took place on a particular day without going through all ledger accounts.

An account is essentially a device for summarizing and classifying transaction information which was recorded within a given journal on a given chronological date. Ledgers in which accounts are maintained are referred to as books of subsequent entry or books of secondary entry. Transferring the summarized and classified financial facts from the journal to a particular ledger is called posting. Although postings are usually made at the end of the month, they can be made at the time the entry is made in the journal or at any convenient time thereafter. No account gets into a ledger account, however, without first appearing in a journal. A check mark is usually placed in a column specially provided for such purpose to indicate that the financial fact has been transferred or copied into the appropriate ledger accounts.

DEBITS AND CREDITS

It is difficult, indeed, to go very far in accounting without running into that inevitable pair "debit and credit." These two elements are included in every financial transaction recorded in the so-called double-entry system of bookkeeping. Jackson[31] declared that "all bookkeeping worthy of the name, since the time of Pacioli (A.D. 1494), has been double-entry bookkeeping." It is contended that the only method to record a transaction completely is to report both its debit and credit effect. To prevent the development of an erroneous conception of double-entry as a system which requires making every entry twice, Jackson[32] suggested that " 'complete-entry' bookkeeping might even be a better name."

Before pinning down the meaning of debit and credit, the definitions of such terms as *asset, liability,*

[31] J. Hugh Jackson, *Accounting Principles,* New York: McGraw-Hill Book Company, 1951, p. 22.
[32] *Ibid.,* p. 22.

and *net worth* must be explored. Anything of value which is owned by a school district or business concern is an asset. There are tangible assets such as cash on hand, bank deposits, office equipment, tuition receivable, land, and buildings. Intangible assets such as patents, copyrights, and good will are usually not recorded as a financial asset to a school, but they are real financial assets to industrial and commercial organizations. Anything which is owed by a school district is a debt or a liability. Short-term loans, bonds, accounts owed to creditors, and tuition payable are the most common liabilities of school districts. Net worth is also referred to as proprietorship or capital. It is the difference between what a business owns and what it owes, or, stated another way, it is the excess of assets over liabilities. As indicated previously,[33] there is no one figure of net worth for school districts. Accounts which express ownership are not required. Surplus accounts showing excess of certain assets over liabilities and reserves would come the closest to being an expression of proprietorship by a governmental body.

The relationship between assets, liabilities, and net worth can be expressed in an algebraic equation. The word form of this equation would be: net worth is equal to assets minus liabilities. This equation is true by definition of the term net worth. Assume that

$$A = \text{Assets}$$
$$L = \text{Liabilities}$$
$$W = \text{Net Worth.}$$

By substitution the equation would be:

$$W = A - L.$$

Then, by algebraic manipulation,

$$A = L + W.$$

This statement of relationship between assets, liabilities, and net worth (or capital) is called the fundamental equation[34] by some, bookkeeping equation[35] by others, and balance sheet equation[36] by still others. The balance sheet, so often referred to in accounting, is the formal financial statement of the value of the assets, liabilities, and net worth of the business. Its relationship to the equation stated above should be obvious. The balance sheet is merely a more formal presentation of the financial facts in the so-called fundamental or bookkeeping or balance sheet equation.

Asset accounts are used to keep track of the vari-

[33] See p. 33.
[34] Tunick and Saxe, *op. cit.*, p. 18.
[35] Hadley Editorial Staff, *Applied Bookkeeping*, New York: McGraw-Hill Book Company, college ed., 1952, p. 3.
[36] Jackson, *op. cit.*, p. 7.

ous kinds of assets. Under the broad classification of asset accounts there would be the cash account, bank account, etc. Similarly, liability accounts are necessary to record the various kinds of liabilities. Net worth accounts are reports of net worth.[37] Debit and credit are simply terms to indicate changes (either increases or decreases) which take place within the various asset, liability, or net worth accounts.

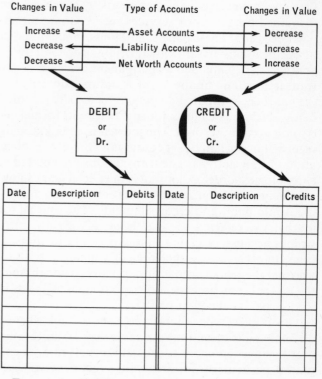

FIGURE 3.   Debits and Credits in Various Types of Accounts

In its simplest form an account is merely a sheet of paper with a line ruled down the middle to create the effect of two columns. One column on one side of the paper is used to record increases in the account and the other side is used to record decreases. Standard practice among bookkeepers and accountants is to refer to the left side of the account form as the debit side and the right side as the credit side. Custom, rather than logical analysis, has arbitrarily determined such designations as debit side and credit side of an account form. The abbreviation used for debit is "Dr." and that for credit is "Cr." There are rules to be followed in determining whether changes in an account caused by a financial transaction shall be called a debit or a credit. The rules for debit and credit notations in asset accounts differ from those in liability and net

[37] See Chart of Accounts for the General Fund of the School District on pp. 39–40 for various Asset, Liability, and Surplus Accounts.

worth accounts. The student has no recourse but to memorize the following rules:

In *asset* accounts:
1. *Increases* in asset accounts are called debits and are recorded on the *left side* of the account form.
2. *Decreases* in asset accounts are called credits and are recorded on the *right side* of the account form.

In *liability* and in *net worth* accounts:
1. *Decreases* in liability accounts are called *debits* and are recorded on the *left side* of the account form.
2. *Increases* in liability and net worth accounts are called *credits* and are recorded on the *right side* of the account form.

It should be noted that what occurs in asset accounts is the reverse of liability and net worth accounts. It should also be clear that regardless of being an increase in asset accounts and a decrease in others, a debit is *always* recorded on the left side of the account form. Likewise, regardless of changes, a credit is *always* recorded on the right side of the account form.

Another way of defining debit and credit would be: *Debits* are *increases* in *asset* accounts or *decreases* in *liability* and *net worth* accounts. *Credits* are *decreases* in *asset* accounts or *increases* in *liability* and *net worth* accounts.

In the double-entry system every financial transaction consists of value received and value surrendered. For every debit recorded there must be a credit in an equal amount recorded in another account. The usual debit balances in asset accounts must be balanced off with credit balances in liabilities and in net worth. Dollar signs should not be used when entering money values into accounts. When an entry is made and the amount involved happens to be in terms of even dollars without any cents, the cents column should not be left blank but two zeros or at least a dash should be written in the cents column.

The opening of the school's financial transactions starts with the authorized school budget which has been spread over the minutes of the board of education. The budget spread on the minutes would indicate the estimated receipts and the budgeted appropriations for expenditures. The "Journal Voucher" is the system employed for transferring the budget from the minute book to the various ledgers. As Fowlkes[38] emphasized, the Journal Voucher is simply a verifying or authorizing memorandum. The closing of the book at the end of the fiscal year is a relatively simple matter if the various account books have been totaled and balanced at the end of each month. The financial report at the end of the school year is made after the actual closing of the school's financial records.

[38] Fowlkes, *op. cit.,* p. 99.

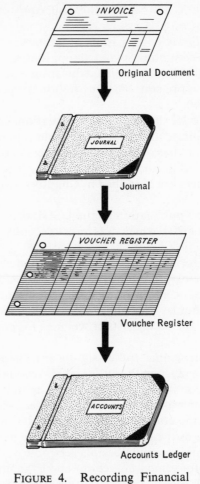

FIGURE 4. Recording Financial Transactions

ATTAINING UNIFORMITY IN THE FINANCIAL ACCOUNTING FOR PUBLIC SCHOOLS

Attaining uniformity in the financial accounting for public schools has been a long-sought goal. The 1957 USOE publication entitled *Financial Accounting for Local and State School Systems, Standard Receipt and Expenditure Accounts* was the result of several years of study by many different educational organizations. Uniformity in school accounting is a major objective of this handbook. This can be seen from the following list of purposes of the 1957 USOE financial accounting manual:
1. To help insure appropriate initial recording of financial data.
2. To improve the accounting for school funds.
3. To improve budgeting.
4. To establish a sound basis for cost accounting.

5. To improve the accuracy of local, state, and national summaries.
6. To facilitate comparisons of financial information among communities and among states.
7. To enable local and state educational authorities to obtain more suitable information for policy determination.
8. To improve the accuracy of educational research.
9. To facilitate and improve reliable reporting to the public on the condition and progress of education.[39]

The detailed accounting procedures for receipts and expenditures are described in Chapters 4 and 7 of this book.

The 1957 publication by the USOE is the successor to Circular 204 which was most recently revised in 1948.[40]

The major emphasis in this 1957 financial accounting handbook put out by the U.S. Office of Education is on the basic accounts used for schools, namely, Receipt Accounts, Expenditure Accounts, and Clearing Accounts. It also suggests procedures for prorating expenditures.

There are some rather significant changes which have taken place in the 1957 USOE accounting handbook. Accounts are given numbers as well as names. Some of the classification titles have been changed. To illustrate, the county unit of school administration is referred to as the intermediate unit. The basic classification of all Revenue Receipts is by source rather than by source for some transactions and by method of production for others. In Expenditure Accounts, the term ADMINISTRATION is used in place of General Control. This particular change in terminology was indicated as early as 1948. Instead of an Auxiliary Services classification several new separate account series for ATTENDANCE AND HEALTH SERVICES, PUPIL TRANSPORTATION SERVICES, FOOD SERVICES, STUDENT BODY ACTIVITIES, and COMMUNITY SERVICES were developed. It can be said that the 1957 USOE financial accounting handbook for schools represents a distinct step forward toward improvement and toward uniformity in financial accounting for local and state school systems.

Although recognizing the contributions of the 1957 USOE financial accounting handbook for public schools in standardizing terminology and describing the accounts, Baughman pointed out the following limitations of this USOE publication:

1. The handbook does not go much beyond outlining expenditure and revenue accounts and, hence, cannot be considered a complete accounting system.
2. The handbook states that the recommended systems of accounts can be used with either the cash or accrual method of accounting, but it neglected to specify or explain the use of receivable and payable accounts which are necessary in the accrual method. In other words, Accounts Payable, Vouchers Payable, Accounts Receivable, Taxes Receivable, and similar accounts were not developed in the 1957 USOE financial accounting manual.
3. The use of the voucher system was not described in the manual.
4. Encumbrance Accounts, which are needed to reflect the exact condition of the budget at a given moment in time, were omitted in the USOE publication.
5. It would be difficult to use the double-entry accounting method with the existing list of recommended accounts found in the manual.
6. Not one Net Worth Account was reported in the handbook. In governmental accounting the use of the Unappropriated Surplus Account together with other surplus reserves are used to record Net Worth.
7. Accounting for the retirement of term bonds in accordance with the USOE handbook procedures leaves much to be desired.[41]

These criticisms reflect, in part, a difference in approaches to school accounting. The 1957 USOE financial accounting manual is designed primarily for single-entry bookkeeping and the cash or modified cash basis of accounting in spite of its statements to the contrary. Baughman calls for, by implication at least, a double-entry system and the complete accrual basis to bring school accounting in line with governmental accounting elsewhere. Many would argue that Net Worth Accounts have little value and would represent little more than "busy work" in public school accounting.

The writers recognize the contributions of the 1957 USOE accounting manual in accomplishing what it set out to do—standardize terminology and certain accounts. This book goes beyond the USOE manual and develops a more complete accounting system to meet the present-day level of public school needs within the degree of acceptance evident in school systems. This chapter has presented the principles to be considered in designing an accounting system. The chapters that follow (particularly Chapters 4 and 7) will develop the voucher system, Receipts Accounts, Expenditure Accounts, Encumbrance Accounting, etc.

SUMMARY

Accounting is one of the steps necessary in the prudent financial management of schools. It is concerned with the summarization, recording, reporting,

[39] Reason and White, *op. cit.*, p. xvi.
[40] Foster and Akerly, *op. cit.*
[41] Morris F. Baughman, "The Financial Accounting Handbook," *American School Board Journal*, February, 1959, *138*:49–52.

and interpretation of the financial transactions of a school system. The fundamental differences between schools and private business concerns make it necessary that school accounting differ in some degree at least from commercial or industrial accounting. Accounting serves best when it communicates an accurate picture of the financial nature of the district. School accounting systems should be flexible to permit shifts in design and operation as educational programs change in character and scope.

School accounting is a means of (1) safeguarding school district funds, (2) achieving budgetary control, (3) providing financial information to management, (4) providing information to the public, (5) providing necessary data for state reports, (6) showing that legal mandates have been satisfied. School accounting is a type of governmental accounting and the principles affecting the design of accounting systems for governmental units can be applied to schools.

Although there has been considerable progress in the past 50 years, there is much more uniformity in theory than in the practice of school accounting. The 1957 USOE financial accounting manual for schools is another large step toward realizing uniformity in accounting classifications and procedures for schools.

Funds are financial resources segregated for the purpose of attaining specific activities. Each fund demands a complete set of self-balancing accounts, and business procedures must guarantee the identity of fund resources and obligations.

Cash accounting is the simplest basis for accounting but does not reveal the true financial condition of the district. In the accrual basis, expenditures are incurred when the benefit is received (no matter when actually paid) and receipts are earned when payment is due (no matter when actually collected). A compromise for schools would be the modified cash basis which calls for recording expenditures when the benefits are received and receipts when actually collected.

Bookkeeping is a part of accounting concerned mainly with maintaining records of financial transactions. Financial transactions are summarized or classified into accounts. Journals are diaries of financial transactions and are referred to as books of original entry. A ledger is a book in which various school accounts are kept. Transferring information from the original document to the journal is called journalizing. Transferring summarized and classified financial facts from a journal to a ledger is called posting.

A debit or "Dr." is an increase in an asset account or a decrease in a liability or net worth account. A credit or "Cr." is the reverse and represents a decrease in an asset account or an increase in a liability or net worth account. An asset is anything of value owned by the district and a liability (or debt) is anything which is owed to someone by the district. The fundamental bookkeeping equation is: net worth equals assets less liabilities.

QUESTIONS

1. What are the purposes of accounting for schools?
2. What are the similarities and differences between accounting for schools and accounting for private concerns?
3. What is a fund? An appropriation? What are the similarities and differences between a fund and an appropriation?
4. What are the fundamental differences between the accrual basis for accounting and the cash basis?
5. What is journalizing? Posting? Give illustrations of each.
6. What is a debit? A credit?
7. What are asset accounts? Liability accounts?
8. Would it be advisable for schools to use the double-entry system of bookkeeping in preference to any others? Justify your stand.
9. Identify the following:
   a. account
   b. ledger
   c. book of original entry
   d. fixed assets
   e. disbursement
   f. expenditure
   g. modified cash basis of accounting
   h. budgetary control
   i. the general ledger

SELECTED REFERENCES

Foster, Emery M., and Akerly, Harold E., *Financial Accounting for Public Schools,* Circular 204, rev. ed., 1948, U.S. Office of Education, Washington, D.C.: U.S. Government Printing Office.

Fowlkes, John Guy, and Hansen, Abner, "Business Management—Accounting, Auditing and Reporting," in R. L. Johns and E. L. Morphet (eds.), *Problems and Issues in Public School Finance,* New York: Teachers College, Columbia University, 1952.

Hadley Editorial Staff, *Applied Bookkeeping,* New York: McGraw-Hill Book Company, College ed., 1952, chaps. 1, 3, 4, and 6.

Jackson, J. Hugh, *Accounting Principles,* New York: McGraw-Hill Book Company, 3rd ed., 1951, chaps. 1, 3, and 14.

Morey, Lloyd, and Hackett, Robert P., *Fundamentals of Governmental Accounting,* New York: John Wiley & Sons, Inc., 1951, chaps. I, II, III.

Morphet, Edgar, "Difference in State School Accounting," *Proceedings of the Association of School Business Officials,* 39th Convention, 1953.

National Committee on Governmental Accounting, *Municipal*

Accounting and Auditing, Chicago: the Committee, 1951, part I.

Reason, Paul L., and White, Alpheus L., *Financial Accounting for Local and State School Systems, Standard Receipt and Expenditure Accounts,* Bulletin 1957, no. 4, U.S. Office of Education, Washington, D.C.: U.S. Government Printing Office, 1957.

Tenner, Irving, *Municipal and Governmental Accounting,* Englewood Cliffs, N.J.: Prentice-Hall, Inc., 3rd ed., 1955, chap. 1.

CHAPTER 4

Management of the
School Income

TOTAL SCHOOL REVENUES HAVE INCREASED markedly since the end of World War II. The low point in more than 25 years was $1.8 billion in 1933. Total revenues for schools were approximately $3 billion in 1945–1946, $6.4 billion in 1951–1952, and had climbed to almost $9.7 billion by 1955–1956. In the space of 25 years school revenues increased by approximately 500 percent. By 1965 revenues for public schools will approximate $20 billion.

Public education became big business in the years following the Civil War. After each succeeding war educational receipts scaled new highs. Growing enrollments, enriched educational programs, and inflation following World War II placed even greater significance on the problems of collection, custody, and disbursement of school funds than ever before.

ACCOUNTING FOR RECEIPTS

There is a difference between receipts and revenues. All school revenues are receipts, but not all receipts are revenues. Receipt is the broad or general term which can be subdivided into revenue receipt and nonrevenue receipt.

Revenue receipts are receipts which produce additions to assets without *increasing* school *indebtedness* and without *reducing* the value or depleting school *property*. Money from taxes and tuition are examples of revenue receipts. Nonrevenue receipts are receipts which accrue to the district as the result of *incurring* an *obligation* which must be met at a future date or *reducing* the value of school *properties* through the exchange of a property asset into a cash asset. Money obtained from the sale of bonds or school property would be classified as a nonrevenue receipt.

Abatements are returns of money to the school district for previously completed expenditures. Abatements which reach the school district in a fiscal year other than the one during which the expenditures being abated were made are considered to be a special type of revenue receipts. If abatements come to the district treasury during the same fiscal year the expenditures abated were executed, a deduction is posted to the appropriate expenditure account. In other words abatements for expenditures which reach the school during the same fiscal year expenditures were executed are not classed as revenue or nonrevenue receipts.

The classification and definition of receipt accounts used in this book are based on *Financial Accounting for Local and State School Systems* issued by the U.S. Office of Education.[1] Henceforth this significant publication is to be referred to as the 1957 USOE financial accounting handbook or the 1957 USOE accounting manual. If financial information among communities and among states is to be comparable, there must be uniformity in the terminology and the accounts used for recording school financial transactions. The authors join the many other educators, school business officials, and state and national organizations in recommending strongly that the 1957 USOE financial accounting handbook be the basis of this uniformity.

FUNDS AND RECEIPT ACCOUNTS

A fund was defined previously as a sum of money or other financial resources segregated for the purposes of carrying on activities within the limits set by laws or

[1] Paul L. Reason and Alpheus L. White, *Financial Accounting for Local and State School Systems, Standard Receipt and Expenditure Accounts,* Bulletin 1957, no. 4, U.S. Office of Education, Washington, D.C.: U.S. Government Printing Office, 1957, pp. 3–20.

regulations. In another sense a fund is a sum of money or financial resource with "strings" attached. The strings attached make it necessary that each fund be an independent fiscal and accounting entity.

An account is a term used to describe financial transactions which are similar to some degree. Receiving money and expending money are illustrations of financial transactions. Money can come from a number of sources. Classifying money received according to the source raising it for schools is an aid in orderly business management. Stated another way, financial transactions which are similar to some degree can be classified to constitute an account.

Any fund can be divided into a number of accounts for the purpose of systematizing the financial transactions that take place within the fund. Those financial activities which are related to receiving money can be grouped into what are called Receipt Accounts. Those related to spending money are classified as Expenditure Accounts. It follows that the Receipt Accounts, such as those to be developed within this chapter, can be used with any kind of fund.

Note that the plural is always used in referring to Receipt Accounts. There are many ways to order financial transactions into accounts. Whatever system of classification is used, more than one account is necessary to describe carefully what transpires within a fund. Note that two accounts already are suggested by subdividing receipts into Revenue Receipt Accounts and Nonrevenue Receipt Accounts. But even these two classes are much too broad to describe satisfactorily financial activity in any kind of fund. Further division of Revenue Receipts into more specific accounts is necessary. This is also true for Nonrevenue Receipts.

The most commonly employed funds are those for current expenses, capital outlay, and debt service. Some school districts have six or more different funds. Multiplicity of funds is not desirable, for it unduly complicates financial operations. Receipt Accounts to be described herein can be adapted to any funds regardless of whether cash or accrual bases of accounting or the double-entry or single-entry bookkeeping systems be employed.

All school systems, regardless of size, should maintain as a minimum the Receipt Accounts identified in the paragraphs that follow. Numbers have been attached to help simplify identification.[2] The numbers can be interpreted as a system of coding to be used with either machine-accounting methods or the traditional pen-and-ink manual system.

Arabic numerals only identify the major account classifications. The major headings can be divided into

more specific accounts which are designated usually by the Arabic numeral followed by a lower case letter such as Account 11-a. Receipt Accounts are assigned numbers ranging from 10 to 90. The number series attached to various accounts are arbitrarily determined. To achieve uniformity it is desirable that all school districts change over to the numbering system developed in the 1957 USOE financial accounting handbook even though it may appear that another set of numbers may work just as well.

REVENUE RECEIPT ACCOUNTS[3]

The 10–40 series of numbers are used to identify the various revenue receipts that accrue to school districts. There are several ways to group public school revenue receipts. The system employed herein is the one recommended in the 1957 USOE accounting manual. All receipts are recorded by (1) source and (2) method of production. Classification of receipts by elementary, secondary, or other program area is not recommended unless used as further subdivision of source or method of production for purposes of unit cost analysis.

Local, intermediate, state, and federal governmental units are the sources of revenues for schools. The revenues from these sources can be produced from property and nonproperty taxation, appropriations, tuition, earnings from permanent funds and endowments, and other means. The several Revenue Receipt Accounts are identified by a given name and also by a series of numbers starting with 10 or 20 or 30 or 40. The methods used to produce revenues are recognized as groupings under each source. Revenue Receipts Accounts start with ACCOUNT SERIES 10—REVENUE FROM LOCAL SOURCES and conclude with ACCOUNT SERIES 40—REVENUE FROM FEDERAL SOURCES.

ACCOUNT SERIES 10—REVENUE FROM LOCAL SOURCES

The revenues produced from local taxation, appropriations, tuition, special fees, and other local sources are posted under this series of accounts. Local revenues continue to provide the largest share of school operating funds in most states. In some agricultural states local revenues yield 80 to 90 percent of the school receipts.

The following major accounts and some subdivisions represent a minimum for the proper recording of revenue transactions from local sources. The major account classifications are based on methods of production of local revenue.

[2] Ibid.

[3] The accounting names and classifications used in this section are adapted from, ibid., pp. 8–17.

A. *Major Account 11—Taxation and Appropriations Received.* This account can be subdivided further to recognize the particular revenues for:

1. Account 11-a—Taxes Received from School District Levies. This in turn can be broken down into:

    a. Subaccount 11-a-1—Property Taxes. Under this heading are posted monies obtained from levies on real and personal property as well as interest and penalties on delinquent property taxes.

    b. Subaccount 11-a-2—Nonproperty Taxes. Within this subaccount is reported income from local district taxes such as poll taxes, local district income taxes, dog taxes, licenses, and permits.

Taxes recorded under *Major Account 11* include only those for which the school district is the final authority within the legal limits on such taxes. The largest entries will probably be made under property taxes although in 1950 almost 190 city school systems had authority to levy some 29 different types of nonproperty taxes.[4]

2. Account 11-b—Taxes Received from Local Governmental Units Other Than School Districts. Earmarked revenues from local sources but for which the school district is not the final authority for levying taxes are reported herein. In 1950, 7 percent of the city school boards could only recommend the amount of the school tax rate to another local governmental unit which had authority to change the tax. In 30 percent of the city school districts the school board has no authority to levy or collect taxes for school purposes.[5] This account can be subdivided as follows:

    a. Subaccount 11-b-1—Property Taxes.

    b. Subaccount 11-b-2—Nonproperty Taxes.

3. Account 11-c—Appropriations Received from Local Governmental Units Other Than School Districts. Included in this account are appropriations from other units of local governments. The appropriations may be used instead of assigning the yield of an earmarked tax for school purposes. The appropriation is voted from the general treasury of the local unit other than a school district.

B. *Major Account 12—Tuition from Patrons.* This account includes monies received from students, their parents, or guardians who may or may not reside within the district but participate in such programs as summer school, regular day school, adult education, and veteran's training. Only tuition for resident or nonresident pupils paid by an individual or from a welfare or similar agency (but not another school district!) is reported in this major account. Tuition for nonresident pupils received from the school boards of other districts is posted in Accounts 80-a and 90-a. Student activity fees are placed in CLEARING ACCOUNT SERIES 1810 and not here. *Major Account 12* can be subdivided into:

1. Account 12-a—Regular Day School Tuition from Patrons. This account includes tuition receipts for resident and nonresident day school students only. All others are reported in the following accounts.

2. Account 12-b—Adult Education Tuition from Patrons. Reported herein is money received from nonresident and resident adult education pupils only but paid by individuals or welfare agencies.

3. Account 12-c—Other Tuition from Patrons. This account includes tuition payments by individuals or other nonschool district agencies for resident and nonresident pupils participating in types of programs other than those listed above in Accounts 12-a and 12-b.

C. *Major Account 13—Transportation Fees from Patrons.* This account includes only money received from students or parents or guardians for transportation. It does not include transportation paid by another school district, for this is reported in Accounts 80-b and 90-b.

D. *Major Account 14—Other Revenue from Local Sources.* This account can be subdivided into:

1. Account 14-a—Earnings from Permanent Funds and Endowments. This includes earnings from the *local* permanent funds. Earnings from property owned by the local school district and held for future school use or disposal rather than as a permanent investment to produce revenue are posted under Account 14-e, rather than here.

2. Account 14-b—Earnings from Temporary Deposits and Investments. It includes net earnings from all deposits and investments except those from permanent funds and endowments.

3. Account 14-c—Net Receipts from Revolving Funds or Clearing Accounts. The excess at the end of the accounting period of gross receipts over gross expenditures in revolving funds (clearing accounts) under the jurisdiction and control

[4] National Education Association, Committee on Tax Education and School Finance, *New Sources of Local Revenues for Public Schools,* Washington, D.C.: NEA, May, 1950, p. 16.

[5] National Education Association, Research Division, "Fiscal Authority of City School Boards," *Research Bulletin,* Washington, D.C.: NEA, April, 1950, 28:60.

of the board of education are entered in this account. The net receipts or balance at the end of the fiscal period for such activities as food services, textbooks, athletics, clubs, and publications which are under the financial control of the board of education and are posted in ACCOUNT SERIES 1810 are closed out to this account.

4. Account 14-d—Rent from School Facilities. This account is necessary to account properly for money received from rental of school property such as the school auditorium or gymnasium.

5. Account 14-e—Rent from Property Other Than School Facilities.

6. Account 14-f—Gifts and Bequests. Income from philanthropic foundations, private individuals, or private organizations for which no recurrent repayment or special service is expected are entered herein.

7. Account 14-g—Miscellaneous Revenue from Local Sources. It includes special assessments, abatements for expenditures made in prior years, and any other revenues from local governmental sources which are not covered by other revenue receipt accounts.

ACCOUNT SERIES 20—REVENUE FROM INTERMEDIATE SOURCES

Recorded herein are monies collected by an intermediate administrative unit and distributed to school districts in amounts different from those which were collected within such districts. The intermediate administrative unit is a political subdivision between the local school district and the state. Previous accounting handbooks have used the term county unit of administration rather than intermediate administrative unit.[6]

The intermediate unit must be more than a mere agent for collecting taxes for the local school districts and returning them in the same amount to local districts if such revenue is to be recorded under this series of accounts. The intermediate administrative unit must gather the school tax and distribute monies collected to local districts as flat grants or equalization aids. If the intermediate unit acts only as a collecting agency for local school districts, such monies are recorded in *Major Account 11.* If the county or intermediate unit is the basic unit of local school administration the revenues it receives are also placed in *Major Account 11.*

[6] Emery M. Foster and Harold F. Akerly, *Financial Accounting for Public Schools* Circular 204, rev. ed., 1948, U.S. Office of Education, Washington, D.C.: U.S. Government Printing Office, p. 7.

ACCOUNT SERIES 30—REVENUE FROM STATE SOURCES

The purpose of this series is to identify funds collected by the state and distributed to local school districts in amounts different from those which were collected within such local units.

A. *Major Account 30-a—State.* Within this classification are posted revenues levied as well as collected by the state for eventual distribution to local school districts. The exception to this is state aid for food services as such aids are accounted for in CLEARING ACCOUNTS SERIES 1700. The state must act in a capacity other than that of a mere agent for gathering certain tax monies for local districts if the state grants are to be recorded herein. State aids must be made to local units on the basis of flat grants or equalization aids to be entered into *Major Account 30-b.*

There has been a distinct trend, nationally, toward increasing state contributions for the support of public elementary and secondary schools in particular. In 1929–1930, 16.9 percent of the total school revenues were derived from state sources, as compared with 37.4 percent of the total revenue derived from state sources in 1953–1954. It is estimated that the percent of total school revenues from state sources will climb above 40 percent in the years ahead. There is considerable variation among the states with respect to the various kinds of aids to local school districts. Some state support is in the form of special-purpose grants, others are flat grants, and still others are equalization grants. Most state aids continue to be flat grants, although there is a distinct trend toward increasing state equalization grants.

As many accounts should be organized as may be necessary to record properly the variety of state aids in each state. The following are illustrations of such accounts.

1. Account 30-a-1—Special-Purpose Grants.
2. Account 30-a-2—Flat Grants.
3. Account 30-a-3—Equalization Aid.

Another approach would be to classify state aids by purposes or programs such as:

1. Account 30-a-1—Elementary School Grants.
2. Account 30-a-2—Secondary School Grants.
3. Account 30-a-3—Junior College Grants.
4. Account 30-a-4—Adult or Evening School Grants.

B. *Major Account 30-b—Federal Money Received Through the State.* Money derived from the federal government but distributed by the state to local districts is entered in this account. The exception to this is federal aid for food services which should be listed under the food services operation accounts in the Clearing Accounts to be described in the last part of this chapter. The various types of federal aids administered through the state and recorded in *Major Account 30-b* can be subdivided as per illustrations in *Major Account 30-a*.

ACCOUNT SERIES 40—REVENUES FROM FEDERAL SOURCES

All federal government grants issued directly to local school districts without going through the state are recorded in ACCOUNT SERIES 40. Excluded are federal food service grants or school lunch aids that may come directly to schools. This series could be divided into:

A. *Major Account 41—Federal Grants for Current Expenses.*
B. *Major Account 42—Federal Grants in Lieu of Taxes.*
C. *Major Account 43—Federal Grants for Capital Improvements.*
D. *Major Account 44—Other Direct Federal Grants.*

NONREVENUE RECEIPT ACCOUNTS[7]

As defined previously, nonrevenue receipts are monies produced as the result of incurring an obligation to the school district which must be amortized at some future date or monies produced from the sale of school property. They include income from loans, sale of bonds, sale of property, and proceeds from insurance adjustments.

The Nonrevenue Receipts Accounts start with ACCOUNT SERIES 50—SALE OF BONDS and conclude with ACCOUNT SERIES 70—SALE OF SCHOOL PROPERTY AND INSURANCE ADJUSTMENTS.

ACCOUNT SERIES 50—SALE OF SCHOOL BONDS

Reported under this series are the proceeds from local school bond sales including premiums, accrued interest, and interest on monies received from the sale of bonds but said monies later invested for short periods. It does not include receipts gathered from bonds issued to refund a previous set of bonds. Receipts from the sale of refunding bonds are recorded in CLEARING ACCOUNT SERIES 1910—REFUNDING BONDS.

ACCOUNT SERIES 60—LOANS

This account series is instituted as a place for posting loans or tax anticipation warrants to be paid in a year other than the fiscal year during which the loan or

[7] The accounting classifications and names used in this section are adapted from Reason and White, *op. cit.*, pp. 17–19.

note was issued. Current loans or tax anticipation notes which will be paid back during the same fiscal year are accounted for in CLEARING ACCOUNT SERIES 1610—CURRENT AND SHORT-TERM LOANS.

A. *Major Account 60-a—Short-Term Loans.* Short-term loans issued for 5 years or less and not repaid during the same fiscal year they were issued are reported herein.
B. *Major Account 60-b—Long-Term Loans.* Posted here are loans in excess of 5 years which are not secured by serial or term bonds.

ACCOUNT SERIES 70—SALE OF SCHOOL PROPERTY AND INSURANCE ADJUSTMENTS

The title of this account series is almost self-explanatory. If the money from such sales does not come to the school treasury, the sum is not posted and the transaction is noted in Memoranda Accounts. Memoranda Accounts are informal records of school transactions that cannot be posted in regular accounts but for which a record is desired or necessary.

A. *Major Account 70-a—Sale of Real Property.*
B. *Major Account 70-b—Sale of Equipment.*
C. *Major Account 70-c—Net Insurance Recovery.* Only the net balance of money remaining at the end of the fiscal year in CLEARING ACCOUNT SERIES 1930—INSURANCE ADJUSTMENTS is entered herein.

INCOMING TRANSFER ACCOUNTS[8]

Incoming Transfer Accounts are necessary to record monies received from other school districts for services rendered. Although tuition receipts from other school districts are income for the receiving district, they can, nonetheless, distort the picture on total school receipts in all school districts of the state or the nation. Incoming Transfer Accounts are necessary to avoid duplication of data on school receipts and, therefore, can help yield more reliable and more comparable state and national figures on educational receipts. The receiving district should identify all receipts coming from other school districts. These Incoming Transfer Accounts start with ACCOUNT SERIES 80—AMOUNTS RECEIVED FROM OTHER SCHOOL DISTRICTS IN THE STATE and end with ACCOUNT SERIES 90—AMOUNTS RECEIVED FROM SCHOOL DISTRICTS IN ANOTHER STATE.

ACCOUNT SERIES 80—AMOUNTS RECEIVED FROM OTHER SCHOOL DISTRICTS IN THE STATE

A. *Major Account 80-a—Tuition.* Keep in mind that this is tuition received from school boards of other *districts.*

[8] The accounting classifications and names used in this section are adapted from *ibid.*, pp. 19–20.

B. *Major Account 80-b—Transportation.* The amount received from other school districts in the state for transportation of pupils is reported herein. Money coming from patrons is posted under *Major Account 13.*

C. *Major Account 80-c—Miscellaneous.* Posted herein are monies received from other school districts in the state for any services rendered to pupils other than payments for tuition and transportation described above. This might be health services or the use of recreational facilities in the receiving district.

ACCOUNT SERIES 90—AMOUNTS RECEIVED FROM SCHOOL DISTRICTS IN ANOTHER STATE

A. *Major Account 90-a—Tuition.*

B. *Major Account 90-b—Transportation.*

C. *Major Account 90-c—Miscellaneous.*

OUTLINE OF RECEIPT ACCOUNTS

A. REVENUE RECEIPT ACCOUNTS—10-40 SERIES

ACCOUNT SERIES 10—REVENUE FROM LOCAL SOURCES
Major Account 11—Taxation and Appropriations Received
  Account 11-a—Taxes Received from School District Levies
    Subaccount 11-a-1—Property Taxes
    Subaccount 11-a-2—Nonproperty Taxes
  Account 11-b—Taxes Received from Local Governmental Units Other Than School Districts
    Subaccount 11-b-1—Property Taxes
    Subaccount 11-b-2—Nonproperty Taxes
  Account 11-c—Appropriations Received from Local Governmental Units Other Than School Districts
Major Account 12—Tuition from Patrons
  Account 12-a—Regular Day School Tuition from Patrons
  Account 12-b—Adult Education Tuition from Patrons
  Account 12-c—Other Tuition from Patrons
Major Account 13—Transportation Fees from Patrons
Major Account 14—Other Revenues from Local Sources
  Account 14-a—Earnings from Permanent Funds and Endowments
  Account 14-b—Earnings from Temporary Deposits and Investments
  Account 14-c—Net Receipts from Revolving Funds or Clearing Accounts
  Account 14-d—Rent from School Facilities
  Account 14-e—Rent from Property Other Than School Facilities
  Account 14-f—Gifts and Bequests
  Account 14-g—Miscellaneous Revenue from Local Sources
ACCOUNT SERIES 20—REVENUE FROM INTERMEDIATE SOURCES
ACCOUNT SERIES 30—REVENUE FROM STATE SOURCES
  Major Account 30-a—State

  Account 30-a-1—Special-Purpose Grants
  Account 30-a-2—Flat Grants
  Account 30-a-3—Equalization Aid
Major Account 30-b—Federal Money Received Through the State
ACCOUNT SERIES 40—REVENUE FROM FEDERAL SOURCES
Major Account 41—Federal Grants for Current Expenses
Major Account 42—Federal Grants in Lieu of Taxes
Major Account 43—Federal Grants for Capital Improvements
Major Account 44—Other Federal Grants

B. NONREVENUE RECEIPT ACCOUNTS—50–70 SERIES

ACCOUNT SERIES 50—SALE OF SCHOOL BONDS
ACCOUNT SERIES 60—LOANS
Major Account 60-a—Short-Term Loans
Major Account 60-b—Long-Term Loans
ACCOUNT SERIES 70—SALE OF SCHOOL PROPERTY AND INSURANCE ADJUSTMENTS
Major Account 70-a—Sale of Real Property
Major Account 70-b—Sale of Equipment
Major Account 70-c—Net Insurance Recovery

C. INCOMING TRANSFER ACCOUNTS—80–90 SERIES

ACCOUNT SERIES 80—AMOUNTS RECEIVED FROM OTHER SCHOOL DISTRICTS IN THE STATE
Major Account 80-a—Tuition
Major Account 80-b—Transportation
Major Account 80-c—Miscellaneous
ACCOUNT SERIES 90—AMOUNTS RECEIVED FROM SCHOOL DISTRICTS IN ANOTHER STATE
Major Account 90-a—Tuition
Major Account 90-b—Transportation
Major Account 90-c—Miscellaneous

The method of accounting of receipts outlined in the preceding paragraphs is a modification of that recommended in the 1948 Circular 204 financial accounting handbook issued by the U.S. Office of Education.[9] Some changes in terminology were noted in the 1957 handbook as compared with the revised 1948 Circular 204.

THE CUSTODY AND COLLECTION OF SCHOOL FUNDS

CUSTODY OF SCHOOL FUNDS

Receipts for public education come from a variety of sources. One of the purposes of the system of Receipt Accounts proposed earlier in this chapter was to identify properly the sources of school monies. Careful accounting is one way to protect funds in the treasury of the school district. The bonding of officials

[9] Foster and Akerly, *op. cit.*, pp. 4–10.

FORM 1 (Front).

FORM NO-3
APR. '57 10M

Receipts by Funds and Sources

DATE	FROM WHOM	CODE	GRAND TOTAL RECEIPTS 10-60	FUND RECEIPTS								SOURCE OF REVENUE RECEIPTS 10-40 SERIES							
				TEACHERS	INCIDENTAL	FREE TEXTBOOK	BUILDING	SINKING	INTEREST										
										CURRENT TAXES 11.1	DELINQUENT TAXES 11.2	INTANGIBLE TAXES 11.3	TUITION 12	TRANSPORTATION 13	OTHER LOCAL RECEIPTS 14.1	FOOD SERVICES 14.2	STUDENT BODY ACTIVITIES 14.3		

LOCAL MONEY – 10 SERIES
RECEIVED FROM PATRONS FOR

	BUDGET ESTIMATE																
1																	
2	BALANCE ON HAND JULY 1																
3	BUDGET ESTIMATE BALANCE																

(Courtesy of the Missouri State Department of Education)

FORM 1 (Back).

FORM NO-2. CONTINUED
APR. '57 10M

Receipts by Funds and Sources, Continued

SOURCE OF REVENUE RECEIPTS - 20 - 40 SERIES

	COUNTY MONEY - 20 SERIES			STATE MONEY — 30 SERIES								FEDERAL SOURCES (DIRECT) 40	NON-REVENUE RECEIPTS 50 AND 70 SERIES			RECEIPTS FROM OTHER SCHOOL DISTRICTS - 80 SERIES	
	FINS. PENS.-TURNS. INTEREST, ETC. 21	R.R. & UTILITY TAXES 22	OTHER COUNTY RECEIPTS 23	E.G., T.I., AND A.A. 31	TRANSPORTATION 32.1	EXCEPTIONAL PUPIL AND ORPHAN AIDS 32.2	BUILDING AIDS 32.3	FOR-DON-INS. (TEXTBOOKS) 33	VOCATIONAL AID 34	FOOD SERVICES 35	OTHER STATE AID 36		SALE OF BONDS 50	SALE OF PROPERTY 71	OTHER NON-REVENUE RECEIPTS 72	TUITION 81	TRANSPORTATION 82
1																	
2																	
3																	
4																	
5																	
6																	
7																	
8																	
9																	
10																	
11																	
12																	
13																	
14																	
15																	
16																	
17																	
18																	
19																	
20																	
21																	
22																	
23																	
24																	
25																	
26																	
27																	
28																	
29																	
30																	
31																	
32																	
33																	
34																	
35																	
36																	
37																	
38																	
39																	
40																	

responsible for managing school funds is of limited value unless the losses can be discovered through the proper accounting, auditing, and reporting.

There are and must be other safeguards against individual dishonesty, carelessness, or mismanagement of school funds besides those related to accounting. It is imperative that all officials having responsibility for the collection or custody of school funds, supplies, or movable equipment be bonded. This includes individuals who hold positions as tax collectors, treasurers, bookkeepers, auditors, etc., and, in short, all persons who collect money, make payments, handle property, or keep financial and property records. The amount of the bond should be equal at least to the amount of money that the official would have on hand during any 30-day period.

Fidelity bonds, corporate surety bonds, and personal bonds for school officials are discussed in Chapter 16 on School Insurance. It is recommended that the boards require corporate surety bonds rather than personal bonds. Unfortunately, there is considerable difference in the extent to which school boards bond various officials responsible for school money and property. Some boards bond nearly all officers, whereas others bond but a few.

In addition to internal checks on personnel and the financial accounting system, certain administrative safeguards, particularly those related to procedures governing the collection and disbursement of money, should receive careful consideration. All checks and vouchers should be countersigned to make more than one person responsible for disbursing money. In 45 percent of the city school systems in which the school board members are appointed, city officials must sign or countersign the school checks. In those with elected school boards, the signatures of city officials go on school checks in only 25 percent of the cases.[10] When only the signatures of school board members appear, that of the president of the board is most frequently required. When both the school board and some local governmental agency must sign, the secretary of the board is most frequently the signer on behalf of the school board and the city or county treasurer on behalf of the other local governmental agency. The larger the city school system, the less likely it is that only the representatives of the school board sign the checks or warrants for school expenditures.

Receipts for school funds should be numbered serially and made out in triplicate—one for the payee, one for the accounting officer, and one for the files of the treasurer.

Burke declared that large losses usually result from

[10] National Education Association, Research Division, *op. cit.,* p. 64.

small defalcations over a long period of time.[11] School officials authorized to receive funds should not have authority to make expenditures. Likewise, those responsible for receiving funds or making disbursements should not carry the additional responsibility of keeping accounts. Publicity through monthly reports as well as occasional spot-audits of monies due, collected, and deposited can be used to discover trouble or embezzlement. The recent recommendations of banking officials that all personnel handling money be required to take a vacation once a year is worthy of serious consideration in all school districts. Administrative safeguards that minimize opportunities for defalcations from school funds can help overcome some of the temptations to embezzle as well as help prevent losses through mismanagement.

THE DEPOSITORY

In some school systems funds which accrue to school districts are deposited the day received and duly reported and entered into the school's financial records. In other districts which have facilities for storing money in schools in new and relatively burglar-proof safes, a deposit schedule of two or three times a week is followed. In any case, large amounts of cash should not be permitted to build up in schools to serve as a temptation to burglars. A problem arises as to just who shall be appointed the custodians of the school funds. The laws as well as practices in many states vary widely with respect to what school officials are charged with the custody of school funds. In a 1930 study, Beach reported the use of four distinct types of custodial agencies for school funds.

1. The school board treasurer system where a member of the school board or an official appointed by the board executes the functions and responsibilities of treasurer of district funds.
2. The clerk-treasurer system, where the clerk of the school board or the superintendent of schools is appointed treasurer. This is a variation of the first type.
3. The governmental treasurer system, where the treasurer of another governmental unit at the local, county, or state level performs as treasurer for the school district.
4. The depository system, where a bank is designated as custodian of school funds.[12]

Few changes in school fund custody took place in

[11] Arvid J. Burke, *Financing Public Schools in the United States,* New York: Harper & Brother, rev. ed., 1957, p. 38.
[12] Fred F. Beach, *The Custody of School Funds,* Contributions to Education no. 577, New York: Teachers College, Columbia University, 1933, pp. 8–12.

districts throughout the United States during the years from 1870–1930. A decrease in the number of school districts in the various states that designated a member of the school board as treasurer and a slight increase in the number of other types of custodial agencies were among the more important changes during this 60-year period.

There is much to be said in favor of the depository system. Under this system, the tax collector, the county treasurer, or the other collecting agency deposits money due to schools directly into a bank previously designated as the depository. Money is released by the bank depository after vouchers approved for payment by the board of education have been received. It is a relatively simple procedure which eliminates the necessity of bonding a treasurer. The risk of loss is reduced by eliminating the treasurer, and the school system receives the benefit of trained personnel in the bank who are responsible for handling large funds.

In spite of the many advantages of other systems, the school board treasurer system is still by far the most prevalent among school districts. The school board treasurer is usually but not necessarily a member of the board. It is his function to receive all monies from the tax collector or state agency disbursing state aids and deposit the same in the bank or trust company designated as the school fund depository. It is not always clearly defined whether this officer is merely the custodian or the custodian and accounting officer. Some are of the opinion that vested interests have developed in this old and widespread system which serve to perpetuate it. This is particularly true where the school board treasurer is paid a salary for his work and discontinuance of this office would deprive an official of a position and a small salary attached thereto.[13]

The school boards in 64 percent of the city school systems in 1950 had custody over their own funds, or, in other words, they received, deposited, and disbursed funds without the help or participation of any other agency. In one-fourth of the states, school boards are responsible for school funds and expenditures in all the city school systems therein. In about one-sixth of the states, however, school boards do not have the custody of school funds in any city school system in these states. In a minority of city school systems where an agency of another local governmental unit has the custody of the school funds, the custodian is most often the city treasurer (in 43 percent of these city systems) or the county treasurer (in 23 percent of these city systems).[14]

The selection of depositories for school receipts is a matter for the school board to determine. Some have recommended the use of bidding with the school depository being selected on the basis of the largest interest rate paid for school funds on deposit. The criteria of security and service receive prime consideration today with little emphasis if any on the amount of interest boards can collect on school funds in a bank. Banks, as school depositories, should be selected in terms of financial standing, convenience, and service, rather than interest paid. It is unfortunate that all too often the criteria used in selecting a depository for funds are more local and personal in nature with slight consideration of security and service. The majority of states have attempted to make some provision for securing public school funds in depositories. In banks subscribing with the Federal Deposit Insurance Corporation, school deposits are insured up to $10,000 for any one account.

State guaranty plans for the protection of public funds in banks were rather popular some years back. The mutual bank deposit insurance organization was among the more common types of guaranty plans. With this system, losses were covered by assessing all other member banks affiliated with the guaranty plan. Oklahoma, Kansas, Nebraska, Mississippi, South Dakota, North Dakota, and Washington organized this type of guaranty plan and required all state banks to be a part of it. An appraisal of guaranty fund plans showed that they had difficulty in achieving their objectives in most states, particularly after 1920 when bank failures became more numerous. When the burden on the member banks in such guaranty fund plans became so great, the plans became inoperative or the law was repealed by the state.[15]

The exception to this was the Iowa State Sinking Fund for Public Deposits, organized in 1925. This fund was developed by diverting the interest earned on public deposits up to 2 percent for about 90 percent of the daily balances in public deposits. This state sinking fund is under the management of the state treasurer and was created through the interest paid on deposits of public monies in state, county, township, municipal, and school corporations. The status of this fund was relatively inactive during the years of the depression but has worked out very satisfactorily subsequent to that period. The plan is still in operation under the

[13] William E. Arnold, William B. Casteter, Walter C. Reusser, and Roman J. Verhallen, "Business Management—Safeguarding School Funds and Property" in R. L. Johns and E. L. Morphet (eds.), *Problems and Issues in Public School Finance,* New York: Teachers College, Columbia University, 1952, pp. 429–463.

[14] National Education Association, Research Division, *op. cit.,* p. 63.
[15] Paul R. Mort and Walter C. Reusser, *Public School Finance,* New York: McGraw-Hill Book Company, rev. ed., 1951, p. 22.

original law, and no interest has been charged on public funds for eight to ten years.[16]

THE COLLECTION OF SCHOOL TAXES

In most school districts the levies on properties are legally authorized by the board of education. In very few, however, do the boards actually collect the tax. In city school systems of a hundred thousand or more in population only one in ten levied and collected its own taxes during 1950. About 60 percent of the city boards and most other nonurban districts are essentially free to establish the local tax rate for school purposes without consultation or interference from nonschool agencies.[17]

Most authorities are in agreement that school taxes can be collected by county or municipal tax collectors without exercising undesirable controls over public education. Wilkins reported that tax delinquency was greater in school systems using special departments to assess and collect school taxes and that it cost more to operate a separate tax department than to rely on municipal tax departments for collections. He concluded that responsibilities for collecting tax monies directly from the taxpayer are better assumed by representatives of general tax collecting agencies than by school districts.[18]

In Arizona, South Carolina, and Texas, school property assessment is computed in part by assessors selected by the board of education. Most authorities are in agreement that for all the shortcomings, the assessment of property in the school district by county assessors and review by state agencies is to be preferred. There are few advantages but many disadvantages in the practice of appointing special assessors for school district property only.

INVESTMENT OF SCHOOL FUNDS

All but ten states authorize the investment of some school money. In 1952 Muelder reported that a sample of 50 school districts studied had invested over $207 million. Most of this was invested in United States government securities with anticipated yields ranging from about 1 to 2 percent annually.[19] Unfortunately, there is little research regarding the investment of school funds. Where school boards are engaged in the

business of investing school monies for the purposes of yielding a profit, the safety of investments should be of primary importance. Needless to say, the identity of the principal of any school fund should be maintained no matter how many or how complex the school investments. The interest earned on investments should be deposited in the account from which the invested money was temporarily withdrawn. Legal prescriptions as well as traditional practices have tended to restrict the investment of most school monies to short-term United States government securities. It is extremely questionable whether the investment of school monies that may be temporarily idle is properly the function of the board of education.

CLEARING ACCOUNTS OR REVOLVING FUNDS

The purpose of Clearing Accounts or Revolving Funds is to record the gross amounts of monies received and paid out for a variety of school activities. Among the activities whose financial transactions are best described through Clearing Accounts are food services, student body activities, the purchase and sale of textbooks, refunding of school bonds, athletics, short-term loans, deductions from payrolls, etc. Without Clearing Accounts or Revolving Funds there is a great likelihood of ending the fiscal year with a distorted picture of the total amount of school receipts and expenditures.

In the conduct of school business affairs certain financial transactions involve a double handling of money. To illustrate, money may be received from the operation of a given activity and then spent again for the same activity in the cycle of operations. If these activities were recorded in the regular Receipts and Expenditure Accounts, there would be a great distortion of financial operations. Revolving Funds or Clearing Accounts make it possible to record gross transactions for certain school activities outside of the regular Receipts and Expenditure Accounts.

The 1948 financial handbook prepared by the U.S. Office of Education used the term "Accounting for Advancements and Revolving Funds."[20] This book will adopt the term "Clearing Accounts" suggested in the 1957 USOE handbook.[21] Henceforth the term "Revolving Funds" will be dropped in favor of "Clearing Accounts."

If it is the policy of the school board to subsidize certain activities, the Clearing Accounts for such activities

[16] Ibid.
[17] National Education Association, Research Division, op. cit., p. 60.
[18] E. G. Wilkins, Public School Tax Management, Contributions to Education no. 703, New York: Teachers College, Columbia University, 1937.
[19] Wallace R. Muelder, "Investment of School District Funds," Proceedings of the Association of School Business Officials, 38th Convention, October, 1952, pp. 226–230.

[20] Foster and Akerly, op. cit., pp. 35–36.
[21] Reason and White, op. cit., pp. 105–139.

should be balanced at the end of the fiscal year and the net expenditures at such time for each activity posted to the appropriate Expenditure Accounts. If there is a balance, the net receipts are recorded in the appropriate Receipt Accounts and, therefore, made available for other general expenditures. If the net receipts are not available for general expenditure either through a policy of the board or its lack of financial control of certain activities listed in Clearing Accounts, the balance is carried forward from year to year for each of the various activities.

If it is not the policy of the board of education to subsidize school activities reported in the Clearing Accounts, then receipts or net expenditures are not recorded in the appropriate Receipt and Expenditure Accounts. The balance or deficit is then carried forward from year to year in each of the activities listed.

Clearing Accounts[22] start with ACCOUNT SERIES 1500—ASSET ACCOUNTS and conclude with ACCOUNT SERIES 1900—MISCELLANEOUS ACCOUNTS. Clearing Accounts are used in conjunction with Receipt and Expenditure Accounts. They include the financial transactions which are related to income as well as outgo.

ACCOUNT SERIES 1500—ASSET ACCOUNTS

Major Accounts for Petty Cash, Stores, Prepaid Insurance Premiums, Prepaid Rent, Securities, and Sinking Fund Accounts make up this series of accounts.

A. *Major Account 1510—Petty Cash Fund.* It includes money set aside for making change or immediate payments of comparatively small amounts. It is not a self-sustaining fund. As money is used, it must be replenished by making charges to the appropriate Expenditure Accounts for the amount to be replenished. *Petty Cash Fund* is considered a part of the current expense fund. At the end of the fiscal year the balance in the *Petty Cash Fund* is included in the cash balance of the current expense fund.

B. *Major Account 1520—Stores.* This major account is employed only in those school districts which have central storage facilities. It is not needed in the school districts where goods are delivered directly by the vendor to schools, individuals, or other organizational units. Expenditures for goods delivered to the central storage space are charged to *Major Account 1520—Stores.* After distribution of materials, charges in the value of the materials delivered are made to the appropriate Expenditures Accounts. The value of the remaining inventory in

the central storage place is reported as an asset in the financial statement.

Major Account 1520 was described as "Accounting for Stores" in Circular 204, the 1948 financial accounting handbook of the U.S. Office of Education.[23] It is considered in this book as one of the several Clearing Accounts that may be necessary in a school district.

C. *Major Account 1530—Prepaid Insurance Premiums.* This account is used only in school districts employing the accrual basis for accounting. Very often the total premium on insurance for a five-year period is paid during a given fiscal year. The part that applies to the first year is recorded under FIXED CHARGES, or *Major Account 820* and the rest is recorded under *Major Account 1530—Prepaid Insurance Premiums.* In preparing the financial statement any balance in this prepaid account is included as an asset.

D. *Major Account 1540—Prepaid Rent.* This account operates very much in the same way as does the account for prepaid insurance. School districts on the cash basis of accounting would not require this account but those on an accrual basis would.

E. *Major Account 1550—Securities.* This account is used to record the purchase and sale of United States government bonds and other securities. Investment of cash in securities or the sale of securities to obtain cash is merely an exchange of one asset for another. The financial condition of the school district is changed through such transactions only insofar as any profit or loss results. If the security is sold for a profit, the excess of money received over the purchase price is recorded under Account 14-b—Earning from Temporary Deposits and Investments. In reporting such financial transactions only the gross amounts received from the sale and gross amounts paid for the purchase of securities should be shown under the following numbered accounts.

1. Accounts 1550-a—Money Received from the Sale of Securities.
2. Account 1550-b—Money Paid Out for the Purchase of Securities.

F. *Major Account 1560—Sinking Fund Account.* Posted in this major classification are monies set aside or invested for the purpose of meeting payments on debts at some future date. Accounted herein are amounts of money which are permitted to accumulate over a period of years and which must be available for the redemption of long-term obligations at the date of maturity. Payments into the sinking funds are reported as expenditures under DEBT

---

[22] The accounting classification and names used in this section are adapted from *ibid.*, pp. 105–124.

[23] Foster and Akerly, *op. cit.*, p. 34.

SERVICE. This is necessary to make certain that the money is not available for other purposes. Without *Major Account 1560* districts could duplicate reports of debt service expenditures at the time money is disbursed from a sinking fund. This major account can be divided into the following numbered accounts:

1. Account 1560-a—Money Received into Sinking Funds from All Sources.
2. Account 1560-b—Money Paid Out from Sinking Funds.
   a. Subaccount 1560-b-1—Bonds.
   b. Subaccount 1560-b-2—Interest on Bonds.

ACCOUNT SERIES 1600—LIABILITY ACCOUNTS

Current and short-term loans and deductions from payrolls are classified as parts of the liability series of accounts. They can be organized as follows:

A. *Major Account 1610—Current and Short-Term Loans.* This account is needed to account for loans payable in the same fiscal year in which the money is borrowed. As defined previously, short-term loans are those with maturities of five years or less. Tax anticipation notes or warrants are treated as current loans if repaid from the very same tax collections anticipated at the times notes were executed. This account can be divided into:
   1. Account 1610-a—Money Received.
   2. Account 1610-b—Money Paid Out.
B. *Major Account 1620—Deductions from Payrolls.* Posted herein are payroll deductions which are to be transmitted to other agencies at periods other than those during which deductions were made. It should be noted that total salaries, including deductions, are recorded in Expenditure Accounts and not in *Major Account 1620.* The need for this account is prompted by the fact that there is a time lag between the payment of salary from which deductions are made and the forwarding of deductions made to the proper payee. By way of illustration federal withholding taxes are deposited in the Federal Reserve Bank monthly even though deducted weekly or biweekly from individual salaries or wages. This major account can be divided into:
   1. Account 1620-a—Money Received.
   2. Account 1620-b—Money Paid Out.

ACCOUNT SERIES 1700—FOOD SERVICES OPERATION

FOOD SERVICES OPERATION accounts are needed if such services are under the financial control of the school board and if the program is financed in whole or in part by revenue produced by this activity. School lunch programs and cafeterias are fairly common in public schools. Substantial federal and state aid in the form of actual cash outlays or food items is available for the support of school FOOD SERVICES. Without a means of recording financial transactions for FOOD SERVICES in this Clearing Account expenditures would be distorted as so much of what is spent is sustained by special receipts collected for such service.

Policy decisions influence what is finally done with net balances or deficits in FOOD SERVICES OPERATIONS at the end of the fiscal period. If, as a matter of policy, the school board agrees to subsidize cafeteria school lunch operations, then the net deficit at the end of the fiscal period is charged to *Major Account 930—Expenditures to Cover Deficit of a Separate Food Services Fund or Account.* On the other hand, if, as a matter of policy, the board does not subsidize FOOD SERVICES, then the net balance or deficit is not closed out to a regular Receipts or Expenditures Account but is carried forward from year to year. This series of accounts is divided into:

A. *Major Account 1710—Money Received.* This account can be further subdivided into:
   1. Account 1711—Money Received from the State for Food Services. This in turn has the following subclassifications:
      a. Subaccount 1711-a—State Aid for Food Services.
      b. Subaccount 1711-b—Federal Aid for Food Services.
   2. Account 1712—Money Received from Other Sources for Food Services. This is subdivided into:
      a. Subaccount 1712-a—Money Received from the Sale of Food
      b. Subaccount 1712-b—Miscellaneous Sources. Money received for food services but not recorded under Subaccount 1712-a.
B. *Major Account 1720—Money Paid Out.* This account includes the self-explanatory accounts:
   1. Account 1720-a—Salaries for Food Services.
   2. Account 1720-b—Food.
   3. Account 1720-c—Additional Equipment for Food Services.
   4. Account 1720-d—Replacement of Equipment for Food Services.
   5. Account 1720-e—Other Expenses for Food Services.

ACCOUNT SERIES 1800—OTHER OPERATION ACCOUNTS

ACCOUNT SERIES 1800 provides the means of recording the financial transactions more or less closely related to instruction. The financial actions of divers activities such as student body activities, school supply sales, textbook sales or rentals, and investment properties are recorded herein. Once again policy decisions influence final dispositions of net balances or deficits. In order to record herein the accounts of any of the following activities, they must be under the financial control of the board and wholly or partially financed by revenue produced from these activities. If the school board subsidizes any of these activities, they are closed out at the end of the fiscal year and balances or deficits are added to Receipts or Expenditure Accounts; otherwise the balance or deficit is carried from year to year.

This series of accounts starts with *Major Account 1810—Student Body Activities* and concludes with *Major Account 1840—Operation of Investment Properties.*

A. *Major Account 1810—Student Body Activities.* If these activities are not under the financial control of the body, these accounts are useful for at least supervisory control. If they are controlled by the board and it is board policy to subsidize such activities, net receipts at the end of the fiscal year are recorded in Account 14-c—Net Receipts from Revolving Funds or Clearing Accounts. Under similar policy conditions, if a deficit exists it is charged to *Major Account 1030—Expenditures to Cover Deficits of Student Body Activities Funds or Accounts. Major Account 1810* can be further subdivided into:
   1. Account 1811—Athletics or Interscholastic Athletics.
      a. Subaccount 1811-a—Money Received.
      b. Subaccount 1811-b—Money Paid Out.
   2. Account 1812—School Entertainments (Plays, Shows, Fairs, etc.).
      a. Subaccount 1812-a—Money Received.
      b. Subaccount 1812-b—Money Paid Out.
   3. Account 1813—School Publications.
      a. Subaccount 1813-a—Money Received.
      b. Subacount 1813-b—Money Paid Out.
   4. Account 1814—School Clubs and Other Cocurricular Activities.
      a. Subaccount 1814-a—Money Received.
      b. Subaccount 1814-b—Money Paid Out.
B. *Major Account 1820—Materials for Resale.* Posted herein are receipts and expenditures for materials or school supplies purchased for resale to students which are under the financial control of the school board. This major account may be subdivided into:
   1. Account 1820-a—Money Received.
   2. Account 1820-b—Money Paid Out.

C. *Major Account 1830—Textbooks.* This major account is used if the school district purchases textbooks and resells or rents them to students. It should not be used if free textbooks are used.
   1. Account 1830-a—Money Received.
   2. Acount 1830-b—Money Paid Out.
D. *Major Account 1840—Operation of Investment Properties.* Recorded herein are income and expenditures from property acquired for investment purposes to produce revenue for the support of the school.
   1. Account 1840-a—Money Received.
   2. Account 1840-b—Money Paid Out.
If the investment is part of the permanent fund, any net balance at the end of the fiscal year is closed out to Account 14-a; otherwise it is closed out to Account 14-e.

ACCOUNT SERIES 1900—MISCELLANEOUS ACCOUNTS

The miscellaneous accounts start with *Major Account 1910—Refunding Bonds* and conclude with *Major Account 1940—Interfund Transfers.* They can be organized as follows:
A. *Major Account 1910—Refunding Bonds*
   1. Account 1910-a—Money Received.
   2. Account 1910-b—Money Paid Out.
B. *Major Account 1920—Abatements*
   1. Account 1920-a—Money Received.
   2. Account 1920-b—Money Paid Out.
C. *Major Account 1930—Insurance Adjustments*
   1. Account 1930-a—Money Received.
   2. Account 1930-b—Money Paid Out.
D. *Major Account 1940—Interfund Transfers*
   1. Account 1940-a—Transfers from Other Funds.
   2. Account 1940-b—Transfers to Other Funds.

OUTLINE OF CLEARING ACCOUNTS

ACCOUNT SERIES 1500—ASSET ACCOUNTS
   Major Account 1510—Petty Cash Fund
   Major Account 1520—Stores
   Major Account 1530—Prepaid Insurance Premiums
   Major Account 1540—Prepaid Rent
   Major Account 1550—Securities
      Account 1550-a—Money Received
      Account 1550-b—Money Paid Out
   Major Account 1560—Sinking Fund Account
      Account 1560-a—Money Received
      Account 1560-b—Money Paid Out
         Subaccount 1560-b-1—Bonds
         Subaccount 1560-b-2—Interest on bonds
ACCOUNT SERIES 1600—LIABILITY ACCOUNTS
   Major Account 1610—Current and Short-Term Loans
      Account 1610-a—Money Received

Account 1610-b—Money Paid Out
Major Account 1620—Deductions from Payroll
Account 1620-a—Money Received
Account 1620-b—Money Paid Out

ACCOUNT SERIES 1700—FOOD SERVICES OPERATION
Major Account 1710—Money Received
Account 1711—Money Received from the State
Subaccount 1711-a—State
Subaccount 1711-b—Federal
Account 1712—Money Received from Other Sources
Subaccount 1712-a—Money Received from the Sale of Food
Subaccount 1712-b—Miscellaneous Sources
Major Account 1720—Money Paid Out
Account 1720-a—Salaries
Account 1720-b—Food
Account 1720-c—Additional Equipment
Account 1720-d—Replacement of Equipment
Account 1720-e—Other Expenses

ACCOUNT SERIES 1800—OTHER OPERATION ACCOUNTS
Major Account 1810—Student Body Activities
Account 1811—Athletics
Subaccount 1811-a—Money Received
Subaccount 1811-b—Money Paid Out
Account 1812—School Entertainments
Subaccount 1812-a—Money Received
Subaccount 1812-b—Money Paid Out
Account 1813—School Publications
Subaccount 1813-a—Money Received
Subaccount 1813-b—Money Paid Out
Account 1814—School Clubs and Other Cocurricular Activities
Subaccount 1814-a—Money Received
Subaccount 1814-b—Money Paid Out
Major Account 1820—Materials for Resale
Account 1820-a—Money Received
Account 1820-b—Money Paid Out
Major Account 1830—Textbooks
Account 1830-a—Money Received
Account 1830-b—Money Paid Out
Major Account 1840—Operation of Investment Properties
Account 1840-a—Money Received
Account 1840-b—Money Paid Out

ACCOUNT SERIES 1900—MISCELLANEOUS ACCOUNTS
Major Account 1910—Refunding Bonds
Account 1910-a—Money Received
Account 1910-b—Money Paid Out
Major Account 1920—Abatements
Account 1920-a—Money Received
Account 1920-b—Money Paid Out
Major Account 1930—Insurance Adjustments
Account 1920-a—Money Received
Account 1920-b—Money Paid Out
Major Account 1940—Interfund Transfers
Account 1940-a—Money Received
Account 1940-b—Money Paid Out

SUMMARY

School revenues have increased by approximately 500 percent in the space of 25 years since 1930. All school revenues are receipts but not all receipts are revenues. Revenue receipts are additions to assets that do not increase debts or deplete property values. Nonrevenue receipts produce money at the expense of incurring an obligation or reducing property values.

It is strongly recommended that the 1957 USOE financial accounting handbook be used as the basis of achieving uniformity in accounting for school receipts. Receipts should be recorded by (1) source (local, intermediate, state, or federal levels of government) and (2) method of production (taxes, appropriations, fees, etc.). Incoming Transfer Accounts are necessary to present a true picture of school receipts for the state or the nation as a whole.

Careful accounting is one method of protecting school district funds. It is imperative that all persons who collect school money or keep records be bonded. All checks and vouchers should be validated by at least two signatures. In general, administrative safeguards should minimize opportunities for defalcations from school funds.

Funds which accrue to the district should be deposited the day they are received. Few changes in school fund custody took place from 1870 to 1930. The school board treasurer system is still most prevalent even though the depository system is more desirable. Selection of school depositories should be based on the criteria of security and service rather than amount of interest on idle funds.

Few school districts collect as well as levy taxes. School taxes can be more efficiently collected by municipal or county tax agencies than school districts.

Clearing Accounts are needed to record gross amounts of monies collected and disbursed. Double handling of some funds can distort the picture of total school receipts and expenditures during a given fiscal year, if Clearing Accounts are not used. Clearing Accounts (formerly known as Revolving Funds) are used in conjunction with Receipt and Expenditure Accounts.

QUESTIONS

1. Identify the following:
   a. revenue receipt
   b. nonrevenue receipt
   c. abatements
2. When is an abatement a revenue receipt?

3. Why is it necessary to separate receipts into revenue and nonrevenue receipts?
4. What are the advantages and shortcomings of the depository system in caring for school funds?
5. What are the advantages and dangers of investing temporarily idle school monies?
6. Why is it desirable to institute a system of Clearing Accounts as well as Receipt and Expenditure Accounts?
7. What procedures should be instituted to safeguard school funds?
8. What in your estimation would be the minimum Receipt Accounts needed in all school systems in the United States?
9. What in your estimation would be the minimum Clearing Accounts needed in all school systems in the United States?

SELECTED REFERENCES

Arnold, William E., Casteter, William B., Ruesser, Walter C., and Verhallen, Roman J., "Business Management—Safeguarding School Funds and Property" in R. L. Johns and E. L. Morphet (eds.), *Problems and Issues in Public School Finance,* New York: Teachers College, Columbia University, 1952.

Beach, Fred F., *The Custody of School Funds,* Contributions to Education no. 577, New York: Teachers College, Columbia University, 1933.

Mort, Paul R., and Ruesser, Walter C., *Public School Finance,* New York: McGraw-Hill Book Company, rev. ed., 1951.

National Education Association, Research Division, "Fiscal Authority of School Boards," *Research Bulletin,* Washington, D.C.: NEA, April, 1950.

Reason, Paul L., and White, Alpheus L., *Financial Accounting for Local and State School Systems, Standard Receipt and Expenditure Accounts,* Bulletin 1957, no. 4, U.S. Office of Education, Washington, D.C.: U.S. Government Printing Office, 1957.

CHAPTER 5

The Purchasing and Management of School Supplies and Equipment

SCHOOL DISTRICTS INCUR LIABILITIES THROUGH purchasing services and materials needed in the educational process. The majority of school expenditures are made for the personal services of teachers, supervisors, principals, superintendents, custodians, clerk-typists, and others. Salary schedules and payroll management for personal services of regular and temporary employees will be reported in the chapter that follows. The emphasis in this chapter will be on business procedures for incurring liabilities through requisitioning, procuring, managing, and inventorying school materials and supplies.

Procurement of school materials begins with the initiation of a request or requisition to supply a certain need and ends with the approval of an invoice or payment. Following procurements comes the management of goods received through functionally designed systems of central storage, distribution, and inventory.

This chapter on purchasing and the one that follows on payroll practices precede the chapter on accounting for school expenditures for several reasons. One is that the purchase act and contracts for personal services supply the original transactions upon which accounting for expenditures is based. A second is that the authorization for fund disbursement or encumbrance accounting is related closely to the purchase act and salary payment.

SUPPLIES AND EQUIPMENT

There is a fine line that separates a school supply item from an item of equipment. The differentiation between the two is an arbitrary one. The 1957 U.S. Office of Education financial accounting handbook developed the following criteria for classifying an item as a supply or equipment.

A supply item is any article or material which meets any *one* or more of the following conditions:
1. It is consumed in use.
2. It loses its original shape or appearance with use.
3. It is expendable. That is, if the article is damaged or some of its parts are lost or worn out, it is usually more feasible to replace it with an entirely new unit rather than to repair it.
4. It is an inexpensive item having characteristics of equipment whose small unit cost makes it inadvisable to capitalize the item.
5. It loses its identity through incorporation into a different or more complex unit of substance.

An equipment item is an immovable or fixed unit of furniture or furnishings, an instrument, a machine, an apparatus or a set of articles which meets *all* of the following conditions:
1. It retains its original shape and appearance with use.
2. It is non-expendable, that is, if the article is damaged or some of its parts are lost or worn out, it is usually more feasible to repair it rather than replace it with an entirely new unit.

3. It represents an investment of money which makes it feasible and advisable to capitalize the item.
4. It does not lose its identity through incorporation into a different or more complex unit or substance.[1]

Another differentiation between the supplies and equipment is based primarily on the cost. If an item purchased costs less than five dollars, it is classified as a supply whereas if it costs five dollars or more, it is an item of equepment. Although this arbitrary cost differentiation is a convenient one, it does not satisfy all the criteria of differentiation listed above. Uniformity in differentiation between supplies and equipment inevitably necessitates the development of a list of what shall be labeled a supply or equipment. Many state accounting handbooks prepare such lists. An alphabetical list of supplies and equipment other than built-in equipment developed by the United States Office of Education is found in the Appendix.[2]

THE REQUISITION

The requisition is a formal written request from a person or department in the school system for the purchase of supplies or equipment. It should be kept in mind that the requisition is a request and not a guarantee that a purchase will actually be made. Whether the requisition shall be translated into a definite purchase order depends upon whether the item requested is not on hand in the central warehouse,

[1] Paul L. Reason and Alpheus L. White, *Financial Accounting for Local and State School Systems, Standard Receipt and Expenditure Accounts,* Bulletin 1957, no. 4, U.S. Office of Education, Washington, D.C.: U.S. Government Printing Office, p. 191.

[2] *Ibid.*, pp. 193–215, or the Appendix, pp. 313–324.

REQUISITION **BOARD OF EDUCATION**
City of Madison 3, Wisconsin.
No.

____________ School

____________ Department Date ____________ 195___

1 Quantity Requested	2 Purchase Order No.	3 Description and Size of Item Name and Address of Dealer	4 Budget Acct. No.	5 Estimated Cost	6 Account No.	7 Budget Yes	No

Approved: ____________ SUPT. OF SCHOOLS ____________ DATE

Approved: ____________ SUPT. OF PURCHASES ____________ DATE

Principal or Supervisor sign below:
(Signed) ____________ PRINCIPAL OR SUPERVISOR

Requisitioning officers will fill in columns 1, 3 and 4 only. Place check mark after period covered by this requisition.

FIGURE 5. Requisition Form. Courtesy of the Madison, Wisconsin, Public Schools

Board of Education, Madison 3, Wisconsin   No.

Office of Secretary and Supervisor of Purchases and Supplies

351 West Wilson Street   Phone ALpine 6-1911

Indicate this Number
on Invoice

Purchase Order

_____19___

TO_____

_____

_____

Please Enter Our Order for Immediate Delivery.

School_____ Account No._____

QUANTITY	DESCRIPTION	TOTAL
	TOTAL	

Send to:

Invoice to: Board of Education
351 W. Wilson St.
Madison, Wis.

Requisition No._____

BOARD OF EDUCATION

By_____
SECRETARY AND SUPERVISOR OF PURCHASES AND SUPPLIES

PLEASE FORWARD INVOICE IMMEDIATELY

No claim will be considered unless
supported by a purchase order.

Per_____

FIGURE 6.   Purchase Order Form. Courtesy of the Madison, Wisconsin, Public Schools

whether it is included in the adopted budget, whether unencumbered funds are available, etc.

As many copies of the requisition should be filed as are needed for the business operation. One copy must be forwarded to the purchasing office in the school system. If the person making the request desires a copy, then at least two must be made. If one copy of the requisition is to be held in the files of the head of the department, three copies are necessary. If it is deemed desirable to keep a copy in the building principal's office, then the requisition must be issued in quadruplicate.

As a general rule, any form filled out in the school system should be written in as few copies as necessary to execute the act and control it. Each copy must be justified in terms of the function to be performed. No fewer than two copies of the requisition are necessary and in large systems as many as four may be necessary for control and complete information. If a requisition must be approved by the head of the department to which the teacher is assigned as well as by the building principal, each person required to pass on the requisition is entitled to a copy for his files.

THE PURCHASE ORDER

The duly approved requisition, in effect, originates the purchase order. The purchase order is a document which authorizes a vendor (seller) to deliver described merchandise or material at a specified price. When accepted by the vendor, the purchase order becomes a contract. The precise number of copies of a purchase order to be executed is determined by the nature of the act, the degree of control, and who should be informed that a purchase was made.

One copy of the purchase order is sent to the vendor to actuate the purchase. One copy should be sent to the accounting department as basic data for encumbrance accounting. A third copy should be sent to the individual who is to receive the goods or to the central warehouse if such exists. A fourth copy will be necessary for the records of the purchasing department. The purchasing department's copy of a purchase order can be filed either by the vendor or by the department or account making the purchase. If there is to be any cross-index filing of the purchase order by the vendor as well as by the department ordering or the account against which it is to be charged, then the purchasing department must keep two copies. This makes a total of five copies of the purchase order and six could be justified if the person who made the request is entitled to formal notice of the purchase. At least five and possibly six copies of the purchase order can be justified in a very large school system. In a small school system, two or three copies of the purchase order may accomplish the same purpose as five or six in the very large system. Each school system must develop a system for executing purchase orders in the numbers required to satisfy local need. "Red tape" is another way of saying more copies than needed are prepared.

Several conditions must be satisfied before the purchase order can be mailed to the vendor. The first step is careful check of inventory to make certain it is not already on hand. Some factors are related to the items to be purchased, some to budgeting, and others to accounting procedures. They will be discussed in that order.

The degree of formality in school purchase orders varies from an informal letter declaring intent to purchase to a notarized and formal purchase order form. Better business practices would dictate the use of some type of purchase order form rather than orders on school letterheads.

SPECIFICATIONS FOR PURCHASING

The specifications for an item to be purchased describe in clear and concise terms the characteristics of what is to be purchased and the conditions under which the purchase is to be made. To be certain that the vendor will send what is requested, there must be mutual understanding between the purchaser and the vendor as to the precise nature of the item in question. This often necessitates the development of a detailed description or specifications. Without a clear understanding of the item to be purchased, the prospective vendors are not in a position to quote prices and fill orders intelligently.

There are many ways to describe the commodity desired. The simplest is designation of one or more brand names. A very common practice is merely naming the item with no further descriptions. The naming can vary from specifying a manufacturer's brand to a catalog number specified by a supplier. Purchasing under such conditions would seldom require testing or checking of the qualities of a sample of the items desired. Where bidding is necessary, the lowest responsible bidder on any of the brands specified is usually acceptable. It is standard procedure to specify more than one brand name for the item named. To illustrate, if all manual standard keyboard typewriters are regarded as equal, then the names Underwood, Remington, Royal, Smith, etc., can be designated for a given model standard 11-inch carriage, pica type machine. When only brand

BOARD OF EDUCATION

Telephone ALpine 6-1911

No.

City of Madison, Wisconsin

351 West Wilson Street

OFFICE OF THE SECRETARY and SUPERVISOR
OF ACCOUNTS, PURCHASES
and SUPPLIES

Date_____

This is not a Purchase Order

To_____

_____

_____

Please quote price to the Board of Education on the material as listed below. Submit quotation on this form, placing price opposite items listed. The right is reserved to accept or reject all or part of proposal submitted.

W. N. McDaniels,

Secretary and Supervisor of Accounts,

Purchases and Supplies

Quotations must be in this office not later than_____

Quantity	Article	If Unable to Furnish Material as Specified, List Substitution Here.	List	Discount	Net

Quote price per_____F. O. B._____

Can Deliver _____ Terms_____

(STATE EXACT DATE.)

Remarks:_____

Date_____ Signed_____

Information regarding disposition will be furnished **only on request.** accompanied by a self-addressed stamped envelope. If you are unable to bid on this material please return quotation.

QUOTATION INQUIRY BD. FORM 2

FIGURE 7.   Quotation Inquiry Form. Courtesy of the Madison, Wisconsin, Public Schools

names with little else are specified, the words "or its equivalent" should be added.

Although specifying by brand name or catalog number is simple, it will not always satisfy the demands of all purchasing situations. This is particularly true for highly specialized equipment which requires special manufacture. Under such conditions accurate specifications or descriptions are necessary for the item desired. The great majority of items purchased by schools are standardized with grades acceptable throughout the industry. Even the federal government with many thousands of different items to buy has only about 1700 formalized specifications outside of those used for the armed services.[3]

Most specifications are based on performance requirements. After the item purchased under performance specifications is received, the board has the obligation to test whether it will meet standards demanded. This can be done either by the scientific laboratory method or by actual tests on the job. To illustrate: a performance test can be made to determine the relative efficiency of samples of stencil correction fluid. This is done simply by using different brands of stencils with some intentional errors cut on each. Various samples of correction fluid are tested by performance in eradicating the error. This involves a visual evaluation of the mimeographed sheet prepared from corrected stencils with an expression of preference from those who are likely to use the correction fluid; namely, qualified typists.

Larger school systems may find it worth while to organize a laboratory for testing purchases. Even in the smaller school system, however, a high school science teacher or a nearby college or university laboratory may be available at little cost for such testing.[4]

A combination of specifications based on the brand name and those developed in greater detail and based on performance can be used as well. In all cases, the supplier should certify that the material sent will live up to the specifications. In case of dispute, the buyer has the right to have the material tested and to charge this to the supplier if the material does not comply with specifications. If it does, the buyer bears the expense.

There is considerable dispute as to the value of full and complete specifications based on performance. With many new products coming out, the file of specifications can become obsolete in a relatively short period of time. This is true even with such standard products as paints. New developments in paints can render all specifications obsolete, and for this reason many superintendents question whether the time and effort placed in developing careful specifications are worth while. Furthermore, it is impossible to write a description of some products as accurately as they can be described by a trade name. For this reason schools have tended, by and large, to purchase on the basis of several trade names or catalog numbers with the usual proviso "or its equivalent" or "its equal" placed in the specification description. There is considerable value to good specifications and it is questionable whether good purchasing can be practiced effectively without them. The danger of rigidity and verbosity is always present.

The preparation of specifications is not the sole function of the purchasing agency. Information from departments which use the item and from the vendors usually contacted for quotations or bids should be solicited during the preparation of specifications. Actually no item should be purchased without checking with the user. The objective of specifications is quality control. Many large school systems prepare a standardized list of supplies and equipment. Teachers use the list to make purchases. Without some degree of standardization of such items as paper the purchasing and inventory problems are greatly compounded.

Most schools lack the facilities for developing detailed specifications. Federal specifications now available for every item of need in every department of the federal government can be a handy reference for schools.[5] The federal government also publishes an extensive list of testing services.[6]

INFORMAL PURCHASING, BIDDING, AND QUOTATIONS

A large share of school purchasing is accomplished in a rather informal manner. A salesman calls and the order is placed at that time or the purchase is made based on catalogs left by salesmen. It is a relatively inexpensive and quick way of making purchases so long as the price is not much more than it would be through competitive bidding on the same number of articles. Going a step further, but still remaining rather informal, is seeking quotations by letter or by telephone and making purchases on this bid. This can be carried still further to purchasing on the basis of rather informal sealed bids where further negotiation is possible.

[3] George S. Frank, "Purchasing Specifications," *School Business Affairs,* Association of School Business Officials, August, 1951, *17:*1–2.

[4] See Monroe Milton, "The Place of Testing and Good Buying Procedures," *School Business Affairs,* Association of School Business Officials, October, 1954, *20:*5, 7.

[5] U.S. National Bureau of Standards, *Federal Standard Stock Catalog of Specifications,* General Service Administration, Washington, D.C.: U.S. Government Printing Office.

[6] U.S. National Bureau of Standards, *Directory of Commercial and College Laboratories,* Washington, D.C.: U.S. Government Printing Office, 1951.

There is nothing fundamentally wrong with informal methods of purchasing executed with the honesty and professional care that purchasing deserves.

The question also arises as to the propriety of patronizing merchants within the local school district. There is nothing fundamentally wrong with this practice particularly if the price offered by local merchants is competitive. On the other hand, there is no reason why all school purchases should be placed with local merchants. This would be particularly true if items of the same quality or better could be purchased at a much lower price from others. All the taxpayers should not be forced to bear an increased burden simply because a local merchant demanding higher profit cries that he is a taxpayer.

Legal requirements in certain states demand that large purchases be on the basis of formal and sealed bids. The original purpose behind bidding requirements was not to increase efficiency of purchasing but rather to prevent fraud. Very often state laws demand formal bids on purchases in excess of certain sums. In Florida, Pennsylvania, and West Virginia formal bids must be submitted for purchases in excess of $300. Other states such as California, Iowa, Massachusetts, Minnesota, New York, Washington, and Wisconsin allow informal purchasing up to $1000 and demand bids at that figure and beyond. On the other hand, Ohio recently passed legislation to permit school purchases up to $6000 before formal bidding is required. Ernst pointed out that the $1000 limit on purchasing without bids was introduced over 25 years ago at a time when the purchasing power of the dollar was only approximately one-half of its value today.[7] The Hoover commission estimated that it costs the federal government $10 for every order written no matter whether the value of the items amounted to $5 or $500. The cost of advertising bids in a newspaper is the same no matter what the size of the purchase. Ernst implied that formal bids on purchases of $1000 or more was too restrictive and that the limit should be raised to more defensible levels. Others argue, however, that at least informal bidding through direct letters to suppliers seeking firm quotations on materials specified should be installed no matter what the legal requirements.

Formal bids must be carefully prepared and duly advertised. Bids can be prepared for a single item or a combination of many items, but the quantities and qualities should be clearly specified. The bid forms prepared by the school and submitted by the bidders should be so prepared that bidders need only fill in the prices. All bids should be sent by registered mail in a sealed container. The bids should not be opened until the advertised date for the opening of bids. Those who bid are entitled to be present at the board meeting during which the sealed bids are opened for inspection. In all cases, the board should advertise its right to reject any and all bids. The supplier winning the bid need not be the lowest bidder but rather the lowest responsible bidder for the quality and quantity of items desired. Samples may be required. The samples become the property of the school district and the buyer reserves the right to retain or destroy the samples for purposes of testing, free of any actions or claims on the part of the contractors. The bidders are expected, however, to assume full responsibility for the delivery and removal of all samples. Needless to say, these samples must be carefully labeled so that the vendor supplying them is properly credited.

As a general rule, bids should be allowed to be withdrawn before they have been opened but not after having been submitted and opened. It is a good procedure to demand that all bids be submitted on the special form provided by the purchasing department. The prices should not include excise or other taxes from which these schools are exempted. It is not desirable that the prices have qualifications such as "insurance and delivery shall constitute additional charges." The F.O.B. delivery point should be the local school or warehouse to avoid embarrassment in the event goods are damaged in transit.

All bidders on supplies and equipment should show their good faith by submitting certified checks or bid bonds along with their bids. The checks or bonds should be made in the name of the board of education. Actually, it is good practice to refuse to accept bids for consideration unless accompanied by a certified check or bid bond equal to no less than 5 percent or more than 10 percent of the bid. Certified checks and bid bonds are returned to those whose bids were not accepted. The board has the authority to cash the certified check or seek recovery on the bid bond if the successful bidder fails to enter into fulfillment of obligations stated in the terms of the bid. When the successful bidder accepts the contract he is asked to file a performance bond equal to 100 percent of the contract. Failure to execute obligations of the contract will precipitate board action to recover damages through action on the performance bond.

COÖPERATIVE PURCHASING

There is evidence that coöperative purchasing is of considerable value. In coöperative purchasing agreements several school districts get together to sub-

---

[7] Joseph L. Ernst, "Remove Legal Barriers to Efficient Purchasing," *School Business Affairs*, Association of School Business Officials, April, 1952, *18*:1, 6, 8.

mit a single large purchase rather than several small purchases of the same items. The objective is savings that result from quantity buying. Coöperative buying can be easily achieved through the intermediate administrative unit which is rapidly becoming a service unit to local school districts. Some states such as North Carolina have a state purchasing system for items such as school buses.

Shaeffer reported that savings of upwards of $100,-000 annually plus indirect savings and other benefits accrued to the city of Cincinnati, the Cincinnati Board of Education, the county of Hamilton, the University of Cincinnati, and the Public Library of Cincinnati in Hamilton County through a Coördinating Committee on Purchasing.[8]

The functions of the Hamilton County Coördinating Committee on Purchasing are (1) to determine which items should be purchased jointly, (2) to ascertain the method of purchase—formal contract, informal agreement, direct purchase, etc., (3) to standardize items purchased to reduce the existing diversity of sizes and types, (4) to formulate standard specifications to be used in soliciting bids, (5) to standardize bid contract agreement forms within legal restrictions imposed on various units, (6) to develop methods of testing and inspecting purchases, (7) to make the necessary joint purchases, (8) to facilitate the adoption of uniform contracting dates.[9]

Such materials as gasoline, fuel oil, automobile lubricating oil, Portland cement, premixed concrete, concrete sewer pipe and fittings, wrought iron and steel pipe and fittings, incandescent and fluorescent lamps, passenger car, truck, bus, and industrial tires and tubes, carbon paper and ribbons, calendar pads, various types of soaps and soap products, and cleaning compounds have been bought through the efforts of the Hamilton County Coördinating Committee on Purchasing. Altogether there are in existence approximately 200 agreements and 50 contracts against which the five independent governmental units may acquire their requirements of approximately 400 odd individual items.

The success of this and other coöperative purchasing agreements clearly indicates their usefulness. Savings can result through buying in carload lots rather than small units. The success of these and other plans clearly indicates a possible trend in coöperative purchasing through informal organizations or through the intermediate unit of school administration.

[8] Robert W. Shaeffer, "Coördinating Governmental Purchases," *School Business Affairs,* Association of School Business Officials, April, 1953, *19*:1, 8.
[9] *Ibid.*

TIMING OF PURCHASES

Considerable evidence points to the fact that only a minority of school districts spread their purchases over the entire fiscal year. About three-fourths of all purchases are made during the months of June, July, and August. Only one school district in ten places orders throughout the school year. Peak purchasing loads create problems for vendors and result in higher costs which are passed on to the buyer. Peak loads also slow down delivery services. Vendors are forced to be extremely busy during a relatively short period of time, which usually lasts no more than three months, and to have a slack season of almost nine months. It would be highly desirable if school districts could schedule their purchases in such a way as to spread them out over the year rather than placing a large load near the end of one fiscal year and the beginning of another.

Slow payments to vendors likewise increase costs to schools. The great majority of schools fail to pay within the 30-day period and most have their accounts payable exceed 90 days. This is not a desirable procedure and is an undue burden upon the vendor. Unless there is a satisfactory explanation or the school requests such service in an effort to reduce the peak buying periods, failure to pay bills when due can only be labeled as unsatisfactory business procedures.

PURCHASING POLICY

It is the function of the board of education to indicate clearly what policy shall be followed in purchasing procedure. The guiding policy should be that all buying shall be done through the executive branch of the school district and not by individual school board members. At the time the budget is presented the board should be informed of proposed purchases during the fiscal year with a justification of each. When the board adopts the budget, it is in effect approving the expenditures plan within which are the items to be bought during the fiscal period. The requirement that the school administrator obtain approval of the board before any purchase previously adopted within the budget is not only frustrating but poor business procedure. The budget, in effect, controls all purchases. After adoption it should be considered the authorization for the executive department to make such purchases as are consistent with budgetary appropriations and the flow of income to the school district during the fiscal year. It follows that any extrabudgetary purchases must of necessity be approved by the board of education prior to execution.

Business has recognized the importance of a specialized purchasing department. The practice of employing purchasing agents is slow in developing even in large school districts. It would be highly unusual if purchasing agents were not confronted by continual calls from salesmen and suppliers. Reputable salesmen and suppliers deserve courteous treatment. They can make the buyers' task easier, but some have also been known to outwear their welcome.

It is inevitable that there will be pressures on purchasing agents from local and other people who have something to sell. The expensive gifts to those responsible for placing school orders on the occasion of a birthday, the start of the school term, Christmas time, etc., are a more subtle form of pressure or means to obtain a more favorable hearing.

Every school district should have a policy statement if not a buying code which covers gifts that may add up to sizable sums. Whether advertising materials such as calendars belong in the category of gifts is open to question but deserves clarification.

It is important that only the highest ethics or principles be followed where expenditure of public funds is involved. The policy which is likely to result in the least amount of embarrassment is one which demands that all gifts sent to school purchasing agents by salesmen or suppliers be returned. Such subtle pressure should not be permitted to influence the activities of school purchasing agents.

A buying and selling code for schools was developed through the efforts of the American Association of School Administrators, The Association of School Business Officials, the National School Board Associations, and the National School Service Institute. Some states have adopted special purchasing codes as well. Some purposes of the national code were to set forth principles designed to promote economy, increase service, insure reliability, facilitate purchase and delivery practices, and establish buying and selling procedures of a highly ethical and mutually satisfying caliber.

Some highlights of this code are:

1. The welfare of children must always come first in the purchase of items. These items must be bought with the idea of fitting the needs of school teachers and the students.
2. The practice of bidding on quantity orders with its many ramifications raises more problems than any other buying and selling activity. It was recommended that boards be delegated authority to buy with certain specified limits and categories. Where bidding prevails, ample time should be allotted for the careful preparation of bids.
3. Specifications should be complete in all details and be based on sufficient knowledge of the use, functional value, and longevity of the product. Thus, specifications should never be so loose that price becomes the only factor, for the cheapest article seldom represents the best value in use.
4. In naming a company product or brand name the qualifying term "or equal" should be avoided unless the "equal" is to be properly tested.
5. Samples received from vendors should be protected against tampering by competitors.
6. Three-fourths of the year's business is delivered within two months and this results in more expensive products, for the seller must hire extra and inexperienced help, schedule overtime, and risk shortages and shipments. Many times materials are ordered for September delivery and not used until January.
7. Good business practices in public schools demand that there be a clear set of policies governing procurement practices in public schools.

MANAGEMENT OF SUPPLIES AND INVENTORY

Buying in large quantities will result in savings only if supported by careful inventory, storage, and distribution. To illustrate, the purchase of a sufficient quantity of mimeograph, hectograph, or other papers to last the entire school year can save money as well as time spent in frequent ordering through the year. However, improper storage or distribution of paper can waste more than what was saved through quantity buying.

Contracts with the vendor calling for even flow of items purchased during the year may minimize the central storage space needed but never eliminates the need for storage. Central storerooms must be properly heated, ventilated, and kept dry.

All items should be placed in a storeroom only after being carefully checked. Checking would include (1) comparison of the invoice sent by the vendor with the purchase order sent by the school, (2) comparison of invoice with the materials received, (3) examination to reveal any damaged or broken materials, (4) execution of the necessary storeroom records to insure proper cataloging and ease of inventory, and (5) placement of materials in the appropriate storage places.

A central warehouse may be necessary in a large school system but at least a single storage place is needed in a smaller one. Decentralized storage in the building where the materials are to be used has the advantage of low overhead through the elimination of deliveries, the original cost and upkeep of central warehouse, and the need for storeroom clerks. In decentralized storage systems employees in each building are usually aware of supplies that they have in their room and are, therefore, more likely to consume them before requesting the purchase of others.

Decentralized storage does reduce red tape, but at the same time it may result in an overabundance of supplies in one building and a lack of supplies in another. The smaller the system, the more effectively decentralized is the storage. At what point central storage and warehousing is more effective is not definitely known. The advantage of central stores becomes more apparent with the addition of each new and separate building.

It is imperative that the requisition be checked against inventory in storerooms before any purchases be made. Purchases should be made only after due determination that the item does not exist in the central warehouse. Withdrawal of items from the central warehouse should follow very much the same procedure as purchasing. Items should be withdrawn only on request in written form. After withdrawal the proper storeroom records must be checked.

Most authorities recommend that there be a continuing inventory system. This is a system based on an actual count of materials as they enter the central storeroom or warehouse. After each withdrawal, the inventory is immediately reduced rather than waiting to post such information at the end of the fiscal year. A continuous inventory system does not do away with the necessity of the annual count. This is particularly true for large items such as furniture. Without careful inventory and inventory practices, considerable waste and inefficient use of materials will result. Purchasing in large quantities can only result in saving if there is adequate storage, careful inventory, and proper distribution of materials to the places where they are needed. Teachers must be continually informed of the procedure for obtaining materials from the central storeroom.

ACCOUNTING PROCEDURES FOR SCHOOL PURCHASING

It was indicated in the opening portion of this chapter that the requisition initiates the purchase order. The purchase order initiates the purchase act by mailing such order to the vendor. No purchase order can be released, however, unless it is ascertained that (1)

funds are available in the school budget for such a purchase; that is, a purchase was authorized in the budget for the school year, (2) that funds were appropriated for the purchase, and (3) that the unencumbered funds are greater than the estimated cost of the item to be purchased. It is only after these checks have been made that the purchase order with a clear specification of items wanted can be released to the vendor.

The purchase order is one of the fundamental or primary accounting transactions. Often a purchase order journal is prepared and regarded as the accounts payable ledger.

The invoice is sent by the vendor to the school district and is a document showing the character, quantity, price, terms, nature of delivery, and other particulars of goods sold or services rendered to the school district. The invoice is sometimes sent with the goods to the school district, or it is sent under a separate cover. After the invoice is matched with the purchase order and the materials received, it is duly marked as approved by the receiving agency of the school district and sent to the accounting department for the payment. The invoice is noted in the encumbrance file and entered on the voucher or check register. The voucher check is sent in original form to the vendor with the duplicate kept in the voucher jacket and used as the entry to the proper Expenditure Account.

AN OUTLINE OF PROCUREMENT PROCEDURE

Steps in procurement can be outlined as follows:

a. Requisition	Initiated by user, sent to purchasing official for approval, one copy retained by the user or the school.
b. Specifications	Prepared in detail by purchasing official and made available to prospective contractors or vendors.
c. Bids or Quotations	Checked and tabulated by a purchasing official and recommendation made to board of education on formal bids.
d. Contract or Purchase Order	Contract signed by designated board official, order signed by purchasing official.
e. Follow-Up by Purchasing Official	
f. Receipt of Goods	Requisitioner signs receipt and sends to purchasing official, indicating whether quantity and quality are satisfactory.

g. Invoice	Check for price, quantity, and extensions by purchasing official.
h. Quality Control	Purchasing official checks to see that item meets specification.
i. Invoice Approved for Payment	Purchasing official and board of education approve invoice after receipt of goods is acknowledged by requisitioner.
j. Payment of Vendor	Accounting and treasury officials pay vendor after due notice in voucher register and issuance of voucher checks.[10]

SUMMARY

The following factors should be considered in making purchases.

1. There should be a standardized list of supplies and equipment, indicating supplies and equipment available per subject per year, which should be subject to annual revision.
2. The kind, quantity, and quality of all equipment and supplies, in any school system, should be justified from the standpoint of improvement of educational or instructional services.
3. Controlled experimental studies, having as their objective the scientific determination of quality and quantity of supplies and equipment required, should be continuous.
4. Requests for new and additional educational supplies and equipment should come from the teacher.
5. These requests for a particular supply or equipment should be based on justifiable needs of desirable activities.
6. Sufficient notice of contemplated change in any equipment or supplies should be given to the purchasing agent to permit the making of arrangements whereby supplies on hand can be used before changes are made.
7. Hoarding of supplies and equipment by teachers and janitors should be prevented.
8. A periodical inspection of the classrooms and individual school storage rooms should be made to see that supplies and equipment are being properly and economically used.
9. Expenditures for supplies and equipment should be in strict accordance with budgetary policies.
10. Purchases should be made at times when best advantages of market prices may be had.
11. All purchases, insofar as possible, should be made from the largest number of competitive closed bids.
12. Purchases should be made from specifications wherever possible.
13. The quality of the material should not be in excess of that which will meet the specific need; neither should it be below such standards.
14. The direct responsibility for the selection of educational supplies and equipment should be lodged with the superintendent or someone responsible to him, those who are to use this equipment, and those assigned purchasing duties.
15. The use of equipment and supplies should determine their selection.
16. The selection of supplies and equipment should be a coöperative task between the user, purchasing agent, committees, and superintendent.
17. A scientific study should be made to determine which material or supply is best.
18. Supplies and equipment should be selected by those who know their value for the purpose for which they are to be used.
19. The purchasing agent should keep an up-to-date file containing names of all reliable vendors handling the various items.
20. A copy of specifications should be available for each vendor requesting it, providing an intention to participate in the bidding is indicated.
21. When bids have been opened and tabulated, consideration should be given in each case to the lowest and best bidder, quality and service considered.
22. It is essential that samples be submitted with bids when substitutes are offered or when specifically requested.
23. All bids should be accompanied by a certified check amounting to not over 10 percent of the bid, assuming a fixed minimum and maximum.
24. The person in charge of purchases should retain supervision and control until the supplies are delivered to the school.
25. All supplies should be kept in and delivered from a central or separate storeroom.
26. The stockroom should have a diagram showing the location of all items stored in it.
27. Coöperative purchasing among school boards is worthy of consideration.
28. An order to purchase should constitute an order to use discounts for prompt payment.[11]

QUESTIONS

1. What are the basic differences between a supply item and an equipment item?
2. What is the relationship between a requisition and a purchase order?
3. What are the advantages and problems in developing and maintaining a file of specifications for purchasing?
4. Identify the following:
   a. coöperative purchasing
   b. vendor
   c. continuous inventory
   d. invoice

[10] University of the State of New York, *School Business Management Handbook*, Purchases and Stores, no. 5, Albany, N.Y.: The State Education Department, 1955, p. 24.

[11] Adapted from National Association of Public School Business Officials, *Selection, Purchase, Storage and Distribution of Supplies*, The Committee on Supply Research, Supply and Equipment, series no. 1, Trenton, N.J.: the Association, 1932, pp. 49–51.

e. purchase order journal

f. performance bond

5. Assume you were a school superintendent. What purchasing policies would you seek the school board to approve?

6. Outline the steps to be followed in calling for formal bids for school purchasing.

7. What are the advantages and disadvantages to establishing a standardized list of school supplies?

SELECTED REFERENCES

Ernst, Joseph L., "Remove Legal Barriers to Efficient Purchasing," *School Business Affairs,* Association of School Business Officials, April, 1952.

Frank, George S., "Purchasing Specifications," *School Business Affairs,* Association of School Business Officials, August, 1951.

Milton, Monroe, "The Place of Testing and Good Buying Procedures," *School Business Affairs,* Association of School Business Officials, October, 1954.

Reason, Paul L., and White, Alpheus L., *Financial Accounting for Local and State School Systems, Standard Receipt and Expenditure Accounts,* Bulletin 1957, no. 4, U.S. Office of Education, Washington, D.C.: U.S. Government Printing Office, 1957.

Shaeffer, Robert W., "Coordinating Governmental Purchases," *School Business Affairs,* Association of School Business Officials, April, 1953.

CHAPTER 6

Salary Schedules and Payroll Management

SCHOOL DISTRICTS INCUR LIABILITIES FOR THE personal services of teachers, supervisors, superintendent and principal, custodians, clerical help, and others through contracts or by hourly, weekly, or monthly wage agreements. By far the greatest proportion of school expenditures are made for services of various personnel. Burke estimated that salaries for instructional personnel approximated nearly 80 percent of the total public school expenditures in 1890, nearly 60 percent in 1910, less than 57 percent in 1930, and less than 52 percent in 1950.[1] If the salaries of superintendents, custodians, maintenance personnel, food services employees, etc., are added to those of instructional personnel, the total payroll would constitute approximately 85 to 90 percent of the current expenses of public school systems. Of the total 1956–1957 disbursements for current expenses in New York City schools, 92.2 percent went for salaries of various personnel.

SALARY SCHEDULES

The authorization of a contract for personal services is the first step in the management of salary payments. All contracts must be issued by the board of education. Where the law requires that contracts be in writing, oral contracts are not recognized as valid legal documents to be used as the basis for salary payments. In the absence of specific statutory commands to the contrary, oral contracts are as valid as written contracts.

One of the most significant developments in personnel administration in recent years has been the growth and use of salary schedules. Salary schedules for instructional personnel are a twentieth century phenomenon. In 1918–1919, less than one-half of the cities had salary schedules. But by 1922-1923 approximately 65 percent of the city schools studied by the National Education Association had schedules for salary payments to instructional personnel. A most prophetic statement issued in 1922–1923 declared: "It is safe to assume that scheduled salaries are to be a permanent element in the administration of American schools."[2] This prophecy is approaching reality, for by 1956–1957, 97 percent of the city school districts had developed and used salary schedules. Many of the smaller school districts do not have schedules for salary payment. It is predicted that within the next 25 years, there will be hardly a school district in the United States without a salary schedule for instructional personnel.

By and large, the salary schedule is a development of local school systems. Some states have statewide salary schedules for teachers. The relative slowness with which statewide salary schedules change has made it necessary for local systems within these states to develop local schedules based on more realistic payments to teachers. In this sense, the state schedule is a minimum salary law rather than a true picture of teachers' salaries in the state. Over two-thirds of the states have minimum salary requirements for teachers but not all of these have salary schedules. A few states have minimum salary regulations which are so low as to make the law obsolete.

The salary schedule is a statement of policy on remuneration for personal services. As a policy adopted

[1] Arvid J. Burke, *Financing Public Schools in the United States,* New York: Harper & Brothers, rev. ed., 1957, p. 103.

[2] National Education Association, Research Division, "Teachers Salaries and Salary Trends in 1923," *Research Bulletin,* Washington, D.C.: NEA, 1923, *1:*36.

by the local board of education in most states, the board has a right to modify or abolish its salary schedule. In the few states having a statewide salary schedule for teachers local board action cannot abolish state schedules or pay below state prescribed minimums. If the salary schedule establishes that teachers of similar qualifications must be given similar salary consideration there can be no discrimination. Salary schedules facilitate to a great degree the administration of salary payments.

Many reasons have been offered for the development of salary schedules. Among these are (1) to secure teachers who are personally competent and professionally well prepared, (2) to encourage professional growth of teachers and, (3) to retain competent teachers. A salary schedule is a formally adopted plan for the payment of the school employees. To a large degree it determines the beginning salary, the amount and number of yearly increases, and the maximum salary to be received by various groups of teachers, or other groups of employees with specified qualifications.

There are many factors involved in the development of a salary schedule. It is not the purpose of this chapter to justify or develop any of the philosophical bases upon which salary schedules are founded but merely to indicate some of the problems in the development and use of salary schedules.

POLICIES AND PROCEDURES RELATED TO SCHEDULE PREPARATION

The action of individuals or groups such as the superintendent, teachers organizations, and lay groups usually motivates the study of salaries with the objective of preparing a new schedule or revising the existing one. Such requests to begin preliminary work should receive the formal approval of the board of education. The appointment of personnel to execute the systematic study preliminary to actually writing a schedule should rest with the board. This group should include the superintendent, representatives of the entire staff, members of the board of education, citizens other than the board members, and special consultants as necessary.

The responsibility for drafting a schedule must be fixed either in the committee making the study or in the executive officer of the school district. Although the primary burden for making the study should rest with a specially appointed committee, the entire teaching staff should be called upon for assistance as needed. The board of education has the ultimate responsibility to adopt and execute the schedule and, therefore,

should be given the opportunity to review and criticize proposed drafts of the schedule.

The committee or individual charged with the responsibility of preparing the salary schedule must assemble and consider certain information germane to the determination of local salary policies. This includes information on (1) the salary schedule already in effect with a review of its strengths and weaknesses; (2) minimum, maximum, median, and average salaries and increments paid in other school systems, particularly those similar to the one under consideration or in close relationship to it; (3) salaries in occupations other than teaching; (4) the age, sex, marital status, living standard, income, expenditures, dependents, etc. of the present teaching staff; (5) the professional preparation and evidence of recent growth among staff members; (6) teacher turnover and teaching load; (7) trends in costs of living; (8) and property assessments, tax rates and collections, municipal expenditures, school expenditures, and other factors related to financing the proposed salary schedule.

Policies must be formulated to stipulate what groups of employees are to have salaries specified by the schedule. It must be determined whether the staff, superintendents, administrative assistants, and others are to be included. Policies on local standards to be used in determining qualifications for appointment to positions of school service—the training, native ability, personality, and experience requirements—must be spelled out in sufficient detail to make the schedule workable.

Among the more important decisions to be made is whether the salary schedule shall be a position type, a professional preparation type, or a combination type of schedule. There is a definite trend toward the professional preparation type of schedules. Whatever the type, the minimum salary and maximum salary to be paid must be stipulated. Most authorities recommend that the maximum be at least twice the minimum salary.

The number of the increments or salary raises a teacher will receive in moving from the minimum to the maximum salary is still another important aspect of the problem. This includes the determination of the total number of increments in each salary class, the spacing of increments at annual or at longer intervals, the size of the increments, and whether there shall be uniform, smaller, or larger sized increments at the beginning or end of the schedule.

Some of the unsettled problems which inevitably create lengthy discussions in schedule development are: (1) Should men and women of equal qualifications be paid equal salaries for equal work? (2) Should merit or teacher efficiency be recognized in the salary schedule? If there is to be a super maximum or merit raise, what should be the size of increment, the maximum salary with efficiency rating, and the super maximum salary granted to teachers of outstanding efficiency? (3) Should special teaching assignments be recognized with special minimums and maximums on a separate schedule or should special assignments for teachers be recognized on the same schedule with a bonus above scheduled amounts? How do you define special assignments such as those for head football coach, director of student plays, or advisor to the school annual staff?

Ample time must be allowed to interpret the statistical findings, deliberate on the proposed policies, and arrive at decisions that seem most appropriate for the school district being served. The salary provisions agreed upon should determine the organization and format of the schedule. The format should include such items as official name of the schedule; name of the district; location of the district, date of adoption; classification of salaries; minimum qualifications for appointment to each salary class; minimum salary for each position; maximum salary for each position; number, size, and scheduling of increments; basis of super maximum when granted; differentials, if any, for sex, race, marriage, and dependents; plan for transfer from old schedule to new schedule; and amount allowed to new teachers for approved experience in other systems.

It must be ascertained that the funds for putting the salary schedule into effect are available. It may be desirable to enlist special public interest in the support of financing the salary schedules. The last stage in putting the schedule into effect is the transition from the old to the new after appropriate board action.[3]

The preparation or single salary schedule and the position type of salary schedule are the two basic types with many variations and combinations possible from these. In the single salary schedule, the basis for variation of salary payments to classroom teachers is preparation and experience. The single salary schedule is a direct contrast with the position type of schedule. In the position type of schedule salary will vary according to the grade level at which the teacher teaches and also with the subject taught. High school teachers receive more than grade school teachers, and band men might receive more than English teachers in a position type of schedule.

In 1918–1919, no city school system had a single salary schedule. As early as 1919, the National Education Association went on record in favoring a single salary schedule for teachers. By 1922–1923, 16 percent of the city school systems had single salary schedules. There was little change in the years that followed, and by 1930–1931, only 17 percent of the city school systems had single salary schedules. In 1940–1941, 31.3 percent of the city systems had single salary schedules, and in 1950–1951, 97.1 percent had them. By 1956–1957, the proportion of any type of schedule other than the single salary schedule in city systems was negligible.[4] There seems little question but that the single salary or preparation type of schedule is now in use in the overwhelming majority of all school systems that have any type of a salary schedule.

Differentiation of salary payments on the basis of sex is one of the more difficult problems in scheduling. The trend is away from differentiation purely on the basis of sex, for less than 5 percent of the city school systems that have a salary schedule pay men more than they do women teachers of equal ability,

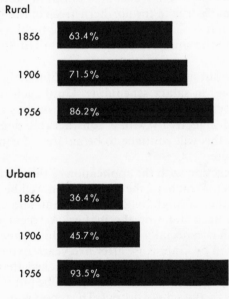

Rural

1856 — 63.4%
1906 — 71.5%
1956 — 86.2%

Urban

1856 — 36.4%
1906 — 45.7%
1956 — 93.5%

FIGURE 8.   Average Salary of Women Teachers as a Percent of Men's Salary
NOTE: Figures for 1856 and 1906 are from W. Randolph Burgess, *Trends of School Costs*, 1920.
SOURCE: National Education Association, Research Division, "The Status of the American Public School Teacher," *Research Bulletin*, Washington, D.C.: NEA, February, 1957, 35:20.

[3] National Education Association, Research Division, "The Preparation of Teacher Salary Schedule," *Research Bulletin*, Part II: Drafting the Schedule, Washington, D.C.: NEA, March, 1936, 14:92–96.

[4] National Education Association, Research Division, "Salaries and Salary Schedules of Urban School Employees, 1956–1957," *Research Bulletin*, Washington, D.C.: NEA, April, 1957, 35:90.

training, and experience. This is reflected in the level of salaries for men and women teachers in 1956–1957. The average salary of a woman teacher in rural areas in 1856 was 63.4 percent of that of the average salary paid to men. In 1906, this figure rose to 71.5 percent. By 1956 the average salary of a woman teacher was 86.2 percent of the average salary paid to men teachers in rural areas. In urban areas the difference is even more striking and the gains more substantial. Thus, in 1856 the average salary of women teachers in an urban area was 36.4 percent of the average salary paid to men. In 1906 this had climbed to be 45.7 percent. By 1956, the average salary paid to a woman teacher in an urban system was 93.5 percent of the man's average.[5] The striking thing about the differences between the average salaries paid to men and women in 1956 is not that they are so great, but that they are no greater. The plain fact is that the single salary schedule has not resulted in one schedule for teachers of one sex and a second for teachers of another sex.

It appears that salary schedules are discriminating less and less between teachers of different races. This is particularly true in the northern areas of the United States, but it is also fast becoming true for the school districts in the southern parts of the United States as well.

The question of merit remains one of the big undecided issues in salary scheduling. Until such time as merit in teaching as well as teaching success can be measured objectively with a considerable degree of accuracy, this will continue to be an area of considerable dispute.

In connection with the application of the merit plan in salaries for teachers, the question can well be raised as to whether enough long-term, patient, and careful work has been done on the matter. A recent report from Utah is especially significant in this connection. As reported by Gale Rose after five years' experience in Utah, the conclusion has been reached that with adequate preparation, merit rating can be put to work effectively in any school district. The report is summarized as follows:

"In summary, the Utah committee's position after nearly five years of intensive study is this: Sound personnel evaluation and merit salary programs for teachers, and others in the schools, are feasible if a district is willing and able to pay the price in terms of leadership, time and effort to develop and use the necessary criteria and procedures. When a district does this, great

[5] National Education Association, Research Division, "The Status of the American Public School Teacher," *Research Bulletin*, Washington, D.C.: NEA, February, 1957, 35:20.

TABLE 3. Salary Differentials Above Teachers' Salary Schedule for Administrators and Supervisors,[a] 1957–1958, Davenport Public Schools, Davenport, Iowa

Senior High School		
Assistant Principal	46 weeks	$2150
Dean of Students	44 weeks	1150
Junior High School		
Principal	44 weeks	1750
Assistant Principal	40 weeks	600
Elementary Schools		
Principal	44 weeks	1750
Assistant Principal	40 weeks	600
Teacher-in-Charge	40 weeks	200
Assistant Supervisor of Physical Education	44 weeks	850
Coördinators of Instruction	44 weeks	1050
Director of Athletics and Supervisor of Physical Education	44 weeks	1050
Director of Adult and Industrial Education	12 months	2250
Head Teacher Oral Deaf	40 weeks	450
Psychologist	44 weeks	1150
Supervisors of Instruction	44 weeks	850
Supervisor of Instrumental Music, High School Band and Orchestra	44 weeks	1350
Supervisor of Special Education and Principal of Special School	44 weeks	1050
Senior High School		
Activities Manager	44 weeks	850
Coördinator of Coöperative Training Program	44 weeks	550
Coördinator of Summer Apprentice Program		150
Counselors	40 weeks	300
Debate Coach	40 weeks	425
Dramatics Coach	40 weeks	175
Heads of Departments	40 weeks	300
Publications Advisor[b]	40 weeks	600
Vocal Music	40 weeks	425
Junior High Schools		
Counselors	40 weeks	300
Coördinator of Civil Defense	40 weeks	400
Head of Home Instruction	40 weeks	200

[a] The Superintendent, Administrative Assistant to the Superintendent, Director of Elementary Education, and High School Principal are in special categories without specific salary differentials.
[b] Receives $300 additional paid from Publications Account.

benefit to the profession and the public will be attained."[6]

Another problem of considerable consequence is that of extra pay for extra work. This implies that the teacher's position can be defined with an accuracy so precise that the exact number of hours spent in a variety of activities can be defined for each teacher. The very nature of the teaching profession makes this next to impossible. School systems continue to argue whether coaches and special teachers of music, dramatics, and so on, deserve more money than teachers in regular positions. Salary differentials above the teacher salary for the Davenport public school, Iowa, for certain assignments and administrators and supervisors are noted in Table 3. It can be seen that these differentials range from $175 above schedule to $2250 above schedule for the director of adult industrial education.

In many cases the salary differentials are justified allegedly on longer working periods than those ascribed to regular teachers. In other cases, special administrative and supervisory duties are recognized as deserving pay above the salary schedule. Salary payments above the schedule for special assignments other than those related to administrative and supervisory duties are often difficult to justify. To illustrate, the head varsity football coach may receive $700 above schedule but the head varsity track coach may receive only $400 above schedule. The fact that a coach of a so-called "minor" varsity sport receives less increment above the salary schedule than the football or basketball coach clearly indicates that more than extra time is involved in determining "extra pay for extra work." If extra time were used to justify bonuses to coaches, then it would follow that assistant coaches should receive as much as head coaches.

It is questionable whether this problem will ever be resolved to the satisfaction of all until such time as a truly professional wage is paid to teachers. As long as teachers' salaries barely continue to keep pace with increases in living costs, the problem of extra pay for extra work will plague the profession. Much the same thing could be said with reference to dependency credit.

MINIMUMS, MAXIMUMS, AND INCREMENTS

The problem of a minimum and maximum salary and the number of increments needed to reach the maximum cannot be neglected in salary scheduling.

[6] Gale Rose, "Preparation Unlocks the Door to Successful Merit Rating," *The Nation's Schools,* October, 1959, *64*:51–53.

There is little question that teachers' salaries have continued to increase in past years. The problem in the post-World War II period is not dissimilar to that which occurred immediately following World War I. Teachers' salaries do not keep pace with the increases in cost of living in the periods immediately following a war. The National Education Association has at various times recommended minimum starting salary schedules for teachers. During the 1930's, $1200 was recommended as a minimum starting wage at a time when many teachers were getting much less than $1000 a year to start. In the early 1940's, $1800 was regarded as an absolute minimum starting wage for teachers. This was then raised to $2400 by the end of World War II. From the writer's experience as an administrator, he can report that many school board members thought $2400 was an outlandish salary to pay a beginning and inexperienced school teacher. Today (1959) any four-year college graduate would be insulted by a beginning offer of only $2400. The minimum was then raised to $3200 in the early 1950's. This was regarded by many at the time as purely visionary with little likelihood of attainment. There are few schools today who would consider offering teachers as little as $3200 as a starting salary. This minimum was moved steadily from $3200 to $3600, $4000, and then to $4500. In July, 1957, the National Education Association recommended that the minimum starting salary for teachers should be $5000. This may be regarded by many as too high for attainment, but there seems to be little question that most of the school systems today, particularly those in cities, are moving toward this minimum. Note the minimum salaries for classroom teachers in 18 of the largest urban school districts presented in Table 4.

It is recommended that the maximum be at least twice the minimum. Clearly, if the minimum is $5000, the maximum should then be at least $10,000, but the NEA went on record for an $11,500 maximum in 1957. There is some justification for this point of view, particularly in view of the fact that school districts have steadily increased the minimum but have not done the same for the maximum. There is justification for at least doubling the minimum for the highest professional class. One of the problems facing the profession is the fact that the maximums are far too low, particularly in relation to the minimums for the inexperienced.

Some recommend that the number and size of increments should be such as to enable a teacher to reach the maximum salary within 15 years of teaching. Others feel that the maximum should be attained

TABLE 4. Rankings of the Eighteen Largest Urban School Districts on Salaries Scheduled for Classroom Teachers, January 1, 1958

AB Degree Minimum Salary

Los Angeles / Detroit / San Francisco	$4500
Chicago	$4250
Cleveland / Milwaukee^a	$4200
Minneapolis^a	$4100
Baltimore^a / Cincinnati^b / New York	$4000
Philadelphia^a / Pittsburgh^a / Washington	$3900
St. Louis	$3800
Boston	$3768
Buffalo^a / Houston	$3600
New Orleans	$3340

AB Degree Maximum Salary

New York	$7600
Detroit	$7000
San Francisco	$6970
Cleveland / Milwaukee^a	$6600
Baltimore^a / Chicago^a / Minneapolis^a	$6500
Los Angeles	$6430
Buffalo^a / Cincinnati^b	$6400
Boston	$6264
Pittsburgh^a / St. Louis	$6200
Philadelphia^a	$6000
Washington	$5800
Houston	$5600
New Orleans	$5264

MA Degree Maximum Salary

New York	$8000
San Francisco	$7630
Detroit	$7250
Cleveland	$7200
Chicago^a	$7000
Milwaukee^a	$6900
Minneapolis^a	$6850
Los Angeles	$6830
Baltimore^a	$6750
Buffalo^a	$6700
Boston	$6612
Cincinnati^b	$6600
Philadelphia^a / Pittsburgh^a / St. Louis	$6400
Washington	$6300
New Orleans	$5946
Houston	$5800

Highest Degree Recognized Maximum Salary

New York	$8400
Los Angeles / San Francisco	$8250
Chicago^a	$8000
Detroit / Milwaukee^a	$7500
Cleveland / Minneapolis^a	$7200
Baltimore^a	$7000
Boston	$6700
Buffalo^a	$6612
Cincinnati^b / St. Louis	$6600
Washington	$6500
Philadelphia^a / Pittsburgh^a	$6400
New Orleans	$6246
Houston	$5800

a Higher schedules have been approved for 1958–1959. Medians based on the January 1 data would be a little higher than the medians in the text, which are based on data received from all cities in September, 1957.
b Board action in Cincinnati, retroactive to January 1, raised all salaries by $50.
SOURCE: National Education Association, Research Division, *Research Bulletin*, Washington, D.C.: NEA, February, 1958, 36:7.

in so short a period as 10 years. The average number of increments seems to be between 13 and 14. Many schedules are so designed that those with only a bachelor's degree receive fewer increments than those who have a master's degree plus 30 hours of extra credit.

It is not necessary that all annual increments be of the same size. Today, most school systems give annual increments of at least $200. This is in contrast to the practice years ago of giving annual increments of between $50 and $100. There is considerable justification for the point of view that the increments should be smaller in the first few years when the teacher is inexperienced and larger in the later years. Such a program would tend to encourage teachers to continue in the system and to continue on in the profession. Some schedules are designed for $150 increments during the first few years and $200 or larger increments in the later periods.

TRENDS IN SALARY SCHEDULES

Reller reported the following trends and issues regarding salary schedules and salaries at the middle of the twentieth century:

1. There is a distinct trend toward using the single salary schedule, especially in the larger cities and school districts.
2. Job evaluations are receiving greater consideration in salary schedules.

3. Cost of living and standard of living increments received considerable attention immediately following World War II but tended to disappear after 1950.
4. Minimum salaries in the schedules have risen more rapidly than maximum salaries.
5. The average number of increments has remained relatively constant with only a slight increase in number.
6. There is a trend toward larger salary increments for teachers and a slight trend toward equal increments from minimum to maximum salary levels.
7. There is a slight trend away from increments based upon merit or efficiency ratings of teachers.
8. There has been a growing awareness that ratings are inadequate and a more comprehensive evaluation of teacher effectiveness must be developed before merit can be successfully included in schedules.
9. Salary differentials between men and women have been disappearing.
10. Dependency load in salary payments continues to be recognized.
11. Extra pay for extra work remains one of the most difficult issues in salary scheduling.
12. Transition from the old to the new schedule continues to remain a major problem in salary schedules.
13. Interest continues in the possibility of employing and paying teachers for a 12-month period which should not be confused with the practice of spreading a 9-month salary over a 12-month period.
14. The number of salary classes to be included in the schedule continues to be an issue in the preparation of a salary schedule.
15. The average salaries paid to teachers as measured by nonadjusted dollars have increased sharply in the last decade.[7]

At the beginning of World War I the average annual salary for teachers was only $525. Average annual wages did not total in four figures until 1920. Between 1930–1931 and 1940–1941 the average annual wage range was small and remained between $1440 and $1470 despite an increase in the qualifications of teachers. It was not until 1949–1950 that average wages exceeded $3000. The most significant gains occurred in the past ten years but these were partially offset by the increase in the cost of living. During the period between 1947–1948 and 1957–1958 the average salary of the instructional staff rose 76 percent in current dollars but only 47 percent in purchasing power.[8] This is shown in Figure 9.

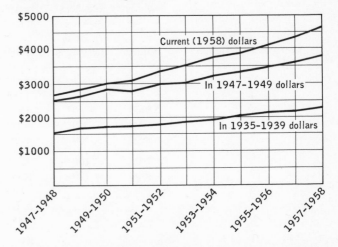

FIGURE 9. Estimated Average Salaries of Instructional Staff Members in Public Schools, 1947–1948—1957–1958
SOURCE: National Education Association, Research Division, *Research Bulletin*, Washington, D.C.: NEA, February, 1958, *36*:5.

The average salary paid to teachers in the United States in 1957–1958 was $4650 compared with $4350 for the previous year. The average for the United States does not show the rather sizable range from $2525 in Mississippi to a high of $5750 in California. In about seven states the average salary of the instructional staff in 1957–1958 was $5000 or larger. In 1957–1958 secondary school teachers had an average salary which was 12 percent higher than the average for elementary teachers. Five years ago the difference between these two averages was 18 percent.

In spite of recent increases, teachers' salaries continue to stay close to the average for all wage and salary workers. Likewise, there seems to be ample evidence to indicate that higher prices and high taxes have whittled down the salary dollar and in effect held down the purchasing power of teachers' salaries. To illustrate, during 1957, the salaries paid to teachers increased 5 percent, but the cost of living ate up 3 percent of this increase, leaving only a 2 percent gain in the real salaries paid to teachers.[9]

HYPOTHETICAL SALARY SCHEDULE

A basic salary schedule for a hypothetical community is presented in Table 5. This salary schedule pro-

---

[7] Theodore L. Reller, "Finance and Personnel" in R. L. Johns and E. L. Morphet (eds.), *Problems and Issues in Public School Finance*, New York: Teachers College, Columbia University, 1952, pp. 359–396.

[8] National Education Association, Research Division, *Research Bulletin*, Washington, D.C.: NEA, February, 1958, *36*:5.
[9] Hazel Davis, "Salaries, Taxes and Prices," *NEA Journal*, March, 1958, *47*:185.

TABLE 5. Basic Salary Schedule for the Smithville Community School District

Salary Steps or Years of Experience	Class D Nondegree Teachers		Class C Bachelor's Degree		Class B Master's Degree		Class A Master's Degree + 30	
	Salary	Annual Increment	Salary	Annual Increment	Salary	Annual Increment	Salary	Annual Increment
1	—	—	$4200	$ 0	$4600	$ 0	$4700	$ 0
2	—	—	4350	150	4750	150	4850	150
3	$3600	$ 0	4500	150	4900	150	5000	150
4	3700	100	4700	200	5200	300	5300	300
5	3800	100	4900	200	5500	300	5600	300
6	3900	100	5000	200	5800	300	5900	300
7	4000	100	5200	200	6100	300	6200	300
8			5450	250	6350	350	6600	400
9			5700	250	6700	350	7000	400
10			6000	300	7050	350	7450	400
11			6300	300	7450	400	7800	400
12			6600	300	7850	400	8200	400
13					8250	400	8600	400
14							9000	400
15							9400	400

vides for four classes of teachers. Class D is for nondegree teachers; class C for teachers with a bachelor's degree; class B for teachers with a master's degree; and class A for teachers with a master's degree and 30 hours of professional work beyond that degree. It should be noted that nondegree teachers are not broken down into those having two and three years of preparation. There is a distinct trend away from employing teachers with less than a bachelor's degree.

This hypothetical schedule includes certain features which are worthy of further explanation. It should be noted that nondegree teachers are not to be appointed henceforth. Class D applies only to those now in service, and new teachers in this class are not anticipated. Teachers in class D reach the $4000 maximum in a hurry with four increments of $100. The purpose behind this is to encourage such people to do the work necessary to move into the class C level. Class C starts at $4200 with a maximum of $6600. This is not twice the minimum, and the purpose behind this schedule is to encourage those with a bachelor's degree to go on to higher professional preparation levels. The annual increment increases for teachers with longer periods of service. The annual increment for steps 1 through 3 is $150; for steps 4 through 7, $200; for steps 8 through 9, $250; and for steps 10 through 12, $300.

The class B teachers start at $400 above those in class C. They receive the same increments for steps 1, 2, and 3 as those in class C. However, at step 4, teachers in class B get $100 more per year in increments that those in class C. Thus the annual increment for class B teachers at steps 4 through 7 is $300; at steps 8 through 10, $350; and at 11 through 13, $400. It should be noted that there is one more annual increment in class B than in class C.

The class A teachers receive $100 more than those in class B. They receive the same increments as those in class B for steps 2 through 7. Starting at step 8, those in class A receive $400 annual increments through step 15, as compared with increments ranging from $350 to $400 for class B. It should be noted that two more steps are provided in class A. The maximum salary at the fifteenth step for class A is twice that of the minimum or starting salary of $4700. This is a basic salary schedule and can be supplemented as the board sees fit for administrators and supervisors in particular. Like most teacher salary schedules, this hypothetical one should be revised to follow NEA recommendations of a $5000 minimum and at least an $11,500 maximum.

The fundamental contribution of the basic salary schedule to business administration is that it presents a picture of what the teachers can expect. It also enables the business manager to compute the teachers' salaries in light of experience and preparation levels.

DIFFERENTIATED SCHOOL STAFFS AND DIFFERENTIATED SALARY SCALES NEEDED

The question can well be raised as to whether the existing concept of the kinds of workers needed in local school systems will ever provide the professional services, or make possible essential or what clearly seems desirable differentiation in payment for workers in schools. Local school systems are the only institutions of comparable social importance, complexity, and size that substantially have only one classification for an overwhelming majority of its workers. In other words, local school systems are suffering from a monolithic classification, and hence a monolithic salary schedule.[10]

The title "teacher" is so broad and diverse in terms of work assignments teachers assume that it is not surprising to find so low a degree of specialization among nearly all of the staffs of local elementary and secondary schools. Teachers are now expected to stimulate and direct learning by children, and at the same time render high-level secretarial, clerical, and mechanical service necessary, toward a level of learning which admittedly with many boys and girls is far short of their capabilities.[11]

It is not surprising that marked differences are found in the competence of teachers to fulfill responsibilities that have been assigned to them. It is not uncommon to find an elementary teacher who will teach the music or art class in another room in exchange for the teaching of arithmetic or science by another fellow teacher. Similarly, members of school custodial staffs particularly are enjoined to "fix" items of instructional equipment ranging from projection machines to impaired globes, because some teachers simply are not "good with their hands."

As a much wider utilization of electronic and other types of learning and teaching machines is made, the importance of what might be called school technicians will become increasingly essential toward maximum effectiveness among teachers and learners. Also, if those who enjoy the tutelage of boys and girls are to serve increasingly as diagnosticians, counselors, resource staff, and advisers as opposed to policemen, nursemaids, prescribers, and exhorters, teachers must be emancipated from secretarial and clerical work which requires peculiar professional skill, if the more specialized teacher functions are to be available to the degree needed.[12]

INSTRUCTIONAL TEAMS SEEM TO BE DEMANDED

In connection with the previous discussion, it seems clear that a different and what promises to be a much sounder approach might well be made on the organization of essential school staffs around what may be called instructional teams. Some experimentation in the direction of organizing instructional teams for teaching has been conducted during recent years with results which suggest that all concerned work more efficiently with more effective learning resulting.[13]

Three illustrative types of instructional teams seem appropriate of mention here:

1. The mere assignment of two present-day workers known as teachers given joint work assignments; as for example, two teachers to two fifth grades; this arrangement while it obviously gives no relief in connection with secretarial, clerical, and technical services needed does seem likely to stimulate a higher level of planning and encourages the fuller utilization of strengths for a pair of teachers working as a team than when they work substantially separately. Also, such an arrangement tends to reduce the excessive effort necessary for a teacher to attempt teaching something for which he, himself, feels his ability and preparation are inadequate.[14]

2. An instructional team composed of what might be called a teacher-chairman or team leader, a teacher associate, an instructional secretary, and the part-time service of a technician in the care and use of instructional and learning equipment. With such a team, recent experimentation has suggested that again more effective work is done by all concerned even when the traditional pupil-teacher ratios of relatively small numbers of children are multiplied from two to four times the ratios usually insisted upon as desirable.[15]

3. If instructional teams are more preferable units of organization than the individul teacher, it seems clear that institutions responsible for the preparation of teachers must include experience in team teaching in connection with what is traditionally called practice teaching. Consequently the instructional team just suggested might be modified to include one or two teaching interns in lieu of the associate teacher.[16]

These are illustrations of what seems to deserve much thinking and actual experimentation in the establishment of instructional staffs in local school systems and the attainment of differentiated staffs and differentiated salary scales or schedules.

[13] *Ibid.*

[14] The National Association of Secondary School Principals, *Bulletin of the National Association of Secondary School Principals,* Washington: D.C., January, 1959, p. 242.

[15] J. Lloyd Trump, *Images of the Future,* Washington, D.C.: The National Association of Secondary School Principals, 1959, pp. 15–18.

[16] Woodring, *op. cit.,* pp. 71–77.

[10] George A. Prescott and Bryce Perkins, "New Careers for Teachers," *The Connecticut Teacher,* April, 1959.

[11] Paul Woodring, *New Directions in Teacher Education,* New York: The Fund for the Advancement of Education, 1957, p. 73.

[12] *Ibid.,* p. 75.

It is apparent that the plan of merit would hold under a policy including instructional teams and hence differentiated salary policy, as well as under the existing prevalent monolithic staff and salary schedule policies. However, it might be that differentiated staffs and corresponding differentiated pay schedules would be highly beneficial toward the recruitment of more competent workers in the classrooms of local school systems and would also make it possible in terms of economics to pay more appropriate salaries to various kinds of workers.[17]

MORE EXACT CLASSIFICATIONS OF SCHOOL STAFFS SEEM NEEDED

It is an established matter that large numbers, particularly of women, even during the time of their college preparation and work toward the gaining of certification, frankly indicate that they do not expect to remain in teaching very long—often for not more than two to five years. Also, no small number of men similarly declare they do not intend to make teaching a career. Many of our young men and women who both by design or the turn of circumstances spend only short periods of time in the classroom are able, professionally minded, and high-level workers. However, those who spend only a short period of time as members of local school staffs hardly seem to deserve salary and welfare policies commensurate with those who intend to make their life's work the role of a school staff member. It would therefore seem, assuming that the beginning salary for all school workers in any connection are of sufficient levels to enable them to live in keeping with their qualifications, that a longer period of service than that now found in most cases might well be required before they are recognized as "career workers."[18]

In this connection, the recommendation has been made that a minimum of five years teaching experience be required before a permanent teaching certificate (or license) is granted.[19]

At any rate, in consideration of the development of a more satisfactory policy in the classification of school staffs and their corresponding remuneration, it seems clear that existing legal requirements in connection with the certifying of teachers should also be examined toward needed revision.

PAYROLL MANAGEMENT

There was a time when the administration of salary payments was fairly simple. The monthly salary accruing to each teacher could be computed at the start of the year with small chance of variation thereafter. This is no longer true. Salary computations at the start of the school year would be subject to many changes as early as the end of the first pay period.

Salary payments to professional and the noncertificated personnel involve careful organization and management. The school department responsible for the preparation of salary payments performs a vital service for the entire professional and nonprofessional staff in an educational system. There is ample evidence to indicate that the method of paying salaries as well as the times at which the salary payments are distributed will influence the morale of all workers. It is imperative that those responsible for the preparation of salary checks follow the service concept and recognize that for all the mechanical operations and computations, they are doing something which has a significant effect on people. The way they meet people with real or imagined salary problems will definitely affect morale. There must be a willingness on the part of those responsible for the preparation of school payrolls to listen carefully to requests, accusations, or demands of the staff. If the employee desires to have his salary payment recomputed this should be done at least as many times as may be necessary within reason. A friendly explanation of the payroll deductions for various purposes may be time consuming but it is necessary. What may seem like small problems to those in the payroll department, such as spelling a name incorrectly on checks, looms large in the minds of some employees. If it is consistent with other legal records, there should be a willingness on the part of the individuals working in the department of salary payments to use the name of Mrs. Anthony J. Thimblebottom on checks if the employee prefers it over Hermina A. Thimblebottom. Sometimes a cordial greeting or a smile settles the ire of those who feel they have been wronged by the checks issued in the payroll department.

If the salary payments are to be made with any degree of efficiency, it is necessary that they be centralized in one office. The timekeeping function where it is necessary is usually a responsibility attached to the individual schools. Policy matters are determined outside the business department. It is advisable to include business department personnel in all policy decisions relating to salary payment to represent at least the practical considerations involved in proposals. The actual preparation of checks, accounting for salary payments and related activities, however, should be centralized in the hands of business personnel rather than building principals or other officials.

[17] Prescott and Perkins, *op. cit.*

[18] The National Commission on Teacher Education and Professional Standards, *The Professional Standards Movement in Teaching: Progress and Projection,* Washington, D.C.: NEA, 1956, p. 94.

[19] *Ibid.*

The school business services primarily concerned with salary payments to professional and noncertified personnel should be assigned the specific functions of (1) preparing and keeping the schedule and systems of salary payments during the course of the fiscal year, (2) determining whether the personal services have been performed by reviewing information supplied by other school officials or by timecards for hourly workers, (3) preparing checks or warrants used in salary payments, (4) developing a system for delivering salary payments, (5) providing the accounting office with salary payments data in such form as to facilitate its posting to appropriate expenditure accounts, and (6) preparing special reports needed for income tax, social security, hospitalization, retirement, and other forms related to salary payments.[20]

BASIC POLICIES FOR SALARY PAYMENTS

There can be no salary payments without prior authorizations and knowledge of administrative policies governing salary payment management. In other words, certain basic information governing salary management must be provided to those in charge of payroll preparations before anything can be accomplished. The services of instructional and noncertificated personnel are procured in departments of school administration other than those directly related to the management of salary payments. Such decisions as length of service, the salary to be paid, and the various welfare provisions to be provided each employee are reached in other departments of school administration. It follows that after vital policies and other decisions affecting payroll have been adopted, they must be made known to the payroll department.

Among the information the payroll department must have for the effective management of salary payments are:

1. The names of those under contract or under hourly, weekly, or monthly wage agreements.

2. The authorization to release salary payments in given amounts and at stated times for those employed on a contractual and a noncontractual basis. This authorization is sometimes little more than knowledge that a valid contract has been executed and spread over the official minutes of the board of education. In certain states, such as Oklahoma, it is illegal to pay any teacher who does not hold a valid certificate to teach in that state. In such cases, the authorization must include a statement by the proper official that either a copy of the teacher's certificate is on file or has been witnessed by a duly authorized person. For

[20] Henry H. Linn (ed.), *School Business Administration*, New York: The Ronald Press Company, 1956, p. 228.

the noncontractual employee, the authorization will consist of timecards or other less formal devices.

3. A clear statement as to the total annual payment or hourly or weekly rate due each employee. It is usually better business practice to inform the payroll department in writing of annual or special salary changes for all included in the officially adopted salary schedule. Usually the director of personnel relays such information to the payroll department.

4. A statement as to whether employees are to be paid weekly, twice a month, or once a month. The majority of school districts pay instructional and other professional personnel once a month. Other school employees may be paid as often as every week. There are arguments to support the payment of school employees twice a month even though this may greatly increase the burden of those responsible for managing salary payments. How many days are included in a salary month must be stipulated. A calendar month is not the same as a teaching month. A teaching month is defined as 20 teaching days, exclusive of any vacations. A teaching month may be four weeks, or if vacations intervene, such as at Christmas time, it may be as long as six weeks. It should be stipulated whether salary payments are to be made at the beginning of the next month or at the end of the present month. Whatever the case, the decision must be made known to the payroll department.

Another problem is the definition of a year for salary purposes. The salary can be paid during the 9 months of the school instructional year or over the entire 12 months of the school fiscal year. There seems to be a trend toward spreading the annual or 9-month salary of teachers over a 12-month fiscal year period. This is not without its problems, particularly if a teacher resigns in June and demands lump sum payment of July and August checks which are due her as her services have been completed at the termination of the school year.

The need for a definite policy statement on such matters should be apparent. It is wise to indicate the method of payment in the contract. Some school districts offer teachers a choice of payment either on the 9-month or 12-month basis. This greatly complicates salary preparation, but if it leads to improved morale of the staff it can be justified.

5. The extent of participation of each teacher in various retirement programs, hospitalization and surgical treatment insurance, accident insurance, life insurance, personal liability insurance, credit union, U.S. saving bond programs, professional association or union dues payments, as well as federal income withholding tax and social security tax, must be made known to the payroll department. The number of deductions have

steadily increased and, as a result, have greatly complicated salary payments.

6. Information on any differentials from the regular monthly salary, such as increases due to overtime, cost of living bonuses, or deductions from regular salary for absence, must likewise be relayed to the business department. Such information is usually supplied by the superintendent, the personnel manager, or the building principal. This includes special stop orders, which preclude either the preparation or the delivery of a check due to sudden termination in employment through death or departure or for attachment of wages by another organization. The decision to increase, decrease, or stop salary payments is reached by officials outside the salary payment department. But each school system must design an effective means of communicating vital information to the payroll department.

PROCESSING THE DATA USED IN PREPARATION OF SALARY PAYMENTS

An Earnings Ledger should be prepared for each employee. This is a special card or ledger which indicates the employee's name and address, date of birth, number of dependents and any other information needed for tax purposes, contractual salary or hourly wage rate, number of pay periods during the fiscal year, date of the monthly or weekly salary payments, and special deductions to be made from his salary for whatever period. In many districts, the fiscal year of the school does not correspond with the calendar year. Taxes paid to the federal and state government on income earned must be paid on the basis of a calendar year. Clearly, then, the Earnings Ledger for each employee should list accumulated earnings during the school's fiscal or instructional year and also during the calendar year if the two are not the same.

The Earnings Ledger for various employees can be grouped according to classifications such as administrative personnel, instructional personnel, custodians, bus drivers, and cafeteria workers. The personnel can also be classified according to whether they are contractual or noncontractual personnel. A third grouping of the individual Earnings Ledgers could be on the basis of pay periods. That is, those that receive payment on the first of each month can be grouped together as well as those who are paid every week, biweekly, or after every 20 teaching days. The particular classification adopted for grouping Earnings Ledgers will depend upon the organization of the school, the pay periods for various personnel, and the type of program.

The Earnings Ledger is a subsidiary ledger. Entries made in the Earnings Ledger are also placed in the Payroll Journal. It is from the Payroll Journal that the Expenditure Accounts for ADMINISTRATION, INSTRUCTION, OPERATION, etc., are debited for salaries paid. It is not necessary to list the individual names of employees who receive salaries in each of the various Expenditure Accounts.

CERTIFICATION OF SERVICES PERFORMED

A record of the number of days worked and those absent, excused or otherwise, for each employee should be maintained in each district. Such records along with contracts form the bases of salary management. This type of record keeping is not necessarily the function of the payroll department. It is the responsibility of the building principal to report the number of days a teacher is absent for excused and unexcused purposes. If the teacher is ill, it must be clearly determined how much of the sick leave during the year has been used. It must likewise be determined what days, if any, the teacher was not present and for which no pay is forthcoming. Although such evidence of service is used by the payroll department, it is gathered and certified in other departments.

Timekeeping for noncontractual employees is the most effective way to determine length of service, information which is necessary in computing wage payments.

PREPARATION OF SALARY PAYMENTS

A calendar can be prepared to show when salary payments are due for the various school employees. Few things are more disconcerting than being kept in ignorance as to when salaries will be distributed. Usually these salaries are received after services have been rendered and not before. On rare occasions, there may be prepayment of salaries but these should be considered as emergency payments and not the rule. Teachers have a right to know just when they can expect salary checks.

It is not unusual for more than one salary payment to be made during a given month. In all but the smallest districts this is the practice when professional and certificated personnel are paid at different periods from the noncertificated personnel.

In small school systems up to 50 employees, the traditional manual pen-and-ink system of preparing payrolls, writing checks, and making accounting entries may be used. When the payroll reaches somewhere between 50 and 100 employees its preparation can be most effectively discharged if the procedures are mechanized. The total number of employees, how payments are spread through the month, and how many payments are made each month are facts to be considered in determining the point at which machines are less costly than manual methods.

There are some aids in payroll preparation based upon manual procedures. One such device is a special board to which the Payroll Journal is fastened. The journal is then covered with carbon paper, and the employee's statement of earnings and deductions (Earnings Ledger) is placed in a clamp after it is aligned with the proper columns of the journal. The check or warrant is placed over the individual Earnings Ledger and the Payroll Journal. This simple device can facilitate payroll procedures in small communities.

In large systems of 100 or more employees, the most effective way of meeting salary payments during the month is by a machine specially designed for such purposes or adapted from the regular general-purpose accounting machines. There are a number of such machines on the market today and each has its advantages and limitations. There are several models of the fundamentally same machine manufactured by a single company. Thus, one model will give gross earnings to date, individual employee's net pay, and accumulated total of net pay. A more elaborate model might include gross earnings to date, individual employee's net pay, total gross pay, total of all deductions, and accumulated total of net pay. Still another will have all those features and include accumulated total of withholding tax as well. Actually, manufacturers of machines which can greatly facilitate the payroll process take pride in the fact that they will develop the machine to suit the particular needs of the district. These needs can be determined either by number of employees or by variety of information necessary.

This implies that school districts which desire to change from the more laborious and time-consuming manual methods of payroll preparation must have a clear concept of what they expect a machine to do, or better, the nature of the payroll problem in that district. Before a machine is purchased, the following information should be obtained:

1. A careful analysis of the number of individuals on the school district payroll and the probable number within the foreseeable future.
2. The frequency of payment and any possible increase in the frequency of salary payments. Although the districts may now issue checks on a monthly basis, there may be some agitation to have bimonthly salary payments.
3. How often there are additions or subtractions from the salary before the standard deductions are made.
4. The number and variety of deductions and the likelihood of an increase in deductions in future years.

To illustrate, federal withholding tax is now standard procedure. Many states are toying with the idea of withholding taxes for state income taxes. This may be more convenient for the employee but more difficult for the payroll department.

5. The records and reports which are now needed or which may be needed in the years ahead.
6. Whether the payroll machine can be used for other accounting operations, either on a regular or emergency basis.
7. The proximity of the service facilities for the machine.
8. The initial cost and price of maintenance.
9. The ease of operation and also the availability of trained personnel incidental to the use of any piece of equipment.[21]

Some machines will do all the necessary calculations but will not include a typewriter with which to enter the name of the person. Others will use the punch-card technique in mechanized payroll accounting. It is imperative that the features of all machines be carefully examined before purchase. Again, it is emphasized that the most important thing is to know your salary payment needs and what the sum is that can be justifiably expended on a machine.

These machines greatly simplify operations because many things can be done at one time. Thus, the Payroll Journal (which includes all salary transactions to all employees during a given pay period), the employees' Earnings Record or Ledger, and an original or carbon copies of the payroll checks can be prepared in one operation. In addition, many of the machines have an error detection device. Illustrations of these forms are provided. More will be said about the use of machines in accounting in the chapter that follows.

METHODS OF PAYMENT

There is little reason to justify any method of payment other than by checks or warrants. For all practical purposes, few if any school district workers today are paid by cash. Payment by check reduces the hazards of payroll robbery, chance of individual loss, difficulty of detecting and recovering salary overpayments, or chance that evidence needed to prove underpayment is missing. It is superior to payment by cash in so many ways that the temptation to belabor the point is extremely great. If there is to be payment by warrants, it is imperative that these warrants be covered by the treasurer by a single check.

The method of delivering checks or warrants to the employees must likewise be carefully planned. These

[21] *Ibid.*, pp. 244–245.

FORM 2.

FORM NO 19a   Page 3
July '57   6M

PERSONNEL PAYROLL

Group employees according to purpose code;
then circle appropriate code group below.

CODE	PURPOSE	CODE	PURPOSE
100	Administration	600	Operation
200	Instruction	700	Maintenance
300	Attendance	900	Food
400	Health	1000	Activities
500	Transportation	1100	Community

FIRST QUARTER

JANUARY, 19 _____

Month begins _____
Month ends _____
Date paid _____

Teacher Retirement	Social Security	Withhold-ing tax	Absence	NET AMOUNT PAID
DEDUCTIONS				

FEBRUARY, 19 _____

Month begins _____
Month ends _____
Date paid _____

Teacher Retirement	Social Security	Withhold-ing tax	Absence	NET AMOUNT PAID
DEDUCTIONS				

MARCH, 19 _____

Month begins _____
Month ends _____
Date paid _____

Teacher Retirement	Social Security	Withhold-ing tax	Absence	NET AMOUNT PAID
DEDUCTIONS				

TOTAL FOR QUARTER
JANUARY–FEBRUARY–MARCH

Teacher Retirement	Social Security	Withhold-ing tax	Absence	NET AMOUNT PAID
DEDUCTIONS				

1
2
3
4
5
6
7
8
9
10
11
12
13
14
15
16
17
18
19
20
21
22
23
24
25
26
27
28
29
30
31
32
33
34
35

(Courtesy of the Missouri State Department of Education)

FORM 2—(Continued)

FORM MO 19 6M
July '57

PERSONNEL PAYROLL

SECOND QUARTER

APRIL, 19 _____
Month begins _____
Month ends _____
Date paid _____

MAY, 19 _____
Month begins _____
Month ends _____
Date paid _____

JUNE, 19 _____
Month begins _____
Month ends _____
Date paid _____

TOTAL FOR QUARTER
APRIL—MAY—JUNE

TOTALS FOR THE YEAR

Group employees according to purpose code;
then circle appropriate code group below

CODE	PURPOSE	CODE	PURPOSE
100	Administration	600	Operation
200	Instruction	700	Maintenance
300	Attendance	900	Food
400	Health	1000	Activities
500	Transportation	1100	Community

DEDUCTIONS: Teacher Retirement | Social Security | Withholding tax | Absence | NET AMOUNT PAID

(Rows numbered 1–35)

FORM 2—(Continued)

FORM MO 19
July '57   6M

Page 1

PERSONNEL PAYROLL

THIRD QUARTER

Group employees according to purpose code; then circle appropriate code group below.

CODE	PURPOSE	CODE	PURPOSE
100	Administration	600	Operation
200	Instruction	700	Maintenance
300	Attendance	900	Food
400	Health	1000	Activities
500	Transportation	1100	Community

TOTAL FOR QUARTER
JULY–AUGUST–SEPTEMBER

JULY, 19 ____
Month begins ____
Month ends ____
Date paid ____

AUGUST, 19 ____
Month begins ____
Month ends ____
Date paid ____

SEPTEMBER, 19 ____
Month begins ____
Month ends ____
Date paid ____

NAME — NUMBER OF DEPENDENTS — POSITION — ANNUAL SALARY — MONTHLY SALARY

DEDUCTIONS: Teacher Retirement — Social Security — Withholding tax — Absence — NET AMOUNT PAID

Rows numbered 1 through 35.

FORM 2—(Continued)

FORM NO. 19a Page 2
July '57 6M

PERSONNEL PAYROLL
FOURTH QUARTER

OCTOBER, 19 _____

Month begins _____
Month ends _____
Date paid _____

NOVEMBER, 19 _____

Month begins _____
Month ends _____
Date paid _____

DECEMBER, 19 _____

Month begins _____
Month ends _____
Date paid _____

TOTAL FOR QUARTER
OCTOBER–NOVEMBER–DECEMBER

Group employees according to purpose code; then circle appropriate code group below.

CODE	PURPOSE	CODE	PURPOSE
100	Administration	600	Operation
200	Instruction	700	Maintenance
300	Attendance	900	Food
400	Health	1000	Activities
500	Transportation	1100	Community

For each month (October, November, December) and for the Quarter Total:

DEDUCTIONS: Teacher Retirement | Social Security | Withholding tax | Absence | NET AMOUNT PAID

Row numbers 1 through 35.

checks can be mailed to the employee's residence or school. They can be sent by messenger to each of the school buildings and then placed in the teacher's regular school mail box. In some very large establishments provisions are made to send the check directly to the bank, whence it is entered into the individual's checking or savings account. The bank, in turn, sends the individual a statement that his account has been credited by the salary payment.

The old procedures of depending upon the principal or even the superintendent to deliver pay checks personally to each of the teachers is a waste of time for an administrator. The practice of some small school districts of expecting teachers to go to a school board member's home and collect salary payments is to be condemned. There remain a few who still desire to let teachers know "who is boss" by expecting them to report to them when salary checks are due.

ACCOUNTING FOR SALARY PAYMENTS

The Payroll Journal or the Salary Payments Journal or Register is a subsidiary record made necessary by the complicated nature of salary payments. It was pointed out previously that one of the basic records in payroll accounting is the individual Earnings Record or Ledger. The individual Earnings Ledger has all the appropriate information necessary for making salary payments.

The voucher or voucher check is evidence of payment. It must be made in duplicate with one carbon copy for the school files as evidence of payment along with the canceled original sent to the employer. In addition, a special journal to record all payments made during any pay period to all employees should be maintained. It is from this overall journal that entries are made to the proper Expenditure Accounts. Except in very small school districts it is not necessary to enter the name and salary of every teacher in the instruction expenditure accounts. Only the totals from the Payroll Register for instructional personnel are needed. The posting under the appropriate Expenditure Account would read: "October payments for instructional personnel." Much the same thing can be obtained from the Payroll Register and carried to the salaries heading of the OPERATION Expenditure Account, the ADMINISTRATION Expenditure Account, etc.

There is the further problem of deductions from employees' checks which are not forwarded immediately to the agencies. To illustrate, withholding tax statements are deposited in the Federal Reserve Bank monthly, and quarterly statements are made to the Bureau of Internal Revenue. Withholding taxes for employees paid weekly or bimonthly must **accumulate** somewhere prior to monthly payments. This creates one of the needs for the establishment of the Clearing Accounts in schools.

Deductions from the payroll are found in the Clearing Accounts and specifically in Account 1620—Deductions from the Payroll. This account is subdivided into 1620-a—Money Received, which includes amounts deducted from salaries for taxes, retirement, insurance, and other purposes and for transmittal to the proper payees. This category can be broken down further into the appropriate subaccounts, such as Subaccount for Federal Withholding Tax, for State Retirement Fund, for Hospitalization Insurance, for Life Insurance, and so on. Account 1620-b—Money Paid Out includes amounts deducted from salaries for taxes, retirement, insurance, and others, which were transmitted to the proper payees. This likewise can be broken down into appropriate subaccounts.[22] Clearly, then, all the deductions made from employees' salaries which are later to be forwarded to the appropriate payee are entered into the Clearing Accounts, until such time as payment from them must be made.

Reconciliation and postauditing are necessary because the preparation of salary payments of any size is often done in an attempt to meet the deadline and, therefore, errors may be present in spite of the very best of precautions. This makes it imperative that there be the proper postaudit of payroll accounts and also reconciliation either with the accounting office or with the treasury.

SUMMARY

School disbursements for various salary payments make up 85 to 90 percent of the current expenditures. One of the most significant developments in school personnel administration in the twentieth century is the salary schedule for instructional personnel. A salary schedule is a formally adopted policy statement for the payment of salaries to personnel.

There is a definite trend toward the development of salary schedules based on the professional preparation and experience of teachers. The "single salary" schedule or preparation type of schedule is now in use in an overwhelming majority of school systems which use a schedule. The questions of merit and extra pay for extra work continue to plague the development and revision of schedules.

[22] Paul L. Reason and Alpheus L. White, *Financial Accounting for Local and State School Systems, Standard Receipt and Expenditure Accounts,* Bulletin 1957, no. 4, U.S. Office of Education, Washington, D.C.: U.S. Government Printing Office, 1957, p. 114.

The minimum salary for teachers has risen steadily in the period following World War II. The changes in the maximum have lagged in comparison. It is recommended that the maximum be at least twice the minimum, but this recommendation is ignored in most systems. The average number of increments in proceeding from minimum to maximum salary is between 13 and 14. It is not necessary that all increments be of the same size. Much of the increase in salary payments to teachers has been dissipated as a result of the reduced purchasing power of current dollars.

Salary payments should be centralized in one office. The payroll department must be kept fully informed on total annual payment, pay periods, participation in the so-called "fringe" benefits, and special bonuses or deductions during the pay period for each employee.

An Earnings Ledger should be prepared for each employee to show all the vital data needed for salary payments during any given period. Smaller systems may meet salary payments by using the traditional or manual methods but most larger systems must rely upon special machines for payroll management.

QUESTIONS

1. Why are salary schedules considered important in personnel administration? In business administration?
2. If you were responsible for the preparation of a salary schedule what would you do about the following?
   a. minimum salary
   b. increments
   c. maximum salary
   d. merit
   e. extra pay for extra work
3. What are the advantages and disadvantages of a preparation type of salary schedule? A position type of salary schedule?
4. What salary payment functions should be assigned to the department of business services? The building principal? The superintendent?
5. Identify the following:
   a. Earnings Ledger
   b. Payroll Journal
   c. voucher
6. What factors should receive consideration in the purchase of a machine for payroll management and accounting?

SELECTED REFERENCES

Linn, Henry H. (ed.), *School Business Administration,* New York: The Ronald Press Company, 1956.

National Education Association, Research Division, "The Preparation of Teacher Salary Schedule," *Research Bulletin,* Part II: Drafting the Schedule, Washington, D.C.: NEA, March, 1936.

National Education Association, Research Division, "The Status of the American Public School Teacher," *Research Bulletin,* Washington, D.C.: NEA, February, 1957.

National Education Association, Research Division, *Research Bulletin,* Washington, D.C.: NEA, February, 1958.

Reller, Theodore L., "Finance and Personnel" in R. L. Johns and E. L. Morphet (eds.), *Problems and Issues in Public School Finance,* New York: Teachers College, Columbia University, 1952.

CHAPTER 7

Accounting for School Expenditures

SCHOOLS INCUR LIABILITIES THROUGH THE purchase act for materials and supplies and contracts for personal services as described in Chapters 5 and 6, respectively. Expenditures are made to liquidate these liabilities. The first portion of this chapter is concerned with another view on meeting liabilities. This is followed by an identification and classification of school Expenditure Accounts. The operational procedures in meeting liabilities through expenditures and accounting for the same is the subject of the last section of this chapter.

MEETING LIABILITIES

The requisition motivates the execution of a purchase order, the purchase order initiates the procurement from the vendor, and the vendor sends an invoice as a demand for payment for goods sold or services rendered. In the same sense the need for teachers prompts the search which terminates in the contract for personal services. Accounting for expenditures becomes a real problem when the contract for services is consummated or after the invoice has been properly checked and it has been determined that the goods or services received are the same as those ordered and the same as those listed on the invoice.

THE VOUCHER SYSTEM

The checked and approved invoice is one of the basic documents in school accounting. It supports the issuance of instruments authorizing payment of funds from the school treasury. The checked and approved invoice is the voucher in the sense that it is the verifying or authorizing document for the disbursement of cash. In a broader sense, the purchase order or the approved requisition are documents which eventually form the basis of authority to make disbursements from the school treasury. A copy of the requisition, the purchase order, and the invoice should be clipped together to show a complete history of the activities that led up to the expenditure. The term "voucher" is best applied to the invoice for it actually precipitates the action which terminates in the liquidation of the liability. Much the same can be said for the legal contract or timecard for personal services.

Payment of the invoice can be by ordinary check, school warrant, or voucher check. A voucher check combines the features of a check, a formal receipt, and a remittance slip.[1] One portion is readily recognized as a check calling for release of funds in the amount stipulated and to the person indicated. Attached to the regular check is a statement which covers the particulars of the check payment, such as the date, the amount of money, the discount or other deductions, invoice numbers, or any other information having to do with the goods or services rendered for the amount released from the school treasury. This is the voucher portion which justifies the preparation of the check.

Information on the financial transaction and the supporting documents involved in meeting liabilities can be clipped to or placed in what is known as the voucher jacket or voucher folder. It is not necessary that this device be a jacket in the sense of being an envelope. A sheet of paper on which is printed the data required to enter an appropriate description of the purchases is all that is necessary to serve as a voucher. The supporting financial documents can be clipped to such a specially

[1] Eric L. Kohler, *A Dictionary for Accountants,* Englewood Cliffs, N.J.: Prentice-Hall, Inc., 1952, p. 446.

printed paper, and the paper can then be folded to the desired size for filing.

Within or attached to the voucher jacket or folder would be such items as the requisition, the duplicate of the purchase order, the invoice, duplicate of a voucher check, and eventually the canceled check. The list of Expenditure Accounts with blank spaces for designation of the amounts disbursed and charged to the various Expenditure Accounts is often printed on the inner side of the voucher jacket. When folded, the outside of the voucher jacket often provides spaces for such information as the voucher number, amount of voucher check, date, name and address of the payee, and the number of the check or warrant issued. The name of the school district and its location are also usually printed on the inside and outside of the voucher jacket. Voucher jackets can be filed numerically or alphabetically. Most systems seem to follow the alphabetical listing by vendor rather than numerical arrangement of voucher jackets.

VOUCHER REGISTER

As the name implies, a Voucher Register is a ledger in columnar form in which all the vouchers are entered. Fowlkes called it a book of original entry in accounting for expenditures.[2] If the accrual system of accounting is followed, an entry is made in the Voucher Register as soon as the invoice has been received, properly checked, and approved. If the cash accounting system of accounting is employed, no entry is made until the voucher check has been prepared. This may take from 30 to 90 days or longer after the receipt of the invoice. It is a desirable procedure to list the invoice in the Voucher Register as soon as received, if there is no other system of encumbrance accounting. With encumbrance accounting used in conjunction with cash systems, the vouchers are not entered until after disbursements have been executed.

As a book of original entry, the Voucher Register can be looked upon as a special type of journal. It is advisable to use the term Voucher Register rather than Voucher Journal, for some authorities use the term Journal Voucher to describe another document often used as a means of opening the books.[3] Although the Voucher Register is a diary of vouchers issued and a device to facilitate posting to other ledgers, it must be regarded, nonetheless, as a special type of journal.

In accounting, items recorded in a journal are referred to as entries and items placed in a ledger are referred to as postings. Entry into a journal or posting in a ledger may occur at the same time or the posting may occur at the end of the month whereas entries into journals occur daily. The posting medium is a book of original entry or journal. In other words, it is the source from which postings to ledgers are made. Keep in mind that a ledger is a book of final entry. No amounts should get into a ledger without also appearing in a journal. A ledger is a group of accounts rather than one account.

IDENTIFICATION AND CLASSIFICATION OF EXPENDITURE ACCOUNTS

The Expenditure Accounts to be enumerated herein can be used with any fund. Keep in mind that a fund is a group of financial resources. Within each fund there can be many kinds and varieties of accounts. All funds will have some accounts to classify properly expenditures made with a particular group of financial resources. Most of the Expenditure Accounts to be identified in subsequent paragraphs will be used in accounting for Current Expenses (expenditures from the so-called General Fund). Fewer of the Expenditure Accounts to be listed can be applied meaningfully in accounting for Schoolhouse Fund expenditures. All of the Expenditure Accounts to be enumerated will not be used in all of the school funds. But some will be necessary in all funds. It is highly unlikely that all accounts enumerated herein will be used in every school district. To be specific, only those systems which operate such community services as public libraries (not school libraries), public recreation programs, and transportation for private school children will have any need for Expenditure Accounts for COMMUNITY SERVICES.

The accounts listed herein can be applied whether the cash or accrual basis of accounting is used. They are necessary whether the double- or the single-entry system of bookkeeping is employed. The 1957 USOE financial accounting handbook[4] makes no recommendations on using the cash or accrual basis for accounting or the double- or single-entry system of bookkeeping. It is recommended in this book, however, that the accrual basis of accounting be used as far as is practicable in public school systems. Likewise, the double-entry system of bookkeeping is recommended for it enables more careful financial control.

---

[2] John Guy Fowlkes, *Principles and Practices of Financial Accounting for Schools,* Eau Claire, Wis.: E. M. Hale and Company, 1934, p. 108.
[3] *Ibid.,* p. 39.

[4] Paul L. Reason and Alpheus L. White, *Financial Accounting for Local and State School Systems, Standard Receipt and Expenditure Accounts,* Bulletin 1957, no. 4, U.S. Office of Education, Washington, D.C.: U.S. Government Printing Office, 1957, pp. 24–25.

THE BASES FOR CLASSIFICATION OF ACCOUNTS

Many different approaches are available to categorize Expenditure Accounts. In the early part of the twentieth century, Case clarified the systematic grouping of school expenditures according to: (1) function, (2) character, (3) object, and (4) location. These four bases provided a means of complete financial record keeping and analysis by:

1. The kind of work helped along by the payment.
2. The financial character of the payment as a fiscal transaction.
3. The object of the expenditure or the actual thing bought or service obtained.
4. The location benefited by the transaction to which the expenditure is chargeable.[5]

Case's well-organized system for recording school expenditures continues in use today with some modification. In addition to the four groups mentioned by Case, expenditures can be classified by fund and educational program area or level (elementary, secondary, or other educational unit).

The most widely accepted means of differentiating among Expenditure Accounts are by character and by function of the financial transaction. The most appropriate term to describe the systematic grouping of Expenditure Accounts under major headings is "functional-character classification." There is a close relationship between the kind of educational work helped by the expenditure (its function) and its financial character. To illustrate, one of the so-called character groupings for expenditures is entitled ADMINISTRATION. This title also suggests functional as well as character groupings, for all financial transactions involved in the execution of activities related to the general regulation, direction, and control of school affairs on a system-wide bases are accounted for under ADMINISTRATION. The same term suggests the function as well as the character of the fiscal transaction.

The word "character" as used in identifying broad accounting classifications is vague. The dictionary defines character, in the sense most likely to be applied in accounting, as "an attribute or quality," "a trait or sum of traits," or "an index of the essential or intrinsic quality." It is suggested by the writers of this book that the term functional-character is much more meaningful. It implies that the index of the essential or intrinsic quality (i.e., character) can be understood best by examining the kind of educational work (i.e., function) helped by the expenditure. In a broad sense the character clas-

[5] Hiram C. Case, *Handbook of Instructions for Recording Disbursements for School Purposes*, Albany, N.Y.: C. F. Williams and Sons, Inc., 1916, p. 7.

sification can be conceived of as a grouping of expenditures necessary to perform functions which are related in the manner suggested by the title of the classification. To be more specific, character is the broad term, and the more specific related functions are organized as parts of the overall pattern. The functional-character system for classifying accounts is most often employed in grouping school fiscal transactions. As will be demonstrated subsequently there are 14 basic functional-character classes around which to group school expenditures.

Classification by object means grouping of transactions by items purchased such as fuel, textbooks, instructional supplies, clerical work and similar rather specific activities, supplies, or materials. The list would be almost inexhaustible. If the objects or services procured were grouped into larger units, the problem of too many groups would not be solved in this approach to account classification. Cost analysis makes it necessary to identify objects through coding of special or subsidiary distribution ledgers. The objects obtained can be identified if first entered in accounts organized by character and function. In other words, the expenditure for an object is placed in an appropriate functional-character class and then later distributed to the subsidiary accounts needed to identify the object for purposes of cost analysis.

Grouping of accounts by location of unit benefited by the expenditure has some value in cost analysis. It is not suggested as a basic approach to classification of fiscal transactions. Under this approach the expenditures are listed by individual schools located within the system. The identification of expenditures with individual schools (this system probably has value only in the case of special schools) can best be accomplished by coding within such educational program areas or levels of classification as elementary, secondary, adult education, etc.

The 1957 USOE financial accounting handbook suggested the following major Expenditure Accounts based on 14 functional-character classifications of AD-MINISTRATION, INSTRUCTION, ATTENDANCE SERVICE, HEALTH SERVICES, PUPIL TRANSPORTATION SERVICES, OPERATION OF PLANT, MAINTENANCE OF PLANT, FIXED CHARGES, FOOD SERVICES, STUDENT BODY ACTIVITIES, COMMUNITY SERVICES, CAPITAL OUTLAY, DEBT SERVICES FROM CURRENT FUNDS, and OUTGOING TRANSFER ACCOUNTS. Each of these 14 major classes will be described in greater detail along with the minimum divisions and subdivisions needed for the proper recording of expenditures in the following pages.

The 14 major character classes differ in some respects from the 8 recommended in previously published financial accounting manuals for public schools issued by the U.S. Office of Education. Circular 204[6] or the 1948 USOE financial handbook called for the following basic account classifications: (1) Administration (General Control), (2) Instruction, (3) Auxiliary Services, (4) Operation of Plant, (5) Maintenance of Plant, (6) Fixed Charges, (7) Capital Outlay, and (8) Debt Service from Current Funds. At one time the term General Control was used to describe the same accounts now grouped under Administration. Many states' accounting handbooks continue to use the older term General Control.

The 1957 handbook recommended a separate account series for each of the following which were previously included under Auxiliary Services: ATTENDANCE SERVICES, HEALTH SERVICES, PUPIL TRANSPORTATION SERVICES, FOOD SERVICES, STUDENT BODY ACTIVITIES, and COMMUNITY SERVICES. There are differences in definitions and directions for posting certain expenditures. The major difference between the 1948 USOE accounting manual and the 1957 USOE financial accounting handbook is the division of what was called Auxiliary Services into six new account series. It is of historical interest that the 1948 USOE manual placed in Auxiliary Services the two separate basic categories of Coördinate Activities and Auxiliary Services.

Circular 204[7] called for eight separate funds to record financial transactions. These were funds for: (1) Current Funds; (2) Capital Funds for new buildings, grounds, and equipment; (3) Revolving Funds, sometimes called Advancement Funds, for commercial operations; (4) Trust Funds established by gift or legacy; (5) "School Funds"—so-called Student or Athletic Funds; (6) Government Funds which are paid by other governmental bodies for school purposes; (7) Imprest or Petty Cash Funds; and (8) Insurance Funds. No specific funds were recommended in the 1957 handbook. Accounting forms were illustrated in the 1948 but not in the 1957 USOE accounting handbook.

State departments of public instruction have influenced the design of local district accounting. It is highly desirable that all state departments of public instruction which have published financial accounting handbooks for local districts carefully reëvaluate their existing pattern in light of the 1957 USOE financial accounting handbook for public schools.

Some degree of arbitrariness is evident in all attempts to define terms, specify posting procedures, and design accounts. If there is to be any comparable data it must be based on uniform terminology as well as on uniform practices and procedures in public school accounting. To promote uniformity in school accounting most of the recommendations in this book coincide with those found in the 1957 USOE financial accounting handbook.[8]

All school systems, regardless of size, should maintain a large portion of the following Expenditure Accounts. Numbers have been attached to the Expenditure Accounts to help simplify identification. The numbers can be interpreted as a system of coding to be used either with machine accounting methods or the traditional pen-and-ink manual systems.

Usually, Arabic numerals only identify the major account classifications. The major headings can then be divided into more specific accounts which are usually designated by Arabic numerals followed by lower-case letters such as 215-a. The Expenditure Accounts are assigned numbers ranging from 100 through 1499. The number series attached to various accounts are arbitrarily determined. To achieve uniformity it is desirable that all school districts change over to the numbering system developed in the 1957 USOE accounting manual, even though it may appear that another set of numbers may work just as well. Receipts Accounts were assigned numbers 10 through 99 and Clearing Accounts numbers 1500 through 1999. The numbers used for the Expenditure Account series start where Receipt Accounts stop and end where the Clearing Accounts begin.

ACCOUNT SERIES 100—ADMINISTRATION

ADMINISTRATION (previously called General Control) is the series of accounts under which are posted expenditures for the general regulation, direction, and control of the educational affairs on a system-wide basis. To be included herein, the administrative activities must influence the school district as a whole and not be confined to a single school building or a school building subject or a narrow phase of school activities. In general, it includes the expenditures for school board salaries and expenses; the superintendent and central office staff salaries and expenses; and salaries and expenses for other activities related to planning organizing, directing, coördinating, and controlling the human efforts and material resources necessary on a system-wide basis. In another sense, all expenditures related to the functions of formulating and executing educational policies for the school system as a whole are

[6] Emery M. Foster and Harold E. Akerly, *Financial Accounting for Public Schools*, Circular 204, rev., 1948, U.S. Office of Education, Washington, D.C.: U.S. Government Printing Office, 1952.
[7] *Ibid.*

[8] The classifications and names for Expenditure Accounts used in this chapter are adapted from Reason and White, *op. cit.*, pp. 36–102.

grouped under this functional-character class of accounts.

Expenditures consummated for the administration of a given school building by a principal or for the supervision of teaching of music throughout the school system are not included herein. These expenditures and others similar to them are judged to be more closely related to INSTRUCTION than ADMINISTRATION. Likewise, the administrative expenses for a narrow phase or specialized area such as attendance, health, transportation, food services, student body activities, and community services are, by definition, recorded elsewhere.

Basically, the various major accounts in this series are organized around three purposes: (1) salaries for personal services, (2) contracted services, (3) other expenses or objects needed. The following accounts and their subdivisions are necessary for the proper recording of expenditure transactions under ACCOUNT SERIES 100.

A. *Major Account 110—Salaries for Administration.* Only the salaries paid to full- or part-time personnel involved in administration of school affairs on a system-wide basis and who are on the regular payroll of the school district are posted in the various subdivisions of this major account heading. The fees paid to special consultants or for contracted services related to general administration are not recorded here but under *Major Account 120.*

1. Account 110-a—Salaries for the Board of Education. The salaries or per diem payments to board of education members and their secretarial or clerical assistants are posted in this account. In states where the board secretary is a business manager or more than a clerk-typist, the salary is recorded in the account that follows rather than herein.

2. Account 110-b—Salaries for the Board Secretary's Office. The full-time, part-time, or pro rata portion of salaries for the office of secretary to the board of education and his secretarial and clerical staff are reported herein. If the secretary to the board is also employed to perform other functions but is paid an additional amount of salary to act as secretary, such extra salary payment is reported in this account.

3. Account 110-c—Salaries for the School District Treasurer's Office. Recorded herein are the full-time, part-time, and pro rata portions of salaries of individuals serving in the treasurer's office. This includes secretarial and clerical staff wages as well as those of the treasurer.

4. Account 110-d—Salaries for School Elections.

The salaries paid to full-time or part-time individuals for services rendered in connection with any school district election such as election of officers or bond elections (that may or may not pass) or budget and appropriation elections (that may or may not pass) are reported herein. If an individual works in another capacity as well as that of an election official, then the pro rata portion of his salary paid for election services only is recorded in this account.

5. Account 110-e—Salaries for Tax Collection. This account is of value only in school districts where the district is actually the collecting agency for school taxes. In most cases taxes are collected by some other agency and turned over to the school district without charge for the collection and, therefore, nothing is charged here or under contracted services for administration. Where there are full-time or part-time personnel involved in school tax collection, their salaries or a pro rata portion of their salaries for such services are posted in this account.

6. Account 110-f—Salaries for Legal Services. Only the salaries paid to full-time or part-time individuals on the school administrative staff and for services involved in the regular operation of the school are recorded under this account. The secretarial and clerical assistants are also included under Account 110-f. Salaries of legal personnel employed for or assigned to specific construction projects are included under the 1200 SERIES of accounts. If the legal services are supplied by firms or individuals not regularly employed by the board, the expenditures made are reported in *Major Account 120 —Contracted Services for Administration.*

7. Account 110-g—Salaries for the Superintendent's Office. The salaries of the superintendent of schools and the immediate personnel who assist him in the general administration of school affairs are posted in this account. If the superintendent is a part-time teacher, then only that part of his salary which is related to administration is reported here, and the remainder is reported in INSTRUCTION. Proration of salary should be based on a proportion of the time spent in teaching and in administration. The salaries of the secretaries and clerks in the superintendent's office are also included in Account 110-g.

8. Account 110-h—Salaries for the Personnel Office. This classification is used in those school systems with a full- or part-time personnel di-

rector and personnel office. If the personnel function is executed by the superintendent of schools only, no such account classification is needed. If a personnel director other than the superintendent is employed, his salary or pro rata portion and the salary paid to the secretarial and clerical assistants are placed under this category.

9. Account 110-i—Salaries for Public Relations. The same comments made with respect to the previous paragraph would apply here. This account heading is used only in those school systems which have a full-time or a part-time person other than the superintendent who is responsible for administering the public relations program for the entire school system.

10. Account 110-j—Salaries for Centralized Research. This account has value in systems employing full- or part-time research personnel performing work of significance to the system as a whole rather than to one segment. Posted herein are the salaries paid to such personnel and their secretaries and clerical assistants. This should not include the salaries paid to individuals in charge of testing programs in specific schools. The cost of the testing programs are included under the 200 SERIES—INSTRUCTION. Where the research is performed on a contractual basis with a university or other agencies, the entire cost is recorded under *Major Account 120.*

11. Account 110-k—Salaries for School Census Enumeration. Posted in this account are salaries paid to full- and part-time personnel who supervise or actually execute the census enumeration as well as the salaries paid to their secretarial or clerical assistants. If the individual who performs this census occupies another position in the school system as well, the pro rata portion of his salary only is reported here.

12. Account 110-l—Salaries for Office of Business Administration. Recorded herein are the salaries of the full-time or part-time chief business officer, general business administrative assistants, and secretarial and clerical help. The business officials concerned with fiscal control, buildings and grounds, purchasing, or personnel administration do not have their salaries reported here but in other accounts which are designed specially for such purposes. These special accounts follow.

13. Account 110-m—Salaries for Fiscal Control. The full-time, part-time, and pro rata portion of salaries of principal accountants, supervisors of accounts, accountants, and auditors who are responsible for controlling the financial operation of the school district are included in this account rather than in the previous one. Posted under this heading are the salaries of the account clerks, bookkeepers, and other clerical personnel employed in fiscal control.

14. Account 110-n—Salaries for the Administration of Buildings and Grounds. Reported under this classification are salaries paid to full- or part-time central office personnel who administer the system-wide plant construction, operation, and maintenance programs; salaries of architects and draftsmen who are on the payroll of the school districts and not assigned to a construction project; and salaries of clerks and secretaries concerned with the administration of buildings and grounds. If the architectural services are purchased from a private concern under a contractual basis they are not included under this account. The salaries of supervisors of custodial or maintenance workers in individual buildings or groups of buildings (less than the entire system) are recorded elsewhere.

15. Account 110-o—Salaries for the Purchasing Office. Posted herein are the salaries paid to full- or part-time purchasing agents; other administrative personnel responsible for system-wide purchasing, storing, and distribution of school supplies and material; and their secretarial and clerical assistants. Salaries of supervisors of warehouses, stock clerks, shipping clerks, and other personnel who operate central storerooms are not included herein but under Account 610-d—Other Salaries for Operation of Plant.

NOTE: An alternative arrangement for Accounts 110-l, 110-m, 110-n, and 110-o is as follows:

12. Account 110-l—Salaries for Office of Business Administration.
   a. Subaccount 110-1-1—Salaries of Chief Business Officer and His Administrative Assistants.
   b. Subaccount 110-1-2—Salaries for Fiscal Control.
   c. Subaccount 110-1-3—Salaries for the Administration of Buildings and Grounds.
   d. Subaccount 110-1-4—Salaries for the Purchasing Office.

This organization differs from that proposed in the 1957 USOE accounting manual but has considerable justification. If used, it would require renumbering the accounts that follow in the remainder of this major account classification.

16. Account 110-p—Salaries for Printing and Publishing. Recorded under this account class are the salaries paid to full-time or part-time personnel for services rendered in connection with the printing or publishing of annual reports, proceedings of the board of education, the school directory, board manuals and any other *administrative* publication of the school district. Expenditures for publications used for school functions and for forms are recorded under the appropriate accounts, according to the purpose for which these items were printed. If the printing and publishing is done on a contract basis, the cost is included under *Major Account 120*.

17. Account 110-q—Other Salaries for Administration. Any other administrative salaries which cannot be recorded under the preceding accounts would be included herein. The salaries of attendance personnel, however, are not recorded here but under *Major Account 310*.

B. *Major Account 120—Contracted Services for Administration*. Recorded in this major classification are expenditures for services necessary for the administration of the school system as a whole but which are rendered by personnel who are not on the regular and continuing payroll of the district. It includes administrative services rendered on a special fee or contract basis. All related expenses covered by the contract as well as salary payments for such services are recorded herein. The subdivisions under this major account could follow many listed in *Major Account 110* such as:

1. Account 120-a—Contracted Services for School Election.
2. Account 120-b—Contracted Services for Tax Collection.
3. Account 120-c—Contracted Services for Legal Services.
4. Account 120-d—Contracted Services for Public Relations.
5. Account 120-e—Contracted Services for Research.
6. Account 120-f—Contracted Services for School Census Enumeration, etc.

C. *Major Account 130—Other Expenses for Administration*. Recorded under this account are expenditures for all expenses *other than salaries* paid to personnel involved in system-wide administration of school district affairs. Posted herein would be expenditures for such items as supplies, repairs to supplies, travel expenses, rental of equipment (but not land or buildings), and administrative in-service training. Freight and cartage costs are recorded with the expenditures for supplies charged to various proper accounts. Membership dues or fees are recorded under the function for which the membership was taken, regardless of whether they are district or individual memberships paid by the district. Expenditures for plant operation, plant maintenance, and rental of land and buildings are not recorded here but under the other appropriate account series. This major account can be subdivided as follows:

1. Account 130-a—Other Expenses for the Board of Education. Membership of the school or individual board members in a state school board association or national school board association would be included herein.
2. Account 130-b—Other Expenses for the Board Secretary's Office. Recorded in this account are only those expenses (and not salaries) used in the board secretary's office.
3. Account 130-c—Other Expenses for the School District Treasurer's Office.
4. Account 130-d—Other Expenses for School Elections.
5. Account 130-e—Other Expenses for Tax Collections.
6. Account 130-f—Other Expenses for Legal Services.
7. Account 130-g—Other Expenses for the Superintendent's Office.
8. Account 130-h—Other Expenses for the Personnel Office.
9. Account 130-i—Other Expenses for Public Relations.
10. Account 130-j—Other Expenses for Centralized Research.
11. Account 130-k—Other Expenses for School Census Enumeration.
12. Account 130-l—Other Expenses for the Office of Business Administration.
13. Account 130-m—Other Expenses for Fiscal Control.
14. Account 130-n—Other Expenses for the Administration of Buildings and Grounds.
15. Account 130-o—Other Expenses for the Purchasing Office.
16. Account 130-p—Other Expenses for Printing and Publishing.
17. Account 130-q—Miscellaneous Expenses for Administration.

It should be apparent that account subdivisions for *Major Account 130* parallel those in *Major Account 110*. The explanations of the subdivisions of *Major Account 130* are similar to those which apply to the subdivisions of *Major Account 110* and hence are not repeated.

ACCOUNT SERIES 200—INSTRUCTION

The purpose of this series of accounts is to group the financial transactions related to activities concerned directly with or aiding in the teaching of students or improving the quality of teaching. This involves the payment of salaries to teachers, principals, supervisors of instruction, and guidance and psychological personnel as well as the textbooks, library books, and other materials and supplies used in the instructional process. Expenditures for supplementary education media such as educational radio or television are posted under the appropriate functional accounts in the same manner as for any other activity of the school. Expenditures for the instructional aspects of educational radio or television are included under the 200 SERIES of accounts whereas those for plant operational aspects are included under the 600 SERIES of accounts. Expenditures for student body activities are not included here but under the 1000 SERIES. Expenditures for recreational activities which are not a part of the regular instructional program or student body activities are likewise recorded under COMMUNITY SERVICES, namely, *Major Account 1100—Recreation.*

By far the largest number and amount of expenditures in the operation of schools are recorded under INSTRUCTION. Approximately two-thirds of all current expenditures are posted under INSTRUCTION. The accounting system can be designed to help analyze different educational program areas such as elementary, secondary, summer, adult education, and community college programs. It was recommended in the 1957 USOE financial accounting handbook that to the extent feasible, expenditures under the INSTRUCTION accounts should be distributed to subsidiary accounts as an aid in analyzing program area costs. This can be accomplished by distributing the expenditures directly to the individual program areas at the time expenditures are recorded in accounts, or by charging expenditures to a total undistributed account at the time of recording and prorating the total account to the different program areas at a later date. The cost analysis can be facilitated through the use of coding. In addition to the numerical code previously explained, letters can be added to designate program areas to be charged. Thus, the letter "E" might be added to identify the cost with the elementary day school, "S" for the costs to second-

ary day schools, "SS" for costs for summer school operations, "CC" for community colleges, and "AE" for adult education programs. In some school districts it may be necessary to go even further and break down costs on the basis of nursery schools, kindergartens, vocational schools, and special education programs. This again can be done either by special coding in the Expenditure Accounts to be listed or by maintaining subsidiary ledgers and accounting classifications.

The following accounts and their subdivisions are necessary for the proper recording of expenditure transactions for INSTRUCTION.

A. *Major Account 210—Salaries for Instruction.*

1. Account 211—Salaries of Principals. The salaries of full-time principals, assistant principals, and any other personnel performing the function of principals are included under this heading. If the principal also teaches, only that part of his salary devoted to administration (as measured by the proportion of the time devoted to the coordination and supervision of the activities) is posted in this account. If teachers or other instructional staff members are assigned administrative duties usually performed by the principal or his assistants and awarded extra salary for these duties, the additional salary for administrative responsibility is also posted herein. The salary of the supervising principal who performs the full-time functions of a superintendent is recorded under Account 110-g—Salaries for the Superintendent's Office rather than here. If the so-called supervising principal performs the functions of the principal as well as the superintendent, that portion of his time and salary devoted to the principal's duties is reported here.

2. Account 212—Salaries of Consultants or Supervisors of Instruction. Recorded under this account are salaries paid to full- or part-time general or subject matter consultants or supervisors of instruction. This includes school library and audio-visual supervisors and consultants. Very often, supervisors of instruction are located in the same building as the superintendent and school board. This has no bearing on the assignment of their salaries to various account classifications. The important thing as far as accounting for salaries is concerned is the function performed. Where outside consultative services are hired in connection with the instructional program, their fees are not recorded here but under Account 250-c—Miscellaneous Expenses for Instruction. Salaries of supervisors for such activities as transportation, food services, health serv-

ices, and attendance services are not recorded herein but elsewhere.

3. Account 213—Salaries of Teachers. Posted in this account class are salaries of full- or part-time personnel rendering teaching services to students in public schools. This includes the salaries of teachers of special classes, such as those for exceptional children, the home-bound, and others. It also includes the salaries paid to substitute teachers. The salaries of department heads are divided between this account classification and Account 212, if they provide teaching services as well as supervisory functions.

Some states require information on salaries paid to men teachers as opposed to women teachers. Under such conditions, the code letters "M" and "W" can be used or the subaccounts can be organized to show salaries of men teachers as opposed to salaries of women teachers. If required, the accounting system could be designed to provide information on salaries paid to teachers of special activities such as football coaches, basketball coaches, dramatic directors, supervisors of school annuals, and so on. Each school will prepare the number of subaccounts necessary beyond the minimum recommended herein to supply the information the board of education and the people of the community desire.

Salaries payments per month can be posted as a lump sum for all teachers or posted to some of the following subaccounts which have some value in computing more reliable cost figures for various program areas.

a. Subaccount 213-a—Salaries of Elementary School Teachers. This in turn can be split into:
213-a-1—Salaries to Nursery School Teachers.
213-a-2—Salaries of Kindergarten Teachers.
213-a-3—Salaries to Other Elementary School Teachers.
b. Subaccount 213-b—Salaries of Secondary School Teachers.
213-b-1—Salaries of Secondary School Music Teachers.
213-b-2—Salaries of Secondary School Art Teachers.
213-b-3—Salaries of English Teachers.
213-b-4—Salaries of Science Teachers.
c. Subaccount 213-c—Salaries of Teachers of Home-Bound Children.
d. Subaccount 213-d—Salaries of Teachers of the Mentally Handicapped.

e. Subaccount 213-e—Salaries of Teachers of Children with Hearing Difficulties.
f. Subaccount 213-f—Salaries of Teachers of the Visually Handicapped.
g. Subaccount 213-g—Salaries of Teachers of the Intellectually Gifted.
h. Subaccount 213-h—Salaries of Substitute Teachers.

4. Account 214—Salaries of Other Instructional Staff.
a. Subaccount 214-a—Salaries of School Librarians. This account includes the full- and part-time public school librarians, excluding audio-visual personnel and excluding the consultants, supervisors, or directors of school libraries.
b. Subaccount 214-b—Salaries of Audio-Visual Personnel. This account includes full- and part-time audio-visual personnel and excludes salaries of consultants or supervisors and television instructional personnel.
c. Subaccount 214-c—Salaries of Guidance Personnel.
d. Subaccount 214-d—Salaries of Psychological Personnel. This account includes the salaries of personnel engaged in psychological services supplied to students by public school psychologists or psychometrists. Salaries of psychiatrists and psychiatric case workers are recorded under Subaccount 410-a-5—Salaries for Other Professional and Technical Health Personnel.
e. Subaccount 214-e—Salaries of Television Instructional Personnel. This includes the salaries paid to personnel engaged in providing educational experiences through the medium of television.

5. Account 215—Salaries of Secretarial and Clerical Assistants.
a. Subaccount 215-a—Salaries for Secretarial and Clerical Services for the Principal's Office.
b. Subaccount 215-b—Salaries for Secretarial and Clerical Services for Consultants or Supervisors of Instruction.
c. Subaccount 215-c—Salaries for Secretarial and Clerical Services for Other Instructional Staff Members. Posted herein are salaries for clerical and secretarial services to school librarians, audio-visual personnel, guidance personnel, psychological personnel, and other such instructional staff.

6. Account 216—Other Salaries for Instruction.

B. *Major Account 220—Textbooks.* This accounting classification is necessary to record expenditures for textbooks furnished *free* to all public school pupils or to certain grades or classes. The binding and other textbook repairs and freight and cartage of books should be included as well. If the texts are purchased and resold or rented to students, only the net cost is reported under this heading. Any profits realized from sale or rental of textbooks are posted under Account 14-c—Net Receipts from Revolving Funds or Clearing Accounts. Expenditures for texts furnished free to indigent pupils are reported in Account 1150-b—Other Expenses for Welfare Activities. *Major Account 220* can be broken down into program areas, as per the following illustrations:

1. Account 221—Textbooks for Elementary Schools.
2. Account 222—Textbooks for Secondary Schools.
3. Account 223—Textbooks Used in the Adult Education Program.
4. Account 224—Textbooks for Exceptional Children.

Further subdivisions by school building can be developed to the extent desired.

C. *Major Account 230—School Libraries and Audio-Visual Materials.*

1. Account 230-a—School Library Books. Posted in this account are expenditures for regular or incidental purchases of school library books available for general use to students as well as binding or other repair costs to existing books. It includes reference books even though they may be used solely in one particular classroom. Not recorded in this account is original purchase of books for a new school library or any material expansion of the library. They are noted under ACCOUNT SERIES 1200—CAPITAL OUTLAY, Account 1230-c.
2. Account 230-b—Periodicals and Newspapers. Recorded herein are expenditures for periodicals and newspapers for general use by the school library. A periodical is defined as any publication appearing at regular intervals or less than a year and continuing for an indefinite period of time.
3. Account 230-c—Audio-Visual Materials. Reported under this account are expenditures for audio-visual materials (not equipment) employed in instruction of students. It includes films, filmstrips, recordings, exhibits, charts, maps, and television and radio materials ob-

tained through outright purchase or by rental. Equipment (not material) rental or purchase is reported under Account 250-c—Miscellaneous Expenses for Instruction.
4. Account 230-d—Other School Library Expenses. Posted in this account are expenditures for library services in place of maintaining a school library and also school library supplies such as paper, pencils, and index cards.

D. *Major Account 240—Teaching Supplies.* This classification is necessary for the posting of expenditures for all supplies which are consumed in the teaching-learning process. Gas and oil for driver education vehicles are charged here. The freight and cartage costs for the delivery of teaching supplies should be included here. A list of teaching supplies would include tests, chalk, paper, test tubes, ink, pencils, paints, paint brushes, crayons, chemicals, shop supplies, oils, cleaners, food used in the instructional program, instructional farming supplies, music supplies, workbooks, physical education supplies, materials for instruction by correspondence, etc. If the supplies are later sold to students, only net costs are reported at this point. Other financial transactions involved in the sale of supplies to students are reported in *Major Account 1820—Materials for Resale* (Clearing Accounts). *Major Account 240* can be subdivided to provide information necessary in cost analysis by program areas. These could be:

1. Account 241—Teaching Supplies for Kindergarten.
2. Account 242—Teaching Supplies for Other Elementary School Classes.
3. Account 243—Teaching Supplies for Secondary School Classes. This in turn could be broken down into as many aspects of the secondary school program as necessary.
4. Account 244—Teaching Supplies for Exceptional Children.
5. Account 245—Teaching Supplies for the Adult Education Program.
6. Account 246—Teaching Supplies for the Community College.

E. *Major Account 250—Other Expenses for Instruction.*

1. Account 250-a—Miscellaneous Supplies for Instruction. The costs of supplies used in the instructional program which are not consumed in the teaching-learning process itself are reported here. Examples of these would be: office supplies, curriculum supplies, professional books and subscriptions for professional magazines for

the instructional staff, supplies for school exhibits, supplies for in-service training of instructional staff, and supplies for the operation of equipment such as ribbons for typewriters in the principal's office and gasoline and oil for vehicles assigned to the instructional personnel. Not recorded here are expenditures for gas and oil for driver education vehicles, school library supplies, and graduation expenses. They are recorded under Account 240—Teaching Supplies; Account 230-d—Other School Library Expenses; and Account 250-c—Miscellaneous Expenses for Instruction, respectively.

2. Account 250-b—Travel Expenses for Instruction. Under this heading are posted expenditures for the travel of all instructional personnel and their assistants, including travel in connection with everyday instructional activities and travel to conventions, meetings, institutes, and workshops. The maintenance of such district-owned vehicles is accounted for under the 700 SERIES of accounts.

3. Account 250-c—Miscellaneous Expenses for Instruction. Reported under this account are outlays for such items as rental of equipment, contracted services for instruction by correspondence, graduation expenses, assembly speakers, membership dues in associations for instructional personnel, and outside consultative services hired in connection with the instructional program. Not recorded herein are costs of tuition, transportation, and other payments to other school districts for tuition to nonpublic schools. They are entered in ACCOUNT SERIES 1400—OUTGOING TRANSFER ACCOUNTS.

ACCOUNT SERIES 300—ATTENDANCE SERVICES FOR PUBLIC SCHOOLS

Financial transactions for those activities whose primary purpose is the promotion and improvement of the attendance of school through the enforcement of compulsory attendance laws or other means are reported under this classification. If the attendance services are for nonpublic schools, charges are made to COMMUNITY SERVICES rather than herein. The major account classifications are divided into two areas: (1) salaries and (2) other expenses.

A. *Major Account 310—Salaries for Attendance Services.*
  1. Account 310-a—Salaries for Attendance Personnel. Reported in this account are salaries of full- and part-time attendance officers, visiting

teachers, home-school counselors, home-school visitors, school social workers, and others whose primary function is to enforce compulsory attendance laws, analyze causes of nonattendance, etc. If these individuals are engaged in other activities, only that part of their salary which is devoted to attendance services is charged to this account. Not included herein are the salaries of teachers of the home-bound or students in hospitals, convalescent homes, and detention homes.
  2. Account 310-b—Salaries of Secretaries and Clerical Personnel for Attendance Services.
  3. Account 310-c—Other Salaries for Attendance Workers.
B. *Major Account 320—Other Expenses for Attendance Services.*
  1. Account 320-a—Supplies for Attendance Services. Posted herein are the costs of forms, office supplies, supplies used in the operation of vehicles, and other equipment and supplies used by attendance personnel and their assistants.
  2. Account 320b—Travel Expenses for Attendance Services. Only the expenditures incurred for travel by attendance personnel in the performance of their everyday activities and for attendance at conventions, meetings, institutes, and workshops are included herein. Maintenance of district-owned vehicles assigned for use by attendance personnel are recorded under ACCOUNT SERIES 700—MAINTENANCE OF PLANT.
  3. Account 320-c—Miscellaneous Expenses for Attendance Services.

ACCOUNT SERIES 400—HEALTH SERVICES FOR PUBLIC SCHOOLS

Physical and mental health services to pupils consist of medical, dental, psychiatric, and nurse care in the form of inspection, treatment, weighing, etc. Posted under this account are expenditures for operation of all health services to public school students and employed personnel (including examinations prior to employment) as well as "health round-ups" for children anticipating enrollment in public schools, etc. Direct instruction in physical or health education are recorded under the 200 SERIES—INSTRUCTION rather than here. Health services to nonpublic schools are charged to COMMUNITY SERVICES. The series consists of two major accounts for (1) salaries of personnel and (2) other expenses.

A. *Major Account 410—Salaries for Health Services.* If the personnel engaged in granting health services also teach, their salaries are prorated in proportion to the time spent in each activity between this group of accounts and those for classroom instruction.

1. Account 410-a—Salaries for Professional and Technical Health Personnel. This can be subdivided into:
   a. Subaccount 410-a-1—Salaries of School Physicians, Including Psychiatrists. Posted in this subaccount are salaries of part- and full-time people on the payroll of the school district. Expenditures for medical services by medical personnel not regularly employed by the school are reported in Account 420-c—Miscellaneous Expenditures for Health Services.
   b. Subaccount 410-a-2—Salaries of School Dentists. Only the salaries of dentists (full- or part-time) regularly employed by the district are listed here. If they are not on the payroll, they are accounted for under Account 420-c.
   c. Subaccount 410-a-3—Salaries of School Nurses. Similar qualifications apply as stated in Subaccounts 410-a-1 and 410-a-2.
   d. Subaccount 410-a-4—Salaries of School Dental Hygienists. Similar qualifications apply as stated in Subaccounts 410-a-1 and 410-a-2.
   e. Subaccount 410-a-5—Salaries of Other Professional and Technical Health Personnel. Posted herein are the salaries of individuals on the regular school payroll who render such health services as optometry, audiometry, psychiatric work, and other therapists.
2. Account 410-b—Salaries of Nonprofessional and Nontechnical Health Personnel. Reported in this account are the salaries of clerks, secretaries, and other assistants performing nonprofessional and nontechnical services.

B. *Major Account 420—Other Expenses for Health Services.*
   1. Account 420-a—Supplies for Health Services. Included here are expenditures for medical and dental supplies, forms, the operation of vehicles and other equipment, and office and other supplies used by health personnel and their assistants.
   2. Account 420-b—Travel Expenses for Health Services.
   3. Account 420-c—Miscellaneous Expenses for Health Services. Posted herein are the costs of health services for public school students and employed personnel that cannot be recorded elsewhere. It also includes health services supplied by individuals who are not on the payroll of the school district.

ACCOUNT SERIES 500—PUPIL TRANSPORTATION SERVICES

The primary purpose of such services is to convey pupils to and from school activities between home and school or on trips for curricular or cocurricular activities. If it is necessary to maintain separate accounts for transportation vehicles used for field trips or cocurricular activities, it is recommended that the appropriate accounts defined below be subdivided to identify such usage. Retirement fund contributions by the district for pupil transportation employees are not posted under these accounts but under ACCOUNT SERIES 800—FIXED CHARGES, Account 810—*School District Contributions to Employee Retirement.* Transportation services for nonpublic school pupils are charged to COMMUNITY SERVICES.

A. *Major Account 510—Salaries for Pupil Transportation.* Posted in this major account are the salaries of full- or part-time transportation personnel regularly employed by the school district. If the individual works in other capacities as well as those of providing transportation services, the salary is prorated among the appropriate accounts in proportion to the time spent in each activity. This major account can be subdivided as follows:
   1. Account 510-a—Salaries of Pupil Transportation Supervisors. Recorded herein are the salaries of full- or part-time supervisors of transportation and other administrative personnel engaged in the administration of pupil transportation.
   2. Account 510-b—Salaries of Drivers for Pupil Transportation Vehicles.
      a. Subaccount 510-b-1—Transportation Between Home and School.
      b. Subaccount 510-b-2—Transportation for Curricular Activities.
      c. Subaccount 510-b-3—Transportation for Cocurricular Activities.
   3. Account 510-c—Salaries of Mechanics and Other Garage Employees. Only the salaries of full- or part-time people regularly employed by the district are recorded here. If such services are contracted the expenditures are reported elsewhere and not here.
   4. Account 510-d—Salaries of Clerks and Other Pupil Transportation Employees.

B. *Major Account 520—Contracted Services and Public Carriers.* Posted in this account are expenditures to owners who operate school buses and small vehicles to transport pupils; to individual contractors who own part of a bus, such as the chassis, even though the school district owns the body; and to parents who transport groups of children (including their own). Outlays for transportation of school children on public carriers are also reported under this classification even though a contract between the school and the public carrier may not exist and payments are made to pupils rather than to the carriers. The rental of school buses operated by school district personnel is reported elsewhere. This major account can be divided into as many headings as may be necessary for purposes of cost analysis. The following are to be regarded as illustrations only:

1. Account 521—Contracted Services to Owners of School Buses.
2. Account 522—Payments to Parents Transporting Children.
3. Account 523—Payments for the Transportation of Pupils Riding Public Carriers.

These in turn could be subdivided to show the costs for transporting elementary school pupils, secondary school pupils, exceptional pupils, etc. Where such services are employed for field trips and cocurricular trips, further subdivisions can be noted in both *Major Account 510* and *Major Account 520*, as per the illustration for Subaccounts 510-b-1, 510-b-2, and 510-b-3.

C. *Major Account 530—Replacement of Vehicles.* The recommended accounting procedure is a departure from previous methods of accounting for replacements. Piece-for-piece replacement, as described in the 1957 USOE financial handbook, is recommended in place of previous methods of computing replacements. The piece-for-piece replacement means replacement of a complete unit of equipment by another complete unit of equipment, serving the same purpose in the same way, even though the new equipment may have features not found on the old or may have a larger capacity. To illustrate, if a 40-passenger bus were replaced by a 54-passenger bus, the entire cost of the new bus (less the trade-in or salvage value of the old) would be recorded under the accounts in this major classification as a replacement outlay (rather than capital outlay), regardless of any difference in purchase prices of the two buses. The payment of notes is not recorded herein but under DEBT SERVICE.

1. Account 530-a—Cash Purchase of Replacements of Pupil Transportation Vehicles. Posted herein are outlays involved in piece-for-piece replacement of pupil transportation vehicles purchased on a cash basis regardless of the relative value of the replaced vehicles and the replacements. The costs for delivery and accessories and special equipment (whether attached at the time of purchase or acquired later) are considered a part of the replacement outlay. Any trade-ins are abated against this account. Not recorded here are the expenditures for additional transportation vehicles. Such acquisitions are charged to CAPITAL OUTLAY.

2. Account 530-b—Lease Purchase and Installment Purchase of Replacement of Pupil Transportation Vehicles. Posted in this account are the piece-for-piece replacement costs for delivered and equipped pupil transportation vehicles acquired on a lease purchase or installment purchase plan. Any trade-in allowances or amounts realized from the separate sale of replaced vehicles are abated against this account.

D. *Major Account 540—Pupil Transportation Insurance.* Recorded herein are premiums paid for various types of insurance such as public liability, property damage, medical care, collision, fire, and theft insurance. For purposes of cost analysis this account class can be subdivided to show pupil transportation insurance on buses owned by the school district and privately owned buses contracted for service in states where laws permit this practice.

E. *Major Account 550—Expenditures in Lieu of Transportation.* In some states room and board charges to maintain children near school or the purchase of boats, sleighs, skis, etc., required for getting children to school may be made in place of transportation costs to the schools. Only districts in sparsely settled regions or where terrain or lack of roads present special problems need be concerned with this major account classification.

F. *Major Account 560—Other Expenses for Pupil Transportation, Operation, and Maintenance.*

1. Account 560-a—Gasoline for Pupil Transportation Vehicles.
2. Account 560-b—Oil, Grease, and Gear Lubricants for Pupil Transportation Vehicles.
3. Account 560-c—Tires and Tubes for Pupil Transportation Vehicles.
4. Account 560-d—Repair Parts and Other Bus Supplies Used in Pupil Transportation Garage.
5. Account 560-e—Supplies and Expenses for Pupil Transportation Garage Operations.
6. Account 560-f—Pupil Transportation Garage and Garage Equipment Repairs.
7. Account 560-g—Maintenance of Pupil Transportation Vehicles by Private Garages.
8. Account 560-h—Rent for Pupil Transportation.

This includes expenditures for rental of land, buildings, and equipment for pupil transportation.

9. Account 560-i—Miscellaneous Expenses for Pupil Transportation and Operation and Maintenance.

ACCOUNT SERIES 600—OPERATION OF PLANT

Activities necessary to keep the school plant in operating condition would include such things as cleaning, disinfecting, heating, lighting, moving furniture, handling stores, caring for grounds, and other such "housekeeping" activities which are repeated somewhat regularly on either a daily, weekly, monthly, or seasonal basis. Repairs and replacement of facilities and equipment, whether used for instructional or other purposes, are charged to MAINTENANCE rather than OPERATION. Posted in the accounts of this series are all current expenses for plant operation except direct expenses for pupil transportation, food services, student body activities, and community services. The operating expenses for such school plants as those for central administration offices, warehouses, garages (but not pupil transportation garages), maintenance shops, teacherages, student dormitories, and other similar buildings are charged to ACCOUNT SERIES 600. Rental fees collected for teacherages and student dormitories are accounted for through Clearing Accounts. Only the net expenditures for operation of facilities where rental charges are made are reported herein.

A. *Major Account 610—Salaries for Operation of Plant.* Posted in this major account class are salaries paid to operational personnel in school plants. Not recorded herein are salaries of members of the central administrative staff who are responsible for the supervision or administration on a system-wide basis for building operation. They are recorded under Account 110-n—Salaries for Administration of Buildings and Grounds.

1. Account 610-a—Salaries of Plant Engineers.

2. Account 610-b—Salaries of Custodial Workers. Recorded in this account are the wages of full- or part-time custodians, firemen, custodians' helpers, matrons, general utility men, dairy men, night watchmen, and other personnel who sweep, clean, polish, mop, care for the building, livestock, operate the heating and ventilating systems, or perform any other housekeeping duties for all purposes (except direct expenses for pupil transportation, food services, student body activities, and community services.)

3. Account 610-c—Salaries for Care of Grounds. Posted herein are the salaries of full- or part-time personnel responsible for the care of grounds (but not repair and replacement) who perform such duties as rake, hoe, water, cut and protect lawns; transplant, trim, and care for shrubbery and sodded play areas; and prepare, plant, and care for flower beds for all purposes except those of direct expenses for pupil transportation, food services, student body activities, and community services.

4. Account 610-d—Other Salaries for Operation of Plant. Recorded in this account are the salaries of full- or part-time telephone switchboard operators, truck drivers, elevator operators, supervisors of warehouses, stock clerks and other personnel who operate a central storeroom, secretarial assistants to the plant operation personnel, and any other plant operation personnel whose salaries cannot be charged to the above accounts for all purposes except direct expenses for pupil transportation, food services, student body activities, and community services.

B. *Major Account 620—Contracted Services for the Operation of Plant.* Costs for plant operation provided by personnel who are not regularly employed by the district and who are not on the district payroll are recorded herein. Contracted services can be procured for washing windows, removing ashes and garbage, moving furniture and equipment, care of grounds, laundry, dry cleaning and linen services, or even complete custodial service. Expenditure for moving portable structures are charged to ACCOUNT SERIES 700—MAINTENANCE rather than here.

C. *Major Account 630—Heat for Buildings.* This major accounting class provides a place for posting all expenditures for the purchase and delivery of all coal, steam, electricity, gas, gasoline, fuel oil, and wood used for heating. If electricity and gas are used for heating as well as other purposes and if the utility bills do not separate costs of heating from others, the expenditure is posted under this major account or *Major Account 640—Utilities, Except Heat for Buildings* depending upon the larger use of the utilities supplied.

D. *Major Account 640—Utilities, Except Heat for Buildings.*

1. Account 640-a—Water and Sewage. Electrical power charges incurred in pumping water in school buildings are reported in the following account and not here.

2. Account 640-b—Electricity. This includes ex-

penditures for electricity for artificial lighting and power (but not for heating buildings).

3. Account 640-c—Gas. Posted herein are outlays for gas for any use other than heating buildings and for all purposes except direct expenses for pupil transportation, food services, student body activities, and community services. These same exceptions apply to all OPERATION accounts.

4. Account 640-d—Telephone and Telegraph. Recorded in this account are the costs for telephone and telegraph, including rental of telephone switchboards.

5. Account 640-e—Other Utilities.

E. *Major Account 650—Supplies for Operation of the Plant, Except Utilities.*

1. Account 650-a—Custodial Supplies. Reported here are the expenditures for brooms, mops, soaps, dusters, electrical fuses, electric light bulbs, paper towels, hand towels, bath towels, paper cups, toilet paper, and other such custodial supplies used by students and district employees for all purposes except direct expenses for pupil transportation, food services, student body activities, and community services.

2. Account 650-b—Supplies for Operation of Vehicles. In this category are posted expenditures for gasoline, lubricants, and other supplies used in the operation of district-owned vehicles for hauling supplies and equipment and by plant operation staff for all purposes except those of pupil transportation, food services, student body activities, and community services. Expenditures for tires, tubes, and replacements of such vehicles are recorded under the ACCOUNT SERIES 700—MAINTENANCE OF PLANT.

3. Account 650-c—Supplies for Care of Grounds. Posted in this account are outlays for care of grounds in the condition found which does not involve regrading sites, reseeding lawns, replacing shrubs, and repairing fences and walks.

4. Account 650-d—Other Supplies for Operation of the Plant.

F. *Major Account 660—Other Expenses for Operation of Plant.* Within this ever present category are recorded expenditures for express, drayage, and freight which cannot be charged to the specific activity for which the expenditure occurred. Also posted herein are expenditures for rental of equipment for plant operation, expenditures for in-service training of operating personnel other than salaries and supplies, and any other expenses incurred by district employees for the operation of the plant.

ACCOUNT SERIES 700—MAINTENANCE OF PLANT

Maintenance is necessary to keep the grounds, buildings, and equipment in their original condition either through repairs or by replacements. A departure over previous accounting practices is recommended through use of the piece-for-piece replacement concept which ignores the relative value of the replaced item of equipment and its replacement. Under other approaches if an item costing $100 was replaced by an item costing $300, $100 was charged to MAINTENANCE and the other $200 to CAPITAL OUTLAY. Under the piece-for-piece replacement point of view, the entire $300 expenditure to replace a $100 piece of equipment is charged to MAINTENANCE. This is true if the equipment purchased serves the same purposes as the equipment replaced. By way of further illustration, if a manual typewriter were replaced with an electric typewriter the entire cost of the electric typewriter would be posted in MAINTENANCE OF PLANT rather than a portion to MAINTENANCE and the additional value of the electric typewriter over the manual typewriter to CAPITAL OUTLAY. Trade-in allowance on old equipment turned in for new or the sale of replaced equipment at a later time is employed to reduce the MAINTENANCE account to which the replacement expenditure was recorded. This can be done by abating directly or after accumulating abatements under *Major Account 1920—Abatements.*

The expenditures for the initial or additional purchase of equipment are not recorded herein but under the 1200 SERIES—CAPITAL OUTLAY. Repairs to building structures which do not add to existing facilities are recorded herein, but if changes of partitions, roof structures, or walls are involved, the expenditures are reported under the 1200 SERIES—CAPITAL OUTLAY as remodeling rather than as maintenance. On the other hand, posted herein are the costs of repairs to the site and repairs and replacement of fixtures built into the grounds.

This group of accounts provides a place for posting all current expenses for maintenance of the plant for the school system except direct expenses for pupil transportation, food services, student body activities, and community services. Rent or fees for teacherages or student dormitories are handled through the Clearing Accounts, and only net expenditures for maintenance are recorded herein. Much the same can be said for investment properties. Insurance adjustments for lost or damaged property are accounted for in *Major Account 1930—Insurance Adjustments.*

The four major accounts in this series are organized on the basis of (1) salaries, (2) contracted services, (3) replacements, and (4) other expenses.

A. *Major Account 710—Salaries for Maintenance of School Plant.* Posted in this grouping are the salaries paid to carpenters, painters, plumbers, electricians, grounds keepers, and similar personnel participating in plant maintenance. If these personnel render other services as well, their salaries are prorated to other accounts in proportion to the time spent on each. Salaries of central office staff personnel responsible for system-wide administration of building operation and maintenance are recorded under Account 110-n—Salaries for Administration of Buildings and Grounds rather than herein. This major account can be divided into groups based on salaries for (1) upkeep of grounds, (2) building repair, (3) equipment repair, and (4) replacement manufacture.

1. Account 710-a—Salaries for the Upkeep of Grounds. Posted in this account are the wages to full- and part-time employees who work to maintain the grounds in their original condition. It includes personnel engaged in repairing and replacing walks, fences, tennis courts, playground surfaces, lawn-sprinkling systems, outside flagpoles, driveways, sewers, and irrigation ditches and personnel engaged in regrading sites, reseeding lawns and replacing shrubs. The initial expenditures for these items are recorded under CAPITAL OUTLAY rather than herein.

2. Account 710-b—Salaries for Repair of Buildings. Recorded under this account are the wages of full- and part-time personnel engaged in the repair and upkeep of buildings for all purposes other than those previously indicated. It would include such personnel as those involved in repainting woodwork; redecorating walls; resurfacing and refinishing floors; shingling; repainting ceilings; repairing foundations; repairing and replacing doors, windows, hardware, gutters, downspouts, window shades, curtains, drapes, and other equipment such as lockers, cabinets, wardrobes, Venetian blinds, swimming pool filtration equipment, soap and towel dispensers, bulletin boards, and door checks; moving portable structures; and repairing and replacing service systems such as boilers, radiators, ventilating ducts; checking and repairing electrical lighting systems, bells, clocks, intercommunication systems, sewers, toilets, fountains, water pipes, tanks, bathroom furnishings, fire plugs, fire hoses, fire sprinkler systems, fire escapes, and elevators.

3. Account 710-c—Salaries for the Repair of Equipment. Reported herein are the salaries of full-

and part-time personnel engaged in repairing equipment which is not built in. For the purposes of cost analysis this account can be subdivided as per the following examples:

  a. Subaccount 710-c-1—Repair of Instructional Equipment.

  b. Subaccount 710-c-2—Repair of Equipment Not Used for Instruction.

4. Account 710-d—Salaries for the Manufacture of Replacements of Equipment. Salaries of full- and part-time district employees who help to manufacture replacements for equipment not built in are recorded herein.

B. *Major Account 720—Contracted Services for Maintenance of Plant.*

1. Account 720-a—Contracted Services for the Upkeep of Grounds. Fees and other contract costs for the labor and other expenses of personnel performing repair and upkeep of grounds similar to those described in the Account 710-a are reported herein.

2. Account 720-b—Contracted Service for Repair of Buildings. Under this category are posted the expenditures for labor and other expenses for the repair of buildings by personnel whose services are contracted for on a special basis and are not ordinarily found on the payroll of the school district. Services rendered by these contracted employees are similar to those described under Account 710-b.

3. Account 720-c—Contracted Service for the Repair of Equipment.

C. *Major Account 730—Replacement of Equipment.*

1. Account 730-a—Replacement of Instructional Equipment. Here, again, the piece-for-piece replacement point of view holds. Recorded herein are the costs of instructional equipment replacements (which are not built in items) which are manufactured by individuals other than district employees. Instructional equipment is equipment purchased for use in the instructional program. Some examples of equipment used for instruction are pupils', teachers', and principals' desks, seats, chairs, tables, bookcases, workbenches, shop machinery and tools, musical instruments and stands, typewriters, business machines, phonographs, radios, motion-picture projectors, sewing machines, refrigerators, science laboratory apparatus, driver education vehicles, farm trucks and tractors, farm livestock, physical education apparatus, motor vehicles for the instructional staff, and other equipment used in the instructional program. It

does not include replacements for school library books which are recorded elsewhere (Account 230-a). The original cost of these items is charged to CAPITAL OUTLAY, but the replacement (regardless of the comparative value of the item being replaced with its replacement) is recorded herein.

2. Account 730-b—Replacement of Noninstructional Equipment. Posted in this account are outlays for piece-for-piece replacement of equipment other than built in items and items manufactured by other than district employees and used for other than instructional purposes.

D. *Major Account 740—Other Expenses for Maintenance of Plant.* Recorded in this major account are the cost of materials and other expenses except salaries for maintenance of plant performed by school district employees. It includes supplies for the operation of vehicles or other equipment used in the maintenance of plant.

1. Account 740-a—Other Expenses for Upkeep of Grounds. In this category are posted expenditures for materials, rentals of equipment, and other incidental expenses (except salaries) for the the repair and upkeep of grounds similar to the activities described in Account 710-a.

2. Account 740-b—Other Expenses for Repair of Buildings. Posted in this account are the monies spent for materials, rental of equipment, repair parts, and other incidental expenses (except salaries) for the repair of buildings by school district employees. The activities included in the repair of the buildings in this account are similar to those previously described under Account 710-b.

3. Account 740-c—Other Expenses for the Repair of Equipment.

4. Account 740-d—Other Expenses for the Manufacture or Replacement of Equipment.

ACCOUNT SERIES 800—FIXED CHARGES

Expenditures which are not readily allocable to other Expenditure Accounts but which are of a generally recurrent nature are posted in the FIXED CHARGES SERIES of accounts.

A. *Major Account 810—School District Contributions to Employee Retirement.*

1. Account 810-a—State, County, or Local Retirement Funds. Included in this heading are expenditures by the school district for retirement funds which have been established by the state or other governmental subdivisions. Such retirement funds are built up through contributions from participants and other sources for the purpose of making payments to those who retire from service in the educational system by reason of age, disability, or length of service. Only the district's contributions are reported herein, and the employee's salary deductions for these retirement funds are posted under the appropriate salary accounts.

2. Account 810-b—Social Security. This category is the appropriate place for posting expenditures of the school district and not the employee's salary deductions to social security.

3. Account 810-c—Pension Payments. Recorded in this account are monies paid by the district for pension payments made directly to individuals from appropriations or to a pension fund. A pension system differs from a retirement plan in that persons terminating service for whatever reasons receive funds to which these persons have not contributed anything.

B. *Major Account 820—Insurance and Judgments.* School districts on the cash basis of accounting record the total premium payment under this account, regardless of whether or not the premium applies beyond the current fiscal year. School systems on an accrual basis post only the part of the premium applicable to the current fiscal year in this account, and the remainder, if any, is posted under *Major Account 1530—Prepaid Insurance Premiums. Major Account 820* can be subdivided according to the type of insurance coverage.

1. Account 820-a—Property Insurance. Under this account are posted premiums paid for all forms of property insurance to cover loss of or damage to property of the district from fire, theft, storm, or other cause. The costs of appraising property for insurance purposes are also included herein.

2. Account 820-b—Employee's Insurance. Posted herein are expenditures for life insurance coverage of employees, workman's compensation, contributions to any state funds for insured employees, or any sickness or accident coverage of persons employed by the school district.

3. Account 820-c—Liability Insurance. In addition to premiums for this type of insurance coverage, the expenditures made in lieu of liability insurance (other than judgments) are posted herein.

4. Account 820-d—Fidelity Bond Premiums.

5. Account 820-e—Judgments Against the School District. Recorded in this account are payments from current funds for all judgments against the school district that are not covered by liability insurance but are of the type that might have

been covered by insurance. Court decisions must force payments for failure to pay bills or debt service or else the amounts are not posted here but under Account 820-c. Legal expenses for defending against judgments are recorded elsewhere.

C. *Major Account 830—Rental of Land and Buildings.* Rental costs for land and buildings for all purposes except direct expenses for pupil transportation, food services, student body activities, and community services are posted in the accounts that follow:

1. Account 830-a—Rent of Land and Buildings for Instructional Purposes. Posted herein are the monies spent for rent of nonpublicly owned school buildings, classroom space, school playground sites, athletic fields, school building sites, and school auditorium and gymnasium facilities. Installment payments to school housing authorities or similar agencies which ultimately result in the acquisition of property are not posted in this account.

2. Account 830-b—Rent for Land and Buildings for Noninstructional Purposes.

D. *Major Account 840—Interest on Current Loans.* Interest payments on borrowed monies paid back during the same fiscal year or on registered warrants are posted in this major division. Tax anticipation notes or warrants paid back from tax collections anticipated with the issuance of the note are treated as current loans. Other interest expenditures are charged to *Major Account 1320* and Accounts 1340-a and 1560-b.

E. *Major Account 850—Other Fixed Charges.* This broad classification covers outlays for special assessments against the school district for the maintenance and operation of nonschool property, any losses resulting from the sale of securities purchased prior to the current fiscal year, and any other expenses of a generally recurrent nature which are allocable to pupil costs and cannot be recorded under any other current expense account. Refunds of taxes, tuition, transportation charges, or other charges which a school district delivers for money received prior to the current fiscal year are also reported here. Refunds made on money received during the current fiscal year are abated against the appropriate Receipt Accounts, either directly or after accumulating in the *Major Account 1920— Abatements.* Not posted in this account are special assessments against the school district for capital improvements, such as curbs, streets, and drains. These are charged to CAPITAL OUTLAY.

ACCOUNT SERIES 900—FOOD SERVICES

Expenditures for activities which have as their purpose the preparation and serving of regular and incidental meals, lunches, or snacks in connection with school activities are posted in FOOD SERVICES. If these services are supported wholly or in part by revenue produced through the operation of the program, the gross expenditures and revenues are accounted for in Clearing Accounts, SERIES 1700—FOOD SERVICES OPERATION. Direct expenses for food services for community activities are reported in ACCOUNT SERIES 1100 —COMMUNITY SERVICES.

A. *Major Account 910—Salaries for Food Services.* Posted herein are salaries paid to part-time or full-time employees for which no reimbursement is to be received.

B. *Major Account 920—Other Expenses for Food Services.*

C. *Major Account 930—Expenditure to Cover Deficit of Separate Food Services Fund or Account.* Posted under this heading is the excess of gross food services costs over the actual reimbursement received from the sale of lunches and state and federal lunch grants. This net expenditure is recorded at the end of the year and transferred from Clearing Accounts, SERIES 1700—FOOD SERVICES OPERATION.

ACCOUNT SERIES 1000—STUDENT BODY ACTIVITIES

The direct and personal adult services rendered to public school pupils for such activities as interscholastic athletics, entertainments, publications, clubs, bands, orchestra, and other affairs managed or operated by the student body which are not a part of the regular instruction program are defined as student body activities. If the activity is financed solely or partly by revenue produced through the operation of the activity, the gross expenditures and gross receipts such as fees from admissions are accounted for in Clearing Accounts, *Major Account 1810—Student Body Activities.*

A. *Major Account 1010—Salaries for Student Body Activities.* Posted herein are the salaries of full- or part-time instructional staff members engaged in guiding student body activities.

B. *Major Account 1020—Other Expenses for Student Body Activities.*

C. *Major Account 1030—Expenditures to Cover Deficit of Student Body Activities or Accounts.* This category provides a place for posting the excess of student body activity expenditures over the actual reimbursement received from other sources. This net expenditure is recorded here at the end of the fiscal year and is transferred from *Major Account 1810—Student Body Activities.*

ACCOUNT SERIES 1100—COMMUNITY SERVICES

Community services are defined as those services provided by the school district for the community as a whole or for some segment of the community other than public school and adult education programs. Under this group of accounts are reported all district monies spent for current expense items for community affairs, except school district contributions to retirement funds and insurance. It would include (1) the prorated salary of full- or part-time regular day school employees, such as the janitor, who work at night cleaning up a school building and may be relieved of such duties for a few hours on different evenings to open up and look after facilities being used by some community activity; (2) the extra salary paid to regular day school employees who perform work for community services in addition to regular school district work; (3) salaries of persons employed specifically for some community activity such as a full-time or part-time playground director. The following series of accounts are useful only in school districts which provide some community services as defined herein.

A. *Major Account 1110—Recreation.* Posted herein are the direct cost for all recreational activities not considered a part of the regular instructional program or student body activities.
   1. Account 1110-a—Salaries for Community Recreation Activities. This includes the salaries only to full- or part-time playground directors, supervisors, assistants, custodians, maintenance staff, and others engaged directly in community recreation programs.
   2. Account 1110-b—Other Expenses for Community Recreational Activities. Posted here are the costs for athletic and other supplies; travel expenses; rent, telephone, heat, electricity, and other operational plant expenses; maintenance of plant expenses, payment to other agencies on the cost-sharing basis; and other direct expenses (except salaries) resulting from community recreational activities.

B. *Major Account 1120—Civic Activities.* Under this account are recorded direct expenses for meetings of lay citizen groups, parent-teacher associations, public forums and elections, civil defense planning, and other civic center activities.
   1. Account 1120-a—Salaries for Civic Activities.
   2. Account 1120-b—Other Expenses for Civic Activities.

C. *Major Account 1130—Public Libraries.* This account is used primarily in those communities where the local public library is operated by the school district. In some communities the school library is open to the public after school hours. This raises the question as to the extent to which the money spent for the school library should be prorated between the school library accounts and this group of accounts. The recommended solution is to post under this account the direct additional cost for providing library services to the community as a whole.
   1. Account 1130-a—Salaries for Public Libraries.
   2. Account 1130-b—Periodicals and Newspapers for Public Libraries.
   3. Account 1130-c—Other Expenses for Public Libraries.

D. *Major Account 1140—Custodial and Detention Care of Children.* Under this series of accounts are posted the direct expenses for the custodial and detention care of children in residential or day school and child care centers.
   1. Account 1140-a—Salaries for Custodial and Detention Care of Children.
   2. Account 1140-b—Other Expenses for Custodial and Detention Care of Children.

E. *Major Account 1150—Welfare Activities.* Within this account are reported direct expenses for the provision of aid to indigent children (for either public or nonpublic students) and adults.
   1. Account 1150-a—Salaries for Welfare Activities.
   2. Account 1150-b—Other Expenses for Welfare Activities.

F. *Major Account 1160—Nonpublic School Pupils.* In certain states public school funds can be spent for certain activities of pupils in nonpublic schools. This account classification is needed for such cases. It can be subdivided as follows:
   1. Account 1160-a—Instructional Services for Nonpublic School Pupils. This in turn can be subdivided into:
      a. Subaccount 1160-a-1—Textbooks for Nonpublic School Pupils.
      b. Subaccount 1160-a-2—Other Expenses for Instructional Services to Nonpublic School Pupils.
   2. Account 1160-b—Attendance and Health Services for Nonpublic School Pupils. This in turn can be subdivided into:
      a. Subaccount 1160-b-1—Attendance Services for Nonpublic School Pupils.
      b. Subaccount 1160-b-2—Health Services for Nonpublic School Pupils.
   3. Account 1160-c—Transportation Services for

Nonpublic School Pupils. Posted in this account are payments for salaries, supplies, and other direct expenses for providing transportation for nonpublic school pupils, including expenditures for transporting nonpublic school pupils by contract with private carriers or by public carriers and payments in lieu of transportation, such as room and board near the school.

ACCOUNT SERIES 1200—CAPITAL OUTLAY

Expenditures which result in the acquisition of fixed assets or additions to fixed assets are posted in this series of accounts. It includes money spent for land for existing buildings, improvement of grounds, construction of buildings, additions to buildings, remodeling of buildings, or initial or additional equipment. The cost of preliminary studies for additions or for a bond election are considered a part of bond elections and are recorded under Administration Account 110-d or 130-d. Repairs to building structures that do not add to existing facilities are charged to MAINTENANCE rather than to CAPITAL OUTLAY. The general rule is that if the repairs to building structures create changes of partitions, roof structures, or walls, they are reported under CAPITAL OUTLAY and not MAINTENANCE. The cost of initial installations or extension of service systems and other built-in equipment in existing buildings is charged to CAPITAL OUTLAY. The repairs and replacement of service systems and other built-in equipment on a piece-for-piece basis are charged to the 700 SERIES—MAINTENANCE OF PLANT. Money to replace a building which has been totally destroyed is charged to CAPITAL OUTLAY. The cost for repair and replacement of lost or damaged school property is posted under MAINTENANCE except that any additions to the plant are recorded in CAPITAL OUTLAY. If insurance adjustments are received, for lost or damaged property, the receipts and expenditures for the repair or replacement of properties are handled through *Major Account 1930—Insurance Adjustments*. Minor collections for loss or damage to school property are abated against the expenditure occasioned by such loss or damage, either directly or after accumulating under *Major Account 1920—Abatements*.

Only the cost of initial or additional equipment is posted in CAPITAL OUTLAY. Expenditures for repair and piece-for-piece replacements are charged to MAINTENANCE.

CAPITAL OUTLAY expenditures may be met by proceeds from current revenues or from the sale of bonds. It may also include installment or lease payments on property, except interest, that have a terminal date and result in the acquisition of property. Although payments to public school housing authorities or similar agencies have certain characteristics of capital outlay, they are not recorded under CAPITAL OUTLAY accounts. Such payments are recorded in the *Major Account 1340—Expenditures to School Housing Authorities or Similar Agencies*. This is done to minimize the danger of duplication and to consolidate the capital outlay figures for states in which public school housing authorities or similar agencies exist.

Separate building funds and capital reserve funds are often established to accumulate monies for future construction or to handle payments for construction in progress. This series of accounts can be used in such funds as well as in the general fund. As indicated previously, the Expenditure Accounts listed in this chapter can be used with any fund rather than with just current expense funds. Money transfers between the general fund and these separate building and capital reserve funds are reported in *Major Account 1940—Interfund Transfers* and not herein.

A. *Major Account 1210—Sites.*
1. Account 1210-a—Professional Services for Sites. The money spent for drawing, specifications, and other fees directly related to the acquisition and improvement of sites, such as landscape architect fees, appraisal fees, search and title insurance, site service, and condemnation proceedings are reported here.
2. Account 1210-b—Site and Site Addition. This includes expenditures for purchase of land excluding expenditures for professional services.
3. Account 1210-c—Improvements to Sites. In this category are posted the costs of improvement of new and old sites and adjacent ways such as grading, landscaping, seeding, and planting of shrubs and trees; constructing new sidewalks, roadways, retaining wall, sewers, and storm drains; installing hydrants; original surfacing and soil treatment of athletic fields and tennis courts; furnishing and installing for the first time fixed playground apparatus, flagpoles, gateways, fences and underground storage tanks which are not parts of building services system; and demolition work. This would include special assessments against the school district for capital improvements such as streets, curbs, and drains.

B. *Major Account 1220—Buildings.* Posted in this group of accounts are the construction costs for buildings and additions. It would consist of all disbursements for general construction and advertisements for contracts, payment on contracts for construction, insulation, plumbing, heating, lighting, ventilating, and electrical systems; built-in lockers, elevators, and other equipment built into the buildings; architectural and engineering services; legal services and travel expenses incurred in connection with the construction; paint and other interior and exterior decorating; and any other cost connected with the planning and construction of buildings and additions to buildings.

1. Account 1220-a—Professional Services for Buildings. This includes money spent for drawings, specifications, and other fees directly related to construction, acquisition, and remodeling a building such as engineering and legal fees and advertisement of contracts. There can be further subdivision of this account to include the cost for each of the buildings under consideration in the district.

2. Account 1220-b—New Buildings and Building Additions. Posted herein are the outlays for the contract for and purchase of buildings being constructed under school board order or agreement and expenditures for outright purchase of buildings, except payments to public school housing authorities or similar agencies. This account can also be broken down into the subaccounts desired to list the various buildings or warehouses.

3. Account 1220-c—Remodeling. Under this heading are posted the expenditures for major permanent structural alterations and initial or additional installation of heating and ventilating systems, electrical systems, plumbing systems, fire protection systems, and other service systems in existing buildings. By definition, remodeling or improvement of buildings refers to changes taking place within the existing floor area, whereas a building addition adds to the floor area.

C. *Major Account 1230—Equipment.* Under this major account are reported monies spent for the initial or additional items of equipment such as furniture, furnishings, machinery, and vehicles that are not an integral part of the building or building services.

1. Account 1230-a—Professional Services for Equipment.

2. Account 1230-b—Equipment for Administration. Posted here are expenditures for initial or additional furniture and equipment for the central administrative office whether housed in school buildings, separate administration buildings, or otherwise. Illustrations of the kinds of equipment to be recorded herein are desks, chairs, bookcases, dictating machines, typewriters, business machines, motor vehicles, and file cabinets.

3. Account 1230-c—Equipment for Instruction. Reported in this account are expenditures for instructional equipment not built in such as pupils', teachers', and principals' desks and seats, chairs, tables, bookcases, workbenches, shop machinery, tools, musical instruments and stands, typewriters, business machines, phonographs, radios, motion-picture projectors, sewing machines, refrigerators, science laboratory apparatus, driver education vehicles, farm trucks and tractors. Also posted in this account are expenditures for new library books for new school libraries and material accessions involving the expansion of the school library.

4. Account 1230-d—Equipment for Attendance and Health Services.

5. Account 1230-e—Equipment for Pupil Transportation.

6. Account 1230-f—Equipment for the Operation of Plant. This includes equipment for central warehouses or storerooms.

7. Account 1230-g—Equipment for the Maintenance of the Plant.

8. Account 1230-h—Equipment for Food Services and Student Body Activities.

9. Acount 1230-i—Equipment for Community Services.

10. Account 1230-j—Equipment for Investment Property.

ACCOUNT SERIES 1300—DEBT SERVICE FROM CURRENT FUNDS

DEBT SERVICE consists of expenditures for the retirement of debt other than current loans. It includes money paid to meet the interest on debt as well as to meet payments on the principal of the debt. Excluded are current loans which are defined as money borrowed and paid back during the same fiscal year. Such loans are accounted for elsewhere. Only debt service paid for out of current funds (not special levies for special funds) are posted in this group of accounts. Current funds are comprised of income collected during the current year from various revenue receipts, and these receipts can be used to pay obligations currently due with any remainder available for reappropriation for other purposes during the current fiscal year. Payment from current funds into a sinking fund is considered a part of DEBT SERVICE in this group of accounts. A fund devoted to the purpose of meeting debt principal payments at some future time is called a sinking fund.

A. *Major Account 1310—Principal of the Debt.*

1. Account 1310-a—Expenditure from Current Funds to Retire Serial Bonds.

2. Account 1310-b—Expenditure from Current Funds to Retire Short-Term Loans. Money expended to meet the principal payments of loans which extend for a period of no more than five years or no less than one year is money used to amortize a short-term loan.
3. Account 1310-c—Expenditures from Current Funds to Retire Long-Term Loans. A long-term loan is one which is amortized during a period of more than five years.
4. Account 1310-d—Warrants or Bills Payable of Preceding Fiscal Year.

B. *Major Account 1320—Interest on the Debt.*
1. Account 1320-a—Expenditures from Current Funds for Interest on Bonds.
2. Account 1320-b—Expenditures from Current Funds for Interest on Short-Term Loans.
3. Account 1320-c—Expenditures from Current Funds for Interest on Long-Term Loans.

C. *Major Account 1330—Amounts Paid into Sinking Funds.* Expenditures from the sinking fund to retire bonds at a future date are made from Clearing Accounts, *Major Account 1560—Sinking Fund Account.*

D. *Major Account 1340—Expenditures to Public School Housing Authority or Similar Agency.* A public school housing authority is a public corporation or a quasi-public corporation which has the power to perform one or more of the following functions: (1) issue authority bonds for public school purposes, (2) acquire and hold property for public schools, (3) construct public school buildings, (4) lease public school buildings to local public school administrative units or transfer titles to such units. Posted herein are all monies paid to such authorities or agencies with similar functions.
1. Account 1340-a—Expenditures for Principal to Public School Housing Authorities or Similar Agency.
2. Account 1340-b—Expenditures for Interest to Public School Housing Authorities or Similar Agency.

E. *Major Account 1350—Other Debt Service from Current Funds.*

ACCOUNT SERIES 1400—OUTGOING TRANSFER FUNDS

Posted within this series of accounts are monies paid to other school districts or administrative units. These expenditures are made for several reasons among which are: (1) the expenditures cut across several accounts and are not readily chargeable to any one classification; therefore, one payment is made in lieu of many different expense items; (2) membership or attendance data needed to relate the expenditures to some classification are lacking in the paying district; and (3) from the standpoint of the nation or the state, such expenditures are actually a transfer of funds between school districts, and in order to avoid duplication and consolidate data for the state or the nation, it is necessary that the paying school district be able to identify such expenditures.

A. *Major Account 1410—Expenditures to Other School Districts or Administrative Units in the State.*
1. Account 1410-a—Tuition. Posted herein are monies sent to other school districts or administrative units in the state for services rendered to pupils residing in the paying district.
2. Account 1410-b—Transportation. This category is for posting expenditures to other school districts or administrative units in the state for transportation of pupils from the paying district to schools in the transporting district or to schools in the paying district.
3. Account 1410-c—Miscellaneous. This account includes the expenditures in the state to another school district for any other services rendered to pupils residing in the paying district, except expenditures for transportation and tuition. This might include health services or the use of recreational facilities.

B. *Major Account 1420—Expenditures to School District or Administrative Units in Another State.* The same comments made under *Major Account 1410* would apply here with the exception that the money is sent to a school district in another state.
1. Account 1420-a—Tuition.
2. Account 1420-b—Transportation.
3. Account 1420-c—Miscellaneous.

C. *Major Account 1430—Tuition to Other Than Public Schools.*
1. Account 1430-a—Tuition to Private Nonsectarian Schools.
2. Account 1430-b—Tuition to Individuals.

SUMMARY OR OUTLINE OF EXPENDITURE ACCOUNTS

The summary is presented with a recommendation for special coding for expenditures by program area. This system of coding is explained as follows: "U" stands for undistributed and indicates that only a total is given. There is no breakdown according to program area. "E" stands for elementary day schools; "S" for secondary day schools; "SS" for summer schools; "CC" for community colleges; and "AE" for adult education. The outline includes a check showing which of the various Expenditure Accounts might well be further coded to show program area distribution.

A rather handy guide for recording any expenditures in Expenditure Accounts identified in this chapter can be found in the 1957 USOE financial accounting handbook.[9]

OUTLINE OF EXPENDITURE ACCOUNTS[10]

Expenditure Accounts	Program Area Distribution					
	U	E	S	SS	CC	AE
ACCOUNT SERIES 100—ADMINISTRATION						
Major Account 110—Salaries	X					
Account 110-a—Board of Education	X					
Account 110-b—Board Secretary's Office	X					
Account 110-c—Treasurer's Office	X					
Account 110-d—School Elections	X					
Account 110-e—Tax Collection	X					
Account 110-f—Legal Services	X					
Account 110-g—Superintendent's Office	X					
Account 110-h—Personnel Office	X					
Account 110-i—Public Relations	X					
Account 110-j—Centralized Research	X					
Account 110-k—Census Enumeration	X					
Account 110-l—Office of Business Administration	X					
Account 110-m—Fiscal Control	X					
Account 110-n—Administration of Buildings and Grounds	X					
Account 110-o—Purchasing Office	X					
Account 110-p—Printing and Publishing	X					
Account 110-q—Other Salaries for Administration	X					
Major Account 120—Contracted Services	X					
Major Account 130—Other Expenses	X					
Account 130-a—Board of Education	X					
Account 130-b—Board Secretary's Office	X					
Account 130-c—Treasurer's Office	X					
Account 130-d—School Elections	X					
Account 130-e—Tax Collection	X					
Account 130-f—Legal Services	X					
Account 130-g—Superintendent's Office	X					
Account 130-h—Personnel Office	X					
Account 130-i—Public Relations	X					
Account 130-j—Centralized Research	X					
Account 130-k—Census Enumeration	X					
Account 130-l—Office of Business Administration	X					
Account 130-m—Fiscal Control	X					
Account 130-n—Administration of Buildings and Grounds	X					
Account 130-o—Purchasing Office	X					
Account 130-p—Printing and Publishing	X					
Account 130-q—Miscellaneous Expenses for Administration	X					
ACCOUNT SERIES 200—INSTRUCTION						
Major Account 210—Salaries		X	X	X	X	X
Account 211—Principals		X	X	X	X	X
Account 212—Consultants or Supervisors		X	X	X	X	X

[9] *Ibid.*, pp. 150–187.
[10] *Ibid.*, pp. 27–35.

Expenditure Accounts	Program Area Distribution					
	U	E	S	SS	CC	AE
Account 213—Teachers		X	X	X	X	X
Account 214—Other Instructional Staff		X	X	X	X	X
Subaccount 214-a—School Librarians		X	X	X	X	X
Subaccount 214-b—Audio-Visual Personnel		X	X	X	X	X
Subaccount 214-c—Guidance Personnel		X	X	X	X	X
Subaccount 214-d—Psychological Personnel		X	X	X	X	X
Subaccount 214-e—Television Instructional Personnel		X	X	X	X	X
Account 215—Secretarial and Clerical Assistants		X	X	X	X	X
Subaccount 215-a—Principal's Office		X	X	X	X	X
Subaccount 215-b—Consultants or Supervisors		X	X	X	X	X
Subaccount 215-c—Teachers		X	X	X	X	X
Subaccount 215-d—Other Instructional Staff		X	X	X	X	X
Account 216—Other Salaries for Instruction		X	X	X	X	X
Major Account 220—Textbooks		X	X	X	X	X
Major Account 230—School Libraries and Audio-Visual Materials		X	X	X	X	X
Account 230-a—School Library Books		X	X	X	X	X
Account 230-b—Periodicals and Newspapers		X	X	X	X	X
Account 230-c—Audio-Visual Materials		X	X	X	X	X
Account 230-d—Other School Library Expenses		X	X	X	X	X
Major Account 240—Teaching Supplies		X	X	X	X	X
Major Account 250—Other Expenses		X	X	X	X	X
Account 250-a—Supplies		X	X	X	X	X
Account 250-b—Travel		X	X	X	X	X
Account 250-c—Miscellaneous Expenses		X	X	X	X	X
ACCOUNT SERIES 300—ATTENDANCE SERVICES						
Major Account 310—Salaries	X					
Account 310-a—Attendance Personnel	X					
Account 310-b—Secretarial and Clerical Personnel	X					
Account 310-c—Other Salaries	X					
Major Account 320—Other Expenses	X					
Account 320-a—Supplies	X					
Account 320-b—Travel	X					
Account 320-c—Miscellaneous Expenses	X					
ACCOUNT SERIES 400—HEALTH SERVICES						
Major Account 410—Salaries	X					
Account 410-a—Professional and Technical Health Personnel	X					
Subaccount 410-a-1—School Physicians, including Psychiatrists	X					
Subaccount 410-a-2—School Dentists	X					
Subaccount 410-a-3—School Nurses	X					

Expenditure Accounts	U	E	S	SS	CC	AE
			Program Area Distribution			

Subaccount 410-a-4—School Dental Hygienists | X

Subaccount 410-a-5—Other Professional and Technical Health Personnel | X

Account 410-b—Nonprofessional and Nontechnical Personnel | X

Major Account 420—Other Expenses | X

Account 420-a—Supplies | X
Account 420-b—Travel | X
Account 420-c—Miscellaneous Expenses | X

ACCOUNT SERIES 500—PUPIL TRANSPORTATION SERVICES

Major Account 510—Salaries | X

Account 510-a—Supervisors | X
Account 510-b—Drivers | X
Account 510-c—Mechanics and Other Garage Employees | X
Account 510-d—Clerks and Other Employees | X

Major Account 520—Contracted Services and Public Carriers | X

Major Account 530—Replacements of Vehicles | X

Account 530-a—Cash Purchase | X
Account 530-b—Lease Purchase and Installment Purchase | X

Major Account 540—Pupil Transportation Insurance | X

Major Account 550—Expenditures in Lieu of Transportation | X

Major Account 560—Other Expenses for Operation and Maintenance | X

Account 560-a—Gasoline | X
Account 560-b—Lubricants | X
Account 560-c—Tires and Tubes | X
Account 560-d—Repair Parts | X
Account 560-e—Supplies and Expenses for Garage Operation | X
Account 560-f—Garage and Garage Equipment Repairs | X
Account 560-g—Maintenance of Vehicles by Private Garages | X
Account 560-h—Rent | X
Account 560-i—Miscellaneous Expenses | X

ACCOUNT SERIES 600—OPERATION OF PLANT

Major Account 610—Salaries | X

Account 610-a—Plant Engineers | X
Account 610-b—Custodial Services | X
Account 610-c—Care of Grounds | X
Account 610-d—Other Salaries for Operation of Plant | X

Major Account 620—Contracted Services | X

Major Account 630—Heat for Buildings | X

Expenditure Accounts	Program Area Distribution					
	U	E	S	SS	CC	AE
Major Account 640—Utilities, Except Heat for Buildings	X					
Account 640-a—Water and Sewerage	X					
Account 640-b—Electricity	X					
Account 640-c—Gas	X					
Account 640-d—Telephone and Telephone	X					
Account 640-e—Other Utilities	X					
Major Account 650—Supplies, Except Utilities	X					
Account 650-a—Custodial Supplies	X					
Account 650-b—Supplies for Operation of Vehicles	X					
Account 650-c—Supplies for Care of Grounds	X					
Account 650-d—Other Supplies for Operation of Plant	X					
Major Account 660—Other Expenses	X					
ACCOUNT SERIES 700—MAINTENANCE OF PLANT						
Major Account 710—Salaries	X					
Account 710-a—Grounds	X					
Account 710-b—Buildings	X					
Account 710-c—Repair of Equipment	X					
Account 710-d—Manufacture of Replacement of Equipment	X					
Major Account 720—Contracted Services	X					
Account 720-a—Grounds	X					
Account 720-b—Buildings	X					
Account 720-c—Repair of Equipment	X					
Major Account 730—Replacement of Equipment	X					
Account 730-a—Instructional Equipment	X					
Account 730-b—Noninstructional Equipment	X					
Major Account 740—Other Expenses	X					
Account 740-a—Grounds	X					
Account 740-b—Buildings	X					
Account 740-c—Repair of Equipment	X					
Account 740-d—Manufacture of Replacement of Equipment	X					
ACCOUNT SERIES 800—FIXED CHARGES						
Major Account 810—School District Contributions to Employee Retirement	X					
Account 810-a—State, County, or Local Retirement Funds	X					
Account 810-b—Social Security	X					
Account 810-c—Pension Payments	X					
Major Account 820—Insurance and Judgments	X					
Account 820-a—Property Insurance	X					
Account 820-b—Employee Insurance	X					
Account 820-c—Liability Insurance	X					
Account 820-d—Fidelity Bond Premiums	X					
Account 820-e—Judgments	X					

Expenditure Accounts	Program Area Distribution					
	U	E	S	SS	CC	AE
Major Account 830—Rental of Land and Buildings	X					
Account 830-a—Land and Buildings for Instructional Purposes	X					
Account 830-b—Land and Buildings for Noninstructional Purposes	X					
Major Account 840—Interest of Current Loans	X					
Major Account 850—Other Fixed Charges	X					
ACCOUNT SERIES 900—FOOD SERVICES						
Major Account 910—Salaries	X					
Major Account 920—Other Expenses	X					
Major Account 930—Expenditures to Cover Deficit of a Separate Food Services Fund or Account	X					
ACCOUNT SERIES 1000—STUDENT BODY ACTIVITIES						
Major Account 1010—Salaries	X					
Major Account 1020—Other Expenses	X					
Major Account 1030—Expenditures to Cover Deficits of Student Body Activities Funds or Accounts	X					
ACCOUNT SERIES 1100—COMMUNITY SERVICES						
Major Account 1110—Recreation	X					
Account 1110-a—Salaries	X					
Account 1110-b—Other Expenses	X					
Major Account 1120—Civic Activities	X					
Account 1120-a—Salaries	X					
Account 1120-b—Other Expenses	X					
Major Account 1130—Public Libraries	X					
Account 1130-a—Salaries	X					
Account 1130-b—Books, Periodicals, and Newspapers	X					
Account 1130-c—Other Expenses	X					
Major Account 1140—Custodial and Detention Care of Children	X					
Account 1140-a—Salaries	X					
Account 1140-b—Other Expenses	X					
Major Account 1150—Welfare Activities	X					
Account 1150-a—Salaries	X					
Account 1150-b—Other Expenses	X					
Major Account 1160—Nonpublic School Pupils	X					
Account 1160-a—Instructional Services	X					
Subaccount 1160-a-1—Textbooks	X					
Subaccount 1160-a-2—Other Expenses	X					

| | Program Area Distribution | | | | | |
Expenditure Accounts	U	E	S	SS	CC	AE
Account 1160-b—Attendance and Health Services	X					
Subaccount 1160-b-1—Attendance	X					
Subaccount 1160-b-2—Health	X					
Account 1160-c—Transportation Services	X					
ACCOUNT SERIES 1200—CAPITAL OUTLAY						
Major Account 1210—Sites	X					
Account 1210-a—Professional Services	X					
Account 1210-b—Sites and Site Additions	X					
Account 1210-c—Improvements to Sites						
Major Account 1220—Buildings	X					
Account 1220-a—Professional Service	X					
Account 1220-b—New Buildings and Building Additions	X					
Account 1220-c—Remodeling	X					
Major Account 1230—Equipment	X					
Account 1230-a—Professional Services	X					
Account 1230-b—Administration	X					
Account 1230-c—Instruction	X					
Account 1230-d—Attendance and Health	X					
Account 1230-e—Pupil Transportation	X					
Account 1230-f—Operation of Plant	X					
Account 1230-g—Maintenance of Plant	X					
Account 1230-h—Food Services and Student Body Activities	X					
Account 1230-i—Community Services	X					
Account 1230-j—Investment Property	X					
ACCOUNT SERIES 1300—DEBT SERVICE FROM CURRENT FUNDS						
Major Account 1310—Principal of Debt	X					
Account 1310-a—Bonds	X					
Account 1310-b—Short-Term Loans	X					
Account 1310-c—Long-Term Loans	X					
Account 1310-d—Warrants or Bills of Preceding Years	X					
Major Account 1320—Interest on Debt	X					
Account 1320-a—Bonds	X					
Account 1320-b—Short-Term Loans	X					
Account 1320-c—Long-Term Loans	X					
Major Account 1330—Amounts Paid into Sinking Funds	X					
Major Account 1340—Expenditures to School Housing Authority or Similar Agency	X					
Account 1340-a—Principal	X					
Account 1340-b—Interest	X					
Major Account 1350—Other Debt Service	X					
ACCOUNT SERIES 1400—OUTGOING TRANSFER ACCOUNTS						

43631

	Program Area Distribution					
Expenditure Accounts	U	E	S	SS	CC	AE
Major Account 1410—Expenditures to Other School Districts or Administrative Units in the State	X					
Account 1410-a—Tuition	X					
Account 1410-b—Transportation	X					
Account 1410-c—Miscellaneous	X					
Major Account 1420—Expenditures to School Districts or Other Administrative Units in Another State	X					
Account 1420-a—Tuition	X					
Account 1420-b—Transportation	X					
Account 1420-c—Miscellaneous	X					
Major Account 1430—Tuition to Other Than Public Schools	X					
Account 1430-a—Private Nonsectarian Schools	X					
Account 1430-b—Individuals	X					

OPERATING PROCEDURES IN FINANCIAL ACCOUNTING

The incurring of liabilities through purchasing and the subsequent meeting of liabilities by releasing to the vendor the authorized voucher check was described in the first part of this chapter. The authorized voucher check was entered into the special type of journal known as the Voucher Register and the expenditure was then posted to the proper Expenditure Accounts (or subaccounts) in a given functional-character grouping of accounts. This would be an oversimplification of accounting procedures if the control aspect of financial accounting is ignored. There is more to school accounting than listing the uniform Receipt Accounts, Expenditure Accounts, and Clearing Accounts. The control through maintenance of a General Ledger and/or Encumbrance Accounts must be explored along with an analysis of operating procedures.

Public school financial transactions should be anticipated in the budget. As stated previously, the budget is the heart of school financial operations. When formally adopted (and spread over the minutes of the board) and supported by the necessary revenue and appropriation acts, it becomes a controlling instrument over all financial transactions and operations. The General Ledger (or Budgetary Accounts) can be used to control expenditures and school monies during the fiscal year so that they reflect the fiscal plan of operation adopted by the board of education.

Encumbrance accounting or the proper encumbering of appropriations when a liability is incurred is a necessary aspect of financial control. Through the practice of encumbering appropriations as liabilities are incurred, an accurate and up-to-date picture of the financial condition of the district can be ascertained without too much difficulty.

THE GENERAL LEDGER—AN ILLUSTRATION

In Chapter 3 it was stated that every account in the school accounting system should be controlled by the General Ledger and every financial transaction should be recorded in summary or in detail therein. The General Ledger can be used as an opening device, a running summary, a controlling instrument, and a closing device. As an opening device and a "book of control," the estimated receipts and appropriations for expenditures must be transferred from the budget to the General Ledger. This is done with the Voucher Journal which is a verifying or authorizing memorandum. Table 6 is an illustration of a portion of the General Ledger to indicate the total anticipated in the Receipt Accounts, the total in the Expenditure Accounts, and only 2 of the 14 Expenditure Accounts, namely, the ADMINISTRATION and the INSTRUCTION accounts. The other account series were omitted to keep the illustration of the operation of the General Ledger as simple as possible.

It can be seen from Table 6 that the budget estimates of receipts for all Receipt Accounts is $3,562,000 of which $356,200 was the cash balance on hand in the

TABLE 6. General Ledger for the Community School District of Smithville, U.S.A.

Steps	Date	Receipts		Expenditures					
				Total for All Expenditure Accounts		100 Series Administration		200 Series Instruction	
		(1) Debit	(2) Credit	(3) Debit	(4) Credit	(5) Debit	(6) Credit	(7) Debit	(8) Credit
	7/1/57	Budget Estimate of Receipts and Budget Appropriations for Expenditure							
		$3,562,000		$3,255,900		$97,677		$2,278,830	
	7/1/57	Cash Balance on 7/1/57							
			$356,200						
1	7/1/57	Money to Be Received and Money to Be Spent During the Year							
		3,255,900		3,255,900		97,677		2,278,830	
2		Money Received and Spent During the First Month							
			162,445		$130,236		$7,814		$22,788
3		Money to Be Received and Spent During Remainder of the Year							
		3,093,455		3,125,664		89,863		2,256,040	
4		Money Received and Spent During Second Month							
			185,876		61,583		7,756		31,874
5		Money to Be Received and Spent During Remainder of Year							
		2,907,579		2,964,081		82,107		2,124,166	
24		Money Received and Spent During Twelfth Month							
			524,876		486,102		7,702		125,732
25		Total Money Received During Year and Total Expenditures Made During Year							
		$3,287,576		$3,255,782		$99,523		$2,253,962	
26		Balance of Receipts Against Expenditures							
		$31,676							
27		Balance of Receipts Received Against Receipts Estimated and Balance of Expenditure Appropriations Against Expenditures Actually Made							
		$31,694	$118	$118		$1,846 Excess		$24,868	

district and carried forward on July 1, 1957. Since it is a desirable policy to operate the budget with approximately the same cash balance at the end of the fiscal year as at the beginning, the cash balance is recorded as a credit in the General Ledger. The estimated receipts other than cash balance at the beginning of the fiscal year are posted in the debit column of Total Receipts.

Budget appropriations for expenditures are posted in the debit column of "Total for All Expenditure Accounts." This is the sum of $3,255,900. This sum for expenditures is divided among the 14 account series. Only the total expenditures for ADMINISTRATION, a sum of $97,677, and for INSTRUCTION, a sum of $2,278,-830 are shown in the illustration. The appropriations for each of the 14 Expenditure Accounts are then transferred from the General Ledger to each of the 14 distribution ledgers.

The total amount estimated to be received during the entire fiscal year in all Receipt Accounts is entered as a debit at step 1 in column 1 of Receipts. The total estimated to be spent during the fiscal year is posted as a debit at step 1 in column 3 of Total Expenditures. The amount in Total Expenditures columns is divided among the 14 Expenditure Accounts. Only two are shown in Table 6 and $97,677 is debited in column 5 under ADMINISTRATION and $2,278,830 is debited in column 7 under INSTRUCTION. In other words, in step 1 of the General Ledger is posted the "Money to Be Received and Spent During the Fiscal Year" which starts on July 1, 1957, for the system used in the illustration.

The "Money Received and Spent During the First Month" is recorded in step 2 of the General Ledger. The information posted in the credit columns for Receipts, Total Expenditures, ADMINISTRATION and INSTRUCTION is gathered from the Receipt Accounts as well as the individual 14 Expenditure Accounts at the end of the fiscal month. In other words, the amounts posted in step 2 of the General Ledger (and all even numbered steps thereafter until the end of the fiscal year) represent a summary of financial transactions for the month. The totals received and spent during the month are recorded in the various distribution ledgers for receipts and accounts and then transferred to the appropriate columns of the General Ledger. In Table 6 $162,445 was received and $130,236 was spent during the month. Of the total for expenditures, $7814 was expended during the month for ADMINISTRATION and $22,788 for INSTRUCTION.

The third step is labeled "Money to Be Received and Spent During the Remainder of the Year." The totals in the debit columns are obtained by subtracting the credits posted in step 2 from the opening debit in step 1. In Table 6, it should be noted that, after what was collected during the first month, $3,093,455 is to be received during the rest of the year. Money to be spent during the remainder of the year equals $3,125,664, and $89,863 of this is allocated to ADMINISTRATION and $2,256,040 to INSTRUCTION. As a running summary, the General Ledger presents a picture of what was received or spent during each month and what remains to be received and spent during the fiscal year. It is a controlling device in the sense that an up-to-date record of what is available for expenditures can forewarn when expenditures are likely to exceed appropriations.

The money received during the second month is (as shown in step 4) exceeded by expenditures. What remains to be collected and expended after the second month is shown in step 5 of Table 6.

The steps 6 through 23 are omitted because they would be repetitious for purposes of illustrations.

Steps 24, 25, 26, and 27 of the General Ledger are shown in the illustration. Money received during the 12 month in the sum of $524,876 was credited in column 2. The total spent during the 12 month in the sum of $486,102 was credited in column 4. In column 6 $7702 was credited to ADMINISTRATION and $125,732 was credited to column 8, INSTRUCTION.

The total received during the fiscal year was $3,287,-576. This is a summation of the postings in the credit column at step 25. Likewise, the total expenditures during the fiscal year of $3,255,782 are the summation (step 25) of postings in credit column 4. The total spent for ADMINISTRATION during the fiscal year was $99,523 and for INSTRUCTION $2,253,962.

The balance of receipts against expenditures for the year was $31,676 as indicated in step 26. In other words, more was received than spent. Step 27 of the General Ledger is a comparison between the receipts received and those estimated and also between budgetary appropriations for expenditures and actual expenditures during the fiscal year. It can be seen that $31,794 more was received than estimated on July 1, 1957. The total expenditures were $118 less than estimated at the beginning of the fiscal year. It should be noted that there were expenditures for ADMINISTRATION which exceeded appropriations during the fiscal year in the amount of $1846. On the other hand, $24,868 less was spent than estimated for INSTRUCTION.

ENCUMBRANCE ACCOUNTING

Encumbrance accounting is of value whether the accrual or cash system of accounting is used. The distinction between expenditures and encumbrances was first reported in Chapter 3. Encumbering an appropriation is not the same as recording an expenditure from an appropriation. An encumbrance merely insures that the amount of money encumbered cannot be used for anything else until the expenditure has been determined or realized and charged against the proper appropriation. An encumbrance is a commitment of resources prior to the actual disbursement of funds to liquidate a liability.

Where the cash system of accounting is employed encumbrances are entered as an estimated cost of the liability incurred, and the estimated amount is deducted immediately from the unencumbered balance of appropriations for a given class of expenditures. The voucher number and the amount of the payment are then entered in the Encumbrance Accounts as soon as the claim is paid. The entire encumbrance associated with a given liability is liquidated when the disbursement is made. If only a part of the order is delivered and partial payment made, the entire encumbrance of the original order is liquidated at the time of the partial payment.

Where the accrual system of accounting is used, fundamentally the same procedure is followed. The encumbrance is recorded as soon as a liability is incurred through the issuance of a purchase order. The encumbrance is liquidated when the invoice is received, checked, and approved rather than when cash is disbursed. It is recommended that expenditures in school be treated as in the accrual system even though receipts must, by law, be accounted for under the cash system of accounting. Some authorities recommend that the expenditures be entered in the Voucher Register as soon as the invoice has been received, checked, and approved.

Encumbrance Accounts can be kept for predeter-mined commitments and for unpredetermined commitments.[11] Table 7 illustrates an Encumbrance Account used for principals' salaries which are commitments during the fiscal year as soon as the contract is in force. In this illustration it is assumed that there are ten principals, each receiving $7000 per year, and the salary payments are made during 10 months of the school year, starting at the end of September and ending the end of June the year following. From Table 7, it can be seen that the appropriations for principals' salaries totaled $70,000 on July 1, 1957. This amount was encumbered immediately through the issuance of contracts for principals' salaries during the fiscal year starting July 1, 1957. The encumbrance is said to be incurred on July 1, 1957, or the start of the new fiscal year. Outstanding Encumbrances on that day became $70,000, and no Unencumbered Balance remained. No payments were made to the principals at the end of July 30, 1957, so the Outstanding Encumbrances remained at $70,000 and the unencumbered balance remained at zero.

On September 30, 1957, $7000 worth of encumbrances were liquidated by paying each of the 10 principals $700 as salary for the month. The Outstanding Encumbrances were, therefore, reduced by $7000 from the July 30, 1957, level and became $63,000 on September 30, 1957. The actual expenditures were $7000. On October 31, 1957, an additional $7000 worth of encumbrances were liquidated so that the Outstanding Encumbrances were reduced to $56,000. If the monthly salary payments continued through May 31, 1958, the Outstanding Encumbrances would be $7000. The last of the encumbrances would be liquidated with the June or final salary payments. In so doing the Outstanding

[11] University of the State of New York, *School Business Management Handbook,* Accounting and Reporting no. 4, Albany, N.Y.: The State Education Department, 1956, pp. 85–89.

TABLE 7.   Encumbrance Account for Principals' Salaries (Predetermined Commitments) for the Community School District of Smithville, U.S.A.

Date	Incurred	Encumbrances Liquidated	Outstanding	Actual Expenditure	Unencumbered Balance
July 1, 1957					$70,000 (Appropriations)
July 1, 1957	$70,000		$70,000		0
July 30, 1957			70,000		
September 30, 1957		$7,000	63,000	$7,000	
October 31, 1957		7,000	56,000	7,000	
May 31, 1958		7,000	7,000	7,000	
June 30, 1958		7,000	0	7,000	

TABLE 8. Encumbrance Account for Instructional Supplies (Undetermined Commitments) for the Community School District of Smithville, U.S.A.

Date	Purchase Order No. (1)	Voucher Number (2)	Encumbrances Incurred (3)	Encumbrances Liquidated (4)	Outstanding (5)	Actual Expenditures (6)	Unencumbered Balance (7)
7/1/57	Appropriation						$289,870
7/10/57	11		$103,780		$103,780		186,090
7/16/57	23		1,586		105,366		184,504
8/1/57	11	33		$103,780	1,586	$103,900	184,384
8/3/57	59		115,800		117,386		68,584
9/1/57	23	87		1,586	115,800	1,500	68,670
10/1/57	59	123		115,800	—	114,900	69,570
10/3/57	111		2,500		2,500		67,070

Encumbrances would be zero. In this particular case, the amount appropriated was precisely the amount expended.

Encumbrance Accounts for instructional supplies are undetermined commitments. An illustration of selected transactions for the first four months of the school year is presented in Table 8. For the purposes of this illustration, it is assumed that $289,870 is appropriated on July 1, 1957, the start of the fiscal year. The first purchase was executed on July 10, with Purchase Order No. 11. This resulted in incurring an encumbrance totaling $103,780 for supplies. On that date, the Outstanding Encumbrances were equal to that one purchase, or $103,780. The Unencumbered Balance was equal to the previous Unencumbered Balance less the amount of Encumbrance Incurred, or $186,090. Another purchase totaling $1586 was made on July 16 with the issuance of Purchase Order No. 23. On that date, the Outstanding Encumbrance (column 5 in Table 8) added up to $105,366 and the Unencumbered Balance (column 7 in Table 8) was reduced to $184,504 ($186,090 − $1586).

A payment of $103,900 was made on August 1, 1957, as Voucher Check No. 33 was issued. This amount was in full payment for materials purchased by Purchase Order No. 11 (issued July 10). Note that the actual expenditure was $120 more than the encumbrance listed in column 3 of Table 8 for July 10. The encumbrance is liquidated (column 4) in the same amount as posted in column 3, but the Unencumbered Balance was reduced by $120 on that date to $184,384 (column 7). In other words, the estimated first encumbrance was less than the actual expenditure and hence the Unencumbered Balance had to be reduced by a greater amount than anticipated. It is difficult to predict exactly what the costs will be particularly if delivery charges are a part of the total cost.

On August 3, with Purchase Order No. 59, there was incurred an encumbrance of $115,800. The Outstanding Encumbrances then totaled $117,386, leaving an Unencumbered Balance of $68,584. On September 1, Voucher Check No. 87 was executed to meet the liabilities incurred when Purchase Order No. 23 was issued. The encumbrances listed on July 16 were liquidated on September 1. It should be noted that the actual expenditure was $86 less than the amount estimated. The Unencumbered Balance was increased by the difference between the Encumbrance Incurred and the Actual Expenditure (or $86).

On October 1, the Encumbrance Incurred by Purchase Order No. 59 was liquidated by issuing Voucher Check No. 123. Once again the Actual Expenditure was less than the Encumbrance Incurred. The Unencumbered Balance was increased by $900 to recognize the difference between the actual and estimated expenditure. Note that in all cases the Encumbrances Liquidated (column 4) are always equal to Encumbrances Incurred (column 3). The difference between Actual Expenditures (column 6) and Encumbrances Incurred is reflected in changes in the Unencumbered Balance (column 7).

On October 3, a new purchase order was issued for $2500, and the Unencumbered Balance on that date was $67,070. The purpose of keeping Encumbrance Accounts is to give a clear picture of the financial obligations of the district at any particular time. There usually is a time lag between the date the purchase order is issued, the date materials are delivered, and the date the invoice is paid. This lag necessitates special accounting procedures, particularly for schools on a cash basis, so that a clear picture of the financial status of the district can be had at any time.

FORMS AND MACHINES

Financial transactions are recorded on specially printed pages called forms. These forms may be developed for use with the manual (traditional pen-and-ink) systems or with machines. The use of me-

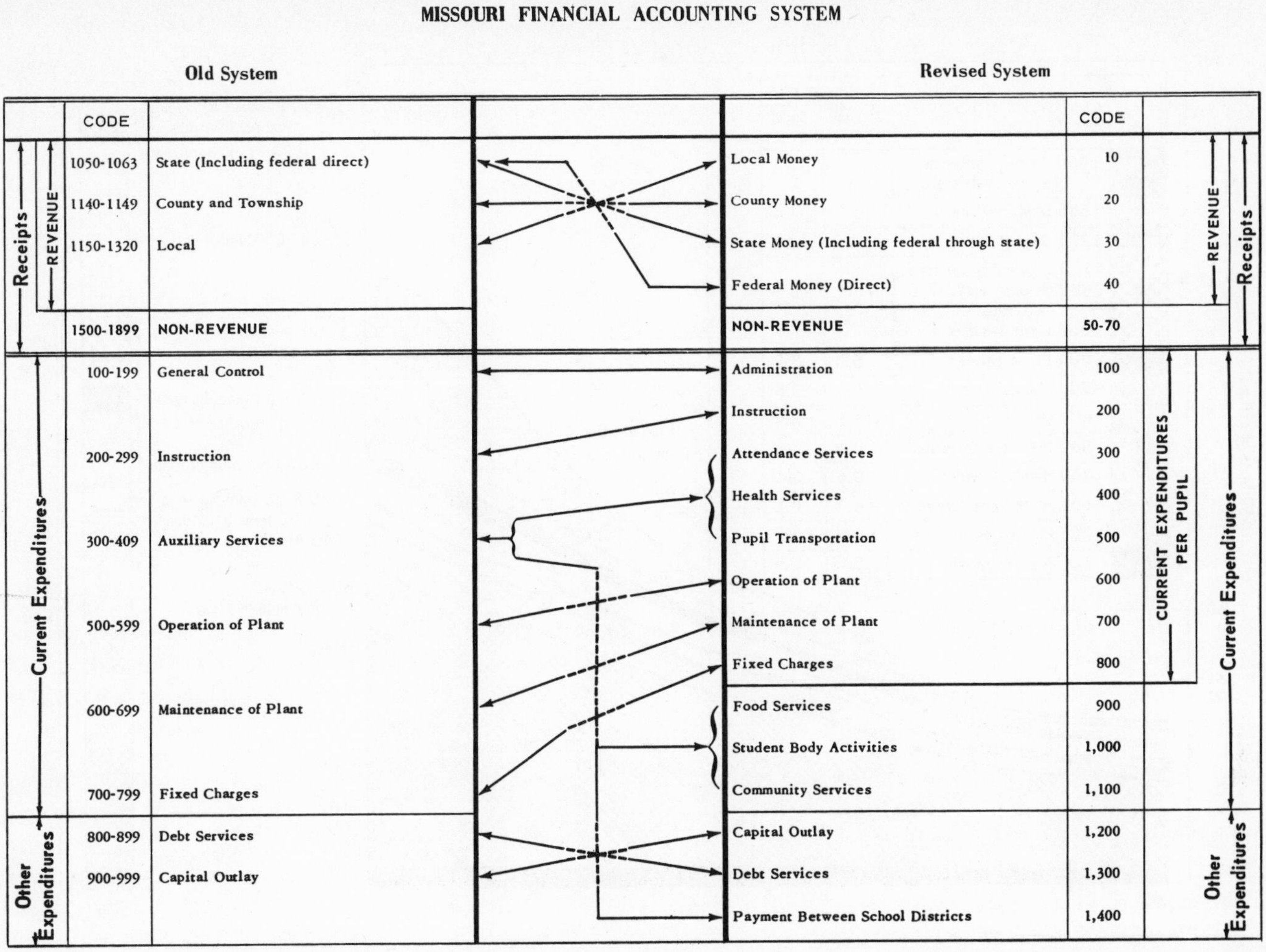
MISSOURI FINANCIAL ACCOUNTING SYSTEM
Old System
Revised System
CODE
Receipts
REVENUE
1050-1063 State (Including federal direct)
1140-1149 County and Township
1150-1320 Local
1500-1899 NON-REVENUE
Current Expenditures
100-199 General Control
200-299 Instruction
300-409 Auxiliary Services
500-599 Operation of Plant
600-699 Maintenance of Plant
700-799 Fixed Charges
Other Expenditures
800-899 Debt Services
900-999 Capital Outlay
Local Money 10
County Money 20
State Money (Including federal through state) 30
Federal Money (Direct) 40
NON-REVENUE 50-70
Administration 100
Instruction 200
Attendance Services 300
Health Services 400
Pupil Transportation 500
Operation of Plant 600
Maintenance of Plant 700
Fixed Charges 800
Food Services 900
Student Body Activities 1,000
Community Services 1,100
Capital Outlay 1,200
Debt Services 1,300
Payment Between School Districts 1,400
CURRENT EXPENDITURES PER PUPIL

FIGURE 10. Comparison Between the Old and Revised Financial Accounting Systems for Schools as Developed in Missouri

SOURCE: Courtesy of the Missouri State Department of Education

chanical devices to speed accounting is of particular significance in this day and age of more complex school business procedures.

School districts in many states continue to follow the procedures outlined in the 1948 USOE accounting manual. The 1957 USOE accounting manual differs in several important respects from the 1948 recommendations. All school districts in the nation should base accounting procedures and terminology on the 1957 USOE manual as soon as it is practicable. Some states have adopted at this writing the recommendations of the 1957 USOE financial accounting handbook. The State Department of Education in Missouri was among the first to recommend utilization of the revised system of accounting in the public schools of that state.

Figure 10 is a diagram used in Missouri to help explain the similarities and differences between the "old system" (1948 USOE accounting manual) and the "revised system" (1957 USOE accounting manual). The terminology or code numbers have changed to some degree in all categories other than INSTRUCTION. It is interesting to note that the annual State Education Department report for Missouri ending on June 30, 1957, used the new accounting classifications to report school expenditures. This is shown in Figure 11.

FORMS

Illustrations of forms employed to account for expenditures as per the 1957 USOE accounting manual are shown as Forms 3 through 10. These are accounting forms used by the public school districts in the state of Missouri. For over 30 years this state has provided accounting forms free of charge to the public school districts. This practice has been an aid in promoting uniform school accounting and rapid implementation of the recommendations of the 1957 USOE accounting manual. It should be noted that these forms

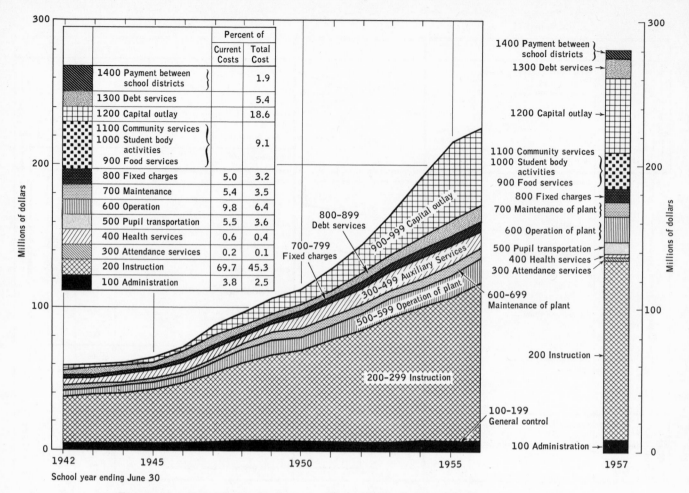

FIGURE 11.   Expenditures by Purpose for the Public Schools of Missouri Since 1942
SOURCE: Courtesy of the Missouri State Department of Education

are of the type for use with manual rather than machine systems of accounting.

Form 3 shows a combination Encumbrance and Voucher Payment Register used in Missouri. The encumbrance is based on voucher jacket information and payment is listed by Warrants Issued. Form 4 is a Distribution Ledger for the ADMINISTRATION series of accounts. The Distribution Ledger for INSTRUCTION is more complex and hence both sides of Form 5 are shown. The three services of ATTENDANCE, HEALTH, and PUPIL TRANSPORTATION are placed on one form—Form 6. Forms 7 and 8 are for OPERATION OF PLANT and MAINTENANCE OF PLANT, respectively. Form 9 is a combination of four different account series and Form 10 is used for three other different account series. The forms are presented for purposes of illustrations only and should not be interpreted as a recommended system of forms for use in all states in exactly the same design and as found in Missouri. Each state should develop forms to be employed by school districts to show

financial transactions in a manner consistent with the 1957 USOE financial accounting manual.

MACHINE ACCOUNTING

Machines can be used as mechanical aids in all phases of the accounting operation. Some accounting machines are mechanical combinations of many adding machines. Others are based on electronic data-processing equipment utilizing punch cards rather than a mechanical combination of adding machines. In the former the information is inserted directly into one machine whereas the latter requires a more indirect approach based on several machines. As indicated previously, a school district with over 50 employees is bordering on a situation where it might well be profitable to utilize some type of machine accounting. It is predicted that within the next 25 years most schools will be using machines to record financial transactions in the accounting system with accuracy and speed. Reorganization of school districts will result in

FORM 3 (Front).

Encumbrance and Voucher Payment Register

Form No. 3 10M
January '53 10M

CURRENT EXPENSE

Date Encumbered and/or Paid	Company or Purpose Listed on Voucher Jacket	Voucher No.	Warrant No.	Code	Grand Total		Total Current Expense		Administration 100		Instruction 200		Attendance Services 300		Health Services 400	
					Encumbered	Paid	Encumbered	Paid	Encumbered	Paid	Encumbered	Paid	Encumbered	Paid	Encumbered	Paid

(Courtesy of the Missouri State Department of Education)

FORM 3 (Back).

Form No. 3, continued
January '58 10M

Encumbrance and Voucher Payment Register, Continued

| | CURRENT EXPENSE, Continued | | | | | | | | | | CLEARING ACCOUNTS | | | | | | OTHER EXPENDITURES | | | | | | | | |
| | Pupil Transportation 500 | | Operation 600 | | Maintenance 700 | | Fixed Charges 800 | | Food Services 900 | | Student Body Activities 1000 | | Community Services 1100 | | Capital Outlay 1200 | | Debt Service 1300 | | Paid to Other School Districts 1400 | | |
	Encumbered	Paid	Encumbered	Paid	Encumbered	Paid	Encumbered	Paid	Encumbered	Paid	Encumbered	Paid	Encumbered	Paid	Encumbered	Paid	Encumbered	Paid	Encumbered	Paid	
1																					1
2																					2
3																					3
4																					4
5																					5
6																					6
7																					7
8																					8
9																					9
10																					10
11																					11
12																					12
13																					13
14																					14
15																					15
16																					16
17																					17
18																					18
19																					19
20																					20
21																					21
22																					22
23																					23
24																					24
25																					25
26																					26
27																					27
28																					28
29																					29
30																					30
31																					31
32																					32
33																					33
34																					34
35																					35
36																					36
37																					37
38																					38
39																					39
40																					40

FORM 4.

FORM MO-6
OCT. '56—5b

Distribution Ledger—Administration

SCHOOL

DATE	TO WHOM	VOUCHER NUMBER	CODE →	TOTAL 100-130	SALARIES 110				SCHOOL ELECTION AND CENSUS 130	AUDIT 130-m	SUPPLIES 130-p	OTHER EXPENSES 130-q		
					SECRETARY BD. OF EDUCATION 110-b	TREASURER BD. OF EDUCATION 110-c	SUPERINTENDENT OF SCHOOLS 110-g	OTHER SALARIES 110-q						
1	BUDGET ESTIMATE													1
2														2
3														3
4														4
5														5
6														6
7														7
8														8
9														9
10														10
11														11
12														12
13														13
14														14
15														15
16														16
17														17
18														18
19														19
20														20
21														21
22														22
23														23
24														24
25														25
26														26
27														27
28														28
29														29
30														30
31														31
32														32
33														33
34														34
35														35
36														36
37														37
38														38
39														39
40														40

(Courtesy of the Missouri State Department of Education)

FORM 5 (Front).

Form No. 7
January '58 10M

Distribution Ledger—Instruction

School _____

| Date | TO WHOM | Voucher No. | Code | Total | SALARIES | | | | | | | Free Textbooks 220 | Library Books, Supplies Periodicals, Etc. 230 | INSTRUCTIONAL SUPPLIES FOR TEACHING | | | |
					Principals 211	Supervisors & Consultants 212	Teachers 213-1	Substitute Teachers 213-2	School Librarians 214	Other Salaries of Instruction 215				Language Arts 240.1	Social Studies 240.2	Mathematics 240.3	
1	BUDGET ESTIMATE																1
2																	2
3																	3
4																	4
5																	5
6																	6
7																	7
8																	8
9																	9
10																	10
11																	11
12																	12
13																	13
14																	14
15																	15
16																	16
17																	17
18																	18
19																	19
20																	20
21																	21
22																	22
23																	23
24																	24
25																	25
26																	26
27																	27
28																	28
29																	29
30																	30
31																	31
32																	32
33																	33
34																	34
35																	35
36																	36
37																	37
38																	38
39																	39
40																	40

(Courtesy of the Missouri State Department of Education)

FORM 5 (Back).

Distribution Ledger—Instruction—Cont.

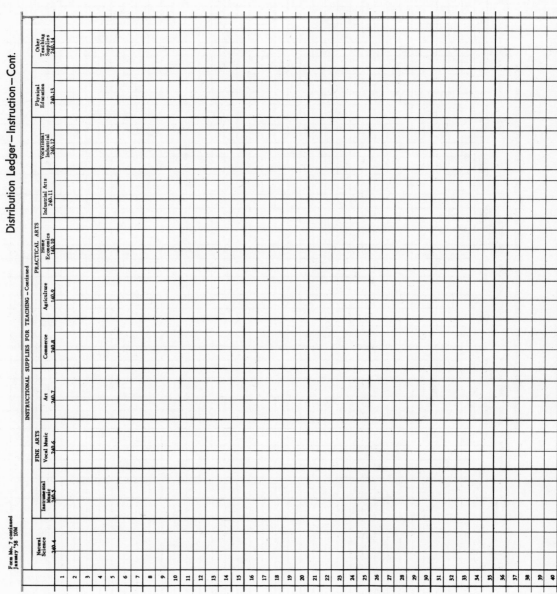

FORM 6.

Distribution Ledgers—Attendance, Health, and Pupil Transportation Services

SCHOOL DISTRICT

DATE	TO WHOM	VOUCHER NO.	CODE→	ATTENDANCE SERVICES 300 SERIES			HEALTH SERVICES 400 SERIES			PUPIL TRANSPORTATION SERVICES 500 SERIES						
				TOTAL 300	SALARIES 310	OTHER EXPENSE 320	TOTAL 400	SALARIES 410	OTHER EXPENSE 420	TOTAL 500	SALARIES 510	REPLACEMENT OF VEHICLES 530	INSURANCE 540	OPERATION AND MAINTENANCE 560	CONTRACTED SERVICES 520	
	BUDGET ESTIMATE															1
																2
																3
																4
																5
																6
																7
																8
																9
																10
																11
																12
																13
																14
																15
																16
																17
																18
																19
																20
																21
																22
																23
																24
																25
																26
																27
																28
																29
																30
																31
																32
																33
																34
																35
																36
																37
																38
																39
																40

(Courtesy of the Missouri State Department of Education)

FORM 7.

FORM MO-7-7
AUG. '59—8M

Distribution Ledger--Operation of Plant

SCHOOL _____

DATE	TO WHOM	VOUCHER NO.	CODE→	TOTAL	SALARIES	FUEL FOR HEATING	UTILITIES (EXCEPT FUEL)	SUPPLIES (EXCEPT UTILITIES)	OTHER EXPENSES						
	BUDGET ESTIMATE									1					
										2					
										3					
										4					
										5					

(Courtesy of the Missouri State Department of Education)

FORM 8.

FORM MO-10-6
AUG. '56—4M

Distribution Ledger - Maintenance of Plant

DATE	TO WHOM	VOUCHER NO.	CODE →	TOTAL	SALARIES	MATERIALS AND OTHER EXPENSES				CONTRACTED SERVICES				REPLACEMENT OF EQUIPMENT								
						UPKEEP OF GROUNDS	REPAIR OF BUILDINGS	REPAIR OF EQUIPMENT		UPKEEP OF GROUNDS	REPAIR OF BUILDINGS	REPAIR OF EQUIPMENT										
1	BUDGET ESTIMATE																					
2																						
3																						
4																						
5																						
6																						
7																						
8																						
9																						
10																						
11																						
12																						
13																						
14																						
15																						
16																						
17																						
18																						
19																						
20																						
21																						
22																						
23																						
24																						
25																						
26																						
27																						
28																						
29																						
30																						
31																						
32																						
33																						
34																						
35																						
36																						
37																						
38																						
39																						
40																						

SCHOOL

(Courtesy of the Missouri State Department of Education)

FORM 9.

Distribution Ledgers–Fixed Charges, Food Services, Student Body Activities, and Community Services

FORM NO 11-O
APRIL '57 8M

SCHOOL DISTRICT _____

DATE	TO WHOM	VOUCHER NO.	CODE→	FIXED CHARGES 800 SERIES				FOOD SERVICES 900 SERIES				STUDENT BODY ACTIVITIES 1,000 SERIES			COMMUNITY SERVICES 1100	
				TOTAL 800	DISTRICT CONTRIBUTION FOR RETIREMENT AND SOCIAL SECURITY 810	INSURANCE 820	OTHER FIXED CHARGES 830	TOTAL 900	SALARIES 910	FOOD EXPENSE 920	OTHER EXPENSES 930	TOTAL 1000	SALARIES 1010	OTHER EXPENSES 1020		
1	BUDGET ESTIMATE														1	
2															2	
3															3	
4															4	
5															5	
6															6	
7															7	
8															8	
9															9	
10															10	
11															11	
12															12	
13															13	
14															14	
15															15	
16															16	
17															17	
18															18	
19															19	
20															20	
21															21	
22															22	
23															23	
24															24	
25															25	
26															26	
27															27	
28															28	
29															29	
30															30	
31															31	
32															32	
33															33	
34															34	
35															35	
36															36	
37															37	
38															38	
39															39	
40															40	

(Courtesy of the Missouri State Department of Education)

FORM 10.

FORM No 13
APRIL '57 8-M

Distribution Ledgers—Capital Outlay, Debt Service, and Payment Between School Districts

SCHOOL DISTRICT _____

DATE	TO WHOM	VOUCHER NO.	CODE→	CAPITAL OUTLAY 1200 SERIES								DEBT SERVICE 1300 SERIES				PAYMENT BETWEEN SCHOOL DISTRICTS 1400 SERIES		
				TOTAL 1200	SITES 1210	BUILDINGS 1220	FURNITURE FOR BUILDING 1231	INSTRUCTIONAL APPARATUS 1232	NEW BUSES 1233	OTHER CAPITAL OUTLAY 1240	TOTAL 1300	RETIREMENT OF BONDS 1310	PRINTING & ENGRAVING OF BONDS 1311	INTEREST ON BONDS 1320	TOTAL 1400	FOR TUITION 1411	FOR TRANSPORTATION 1412
	BUDGET ESTIMATE																
1																	
2																	
3																	
4																	
5																	
6																	
7																	
8																	
9																	
10																	
11																	
12																	
13																	
14																	
15																	
16																	
17																	
18																	
19																	
20																	
21																	
22																	
23																	
24																	
25																	
26																	
27																	
28																	
29																	
30																	
31																	
32																	
33																	
34																	
35																	
36																	
37																	
38																	
39																	
40																	

(Courtesy of the Missouri State Department of Education)

larger districts with more employees per district. This plus more complex educational programs will call for larger budgets which, in turn, will precipitate more accounting problems.

Some of the factors that should be considered in the selection of accounting machines are (1) the use of the equipment to integrate purchasing, accounting, inventorying, and auditing procedures; (2) the initial cost of the machine; (3) the complexity of the educational program; (4) special procedures likely to be encountered and the amount of equipment or auxiliary equipment that may be necessary for such procedures; (5) the flexibility of the equipment, particularly in executing such tasks as detailed cost analysis or research analysis; (6) the cost of forms used in the machine; (7) the availability of service and service expense in event of breakdowns; (8) length of time to complete the cycle of operations; (9) the availability of equipment; (10) the number and preparation level of personnel required to man the equipment; (11) the use of equipment in the preparation of reports; (12) the flexibility of equipment for use in diversified tasks such as preparation of assessment rolls, tax lists, etc.; (13) the capacity of equipment as related to possible expansion in accounting requirements in the school district; (14) mechanical durability; (15) the number of automatic operations performed and the ease of changing from one operation to the other; (16) the degree of visibility of postings; (17) electrification of alphabet and numeral keys; (18) noise created; (19) ease in making simple operating changes such as inserting forms, changing dates, changing program hours, and correcting errors.[12]

What a machine is expected to do in a given accounting program must be spelled out prior to actual purchase. There are many types of machines, and they vary in capacity to execute accounting procedures as well as in cost. Machine accounting is still relatively new, and improvements in manufacture and technical aspects which affect cost as well as ability to perform various tasks with greater speed and accuracy appear frequently. The most expensive and complicated is not always the most efficient, particularly in small districts where the accounting problems are less complex and fewer in number, and accounting personnel are not in short supply. The illustrations of machine accounting in the following paragraphs are based on the direct feed type of machines.

Machine accounting operations can now be used for appropriation accounting, revenue accounting, and payroll accounting. Some of the simpler operating procedures rather than individual machines will be de-

[12] University of the State of New York, *op. cit.,* pp. 90–91.

scribed. Encumbrance and Expense Ledgers for each of the 14 functional-character Expenditure Accounts and for each line item of the budget can be treated by machine techniques. Usually a flexible form on heavy bond paper and printed to show columns for the name of the vendor, description of the transaction, date, check number, purchase order number, invoice number, appropriation adjustments, encumbrances incurred, encumbrances liquidated, outstanding encumbrances, expenditures to date, unencumbered balance (or unexpended balance), and total appropriations can be prepared. Since the Encumbrance and Expense Journals contain accounts with the same information as the Encumbrance and Expense Ledgers, plus additional margin space to prove balance pickup before posting of entry, these operations can be done at one time with a machine. The precise design of forms varies with the particular machine and the nature of the task.

One of the many advantages of machine accounting is the ability to print the voucher check, make the entry into the chronological journal record, and post the expenditure to the desired Distribution Ledger in one operation. In other words, in one operation, the machine will print the voucher check, enter the information into the Voucher Register, and post the facts in *Major Account 240—Teaching Supplies,* if the invoice called for the payment of crayons purchased. The machine will, in effect, print the same information on the distribution ledger as it does on the chronological journal records. Some may question, therefore, as to whether it is necessary to have the journal unless someone becomes interested in a diary of financial activities on the daily basis.

As in the case of the traditional manual or pen-and-ink accounting procedures, the purchase order initiates the encumbrance against an appropriation. The invoice is the basis for liquidating the encumbrance, authorizing an expenditure, and influencing the unencumbered balance in a particular account. With a manual or pen-and-ink method of posting, it was necessary to enter each item in several columns of the journal, Encumbrance Account, and ledger in a laborious but not necessarily accurate fashion. The machine produces all the balances automatically upon the depression of one key. It is becoming more and more evident that accounting machines provide the most economic, efficient, and time-saving operation in those systems which are using encumbrance accounting methods. There is little excuse for avoiding encumbrance accounting with machines available at the present time. There was some excuse for eliminating encumbrance accounting in years gone by, for without machines it required far more man power than cash expenditure accounting. Machines can be a decided asset in improving accounting procedures for schools.

Much the same advantages in machine accounting operation can be listed for revenue accounting and payroll accounting. The Revenue Ledgers can be inserted in the machine. The information posted on the Revenue Ledgers can be immediately placed upon the Revenue Journal which remains in the machine and is covered with a carbon, which causes the posting made on the ledger to be carbonized onto the journal. In other words, any number of Revenue Ledgers for the various Revenue Accounts can be inserted into the machine, but the Revenue Journal remains in the machine until all revenue postings are complete. At the end of the posting period for revenues, the total of transactions listed in the Revenue Journal should equal the total of transactions registered on the various ledgers for Revenue Receipts.

A quick change of stops and bars in the machines can make it perform for payroll preparation as well as in other accounting operations. Descriptive accounting machines have the capacity to process Payroll Journals, Earnings Ledgers, and voucher checks simultaneously and without the aid of auxiliary equipment. Carbonization of forms and machine capacity make such an operation possible. As indicated previously in the chapter on payroll management, an individual Earnings Record or Ledger is maintained for each employee. The individual Earnings Ledger is inserted in the machine. The information placed on the Earnings Ledger by the machine is carbonized onto the Payroll Register and the Payroll Journal. The journal is placed in the accounting machine and remains until the entire payroll is completed. The other insertions are fairly simple. The employee's individual record is inserted in the machine and the payroll check (or voucher check) is placed over it with the remittance advice section of the check (which has a carbon between the check and its duplicate and also between the duplicate and the Earnings Ledger) over the Earnings Record. The completed check and posted Earnings Record card are removed from the machine and a new check and the next employee's Earnings Record card are inserted. This procedure is followed until all Earnings Record cards are posted and all salary checks are completed. The machine then prints the total in each column of the Payroll Journal. The total of the gross earnings entry should equal the net pay column plus deduction column total.

At the end of the payroll operation the machine provides the total gross payroll, the total gross earnings to date, the total withholding tax for payroll period, the total withholding tax to date, the total retirement deduction, the total Blue Cross and Blue Shield deductions, and any and all deductions and then proves them correct.

PUNCH-CARD MACHINE ACCOUNTING

The previous paragraphs have been concerned with mechanical accounting devices based on several banks of electrically powered adding machines. They could also be identified as machines for direct entry of accounting information. In other words, the information is fed directly into the accounting machine and, therefore, entered and posted directly to the financial records. In contrast to this are the indirect information entry accounting machines based on punched cards and electronic data-processing machines. The financial facts are first punched or coded into specially designed cards. The cards are then processed by electronic devices to transfer information to the financial records. Where the punched-card machine methods are employed, the procedure is somewhat indirect, and at least three different machines are required to enter and post financial data into journals or ledgers. Strange as it may appear, the indirect accounting machines are often faster than direct information entry machines, particularly for very large and complex operations.

The punched-card system or electronic processing of accounting data is often referred to as the IBM system. The three basic or minimum number of machines needed for electronic processing of accounting data are the Printing Card Punch, Sorter, and Accounting Machine.

The Printing Card Punch is utilized for recording numerical or other data into special cards. Keyed or coded information is punched and at the same time printed along the top edge of the cards.

The Sorter groups cards of similar classifications to yield the numerical or alphabetical sequence desired. This machine comes in various speeds. Some can sort 650 and others 1000 cards per minute per card column.

The Accounting Machine is the device used to transfer data from the punched cards to the reports and records. This machine reads 80-column cards, records details, adds, subtracts, and prints any desired combination of totals. There are many models of this machine that vary in speed and ability to perform various tasks. In summary, various financial facts are keyed and punched into specially designed cards. The cards are arranged into the particular alphabetical or numerical or other sequence by means of the sorter.

The sorted cards are fed into the accounting machine which prepares reports and records from punched cards.

The battery of data-processing equipment described represents a minimum required. Additional types are available for specific tasks. This is essentially the same type of equipment which could be used for other school purposes such as the preparation of report cards, class schedules, class lists for teachers, attendance reports, transcripts, test scores, and pupil personnel records. The difference lies in the preparation of the punched card.

There are many different business management chores which can be accomplished by electronic data-processing equipment. Some applications of punched-card machine accounting in Baltimore schools were for:

1. Tabulation of supplies and equipment needs.
2. Inventory control.
3. Payrolls.
4. Budget expenditures.
5. Financial reports to the state education department.
6. Tuition billing.[13]

Albright[14] declared that school systems with central business and educational administration and with a pupil population of 10,000 or more will have enough volume of detail work to warrant the installation of electronic data-processing equipment. The machines may be purchased or rented. Monthly rental costs for installations of various capacity vary from approximately $360 to $1500. Salaries of personnel to operate data-processing machines range from a low of $2600 per year for a key punch operator to a high of $8000 for a supervisor of machine accounting.[15]

Smaller city school systems find it difficult to justify monthly rentals or outright purchase of electronic data-processing equipment. The Keokuk public schools employ a commercial data-processing service unit for approximately $65 a month to punch cards used in accounting from source documents such as voucher jackets and also to prepare financial reports from the cards.

There is little question that the machine operation for accounting is one of the most promising developments in improving school accounting procedures in small and large districts alike. With the advent of machines, there is no excuse for keeping only minimum or

[13] O. Eugene Albright, "Application of Machine Accounting in the Field of Public Education," *Proceedings of the Association of School Business Officials,* 43rd Annual Convention, 1957, pp. 199–209.
[14] *Ibid.*
[15] *Ibid.*

inadequate financial records. The old argument that too many personnel workers are needed has disappeared.

SUMMARY

Expenditures are made to liquidate liabilities. The checked and approved invoice is a basic accounting document which supports the issuance of instruments authorizing payment of funds from the school treasury. The voucher check combines the features of a check, a formal receipt, and a remittance slip. The supporting documents involved in meeting liabilities should be placed in the voucher jacket or voucher folder.

The Voucher Register is a special type of journal into which all vouchers are entered. It is a posting medium for various Expenditure Accounts.

There are many different ways to categorize Expenditure Accounts. The functional-character classification was employed in this chapter. In a broad sense, classification by character of the financial transactions can be conceived of as a grouping of expenditures according to functions performed. The Expenditure Accounts for schools were classified into 14 account series recommended in the 1957 USOE financial accounting manual. The accounts could be used with any fund, but not all Expenditure Accounts enumerated in this book will be needed for all school funds.

There are some differences between the 1948 and 1957 USOE accounting manuals for schools. What was called previously Auxiliary Services has been organized into six separate accounting series of ATTENDANCE SERVICES, HEALTH SERVICES, PUPIL TRANSPORTATION SERVICES, FOOD SERVICES, STUDENT BODY ACTIVITIES, and COMMUNITY SERVICES. The term ADMINISTRATION is now used in preference to General Control. The piece-for-piece replacement concept is recommended over other approaches.

Every account should be controlled by the General Ledger. Encumbrance accounting is likewise a necessary aspect of financial control. An encumbrance is a commitment of resources prior to the actual disbursement of funds to liquidate a liability. It insures that the amount of money encumbered cannot be used for things others than its designated purpose.

Financial transactions are recorded on specially printed pages called forms. Some states, such as Missouri, have already issued forms following the recommendations of the 1957 USOE accounting handbook. Each state should change to this recent accounting manual and develop forms consistent with it and yet applicable to the state educational problems.

There are direct and indirect information entry accounting machines. Direct fed machines are based on several banks of electrically powered adding machines. The indirect fed machines use punched cards with specially keyed information which require processing by electronic data-processing equipment. What a machine is expected to do in school accounting should be spelled out prior to actual purchase. One of the most promising developments in improving school accounting is the ever increasing use of accounting machines.

QUESTIONS

1. What is the function of a Voucher Register?
2. What information or documents should be placed in a voucher jacket?
3. What are the 14 functional character classifications for Expenditure Accounts?
4. What is meant by the piece-for-piece replacement concept?
5. What is the difference between:
   a. An encumbrance and an expenditure?
   b. A journal and a ledger?
   c. OPERATION OF PLANT and MAINTENANCE OF PLANT?
   d. CAPITAL OUTLAY and DEBT SERVICE?
   e. The cash system and the accrual system of accounting?
6. When is an encumbrance incurred? Liquidated?

7. To what accounts would you post the following expenditures?
   a. $750 monthly salary of a superintendent who spends 30 percent of his time teaching in the high school.
   b. $6000 for a new 50-passenger school bus to replace an obsolete 36-passenger bus which originally cost $3600.
   c. A $25 monthly gasoline bill for operation of a car used for driver education.
   d. A $500 property insurance premium to pay in full insurance for five years.
   e. $1000 paid to district A for tuition of high school pupils.
   f. Magazine subscriptions totaling $25 for the public library operated by the school district.

SELECTED REFERENCES

Albright, Eugene O., "Application of Machine Accounting in the Field of Public Education," *Proceedings of the Association of School Business Officials,* 43rd Annual Convention, 1957, pp. 199–209.

Reason, Paul L., and White, Alpheus L., *Financial Accounting for Local and State School Systems, Standard Receipt and Expenditure Accounts,* Bulletin 1957, no. 4, U.S. Office of Education, Washington, D.C.: U.S. Government Printing Office, 1957, chaps. 3, 4, and 10.

University of the State of New York, *School Business Management Handbook,* Accounting and Reporting no. 4, Albany, N.Y.: State Education Department, 1956.

CHAPTER 8

The Auditing of Public School Financial Transactions

AN AUDIT IS A SYSTEMATIC INVESTIGATION, verification, and critical review of financial operations within a school district. It is one of the culminating steps in the process of controlling the fiscal affairs of any type of institution. The primary purpose of an audit is to verify or substantiate the financial status of the school system. Through the audit the accuracy, integrity, and authenticity of accounting, vouchers, and other financial records and documents of a business organization can be ascertained. It is a means of inquiring into the stewardship of public monies and other assets by officials entrusted with their collection, safekeeping, and disbursement. The auditor's report should be an expression of an informed opinion on the propriety of transactions as well as fiscal condition.

The process of auditing is based on an analysis and critical review of various items involved in financial transactions, such as documents, records, systems of internal control, and accounting procedure. The aims of the systematic examination are to verify (1) that financial operations are proper, legal, and mathematically accurate, (2) that all financial transactions have been recorded, and (3) that the transactions are accurately reflected in accounts and statements drawn therefrom in accordance with accepted accounting principles.

It is difficult to arrive at one satisfactory scientific definition of auditing which will satisfy all authorities. The variations and modifications are too numerous and too great to permit adequate description of auditing in a single statement or two. The auditing terminology employed in this chapter will follow, in the main, the accepted definitions of the National Committee on Governmental Accounting.[1]

PUBLIC SCHOOL AUDITING COMPARED WITH COMMERCIAL AUDITING

The auditing of financial operations of a school district involves many of the procedures used in business and industry. The unique nature of education separates it in some ways from accepted auditing practices in private business and industry. In most industrial and commercial enterprises the top echelon of people who control corporate affairs and are directly responsible for the management of financial operations are changed less frequently than are school boards and superintendents. This condition makes auditing of a school district even more necessary than in business or industry.

Certain factors make auditing of schools more complex but others make it simpler than in commercial enterprises. Accounting procedures of governmental bodies such as school districts are often controlled by law. The audit is often a legal requirement. Compliance with constitutional and statutory restrictions (some of which are specific and others obscure) imposed upon the financial management of local school

[1] National Committee on Governmental Accounting, *Municipal Accounting and Auditing*, no. 14, Chicago: the Committee, September, 1951, pp. 185–220.

...icts makes auditing in educational institutions ...ore difficult than in private institutions. To perform an effective service auditors engaged in public school assignments must become familiar with the major features of laws and court decisions affecting the financial operations of a school system. On the other hand, the absence of profit and loss accounts found in private enterprise makes school auditing somewhat simpler. Adjusting entries, such as adjustments for depreciation, accruals, and deferred items, which are usually considered in auditing private firms to determine a correct profit and loss figure, are not considered in public school auditing. Instead, so-called "operating statements" are found, which are often nothing more than statements of cash operations.[2] Ownership accounts found in private establishments are absent in governmental units, and this has a tendency to simplify school auditing. The multiplicity of funds with special regulation of receipts and expenditures controlling each fund found in school districts makes the auditing more complex. The same careful examination and verification is necessary in both, but insofar as the functions of schools differ from those of commercial enterprises, school audit procedures and reports will differ from those in private business and industry.

AUDITING TERMINOLOGY

The term "auditing" is a general one. Its meaning is vague unless properly modified. Furthermore, there is no absolute uniformity of definitions for the names attached to various types of audits. A description of what is involved in a type of audit is necessary to judge accurately its character, for the names assigned to it by different authorities may not have the same meaning. The terminology to be employed in this chapter is based primarily on the reports of the National Committee on Governmental Accounting.[3]

There are many ways to classify the various types of audits. The classification of audits into *general* and *special* audits is based on scope. These two broad classifications can be further broken down into *complete* and *limited* audits. The differentiation between the two subclassifications is found in the intensity of investigation of financial records and documents during the auditing process.

[2] Lloyd Morey and Robert P. Hackett, *Fundamentals of Governmental Accounting*, New York: John Wiley and Sons, Inc., rev. ed., 1951, p. 320.

[3] National Committee on Governmental Accounting, *op. cit.*

GENERAL AND SPECIAL AUDITS

A general audit embraces *all* fiscal transactions and records in *every fund* in the district. It is a most comprehensive examination of finances and is usually made at the end of an accounting period, which is most commonly the end of a fiscal year. A special audit is one which is confined to some particular phase of the school district's financial activities. It differs from the general audit in being less comprehensive in scope. An audit of the schoolhouse fund only is an illustration of a special audit. The special audit may cover a period of time which is longer or shorter than a given fiscal year. Suspicion of malpractice often prompts a special audit in one phase of school financial operations. This may occur at any time during the fiscal year and may necessitate examination and verification of records and documents in several past fiscal years as well. The term "specific audit" is probably a more accurate contrast to the term "general audit" than is special audit.

COMPLETE AND LIMITED AUDITS

A complete audit is an intensive examination of financial operations. It involves a detailed study of the system of internal control and of all books and accounts, including subsidiary records and supporting documents, to determine the legality, mathematical accuracy, complete accountability, and application of accounting principles. All or substantially all entries and transactions are reviewed and verified. Under such conditions, the auditor is not expected to make qualifications in his report, other than those which may be imposed upon him by lack of information, that is, inability to get at the facts. It is sometimes referred to as a detailed audit. It is more appropriate to use the word "complete" as a second modifier rather than a single modifier. To illustrate, there are *complete general* audits and *complete special* audits.

In contrast to the complete audit, a limited audit is confined to checking or examining only selected items. The effectiveness of the system of internal control and the mathematical accuracy, legality, propriety, and completeness of all financial transactions is judged by reviewing and verifying only a given sample of entries and transactions. It is assumed the sample of financial transactions analyzed and verified is representative of all financial transactions in the school district. It would follow that the unchecked items will reflect the same pattern of accuracy or errors as those which were checked. This approach to auditing based on the test check or sampling requires less time and, therefore, less cost than one based on a more intensive or complete check of all financial transactions in the school district. The term "limited" is likewise used more appropriately as a second rather than lone modifier to the word "audit."

A complete general audit is one whose scope includes all funds or financial transactions in the district and is based on an intensive review and verification of all items during a given accounting period. It is broad in scope and exhaustive in analysis. The auditor makes few if any qualifications in a complete general audit.

A limited general audit has the same broad scope, but the approach used to substantiate or verify the financial condition of the district is based on a test check or sampling of financial items. The auditor is expected to certify, however, concerning all of the transactions and records in a limited general audit, even though he has examined only some of them. He is entitled to make the qualifications deemed necessary in reaching conclusions and recommendations.

A complete special audit is narrower in scope than a complete general audit but is based on the same exhaustive analysis and verification of all financial transactions. A limited special audit is confined to a specific phase of a school district's financial operation and is based on review and verification of only selected financial items within the phase of financial operation under consideration.

TIME AND AUDITS

An audit can occur at various times. Audits can be classified according to the time they take place. Preaudits, continuous audits, and postaudits are types whose classification is based on time. Time can be measured in terms of a stipulated accounting period or fiscal year. Time can also be measured in terms of rather vague and indefinite periods related to before or after the consummation of a financial transaction during a given fiscal year.

PREAUDIT

A preaudit is an investigation and critical review made prior to the consummation of a financial transaction. The purposes behind a preaudit are:
1. To determine the propriety of the proposed transaction.
2. To determine whether it is authorized in the school budget.
3. To determine whether unencumbered funds remain in the appropriations made for such purposes.

Basically, preauditing is a special part of the control aspect of accounting. A great deal of it takes place in the normal careful accounting routine, rather than with the help of specialized auditing personnel. In many school systems preauditing is highly informal, consisting of little more than the initialing of a purchase order by the superintendent or business manager before the purchase order is mailed. In contrast, preauditing in many large governmental institutions may become formalized and a function of the comptroller. Preauditing is of greater importance in governmental affairs than in private business because of numerous, detailed technical restrictions placed upon the use of funds and the budgeting of amounts for designated purposes.

The preaudit is one way to avoid expenditures of borderline validity. It also prevents money appropriated for one purpose from being used for some other purpose which may be more or less loosely related to it. In this way, the unauthorized shifting of appropriations is avoided.

Preauditing is rarely, if ever, performed by outside, independent, or private agencies. Most authorities recommend that this function be performed by school business personnel rather than by persons independent of the executive of the school system. Considerable difficulty and inefficiency in school operation would result if every purchase, for example, had to be preaudited by some outside agency such as the state department of education or the state comptroller general.

The preaudit is sometimes called the administrative audit or voucher audit. Formal written reports on preaudit activities are the exception and not the rule in most organizations. If disputes arise with respect to the propriety or authority to make a given financial transaction, they are usually submitted to a higher authority within the system for decision. Such conditions may be the occasion for a written report of a given preaudit activity.

It is important to keep in mind that preauditing occurs *before* the act. It is a system of control based on prevention of unauthorized or illegal expenditures. Preauditing is a necessary and useful activity in all school systems of whatever size. Those in charge of school management are responsible for making preaudits of all proposed financial liabilities or commitments. In the very small school system, the superintendent, who must also serve as business manager, or his competent clerk-secretary, should be responsible for preauditing. In larger and more complex school systems, this function should rest with business personnel primarily responsible for budget making and budget execution or a comptroller. It could be performed by a special auditing staff within the system or by the regular accounting personnel. The final decision as to the need or justification of the expenditure should rest with one who is familiar with the total *educational* needs of the school system.

The term "preaudit" is sometimes inappropriately used as a synonym for internal audit. As will be developed later, an internal audit occurs *after* financial transactions during a given accounting period have been consummated.

THE CONTINUOUS AUDIT

The *continuous* audit is in the grey area between auditing and accounting. There is some question as to whether this is a recognized classification of auditing or primarily a system of internal accounting control. In some governmental units there is a failure to distinguish between those operations which are accounting and those which are auditing. Records, items, transactions, entries, and statements are scrutinized continually to determine accuracy, but it is often impossible to determine where accounting ceases and auditing begins.[4]

In the continuous audit, the subsidiary records are closed (for example, weekly or monthly) and made available for audit in a controllable form. Under such an arrangement, the records, transactions entries, and statements are constantly being scrutinized for regularity and accuracy by a special internal auditing personnel. It is valuable in preventing errors but should not be regarded as a substitute for postauditing. The continuous audit is an internal audit. It is performed by personnel employed by the school district. There is no continuous audit report unless irregularities are detected and adjustments found necessary. The continuous audit does not have to be a complete general or special audit but may be limited to satisfy the needs of the occasion. The term "concurrent audit" is used on occasions in place of continuous audit.

POSTAUDIT

The *postaudit* is one performed after the fiscal transactions have been completed during an accounting period or fiscal year. Usually, when one speaks of auditing school accounts, he is referring to the postaudit. The postaudit takes place shortly after the end of a given financial period, which is usually the end of the fiscal year. The so-called annual school audit is a postaudit which takes place at the end of a given calendar or fiscal year. In contrast with the preaudit, which should be accomplished by an individual within the

[4] R. M. Mikesell, *Governmental Accounting*, Homewood, Ill.: Richard D. Irwin, Inc., 1951, p. 632.

system, the postaudit should be performed by an individual from without the system.

The postaudit can be a complete or limited general audit, or it can be a complete or limited special audit. Most state audit laws refer to the postaudit by implication but seldom define the scope and intensity of the audit. The description of auditing procedures in subsequent paragraphs will elaborate further the postaudit.

INTERNAL AND EXTERNAL AUDITS

Audits can be classified in terms of whether they are performed by personnel from within the school system or from without. An audit which is performed by an employee of the school district for the purposes of internal control is called an internal audit. An internal audit is often limited in intensity of investigation but usually involves: (1) verification and appraisal of the reliability of accounting records and statistical data, (2) ascertainment that assets of all kinds are safeguarded and have been properly accounted for and that the accounting process provides information that discloses losses and wasteful practices, (3) determination that operating units are complying with management-prescribed plans, policies, and procedures, and (4) reporting of observations with recommendations for improvement.[5] Internal audit activity is concerned primarily with the verification and critical review of the *completed* financial transactions and records. It is a way of developing improvements in the accounting system.

The internal auditor of an institution is often called upon to make special studies, covering such divers matters as a review of methods of accounting for control and an analysis of plans of accounting and other responsibilities. The internal auditor's responsibility in the development, maintenance, and appraisal of adequate internal checks is his principal contribution toward making fraud difficult and toward the early discovery of frauds in the process of daily methods and control. His concern is not only with the amount involved in a fraud, but also with fraudulent devices used and ways to check and control such devices in the future.

As one of the elements of managerial control, internal auditing is receiving increasing recognition and management acceptance in fields outside education. There is little evidence available on the status of internal auditing in public schools at this writing. In any

[5] Erich Kohler, *A Dictionary for Accountants*, Englewood Cliffs, N.J.: Prentice-Hall, Inc., 1952, pp. 228–230.

school system of moderate to large size, it can prove to be an effective aid, which is limited only by the abilities and background of the internal auditor himself. The internal audit is similar to the continuous audit, which was defined previously as an audit which is performed continuously or at intervals during the fiscal period with the purpose of uncovering and correcting any undesirable practices and errors before the end of the year. In substance, the internal audit is one made by persons on the staff of the school district whose accounts are being audited primarily for purposes of internal control.

As the name implies, an external audit is one performed by an individual not employed by the school district. The term "independent audit" is synonymous with external audit and indicates that the person doing the audit is independent from the usual controls of the executive head of the school unit. An audit by the state department of public instruction or by the state financial examiner is one type of external or independent audit. An audit of school district financial transactions by a private firm or a certified public accountant is another illustration of an external or independent audit. The external or independent audit usually takes place after the conclusion of the fiscal year or other accounting period. In special cases, of course, it can also take place during the fiscal year, if unusual circumstances indicate that fraud or collusion is suspected. It is highly desirable that all postaudits be accomplished by external or independent auditors. On the other hand, audits designed primarily for internal control should be accomplished by employees of the school district.

A FINAL WORD ON VARIOUS
TYPES OF AUDITS

Unfortunately there is much confusion in the usage of auditing terminology in school business affairs. The classification offered is aimed at minimizing such confusion. Auditing, by definition, is an activity which involves systematic investigation, verification, and critical review of financial operations. This definition does not describe the scope, intensity, or time of the audit or by whom it should be carried out. To some the term implies a postaudit only and, therefore, a question is raised with reference to the propriety of such terms as preaudit or continuous audit. But any modifier for the term "audit" is acceptable so long as it describes a financial activity which is concerned with systematic investigation, verification, and critical review of entries

and transactions. Time, whether it is relative to the consummation of a single transaction during the fiscal period or after the fiscal period, is not a limiting factor in the definition of auditing in general.

POSTAUDIT PROCEDURES

There are many ways of examining and verifying the financial records and documents of the school district at the close of the fiscal period. It is necessary, therefore, that there be a clear understanding between the school district and its auditor on important points to be included in the independent postaudit. It is highly desirable that there be a written contract between the school district and the independent or external auditor. This contract should define the scope and intensity of the postaudit and when it is to begin. It is recommended that the postaudit commence no later than 60 days after the close of the school fiscal year and that the independent auditor's report be filed with school officials within 30 days after completion of work.[6]

For every fund classification in the school district to be examined in the postaudit there must be a study of its revenues or receipts, expenditures, assets, and liabilities. A very general list of activities performed in a postaudit would include:
1. Verification of opening balances.
2. Verification, analysis, and examination of sources of income and their proper posting.
3. Verification of disbursements.
4. Reconciliation of budget items with receipts and disbursements.
5. Examination of legal authorization for all expenditures.
6. Examination and analysis of budgeting procedures employed.
7. Verification of all accounts recorded.
8. Reconciliation of all invoices paid, with expenditures accounted for.
9. Examination of board of education minutes, insurance policies, contracts, and deeds (titles) to real estate.
10. Verification of assets and liabilities, bank balances, and so on.
11. Analysis and examination of bonded indebtedness.
12. Examination of capital assets, inventories, surplus accounts, vouchers payable, and so on.
13. Reporting of errors of method and method of recording uncovered in the course of the auditing.

[6] Loyal V. Norman, "Scope, Conduct, and Report of the School Audit," *American School Board Journal*, October, 1953, *127*:44–45.

14. A report on the accounting system employed, with recommendations for desirable and necessary changes if any.

A more specific outline of some of the major steps an auditor might follow in a complete general audit of expenditures, which represents only one aspect of the total audit problem, can be stated in the following manner.

C. Steps in Auditing Expenditures
1. General
   a. Check to determine if expenditures were properly authorized and incurred and properly charged to the appropriate fund and appropriations.
   b. Determine if expenditures are supported by itemized invoices, vouchers, contracts, or other supporting documents approved by the proper school official and they are so marked to prevent re-use.
   c. Determine if disbursements were made by checks which were properly signed against the school depository for authorized purposes.
   d. Carefully scrutinize the endorsements on checks.
   e. Verify the accuracy of disbursement records.
   f. Be on the alert for duplicate payments.
   g. Verify noncash expenditures; that is, in a departmental transfer and interdepartmental transactions, see that all expenditures are supported by vouchers properly authorized and that charges have been made to the proper accounts.
2. Appropriations
   a. Check appropriation ordinances to determine if they comply with those granted boards of education.
   b. Scrutinize appropriation authorizations.
   c. Test check charges to determine if made to proper appropriations.
   d. Examine appropriations to determine if they are properly encumbered. Determine if expenditures plus encumbrances are within appropriations.
3. Purchases (see also inventories of materials and also accounts or vouchers payable)
   a. Check purchasing procedures.
   b. Check prices paid against contracts issued.
   c. Test check footings, extensions, and discounts of invoices.
   d. Test check propriety of prices and methods of awarding of purchases.
   e. Determine if purchases are charged against proper appropriations.
   f. Note vendor's name and watch for irregularities such as false names and names of school officials and employees.
4. Payrolls
   a. Check salaries paid against salary schedule or contracts and also appropriations.
   b. Test check accuracy of payroll computations.
   c. Check payroll receipts or payroll checks against the payroll and scrutinize endorsements.

   d. Check retirement fund, garnishee, withholding tax, hospitalization insurance, and other deductions. Test check funds held for such purposes.
   e. Investigate uncommon methods of delivering pay to employees.[7]

LIMITATIONS OF THE INDEPENDENT ANNUAL POSTAUDIT

The primary purpose of an audit is to show financial status. At no time should the judgment of auditors regarding the desirability of educational expenditures be substituted for the judgment of school officials. It is not within the province of auditors to look into curriculum matters, educational policy, and attendance records of schools. A professionally prepared auditing specialist is an authority in accounting and auditing but not in education. An auditing official who refuses to stay within the bounds of financial advice oversteps his prudential function. There is a danger that certain auditing may produce undesirable controls over educational policies.

The limited knowledge an auditor may have of the legal aspects of public education may often result in his preparing a long list of illegal transactions. A more thorough understanding of the implied and discretionary powers of boards of education could prevent such embarrassment to both parties. An auditor who assumes the power to disallow educational expenditures made in good faith by the board of education, on the grounds that the expenditures are not specifically authorized by law, can definitely handicap at least for a time the actions of school boards attempting to find better practices through experimentation. "The control of educational policy should never be exercised through school fund audits."[8] It is not a legitimate function of auditors to enforce laws or to substitute their opinions for those of attorney generals. In matters of discretion and judgment on purely educational matters, auditors must yield to school boards.

One way of preventing independent auditors from assuming the role of judge and jury in determining the legality of educational expenditures is through state laws which specifically define what shall and shall not be the scope of the audit and the nature of the auditor's investigation and report. Some writers have noted that the various types of state auditors have a greater propensity to become "walking courts" than private or

[7] Adapted from National Committee on Governmental Accounting, *op. cit.*, pp. 215–216.

[8] National Education Association, Committee on Tax Education and School Finance, *Guides to the Development of State School Finance Programs*, Washington, D.C.: NEA, 1949, p. 9.

commercial auditing firms.[9] The tendency for state auditors to go beyond the bounds of financial examination and verification plus the cost of state audits prompts the recommendation that public schools be required to employ commercial or private auditors.

THE STATUS OF AUDITING IN
PUBLIC EDUCATION

The most common type of audit required by state laws is the annual independent audit. It is a post-audit requirement, either by stipulation or implication. In 1953–1954 the school districts in the following nine states were not required by law to have periodic financial audits: Arizona, Illinois, Kansas, Minnesota, Mississippi, Nebraska, Rhode Island, South Carolina, and Texas.[10] In Colorado, Iowa, Missouri, Montana, North Dakota, South Dakota, and Tennessee, some but not all school districts were required to have periodic financial audits. Local school financial accounting records were required to be audited in *all* districts in 32 states. In about two-thirds of the states where at least some of the school districts were compelled by law to have a financial audit of accounts, such audits were required annually. In one state, schools were required to have their accounts audited every three years, and in another state, audits were required every four years. Most state statutes are either vague or silent as to the scope of the school district audit. What accounts, items, records, documents, are to be verified, examined, and analyzed is usually left in the hands of the auditor rather than prescribed by law.

There seems to be little improvement in state statutes governing school-auditing practices. A recent study showed that 9 states made no mention of audits of school accounts in their laws.[11] In 1925, Smith reported that 11 states made no satisfactory provisions for auditing.[12] In 1935, Campbell[13] concluded that auditing requirements were satisfactory in only 15 of the 35 states he studied.

Chase and Morphet reported in 1949 that in some cases the costs of all audits are borne by the state

whereas in others it is borne by the local district.[14] After evaluating the school audit law in the 36 states of Alabama, Arkansas, California, Colorado, Connecticut, Delaware, Florida, Georgia, Idaho, Indiana, Iowa, Kentucky, Louisiana, Maine, Maryland, Massachusetts, Montana, New Hampshire, New Jersey, New Mexico, New York, North Carolina, North Dakota, Ohio, Oregon, Pennsylvania, Rhode Island, South Dakota, Tennessee, Utah, Vermont, Virginia, Washington, West Virginia, Wisconsin, and Wyoming, Norman concluded that no state had a school audit law which embodied all possible desirable features.[15] Relatively few states stipulate when the school audit is to commence. Only one state, Idaho, provides by law for the employment of school auditors under written contractual basis. Of the 36 states where specific school audit laws were found by Norman, only 19 required that a report be made of such school audits. Too much generality and indefiniteness existed among state statutes with respect to when the school audit should be made and when and to whom the reports of it should be rendered.[16]

AUDITING AGENCIES

According to a recent study auditing of school accounts was placed in the hands of 20 different agencies, ranging from the local school board to the state department.[17] The local school district was the agency most frequently charged with responsibility in school audit laws. In 29, or 72 percent, of the 40 states where at least some of the school districts were required to have periodic financial audits, the auditor designated was usually some official of the state government, such as a state auditor, state finance or tax agent department official, state comptroller, state examiner, or state department of education official.[18] A county official was recognized in only three states. Independent or certified accountants were recognized as auditors in 21 of the 40 states.

It can be said that a great variation exists in the auditing agencies employed by public schools. In many school systems laymen are used or appointed as auditors of the school district accounts. Usually it is a committee appointed by the local school board. Although

[9] Paul R. Mort and Walter C. Reusser, *Public School Finance,* New York: McGraw-Hill Book Company, rev. ed., 1951, pp. 194–195.

[10] Clayton D. Hutchins and Albert R. Munse, *Public School Finance Programs of the United States,* Misc. no. 22, U.S. Office of Education, Washington, D.C.: U.S. Government Printing Office, 1955, pp. 53–54.

[11] *Ibid.,* p. 54.

[12] J. E. Smith, *Current Practices and Procedures Relating to Financial Responsibilities and Accountability of Public School Funds,* Master's Thesis, Minneapolis: University of Minnesota, 1925.

[13] Raymond Guy Campbell, *State Supervision and Regulation of Budgetary Procedure in Public School Systems,* New York: Teachers College, Columbia University, 1935, pp. 94–95.

[14] Francis S. Chase and Edgar L. Morphet, *The Forty-Eight State School Systems,* Chicago: Council of State Government, 1949, p. 157.

[15] Loyal V. Norman, *Statutory Provisions for Public School Auditing in the United States,* Doctoral Dissertation, Nashville, Tenn.: George Peabody College for Teachers, 1953.

[16] *Ibid.*

[17] *Ibid.*

[18] Hutchins and Munse, *op. cit.,* p. 53.

such a committee of laymen would make no charge for services rendered, they are not in a position to perform professional auditing. There is evidence that the examination of school funds in some school districts is so superficial that it can hardly be described accurately as a postaudit. It is recognized as highly desirable that school districts use a professional auditor or a certified public accountant to execute postaudits.

The local school board is the most suitable instrumentality for directing an audit of the financial accounts of the district. The state should require an annual, complete general audit of all school transactions to be performed by an independent auditor. Furthermore, the school auditor should be required by law to file a written audit report. The law should further indicate the scope of the work to be completed and the areas outside of the domain of the school auditor.[19] The auditors should be employed on the basis of professional qualifications and experience in school accounting rather than on the basis of bids. Certified public accountants with experience and knowledge of school affairs should be given precedence over those lacking such preparation or experience.

The written contract between the school system and the auditor should include such things as:

1. Names of parties.
2. Date of contract.
3. Scope of the audit.
4. Period to be covered.
5. When work is to begin.
6. Action to be taken if accounts are not in condition for satisfactory audit at the time stipulated.
7. When the report is to be filed and to whom the report is to be sent.
8. Space and equipment to be provided for the auditor at the school.
9. The compensation.
10. Other items of interest in the conduct of the audit.

THE AUDIT REPORT

The National Committee on Governmental Accounting recommended the following outline for an auditing report which could be used for public school reports.

1. Letter of transmittal which should include (a) a statement of the scope and limitations of the audit; (b) a summary of the findings of the audit; (c) recommendations for changes in general accounting procedures; (d) commendation, if any, for efficient methods, procedures, and systems found in the financial system in operation; (e) criticisms as necessary of practices, procedures, policies, and facilities employed in executing financial transactions, (f) statement of errors in method or fact that were uncovered and auditor's judgment on such errors; (g) recommendations for improvements in the school's fiscal operation.
2. A financial section which contains the appropriate financial statements to support the summary and recommendations made in the report.
3. A statistical section to contain the statistical data on such items as cash receipts and disbursements, statement of bonds authorized but unissued by funds, statement of changes in bonds payable, tax rates and tax levies, and so on.[20]

The purpose of the report should be to convey to the public generally such information as it needs to judge the work of its selected and appointed representatives. It would be highly desirable to have at least a summary of the report published in a newspaper of local circulation.

There is no one form which all audit reports should follow. The following is the form and content of an annual postaudit for the Community Consolidated Schools of Evanston, Illinois.

1. *Table of Contents*
2. *Auditor's Certificate*
3. *Cash and Securities*—Summarized statement of the cash balance and short-term securities of various funds.
4. *Taxes Receivable*—Detailed tabulation of uncollectable taxes and the new levy.
5. *Monies Due from the State*—A tabulation of uncollected claims and transactions during the fiscal year.
6. *School Properties*—Tabulation of changes in school properties during the year.
7. *Insurance Coverage*—A tabulation of insurable values on buildings and contents in the district.
8. *Indebtedness*—A table of outstanding bonds and interest thereon.
9. *Comments on Operation*
   a. Revenues and expenditures of the various funds for the present year compared with those of preceding years.
   b. Comparison of rental income between the present year and those of past years.
   c. Tuition and fees of past years compared with those of the present year.
   d. Miscellaneous revenue trends.
   e. Comparison of average cash operating cost and cost per pupil by major budget items between the present and past fiscal year.
   f. Salaries and wages and other operating expenses by ma-

---

[19] Norman, *Statutory Provisions for Public School Auditing in the United States, op. cit.*

[20] National Committee on Governmental Accounting, *op. cit.*, pp. 210–211.

jor budget items for this year as compared with last year.

    g. Total number of teachers, salary range, and average salary of present year as compared with those of the previous year.

    h. Summary of capital outlay expenditures by schools.

    i. Adjustments of prior years.

10. *Exhibit 1*—Balance sheet showing assets, liabilities, and fund balances at the end of the fiscal year.

11. *Exhibit 2*—Statement of revenues and expenditure for present and previous years.

12. *Exhibit 3*—Statement of operating expenses by account numbers for present and previous years.

13. *Exhibit 4*—Summary of bonded indebtedness and interest payable.

14. *Exhibit 5*—Schedule of bond maturities and interest for the present and two future years.

15. *Exhibit 6*—Summary of amount available for construction purposes and other related commitments for the fiscal year.

16. *Appendix* with suggested changes in accounting procedures.[21]

To summarize, the report is a statement of the auditor's work and his expression of belief or opinion as to the propriety of financial statements.

SUMMARY

Auditing is a systematic means of determining the accuracy, integrity, and authenticity of accounting, vouchers, and other financial records and documents. Insofar as the functions of public education differ from private enterprises, school audit procedures and reports will differ from those of business and industry.

There are various types of audits. A general audit is comprehensive in scope whereas the special audit is narrower in range. A complete audit is intensive in analysis of transactions whereas a limited audit is based on a test check or sampling of financial events and documents. A preaudit is a critical investigation before transactions are consummated in contrast to a postaudit which takes place after the fiscal act. Time is not a limiting factor in auditing. Audits can be made before or after the consummation of a transaction or during or after the fiscal period.

Audits can be performed by district employees as in internal audits or by agencies independent of the dis-

[21] Oscar Lanphar, "An Adequate School Audit," *School Business Affairs,* Association of School Business Officials, June, 1954, *20:4.*

trict as in external audits. The so-called annual school audit is a postaudit. It is the most common type of audit required by statutory legislation.

An auditor functions most effectively as an expert in accounting or auditing and least effectively as an expert in educational philosophy and curriculum. Educational policy should never be exercised through school audits. On the other hand, lay committees seldom have the professional qualifications to perform audits.

There is evidence to indicate the need for improvement in school district audit laws. Relatively few laws stipulate when the school audit is to commence, the scope of the audit, and the qualifications of school auditors. The school district is the most suitable instrumentality for directing the school audit.

QUESTIONS

1. Why should preauditing be performed by a school employee instead of outside agencies?
2. Why should a postaudit also be an external audit?
3. What values would there be in employing an internal auditor in large school systems?
4. When is a complete special school audit justified?
5. What, if any, limitations and qualifications should be imposed upon an external auditor performing a postaudit?
6. Assume that you were given the responsibility for developing a school audit law in your state. What would you specify to be included in the new law and what would you modify or delete from the existing law in your state?

SELECTED REFERENCES

Hutchins, Clayton D., and Munse, Albert R., *Public School Finance Programs of the United States,* Miscellaneous no. 22, U.S. Office of Education, Washington, D.C.: U.S. Government Printing Office, 1955.

Mikesell, R. M., *Governmental Accounting,* Homewood, Ill.: Richard D. Irwin, Inc., 1951, chap. 22.

Morey, Lloyd, and Hackett, Robert P., *Fundamentals of Governmental Accounting,* New York: John Wiley and Sons, Inc., rev. ed., 1951, chap. 20.

Mort, Paul R., and Reusser, Walter C., *Public School Finance,* New York: McGraw-Hill Book Company, rev. ed., 1951, chap. 10.

National Committee on Governmental Accounting, *Municipal Accounting and Auditing,* no. 14, Chicago: the Committee, September, 1951, part 3.

Norman, Loyal V., "Scope, Conduct, and Report of the School Audit," *American School Board Journal,* October, 1953.

CHAPTER 9

Cost Accounting and Unit Cost Analysis for Public Schools

PUBLIC SCHOOL COSTS HAVE CONTINUED TO rise at a fairly rapid rate during the years following World War II. The interest of the public in educational costs has never been greater. Estimated total current expenditures for 1957–1958 were approximately $9.5 billion, a rise of 10 percent from the previous year. This compares with total current expenditures of approximately $2.7 billion for 1945–1946.

Except for the period of 1930–1940, public school costs have practically doubled every decade since 1910. Burke identified the following four factors to help explain the steady upward trend of public school expenditures:

1. Those related to attendance such as increased enrollments, longer terms, and improved attendance at schools. Over half the increase between 1910 and 1955 could be traced to attendance factors.
2. Those related to educational services offered and reflected in more comprehensive education programs and higher educational standards of people.
3. Those related to changes in price, particularly the value of the dollar. It took $2.74 to buy the same goods in 1955 that could be purchased with $1.00 in 1910.
4. Those related to economic changes such as rising living standards, income, and improved economic status of women. Salaries paid to public school teachers increased over 700 percent between 1910 and 1955.[1]

Cost accounting can be defined as that branch of accounting concerned with searching out and reporting all elements of the cost incurred in executing a specific activity or a unit of work. The Expenditure Accounts provide the basic data for reporting how much was spent on a given educational function. In a very broad sense, classifying expenditures under various account headings may be called cost accounting. Organized cost data have their origin in accounting systems. Total cost figures for current expenses, debt service, and capital outlay are obtained from Expenditure Accounts and comprise the basic or raw data for further cost analysis. In a strict sense there is more to cost accounting than classifying expenditures under various headings. As Kohler declared: "Included in the field of cost accounting are the design and operation of cost systems and procedures; the determination of costs by departments, functions, responsibilities, activities, products, territories, periods, and other units of forecasted future costs and standard or desired costs, as well as historical costs; the comparison of costs of different periods, of actual with estimated or standard costs, and of alternative costs; the presentation and interpretation of cost data as an aid to management in controlling current and future operations."[2]

Cost accounting for schools endeavors to ascertain and evaluate the cost of units of service performed for or units of benefits received by the public. The extreme difficulty of objectively measuring educational services or benefits forces public school cost accounting to be confined to recording how much was spent for definable areas or programs. Where the accounting systems are well designed and carefully maintained, the determination of costs of various educational programs is no great problem. The great errors and misinterpretations are found in attempts to evaluate the significance

[1] Arvid J. Burke, *Financing Public Schools in the United States,* New York: Harper & Brothers, rev. ed., 1957, pp. 105–111.

[2] Eric L. Kohler, *A Dictionary for Accountants,* Englewood Cliffs, N.J.: Prentice-Hall, Inc., 1952, p. 127.

of cost data. Cost figures can easily delude those who have but a smattering of knowledge of educational institutions and their systems of financial accounting.

Unit cost analysis or unit cost accounting goes a step further in an attempt to measure how much was accomplished at a given price.[3] Unit cost accounting attempts to determine output per standard measurable unit. This calls for well-designed and carefully maintained financial records as well as meaningful units to measure output. Unit cost analysis is a variation or refinement of cost accounting.

The fundamental purpose of unit cost analysis is to present and interpret cost data as an aid to management and administration in controlling current and future operations. This would include unit cost analysis for:

1. Ascertaining costs of operating a given school facility such as gymnasium or auditorium. Such measures are necessary if the rental charges to the public for using such facilities for noninstructional purposes are to be based on actual operating costs rather than merely nominal fees.
2. Judging the efficiency and practicality of certain school activities. Unit cost analysis can help to answer the question of whether it is cheaper to build custom furniture using district employed labor and facilities than to purchase such items on the open market. Unit cost analysis can be used to judge accurately the performance and operation of automotive and other school equipment.
3. Preparing the school budget for those activities which can be reduced to measurable units. More dependable budget estimates are possible where unit cost analysis of building operation and maintenance, in particular, have been carried out.
4. Estimating costs of proposed capital improvements.
5. Estimating costs within the school system of operating various educational services or programs, be they examined on the basis of departments or single subjects taught. There are dangers in interpreting the significance of such unit cost analysis. The fact that unit costs for music education at the high school level are higher than those for Latin instruction is no argument whatsoever for increasing, decreasing, or keeping stable the costs for music education. Such decisions must be settled on the basis of philosophical or educational values rather than unit costs. Unit cost analysis can be used to estimate fairly accurately what the expansion costs would be if expansion were deemed desirable.

[3] R. M. Mikesell, *Governmental Accounting*, Homewood, Ill.: Richard D. Irwin, Inc., 1951, p. 597.

6. Comparing educational costs in one community with another. Obtaining a cost figure is fairly simple but the dangers of misinterpretation of the significance of comparative educational costs are staggering. Much will be said about this in subsequent portions of this chapter.

It is the purpose of this chapter to review the fundamental factors to be considered in designing a system of cost accounting for schools as well as the difficulties encountered in any cost analysis of educational activities.

ALL COST STUDIES HAVE THEIR BASE IN ACCOUNTING

Sooner or later any attempt to study costs in public education must look to the system of accounting for the basic or raw data. The problems of selecting the appropriate unit for expressing costs will be discussed in a subsequent portion of this chapter. All unit cost analyses will reflect the limitations of the financial data available, particularly the design of the accounting system in use. This must be recognized in all attempts to compare costs among school systems in the same state and those in other states. To begin with there can be no meaningful and comparable data on educational costs among school systems within or without states unless there is a uniformity in accounting terminology and procedures. To illustrate, there can be no meaningful cost analyses on administrative costs among school systems unless there is agreement as to what shall and what shall not be included under the functional-character classification of ADMINISTRATION. There must be complete agreement that the salary paid principals is posted in the INSTRUCTION Expenditure Accounts rather than under ADMINISTRATION accounts. Likewise, without Clearing Accounts (or, as they were formerly referred to, Revolving Fund Accounts) considerable confusion will result. To illustrate, the costs of operation of the school lunch program will be extremely high in one school system if such expenditures are listed directly in Expenditure Accounts as compared with another which maintains a system of Clearing Accounts for posting income and expenditures for FOOD SERVICES.

It would be extremely difficult, if not impossible, to have meaningful unit cost analysis without designing an accounting system to satisfy such purposes. Unit cost of textbooks used in elementary schools as compared with those in secondary schools would involve laborious review of all transactions if there were no adequate distribution accounts or coding to identify actual costs for elementary school and secondary school textbooks. The unit cost of operating a school bus with one make of chassis and body as opposed to another can be facilitated if the accounting system is designed to identify individual bus expenditures readily as well as all expenditures for the entire transportation fleet. These factors point to the necessity of thinking through what financial information is desired before designing the detailed or distribution ledgers in the school accounting system. Unnecessarily detailed information or the recording of information not likely to be used in cost analysis is just so much "red tape." On the other hand, without detailed accounts careful unit cost studies are seriously hampered. Each school system must design the additional accounts needed beyond the minimum recommended in Chapter 7.

It is almost axiomatic that there can be no accurate cost accounting or unit cost analysis without planning an accounting system to accomplish such purposes. Sloppy or inconsistent posting of financial transactions in school accounts in one system as compared with careful posting in another makes it impossible to compare unit costs for educational services between the two systems since the basis used in arriving at such a cost cannot by definition be similar.

THE EDUCATIONAL PROGRAM AND COST ANALYSIS

The temptation to analyze the costs for educational programs is very great in spite of many pitfalls and great dangers of misinterpretation. One of the most common units of expressing costs of operating public schools is the total current expenditures per pupil in average daily attendance. These figures for the years 1933–1934 and for 1939–1940 through 1957–1958 are presented in Table 9. Of particular significance is the percent of increase over 1947–1948 figures. It can be seen that current expenditures for pupils in average daily attendance rose from $181.48 in 1947–1948 to an estimated $320.00 in 1957–1958. The estimated figures for 1957–1958 represent an increase of 76.3 percent over those for 1947–1948. But even such figures, although seemingly authoritative and prepared by officials at the U.S. Office of Education or estimated by the National Education Association Research Division, are open to serious questions

TABLE 9.   Total Current Expenditure per Pupil in Average Daily Attendance[a]

Year	Current Expenditure per Pupil in ADA	Percent Increase Over Previous Year	Percent Increase Over 1947–1948
1933–1934	67.48	—	—
1939–1940	88.09	—	—
1940–1941	92.38	—	—
1941–1942	98.31	—	—
1942–1943	104.85	—	—
1943–1944	116.99	—	—
1944–1945	125.41	—	—
1945–1946	136.41	—	—
1946–1947	152.80	—	—
1947–1948	181.48	—	—
1948–1949	197.65	8.9	8.9
1949–1950	210.34	6.4	15.9
1950–1951	224.23	6.6	23.6
1951–1952	247.36	10.3	36.3
1952–1953[b]	235.48	−4.8	29.8
1953–1954	268.42	14.0	47.9
1954–1955[b]	264.58	−1.4	45.8
1955–1956[b]	280.00	5.8	54.3
1956–1957[b]	300.00	7.1	65.3
1957–1958[b]	320.00	6.7	76.3

[a] Current costs (excluding capital outlay, interest, and debt retirement) divided by average daily attendance.
[b] National Education Association, Research Division, estimates.

as to the fundamental meaning and significance. Implicit in unit cost figures is the belief that the educational program or results are precisely the same in all school districts in all states. This is one of the fundamental fallacies in interpreting cost figures such as current expenditures per pupil in average daily attendance. No matter what degree of uniformity in the accounting systems in use, no matter what degree of care is taken in posting expenditures to the appropriate accounts, and no matter how precise is the unit for measuring educational load, the unit cost figures are subject to significant qualifications if they are not expressions of the same educational program or results. The truth of the matter is that educational programs in all school systems in the United States are not the same, which means that all unit cost figures so often used for comparative purposes must be duly qualified to have any value whatsoever. To say that so much per pupil in average daily attendance was spent in one system as compared with another is to beg many questions, not the least of which is "Why?"

To illustrate, one school system may include within its educational costs the service of guidance personnel or school psychologists and the other may not because such services are not available. One school system may operate a summer school program and the other does not. Not all school systems operate junior colleges or adult education programs. These are some of the more obvious differences in educational programs among school districts in one state or among states.

Cost figures for elementary education in one school are not always comparable with elementary education in another. In some school districts, elementary education consists of grades one through six only, whereas other states include kindergarten experiences and still others may think of grades seven and eight as belonging in the elementary school operation. Some schools operate for ten months and others operate for only nine months. Even if we assume that the same number of grade levels and the same period of operation are maintained, some elementary education programs are confined to the three R's alone, whereas others include the three R's plus enriched experiences in art, music, physical education, etc. If there is to be a defensible comparison of unit costs for elementary education, there must be supporting evidence that the grades included and the educational experiences offered are similar. And even where this is true, the educational experiences of children in one elementary school may not be of the same quality as those in another school. Some elementary schools are staffed with immature and inadequately prepared teachers—individuals with scarcely more than two years of professional preparation beyond high school —whereas in other schools elementary school teachers hold at least a bachelor's degree and many have earned master's degrees. Differences in professional preparation often result in differences in the salaries paid. One can presume that the better teachers will migrate to schools where higher salaries are found, and, therefore, there is the likelihood of an improved quality of education in elementary schools which have better prepared and better paid school teachers.

One could go even further and say that some elementary schools have professionally prepared principals at the helm with supervisors or consultants as resource persons to help the elementary school teachers do a more effective job in the classroom. Such services are aimed at improving instruction but are of necessity also more expensive. There is no more pernicious assumption in cost analysis than the one based on the premise that the educational program being measured in the unit cost study is precisely the same in all systems under consideration.

The same comments could be made with reference to a program of secondary education. Not all schools provide vocational agriculture or vocational home economics programs. Some schools have an extensive music program including vocal music, band instruction, and orchestra work. Others are fortunate if they have a person to direct the band a few periods a week. The great differences in educational programs in secondary schools make the average cost per pupil in average daily attendance of questionable value.

This can be illustrated by the information presented in Table 10. The number of pupils in average daily attendance, unit costs per pupil in average daily attendance, and units of educational opportunity in 831 Iowa high schools in 1950–1951 are presented in this table. The average cost per pupil in average daily attendance in Iowa high schools in 1950–1951 that have an average daily attendance of from 0–25 pupils was $459.18. This average unit cost figure declined as the number in average daily attendance in the high school increased until a high school size of between 401–425 in average daily attendance was reached. It then began to climb so that in the large high schools of over 500 the average cost per pupil in average daily attendance was $282.67. Now this average unit cost is about one-half the average cost in the very small high schools with average daily attendances of 0–25 pupils.

In column four of this table is presented the average number of units of educational opportunity for each high school size. The unit of educational opportunity is defined as the offering of one subject matter unit for one full year. If the subject matter unit was offered for only one semester of the year, it was the equivalent of one-half unit. The very small high schools in Iowa had 17 units of educational opportunities as compared with 51.9 units of educational opportunity in the very large high schools (average daily attendance of 500 and above). A new cost unit could be computed based on the three factors of (1) total cost for current expenses, (2) number of pupils in average daily attendance, and (3) the average number of units of educational opportunity. The average cost per pupil in average daily attendance per unit of educational opportunity in very small high schools (average daily attendance of 0–25) is about five times that of very large high schools (average daily attendance of 500 and above). Unit cost analysis based on some measure of equality of the educational program (no matter how crude) as well as the cost per given pupil unit buttresses the argument that small schools not only cost more per pupil unit but offer less for this high cost.

Again it is emphasized that it is wrong to assume that the educational program purchased through the expenditures of monies from the general fund, excluding capital outlay, debt service, and interest, is precisely the same in all school districts being measured. It does not necessarily follow that a school with a lower cost per pupil unit is a better or more efficient school than one with a higher cost. The scope and quality of the educational program must be known to place unit costs in perspective.

Unit costs for elementary school operation will be lower than those for secondary schools, so long as different certification standards for elementary and secondary teachers prevail and so long as there are differences in the scope of these programs. Unit costs for public school districts where large numbers of pupils are enrolled in elementary but not secondary parochial schools will be higher than usual because of a pre-

TABLE 10. Costs per Pupil in Average Daily Attendance and Units of Educational Opportunity in 831 Iowa High Schools in 1950–1951

No. of Schools (1)	ADA in High School (2)	Average Cost per Pupil in ADA (3)	Average No. of Units of Educational Opportunity (4)	Average Cost per Pupil in ADA per Unit of Educational Opportunity (5)
50	0–25	$459.18	17.0	$27.31
237	26–50	384.86	19.1	20.05
202	51–75	341.35	21.5	15.94
102	76–100	302.83	23.4	13.00
76	101–125	309.81	25.6	12.17
32	126–150	288.73	27.6	10.52
22	151–175	290.20	29.4	9.91
15	176–200	299.83	30.4	9.94
10	201–225	279.38	31.7	8.83
11	226–250	284.36	33.5	8.49
9	251–275	281.36	34.6	8.13
9	276–300	271.79	34.5	7.92
13	301–325	282.67	37.1	7.66
2	326–350	321.59	42.8	7.54
8	351–375	247.48	36.1	6.94
3	376–400	287.60	37.8	7.61
1	401–425	216.32	34.0	6.36
5	426–450	264.51	40.9	6.59
2	451–475	273.03	40.5	6.75
1	476–500	258.80	37.5	6.90
21	500 & Above	282.67	51.9	5.61
831				

SOURCE: Roderick B. Peck, *Influence of Enrollment and Expenditures upon Quality of Education in Iowa High School Districts*, Master's Thesis, Ames, Iowa: Iowa State College, 1952.

ponderance of public secondary school students as compared with public elementary school students.

SELECTING APPROPRIATE UNITS FOR COST ANALYSIS

The most frequently used unit in cost analysis is one of many per pupil units. To say that the annual public school current expenditures totaled $250 per pupil is to beg the question "what kind of pupil?" The pupil who attends school half-days is not similar to one who attends school all day. A high school pupil is not the equivalent of an elementary school pupil. A pupil who attends school in a densely populated school district is not the same as one who attends school in a sparsely populated school district. A handicapped pupil or a gifted pupil requires services different from those of large numbers of pupils in the normal range.

In addition, the unit may be based on the number of pupils in the school census, in the enrollment, in average daily attendance, or in average daily membership. Each of the various per capita units has its advantages and disadvantages. They do not reflect the educational load or program to the same degree. To illustrate, the number of pupils in the school census is subject to the following criticisms:

1. The school census is taken at a certain date during the year. Following the original canvass few school systems accurately account for in-migration or out-migration. School census taking is notorious for inaccuracies.
2. It fails to measure adequately the public school load as there is no allowance for pupils of school census age who attend private schools or schools in other districts.
3. The age limits (most commonly between the ages of 5 and 21) may include children who are not yet in school or those who have already completed school.
4. It ignores differences in length of term and pupil-teacher ratios.[4]

The other per pupil units are more refined measures as compared with the pupils of school age but are subject to many variations.

The most frequently used raw per capita unit is the per pupil unit in average daily attendance. This per pupil unit is computed by adding the aggregate days of attendance of all pupils and dividing this by the number of days school was actually in session. The number of pupils in average daily attendance is divided into the total educational costs to obtain the cost per pupil in

[4] Burke, *op. cit.*, p. 414.

average daily attendance. Although the mathematics is precise in computing such unit costs, there is no universally accepted definition of average daily attendance. Some states permit all pupils to be counted in attendance and school in session when teachers attend the state teachers' meeting. Others rule that the child is in attendance if he reports during the first one-half hour of the day even though he may be excused later to go home. Others require attendance for the full morning before half-day credit for attendance is given. Some laws permit the school districts to eliminate certain days, such as those when attendance is low because of bad weather or epidemics, in computing averages of attendance. Other states allow districts to compute the average daily attendance on the basis of their best 100 or more days or best attendance months during the school year.

As a raw measure of educational burden, the average daily membership is a better unit than the average daily attendance. The teacher's salary must be paid whether the pupils are in 85 or 100 percent attendance. The desk and school books must be available to all students who are in membership, whether they are in attendance or not. As raw per capita units go, the average daily membership is a better unit to measure educational burden than the more commonly used average daily attendance unit. Tradition has favored the average daily attendance unit over that of average daily membership.

All raw per capita units for measuring costs in the system as a whole are subject to limitations because educational programs for elementary and secondary students are not the same. Usually little recognition is given to the number of handicapped, part-time, or other special types of pupils in attendance. Weighting can be used to overcome some of the disadvantages of raw per pupil units employed in educational cost analysis. The weighting should give recognition to cost differences between elementary and secondary pupils, price levels in various communities, sparsity, and other factors in programs for special pupils. Often this requires careful statistical analysis. One of the most pressing needs in cost analysis is the development of a weighted pupil unit which more accurately reflects the educational burden of the school district, which is easy to compute, and which will be uniformly accepted throughout the nation.

Burke reported a simple but rough weighting procedure which acknowledges different proportions of elementary and secondary school pupils only in the district as follows:

1. Divide the number of pupils in half-day attendance by two.

2. Multiply the secondary school attendance (grades seven through twelve) by 1.25 or some other ratio on the assumption that secondary school costs are at least that percent higher than elementary school costs.
3. Add (1) and (2) to the number of pupils in full-day attendance in grades kindergarten through six.
4. Divide the net current expenditures by (3) above.[5]

OTHER UNITS USED IN UNIT COST COMPARISONS

For all its limitations, the per pupil in average daily membership or average daily attendance is probably best adapted to measure total educational costs or many costs per functional-character classification. There are limitations to the various refined

[5] *Ibid.,* p. 129.

and crude per pupil units. Per pupil units are not as satisfactory as other units, particularly in measuring the operation and maintenance of school plants.

The most frequently mentioned tabulation of cost units was prepared by Engelhardt and Engelhardt in 1927. It is shown below.[6]

The numerator and denominator used in computing unit costs must be compatible and comparable.

JOB ORDER UNIT COST ANALYSIS

Operation and maintenance often involve many activities whose analysis into cost units can be executed on the basis of the specific job performed. Schools having combination gymnasium-auditoriums

[6] N. L. Engelhardt and Fred Engelhardt, *Public School Business Administration,* New York: Teachers College, Columbia University, 1927, p. 789.

Item	Suggested Unit of Cost
1. Total Educational Cost	Per pupil in ADA
2. Building Cost	Per cubic foot
3. Administrative Cost	Per pupil in ADA
4. Instructional Cost	Per pupil in ADA
5. Supervision Cost	Per teacher supervised
6. Attendance Cost	Per pupil in ADA
7. Instructional Supply Cost	Per pupil in ADA
8. Special Activities	Per pupil in ADA
9. Janitorial Supply Cost	Square feet of floor space
10. Sanitary Supply Cost	Per pupil in ADA
11. Maintenance Cost	Square feet of floor area or value
12. Operation Cost (Cleaning)	Square feet of floor area or value
13. Auxiliary Agencies	Per pupil in ADA
14. Janitor Service	Square feet of floor area
15. Teaching a subject	Per pupil-hour or per pupil in ADA

Some of these units have been modified. Some new units often used are:

Item	Suggested Unit of Cost
a. Transportation Costs	Per pupil or per bus mile or per pupil bus mile
b. Cafeteria Costs	Per meal or per pupil served
c. School Building Cost	Per square feet or per square foot of instructional floor area or per elementary classroom unit
d. Instructional Cost	Per teacher or per classroom unit or per weighted teacher or classroom unit
e. Administrative Cost	Per teacher or per classroom unit
f. Heating Costs	Per cubic foot
g. Total Value of School Property	Per pupil enrolled
h. Educational Costs	Total expenditures per capita, or total expenditures per pupil in ADA or ADM, or current expenditures per pupil in ADA or ADM

find it frequently necessary to set up chairs when this combination facility is used for auditorium purposes. By keeping records such as work orders, the estimated time to complete such work and its cost equivalent can be readily computed. Such cost analysis can be used as the basis for assessing rental or set-up costs to non-school groups (or student body activities) using such facilities during or after school hours.

The job order unit cost analysis is also of value where a specific department, such as an equipment repair department, does repairing, remodeling, or over-hauling of equipment for other departments. Through a job cost sheet the amount of labor and equipment can be computed for each piece of equipment fixed by the repair department. In addition to materials and labor, overhead costs to cover supervisory or administrative or other general costs in operating repair departments are often assessed.

Where a unit cost analysis of specific activities is desired, it is recommended that a requisition for repair or set-up or other services be filed with business officials. This request activates the execution of a work order to direct personnel in school transportation or building operation and maintenance to perform some duty. These workers charged with the responsibility would then complete a job cost record to report on costs involved. Illustration of these forms follow.

COST-QUALITY COMPUTATIONS IN EDUCATION

One of the more intriguing problems in education is to determine the relationship between the costs of an educational program and its quality. Paul R. Mort and his associates have done a considerable

FORM 11.

ORDER FOR SPECIAL WORK FOR THE SCHOOL DISTRICT OF SMITHVILLE, U.S.A.

To _____ (Person or Department)   No. _____

For _____ (Person or Department)   Date _____

Please perform the following work:

_____

(A Description of the Work Desired)

_____

Work to Start _____ (Time and Date)

Estimated Completion Date _____ (Time and Date)

Signed _____ (Authorized Business Official or Superintendent)

Please prepare cost record for materials, labor, and overhead.

amount of research in this area.[7] Several instances have been reported of the positive relationship between cost and quality of education. In many such cases, it has been emphasized that causal relationships cannot be inferred but the writer proceeds to elaborate in such a way as to smother the effect of the caution. Perhaps the most perplexing problem in cost-quality studies is the extreme difficulty in measuring educational outcome. Observers of an educational scene have used direct observation as a means to discern changes that have taken place within the classroom or within the pupils. Achievement test results are fairly objective and can be used for comparative purposes

[7] Paul R. Mort, "Cost-Quality Relationships in Education" in R. L. Johns and E. L. Morphet (eds.), *Problems and Issues in Public School Finance,* New York: Teachers College, Columbia University, 1952, pp. 9–64.

FORM 12.

JOB COST RECORD FOR THE SCHOOL DISTRICT OF SMITHVILLE, U.S.A.

Job No. _____

Description of Work Performed _____

For _____ (Name of Requesting Department)

Completed _____

Date	Explanation	Materials	Labor	Overhead	Total Costs

TOTALS _____

Signed _____ (Worker)   Checked by _____

to some degree. On the other hand, what a person does in a test may not indicate what he is likely to do in life. Furthermore, it is hoped that education can yield better health, emotional stability, the desire to learn, etc. At present it is extremely difficult, if not impossible, to measure precisely such qualities and to relate them to expenditures for education.

Most of the cost-quality studies must of necessity, therefore, be interpreted with care lest zealousness replace the scientific attitude. What is lacking is the development of precise instruments to measure quality in education. The best we have at the present time are instruments which measure certain factors such as length of school term, the professional preparation of teachers, the availability of equipment, and so on, which can be used to good advantage when one presumes that such factors will result in a higher quality of education than if these factors did not exist.

This is not to imply that cost-quality studies should cease. There is a need for seeking answers in this vital area. Through continuing efforts in this complex area, more precise instruments for measuring quality in education may be developed. When quality in education can be directly and objectively measured, unit cost analysis of quality and educational expenditures will become more meaningful.

ANALYSIS OF TOTAL CURRENT EXPENDITURES BY EACH OF THE SIX MAJOR ACCOUNT CLASSIFICATIONS

For various reasons analyses have been made of the percent of the total current expenses of the schools that have been devoted to the previously defined six major accounting classifications of Administration, Instruction, Auxiliary Services, Operation of Plant, Maintenance, and Fixed Charges. The recency of the revised accounting classifications recommended in Chapter 7 and in the 1957 USOE financial handbook for public schools precludes analyses on the basis of 14 functional-character classifications. What has been referred to as Auxiliary Services (or Other Services) is considered in Chapter 7 as six different account series of ATTENDANCE SERVICES, HEALTH SERVICES, PUPIL TRANSPORTATION SERVICES, FOOD SERVICES, STUDENT BODY ACTIVITIES, and COMMUNITY SERVICES. A relatively small portion of the school budget is presently devoted to these six new account series specified in the previous sentence, and analyses of total current expenditures remain of significance even though the term "Auxiliary Services" is used.

The percent of 1956–1957 total current expenditures in each of the previously designated six major account classifications for 789 Iowa school districts maintaining high schools is presented in Table 11. The enrollment data are based on high school students only, although the computations were based on high school and elementary school students. It can be seen that the smaller the school, the larger the percent of the total current expenditures devoted to such accounting classifications as Administration, Auxiliary Services, and Fixed Charges. The percent of the total current expenditures spent for Maintenance and Operation is fairly constant. It should likewise be noted that the smaller the enrollment classification of the high school, the smaller the percent of the total current expenditures devoted to Instruction. Thus, in the schools with high school enrollment of less than 100, 60.5 percent of the total current expenditures is devoted to Instruction; whereas in schools having high school enrollments of 600 or more, 74.4 percent of the total current expenditures is devoted to Instruction. For this state as a whole, 4.84 percent of the total current expendiures was devoted to Administration, 67.54 percent to Instruction, 6.8 percent to Auxiliary Services, 10.97 percent to Operation of Plant, 4.32 percent to Maintenance of Plant, 5.45 percent to Fixed Charges. This is a picture of the distribution of expenditures in a state characterized by many school districts with small enrollments. In the following paragraph the same analysis is made for the small, medium-sized, and large city school districts.

The trends in the percent of the total current expenditures in each of the previously designated six major account classifications in various size cities are presented in Table 12. It can be seen that during the 20-year period from 1935–1936 to 1955–1956, the percent devoted to total current expenditures in each category appears to be fairly constant. Very small changes took place in Administration, Operation, Maintenance, and Auxiliary Services in the city systems studied. Some changes, but with varying magnitude, were noted in the percent of current expenditures devoted to Instruction and Fixed Charges.

The experiences of individual states are not reflected in national figures for cities. McClure reported trends in current operating expenditures in Illinois public elementary and secondary schools for the years 1933–1934 to 1954–1955.[8] In the Illinois schools the percent of the total current operating expenditures during the 20-year period increased from 2.2 percent to 4.0 percent for General Control; decreased from 70.9 percent

[8] William P. McClure, *Educational Cost Analysis*, Bureau of Educational Research, Urbana, Ill.: College of Education, University of Illinois, March, 1957, p. 19.

TABLE 11. Percent of Total Current Expenditures[a] in Each of the Six Major Accounts in 789 Iowa School Districts Maintaining High Schools in 1956–1957

Number of Districts	Enrollment of High School Only	Administration	Instruction	Auxiliary[b] Services	Operation of Plant	Maintenance	Fixed Charges	Total per Pupil Cost in ADA
25	600 & Above	2.9	74.4	4.9	11.4	4.5	4.1	$287.21
8	500–599	3.5	70.8	4.9	10.9	4.5	5.4	262.99
15	400–499	4.2	70.0	5.4	10.8	4.2	5.4	267.09
31	300–399	4.9	68.7	6.4	10.8	4.0	5.2	283.62
48	200–299	5.5	65.2	9.6	10.2	4.0	5.5	287.01
65	150–199	7.1	63.3	9.6	10.1	3.7	6.2	293.73
144	100–149	6.4	62.9	10.2	10.7	3.7	6.1	299.20
453	0–99	6.4	60.5	10.3	11.2	4.8	6.9	336.82
789		4.85	67.54	6.87	10.97	4.32	5.45	$297.30

[a] Excludes capital outlay, debt service, interest, and so-called "special courses" fund.
[b] This classification is presently broken down into Attendance Services, Health Services, and Pupil Transportation Services.

TABLE 12. Trends in Percent of the Total Current Expenditures

Year	Administration in City Group[a]				Instruction in City Group[a]				Operation in City Group[a]			
	I	II	III	IV	I	II	III	IV	I	II	III	IV
1936–1937	3.1	3.3	3.7	5.4	77.7	77.5	75.3	72.7	9.0	10.9	11.7	11.7
1940–1941	3.1	3.4	4.1	5.6	77.1	77.4	75.2	72.5	9.4	11.8	12.4	12.1
1945–1946	3.2	3.3	4.2	5.6	73.8	74.8	73.4	71.2	11.1	10.4	12.0	12.1
1950–1951	3.3	3.0	3.5	4.5	72.6	76.1	75.4	74.3	9.9	10.8	11.3	10.3
1955–1956	2.9	2.8	3.2	4.0	72.6	76.1	75.4	73.8	9.8	10.8	10.7	10.3
20-Year Change in Percent	−0.2	−0.5	−.05	−1.4	−5.1	−1.4	+0.1	+1.1	+0.8	−0.1	−1.0	−1.4

Percent of Total Current Expense Dollar Used for

[a] Group I cities have populations of 100,000 or more.
Group II cities have populations of 25,000 to 100,000 (in 1950 and before the range for this group was 30,000 to 99,999).

to 65.1 percent for Instruction; increased from 17.6 percent to 18.7 percent for Operation and Maintenance; increased from 3.5 percent to 11.0 percent for Auxiliary Services; increased from 0.6 percent to 0.9 percent for Fixed Charges; and decreased from 5.2 percent to 0.3 percent for Interest Charges. McClure's grouping was a little different from those specified in the previous paragraph. In the Illinois schools and in the city schools of the nation the percent devoted to Instruction declined.

There is no one optimum percent level that should be spent for Administration, Instruction, Operation, Maintenance, Auxiliary Services, or Fixed Charges. There is considerable variation in the percent of amounts allocated to each major expenditure classification as indicated in Table 13. The percents allocated to Administration in very large cities with populations of 100,000 or more vary from 1.1 percent to 6.2 percent. Variation in expenditures for Instruction in these same large cities ranges from 63 percent to 86.6 percent. The evidence is clear that there is a considerable variation among cities of all sizes in the percent of the total current expenditures devoted to each of the six previously designated major account classifications.

PRORATING AND EXPENDITURE ANALYSIS

Unit cost analysis is more meaningful when based on careful prorating of expenditures. This is no problem if the expenditure can be classified in one account. Thus, the salary of a full-time secondary school teacher is posted to the INSTRUCTION account under the subaccount for salaries paid to secondary school teachers. On the other hand, it often happens that the building custodian is also the bus driver. What part of the salary of the custodian-bus driver shall be devoted to TRANSPORTATION and what part to OPERATION? If he does maintenance work as well, what part shall be devoted to MAINTENANCE? Likewise, an itinerant music teacher may teach music to secondary and to elementary school students. How much of this teacher's salary shall be prorated to elementary school teachers' salaries and how much to secondary school teachers' salaries?

Prorating school expenditures to various accounting classifications is of major concern in this day and age of expanding educational programs and increased use of educational facilities for adult education and community purposes. This is particularly true in the small school system where so many staff members must "double-in-brass." Heating, lighting, janitorial services, supervision, administration, etc., must be prorated carefully if there is to be any hope for a meaningful unit cost analysis. Uniformity in prorating procedures is necessary if there is to be any significance attached to unit cost figures for school systems from within or without the state.

It is easy to ignore the problem of prorating expenditures. It is not unusual to find school systems charging the entire salary of the bus driver-custodian to OPERA-

Percent of Total Current Expense Dollar Used for

Maintenance in City Group[a]				Auxiliary Services in City Group[a]				Fixed Charges in City Group[a]			
I	II	III	IV	I	II	III	IV	I	II	III	IV
3.9	3.7	4.2	4.0	2.4	2.5	3.4	4.2	3.9	2.1	1.7	2.0
3.9	3.9	3.9	4.1	1.6	2.0	2.9	3.9	4.9	1.5	1.5	1.8
4.3	4.4	4.1	3.9	2.9	3.1	3.8	5.2	5.4	2.4	2.4	2.6
5.4	5.6	4.9	5.1	2.9	2.3	1.8	3.6	5.9	2.2	3.1	2.2
4.7	4.8	4.1	4.0	3.3	2.6	3.4	4.9	6.7	2.9	3.2	3.0
+0.8	+1.1	−0.1	—	+0.9	+0.1	—	+0.7	+2.8	+0.8	+1.5	+1.0

Group III cities have populations of 10,000 to 25,000 (in 1950 and before the range for this group was 10,000 to 29,999).
Group IV cities have populations of 2500 to 10,000.

TABLE 13. Range in Percent of Total Current Expenditure in Each of the Six Major Accounts for Various Sized Cities

Major Account	Range in Percent of Amount Allocated in Each City Size			
	Group I (Over 100,000)	Group II (25,000– 100,000)	Group III (10,000– 25,000)	Group IV (2500– 10,000)
Administration	1.1– 6.2	1.4– 4.7	1.2– 7.9	1.4–10.5
Instruction	63.3–86.6	64.5–87.7	56.6–91.1	60.3–90.8
Operation of Physical Plant	6.2–17.4	6.5–14.9	4.0–21.3	4.0–17.5
Maintenance of Physical Plant	0.6– 9.8	1.4–13.0	0.4–14.5	0.2–17.9
Other School Services[a]	0.2–15.0	0.0–12.5	0.0–21.0	0.0–16.4
Fixed Charges	0.1–14.3	0.1– 9.7	0.0–10.6	0.0–10.9

a Previously called Auxiliary Services. Soon to be broken down into Health, Attendance, Transportation, and Other Services.
SOURCE: Lester B. Herlihy and Joel Williams, *Current Expenditures per Pupil in Public School Systems*, Large Cities, 1955–1956, Circular no. 500; and Small and Medium-Sized Cities, 1955–1956, Circular no. 501; U.S. Office of Education, Washington, D.C.: U.S. Government Printing Office, 1957.

TION since the janitor spends comparatively little time in driving the bus. Also, if the music teacher spends a major portion of time teaching secondary school pupils, the salary is usually assigned to secondary school expenditures rather than to elementary school expenditures. Although this procedure is a simple one, it will show excessive sums of money being spent on certain activities and almost little or no money for others. Likewise, it can hardly be called an accurate way to provide information on school costs for various purposes.

The method of proration recommended in the 1957 USOE financial accounting handbook for local and state school systems is strongly recommended for all school systems.[9] The seven methods of proration recommended in this handbook are based on (1) time, (2) average daily membership or average daily attendance, (3) time-floor area, (4) hour consumption, (5) number of pupils, (6) mileage, and (7) quantities consumed.

The time method of prorating is based on allocating the expenditures in proportion to the time spent in each of the various activities. To illustrate, if a teacher of music spends 60 percent of her time with elementary

9 Paul L. Reason and Alpheus L. White, *Financial Accounting for Local and State School Systems, Standard Receipt and Expenditure Accounts*, Bulletin 1957, no. 4, U.S. Office of Education, Washington, D.C.: U.S. Government Printing Office, 1957, pp. 130–139.

school pupils and 40 percent with secondary school students, 60 percent of her salary would be recorded under Salaries for Elementary Teachers and 40 percent would be posted under Salaries for Secondary School Teachers. Likewise, if a teacher in a high school spent 80 percent of her time teaching and 20 percent of her time in directing the student council, 80 percent of her salary would be recorded in INSTRUCTION accounts and 20 percent under STUDENT BODY ACTIVITIES.

The method of proration based on average daily membership or average daily attendance consists of allocating a part of an expenditure in proportion to the average daily membership or attendance of pupils engaged in the activities. Time spent by the pupils in these activities is also given recognition. It would be more accurate to refer to this as the average daily membership time or average daily attendance time method of proration. Assume for purposes of illustration that a superintendent is paid $16,000 a year and administers the adult education program as well as the regular day school. Assume further that the regular day school has an average daily membership of 3000 pupils and the adult education program has an average daily membership of 1000 adults. The regular day school operates 5 hours a day, 5 days a week, or 25 hours per week. On the other hand, the adult education program is in session 2½ hours a night for two nights, or 5 hours per week. The adult education classes are in session only one-fifth (5 hours as compared with 25) of the time the regular day school is. The adjusted average daily membership for adult education is 1000 divided by 5, or 200. The adjusted average daily membership for the school system as a whole would be 3000 (regular day school) plus 200 (adjusted adult education) or 3200. The part of the $16,000 salary to be charged for the administration of the regular day school is the ratio of 3000 average daily membership to 3200 average daily membership. The computation would be:

Administrative Costs for Regular Day School =
$$\frac{3000}{3200} \times \$16,000 = 15 \times \$1000 = \$15,000.$$

In other words, $15,000 would be charged to regular day school administrative salary costs and $1000 to adult education. The same approach would be followed if average daily attendance were used in place of average daily membership.

In the time-floor area method expenditures are allocated to various accounts in proportion to (1) the gross floor area used by the activity and (2) the length of time the floor area is used. Assume for purposes of argument that the custodial costs for a building used by secondary school students and an adult education program totaled $15,000. Assume further that the secondary school opens at 8:00 A.M. and the students must leave the building at 5:00 P.M. The building is used by secondary school students for various purposes for 9 hours a day, 5 days a week, or 45 hours per week. The evening school, on the other hand, starts at 6:30 P.M. and closes at 9:30 P.M., or 3 hours a night for 5 nights a week, a total of 15 hours per week. The entire 60,000 square feet in the building is used by the secondary school students whereas the adult education programs utilize only 18,000 square feet. In other words, the high school uses 60,000 square feet for 45 hours a week and the adult education program utilizes 18,000 square feet for 15 hours a week. Based on the floor area alone the part of the $15,000 that would be charged to adult education accounts would be the ratio of 18,000 square feet to 60,000 square feet, or 30 percent of the $15,000. Thirty percent of the $15,000 is $4500. On the other hand, the adult education program makes use of the floor space only one-third of the time high school students do. An additional correction must be allowed. The amount chargeable to the adult education program would be one-third of the $4500 or $1500. In other words, the $15,000 for custodial services would be prorated on the following basis: $1500 to the adult education program and $13,500 to the secondary education program.

The hour-consumption method for prorating involves allocating the expenditures in proportion to the length of time used and the hourly rate at which materials, utilities, or services are consumed. It is most useful for computing expenditures for water, electricity, and gas except for heating. Where the adult education program uses school shops, the hourly rate of consumption of utilities would be multiplied by the number of hours the shops were used by adult education classes. Precise unit cost analysis is possible if the shops and other facilities likely to be used in adult or community programs are metered separately. The hourly rate of consumption can be determined from a study of meter readings over an extended period of time. It is necessary to estimate the hourly rate of consumption if there are no separate meters. The local utility company is often available to help in making such estimates.

The number-of-pupils method of prorating is based on allocating expenditures in proportion to the actual number (not average daily membership or average daily attendance) of pupils. This method of prorating is used primarily where special groups of pupils (such as non-public school pupils) are transported in regular public school buses. For example, if 1000 pupils were transported at public expense over regular bus routes and in this total were 200 who were not public school pupils, the expenditures could be prorated as follows: one-fifth charged to COMMUNITY SERVICES accounts and four-fifths charged to PUPIL TRANSPORTATION SERVICES accounts.

The mileage method for prorating consists of allocating the expenditure to a given activity in proportion to the mileage traveled. As is obvious, this is most useful for expenditures for special kinds of transportation services such as field trips or athletic contests.

The quantity-consumed method is based on the actual consumption of supplies or commodities in the given activity. With such a procedure it is necessary to

TABLE 14, I.   Methods for Prorating Between Program Areas

Expenditure Accounts (1)	Methods for Prorating						
	Time (2)	Time-Floor Area (3)	ADM or ADA (4)	Hour Consumption (5)	Number of Pupils (6)	Mileage (7)	Quantity Consumed (8)
ADMINISTRATION							
Salaries	P	—	A	—	—	—	—
Other Expenses	—	—	P	—	—	—	—
INSTRUCTION							
Salaries	P	—	A	—	—	—	—
Other Expenses	—	—	A	—	—	—	P
ATTENDANCE AND HEALTH							
Attendance Services	—	—	P	—	A	—	—
Health Services	—	—	P	—	A	—	—
TRANSPORTATION SERVICES	—	—	—	—	P	P[a]	—
OPERATION OF PLANT							
Salaries	P	A	—	—	—	—	—
Heat for Buildings	—	P	—	—	—	—	—
Electricity	—	A	—	P	—	—	—
Gas (not heat)	—	—	—	P	—	—	—
Water	—	—	—	P	—	—	—
Other Expenses	—	A	—	—	—	—	P
MAINTENANCE OF PLANT							
Salaries	P	A	—	—	—	—	—
Other Expenses	—	A	—	—	—	—	P
FIXED CHARGES							
Retirement	P	—	A	—	—	—	—
Rent	—	P	A	—	—	—	—
Property Insurance	—	P	A	—	—	—	—
Other Fixed Charges	—	—	P	—	—	—	—
FOOD SERVICES AND STUDENT BODY ACTIVITIES							
Food Services	—	—	A	—	P	—	—
Student Body Activities							
Salaries	P	—	A	—	—	—	—
Other Expenses	—	—	A	—	—	—	P
COMMUNITY SERVICES	Not Allocable to Program Areas						

For special transportation services, such as transporting pupils on field trips.
LEGEND: P = preferred method; A = alternate method.
SOURCE: Adapted from Paul L. Reason and Alpheus L. White, *Financial Accounting for Local and State School Systems, Standard Receipt and Expenditure Accounts*, Bulletin 1957, no. 4, U.S. Office of Education, Washington, D.C.: U.S. Government Printing Office, 1957, pp. 138–139.

TABLE 14, II. Methods for Prorating to Community Services Accounts

Expenditure Accounts (1)	Methods for Prorating				
	Time (2)	Time-Floor Area (3)	Hour Consumption (4)	Number of Pupils (5)	Quantity Consumed (6)
COMMUNITY SERVICES (except any services for nonpublic school pupils)					
Salaries	P	—	—	—	—
Heat for Buildings	—	P	—	—	—
Electricity	—	A	P	—	—
Gas (not heat)	—	—	P	—	—
Water	—	—	P	—	—
Other Expenses	—	—	—	—	P
NONPUBLIC SCHOOL PUPILS					
Textbooks and School Supplies	—	—	—	—	P
Attendance and Health Services					
Salaries	P	—	—	A	—
Other Expenses	—	—	—	A	P
Transportation Services	—	—	—	P	—

LEGEND: P = preferred method ; A = alternate method.

keep an accurate count of materials employed in any activity. A part of the total expenditure for the materials is charged to a given account on the basis of the amount used.

It is imperative that there be a relationship between the pro rata procedure and the activity to which the expenditure is prorated. To illustrate, it makes little sense to use the time-floor area method in prorating teachers' salaries since there is very little relationship between the work load of the teacher and the floor area. It is far more meaningful to use time spent in various activities in prorating salary expenditures of teachers. For some activities average daily membership or average daily attendance may be the most satisfactory alternate prorating method. In other words, there is more than one way to do the prorating. Prorating can be greatly facilitated if the accounts are so designed for such purposes. Another aid in prorating is careful coding of accounts. But whatever method of prorating is used, it is important that the same method be used for prorating salaries as is used in prorating personal services in the personnel record. The standard ratios for prorating should be established early in the fiscal year and applied consistently throughout the term.

A summary of the methods of prorating adapted from the 1957 USOE financial accounting handbook is presented in Table 14.

SUMMARY

Increasing public school costs can be traced to better attendance for longer periods, more comprehensive educational programs, rising price levels, and the improved economic status of the professional staff in public schools. Cost accounting for schools endeavors to ascertain and evaluate the costs of operating various phases of the educational program. Unit cost analysis goes a step further in attempting to relate what was accomplished to the price paid. The fundamental purpose of cost accounting or unit cost analysis is to aid management in controlling current and future operations.

All cost studies originate in the accounting system. All unit cost analyses will reflect the limitations and advantages of the financial information available and the design and procedures in accounting.

A well-designed and well-kept account system will facilitate gathering cost data but cannot guarantee the correct interpretation of such information. Unit cost figures for school systems should be qualified if they are not based on the same educational programs. It is erroneous to assume that the same educational program is being purchased with the same or differing amounts of money in all school systems. Further confounding the problem is the selection of the appropriate unit for cost analysis.

Job order unit cost analysis is of value when a specific task is involved. Certain records such as work order requisitions, work orders, and work completed reports are necessary in this approach.

The percent of the total current educational expenditures devoted to Administration, Operation, Maintenance, and Auxiliary Services has remained fairly constant during the past 20 years in city school systems. Some changes were noted in the percent spent on Instruction and Fixed Charges. There is considerable variation among cities in the percent of total current expenditures allocated to various accounting classifications.

Prorating of school expenditures to various accounting classifications can be accomplished by the seven different methods of time, average daily membership or average daily attendance, time-floor area, hour consumption, number of pupils, mileage, and quantity consumed.

a. A school nurse spends one morning in each of five different elementary schools, an afternoon in each of four different junior high schools, and one afternoon a week in the senior high school.
b. The secondary school building custodian spends three-fourths of his time during regular school hours and one-fourth of his time during the hours the night school classes meet.
c. The vocational agriculture instructor teaches three classes of high school students and two classes of adults.
d. Of the 400 children transported, 50 attend a parochial school and 350 attend public school.
e. An adult education class uses the shops which are also used by day students during the school day.
f. The physical education supervisor for secondary schools spends 3 nights a week supervising evening recreation programs.

7. Prorate the following custodial expenses in appropriate amounts to secondary school and adult education accounts:

The total cost of custodial services for secondary and adult education programs using the same building is $25,000. The secondary school uses the building eight hours a day for five days a week. The adult education meets four hours a night for four nights a week. The 72,000 square feet are utilized for secondary education but only 18,000 square feet are employed in adult education programs.

QUESTIONS

1. What are the values and limitations of unit cost analysis in public education?
2. What would be appropriate units for a cost analysis of the following school functions?
   a. The manufacturing of furniture in a shop operated by district employers.
   b. The teaching of vocational agriculture.
   c. The custodial service in a school building.
   d. Heating a school building.
   e. Providing a full-time principal in each building.
3. What kind of records must be maintained for effective job order unit cost analysis?
4. How can you explain the declining percent of the total current expenditures allocated to Instruction during the past years?
5. When is prorating of expenditures necessary? Of what value is prorating?
6. What particular prorating method should be applied in the following situations?

SELECTED REFERENCES

Burke, Arvid J., *Financing Public Schools in the United States,* New York: Harper & Brothers, rev. ed., 1957, chaps. IV, V, and XV.

Engelhardt, N. L., and Engelhardt, Fred, *Public School Business Administration,* New York: Teachers College, Columbia University, 1927, chaps. XXX and XXXI.

McClure, William P., *Educational Cost Analysis,* Urbana, Ill.: University of Illinois, March, 1957.

Mikesell, R. M., *Governmental Accounting,* Homewood, Ill.: Richard D. Irwin, Inc., 1951, chap. XXI.

Mort, Paul R., "Cost-Quality Relationships in Education" in R. L. Johns and E. L. Morphet (eds.), *Problems and Issues in Public School Finance,* New York: Teachers College, Columbia University, 1952, chap. II.

Reason, Paul L., and White, Alpheus L., *Financial Accounting for Local and State School Systems, Standard Receipt and Expenditure Accounts,* Bulletin 1957, no. 4, U.S. Office of Education, Washington, D.C.: U.S. Government Printing Office, 1957, chap. VIII.

CHAPTER 10

Financial Reporting

FINANCIAL REPORTS ROUND OUT THE INSTRUMENTS essential for effective financial administration of public schools. The budget, the accounts, and the audit were described previously as necessary to fiscal management. Financial reporting is a means of informing the school board, professional administrators, the public, and state officials of plans and transactions contained in the budget and accounts.

Reports serve many different functions. The precise form, content, and method of presentation is determined by purposes. Financial reports help those responsible for school management to determine if funds have been safeguarded from loss, theft, waste or misuse; if the limits set by the budget were followed; and if the district is in a financially sound position. In this sense it is a device for exercising local control and supervision over financial activity.

State and national educational agencies require or seek financial information from school districts. State reports are useful to depict local operating conditions and to ascertain if legal mandates have been complied with. Local reports prepared for a state agency are the basis of state and national educational summaries.

Reports to the public differ in many ways from those necessary for local school management and for state and federal summaries. A clear and authoritative concept of public school income and expenditures for various educational services should be presented to the public. Reports to the public are usually issued on an annual basis after the close of the fiscal year, or if the report is related to the budget, it should be issued just prior to the start of the fiscal year. Technical information presented in formal tables may be meaningful to administrators and state officials but it is difficult to interpret by lay people. Monthly or annual reports that may be most valuable to local school administrators or state or federal agencies are not necessarily effective tools for public relations.

The many and different financial reports prepared by school districts in New York are summarized in Table 15. Although this table is a formal statement of what is practiced in the state of New York, many of the reports listed would be demanded in other states as well. To facilitate the preparation of reports at the time required, it is suggested that all school districts make a list of the fiscal data which must be forwarded to different agencies during the course of the fiscal year. This compilation should show the title of the report; its fundamental nature; the period covered; the date it is to be filed; by whom it is prepared; by whom it is signed; to whom it is sent; and any other pertinent information. A sufficient number of copies of this master list should be made so that it can be distributed as a reminder to all officials preparing and receiving the reports, thus minimizing forgetfulness or delays.

MONTHLY FINANCIAL REPORTS

Monthly financial reports are usually the responsibility of school business officials. They are necessary to portray the status of receipts and expenditures and their relationship to budgeted amounts for each fund. The fiscal data of monthly reports are of value to administrators and others responsible for keeping the financial pulse of the school district. They are sometimes referred to as monthly financial statements. Further detail on receipts, expenditures, and disbursements summarized in monthly statements is developed in the following paragraphs.

What happened to school receipts during a given period of the fiscal year can be presented in many ways. It is almost standard procedure to start the report by showing total receipts at the end of the previous month. The next step is identification of total school receipts collected during the period in question. This gives rise to a new grand total up to the end of the monthly reporting period. Monies collected from various sources during the month can be compared with similar periods in previous years of significance and particularly with the last two years. The monthly statement should be sufficiently detailed to show the type of receipt such as taxes collected, tuition paid, fees collected, or state aids received during the fiscal period. Any unusual conditions, such as receiving aids or tax receipts prior to anticipated dates or failing to receive such receipts on schedule, should be explained. Interpretation of the monthly statement on school receipts is facilitated greatly by comparisons with similar experiences in past fiscal years and with anticipations for the present year as disclosed by the budget.

The monthly summary for the Expenditure Accounts has a pattern similar to that for receipts. It should begin with total expenditures made prior to the period under consideration. Following this would be the money expended during the given fiscal period for each of the functional-character accounting classifications. In addition, the encumbrances for various expenditure classifications should be revealed. The danger spots (that is, those classifications where financial transactions are likely to exceed budgeted amounts) should be emphasized. The need for a transfer of appropriations from one classification to another in the same fund can be determined by the board on the basis of financial information in the report. As in the case for receipts, the financial experience in previous years should be included to place present expenditures in perspective.

A suggested form for monthly reporting of school receipts is shown in Form 13. It is based on the standard Receipt Accounts in the 1957 USOE financial accounting manual and Chapter 4 of this book. It can be expanded or condensed to meet the local situation and applied to any school fund.

A suggested form for monthly reporting of expenditures is illustrated in Form 14. It is based on the standard Expenditure Accounts presented in the 1957 USOE financial accounting manual and Chapter 7 of this book. It can be used with a separate statement for each fund.

A summary statement on disbursements for the fiscal period is necessary to show the balance on hand in the treasury at the start of the period, warrants paid during the month, outstanding warrants (if any), and the reconciliation of the receipts recorded in the school district records with those of the school depository or bank. It is frequently called the treasurer's report. Reconciliation of school records with bank records is extremely important. Any loans issued in anticipation of current receipts are likewise designated in such a report. Disbursements and final balance should harmonize with the reports of school receipts and also with school expenditures and encumbrances.

Internal auditors in school systems (where such officials exist) may also issue a review of financial operations to satisfy administrative purposes for periods less than the fiscal year. The function of such a statement would be to spotlight significant financial accounting problems. It is highly unlikely that it would be prepared on a regular or monthly basis. The internal auditor's report and others belong in the category of special reports. It is more than likely that it would be issued at irregular times and as problems are experienced.

The development of monthly reports need not be a laborious task if accounts are properly classified and maintained. Machine accounting greatly facilitates the preparation of the types of financial information the board may desire in order to keep abreast of financial transactions. Each system should prepare forms for monthly reports in line with the information requested for administrative control of financial activities but which are consistent with uniform or standard accounting procedures.

It would be highly desirable to have financial reports executed far enough in advance of administrative staff or board meetings to permit their study prior to the meeting. In many cases it will mean closing books at the end of the fiscal accounting period or month and preparing the reports almost immediately. It follows that all such monthly reports should be written and considered as part of the minutes of the school board. The board speaks through its minutes and it is highly desirable that financial reports be recognized in the board's minutes.

The information presented in monthly reports over a period of years can help in the formulation of future budgets. This is particularly true in developing estimates of school receipts and expenditures for each month of the school year. It is often necessary to determine the amount of money needed to operate through the fiscal year without borrowing. If it is obvious that the total expenditures scheduled are greater than the anticipated receipts during a given period (plus the operating cash balance), then steps must be taken either to borrow money in anticipation of current receipts or to issue nonpayable school warrants. Such a condition can be forecasted with some degree of success through careful maintenance of monthly reports on receipts and expenditures in all of the various school funds.

The preparation of monthly statements on receipts, expenditures, and disbursements is an indispensable

TABLE 15. School District Financial and Statistical Reports

Title	Nature	Period Covered	Prepared by	Signed by	Destination	Remarks
Clerk's Report	Receipts, disbursements and balances	Month	School business official (clerk)	Clerk	A	
Minutes	Action by Board of Education	Each meeting	School business official (clerk)	Clerk	A	
Schedule of Bills	List of bills for board approval (in cities, a warrant on treasurer)	Before each board meeting; in cities as often as necessary	School business official; auditor in cities	Same		Copy to treasurer; referred to by schedule no. in minutes or may be made a part of the minutes
Annual Financial Report	Receipts and expenditures on general and all other funds; statement of indebtedness; assessed valuation; report of tax collection; reconciliation of bank balances	Fiscal year	School business official (clerk) and treasurer	President of board or trustees	B D E F	Two copies to Educational Department; yellow copy to Audit and Control
Teacher List	List of teachers employed during year—salaries, retirement deductions	Fiscal year	School business official	Superintendent of schools or president of board	B L	Financial statement may be signed by president of the board or superintendent; annual report of members signed by superintendent
W2 (Federal)	Total on income tax withheld during calendar year for each employee	Calendar year	School business official	No signature required	I	Internal Revenue Department; two copies to each employee
105 (New York State)	Total wages and salaries	Calendar year	School business official	School business official	G	N.Y. State Department of Taxation and Finance for each employee
106 (New York State)	Summary of all 105 forms	Calendar year	School business official	School business official	G	Same
Transportation Quota Application	Report on bus mileage, pupils transported, costs, etc.	Fiscal year	School business official	President of board	B C	
Report on Tax Levy	Amount of tax levy and tax rate by towns	Current tax collection period	School business official (clerk)	Trustee or clerk	B F	Two copies to state Educational Department
Transportation Routing Data Form	Report on bus routes and pupils transported	Fiscal year	School business official	President of board or clerk	B C	Three copies to superintendent for approval, two of which are forwarded to Educational Department

Report	Contents	Period	Prepared by	Approved by	Codes	Remarks
Final Report on Construction	Recapitulation of entire costs of a construction program	Entire period of construction	School business official (clerk)	Clerk	B K	
Certification of Completion	Certification that building is completed in accordance with plans and approved changes		School business official	President of board and architect	B K	
Debt Statement	List of outstanding obligations and property valuations	Not more than 15 days, nor less than 3 days prior to public bond sale	School business official (clerk)	President of board	B F	Central schools must attach an estimate of building quota percentage provided by the commissioner of education
Treasurer's Monthly Report	Receipts, disbursements, and reconciliation of book balance with bank balance, all funds	Month	Treasurer	Treasurer	A	Certified by treasurer
Central Treasurer Activity Fund	Balance in each activity account and bank reconciliation	Month and fiscal year	Central treasurer	Central treasurer and auditor or controller	A B C F	Annual reports only to Educational Department and Audit and Control
Capital Reserve Fund	Receipts and disbursements; types and amounts of securities held; reconciliations of bank balance	Fiscal year	Treasurer	President of board or trustees	B D E F	Two copies to Educational Department; yellow copy to Audit and Control (part of annual financial report)
Monthly Attendance Report	Total attendance of all pupils for period	Month or every five weeks of school	Principal	Principal	B	These reports are basis for average daily attendance computations and state aid
Statistical Report	Property owned by district; session computation of average daily attendance; number of teachers; special schools	Fiscal year	Superintendent or principal	Superintendent and president of board	B E	Two copies to state Educational Department; villages file one with county clerk
Certificate of Approval of Treasurer's Bond	Names of district officers and statement that appropriate bonds have been filed	Fiscal year	Superintendent	Superintendent		To county treasurer
Budget	Appropriations for fiscal year and comparative data for previous years	Fiscal year	Chief school officer and school business official	Chairman and clerk of annual meeting	B C	Copy of budget must be made available for any legal voter prior to annual meeting

LEGEND:
A = Board of Education Minutes.
B = Superintendent of Schools.
C = Bureau of Field Financial Services.
D = Division of School Financial Aid.
E = Bureau of Statistical Services.
F = Department of Audit and Control.
G = Department of Taxation and Finance.
H = State Employees' Retirement System.
I = Director of Internal Revenue.
J = Department of Civil Service.
K = Division of School Buildings and Grounds.
L = State Teachers' Retirement System.

TABLE 15 (*Continued*). School District Financial and Statistical Reports

Title	Nature	Period Covered	Prepared by	Signed by	Destination	Remarks
Report on Tax Collections	Amount of tax collected by towns	Current tax collection period	Collector	Collector	A B	
Returned Taxes	List of unpaid taxes	Same	Collector	President and clerk of board		To county treasurer
Payroll	List of employees, wages, deductions	Payroll period	School business official	Chief school officer		Distribution ledger; must be certified
Form 103	Nonteaching employees in State Employees' Retirement System, wages, deductions	Same	School business official	School business official	H	State Employees' Retirement System; school district may use its own form
SD-30, October Payroll	All noncertificated personnel, annual salary, October salary	October	School business official	School business official	J	
SD-26, Personnel Report	Any change in status of noncertificated personnel (wages, title, hours, etc.)	Immediately upon such change	School business official	School business official	J	
SA-602 Monthly Claim for Reimbursement	Receipts and expenses of cafeteria	Month	School business official	School business official	D	
Bank Certification	Certificate by officer of official depository of balance in each account maintained by school district	Fiscal year	Bank	Bank officer and district treasurer	B D E F	Part of annual financial report
Final Financial Report	A closing financial statement for a district which has been absorbed by district reorganization	Month following effective date of reorganization	Former trustee or board president	Former trustee or board president and superintendent	B C	One copy to superintendent; two copies to Bureau of Field Financial Services

LEGEND:
A = Board of Education Minutes.
B = Superintendent of Schools.
C = Bureau of Field Financial Services.
D = Division of School Financial Aid.
E = Bureau of Statistical Services.
F = Department of Audit and Control.
G = Department of Taxation and Finance.
H = State Employees' Retirement System.
I = Director of Internal Revenue.
J = Department of Civil Service.
K = Division of School Buildings and Grounds.
L = State Teachers' Retirement System.

SOURCE: University of the State of New York, *School Business Management Handbook, Accounting and Reporting*, no. 4, Albany, N.Y.: The State Education Department, 1956, pp. 107–111.

FORM 13.

MONTHLY FINANCIAL REPORT OF RECEIPTS
COMMUNITY SCHOOL DISTRICT OF SMITHVILLE, U.S.A.

For the Period Beginning ———————, 19——— and Ending ———————, 19———

For ——————— Fund

Receipts

Source of Receipt (1)	Estimated Receipts for the Year (2)	Total Receipts Previously Received This Year (3)	Receipts Received During Month (4)	Total Receipts to Date (5)	Estimated Receipts During Remainder of the Year (6)	Total Receipts Received During Same Month Last Year (7)	Special Comments (8)
A. Revenue Receipts							
11—*Local Taxes*							
12—*Tuition from Patrons*							
13—*Transportation from Patrons*							
14—*Other Local Revenue*							
10—*Total Local Revenue*							
20—*Total Revenue from Intermediate Sources*							
30—*Total Revenue from State Sources*							
40—*Total Revenue from Federal Sources*							
Total Revenue Receipts							

FORM 13—(Continued).

MONTHLY FINANCIAL REPORT OF RECEIPTS
COMMUNITY SCHOOL DISTRICT OF SMITHVILLE, U.S.A.

For the Period Beginning _____ Fund _____ , 19___ and Ending _____ , 19___

For _____

Receipts

Source of Receipt (1)	Estimated Receipts for the Year (2)	Total Receipts Previously Received This Year (3)	Receipts Received During Month (4)	Total Receipts to Date (5)	Estimated Receipts During Remainder of the Year (6)	Total Receipts Received During Same Month Last Year (7)	Special Comments (8)
B. Nonrevenue Receipts							
50—*Sale of Bonds*							
60—*Loans*							
70—*Sale of School Property and Insurance Adjustments*							
Total Nonrevenue Receipts							
C. Incoming Transfer Accounts							
80—*Tuition, Transportation, and Miscellaneous from School Districts in State*							
90—*Tuition, Transportation, and Miscellaneous from School Districts in Another State*							
Total from Incoming Transfer Accounts							
Total Receipts in General Funds							

FORM 14.

MONTHLY FINANCIAL REPORT OF EXPENDITURES
COMMUNITY SCHOOL DISTRICT OF SMITHVILLE, U.S.A.

For the Period Beginning _____, 19___ and Ending _____, 19___
For _____ Fund

Expenditures

Classification (1)	Estimated Expenditures for the Year (2)	Total Expenditures Previously Made This Year (3)	Expenditures During Month (4)	Total Expenditures to Date (5)	Encumbrances (6)	Estimated Expenditures for Remainder of the Year (7)	Total Expenditures During the Same Month Last Year (8)	Special Comments (9)
A. Administration								
110—*Salaries*								
120—*Contracted Services*								
130—*Other Expenses*								
100—TOTAL EXPENDITURE FOR ADMINISTRATION								
B. Instruction								
210—*Salaries*								
220—*Textbooks*								
230—*School Libraries, etc.*								
240—*Teaching Supplies*								
250—*Others*								
200—TOTAL EXPENDITURE FOR INSTRUCTION								
C. Attendance and Health Services								
300—*Attendance Services*								
400—*Health Services*								
D. Pupil Transportation Services								
510—*Salaries*								
520—*Contracted Services and Public Carriers*								
530—*Replacement of Vehicles*								
540—*Insurance*								
550—*Expenditures in Lieu of Transportation*								
560—*Others*								

FORM 14—(Continued).

MONTHLY FINANCIAL REPORT OF EXPENDITURES
COMMUNITY SCHOOL DISTRICT OF SMITHVILLE, U.S.A.

For the Period Beginning _____ , 19___ and Ending _____ , 19___

For _____ Fund

Expenditures

Classification (1)	Estimated Expenditures for the Year (2)	Total Expenditures Previously Made This Year (3)	Expenditures During Month (4)	Total Expenditures to Date (5)	Encumbrances (6)	Estimated Expenditures for Remainder of the Year (7)	Total Expenditures During the Same Month Last Year (8)	Special Comments (9)
500—TOTAL EXPENDITURE FOR TRANSPORTATION SERVICES								
E. Operation of Plant								
610—*Salaries*								
620—*Contracted Services*								
630—*Heat*								
640—*Utilities, Except Heat*								
650—*Supplies, Except Utilities*								
660—*Others*								
600—TOTAL EXPENDITURE FOR OPERATION								
F. Maintenance of Plant								
710—*Salaries*								
720—*Contracted Services*								
730—*Replacement of Equipment*								
740—*Others*								
700—TOTAL EXPENDITURE FOR MAINTENANCE								
G. Fixed Charges								
810—*Retirement*								
820—*Insurance and Judgments*								
830—*Rentals*								
840—*Interest on Current Loans*								
850—*Others*								

FORM 14—(Continued).

MONTHLY FINANCIAL REPORT OF EXPENDITURES
COMMUNITY SCHOOL DISTRICT OF SMITHVILLE, U.S.A.

For the Period Beginning _____, 19__ and Ending _____, 19__

For _____ Fund

Classification (1)	Estimated Expenditures for the Year (2)	Total Expenditures Previously Made This Year (3)	Expenditures During Month (4)	Total Expenditures to Date (5)	Encumbrances (6)	Estimated Expenditures for Remainder of the Year (7)	Total Expenditures During the Same Month Last Year (8)	Special Comments (9)
800—Total Expenditure for Fixed Charges								
H. Food Services and Student Body Activities								
900—Food Services								
1000—Student Body Activities								
900–1000—Total Expenditure for Food Services and Student Body Activities								
I. Community Services								
1110—Recreation								
1120—Civic Activities								
1130—Public Libraries								
1140—Care of Children								
1150—Welfare Activities								
1160—Nonpublic School Pupils								
1100—Total Expenditure for Community Services								
J. Capital Outlay								
1210—Sites								
1220—Buildings								
1230—Equipment								

FORM 14—(Continued).

MONTHLY FINANCIAL REPORT OF EXPENDITURES
COMMUNITY SCHOOL DISTRICT OF SMITHVILLE, U.S.A.

For the Period Beginning _____, 19___ and Ending _____, 19___

For _____ Fund

Classification (1)	Estimated Expenditures for the Year (2)	Total Expenditures Previously Made This Year (3)	Expenditures During Month (4)	Total Expenditures to Date (5)	Encumbrances (6)	Estimated Expenditures for Remainder of the Year (7)	Total Expenditures During the Same Month Last Year (8)	Special Comments (9)
1200—TOTAL EXPENDITURE FOR CAPITAL OUTLAY								
K. Debt Service								
1310—*Principal on Debt*								
1320—*Interest on Debt*								
1330—*Sinking Funds*								
1340—*School Housing Authority*								
1300—TOTAL EXPENDITURE FOR DEBT SERVICE								
L. Outgoing Transfer Accounts								
1410—*Expenditures to School Districts in State*								
1420—*Expenditures to School Districts in Another State*								
1430—*Tuition to Other Than Public Schools*								
1400—EXPENDITURE IN OUTGOING TRANSFER ACCOUNTS								
Total All Expenditures								

tool of financial control in all districts. It should be a matter of standard operating procedure to prepare such records in all school districts no matter how small or how large.

ANNUAL REPORTS ON THE FINANCIAL CONDITION OF THE SCHOOL SYSTEM

It is usually the function of the superintendent of the schools with the assistance of his business department to prepare an annual report for the board and the people. A portion of this yearly summary of educational accomplishments is devoted to financial transactions during the fiscal year. The annual report can be as technical as the monthly reports, or it can be condensed and produced in a more popularized form. The popularization of reports, particularly through the use of graphs, charts, and pictorial diagrams, requires more time and ingenuity for preparation but a popularized report can also convey facts in a more dramatic fashion.

The annual reports of city superintendents to boards of education had their start in many of the large school systems prior to the Civil War. But at least informal or oral school reports were made to the public during colonial times.[1] Today, even many of the very small school systems have superintendents who carefully prepare an annual report, part of which is devoted to the financial aspects of public school operation. These reports vary considerably in content and in presentation.

Reeder declared that the purposes of the annual reports were to inform, to appraise, and to preserve the history of school activities.[2]

It is unfortunate that most annual summaries of financial activities continue to be primarily technical in nature and are presented in a most uninteresting manner. The literature in reporting is full of criticisms of the inadequacies of annual reports. Many reports are little more than a collection of tables that are extremely difficult to interpret and are confined to information for the current year only.

There is a great need for popularization and a reformulation of the fundamental purposes of such reports. There is a difference between reports needed by technicians in charge of operating a program and those aimed at giving the board of education and the public

an understanding of what occurred in the school district during the year, particularly insofar as finances are concerned. Technical reports can best be understood by those with a technical background based on professional preparation or experience. It is simply expecting too much to ask the general public to interpret statistical tables or even to expend the necessary effort to review such information and obtain a point of view about school operations.

The remarks herein concerning the need for popularizing annual reports are not a new point of view. Fowlkes examined the reports of 35 city superintendents issued in the mid-1920's and found many deficiencies.[3] At that early date he recommended that annual reports by superintendents be improved by:
1. Addressing the report to the people rather than to the board alone.
2. Simplifying and reducing to a minimum technical information.
3. Keeping definite objectives in mind while preparing the report.
4. Using illustrations.
5. Keeping mechanical construction of the report at a high level.
6. Using an attractive cover stock.
7. Developing a table of contents and an index.
8. Holding the report to approximately 100 pages or less.

The topics discussed and the manner of presentation are summarized in Table 16, page 183.

Before and since Fowlkes' analysis, writers have called for more illustrations and carefully edited copy for annual reports. There are some good examples of well-prepared superintendents' reports to the people but they are outnumbered by those that leave much to be desired. Perhaps lack of time or lack of funds to do an adequate job can explain the slowness of improvement. It could also be a failure to comprehend the importance of reporting to the public.

There is little question that industry today has made great strides toward improving the format of its annual reports to stockholders. Many reports such as those prepared by the Standard Oil Company of New Jersey and the Nekoosa-Edwards Paper Company of Wisconsin are based on a very colorful format which at least invites perusal if not a careful study. Annual reports by industry emphasize pictures, colorful graphs, maps, and charts to communicate vital financial information to the public. School superintendents can gather many ideas on presenting financial infor-

[1] M. G. Neale, *School Reports As a Means of Securing Additional Support of Education in American Cities,* Columbia, Mo.: The Missouri Book Co., 1921.

[2] Ward G. Reeder, *An Introduction to Public-School Relations,* New York: The Macmillan Company, 1953, chap. 5.

[3] John Guy Fowlkes, "The City Superintendents' Annual Report," *The Nation's Schools,* September, 1928, 2:62–67.

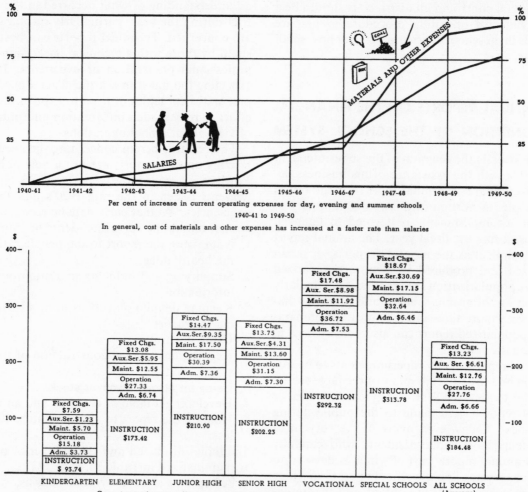

Per cent of increase in current operating expenses for day, evening and summer schools
1940-41 to 1949-50

In general, cost of materials and other expenses has increased at a faster rate than salaries

Current operating expenditures per pupil in average daily attendance, regular day school, 1949-50

Instructional cost is the largest single item of expenditures in any program

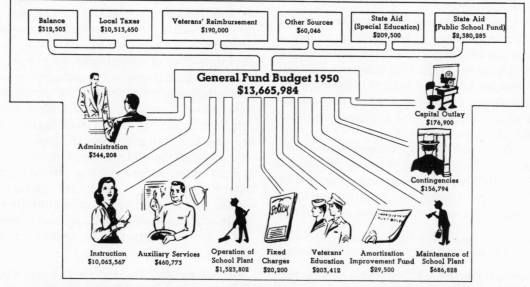

FIGURE 12.   Excerpts from the Cincinnati Superintendent's Annual Report for 1950
SOURCE: Claude V. Courter, *The Cincinnati Public Schools: A Vast Community Enterprise,*
Annual Report of the Superintendent, Cincinnati: Office of the Superintendent, 1950.

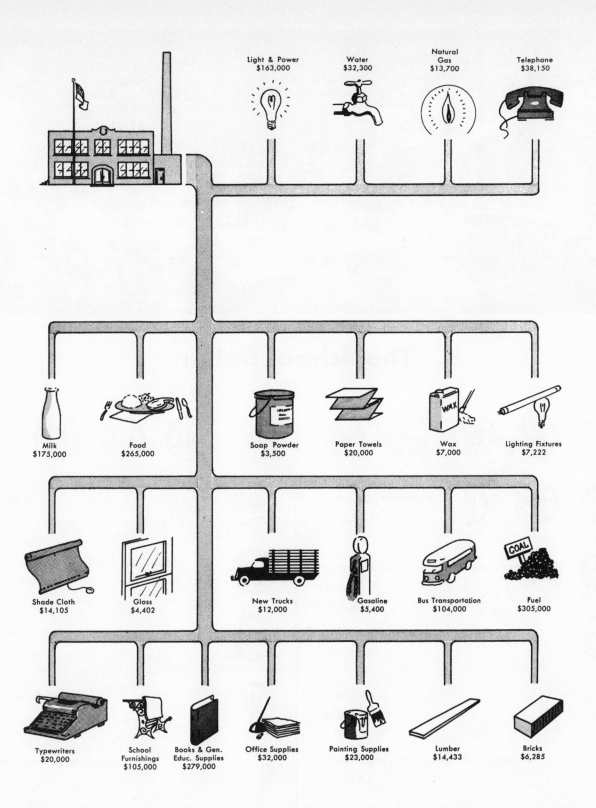

Light & Power $163,000 Water $32,300 Natural Gas $13,700 Telephone $38,150

Milk $175,000 Food $265,000 Soap Powder $3,500 Paper Towels $20,000 Wax $7,000 Lighting Fixtures $7,222

Shade Cloth $14,105 Glass $4,402 New Trucks $12,000 Gasoline $5,400 Bus Transportation $104,000 Fuel $305,000

Typewriters $20,000 School Furnishings $105,000 Books & Gen. Educ. Supplies $279,000 Office Supplies $32,000 Painting Supplies $23,000 Lumber $14,433 Bricks $6,285

These are but a few of the hundreds of items annually purchased for the Milwaukee Public Schools. Most of these purchases are made locally. Their magnitude can be seen from the fact that coal alone, purchased from local vendors, would fill almost 6,000 trucks. If these were placed in line at a distance of five feet, they would extend about 30 miles, or from Milwaukee to about Port Washington.

FIGURE 13. Excerpts from the Milwaukee Superintendent's Annual Report for 1951
SOURCE: Harold C. Vincent, *Our Best Investment*, 92nd Annual Report of the Superintendent of Milwaukee Public Schools, Milwaukee: Office of the Superintendent, 1951, p. 20.

Money for schools is invested, not spent.

The School Dollar

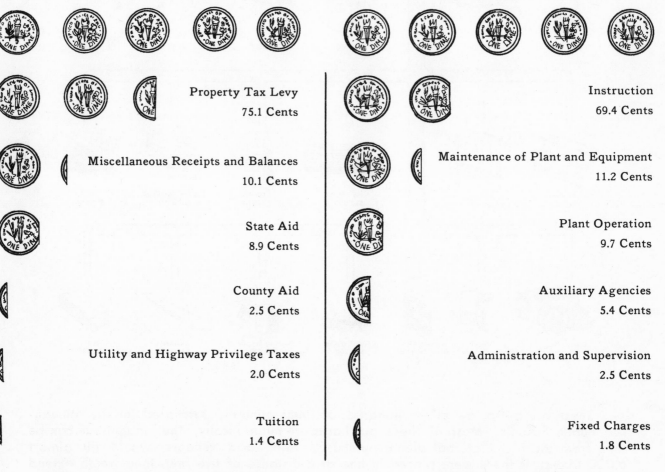

Where It Comes From	Where It Goes
Property Tax Levy 75.1 Cents	Instruction 69.4 Cents
Miscellaneous Receipts and Balances 10.1 Cents	Maintenance of Plant and Equipment 11.2 Cents
State Aid 8.9 Cents	Plant Operation 9.7 Cents
County Aid 2.5 Cents	Auxiliary Agencies 5.4 Cents
Utility and Highway Privilege Taxes 2.0 Cents	Administration and Supervision 2.5 Cents
Tuition 1.4 Cents	Fixed Charges 1.8 Cents

Where It Comes From   Where It Goes

FIGURE 14.   Excerpts from the Milwaukee Superintendent's Annual Report for 1957
SOURCE: Courtesy of the Milwaukee, Wisconsin, Public Schools

TABLE 16.   Manner of Presenting Major Topics in the Reports of 35 Superintendents
of Schools

Topic	Number of Reports Which Include the Topic	How the Topic Is Treated[a]		
		D	S	DS
Attendance and Enrollment	26	2	11	13
Buildings—Programs, and Use of	23	13	3	7
Teachers—Salary, Tenure, etc.	22	9	5	8
Extension Activities	20	9	4	7
Educational Costs, Finance	18	3	5	10
Health	16	8	2	6
Special Classes—Blind, etc.	16	12	1	3
General Educational Programs	16	13	0	3
Vocational Education	13	9	0	4
Senior High School	12	9	1	2
Elementary Schools	11	7	1	3
Special Subjects	11	9	0	2
Junior High Schools	10	6	1	3
Miscellaneous Activities	10	7	3	0
Supervision Program	9	7	0	2
Curriculum	8	8	0	0
Administrative Program	7	4	0	3
Department of Research	7	6	0	1
Business Department	7	0	6	1
Progress of Schools	7	3	1	3
School Savings	6	3	2	1
City Colleges	6	6	0	0
Extracurricular Activities	5	4	1	0
Total	286	157	47	82

[a] LEGEND: D = discussion; S = statistical; DS = discussion and statistical.
SOURCE: John Guy Fowlkes, "The City Superintendent's Annual Report," *The Nation's Schools*, September, 1928, *2*:64.

mation about schools in a most interesting fashion from the annual reports of industry. Keep in mind that the information must be presented so that it will be intelligible to individuals who do not have professional understanding and experience in public education. Color can contribute much as can well-edited copy. Better understanding is a step in the direction of better support of schools. The annual report of the superintendent to the board of education and the people should be looked upon as an instrument to promote better understanding of the local educational program and its accomplishments.

It is beyond the scope of a book on business management to present criteria for a report most likely to impress the public. There is a need to present the facts in a convenient form with careful explanations and diagrams to convey information needed to the public in a dramatic form.

One illustration of a very well-developed report on the finances in a large city school system is that presented by the superintendent of the public schools in Cincinnati. Figure 12 gives an indication of the judicious use of charts, pictures, and pictograms to present vital financial data to those people of Cincinnati who are interested in their public schools. A most intriguing annual report was prepared by Superintendent Harold S. Vincent of Milwaukee for the year ending 1951. It featured cartoons and well-edited copy. Excerpts from the 1951 and 1957 Milwaukee reports are illustrated in Figures 13 and 14.

BUDGET REPORTS

A fairly common practice is the preparation of a budget prior to its adoption by the board and its approval by the public. The budget document must of necessity be an elaborate document if it is to serve

WHERE YOUR STATE TAX DOLLAR GOES

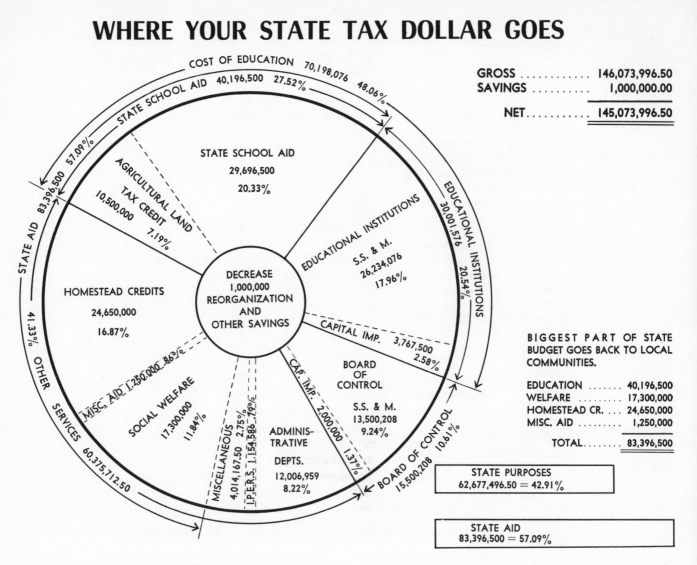

GROSS	146,073,996.50
SAVINGS	1,000,000.00
NET	145,073,996.50

BIGGEST PART OF STATE BUDGET GOES BACK TO LOCAL COMMUNITIES.

EDUCATION	40,196,500
WELFARE	17,300,000
HOMESTEAD CR.	24,650,000
MISC. AID	1,250,000
TOTAL	83,396,500

STATE PURPOSES
62,677,496.50 = 42.91%

STATE AID
83,396,500 = 57.09%

FIGURE 15. Iowa State Budget for 1955–1957—Expenditures
SOURCE: *Mr. and Mrs. Iowa Taxpayer*, *This Is Your State Budget for 1955–57*, Des Moines, Iowa (state government publication)

as a controlling instrument in financial management. The technical document which is prepared by the chief executive and examined by the school board need not be the same one used to inform the public about future school financial operations.

Once again it is emphasized that the function of the financial report should determine its method of presentation, format, and content. The legal requirement of publishing the budget in a newspaper of current circulation in the district can be satisfied by a format and technical summary. Effective communication with the public on school budgets must be carefully designed to convey technical financial information dramatically. One approach is the illustration based on the budget for the state of Iowa presented in Figures 15 and 16.

PRESERVATION AND DESTRUCTION OF REPORTS AND RECORDS

School records, particularly accounting and auditing records, form the basis of financial reporting to serve management functions and public information. Year after year the records accumulate. The larger the system, the more elaborate the records and the faster the accumulation. Many school districts have failed to develop an adequate policy to determine what records should be kept and which should be destroyed, when a record becomes noncurrent and ready for storage, and how long it should be retained in storage before it is to be disposed of. The following school financial records

REVENUE DOLLARS — GOVERNOR'S RECOMMENDATION
$146,214,000

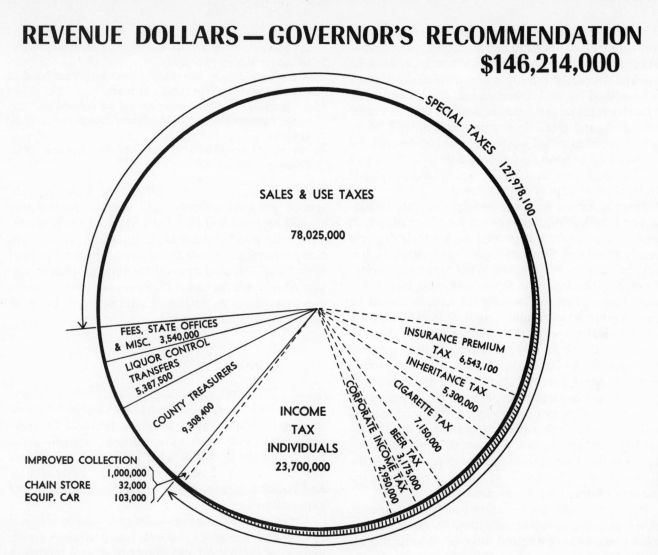

SPECIAL TAXES 127,978,100

SALES & USE TAXES

78,025,000

FEES, STATE OFFICES
& MISC. 3,540,000

LIQUOR CONTROL
TRANSFERS
5,387,500

COUNTY TREASURERS
9,308,400

INCOME
TAX
INDIVIDUALS
23,700,000

INSURANCE PREMIUM
TAX 6,543,100

INHERITANCE TAX
5,300,000

CIGARETTE TAX
7,150,000

CORPORATE INCOME TAX
2,950,000

BEER TAX 3,175,000

IMPROVED COLLECTION
1,000,000
CHAIN STORE 32,000
EQUIP. CAR 103,000

FIGURE 16.   Iowa State Budget for 1955–1957—Revenues
SOURCE: *Mr. and Mrs. Iowa Taxpayer, This Is Your State Budget for 1955–57,* Des Moines, Iowa (state government publication)

and documents were reported to accumulate annually in Dallas, Texas.

1. 80,000 canceled checks.
2. 53 standard drawer files of vouchers, with invoices attached to vouchers.
3. 16 volumes of ledgers, financial reports, and payrolls of average size (14 × 17).
4. 6500 earnings cards.
5. 1500 cash reports, sized 11 × 17.
6. 60,000 receipts for money.
7. 3600 deposit warrants and deposit slips.
8. 30,000 canceled bonds and coupons.[4]

School business affairs in future years are likely to require more complex record keeping rather than less

[4] Leon G. Hoseck, "Record Destruction and Preservation," *School Business Affairs,* Association of School Business Officials, March, 1954, 20:3–4, 6, 7.

and, hence, multiplying the above by 25 or 50 would be a conservative estimate of the magnitude of the problem within the next 25 to 50 years.

Microfilming of documents, records, and reports can reduce the amount of storage space. It is estimated that a microfilm will require up to 98 percent less space and equipment for storage than will the original document. Nine hundred 100-foot rolls of 16 millimeter film will photograph 3 million letter-sized documents and require little more floor space for storage than a standard four-drawer file cabinet.[5]

On the other hand, the cost and legal requirements on record storage cannot be ignored. Hoseck observed that "the cost involved in preparing papers and records for microfilming made the operation of microfilming

[5] *Ibid., p. 4.*

of records less than five years old very expensive." [6] Some difficulties encountered in microfilming preparation are: papers in poor physical condition must be repaired—turned down edges or crumpled sheets must be smoothed out and tears mended; staples and other fasteners must be removed; and colors such as violet, blue, pink, and green do not photograph well. Some cases have been noted where microfilmed records did not stand up in court, and it would be wise to consult an attorney before large-scale microfilming of records which must be kept is contemplated. [7]

There is a need for more widespread state legislation on length of time and the nature of records which must be kept intact with procedures for their disposal clearly stipulated. Some states such as California, Illinois, Indiana, New York, and Wisconsin have statutes governing the disposal of school and other public records. The reasons for keeping old records should be kept in mind when formulating such laws. If they are for historical purposes, then summary rather than detailed records are all that are needed. If they are to be the basis for possible prosecution of those whose embezzlements were not immediately apparent, then detailed records must be kept. Even in such cases requirements of perpetual storage of financial records will be of small value after the statute of limitations has expired. The statute of limitations varies in different states. There is good reason for permitting the disposal of detailed records of school finances after the statute of limitations has expired.

Records should not be destroyed without specific board of education authorization to do so. Many school boards have directed disposal of some records that are seven years old or older. In some states the disposal can be accomplished after five years. In the absence of specific statutory requirements to the contrary, the burning of school records that are 10 years old or older would be a very conservative step.

On the basis of what he called "practical common sense and experience of others," Hoseck declared:

1. There is nothing wrong with burning canceled bonds and interest coupons returned to the school as paid. A wise procedure would be to list the number of canceled bond issues directed to be destroyed by board of education order.
2. Many auditors recommend disposal of detailed school payroll records after seven years have elapsed. Summary information needed to ascertain longevity pay and service records which will have an effect on retirement or disability programs should be preserved in permanent records.
3. All records of school owned property should be kept in permanent records.

6 *Ibid.*
7 *Ibid.,* p. 6.

4. The last fidelity bond of an employee or officer which was in effect at the time service was terminated should be preserved for at least 15 years.
5. Accounting ledgers, cash receipt book, and similar financial records should be kept at least 15 years.
6. All journals of original entry should be indexed and preserved permanently to facilitate future inquiries and investigations.
7. No records should be destroyed until there has been an independent postaudit. [8]

School board minutes, annual financial reports, school property records, and similar information should be preserved in original form or microfilmed. There are good reasons for maintaining some summary reports on school financial reports on a permanent basis. Detailed financial records of ancient vintage which were the basis of approved summary reports can and should be destroyed after seven or no more than ten years have elapsed.

SUMMARY

The form, content, or presentation of a report varies with its purpose. Reports are used to help professional administrators keep the pulse of financial operations. They also have value in informing the board and the public of what is being accomplished and at what cost. Local reports are the basis of state and national summaries of educational receipts and expenditures.

There are many reports to be prepared in a school system and it is good procedure to prepare a classified list of the nature and timing of school reports in each system. Monthly statements of receipts, expenditures, and disbursements are an indispensable tool for the financial administration of schools.

An annual summary of financial transactions is usually a part of the superintendent's annual report. The professional literature is replete with criticisms of the dull or uninteresting annual report which receives small attention in proportion to the effort expended on its preparation. The suggestions to popularize such reports through carefully edited copy and the use of illustrations to dramatize facts presently buried in statistical tables have not been utilized to the extent desirable. Industry has moved far ahead of schools in producing more interesting and more useful annual reports.

School records accumulate fast. There is a need for legislation and policy to determine which records should be kept and which destroyed. Microfilming is a

8 *Ibid.*

help in reducing storage requirements of permanent records, but the high cost and possible legal problems should not be overlooked. In the absence of specific statutory requirements to the contrary many school records and reports could be disposed of after ten years without limiting school administration.

QUESTIONS

1. What are the essential differences in reports needed by professional personnel and those aimed at improving public understanding?
2. Who should be responsible for preparing monthly financial reports? Annual reports? Special financial reports?
3. When should school financial records be destroyed? Justify your position.
4. What financial records should be permanently preserved?

SELECTED REFERENCES

Fowlkes, John Guy, "The City Superintendent's Annual Report," *The Nation's Schools,* September, 1928.

Hoseck, Leon G., "Record Destruction and Preservation," *School Business Affairs,* Association of School Business Officials, March, 1954.

Neale, M. G., *School Reports As a Means of Serving Additional Support of Education in American Cities,* Columbia, Mo.: The Missouri Book Co., 1921.

Reeder, Ward G., *An Introduction to Public-School Relations,* New York: The Macmillan Company, 1953, chap. 5.

University of the State of New York, *School Business Management Handbook,* Accounting and Reporting, no. 4, Albany, N.Y.: The State Education Department, 1956.

CHAPTER 11

Managing and Accounting for Student Body Activity Funds

AT ONE TIME OR ANOTHER STUDENT BODY ACtivities have been called cocurricular activities, extraclassroom activities, extracurricular activities, student activities, or allied activities. Recently there has been a tendency to favor the terms "student body activities" or "student activities." Each term has desirable and undesirable connotations. Student body activities or student activities will be used in the main throughout this chapter.

Several decades ago, it was comparatively simple to define student body activities. Such activities were in the process of formation early in the twentieth century. They were prompted largely by students and received little recognition and assistance from teachers and administrators. During this period they were truly organizations outside the formal courses offered for credit and not included as part of the regular class instructional schedule. The curriculum was one aspect of the school program and student organizations were extra or "outside" the curriculum.

Today the difficulties of differentiation have been compounded. It is not unusual to find many teachers on the regular school payroll who devote a considerable portion of their efforts to the direction of student activities. In addition, time may be provided during the regular school schedule for meeting of student organizations or athletic team practice sessions. Many schools provide and pay for special equipment and materials to stimulate student participation in clubs, interscholastic athletics, etc.

There seems to be little question that today the line that separates curricular activities from extracurricular activities is a very faint one, if it exists at all. It may well be that within the next generation, we shall cease the arbitrary designation of student body activities as something outside the regular curricular experiences of

the school. Student clubs, athletic teams, etc., shall be recognized for the contribution they make to educational experiences needed for the complete growth and development of children and youths.

Student clubs, organizations, athletic teams, and other events are the product of the "roaring twenties." Although many organizations and functions can be traced far back in history, pupil activities as we know them today are a product of the twentieth century. Their acceptance in such variety and among so many schools in America can be traced to the years following 1920 when they were actually stimulated by professional educators and lay citizens. Stimulation of student activities did not always exist. As late as the turn of the twentieth century, coaching a sport, directing a student play, or sponsoring a club was not considered a fit occupation for teachers.[1] Today coaches of interscholastic sports or directors of class plays occupy positions of glamour in school and are given special recognition by students and the lay public as well.

GENERAL BUSINESS PROCEDURES

It is as difficult to define student body activity funds as it is to separate student sponsored events and functions from regular curricular experiences. Student body activity funds are those whose receipts are obtained from or for functions sponsored in the name of or controlled essentially by the pupils of a school and whose expenditures are for student sponsored or controlled events. Essentially, the income comes from nontax sources and as a result of functions such as games, class plays, and carnivals sponsored by the pupils of

[1] Paul B. Jacobson, William C. Reavis, and James D. Logsdon, *The Effective School Principal,* Englewood Cliffs, N.J.: Prentice-Hall, Inc., 1954, p. 301.

the school. In some schools, the board of education appropriates money for student activities. Income from school cafeteria operations, stores operated by the school for student benefit such as those selling materials and supplies to the student body, PTA funds, etc., are excluded by definition. In most schools such funds are not controlled by students. They may be temporarily housed in the individual school building accounts. Cafeteria, school stores, PTA, etc., monies are usually accounted for in Clearing Accounts of student activity accounts, for they are remitted to the board or to the PTA groups at the close of the fiscal period.

McKown's study in 1926 of 268 schools with enrollments varying from 30 to 4700 pupils reported that the amount of money handled through the actvity funds ranged from $300 to $125,000 per year.[2] These are unusually large sums for an early period in the history of student activities. The receipts and expenditures for student activities have swelled beyond those of 1926, creating an irrepressible demand for proper accounting. It is not unusual today to find schools where the total amount of money raised and spent in all of the various student body activities exceeds $100,000 per annum. Davis estimated that student activitiy funds in Los Angeles public schools would reach $7 million in 1957–1958.[3]

The very size as well as the complexity of such funds demands careful design and attention to their business management. The custody of student organization monies has long outgrown the practice of storage in fruit jars, filing cabinets, personal checking accounts, or even the left-hand pocket of the activity sponsor. Cash disbursements of sizeable amounts have been made in an equally informal fashion. The amount of money received during the fiscal period demands that receipts be placed in a well-protected depository and that they be properly accounted for. Expenditures should follow accepted business procedures. Student body activity funds are now big business in large secondary schools. As will be developed later, one of the most urgent business management needs in public school administration is the development of prudent management of student body activities.

LEGAL STATUS OF STUDENT BODY ACTIVITIES

Student body funds have grown like Topsy. The little direction and attention given to such school funds are indicated by the fact that presently only one-half the states have laws bearing upon student body activity funds. In the states having such laws, there is considerable variance, ranging from rigid controls to perfunctory attention. It is only within the last 25 years that some state departments of education have issued regulations, advisory bulletins, manuals of accounting, and the like, to help districts maintain more careful records of financial transactions of activity funds.

A question arises as to whether these are public or nonpublic funds. In reviewing some legal disputes on the matter, Hamilton submitted the opinion that student activity funds are definitely public funds. Their source is from public and not private activities, they involve the use of public property, and they utilize services of teachers paid for by public money.[4] In perhaps one of the more emphatic statements on the subject, Hamilton put such funds in the following perspective: "You would be well-advised to place all funds in the hands of the board and let it approve and pay all bills. The practice of setting up special funds to be spent by organizations upon the signature of its officers is definitely illegal. So also is the practice of some boards to pay to the administrator a fund upon which he may write checks. *Keep your hands off public money!* Let those the law charges with responsibility of protecting and disbursing such money discharge that responsibility."[5]

On the other hand, the state of Indiana defines student body activity funds as quasi-public funds. It is the opinion of the writers that student body activity funds are public monies and should be treated accordingly. The income is derived from functions sponsored directly by the school. It is of little import that the monies in such a fund were obtained by donations, class dues, sale of concessions, carnivals, etc. The income is produced under the direct sponsorship of the school with professional staff members of the school district in positions of supervisory responsibility. The fact that they are nontax funds does not make them nonpublic funds.

The concept of student body activity funds as public funds is of major significance in designing business procedures. By implication the board of education has control over student body activity funds even though the laws may be silent on the matter. The school board has control over all public funds within the school district unless the laws state to the contrary. The fact that the board of education has not appropriated money for the operation of the various student body functions or

[2] H. C. McKown *et al.,* "Financial Administration of Extra-Curricular Activities," *25th Yearbook, Part II,* National Society for the Study of Education, Chicago: The University of Chicago Press, 1926, p. 116.

[3] Clifford M. Davis, "Supervision and Control of Student Body Finances," *Proceedings of the Association of School Business Officials,* 43rd Convention, October, 1957, pp. 210–215.

[4] R. R. Hamilton, "The Legal Status, Control and Use of Athletic and Other Extra-Curricular Funds," *The Bi-Weekly School Law Letter,* September 18, 1953, 2:57–60.

[5] *Ibid.,* p. 60.

has failed in the years past to exercise the control it should have over such funds is beside the point. The special income that accrues as the result of student controlled functions is essentially similar in character to that raised by the board of education through taxations, fines, forfeitures, and grants and is hence subject to the same control.

The 1942 Pennsylvania case, known as the "German Township Case," established the principle that it is illegal to spend athletic or extracurricular funds without board approval of the various items.[6] In another Pennsylvania case some five years later, the school board refused to permit auditors to audit the activities accounts on the grounds that they were not regular school funds and, therefore, not subject to audit. The suit brought by the auditor to force the board to produce the activity fund records and accounts for audit was successful. In this so-called Hatfield Township Case, the court declared that all activity funds were under the control of the board of education.[7] Hamilton was of the opinion that the Hatfield Township Case would be followed generally in other states if the question of the control of the board of education over activity accounts should arise there.[8]

Further examination of the operation of student body activities would indicate that a sizable portion of school district tax funds are utilized in the sponsorship and direction of student activities. To illustrate, coaches' or sponsors' salaries are paid for out of district funds. Unfortunately, failure to prorate salaries of teachers correctly between instructional services rendered (ACCOUNT SERIES 200) and student body activities has made it difficult to produce evidence on the actual amounts of district money spent on student functions. Likewise, school football fields and gymnasiums are used for football games and basketball games. More often than not no charges whatsoever are made against activities by the school board for use of fields or gyms. The costs of installing and operating the lighting of the football field and the heating and lighting of gyms for basketball games are borne by regular school taxes. To argue that admissions charged belong to athletics or students in a particular school building rather than to the district as a whole has little basis in fact.

The state of Oklahoma clearly specifies board control over student body activity funds. It would be highly desirable that all states have similar laws to put these funds in proper perspective. The Oklahoma law is quoted to indicate the definitions that are desirable.

[6] *In re German Township School Directors,* 46 D and C, 562. See *ibid.,* p. 58.

[7] A Petition of Auditors of Hatfield Township School District, 161 Pa. Super, 388 54 A. 2d 833.

[8] Hamilton, *op. cit.,* p. 59.

Section 70. Control—Rules and Regulations: The board of education of each school district shall exercise complete control over all funds on hand or hereafter received or collected from all student activities conducted in such school district, including all funds received or collected from students and others as admission charges to athletic contests, school plays and any and all other school activities and from the sale of student activity tickets.

The board of education of each school district is hereby authorized and directed to adopt appropriate rules and regulations governing the handling and expenditure of such funds and shall require the custodian or custodians thereof to make a full and true accounting for all funds which may come into their possession or into their control and shall require such custodians to give a bond in such amount as the board may deem necessary, provided, however, the cost of the bond shall be paid out of such activity funds.

Section 71. Student Activities Funds—Annual Audit: The board of education of each school district shall likewise provide for annual audit of all such student activity funds, the cost to be paid out of such funds. The original report of such audit shall be delivered to the board of education, and a copy thereof shall be furnished to the treasurer of the school district.[9]

Such laws are needed to remove the last vestige of doubt that the control of student activity receipts and expenditures belongs under the jurisdiction of the board of education. Student control can be continued in the sense of formulating policies, recommending the disposition of receipts and expenses, etc. But in no way should the student control extend to actual business management responsibilities. The expenditures from the funds should be by checks signed by personnel authorized by the board of education. Board approval of all expenditures is necessary. Hamilton emphasized the dangers of expending school activity funds in any other way. "The common practice of setting up special funds and expending them upon checks signed by a teacher, or a pupil and a teacher, is clearly under the authority of this case [German Township Case] illegal. *If this practice is continued, legal involvement is being invited.* The same may be said of sums paid by the board to the coach or administrator to be spent in the discretion of the latter—the so-called miscellaneous funds! If you would be safe, *treat all school funds alike.* Do not touch them or sign your name to checks on school funds unless you are certain the law expressly authorizes you to do so, and it seldom does."[10]

THE STATUS OF BUSINESS MANAGEMENT OF STUDENT BODY ACTIVITY FUNDS

A sizable literature on student body activity fund accounting and other business management problems

[9] *School Laws of Oklahoma,* 1953, secs. 70 and 71.

[10] Hamilton, *op. cit.,* pp. 58–59.

has been developed within the last 35 years. Most writings in professional magazines or books describe the many shortcomings in the business management of student activities. The following practices characterized the business management of student activity funds as late as 1955: (1) careless handling of receipts; (2) poorly trained personnel charged with business responsibilities; (3) inadequate storage vaults for temporary housing of funds; (4) poor financial records; (5) absence of central control agencies; and (6) insufficient accounting and budget forms.[11] Such charges are well documented by many published writings on this subject.

There is little uniformity among schools in accounting for financial transactions for student organizations. The U.S. Office of Education has developed a special manual in this area which was released late in 1959. This should prove to be a big step toward uniformity. Ignorance of the laws dealing with public funds or ignorance of proper business management is hardly a satisfactory defense for the continuance of bad practices. There is evidence of a growing concern over the informal and ill-conceived methods of managing the school business affairs of student activities.

At present only a handful of school systems prepare a budget, keep accurate accounts, or call for an independent professional audit of activity funds. One of the pressing problems in school business administration is the establishment of justifiable business practices for student body activity funds.

DESIGNING BUSINESS MANAGEMENT PROCEDURES FOR STUDENT BODY FUNDS

Careful budgeting, a centralized treasury system, centralized accounting, defensible procedures for incurring and meeting liabilities, auditing of financial transactions, and reporting at stipulated intervals can be applied to student body funds as well as to other public school operations. The specific applications of these to the business management of student body funds will be developed in subsequent portions of this chapter.

The 1957 USOE financial accounting handbook presented a basis for accounting for student activity funds. Special recognition of these funds was given in the Clearing Accounts, particularly *Major Account 1810—Student Body Activities*.[12] It was recommended that

these Clearing Accounts be used when the student body activities are under the *financial control of the school board* and are financed wholly or partly by revenue produced by the functions. The accounts under this major heading would serve whether or not it is the policy of the school board to subsidize student body functions. This major account classification could be used even though the legal fiction were continued that the student body activities are not under the financial control of the school board. Such accounts could be used for supervisory control in such cases. The last portion of this chapter is devoted to accounting procedures for student funds regarded in some districts as outside school board jurisdiction.

The money received and money paid out for the following accounts under board jurisdiction could be established under *Major Account 1810—Student Body Activities*. This would include:
1. Account 1811—Athletics.
2. Account 1812—School Entertainments.
3. Account 1813—School Publications.
4. Account 1814—School Clubs and Other Cocurricular Activities.

Illustration of detailed accounts for:
1. Account 1811—Athletics.
   a. Subaccount 1811-a—Money Received.
      1) 1811-a-1—Money Received from Football Gate Receipts, Radio and Television Rights, Guarantees, and Other Sources.
      2) 1811-a-2—Money Received from Basketball Gate Receipts, Radio or Television Rights, Guarantees, and Other Sources.
      3) 1811-a-3—Money Received from Track and Field Events
      4) 1811-a-4—Money Received from Baseball Events.
      5) 1811-a-5—Money Received from Other Athletic Contests.

   Subaccount 1811-a could be coded to show monies received from each secondary school in the district.
   b. Subaccount 1811-b—Money Paid Out.
      1) 1811-b-1—Money Paid Out for Football Activities. This in turn could be subdivided to show the cost of officials, game balls, equipment, and other objects, if such information is useful for unit cost analysis.
      2) 1811-b-2—Money Paid Out for Basketball Activities.
      3) 1811-b-3—Money Paid Out for Track and Field Events.
      4) 1811-b-4—Money Paid Out for Baseball Activities.

[11] Jacob D. Rieger, *A Critical Analysis of the Administration of Internal Accounts in Secondary Schools,* Doctoral Dissertation, Storrs, Conn.: University of Connecticut, 1955.

[12] Paul L. Reason and Alpheus L. White, *Financial Accounting for Local and State School Systems, Standard Receipt and Expenditure Accounts,* Bulletin 1957, no. 4, U.S. Office of Education, Washington, D.C.: U.S. Government Printing Office, pp. 117–120.

5) 1811-b-5—Money Paid Out for All Other Athletic Activities.

Here again, coding or further detailed accounts could be used to record expenditures for athletic purposes in the various secondary schools. The same purpose can be accomplished by coding.

2. Account 1814—School Clubs and Other Cocurricular Activities. This account could be subdivided to show as much detail as is necessary for the system as a whole or each of the secondary school buildings of the district.

   a. Subaccount 1814-a—Money Received.

      1) 1814-a-1—Money Received from the Pep Club.

      2) 1814-a-2—Money Received from the Freshman Class.

      3) 1814-a-3—Money Received from the Sophomore Class.

      4) 1814-a-4—Money Received from the Junior Class.

      5) 1814-a-5—Money Received from the Senior Class.

      6) 1814-a-6—Money Received from the Science Club.

   Much the same division and detailed accounts can be used for Subaccount 1814-b—Money Paid Out.

The Clearing Accounts presented in the 1957 USOE accounting manual could serve as the base for recording receipts and expenditures of student body funds either as controlling records or as supervisory records.

In this book, it is recommended that the Petty Cash Fund, Stores Fund, Food Services Operation Accounts, Materials for Resale, and Textbooks for Resale or Rent should not be included as part of the student body funds. The financial transactions for these purposes can be recorded within the Clearing Accounts described on pp. 57–61 of Chapter 4.

It should be noted that the *net* expenditures for student body activities supported by the board of education are recorded in ACCOUNT SERIES 1000—STUDENT BODY ACTIVITIES described in greater detail in Chapter 7. Likewise, any excess of receipts over expenditures for *Major Account 1810—Student Body Activities* is closed out at the end of the year to Account 14-c— Net Receipts from Revolving Funds or Clearing Accounts. The other phases of student fund accounting can be designed to follow the regular business procedures for ordinary school financial transactions.

There is considerable merit to the idea that student body activities have developed to the point where they should be controlled and also supported with appropriations from the board of education. This would mean that high school students could be admitted to all school activities free of charge or for a nominal sum. All receipts would be placed in the general fund and all expenditures would be accounted for as per other school fiscal transactions. Clearing Accounts could be used to identify gross receipts and gross expenditures and only the net expenditure or receipts at the close of the fiscal year would be transferred to the appropriate Expenditure or Receipt Accounts.

If the business transactions of student body activities are to be executed outside of the jurisdiction of the school board but within each building, the following descriptions of budgeting, centralized treasury system, procedures for incurring and meeting liabilities, and systems of accounting, auditing, and reporting would apply.

BUDGETING FOR STUDENT BODY ACTIVITY FUNDS

Judging by the number of articles appearing in professional journals and books, the establishment of a budget for student activities appears to be one of the more popular topics. A budget for school organizations has the same value as for other areas of school business management. In its simplest form it would show estimated receipts and estimated expenditures for all functions. The receipts should be in sufficient detail to depict the amount anticipated from all sources and for each activity. Expenditures can be grouped by functions such as programs, parties, banquets, stock for concessions, special projects, and class activities. As in all budgets, the balance at the end of the fiscal year should approximate that found at the beginning.

The budget fiscal year should begin September 1 and end on the following August 31. The budgetary need for various programs is an aid in determining the admission prices of student events if no other means of support are available. The student representatives from each organization can be granted the opportunity to participate in the formulation of the budget. The authority to adopt the budget and put it into operation is often lodged with the student council with or without faculty council concurrence. It is desirable to have the principal participate in the policies and procedures affecting student funds, and this includes budget preparation and adoption. Budgeting lessens the likelihood of deficits and can help to promote economy and thrift. If receipts through the sale of student activity tickets are deposited in a general use fund, the budget can be used to stimulate student events and organizations which are desirable but which do not have the potential of raising sufficient funds to be self-supporting.

The development of budgets for student body activities can be interpreted as one sign of improved business management practices in this area, for it is the heart of financial management. Budgetary controls aid progress toward the goal of sound business management.

THE CENTRALIZED TREASURY SYSTEM FOR ACTIVITY ACCOUNTING

The early years of financial management of receipts for student groups was characterized by a highly decentralized and highly informal treasury system. Each club or organization had its own treasurer who collected and paid out monies with little regard to careful record keeping. Thus, the treasurer of the pep club was responsible only to the pep club members and was usually independent of any supervision other than that of the club sponsor. It is an approach characterized by considerable confusion, mismanagement, and inept record keeping. In many cases, money was not even deposited in a bank, but was kept in desk drawers or fruit jars. If the receipts were in a bank, they were likely to be in somebody's personal checking account.

Most authorities are in agreement that in each school building there should be one central treasurer to receive and deposit the receipts for all student organizations. The treasurer should be a responsible individual, preferably a member of the school staff. This procedure would help eliminate some of the charges of malpractice and inefficiency lodged against those responsible for the accounting and custody of student funds. The literature is replete with descriptions of school systems that use the centralized treasury system and report with enthusiasm of its practicality and success.

It would be the function of the treasurer to maintain all Receipt Accounts and other records of the central treasury, prepare financial statements of all Receipt Accounts, sign or countersign all checks disbursing funds from the treasury, and audit the financial records of the various student treasurers. Insofar as possible, all cash should be collected in the central treasurer's office. A cash register supplying cumulative readings would be desirable to facilitate such collections.

Prenumbered receipts should be issued at least in duplicate, one to the payee with the other kept for the accounting records of the central treasury. The receipts should indicate the date, the amount being deposited in the central treasury, the name of the individual making the deposit for the organization, and the account to be credited with the deposit. All receipts should be signed by the duly authorized collector of receipts for student funds.

Disbursements from the central treasury should only be made by checks that are signed or countersigned by the central treasurer. The central treasurer should be bonded in an amount at least equal to the money on hand during any 30-day period. Cash receipts should not be kept overnight on school premises but should be deposited in the bank designated as the depository.

It is questionable if there is any great advantage in burglary protection in a huge wall safe that is opened only through knowledge of the combination. Breaking and entering into school safes is not uncommon. The practice of depositing all school receipts in a bank at the end of the school day would tend to discourage burglaries of the school safes. Very often the damage done to the safe door is far greater than the amount of money lost. A good temporary storage space is needed. The door to the space used for the temporary storage of funds during a school day can be a strong steel door of fireproof construction having a well-constructed lock with limited number of keys available. Experience has shown that the traditional heavy safe door with a combination lock is a small deterrent to those bent on burglary.

Student organizations are characterized by the many ways to gain income. Among these are the sale of tickets, guarantees from other schools, television and radio rights, program and concession sales for the various athletic events, pay entertainments, sale of student body publications, salvage drives, vending machine profits, gifts, profits from general student body activities, special fund raising events, and class dues.[13] It can be said that the manner of obtaining income varies from little more than outright begging to donations to special dues to admission charges. It is beyond the scope of this book to evaluate the various devices for raising student funds. It is recommended, however, that each school system develop written policies to define approved and disapproved procedures for raising money for student activities. In general the raising of funds should contribute to the educational experiences of pupils.

INCURRING AND MEETING LIABILITIES

Incurring liabilities for student activities should follow business procedures similar to those recommended

[13] Association of School Business Officials, "Special Committee Report: Regulation Supervision of Student Body Expenditure Committee," *A Manual of Accounting Principles and Procedures for Student Activity Funds*, Bulletin no. 17, Evanston, Ill.: the Association, 1957, pp. 11–12.

for the General Fund of the school system. A requisition from the student organization approved by the faculty sponsor initiates the purchase act. To indicate approval the requisition is signed by the student president of the organization as well as by the faculty sponsor. The purchase act should be consummated by the school's centralized purchasing office rather than by students or through other informal approaches. Considerable savings will result where the regular school purchasing department is involved. The purchase order authorizes the procurement from the vendor. The purchase order, however, should not be mailed to the vendor unless unencumbered funds are available to meet the liability.

The receipt of the invoice and the materials or services starts the procedures for meeting the liability. It is the responsibility of the faculty sponsor to check goods received against the invoice and then approve the invoice for payment. Such approval can be registered through the issuance of a pay order which is a request to the central treasurer to pay the given invoice.

The following information is needed for the preparation of the pay order: name of school; date issued; request number; name and address of payee; amount of money; description of item or service purchased; name of activity to be charged; signature of student treasurer, faculty sponsor, business office representative; and check number and date.

The disbursement of funds from the central treasury is made by check only. Keep in mind that the check is prepared only upon presentation of the organization's pay order and the invoice or voucher document to the central treasurer. The signatures of the central treasurer and the individual authorized by the board to make expenditures validate the check. At least two signatures should be required before funds are released from the central treasury. The authority to expend money should be distinct and separate from the authority to collect and deposit monies. The student functions are limited to the authorization for disbursement by preparation of the pay order, signed by the student treasurer and faculty sponsor.

As a matter of policy and in accordance with the authority delegated to him by the school board, the superintendent should demand prior approval of activity fund expenditures to the extent necessary to insure adequate protection of student body funds. The Association of School Business Officials recommended that expenditures for the following items be permitted without prior authorization of the superintendent of schools as the executive officer of the school board. It is assumed that amounts are within an approved budget.

1. The purchase of equipment costing less than $300 (except that which is to be attached to the building or requires the use of public utilities); supplies, forms, and postage used exclusively by student organizations or for student events.
2. The repair, moving, and maintenance of any equipment (other than board of education equipment) used by student organizations or events.
3. The purchase of merchandise to be sold later in student body stores (including confections) or to accommodate classes and clubs.
4. Welfare expenditures (other than for family relief) not to exceed $200 per year.
5. Hospitality expenditures for those who have performed a service to the student body but not to exceed $200 per year.
6. Expenditures for entertainments.
7. Expenditures for publications.
8. The purchase of materials for sale to shops and art and crafts classes.
9. The purchase of athletic supplies and equipment.
10. The cost or purchase of laundry and towel service.
11. The purchase of towels.
12. The purchase of sanitary service.
13. General student body expenses not otherwise restricted.[14]

Expenditures which should require prior authorization would include those exceeding the amounts specified in (1), (4), and (5) above as well as the following:

1. All equipment, whether purchased, rented or borrowed, which is to be attached to the building or which would utilize public utilities.
2. Expenditures for plants and trees to be placed in special student areas.
3. The purchase of buildings, bulletin boards, or other structures.
4. The purchase of risers and bleachers.
5. Purchases made from any employee of the school district.
6. Salaries to student body employees.

Going a step further, the Association of School Business Officials recommended that the following expenditures be prohibited from student activity funds:

1. The purchase of equipment, supplies, forms, and postage used for regular classroom use or board of education business.
2. Expenditures to repair or maintain equipment owned by board of education (except certain jointly used equipment).
3. Expenditures for professional books and magazines and memberships in professional organizations.

[14] *Ibid.*, pp. 19–20.

4. Payments for memberships in and contributions to any out-of-school organizations.
5. The purchase of custodial supplies and equipment.
6. Salaries paid for services which are the responsibility of the board of education or result from board of education assignments.
7. The purchase of plants and trees for general landscaping of school grounds.
8. The purchase of flowers and plants for offices, classrooms, and other areas when these facilities are not used primarily for student organizations and events.
9. The purchase of articles for the personal use of board of education employees or other persons.
10. Expenditures for merchandising accommodations and loans and credit to board of education employees or other persons.
11. The purchase of equipment, supplies, and services for rooms and areas not used primarily by student organizations and events.
12. Contributions to fund-raising drives from general student activity funds.

In all cases, however, the purchases are based on formal purchase orders and payment is made only after careful documentation. In general, student body funds are used to finance student functions which augment but are not intended to replace the regular curricular or teaching functions supported by district funds.

ACCOUNTING FOR COCURRICULAR ACTIVITIES

Accounting for cocurricular activities can follow the design of *Major Account 1810,* previously described. A Voucher Register is needed to enter all the voucher checks. Supporting payment orders are filed in appropriate voucher jackets. Sufficient records are maintained for all the various student activities to record accurately the financial transactions.

There is a need for regular and professional audit of all student body funds. Auditing should take place on at least an annual basis and should be performed, preferably, by an independent certified public accountant. In all cases where tickets are used, ticket reports and unsold tickets must be available for audit. Student help in the business management is used to supplement rather than substitute for mature and specially prepared business personnel.

The suggested general ledger classifications for student funds recommended by the Association of School Business Officials are:
1. Agriculture.
2. Arts and Crafts.
3. Athletics.

4. Cash (all cash received is debited and all cash disbursed is credited to this account).
5. Clearing Accounts (for funds that are merely collected and are then disbursed in the same amount, such as funds for the Red Cross, the Community Chest, etc.).
6. Concessions.
7. Entertainments.
8. Equipment.
9. Expense.
10. Fines.
11. Inventories.
12. Investments.
13. Net Worth.
14. Clubs and Classes, Activities.
15. Payables.
16. Publications.
17. Receivables.
18. Reserves.
19. Shops.
20. Student Store.
21. Trust—Board of Education.
22. Trust—Student Activity.[15]

Many of the above classifications are similar to the recommendations of the U.S. Office of Education reported in the last portions of this chapter.

OPERATIONAL PROCEDURES

Davis[16] recommended an administrator of student finance to control the business procedures on a system-wide basis and a local school agent for each building. This approach has considerable merit in large school systems with two or more secondary school buildings. In addition, each school should develop a written statement of policies and regulations to govern the financial transactions of student body activities. These statements can be supplemented by a complete accounting manual to be used in all school buildings in the system. Carefully formulated regulations formally adopted by the board can help to minimize the possible misuse of student funds.

Incurring and meeting liabilities should follow established procedures for regular school affairs. Financial reporting is the culminating step of business management which previously included budgeting, accounting, incurring and meeting liabilities, and auditing. The report for the system as a whole should include the following information.[17] Each local school building should prepare monthly and annual financial

[15] *Ibid.,* pp. 34–38.
[16] Davis, *op. cit.*
[17] *Ibid.*

reports to portray the financial condition of student activity accounts in each building.

USOE HANDBOOK ON STUDENT ACTIVITIES ACCOUNTING

The U.S. Office of Education has developed a handbook called *Financial Accounting for School Activies* in coöperation with the American Association of School Administrators, the Association of School Business Officials, Council of Chief State School Officers, National Association of Secondary School Principals, National Association of Elementary School Principals, and the Research Division of the National Education Association.[18]

The 1959 USOE financial accounting handbook for school activities will fulfill a great need to standardize accounts and terminology in school activity accounting as well as to suggest and promote a system of accounting which will provide safe, economical, and efficient handling of student activity funds. The purposes of this standard accounts and terminology handbook are: (1) to help insure the proper initial recording of financial transactions; (2) to improve accounting for school activity money; (3) to improve school budget making; (4) to provide information for policy determination for school activities; (5) to facilitate comparisons of financial information among communities and states; (6) to facilitate reliable reporting to the board of education and the public concerning the financial condition of school activities; (7) to improve the accuracy of local, state, and national summaries; and (8) to serve as a protection for those individuals responsible for student funds. It is a practical guide recommended for use in all school systems.

It would be cumbersome in most schools to handle all financial transactions for student activities in a single fund. For this reason, the 1959 USOE accounting manual for school activities recommended the six basic funds entitled: Athletic Fund; Merchandise Fund; Student Organization Fund; Publications Fund; Instructional Fees and Rental Fund; and Miscellaneous Fund. In the previous sections it was pointed out that Food Services should be handled in the Clearing Accounts for the regular funds of local school systems. The standard Receipts and Expenditure Accounts to be developed in the subsequent portions of this chapter can be adapted to establish a Food Services Fund if this procedure is necessary in a given school system.

[18] Everett V. Samuelson, George G. Tankard, Jr., and Hoyt W. Pope, *Financial Accounting for School Activities,* Bulletin 1959, no. 21, U.S. Office of Education, Washington, D.C.: U.S. Government Printing Office, 109 pp.

Many of the principles governing activity fund accounting, including recommendations for a centralized treasury and accounting system, proper procedures for recording cash receipts, and incurring and meeting liabilities recommended in the previous portion of this chapter, are in accord with those in the forthcoming USOE financial accounting handbook for school activity funds. The standard Receipt Accounts, Expenditure Accounts, and Clearing Accounts to be described are based on the 1959 USOE handbook of *Financial Accounting for School Activities* and can be applied to the degree desirable in any of the five funds previously enumerated.

RECEIPT ACCOUNTS

The income for student body activities is derived from various sources. They include ticket sales or admissions, dues and fees, general activity tickets, sale of merchandise, advertising, guarantees, rentals, and others. The following Receipt Accounts will apply if the specific activities are financed wholly or in part by revenue directly obtained from the operation of that activity. The accounts in this portion of the chapter would not apply if the school activity is financed entirely by money appropriated by the school district and the school district receives no reimbursement from the operation of that activity. The approach to such accounting was described in an earlier portion of this chapter. It is strongly recommended that all schools, regardless of size, maintain the Receipt Accounts which apply to the given school system. Uniformity is to be strongly recommended but only those minimum Receipt Accounts which apply to the school situation should be used.

The Receipt Accounts can be divided basically into: (1) ACTIVITY INCOME, (2) GRANTS FROM THE SCHOOL DISTRICT, (3) GRANTS FROM OTHER SOURCES, and (4) OTHER RECEIPTS. The Receipt Accounts are given numbers ranging from 10 to 99.

ACCOUNT SERIES 10—ACTIVITY INCOME

Posted within these accounts are all monies which accrue in any of the five funds as the result of operation of the various student activities, contests, publications, organizations, services, etc. This account series can be divided into the following major accounts:

A. *Major Account 11—Admissions.* As the term implies, posted herein is the money received from the sale of tickets or from other admission charges for any activity. It includes pregame and season ticket sales. The total receipts less admission taxes, which must be paid, are reported here. The sums which must be remitted to pay taxes are placed in the Clearing Accounts and not herein.

B. *Major Account 12—Prorated Share of General Activity Tickets.*

C. *Major Account 13—Dues and Fees.* If the exact amount of dues and fees collected is to be turned over to the board of education, they are recorded in the Clearing Accounts and not herein. Dues and fees are posted here if used by student organizations.

D. *Major Account 14—Sales.* This, in turn, can be subdivided to reflect a particular type of sales:
   1. Account 14-a—Books and Periodicals.
   2. Account 14-b—Confections, Foods, and Beverages.
   3. Account 14-c—Other Merchandise.

E. *Major Account 15—Student Rentals from Materials.* This includes rental for books and supplies to students and not rentals which must be turned over *in toto* to the board of education. If the funds are to be returned to the board of education, they are recorded in the Clearing Accounts.

F. *Major Account 16—Advertising.* Recorded here is money received from the sale of advertising space in a school annual, paper, program, or other school property.

G. *Major Account 17—Guarantees.* Guarantees represent income received from a public performance of athletic teams or from musical or dramatic organizations that appear elsewhere.

H. *Major Account 18—Other Activity Income.*

ACCOUNT SERIES 20—GRANTS FROM THE SCHOOL DISTRICT

Within this series of accounts would be posted receipts in the form of appropriations from the General Fund of the school district for the support of student activities.

ACCOUNT SERIES 30—GIFTS FROM OTHER SOURCES

ACCOUNT SERIES 40—OTHER RECEIPTS

STANDARD EXPENDITURE ACCOUNTS

The standard Expenditure Accounts can be divided into major classifications of (1) ACTIVITY EXPENSE and (2) CAPITAL OUTLAY. Activity Expense is defined as any expenditure from an activity fund for the operation of student programs. Most expenditures generally incurred by all schools are grouped in *Major Account 110.* Supplemental expenses can be posted

to *Major Account 120.* The Expenditure Account series are given the numbers 100 through 900 but only those accounts in the 100 and 200 series are developed herein.

ACCOUNT SERIES 100—ACTIVITY EXPENSE

Within this series of accounts are included expenditures directly connected with the operation of school activities. Posted in the *Major Accounts 100–120* are expenditures for athletic contests, entertainment events, publications, student organizations, instructional services, merchandising activities, and items of a similar nature.

A. *Major Account 110—Basic Operating Expenditures.*
   1. Account 111—Personal and Contracted Services. Posted herein are expenditures for the services of assembly speakers, chaperons, ticket sellers, and police guards, as well as the salaries of all district personnel directly connected with the operation of the school activity program such as coaches, activity directors and advisors, sponsors, leaders, teachers, trainers, secretaries, clerks, and similar personnel. This assumes that the salary is paid for out of such activity funds rather than out of board of education funds.
   2. Account 112—Supplies.
   3. Account 113—Purchases of Merchandise.
      a. Subaccount 113-a—Books and Periodicals.
      b. Subaccount 113-b—Confections, Foods, and Beverages.
      c. Subaccount 113-c—Other Merchandise.
   4. Account 114—Other Activity Expense.
      a. Subaccount 114-a—Advertising.
      b. Subaccount 114-b—Guarantee.
      c. Subaccount 114-c—Travel Expense.
      d. Subaccount 114-d—Miscellaneous Expense.

B. *Major Account 120—Supplemental Operating Expenditures.*
   1. Account 121—Health Services. This major category starts the Supplemental Accounts which are those accounts that are not necessary in all schools or funds.
      a. Subaccount 121-a—Personal and Contracted Services.
      b. Subaccount 121-b—Other Expenses.
   2. Account 122—Pupil Transportation. These are expenditures or expenses related to transporting pupils to various school activities.
      a. Subaccount 122-a—Personal and Contracted Services.
      b. Subaccount 122-b—Other Expenses.
   3. Account 123—Operation of Plant. Placed herein are expenditures from the activity fund for the

various housekeeping activities necessary to keep the physical plant open and ready for use by student activities.

  a. Subaccount 123-a—Personal and Contracted Services.
  b. Subaccount 123-b—Other Expenses.

4. Account 124—Maintenance of Plant.

  a. Subaccount 124-a—Personal and Contracted Services.
  b. Subaccount 124-b—Other Expenses.

5. Account 125—Fixed Charges. Recorded herein are expenditures not readily allocable to other accounts such as contributions to retirement, insurance premiums, etc.

  a. Subaccount 125-a—Employer Contributions to Retirement Systems.
  b. Subaccount 125-b—Insurance.
  c. Subaccount 125-c—Rental of Land and Buildings.
  d. Subaccount 125-d—Other Expenses for Fixed Charges.

ACCOUNT SERIES 200—CAPITAL OUTLAY

Posted herein are all expenditures from the activity fund which result in the acquisition of initial or additional equipment for any activity or organization. To illustrate, the initial purchase of a basketball scoreboard or photographic equipment would be placed in this series of accounts.

CLEARING ACCOUNTS FOR STUDENT ACTIVITIES

Clearing Accounts are as necessary for school activities as they are for the General Fund. They help to present a true picture of the financial condition of the school and prevent distortion that would result if the receipts and expenditures were reported in the regular Receipt and Expenditure Accounts.

The Clearing Accounts recommended in the 1959 USOE financial accounting handbook for student activity funds are classified into the two general types of (1) money collected and held for the board of education and out-of-school organizations which must be turned over to such agencies in the exact amount collected, and (2) money collected and held for individual or group activities of the school which should be accounted for apart from the regular accounts of student activities and organizations.

Placed within the first category are collections that must be turned over to the board such as fees, rentals, and fines; monies belonging to special drives or campaigns such as the Red Cross; collections for taxes and payroll deductions; other miscellaneous activities of the in-and-out nature such as student insurance premiums and individual bus fares.

The second category would include (1) collections from students, a portion of which is to be returned at a later date, such as deposits on lockers, towels, gym suits, and laboratory fees; (2) unprorated portions of the general activity ticket; (3) refunds, rebates, and collections for loss and damage to school property; (4) loans from the school district; (5) interfund transfers; (6) advancements such as those made for Petty Cash; and (7) receipts from state or conference meets or tournaments.

In using Clearing Accounts, several rules are recommended: (1) each account should be kept separate and distinct within itself; (2) all monies received by the school, which are not part of the regular Receipt Accounts, are recorded initially in the appropriate Clearing Accounts as money received; (3) all monies paid out are reported in the appropriate Clearing Account; (4) when all of the money in a particular account has been paid out, the account is cleared; (5) with few exceptions, all Clearing Accounts should be cleared at the end of the fiscal year.

ACCOUNT SERIES 1000—CLEARING ACCOUNTS

Accounts are required to house temporarily income for activities in individual schools which are sent at a later date to such outside groups or organizations as the board of education, a state or federal tax department, commercial firms, etc. The school operates essentially as a collecting agency for funds which are later turned over to groups at designated periods in the exact amount collected. In all cases further subdivisions of the accounts listed below would show Money Received and Money Paid Out, i.e., *Receipts and Expenditures.*

A. *Major Account 1010—Board of Education.* Money collected for the board of education for instructional fees, fines, payments, the repair and replacement of books and property, and any other purposes and which is to be remitted to the board of education at some future date is posted herein.

B. *Major Account 1020—Out-of-School Campaigns.* Posted herein is money collected for the various campaigns sponsored by local and national organizations such as Red Cross, Cancer Fund, and Community Chest. Appropriate subaccounts would be necessary for each campaign held in the school.

C. *Major Account 1030—Taxes and Deductions.* Recorded in this account are monies deducted from the salaries of employees of student activity accounts. Such monies are usually remitted to the federal government or the state agency for which purpose it was withheld.

D. *Major Account 1040—Nonstudent School Organizations.* Included here are monies belonging to

TABLE 17. Applications of Accounts to the Athletic Fund

REGULAR ACCOUNTS	
Receipts 10–99 Series	Expenditures 100–200 Series

ACCOUNT SERIES 10—ACTIVITY INCOME
 	
Major Account 11—Admissions
 	
Major Account 12—Prorated Share of General Activity Tickets
 	
Major Account 13—Dues and Fees
 	
Major Account 16—Advertising
 	
Major Account 17—Guarantees
 	
Major Account 18—Other Activity Income
 	
ACCOUNT SERIES 20—GRANTS FROM THE SCHOOL DISTRICT
 	
ACCOUNT SERIES 30—GIFTS FROM OTHER SOURCES
 	
ACCOUNT SERIES 40—OTHER RECEIPTS
	ACCOUNT SERIES 100—ACTIVITY EXPENSE
	
	A. *Major Account 110—Basic Operating Expenditures*
	  1. *Account 111—Personal and Contracted Services*
	  2. *Account 112—Supplies*
	  3. *Account 114—Other Activity Expense*
	    Subaccount 114-a—Advertising
	    Subaccount 114-b—Guarantees
	    Subaccount 114-c—Travel Expense
	    Subaccount 114-d—Miscellaneous
	
	B. *Major Account 120—Supplemental Operating Expenditures*
	  1. *Account 121—Health Services*
	    Subaccount 121-a—Personal and Contracted Services
	    Subaccount 121-b—Other Expense
	  2. *Account 122—Pupil Transportation*
	    Subaccount 122-a—Personal and Contracted Services
	    Subaccount 122-b—Other Expense
	  3. *Account 123—Operation of Plant*
	    Subaccount 123-a—Personal and Contracted Services
	    Subaccount 123-b—Other Expense
	  4. *Account 124—Maintenance of Plant*
	    Subaccount 124-a—Personal and Contracted Services
	    Subaccount 124-b—Other Expense
	  5. *Account 125—Fixed Charges*
	    Subaccount 125-a—Employer Contributions to Retirement Systems
	    Subaccount 125-b—Insurance
	    Subaccount 125-c—Rental of Land and Buildings
	
	ACCOUNT SERIES 200—CAPITAL OUTLAY (Initial and Additional Equipment)

ACCOUNT SERIES 1000—CLEARING ACCOUNTS
Money Received and Paid Out
Major Account 1030—Taxes and Deductions *Major Account 1070—Abatements* *Major Account 1090—Interfund Transfers* *Major Account 1100—Petty Cash*

TABLE 18.   Application of Accounts to the Merchandise Fund

REGULAR ACCOUNTS	
Receipts 10–99 Series	Expenditures 100–200 Series

ACCOUNT SERIES 10—ACTIVITY INCOME
 	
Major Account 14—Sales
 	
Major Account 18—Other Activity Income
 	
ACCOUNT SERIES 20—GRANTS FROM THE SCHOOL DISTRICT
 	
ACCOUNT SERIES 30—GIFTS FROM OTHER SOURCES
 	
ACCOUNT SERIES 40—OTHER RECEIPTS
	ACCOUNT SERIES 100—ACTIVITY EXPENSE
	
	A. *Major Account 110—Basic Operating Expenditures*
	  1. *Account 111—Personal and Contracted Services*
	  2. *Account 112—Supplies*
	  3. *Account 113—Purchase of Merchandise*
	    Subaccount 113-a—Books and Publications
	    Subaccount 113-b—Confections, Foods, and Beverage
	    Subaccount 113-c—Other Merchandise
	  4. *Account 114—Other Activity Expense*
	
	B. *Major Account 120—Supplemental Operating Expenditures*
	  1. *Account 123—Operation of Plant*
	    Subaccount 123-a—Personal and Contracted Services
	    Subaccount 123-b—Other Expense
	  2. *Account 124—Maintenance of Plant*
	    Subaccount 124-a—Personal and Contracted Services
	    Subaccount 124-b—Other Expense
	  3. *Account 125—Fixed Charges*
	    Subaccount 125-a—Employer Contributions to Retirement
	    Subaccount 125-b—Insurance
	    Subaccount 125-c—Rental
	
	ACCOUNT SERIES 200—CAPITAL OUTLAY (Initial and Additional Equipment)

ACCOUNT SERIES 1000—CLEARING ACCOUNTS
Same as in Table 17

TABLE 19. Application of Accounts to the Publication Fund

REGULAR ACCOUNTS	
Receipts 10–99 Series	Expenditures 100–200 Series

ACCOUNT SERIES 10—ACTIVITY INCOME

   Major Account 12—Prorated Share of General Activity Tickets

   Major Account 13—Dues and Fees

   Major Account 14—Sales

   Major Account 16—Advertising

   Major Account 18—Other Activity Income

ACCOUNT SERIES 20—GRANTS FROM THE SCHOOL DISTRICT

ACCOUNT SERIES 30—GIFTS FROM OTHER SOURCES

ACCOUNT SERIES 40—OTHER RECEIPTS

ACCOUNT SERIES 100—ACTIVITY EXPENSE

  A. *Major Account 110—Basic Operating Expenditures*
    1. *Account 111—Personal and Contracted Services*
    2. *Account 112—Supplies*
    3. *Account 114—Other Activity Expense*
      Subaccount 114-c—Travel Expense
      Subaccount 114-d—Miscellaneous

  B. *Major Account 120—Supplemental Operating Expenditures*
    1. *Account 123—Operation of Plant*
      Subaccount 123-a—Personal and Contracted Services
      Subaccount 123-b—Other Expense
    2. *Account 124—Maintenance of Plant*
      Subaccount 124-a—Personal and Contracted Services
      Subaccount 124-b—Other Expense
    3. *Account 125—Fixed Charges*
      Subaccount 125-a—Employer Contributions to Retirement
      Subaccount 125-b—Insurance
      Subaccount 125-d—Other Fixed Charges

ACCOUNT SERIES 200—CAPITAL OUTLAY (Initial and Additional Equipment)

ACCOUNT SERIES 1000—CLEARING ACCOUNTS

Money Received and Paid Out

   Major Account 1030—Taxes and Deductions
   Major Account 1070—Abatements
   Major Account 1090—Interfund Transfers
   Major Account 1100—Petty Cash

TABLE 20. Application of Accounts to the Student Organization Fund

REGULAR ACCOUNTS

Receipts 10–99 Series	Expenditures 100–200 Series
ACCOUNT SERIES 10—ACTIVITY INCOME	ACCOUNT SERIES 100—ACTIVITY EXPENSE
Major Account 11—Admissions	A. *Major Account 110—Basic Operating Expenditures*
Major Account 12—Prorated Share of General Activity Tickets	1. *Account 111—Personal and Contracted Services*
Major Account 13—Dues and Fees	2. *Account 112—Supplies*
Major Account 14—Sales	3. *Account 113—Purchase of Merchandise*
Major Account 16—Advertising	4. *Account 114—Other Activity Expense*
Major Account 17—Guarantees	Subaccount 114-a—Advertising
Major Account 18—Other Activity Income	Subaccount 114-b—Guarantees
ACCOUNT SERIES 20—GRANTS FROM THE SCHOOL DISTRICT	Subaccount 114-c—Travel Expense
	Subaccount 114-d—Miscellaneous
ACCOUNT SERIES 30—GIFTS FROM OTHER SOURCES	B. *Major Account 120—Supplemental Operating Expense*
ACCOUNT SERIES 40—OTHER RECEIPTS	1. *Account 122—Pupil Transportation*
	Subaccount 122-a—Personal and Contracted Services
	Subaccount 122-b—Other Expense
	2. *Account 123—Operation of Plant*
	Subaccount 123-a—Personal and Contracted Services
	Subaccount 123-b—Other Expense
	3. *Account 124—Maintenance of Plant*
	Subaccount 124-a—Personal and Contracted Services
	Subaccount 124-b—Other Expense
	4. *Account 125—Fixed Charges*
	Subaccount 125-a—Employer Contributions to Retirement Systems
	Subaccount 125-b—Insurance
	Subaccount 125-c—Rental
	ACCOUNT SERIES 200—CAPITAL OUTLAY (Initial or Additional Equipment)

ACCOUNT SERIES 1000—CLEARING ACCOUNTS

Money Received and Paid Out

Major Account 1030—Taxes and Deductions
Major Account 1070—Abatements
Major Account 1090—Interfund Transfers
Major Account 1100—Petty Cash

TABLE 21. Application of Accounts to the Miscellaneous Fund

REGULAR ACCOUNTS

Receipts 10–99 Series	Expenditures 100–200 Series

ACCOUNT SERIES 10—ACTIVITY INCOME
 	
  Major Account 12—Dues and Fees
 	
  Major Account 18—Other Activity Income
 	
ACCOUNT SERIES 20—GRANTS FROM THE SCHOOL DISTRICT
 	
ACCOUNT SERIES 30—GIFTS FROM OTHER SOURCES
 	
ACCOUNT SERIES 40—OTHER RECEIPTS
	ACCOUNT SERIES 100—ACTIVITY EXPENSE
	
	A. *Major Account 110—Basic Operating Expenditures*
	  1. *Account 111—Personal and Contracted Services*
	  2. *Account 112—Supplies*
	  3. *Account 114—Other Activity Expense*
	
	B. *Major Account 120—Supplemental Operating Expenditures*
	  1. *Account 123—Operation of Plant*
	    Subaccount 123-a—Personal and Contracted Services
	    Subaccount 123-b—Other Expense
	  2. *Account 124—Maintenance of Plant*
	    Subaccount 124-a—Personal and Contracted Services
	    Subaccount 124-b—Other Expense
	  3. *Account 125—Fixed Charges*
	    Subaccount 125-a—Employer Contributions to Retirement Systems
	    Subaccount 125-b—Insurance
	    Subaccount 125-c—Rental
	
	ACCOUNT SERIES 200—CAPITAL OUTLAY (Initial or Additional Equipment)

ACCOUNT SERIES 1000—CLEARING ACCOUNTS

Money Received and Paid Out

  Major Account 1010—Board of Education
  Major Account 1020—Out-of-School Campaigns
  Major Account 1030—Taxes and Deductions
  Major Account 1040—Nonstudent School Organizations
  Major Account 1060—General Activity Tickets
  Major Account 1100—Petty Cash

FORM 15.

RECEIPTS DISTRIBUTION LEDGER

| | | | | | RECEIPT ACCOUNTS | | | | | | |
| | | | | | 10. Activity Income | | | | | | |
No.	Date	Receipt No.	Amount	Explanation	Admissions 11	Prorated Activity Tickets 12	Dues and Fees 13	Sales 14	Advertising 16	Guarantees 17	Other Income 18
(1)	(2)	(3)	(4)	(5)				(6)			
1	10/2	100	$500	Junior Class Play	$490						
2	10/3	103	100	Assembly Program	100						
3	10/5	105	25	Dramatic Club			$25				
4	10/7	107	600	School Carnival	196			$392			
5	10/9	108	50	Y-Teens			50				
6	10/10		400	Transferred from Miscellaneous Fund ↰ ↲ Sale of Magazine to Senior Class							
7	10/10		100	Prorated Share of General Activity ↰ ↲ Tickets, Student Council		$100					
			$1775	Totals	$786	$100	$75	$392			

FORM 15—(Continued).

				CLEARING ACCOUNTS				
Grants 20	Gifts 30	Other Receipts 40	Total Receipts	Taxes and Deductions 1030-a	Deposits 1050	Interfund Transfers 1090-o	Petty Cash 1100-o	Total Clearing Receipts
(7)	(8)	(9)	(10)	(11)	(12)	(13)	(14)	(15)
			$ 490	$10				$ 10
			100					
			25					
			588	12				12
			50					
						$400		400
			100					
			$1353	$22		$400		$422

FORM 16.

EXPENDITURES DISTRIBUTION LEDGER

					EXPENDITURE ACCOUNTS							
					100. Activity Expense							
					110. Basic Operating Expenditure					120. Supplemental Operating Expenditure		
No.	Date	Check No.	Amount	Explanation	Personal & Contracted Services 111	Supplies 112	Purchases of Merchandise 113	Other Activity Expense 114	Transportation 122	Operation of Plant 123	Maintenance of Plant 124	Fixed Charges 125
(1)	(2)	(3)	(4)	(5)	(6)							
1	10/3	21	$ 20	Junior Class Playbooks		$20						
2	10/4	23	50	Junior Class Rental of Costumes				$50				
3	10/5	25	100	Junior Class Carnival Sup.			$100					
4	10/7	26	15	Junior Class Play Newspaper Ad				15				
5	10/8	27	20	Sales Tax								
6	10/9	28	150	Dramatic Club Tape Recorder								
7	10/10	29	25	Junior Class Play Custodian						$25		
			$380			$20	$100	$65		$25		

		CLEARING ACCOUNTS				
Capital Outlay 200	Total Expenditures	Taxes and Deductions 1030	Deposits 1050	Interfund Transfers 1090	Petty Cash 1100	Total Clearing Expenditures
(7)	(8)	(9)	(10)	(11)	(12)	(13)
	$ 20					
	50					
	100					
	15					
		$20				$20
$150	150					
	25					
$150	$360	$20				$20

FORM 17.

FUND LEDGER

Senior Class

Student Organization Fund

Date	Explanation	Receipt No.	Check No.	Receipts	Expenditures	Balance
	Balance, 10/1/58					$ 50.00
10/5	School Carnival	107		$588.00		638.00
10/7	Merchandise Sold at Carnival		25		$100.00	$538.00
10/10	Profit from Sale of Magazine Transferred from Merchandise Fund			400.00		938.00

Junior Class

Date	Explanation	Receipt No.	Check No.	Receipts	Expenditures	Balance
	Balance, 10/1/58					$100.00
10/2	Junior Class Play	100		$490.00		590.00
10/3	Playbooks		21		$ 20.00	570.00
10/7	Advertising		26		15.00	555.00
10/4	Rental of Costumes		23		50.00	505.00
10/10	Custodian Fee for Play		29		25.00	480.00

Student Council

Date	Explanation	Receipt No.	Check No.	Receipts	Expenditures	Balance
10/3	Assembly Program	103		$100.00		$100.00
10/10	Prorated Share of General Activities Tickets			100.00		200.00

Dramatic Club

Date	Explanation	Receipt No.	Check No.	Receipts	Expenditures	Balance
10/1	Balance					$125.00
10/5	Club Dues	105		$ 25.00		150.00
10/9	Purchased Tape Recorder		28		$150.00	——

Y-Teens

Date	Explanation	Receipt No.	Check No.	Receipts	Expenditures	Balance
10/9	Club Dues	108		$ 50.00		$ 50.00

Sales Tax Payable

Date	Explanation	Receipt No.	Check No.	Receipts	Expenditures	Balance
10/2	Tax on Junior Class Play	100		$ 10.00		$ 10.00
10/5	Tax on School Carnival	107		12.00		22.00
10/8	Paid Tax Commission		27		$ 22.00	——

FORM 18.

MONTHLY FINANCIAL STATEMENT

_____ Fund

Balance, 10/1/57		$ 275.00

RECEIPTS
Regular Receipts — $1,353.00
Clearing Receipts

Transfers from Other Funds	$ 400.00	
Other Clearing Receipts	22.00	

Total Clearing Receipts — 422.00
Total Receipts — $1,775.00

EXPENDITURES
Regular Expenditures — $ 360.00
Clearing Expenditures

Transfers to Other Funds	$ ———	
Other Clearing Expenditures	22.00	

Total Clearing Expenditures — 22.00
Total Expenditures — $ 382.00

Balance — $1,393.00
Total Cash for Fund, 10/31/57 — $1,668.00

Detailed Monthly Financial Statement

Activity	Balance 10/1/57	Receipts	Expenditures	Balance 11/1/57
Senior Class	$ 50.00	$ 988.00	$100.00	$ 938.00
Junior Class	100.00	490.00	110.00	480.00
Student Council		200.00		200.00
Dramatic Club	125.00	25.00	150.00	
Y-Teen Club		50.00		50.00
State Sales Tax		22.00	22.00	
Total	$275.00	$1,775.00	$382.00	$1,668.00

FORM 19.

MONTHLY SUMMARY STATEMENT FOR ALL FUNDS

Balance, 10/1/57	$1,000.00	
Total Deposits Nos. 10–13	2,490.00	
Total	$3,490.00	
Less Checks Nos. 21–29	815.00	
Balance, 11/1/57		$2,675.00

Fund	Balance 10/1/57	Regular Receipts	Clearing Receipts	Regular Expenditures	Clearing Expenditures	Balance 11/1/57
Athletic	$ 250.00	$ 392.00	$ 8.00	$ 75.00	$ 8.00	$ 567.00
Merchandise	200.00	750.00		350.00	400.00	200.00
Publications	100.00	25.00				125.00
Student Organization	275.00	1,353.00	422.00	360.00	22.00	1,668.00
Miscellaneous	175.00		40.00		100.00	115.00
Total	$1,000.00	$2,520.00	$470.00	$785.00	$530.00	$2,675.00

nonstudent organizations such the faculty club, PTA, alumni organizations, etc.

E. *Major Account 1050—Returnable Deposits.* Posted herein are monies collected from students to guarantee the safe return of books, keys, uniforms, laboratory equipment, etc., which have been furnished to students by the school or student activity. Subaccounts should be maintained for each type of deposit.

F. *Major Account 1060—General Activity Tickets.* Posted herein are monies received from the sale of general activity tickets which are to be prorated on the percentage basis to various student activities. Season tickets are not included herein but under *Major Account 11—Admissions.*

G. *Major Account 1070—Abatements.*

H. *Major Account 1080—Loans from the School District.*
   1. Account 1080-a—Receipts. This includes money received as a loan from the school district for the junior class yearbook, student council, etc.
   2. Account 1080-b—Expenditures.

I. *Major Account 1090—Transfers.* The purpose here is to record transfers from one activity fund to another. An interfund transfer is a receipt or expenditure of the fund to which or from which it is transferred; it is not a receipt or expenditure for the total activity funds of the school.
   1. Account 1090-a—Transfers from Other Funds.
   2. Account 1090-b—Transfers to Other Funds.

J. *Major Account 1100—Petty Cash.*

APPLICATION OF RECEIPT AND EXPENDITURE ACCOUNTS TO THE VARIOUS ACTIVITY FUNDS

1. *Athletic Fund.* The Athletic Fund is necessary to account for the financial transaction of various interscholastic programs for football, basketball, track, or other sports. The general standard Receipt, Expenditure, and Clearing Accounts to be maintained are summarized in Table 17. If more specific information is needed to cover the finances of each sport, Receipt, Expenditure, and Clearing Accounts can be had under separate headings or categories or through coding.

2. *Merchandise Fund.* The Merchandise Fund is used to account for the merchandising activities of the school directed primarily toward satisfying purchasing needs of students, teachers, and the general public. The standard Receipt, Expenditure, and Clearing Accounts which can be easily applied to this fund are presented in Table 18.

3. *Publications Fund.* The financial transactions necessary in the preparation, production, and distribution of student-produced publications such as the paper, yearbook, or magazine can be posted in the Publication Fund. The application of standard Receipt, Expenditure, and Clearing Accounts to the Publication Funds is summarized in Table 19.

4. *Student Organization Fund.* All the money used to finance the activities of clubs, classes, and similar organizations under the supervision of the schools is posted in the Student Organization Fund. Nonschool student organizations, such as boy scouts and girl scouts and 4-H Clubs, are handled through the Miscellaneous Fund or Clearing Accounts. The application of the standard Receipt, Expenditure, and Clearing Accounts to the Student Organization Fund is presented in Table 20.

5. *Instructional Fees and Rental Fund.* Included herein are the transactions for activities primarily of a classroom nature, such as instructional aids and fees.

6. *Miscellaneous Fund.* The Miscellaneous Fund consists of financial transactions of student-related activities unaccounted for in other funds. The application of the standard Receipt, Expenditure, and Clearing Accounts to this fund is reported in Table 21.

7. *Forms.* A variety of forms are suggested for receipts, checks, registers, and distribution ledgers. Included herein are forms to serve as the Receipts Distribution Ledger, Expenditures Distribution Ledger, and a Fund Ledger. These are adapted from the U.S. Office of Education handbook on *Financial Accounting for School Activities.*

In addition, the suggested forms for monthly financial statements were presented in the U.S. Office of Education financial accounting manual for school activities.

SUMMARY

The tremendous growth of student body activities is a product of the twentieth century, particularly the period following 1920. It is no simple matter today to distinguish between what is curricular and what is extracurricular. Today student body activity funds must be classed as big business and managed accordingly. There is legal support to the contention that student activity funds are public rather than nonpublic funds. Legislation to define clearly the responsibility of school boards with reference to student activity funds is needed in most states.

Student body funds under school board jurisdiction can be accounted for under *Major Account 1810—Student Body Activities* of the regular school Clearing Accounts. The USOE financial accounting handbook for student body activities is a big step toward uniformity in student activity accounting. Budgeting and the centralized treasury system have considerable merit in the business operations of student organizations and events.

Students can help to formulate policies related to business management of student body activity funds, but the actual business operations such as performing the duties of the treasury, purchasing, disbursing, accounting, and reporting should be performed by a professionally prepared adult member of the school's professional staff.

QUESTIONS

1. What are the arguments that tend to establish student body activity funds as public rather than nonpublic funds? As nonpublic rather than public funds?
2. What in your opinion would be justifiable school board controls over student funds?
3. What are the advantages and problems of a central treasury system for the collection and custody of student body funds?
4. Who should participate in the formulation of a budget for student activities? Who should adopt it? Who should execute it?
5. How should funds be disbursed from the student activity treasuries?
6. What are the advantages and problems encumbered in various procedures used to raise money for student organizations?

7. What are the essential elements in a defensible accounting system for student body activities?

SELECTED REFERENCES

Association of School Business Officials, "Special Committee Report: Regulation Supervision of Student Body Expenditure Committee," *A Manual of Accounting Principles and Procedures for Student Activity Funds,* Bulletin no. 17, Evanston, Ill.: the Association, 1957.

Davis, Clifford M., "Supervision and Control of Student Body Finances," *Proceedings of the Association of School Business Officials,* 43rd Convention, October, 1957.

Hamilton, R. R., "The Legal Status, Control and Use of Athletic and Other Extra-Curricular Funds," *The Bi-Weekly School Law Letter,* September, 1952.

Jacobson, Paul B., Reavis, William C., and Logsdon, James D., *The Effective School Principal,* Englewood Cliffs, N.J.: Prentice-Hall, Inc., 1954, chaps. 14, 15.

McKown, H. C., *et al.,* "Financial Administration of Extra-Curricular Activities," *25th Yearbook, Part II,* National Society for the Study of Education, Chicago: University of Chicago Press, 1926.

Reason, Paul L., and White, Alpheus L., *Financial Accounting for Local and State School Systems, Standard Receipt and Expenditure Accounts,* Bulletin 1957, no. 4, U.S. Office of Education, Washington, D.C.: U.S. Government Printing Office, 1957, chap. 5.

Samuelson, Everett V., Tankard, George G., Jr., and Pope, Hoyt W., *Financial Accounting for School Activities,* Bulletin 1959, no. 21, U.S. Office of Education, Washington, D.C.: U.S. Government Printing Office, 109 pp.

CHAPTER 12

School Indebtedness and Capital Outlay Financing

THE GROWING SCHOOL DEBT, THE INCREASING expenditures for interest, and the expanding debt service payments attest to the continuing importance of prudent debt management for public schools. The total school indebtedness in 1929–1930 was approximately $2.4 billion. The debt rose during the first few years of the 1930's and then started a downward trend to hit a low of approximately $1.89 billion in 1944–1945. The feverish school plant construction during the post-World War II period reversed the downward trend and a new period of increasing school debt started in 1945–1946. By 1949–1950 the public school debt reached $3.13 billion. At the beginning of the school year 1952–1953, the school debt exceeded $4 billion for the first time as it totaled $4.4 billion.[1] It is estimated that by no later than 1960 the total school indebtedness will exceed $5 billion.

The size of this debt must be put in perspective. The gross national debt of the United States increased from $1 billion in 1910 to a high of $269 billion in 1946. In 1958 the national debt ceiling of $275 billion was raised temporarily to $280 billion. State and local debts likewise grew in the postwar period. In 1945 the total state and local debt was $13.7 billion. It topped $20 billion in 1950, was greater than $30 billion in 1954, and exceeded $40 billion for the first time in 1956. The private debt of corporations and individuals also scaled new highs in the post-World War II period. Thus, in 1945 the total private debt amounted to something less than $140 billion. The private debt was greater than $200 billion in 1948, exceeded $300 billion for the first time in 1952, and topped $400 billion for the first time in

1956. Since 1945 the net private debt has nearly tripled whereas the school debt was increased by less than two and one-half times during the same period.

The percent of the total local governmental indebtedness incurred for public educational purposes has remained less than 20 percent of the total debt of local governments through the early part of the 1950's. In 1931–1932, the school indebtedness was approximately 19.1 percent of the total debt of local governments. This is about the same as it was in 1951–1952.[2]

In 1929–1930 public elementary and secondary school interest payments were less than $100 million. From 1930 to 1942 school interest payments per year were more than $100 million but less than $141 million. During 1943 and 1948 expenditures per year for interest on existing debt were at a low ebb as they fell considerably below $100 million and 1929–1930 levels. In 1949 the interest payments exceeded $100 million per year once again.[3] By 1955–1956 school interest payments reached $209,108,000.[4] It is estimated that interest payments per year will continue at high levels of $200 million or more. Expenditures for interest have varied from 3 to 5 percent of the school debt. The ratio of interest payments to total school indebtedness has exhibited a distinct downward trend since 1929.

In 1953–1954 the total debt service expenditures for public schools reached a new high of $667,346,295. Debt service is defined as expenditures for the retirement of debt principal and expenditures for interest on the debt. Expenditures made at the time a building is erected are classed as capital outlay and not debt serv-

[1] Clayton D. Hutchins, Albert R. Munse, and Edna D. Booher, *Trends and Significant Facts on School Finance, 1929–1930—1953–1954,* Circular no. 498, U.S. Office of Education, Washington, D.C.: U.S. Government Printing Office, 1957, p. 73.

[2] *Ibid.*
[3] *Ibid.* p. 74.
[4] U.S. Department of Health, Education, and Welfare, *Preliminary Statistics of State School Systems, 1955–1956,* Circular no. 58, U.S. Office of Education, Washington, D.C.: U.S. Government Printing Office, October, 1957.

ice. Expenditures for debt services totaled approximately $251 million in 1929.[5] Although the debt service expenditures have increased in amount, they have decreased as a percent of the total expenditures for public schools. To illustrate, total dollars expended on debt service totaled less in 1929 than in 1953–1954. But the debt service expenditures were 10.9 percent of the total expenditures for schools in 1929–1930 as compared with 7.4 percent in 1953–1954. In 1933–1934, the debt service expenditures for public elementary and secondary schools reached a peak ratio of 21.4 percent of the total expenditures for schools. It is estimated that although expenditures for debt service will continue to increase in amount, they will constitute between 7½ to 10 percent of the total expenditures for the public schools.

There are indications that the school debt will continue to rise unless substantial school construction aid in the form of outright grants are forthcoming from state and federal governmental agencies. Most of the school debt is the direct result of financing schoolhouse construction. Large-scale construction and expenditures for new public school buildings continue during the middle part of the 1950's. In 1954 there was constructed a total of 7567 elementary, secondary, and combination-type public school buildings for which $2.264 billion was expended. There were 7836 buildings completed in 1955 with a total value of $2.44 billion. In 1956 new public school plant construction in the United States totaled 8211 buildings at a cost of $2.547 billion.[6]

The tremendous spurt in school building expenditures in the second half of the twentieth century is further indicated by the fact that $1.03 billion was spent on public school plant construction in 1949, as compared with $2.547 billion in 1956. It is estimated that in 1958 the total public school plant construction will cost $3 billion. Education construction cost rises have not been disproportionate to that of similar construction costs, which have increased more than 150 percent since 1939.

Very large expenditures for capital improvements since World War II made prudent management of indebtedness more imperative than ever before. Most school plant construction must be financed through the sale of bonds. A very large share of the schools' indebtedness is incurred to provide needed capital improvements such as school buildings and large equipment. Some of the school debt is the result of refunding old debts or emergency payments which cannot be met through budgetary appropriations during a given fiscal period. Management is of critical importance in the amortization of a long-term debt. There are indications that the short-term debt problem will demand the same careful management, since school expenditures for current operations increase faster than working capital.

PAY-AS-YOU-GO METHOD OF FINANCING CAPITAL OUTLAYS

Bonds are not the only way to finance capital outlays. There are other ways to finance improvements such as the pay-as-you-go plans. Under the pay-as-you-go plan the annual yield of a dedicated tax is used to pay for the cost of new school facilities. This tax is usually a relatively small millage but when applied to a relative large tax base it produces sufficient revenue to pay for the school building during the period of construction. It should be apparent that a pay-as-you-go plan is not practical in small school districts or in districts with a limited property tax base. Larger cities, which have sizable property tax valuations and where building construction is likely to be carried on more or less continuously, have been known to levy a relatively small tax of 1 to 3 mills to produce a million or more dollars to finance buildings under construction.

The pay-as-you-go plan has the advantage of immediate payment for the school building without incurring additional costs such as interest, bond attorney fees, and other costs incidental to financing capital outlay through bonding. Essex investigated the relative merits of pay-as-you-go plans as compared with bonding as a means of financing building programs.[7] He reported the difficulties experienced by some large communities as well as those of small communities that attempted to finance capital improvements on an annual basis. Perhaps the most serious difficulty with a pay-as-you-go plan is that it does not produce sufficient revenue to finance school plant construction during periods of great demand for schoolhouses. Very few school districts during the period of tremendous school plant construction following World War II were able to pay for the needed construction out of current receipts.

Current tax receipts earmarked for schoolhouse construction in most communities must be regarded in periods of considerable construction as a supplemen-

[5] Hutchins, Munse, and Booher, *op. cit.,* p. 71.
[6] The Editors, "Educational Building in 1956," *American School and University, 1957–1958,* 29th ed., vol. 1, *School Plant Reference,* New York: American School Publishing Corporation, pp. 8–20.

[7] Don L. Essex, *Bonding vs. Pay-As-You-Go in the Financing of School Buildings,* Contributions to Education no. 496, New York: Teachers College, Columbia University, 1931.

tary source rather than as a substitute for bonding. Even larger cities like Milwaukee, which for many years satisfied school plant requirements by using the proceeds of a very small annual tax, found it necessary in the post-World War II period to issue bonds to finance the tremendous school plant needs faced in this growing and dynamic community.

The city of Portland, Oregon, is perhaps unique in that it has successfully employed the pay-as-you-go plan to finance school construction since 1945.[8] Between 1947 and 1957 the school enrollment in this city increased from 49,814 to 70,210 or about 2000 per year. All of the new schools constructed since 1947 were financed on a pay-as-you-go basis. This was accomplished through a series of three tax levies approved by the voters. The first approved $1 million a year for five years to build elementary schools. It became apparent that this $5 million was not enough so in 1948 the voters approved a second levy providing $2½ million a year for ten years. The need for additional high schools required a third serial levy in 1951, totaling $2.78 million for ten years. The three special levies which provided the financial resources to construct new school buildings totaled $57 million. An additional sum of money was carried in the operating budget to remodel some existing plants. During the ten years of 1947 to 1957 remodeling expenditures totaled an additional $3.6 million. It was estimated by DeBernardis and Baker that this system of financing saved the people of Portland an estimated $14 million. This saving was based on the assumption that 3 percent interest on 20-year serial bonds would have been paid if the pay-as-you-go plan had not been used.[9]

THE BUILDING RESERVE PLAN

The building reserve plan is another variation of pay-as-you-go plans. It is sometimes referred to as the sinking fund plan. Under this approach a special tax is voted for a given number of years. The annual proceeds of the voted tax are permitted to accumulate in a fund specially created to finance school plant construction. The annual tax proceeds are large enough and immediately available to cover the cost of a building in the pay-as-you-go plan described in the previous paragraphs as compared with the necessity of accumulating annual tax proceeds in the building reserve plan. At times it is impossible to distinguish be-

tween the two types of pay-as-you-go plans, particularly when the financing of additions to several buildings costs about as much as is received annually from the special school construction tax.

In some states the annual accumulations of special school construction tax can be used for new school construction, additions, or remodeling but in others it is limited to new construction only. The duration of the special tax is decided by ballot and can last one year, five years, or ten years. Often a maximum tax rate is stipulated such as 2½ mills in Iowa. The building reserve fund is practical where time permits the accumulation of additional funds. In most districts the annual proceeds from a tax limited to 1 to 3 mills are too small to finance any sizable building or addition. However, in many communities where far-sighted planning anticipates school building needs, the building reserve plan can prove most effective.

There is considerable merit to the building reserve plan as a means of accumulating funds to replace buildings whose physical or educational obsolescence can be forecasted. The reserves must be carefully managed and held for construction or remodeling only. Special legal and accounting safeguards must be instituted to prevent the shifting of building reserves to uses other than the original purpose.

BONDING

Bonding is most often used to finance large capital outlay programs in public schools. A school bond is similar in some ways to the private corporation bond but different in others. A bond can be defined as *a written financial instrument issued by a corporate body to borrow money with the time and rate of interest to be charged, method of principal payment, and the term of the debt clearly expressed.* The maximum amount of interest payments, the length of term of the issue, the size of bond denominations, school bond elections, etc., are regulated carefully by law in most states.

The bonds of a private corporation are secured by its property. In case of default, the physical assets, particularly those purchased with the bonds, can be taken over. This is not true in school districts. Courts will not permit bond holders to foreclose and take over the physical assets of a defaulting school district. It has been held that to close a school to satisfy bondholders would be contrary to the public good. In this sense, a school bond cannot be looked upon as a mortgage on the real or personal property of the district. To compensate for this, the statutes and courts have ear-

[8] Amo DeBernardis and L. J. Baker, "Paid in Full—Portland $57,-000,000 New School Program," *The American School Board Journal,* February, 1958, *136*:42–44.
[9] *Ibid.*

marked for bondholders a part of the taxable income accruing to defaulting districts until the debt settlement is reached. It is interesting to note that very few school districts have defaulted, and most of those that have defaulted have payed the debt at a later date.

Often the restrictions placed upon bonding appear to be onerous and unnecessary. A review of the history of state and municipal borrowing in particular supports the contention that many of the restrictions were necessitated by previous questionable practices and poor management. Groves pointed out that in the financial history of states and municipalities there were three principal periods in which they plunged recklessly into debt and which ended with much financial distress and defaulting.[10] One such period started in 1820 and ended with the panic in 1837. It was during this time that states and municipalities borrowed heavily to finance canals, railroads, and turnpikes. The total state debt in the United States rose from $26 million in 1830 to $175 million at the close of that decade. By 1852, eight states were in default, six of which later made good on their obligations. The constitutional restrictions on state borrowing became a feature of most state constitutions by 1857 as a result of these excesses.

A second period preceded the panic of 1873. Following this second period of careless financing, state governments borrowed little from 1875 to 1914. The third period of considerable public borrowing occurred during the period from 1920 to 1930. The depression of 1929 brought about tremendous problems. By April of 1933, three states and over 1000 municipalities were technically insolvent. It is characteristic of American states and cities to borrow when times are good and taxes are comparatively easy to raise and to pay off their bonds when times are bad and tax collection is difficult. This appears to be the pattern in school indebtedness as well. As was pointed out previously, the school debt was declining during the depression years, but during the very prosperous times of the 1940's and 1950's, the school debt increased significantly.

Although legal restrictions on incurring indebtedness are onerous, they are not necessarily bad in themselves. Those that promote better management, such as the requirement that only serial bonds can be issued, are commendable. Statutory or constitutional requirements which promote the careful regulation of the school's debt can make bonds easier to market and command a more favorable rate of interest. Legal restrictions, such as holding the debt limitation of schools to an unrealistically low percent of the assessed valuation of property, can result in the impairment of the

[10] Harold M. Groves, *Financing Government*, New York: Henry Holt & Co., Inc., rev. ed., 1945, pp. 540–541.

fundamental purposes of the school district. This is particularly true in states where property assessed by local or county assessors is set at a mere fraction of its true or full value and no effective means are taken at the state level to correct the gross underassessment of property in a school district.

LIMITATIONS ON SCHOOL INDEBTEDNESS

The limitations on indebtedness through the issuance of school bonds vary greatly among the states. Usually these limitations are expressed in terms of assessed value of taxable property in the district. The debt limits as percent of assessed value of taxable property range from 2 percent for Indiana and Kentucky up to 50 percent for certain school districts in Minnesota.[11] In Maryland there is no limit, but all the bond issues in the 24 school districts of the state must be presented for the consideration of the state legislature of Maryland. Approximately one-fourth of the states in 1953–1954 placed a limitation of 5 percent or less of the taxable assessments. About one-half of the states set the debt limitation of 9 percent or less of the assessed value of taxable property. The nine states of Arkansas, California, Louisiana, Michigan, Minnesota, Mississippi, Nebraska, Nevada, and Virginia permit at least some of the school districts to issue bonds up to 12 percent or more of the taxable valuations of property. The legal limitations on school bond indebtedness are more often to be found in the statutes than in the constitutions although the constitutions of 20 states prescribe the limitations on school bond indebtedness. There is a trend toward raising the debt limitations.

Other limitations may also prevail. To illustrate, in Iowa the debt service for the retirement of bond issues cannot be larger than the amount of money that can be raised by 7 mills in one year. During periods of high interest rates, this tends to reduce further the amount of bonds which can be issued in that state.

State law also determines the maximum number of years a school bond may run, what type of bonds may be issued, and what agency may issue the bonds. School bonds may be issued by local school boards in 41 states. But in ten states a nonschool agency may issue school bonds. Of these ten, Georgia, New Jersey, and Wisconsin permit school bonds to be issued by

[11] Clayton D. Hutchins and Albert R. Munse, *Public School Finance Programs of the United States*, Miscellaneous no. 22, U.S. Office of Education, Washington, D.C.: U.S. Government Printing Office, 1955, pp. 45–49.

school agencies as well as by nonschool agencies, but in the remaining seven states bonds for school constructions are issued exclusively by nonschool agencies.[12]

The state laws in 34 states indicate that only serial bonds may be issued. The maximum number of years a school bond may run varies from 15 years in some school districts in Maryland and New Jersey to no limit in Arkansas, Indiana, Nebraska, Pennsylvania, Rhode Island, and South Dakota. The average term for school bonds is approximately 26 years.[13] Most states set the maturity limits for school bonds at between 20 and 25 years. There are grounds for considerable argument as to what is the proper length of a term in years for a school bond. The length of term is more often determined arbitrarily rather than through a carefully developed understanding of the life span of the capital improvement which the bond issue finances. With school buildings constructed to last from 50 to 75 years, it appears reasonable that the length of the bond term could well be at least half as long as the life of the building. This would indicate that the period for amortization of a bond could justifiably range from 25 to 37½ years. Some states like New Jersey vary the total amortization period for school bonds according to the type of construction. To illustrate, frame buildings will become physically obsolete before a building constructed primarily of steel and masonry and hence bonds on frame buildings should be amortized 10 to 20 years before those issued to finance steel and masonry structures.

Some states have additional restrictions, such as state approval of local issues, either before or after elections. State approval is required in less than one-half or 21 states of the Union. Relatively few require that the bonds must first be offered to a state agency, and fewer still demand that the state assist with the sale of bonds.[14]

Property valuations for tax purposes are not assessed at the same rate in all states. It is estimated that the value of taxable properties as expressed on assessment roles varies from 10 to 90 percent of true value. In 21 states the property assessments for tax purposes are lower than 40 percent of true values. Only six states report estimates as high as 60 percent. It can be seen that this tendency to underassess property values in school districts is a further limitation on the amount of money school districts can borrow for construction purposes.

Another legal limitation which cannot be ignored is that all bond issues have to be submitted for approval to a vote of the people. There appears to be a reduction in the requirement for approval since Smith's study in 1930.[15] In a 1949 study, it was reported that requirements for bond elections in 45 states specify that the issue must carry by a simple majority in 34 states, by 60 percent in 4 states, and by approximately two-thirds in 7 states.[16] Smith's study in 1930 indicated that 5 states required a three-fourths vote, but a study of the 48 state school systems in 1949 indicated that no states had a requirement as rigid as a three-fourths approval for school bond elections. It is questionable whether any more than a simple majority for approval is necessary. Where a 60 percent majority must prevail for a school bond issue to be approved by the electorate, a minority of a little more than 40 percent of the people can dictate the course of indebtedness.

It is heartening to note that school bond issues submitted to a vote of the people have more often met with success than failure. In Iowa during 1950–1955, three out of every four bond issues were approved at the first ballot. All that failed were resubmitted with or without modifications and were subsequently approved. It appears that the initial disapproval merely delayed for a period rather than completely defeated the bond proposal. Other states reported approval of from 80 percent to 90 percent of school bonds submitted to an election during a given fiscal period.

TYPES OF BONDS

There are many ways to classify bonds. They can be labeled according to the agency issuing the bonds. All school bonds are public or governmental bonds issued, in most cases, by the school district or, in a minority of states, by the municipality or state. Bonds have also been categorized according to whether they are secured or unsecured; the procedures for paying interest; and the method of retirement of the principal.

School bonds are unsecured bonds. In this sense, all school bonds are debenture bonds or a type of bond not secured by collateral or the tangible assets of the school district.

The methods of paying interest suggest several categories. In a coupon bond interest is paid when a coupon for a stated maturity date is clipped from the many coupons attached to the bond document and

[12] Ibid.
[13] Ibid.
[14] Ibid.

[15] James H. Smith, *Legal Limitations on Bonds and Taxations for Public School Buildings,* Contributions to Education no. 453, New York: Teachers College, Columbia University, 1930, pp. 71, 112–113.
[16] Francis S. Chase and Edgar L. Morphet, *The Forty-Eight State School Systems,* Chicago: The Council of State Governments, 1949, table 42, p. 215.

surrendered to the bank or trust agency designated to pay interest. Each coupon on the bond document reaches maturity at a different time and hence is redeemable for a specific amount on a specific interest date. Coupon bonds are negotiable and the interest is paid to any person who presents the coupon for payment.

Registered bonds carry the provision that principal and interest payments shall be paid to registered owners only. The issuing school district must keep a register of ownership. Transfers are recorded at the issuing office. If the bonds are registered as to interest payment, no coupons are provided and interest is paid at stated periods to the individual who is registered as the owner of the bond. Most authorities recommend that school bonds be unregistered for greater negotiability. Registered bonds are inconvenient for investors who desire negotiability without the bother and expense of registration fees and transfer procedures.

Some bonds are registered as to principal payments only but have coupons for interest payment attached. They are called registered coupon bonds.

Bonds are most frequently classified according to maturity of principal or method of making principal payments. The straight term bond was widely used in the financing of school buildings a generation ago. Interest was paid at stated intervals on the term bond. Principal payments do not fall due until the complete issue reaches maturity. In other words, the entire bond principal payment is paid at maturity. Unless the school district has carefully set aside sufficient funds each year and permitted such funds to accumulate to pay the principal at maturity, there may not be sufficient money at maturity to pay the total principal due. The failure to set aside money each year for principal payment or the mismanagement of whatever sums were accumulated often necessitated refunding or issuance of a new set of bonds to pay the principal on the old, previously issued bonds. Straight term bonds received a rather undesirable reputation simply because of poor planning and inability to meet total principal payments at maturity.

One attempt to correct the principal payment difficulties experienced with the term bond was to require by law the establishment of a sinking fund. The sinking fund type of bond is a term bond where once again the total principal is deferred until the end of the maturity period. However, legal requirements specified the levy of an irrevocable tax, the annual proceeds of which must be placed in a specially designated sinking fund for the payment of principal at maturity. The management of sinking funds often became a problem.

Rather than permit the accumulated funds earmarked for principal payments to remain idle in the bank, school boards played the role of investment experts. Mismanagement of the sinking funds through poor investments or transfer or loans to meet other school costs defeated the very purpose of this type of bond. The management of the accumulated annual principal payments in the sinking fund can be a problem.

The unhappy experiences with the straight term bond and sinking fund bond made serial bonds the most popular type in school use today. The serial bond is the only type permitted to be issued by schools according to school laws in approximately two-thirds of the states. In this type of bond the principal is amortized in installments over a number of years rather than in one lump sum at maturity date. It is, in effect, a series of separate bond issues which mature at different times with principal payments scheduled for a number of years during the lifetime of the issue. It has the advantage over other bonds in that there is systematic payment of principal as well as interest. It also frees a greater portion of the bonding capacity of the district as soon as principal payments on one series fall due.

The serial bond can be regarded as a collection of many term bonds with a certain number of the term bonds reaching maturity each year. The total issue is broken down into several bonds which are numbered serially and are called or mature in that order. No annual payments are placed in a sinking fund under this plan. These bonds are, in effect, a callable type of bond with the date of calling for each series within the total issue clearly indicated. To illustrate, assume a $20,000 bond issue of 20 years with equal annual principal payment. The single issue of $20,000 could be broken up into a series of twenty $1000 bonds and lettered as Series A, Series B, and so on, up to Series T. If the total issue were sold in January 1, 1955, the $1000 Series A could be scheduled to fall due on January 1, 1956. A $1000 principal payment plus the usual interest payment for all existing series bonds would be paid on January 1, 1956. The tax for bond retirement would have to be large enough to pay the $1000 in principal falling due on January 1 of each year plus interest payments. The $1000 Series B bond could be scheduled to mature on January 1, 1957, and the principal of $1000 plus interest payments would be payed on that date. Each of the twenty $1000 bonds would mature in order, or serially, until the last $1000 Series T bond would fall due on January 1, 1975. Note that the bonding capacity of the district is increased by $1000 each year as that amount of principal is retired. This illustration is not intended to convey the idea that all serial bonds must be scheduled for equal annual principal payments during the life of the issue. Nor is it always possible to start retiring part of the principal of the total issue within a year after the bonds are sold. The first payment of principal may be started within three to five years after the sale of the issue, but all must be retired within the maximum term required by state law. The scheduling of principal payments in a serial bond issue is very important in prudent business management of the indebtedness program. It will be developed at greater length in a subsequent portion of this chapter.

Bonds can also be dichotomized into callable and noncallable bonds. Callable bonds include a special provision which gives the district the privilege of paying the entire debt earlier than the maturity stipulated at the time of sale of the issue. Noncallable bonds cannot be called in (the total principal paid, that is) until the stipulated date of maturity. Usually a district will have to pay from ¼ to ½ percent more interest for callable bonds than for noncallable bonds. Callable bonds have a distinct advantage during periods of very high interest rates. Thus, if bonds were issued when high interest rates of 4 or 5 percent prevailed, it would be to the advantage of the district to issue callable bonds, even though this may necessitate an additional ¼ or ½ percent over noncallable bonds. The district has the option to call or not to call any or all bonds after a certain number of years have passed. Assume for purposes of argument that prevailing interest rates dropped to 2 percent some ten years after the 4½ percent callable bonds were sold. It would be to the advantage of the district to recall the entire issue and refinance it at the much lower prevailing rate of interest. There is little advantage to issuing callable bonds sold for a rather low rate of interest of 1 or 2 percent. The only advantage to callable bonds sold at a low rate of interest would be accumulation of considerable unexpected tax funds which would permit the earlier retirement of the debt to procure savings on interest payments.

Refunding bonds are, as the name implies, bonds issued to refund an existing debt which is in callable bond form or which reaches maturity. Refunding bonds are issued when and if interest rates are favorable to consolidate three or four or more callable issues which required several different payments. The unfortunate use of refunding bonds to create a continuing debt when the principal payments of a maturing bond issue cannot be met is difficult to justify even though the necessity may be recognized. It is not necessary to have a special vote of the people to refund existing obligations.

During the depression of the 1930's a school bond known as the *serial-redemption sinking fund bond* was used in refunding programs. It is a callable issue in which the obligations are paid off in serial order as rapidly as accumulations from a continuing levy will permit. It is a term bond with a callable feature in the sense that the entire issue is scheduled to mature on the same date. As a flexible instrument it allows the acceleration of redemption in good times and deceleration when revenues decline. This type of school bond has the advantages of both serial and sinking fund bonds and the disadvantages of neither. A provision in the deed of trust requires that the school district vote a continuing tax levy for the life of this issue. The annual proceeds from this irrevocable annual levy are pledged to a sinking fund, but the nature of the bond requires that the sinking fund be exhausted annually by the call and payment of principal of bonds in serial order. Under this type of debt programming, the district votes an annual tax for debt amortization with as much of the issue called each year as can be raised by the tax rate. Insurance organizations have appeared more willing to purchase the combination type of bond than have banks which seem primarily interested in bonds that definitely mature within ten or twelve years.[17]

Bonds are often called premium or discount bonds. If the bond is sold at a figure higher than par value (or the value stipulated on the face of the bond), it is known as a premium bond. If it is sold for less than par value, it is referred to as a discount bond. The term "premium" is also used at the time of the initial bond sale. A premium is the amount of money offered in excess of the par or face value of the bonds offered for sale.

INTEREST ON SCHOOL BONDS

School bond interest rates have varied through the years. In January of 1951, the average interest rate on all school bonds sold was a very low 1.87 percent. By the end of 1957, however, the school bond interest rates exceeded 4 percent.[18] School interest rates reflect economic conditions. The Korean War, as an illustration, affected school bond interest rates. The actions of the Federal Reserve Board influence interest rates at all times. Clark stressed that for the last 25 years school boards have been able to borrow money at artificially

[17] American Association of School Administrators, *American School Buildings,* 27th Yearbook, Washington, D.C.: the Association, 1949, p. 298.

[18] Harold F. Clark, "Bond Rates, Building Costs, and School Plant Financing," *American School and University, 1957–1958,* 29th ed., vol. 1, *School Plant Reference,* New York: American School Publishing Corporation, pp. 262–266.

low rates. These low rates were established in the 1930's in an effort to encourage business expansion and were continued during the war while the sale of war bonds at low rates was encouraged.[19]

The average rate of interest for school bonds was 4.81 percent in 1929 as compared with 4.48 percent in 1927. There was no month in 1927 when the interest rates were as low as the highest month in 1956, a year during which school bond interest rates were climbing. During 1957 and the early part of 1958 school bond rates approximated the predepression levels. The threat of a rather serious recession during the latter part of 1957 and the early part of 1958 prompted the Federal Reserve Board to lower the member bank reserve requirement and rediscount rates, and this turned the tide, for school bond interest rates began to fall from their 25-year highs.

During the depression it was not unusual for school districts to pay as high as 6 percent interest. This prompted many states to set a maximum of 6 percent on school bonds. Following World War II up through 1957, the free bond market was such as to keep most school bond interest rates below the 4 percent level. Bond interest rates will continue to fluctuate, and only the very careful and astute students of the bond market or those endowed with a good measure of luck are in a position to predict whether it is most prudent to withhold bonds for a month or two in anticipation of the rates going down or to sell them immediately before rates continue to climb. Hindsight gives a much better answer than careful study before the act.

This is not to infer that the credit rating of the school has nothing to do with the interest rate demanded for its bonds. Actually, the credit rating of the district has a considerable amount to do with the specific interest rate on its bonds. Such agencies as Dunn and Bradstreet, Moody's Investor Service, and Poor's Publishing Company maintain credit rating on political subdivisions, including some school districts. The establishment of a sound credit rating should be given careful attention by school administrators early in any program that may necessitate the borrowing of funds.

Some factors which influence the credit rating of a school district are:

1. The amount and nature of the existing local debt.
2. Favorable or unfavorable market reaction to the given local unit. This is based on the frequency with which it borrows; its size; availability of information on its financial status; etc.
3. The present and future financial soundness of the school district. This is judged by its ability to live within its income; the status of its major source of

[19] Ibid.

local revenue, namely, the local assessed taxable property; state aids on debt retirement; contingent liabilities, etc.
4. The status of the district structure, organization, and administration. This involves judgment on the character and legal status of the district; how efficiently, honestly, and intelligently it is administered; the law on debt limitations which apply to the district; tax calendar; bondholder's remedies in case of default, etc.
5. The economic and social conditions of the community in which the school district is located. This is derived from a knowledge of the community, its strategic location, character of the population, economic resources, stability, etc.[20]

THE SALE OF BONDS

There are a number of legal restrictions and procedures which must be followed in all aspects of school bonding from the formulation of the petition calling for an election, to the performance of the election, to the ultimate sale of the bond issue. The well-known legal maxim that "the statutory mode is the measure of power" of the district applies in all matters of incurring indebtedness. Either a bond attorney or a reputable bond house with which the bonds are to be marketed should be consulted on the various steps of bonding. If there is an attorney involved, it is well to keep in mind that a bond attorney is a specialized individual whose competence extends beyond that of the ordinary attorney for the school district. Fees for bond attorneys usually vary with localities, but they are calculated, by and large, on the basis of $1 per $1000 on large issues and a fixed minimum on small issues.

A bond attorney or the services available from a reputable financial house specializing in bonding will usually provide advice on the type of information needed to certify the authenticity of a bond issue. These might include documents which show:

1. The assessed valuation of the district.
2. An affadavit of the existing school debt.
3. The minutes of the school board meeting at which resolution to borrow was passed.
4. A citation of statutory or constitutional sources giving legal authority to the district to borrow.
5. The necessary resolution which authorized the calling of a school election to approve the bond issue.

[20] Carl H. Chatters and A. M. Hillhouse, *Local Government Debt Administration*, Englewood Cliffs, N.J.: Prentice-Hall, Inc., 1939, pp. 282–287.

6. The election notice and manner and dates of posting.
7. Certificate of publication of election notice.
8. The form of ballot used in the election.
9. The proceedings canvassing election returns.
10. The certificate of a duly authorized public official showing that election returns are certified public record.
11. The advertisement of sale of bonds.
12. The certificate of publication of the bond sale notice.
13. The certificate of bond sale and to whom awarded.
14. The resolution confirming the bond sale.
15. The certificate of signatures on bonds.
16. The copy of the bond form employed.
17. The nonlitigation certificate.
18. The treasurer's receipts for payment for bonds.[21]

There are several ways to sell bonds. Bonds can be sold "over-the-counter" but most authorities feel this is not the most successful way. "Over-the-counter" sales are direct sales to the public.

The most satisfactory method is marketing through the commercial bonding houses. It is imperative that the most favorable time for marketing bonds be carefully ascertained to prevent flooding of the bond market with similar issues. The time, place, and manner of receiving the bids from the various bond houses should be advertised in the financial journals and in newspapers of wide circulation. These bonds are generally sold by sealed bids or at an auction sale with split-rate premiums, or discounts offered by the bidder. It is often a difficult but necessary task to calculate the best bid. It is advisable that the board seek assistance from a financial expert who will be present to help the board determine the most satisfactory bond bid. In addition to low interest rates, the premiums offered must be given consideration. Most of the states prohibit the sale of school bonds for less than par value.

BOND RETIREMENT SCHEDULES

Serial bonds have a distinct advantage over the other types, but this advantage may be dissipated without careful scheduling of debt amortization. In a stable school district where there is little likelihood of significant enrollment expansion and, therefore, a small chance of future bond issues, almost any type of scheduling could prove to be acceptable. In such situations, the important things are to meet legal requirements on

[21] American Association of School Administrators, *op. cit.*, pp. 303–304.

the term of the bond and to satisfy the demands that the tax rate for annual debt retirement be within the promises made to voters or the board's desires. Usually the board will attempt to spread the debt retirement costs evenly during the term of the bond issue. The objective is to have equal annual total payments for debt retirements, which include payment of interest as well as principal.

In more dynamic school communities, where not all future capital improvements can be financed from a single bond issue or where there is an existing debt retirement schedule or where there is a strong likelihood of future bond issues, careful scheduling of the amortization of serial bonds is of importance. To illustrate, if the present bond issue is used to satisfy relatively minor capital improvements, but with a clear indication that a second and much larger bond issue must be sold within a five or ten-year period, it would be desirable that the amortization of the present small issue be scheduled with large principal payments at the beginning of the specified term and smaller principal payments during times when the principal payments on future issues fall due.

On the other hand, if there is an existing debt load which demands a relatively high tax rate, the amortization schedule for the new issue should allow small principal payments or even deferred principal payments during the early years, until most of the previous debt principal and interest payments are satisfied.

There is no one formula or one schedule which can apply to all communities. In designing a retirement pattern for a new issue each school administrator or business manager must of necessity determine not only the past debt retirement pattern but also what future bond issues may be necessary. Without a knowledge of future school-building demands and the availability of resources for financing, the district will be involved in blind scheduling of bond retirements. Prudent planning of the indebtedness program involves a careful survey of all school district capital improvement requirements. Improperly developed serial bond retirement schedules can prove most embarrassing in financing future capital improvements.

SINKING FUND AND SERIAL BOND COSTS

The debt retirement costs for a $1000 sinking fund bond for various terms and at varying interest rates are summarized in Table 22. The same information could be used to estimate costs of sinking fund

TABLE 22.   Debt Retirement Costs per $1000 Sinking Fund Bond for 15-, 20-, and 30-Year Terms at Varying Interest Rates[a]

Bond, by Length of Term	Cost of Bonds at Interest Rate of			
	1 Percent	2 Percent	3 Percent	4 Percent
15 Years				
Total Interest Cost	150.00	300.00	450.00	600.00
Total Principal and Interest	1150.00	1300.00	1450.00	1600.00
Average per Year	76.67	86.67	96.67	106.67
20 Years				
Total Interest Cost	200.00	400.00	600.00	800.00
Total Principal and Interest	1200.00	1400.00	1600.00	1800.00
Average per Year	60.00	70.00	80.00	90.00
30 Years				
Total Interest Cost	300.00	600.00	900.00	1200.00
Total Principal and Interest	1300.00	1600.00	1900.00	2200.00
Average per Year	43.33	53.33	63.33	73.33

[a] Interest is paid annually; sinking funds are collected annually but principal payment is deferred to one maturity date.

SOURCE: Adapted from N. E. Viles, *Local School Construction Programs*, Bulletin 1957, no. 20, U.S. Office of Education, Washington, D.C.: U.S. Government Printing Office, 1957, p. 51.

TABLE 23.   Debt Retirement Costs per $1000 Serial Bond Scheduled with Equal Annual Principal Payments for 15-, 20-, and 30-Year Terms at Varying Interest Rates[a]

Bond, by Length of Term	Costs at Interest Rate of			
	1 Percent	2 Percent	3 Percent	4 Percent
15 Years				
Total Interest to Pay	80.00	160.00	240.00	320.00
Total Principal and Interest to Pay	1080.00	1160.00	1240.00	1320.00
Average Annual Payment	72.00	77.33	82.67	88.00
Maximum Annual Payment	76.67	86.67	96.67	106.67
Minimum Annual Payment	67.34	68.00	68.67	69.33
20 Years				
Total Interest to Pay	105.00	210.00	315.00	420.00
Total Principal and Interest to Pay	1105.00	1210.00	1315.00	1420.00
Average Annual Payment	55.25	60.50	65.75	71.00
Maximum Annual Payment	60.00	70.00	80.00	90.00
Minimum Annual Payment	50.50	51.00	51.50	52.00
30 Years				
Total Interest to Pay	155.00	310.00	465.00	620.00
Total Principal and Interest to Pay	1155.00	1310.00	1465.00	1620.00
Average Annual Payment	38.50	43.33	48.83	54.00
Maximum Annual Payment	43.33	53.33	63.33	73.33
Minimum Annual Payment	33.67	34.00	34.33	34.67

[a] Interest and total annual debt retirement costs decrease as the amount of unpaid debt principal decreases.

SOURCE: Adapted from N. E. Viles, *Local School Construction Programs*, Bulletin 1957, no. 20, U.S. Office of Education, Washington, D.C.: U.S. Government Printing Office, 1957, pp. 52–53.

TABLE 24. Debt Retirement Costs per $1000 Serial Bond Scheduled with Equal Annual Total Payments for 15-, 20-, and 30-Year Terms at Varying Interest Rates[a]

Bond, by Length of Term	Costs at Interest Rate of			
	1 Percent	2 Percent	3 Percent	4 Percent
15 Years				
Total Interest to Pay	80.89	166.97	255.65	348.83
Total Interest and Principal	1080.89	1166.97	1255.65	1348.83
Annual Payment Schedule				
Used	73.00[b]	78.00	84.00	90.00
Average Annual Cost	72.06	77.80	83.71	89.92
20 Years				
Total Interest to Pay	107.14	219.50	338.94	467.54
Total Interest and Principal	1107.14	1219.50	1338.94	1467.54
Annual Payment Schedule				
Used	56.00	62.00	68.00	74.00
Average Annual Cost	55.36	60.98	66.95	73.38
30 Years				
Total Interest to Pay	161.26	335.78	513.36	730.40
Total Interest and Principal	1161.26	1335.78	1513.36	1730.40
Annual Payment Schedule				
Used	39.00	45.00	52.00	58.00
Average Annual Cost	38.71	44.52	50.44	57.68

[a] As interest payments decrease, principal payments increase.

[b] Payment schedule used—next whole dollar above minimum required to amortize. Average annual costs shown here are slightly less than required annual amortizing payments, since larger payments (next dollar) are cumulative and leave smaller last year payment. For instance, the required amount to amortize a 20-year, 2 percent bond is $61.16 per year, but when the even dollar ($62.00) annual payment is used, the average annual cost is only $60.98.

SOURCE: Adapted from N. E. Viles, *Local School Construction Programs*, Bulletin 1957, no. 20, U.S. Office of Education, Washington, D.C.: U.S. Government Printing Office, 1957, p. 55.

bonds issued in multiples of $1000. As would be expected the average cost of debt retirement increases as the amount of interest increases. It is also evident that the average debt retirement costs per year decrease as the length of term of the bond increases, but the total principal and interest costs increase as the length of term of the bond increases.

Tables 23 and 24 show debt retirement costs per $1000 serial bond using two different methods of scheduling. In Table 23 the objective was equal annual principal payments. The interest costs and total annual payments for both interest and principal decreased as the amount of unpaid principal decreased. By way of illustration, the maximum annual payment for a 3 percent, 20-year term, $1000 serial bond scheduled for equal annual principal payments will be $80. This will drop to $51.50 during the last year. The average annual payment will be $65.75 per $1000 bond. If the total bond issue were $100,000 instead of the $1000 used in Table 23, the average annual debt retirement payment for interest and principal would be $6575.

On the other hand, if the objective, as in Table 24 is equal annual total payments (which include principal and interest), theoretically there would be no variation whatsoever. Rounding off to the next whole dollar above the minimum required to amortize the debt during the term makes the final payment smaller than the other equal annual payments. By way of illustration, the equal annual total payments on principal and interest for 19 years of a 20-year $1000 bond, bearing a 3 percent interest rate, would be $68. This is given in Table 24. A lesser payment in the twentieth year would reduce the average annual cost to $66.95. Once again, if the total bond issue were $100,000 rather than $1000, the average annual payment would be $6800 for 19 years, with the last year's payment being less to reduce the average annual cost to $6695.

The debt retirement costs per $1000 sinking fund bond, per $1000 serial bond with equal annual principal but variable interest payments, and per $1000 serial bond with equal annual principal and interest payments are compared in Table 25. Information in-

TABLE 25. Comparative Debt Retirement Costs per $1000 Sinking Fund Bond and Serial Bond for 15-, 20-, and 30-Year Terms at Varying Interest Rates

Bond, by Length of Term	Costs at Interest Rate of			
	1 Percent	2 Percent	3 Percent	4 Percent
15 Years				
Sinking Fund	1150.00	1300.00	1450.00	1600.00
Serial-Equal Principal, Variable Interest Payment	1080.00	1160.00	1240.00	1320.00
Serial-Equal Total Principal and Interest[a] Payment	1080.89	1166.97	1255.65	1348.83
20 Years				
Sinking Fund	1200.00	1400.00	1600.00	1800.00
Serial-Equal Principal, Variable Interest Payment	1105.00	1210.00	1315.00	1420.00
Serial-Equal Total Principal and Interest[a] Payment	1107.14	1219.50	1338.94	1467.54
30 Years				
Sinking Fund	1300.00	1600.00	1900.00	2200.00
Serial-Equal Principal, Variable Interest Payment	1155.00	1310.00	1465.00	1620.00
Serial-Equal Total Principal and Interest[a] Payment	1161.26	1335.78	1513.36	1730.40

[a] Total costs for equal total annual payments—principal and interest—are, as computed for the illustrations, on the basis of the next whole dollar above the minimum. Total costs are slightly less than those shown in Table 21, and the difference is greater or less as the amount of the next whole dollar varies from the minimum as derived from the index.

SOURCE: Adapted from N. E. Viles, *Local School Construction Programs*, Bulletin 1957, no. 20, U.S. Office of Education, Washington, D.C.: U.S. Government Printing Office, 1957, p. 56.

cludes 15-, 20-, and 30-year maturities with interest rates at 1, 2, 3, and 4 percent. By way of illustration (and using the figures quoted in Table 25), the total debt retirement cost of a $1000 sinking fund bond scheduled for 20 years at 3 percent interest is $1600. A 20-year, 3 percent $1000 serial bond, scheduled with equal annual principal payments but variable interest costs, is $1315. A 20-year, $1000, 3 percent serial bond scheduled with equal annual total principal and interest costs would require the expenditure of $1338.94.

Serial bonds actually cost less to amortize than sinking fund bonds of equal amounts for equal terms and bearing equal interest rates. This is not surprising, for with sinking fund bonds, interest is paid on the total principal borrowed for the entire term. On the other hand, various portions of the principal are retired during the term of the serial bond, with the result that interest paid each year becomes smaller as the unpaid balance of the debt shrinks. Funds accumulated in a sinking fund can be invested to bear interest, and such investment return should be subtracted from the total cost of the sinking fund bond. If a special investment counselor must be retained or a school administrator spends a portion of his time administering the investment of sinking funds, such added costs should be subtracted from the total earned in sinking fund investment.

INDEX OF AMORTIZATION

Boards of education often desire an estimate of debt retirement costs per year and total cost over the entire term. There are indices of amortization for bonds issued at specified interest rates and maturities which can be used to compute such estimates. Indices for estimating average annual or total costs for bonds scheduled at 1, 2, 3, and 4 percent interest rates and for maturity periods of 10, 15, 20, and 30 years can be found in Table 26. The indices are derived from mathematical formulas found in texts on business mathematics.

TABLE 26. Indices for Estimating Amortization Schedules Showing the Average Annual and Total Debt Retirement Costs per $1000 Bond

Schedule	10 Years	15 Years	20 Years	30 Years
1 Percent				
Index of Amortization	0.1055820	0.0721237	0.0554153	0.0387481
Average Annual Debt Retirement Cost per $1000 Bond[a]	$105.58	$72.12	$55.42	$38.75
Total Costs for the Full Term of a $1000 Bond[a]	$1055.80	$1081.80	$1108.40	$1162.50
2 Percent				
Index of Amortization	0.1113265	0.0778254	0.0611567	0.0446499
Average Annual Debt Retirement Cost per $1000 Bond[a]	$111.33	$77.83	$61.16	$44.65
Total Costs for the Full Term of a $1000 Bond[a]	$1113.30	$1167.45	$1223.20	$1339.50
3 Percent				
Index of Amortization	0.1172305	0.0837665	0.0672157	0.0510192
Average Annual Debt Retirement Cost per $1000 Bond[a]	$117.23	$83.77	$67.22	$51.02
Total Costs for the Full Term of a $1000 Bond[a]	$1172.30	$1256.55	$1344.40	$1530.60
4 Percent				
Index of Amortization	0.1232909	0.0899411	0.0735817	0.0578300
Average Annual Debt Retirement Cost per $1000 Bond[a]	$123.29	$89.94	$73.58	$57.83
Total Costs for the Full Term of a $1000 Bond[a]	$1232.90	$1349.10	$1471.60	$1734.90

[a] Includes interest and principal payments.

SOURCE: Adapted from N. E. Viles, *Local School Construction Programs*, Bulletin 1957, no. 20, U.S. Office of Education, Washington, D.C.: U.S. Government Printing Office, 1957, p. 54.

An illustration of how an index of amortization can be used to estimate debt retirement costs follows. Assume that $100,000 in bonds are marketed at 3 percent for 20 years. From Table 26 the index of amortization is found to be .0672157. The average annual debt requirement costs for a $1000 bond at 3 percent for 20 years would be 1000 times the index quoted or $67.22 and for a $100,000 bond issue 100,000 times the index of .0672157 or $6721.57. The total cost for the full term of the 20-year bond would be 20 times the average cost per year or $1344.40 for the $1000 bond and $134,-431.40 for a $100,000 issue. Debt retirement costs for any size bond with a maturity period of 10, 15, 20, or 30 years and with interest rates of 1, 2, 3, or 4 percent can be computed with the help of the indices in Table 26. The general procedure is to locate the appropriate index of amortization for the given percent of interest and maturity in Table 26. The appropriate index is multiplied by the amount of the bond issue for the average annual cost and then in turn by the maturity period if total debt retirement costs are desired.

SCHEDULING EQUAL ANNUAL TOTAL PAYMENTS FOR SERIAL BONDS

Equal annual total debt retirement payment schedules for the amortization of a $1000 bond for 15-,

TABLE 27. Equal Annual Total Debt Retirement Payments Schedule for the Amortization of 15-Year Bonds at 3 Percent Interest

Years	Principal Due	Interest to Pay	Payment on Principal	Total to Pay	Balance Due
1	$1000.00	$30.00	$54.00	$84.00	$946.00
2	946.00	28.33	55.62	84.00	890.36
3	890.38	26.71	57.29	84.00	833.09
4	833.09	24.99	59.01	84.00	774.08
5	774.08	23.22	60.78	84.00	713.30
6	713.30	21.40	62.60	84.00	650.70
7	650.70	19.52	64.48	84.00	586.22
8	586.22	17.59	66.41	84.00	519.81
9	519.81	15.59	68.41	84.00	451.40
10	451.40	13.54	70.46	84.00	380.94
11	380.94	11.43	72.57	84.00	308.37
12	308.37	9.25	74.75	84.00	233.62
13	233.62	7.01	76.99	84.00	156.63
14	156.63	4.70	79.30	84.00	77.33
15	77.33	2.32	77.33	79.65[a]	—
Total	—	255.65	1000.00	1255.65	—

[a] Last payment is not equal to others but is smaller as payments were rounded off to the next whole dollar above the minimum annual amount required to amortize a $1000 bond.

SOURCE: Adapted from N. E. Viles, *Local School Construction Programs*, Bulletin 1957, no. 20, U.S. Office of Education, Washington, D.C.: U.S. Government Printing Office, 1957, p. 63.

TABLE 28. Equal Annual Total Debt Retirement Payments Schedule for the Amortization of 20-Year Bonds at 3 Percent Interest

Years	Principal Due	Interest to Pay	Payment on Principal	Total to Pay	Balance Due
1	$1000.00	$30.00	$38.00	$68.00	$962.00
2	962.00	28.86	39.14	68.00	922.86
3	922.86	27.69	40.31	68.00	882.55
4	882.55	26.48	41.52	68.00	841.03
5	841.03	25.23	42.77	68.00	798.26
6	798.26	23.95	44.05	68.00	754.21
7	754.21	22.63	45.37	68.00	708.84
8	708.84	21.26	46.74	68.00	662.10
9	662.10	19.86	48.14	68.00	613.96
10	613.96	18.42	49.58	68.00	564.38
11	564.38	16.93	51.07	68.00	513.31
12	513.31	15.40	52.60	68.00	460.71
13	460.71	13.82	54.18	68.00	406.53
14	406.53	12.20	55.80	68.00	350.73
15	350.73	10.52	57.48	68.00	293.25
16	293.25	8.80	59.20	68.00	234.05
17	234.05	7.02	60.98	68.00	173.07
18	173.07	5.19	62.81	68.00	110.26
19	110.26	3.31	64.49	68.00	45.57
20	45.57	1.37	45.57	46.94[a]	—
Total	—	338.94	1000.00	1338.94	—

[a] Last payment is not equal to others but is smaller as payments were rounded off to the next whole dollar above the minimum annual amount required to amortize a $1000 bond.

SOURCE: Adapted from N. E. Viles, *Local School Construction Programs*, Bulletin 1957, no. 22, U.S. Office of Education, Washington, D.C.: U.S. Government Printing Office, 1957, p. 69.

20-, and 30-year maturities at 3 percent interest are summarized in Tables 27, 28, and 29 respectively. Table 28 can be used for more specific illustration and is based on the amortization of a $1000 bond for a 20-year period and bearing 3 percent interest. The objective is to schedule equal annual total debt payment of interest and principal. This goal can be reached by paying $68.00 a year for 19 years, with the last payment on the twentieth year being only $46.94. The reason for the last payment being smaller than others is that previous payments were rounded off to the next whole dollar above the minimum annual amount necessary to amortize the $1000 bond for 20 years at 3 percent interest. It should be noted from Table 28 that the interest payments are high during the early years and low during the later years of the maturity. Principal payments show the reverse, being low during the first part of the term and high during the last years.

There is no great financial advantage to serial bond debt retirement schedules based on total equal annual payments for principal and interest. Debt retirement programs scheduled with equal annual principal and variable interest payments actually cost less than amortization schedules calling for equal total payments of principal and interest each year. Debt service costs will be even smaller if heavy principal

TABLE 29. Equal Annual Total Debt Retirement Payments Schedule for the Amortization of 30-Year Bonds at 3 Percent Interest

Years	Principal Due	Interest to Pay	Payment on Principal	Total to Pay	Balance Due
1	$1000.00	$30.00	$22.00	$52.00	$978.00
2	978.00	29.32	22.66	52.00	955.34
3	955.34	28.66	23.34	52.00	932.00
4	932.00	27.96	24.04	52.00	907.96
5	907.96	27.24	24.76	52.00	883.20
6	883.20	26.50	25.50	52.00	857.70
7	857.70	25.73	26.27	52.00	831.43
8	831.43	24.94	27.06	52.00	804.37
9	804.37	24.13	27.87	52.00	776.50
10	776.50	23.30	28.70	52.00	747.80
11	747.80	22.43	29.57	52.00	718.23
12	718.23	21.55	30.45	52.00	687.78
13	687.78	20.63	31.37	52.00	656.41
14	656.41	19.69	32.31	52.00	624.10
15	624.10	18.72	33.28	52.00	590.82
16	590.82	17.72	34.28	52.00	556.54
17	556.54	16.70	35.30	52.00	521.24
18	521.24	15.64	36.36	52.00	484.88
19	484.88	14.55	37.45	52.00	447.43
20	447.43	13.42	38.58	52.00	408.85
21	408.85	12.27	39.73	52.00	369.12
22	369.12	11.07	40.93	52.00	328.19
23	238.19	9.85	42.15	52.00	286.04
24	286.04	8.58	43.42	52.00	242.62
25	242.62	7.28	44.72	52.00	197.90
26	197.90	5.94	46.06	52.00	151.84
27	151.84	4.56	47.44	52.00	104.40
28	104.40	3.13	48.87	52.00	55.53
29	55.53	1.67	50.33	52.00	5.20
30	5.20	.16	5.20	5.36[a]	—
Total	—	513.36	1000.00	1513.36	—

[a] Last payment is not equal to others but is smaller as payments were rounded off to the next whole dollar above the minimum annual amount required to amortize a $1000 bond.

SOURCE: Adapted from N. E. Viles, *Local School Construction Programs*, Bulletin 1957, no. 20, U.S. Office of Education, Washington, D.C.: U.S. Government Printing Office, 1957, p. 75.

Retirement of 1948 or First Issue of $135,200

1949	1950	1951	1952	1953	1954	1955	1956	1957	1958
$14,000	$14,000	$14,000	$14,000	$14,000	$14,000	$14,000	$14,000	$14,000	$9,200

Retirement of 1949 or Second Issue of $60,000

1949	1950	1951	1952	1953	1954	1955	1956	1957	1958	1959	1960	1961
$1,000	$2,000	$2,000	$2,000	$2,000	$2,000	$2,000	$2,000	$2,000	$8,000	$14,000	$14,000	$9,000

Retirement of 1951 or Third Issue of $48,000

1962	1963	1964	1965	1966	1967
$8,000	$8,000	$8,000	$8,000	$8,000	$8,000

Graph of Annual Principal Payments Due

Principal Due 1949 1950 1951 1952 1953 1954 1955 1956 1957 1958 1959 1960 1961 1962 1963 1964 1965 1966 1967
$18,000
17,000
16,000
15,000
14,000
13,000
12,000
11,000
10,000
9,000
8,000
7,000

Other Pertinent Data

	Issue No. 1	Issue No. 2	Issue No. 3
Original Issue Date	1948	1949	1951
Interest Rate	1¾ Percent	2½ Percent	2½ Percent
Total Amount of Original Issue	$135,200	$60,000	$48,000
Paid on Principal (2/1/58)	126,000	15,000	None
Left to Pay on 2/1/58	$9,200	$45,000	$48,000

Total Bonded Indebtedness $102,200
Compiled by W. Fredrick, Superintendent

FIGURE 17. Bond Retirement Schedule Chart for the Garnavillo Community School, Garnavillo, Iowa

payments are scheduled during early portions of the maturity span. On the other hand, schedules which defer large principal payments until the latter portions of the bond term cost more than those scheduled for equal annual total payments of interest and principal.

Only in theory and never in practice can exactly equal annual total payments, as shown in Tables 27, 28, and 29, be attained. It should be noted that in these tables, the payment on the principal fluctuates and does not lend itself readily to retirement of units of $1000 or even $100 in many cases. Many states require that bonds be issued in denominations of no less than $1000. Employing the figures in Table 28 as an illustration, even on a million dollar issue, the principal payments in the second year and thereafter would call for bond denominations in odd lots. Thus, in the second year of a million dollar issue it would be necessary to pay $39,140 on principal. This could be met partially by retiring thirty-nine $1000 bonds, but there must also be one for $140. To meet the principal payment you must call in all bonds in a series which fall due. To retire a $1000 bond you must pay $1000. You cannot retire it through a number of partial payments over several years. Only in states which permit the sale of school bonds in units smaller than $100 would it be possible to obtain equal annual total payments of principal and interest. In a practical sense, it can be said that it is impossible in states requiring school bonds to be issued in denominations of $1000 or multiples thereof to have equal annual payments. There can be only an approximation of equality in annual payments. Very little can be gained through precise equality of total annual payments, but a considerable amount can be lost in the ease of marketability of school bonds when they are issued in odd dollars and cents, particularly if they are issued in units of less than $1000. The objective of equal annual total payments is not a particularly important one in prudent scheduling or management of the indebtedness. The important thing in debt retirement management is that the bond issue to be scheduled fit into previous patterns of existing debt amortization and be so designed as to minimize the scheduling problems of debts which may be incurred in the foreseeable future.

Figure 17 is a graphic presentation of a bond retirement schedule taken from the Garnavillo Community School District of Garnavillo, Iowa. It can be seen that the three bond issues have different terms and the principal payments are not all equal. This graphic method of presenting a bond retirement schedule is easily understood by the lay public and merits consideration by those desiring simple ways of presenting financial facts to the people of the community.

ACCOUNTING FOR SCHOOL BOND PAYMENTS

The sale of school bonds results in the creation of a liability which must be amortized according to a given schedule made known to those who purchase the bonds. It is often unwise to sell immediately the total amount authorized if the capital improvements to be constructed from authorized bond funds will not require payment until one to three years after the bond election. It is not unusual to find school districts approving a $10 million bond issue to finance school construction that may take three to five years for completion. It is questionable whether the bonds should be sold immediately after authorization at the ballot box, that is, before the money from the sale is actually needed to pay construction costs. In most cases, it is more prudent to withhold sale until contractors have reached a stage where payment is necessary. It usually takes a year to prepare plans in sufficient detail to permit bidding by contract. In large buildings, an additional year and sometimes three is needed to complete construction. It is better to withhold the marketing of bonds until construction demands make it necessary.

There are exceptions to this practice, one of which is related to the interest trends. When interest rates are at a low point and signs seem to indicate a definite increase, it might be more prudent to sell the entire issue even though the proceeds may not be needed for another year. This, of course, is a calculated risk. On the other hand, there is little advantage to selling the total issue at a time when the interest rates for schools are reaching new highs. There have been some unusual situations where a district has approved a school bond issue, marketed part, and withheld the other part from sale, pending completion of slow-moving constructions. During the interim between the first sale of the authorized bonds and the time the remainder were to be marketed, the district boundary lines were altered to include new territory. A conservative legal opinion demanded a new approval vote by the entire district on the previously authorized but unissued amounts. This is an exception but one which merits the careful attention of business managers in school districts undergoing reorganizations.

It is imperative that records for each bond issue be kept so that the financial resources and expenditures from each issue can be clearly identified. The receipts from all school bond issues should be deposited in a separate fund, designated simply as the "bond" or the "schoolhouse" fund. The accounts must show the resources and obligations for each and every separate bond issue.

The usual resources of a bond fund are cash from the sale of issues, amount due from other funds, and bonds authorized but unissued. Receipts from the sale of a bond issue are classed as nonrevenue receipts as they result from the creation of an obligation which must be met at some future date. The obligations of funds are accounts payable, temporary loans payable, amount due to other funds, and reserves for encumbrances. Accounts of Cash Due from Other Funds, Accounts Payable, Due to Other Funds, and Reserve for Encumbrances operate in the same way as those for revenue funds based on accrual and encumbrance accounting procedures. An account known as Bonds Authorized and Unissued should be opened as soon as the bond issue is authorized by proper election. This account is debited with total par value of bonds authorized and the Bond Fund balance is in turn credited with the same amount. When the bonds are sold, the Cash Account is debited, and the Bonds Authorized and Unissued Account is credited in the same amount, with discount or premium being charged or credited to the Bond Fund Balance Account or otherwise disposed of.[22]

Refunding bonds exchange one liability for another and do not change the condition of the school district with respect to assets and liabilities.

To summarize, bonds should be recorded in a self-balancing group of accounts. A special fund is necessary where capital improvements are to be financed through sale of bonds specifically authorized by the vote of the people. Expenditures to meet construction costs are made from the Capital Outlay Account of this fund. Payment of principal and interest on bonds are charged to the debt service classification of the same fund. The receipts to meet capital outlay payments are nonrevenue receipts accruing primarily from the sale of bonds. The receipts to meet debt service expenditures are derived from the special annual taxes earmarked for debt amortization. The capital outlay and debt service costs in a bond or schoolhouse fund should not be confused with the classifications of the same titles in the General or Current Expense Funds.

SHORT-TERM INDEBTEDNESS

Short-term indebtedness is arbitrarily defined as that debt incurred for a period of five years or less. In many cases the short-term debt exists for less than one year. Short-term indebtedness is often necessary in school districts where the flow of income during a given fiscal year does not coincide with the flow of expenditures. The greater the number of separate and distinct funds, the greater the necessity for borrowing. Short-term indebtedness needs can be reduced to a minimum when few funds are in operation.

It often occurs that state aids and tax monies during a given fiscal years are not coördinated with such constant and large expenditures as payrolls which cannot be deferred. The expenditures must be met, but funds are lacking. This is usually a temporary situation during a given fiscal year and not necessarily an indication of bad budgeting. Short-term borrowing can be eliminated if a large operating balance is maintained to cover the necessary expenditures until the aids and tax funds come to the school treasury. In many school districts, the fiscal year for the school district begins operation some six months before the calendar or tax years of governmental units which either collect taxes or grant special aids for school districts.

In the absence of a large operating balance, the most effective way of controlling short-term debt is to permit the school to borrow for a limited period of time. Notes or loans issued in anticipation of current receipts should be permitted up to no more than 50 percent of current receipts. Some authorities actually recommend short-term borrowing as preferable to the maintenance of large working balances. Short-term borrowing is permissive in 41 states, and in all but two of these, the amount is restricted to the amount of anticipated revenues.[23]

Some school districts create short-term indebtedness through the issuance of vouchers payable, warrants payable, tax and revenue anticipation notes, judgments payable, and accrued liability. Warrants payable are related to vouchers payable and are usually in the form of written orders or warrants issued against the funds of the district. If the district does not have the cash, the warrants are registered, and the warrant payable becomes a short-term liability. The law usually prescribes the method by which warrants can be registered and the order in which they shall be paid. This is, in effect, an I.O.U. issued by the school district, indicating that it is short of cash but that as soon as the cash becomes available, the warrant will be paid. The holder of the warrant can charge interest only from the day the warrant is registered. To register a warrant, one merely presents it to the school treasurer for payment. The laws of most states prescribe the maximum amount of interest that shall be charged on warrants payable.

[22] Lloyd Morey and Robert P. Hackett, *Fundamentals of Governmental Accounting*, New York: John Wiley & Sons, Inc., rev. ed., 1951, pp. 259–269.

[23] R. W. Holmstedt, "Fiscal Controls" in R. L. Johns and E. L. Morphet (eds.), *Problems and Issues in Public School Finance*, New York: Teachers College, Columbia University, 1952, pp. 276–323.

SUMMARY

Total school debt hit a low of $1.89 billion in 1944–1945 and started a rapid climb the next year in the period following World War II. School indebtedness will exceed $5 billion by no later than 1960. The increases in private debt since 1945 have exceeded the increases in school debt for the same period. Interest payments by schools will be in excess of $200 million annually in the years ahead. Although total debt services costs are higher than ever, they represent a comparatively small percent of total expenditures for education.

Pay-as-you-go plans for financing school construction are based on the annual yield of a tax dedicated for building purposes. Under the building reserve plan the yearly proceeds of a tax are permitted to accumulate until enough money is available to help finance school plant construction. Special legal and accounting safeguards should be instituted to prevent the shifting of building reserves to other than original purposes. Current tax receipts earmarked for new buildings must be regarded in most communities during times of considerable construction as a supplementary financing source rather than as a substitute for bonding.

A bond is a written financial instrument issued by a corporate body to borrow money with the time and rate of interest to be charged, the method of principal payment, and the maturity of the debt clearly expressed. School bonds are unsecured or debenture bonds. Bondholders cannot take over the physical assets of the district in cases of default on bonds.

Many restrictions on governmental borrowing were made necessary by previous questionable practices and poor management. Legal demands which promote better management and careful regulation of debt help to make school bonds easier to market and command a more favorable rate of interest. Debt limitations based on unrealistically low percentages of property valuations can interfere with the satisfaction of needs and desirable improvements in education.

Limitations on indebtedness vary greatly among the 50 states. Most states set bond maturity limits at from 20 to 25 years. Bond issues in all states must be submitted to a vote of the electorate, and in most states they must be approved by at least a 60 percent majority. Recently, school bond issues submitted to a vote of the people have received favorable reception in at least three-fourths of the cases. About two-thirds of the states require the issuance of serial school bonds only.

The serial bond provides for systematic payment of principal as well as interest. The advantage of issuing serial bonds can be minimized if careful scheduling of deft amortization is neglected. Prudent debt management is based on knowledge of existing and future debt requirements as well as the size of the issue to be amortized.

School bond interest rates reflect economic conditions and the credit rating of the district. Interest rates in 1957 were high but not as high as during the pre-1930 years. During most of the period following World War II, school bond interest rates were below the 4 percent level.

Short-term indebtedness is defined as a debt lasting five years or less. Such indebtedness is often necessary where the flow of income does not coincide with the flow of expenditures and small working capital is available. In the absence of large operating balances, the most effective way to control short-term debt is to permit schools to borrow in anticipation of current revenues for the fiscal year.

QUESTIONS

1. Why is the school debt continuing to increase in the face of larger debt service payments than ever before?
2. What are the similarities and differences between debts for schools and debts for private corporations?
3. How would you answer an angry patron in your school district who declared, "School debts have more than doubled since the end of World War II. We must vote down the proposed school bond issue and keep the school debt at manageable levels!"
4. What are the advantages and shortcomings of using pay-as-you-go plans to finance school construction?
5. What is a defensible or optimum maturity period for school bond issues?
6. Identify the following:
   a. coupon bond
   b. sinking fund bond
   c. registered bond
   d. callable bond
   e. serial-redemption sinking fund bond
7. Why do you suppose so many states require that schools issue serial bonds only?
8. What factors affect the interest rate for school bonds?
9. What factors must be taken into consideration in the scheduling of bond amortization?
10. What would be the estimated annual debt retirement costs of a $775,000 bond issue for 30 years and bearing 2 percent interest? What would be the total debt retirement costs over the maturity period of these same bonds?

SELECTED REFERENCES

American Association of School Administrators, *American School Buildings,* 27th Yearbook, Washington, D.C.: the Association, 1949, chap. 17.

Chase, Francis S., and Morphet, Edgar L., *The Forty-Eight State School Systems,* Chicago: The Council of State Governments, 1949.

Clark, Harold F., "Bond Rates, Building Costs, and School Plant Financing," *American School and University, 1957–1958,* 29th ed., vol. 1, *School Plant Reference,* New York: American School Publishing Corporation.

DeBernardis, Amo, and Baker, L. J., "Paid in Full—Portland $57,000,000 New School Program," *The American School Board Journal,* February, 1958.

Holmstedt, R. W., "Fiscal Controls" in R. L. Johns and E. L. Morphet (eds.), *Problems and Issues in Public School Finance,* New York: Teachers College, Columbia University, 1952.

Hutchins, Clayton D., and Munse, Albert R., *Public School Finance Programs of the United States,* Miscellaneous no. 22, U.S. Office of Education, Washington, D.C.: U.S. Government Printing Office, 1955.

Morey, Lloyd, and Hackett, Robert P., *Fundamentals of Governmental Accounting,* New York: John Wiley & Sons., Inc., rev. ed., 1951, chap. 16.

Viles, N. E., *Local School Construction Programs,* Bulletin 1957, no. 20, U.S. Office of Education, Washington, D.C.: U.S. Government Printing Office, 1957.

CHAPTER 13

Efficient Operation and
Maintenance of School Plants

THE TOTAL VALUE OF SCHOOL PROPERTY IN the United States in 1929–1930 was approximately $6.2 billion. In 1939–1940, the buildings and equipment were appraised at approximately $7.6 billion, or approximately $1.4 billion more than in 1929–1930. By 1949–1950, school property totaled almost $11.4 billion, or almost $3.7 billion more than in 1939–1940.

School property values increased slowly from 1929–1930 to 1945–1946. Very large gains occurred in the years following the end of World War II. By 1951–1952, the estimated worth of school properties climbed to almost $14 billion.[1] New construction since 1951 is proceeding at a rate which will make the total value of school plants and equipment by 1960 more than double the 1951 figures. This is indeed a sizable investment of public funds in school property.

The time it takes for a building to become obsolete from a physical standpoint varies with the quality of the original construction and materials as well as the quality of the housekeeping and maintenance during the lifetime of the structure. Some buildings have a useful physical life of less than 50 years whereas others function effectively for more than 75 years. The program of maintenance and operation has a considerable effect upon the physically useful life of a school building.

As Worth McClure stated:

School buildings deteriorate with age. Equipment and appliances get out of adjustment. Dust accumulates. Classroom furnishings are soiled through the activities of children and teachers. The tread of many small feet wears the protective covering on floors to a thread-bare appearance. Educational programs change and plant facilities need to be brought up to date.

These are but natural developments in the operation of the school plant. The superintendent must be responsible for all that is necessary to meet them. Without this kind of care, real education is impossible, and the community's investment in its school plant is not safe.[2]

School plant operating services have experienced considerable improvement in past years. Viles declared that such services are too often far below acceptable standards:

Desk tops are usually dark and are often carved. Accumulations of perspiration and dirt leave dark spots on desks and chair arms. Some floors are dark and unsightly. Unfilled floor cracks may make it impossible to maintain clean floors. Walls above radiators may show dirt streaks to the ceilings.

Toilet rooms often reek from the fumes of disinfectants and deodorants which are little less offensive than the odors they are supposed to cover. Pervious toilet room floors and walls are not treated to make them less absorbant of odors. Yards are often unsightly; hedges are not maintained. Holes and ditches create playground hazards for the pupils. Mud from unsurfaced playgrounds clings to the children's shoes and, if not stopped at the door by shoe cleaning facilities and teacher control, is carried into the rooms where it may injure floor surfaces and provide quantities of dust to float in the air the pupils must breathe. Ventilating ducts and fans are sometimes shut off to conserve fuel or power.

These are only a few of the illustrations of inadequate school building care. School officials and all others having any responsibility for school plants have an obligation to help provide and maintain safe, healthful, attractive environments for children required to attend school. A housekeeping program that insures clean, sanitary and attractive surroundings

---

[1] Clayton D. Hutchins, Albert R. Munse, and Edna D. Booher, *Trends and Significant Facts on School Finance, 1929–1930—1953–1954.* Circular no. 498, U S. Office of Education, Washington, D.C.: U.S. Government Printing Office, 1957, p. 69.

[2] American Association of School Administrators, *School Plant Maintenance,* Washington, D.C.: the Association, 1951, pp. 3, 4.

should be the goal of every school official and custodian, and the reduction of all physical hazards to a minimum should be a *must* in and around all school buildings.[3]

Activities such as cleaning, disinfecting, heating, caring for grounds, and similar housekeeping duties which are repeated somewhat regularly are necessary to keep the physical plant in operating condition. In the strict sense, repairing or replacing is not a part of operation but of maintenance.

Activities concerned with keeping the grounds, buildings, and equipment at the original condition of completeness or efficiency are a part of maintenance. Repairs or replacements of property are an essential part of maintenance.

There is a difference between operation and maintenance. In a practical sense, particularly in small schools, the two are closely related and may be performed by one and the same person. When the employed person pulls a dust rag out of his pocket and dusts a door, he is performing operating functions. If he goes to his pocket and pulls out a screwdriver to tighten or replace the locks on the door, he is involved in maintenance. It is often difficult for a custodian to distinguish between maintenance and operation tasks in developing a work schedule. It is questionable if such minute differentiation is necessary or valuable. Operation and maintenance have the common objective of keeping the school property in the best possible condition at all times for effective education. Preservation of property is dependent upon efficient operation as well as maintenance.

EFFICIENT OPERATION OF SCHOOL PLANTS

SCHOOL CUSTODIANS

People given the primary responsibility for the care of school buildings and grounds are known by many names. Men are called janitors, custodians, porters, and cleaners. Women are referred to as maids, janitresses, matrons, cleaners, scrubwomen, or charwomen. The present writers have a preference for the term "custodian" when applied to men and "matrons" when applied to women. There appears to be little question that custodians and matrons have an important role to play in school plant and property management. Their functions are many and varied and

include such things as: (1) preventing fire and maintaining safety, which involves inspecting and removing possible fire hazards, testing, maintaining, and operating fire alarm and fire-fighting equipment, and coöperating with civilian defense programs; (2) sweeping classroom floors, corridors, stairways, and other parts of the building; (3) dusting; (4) scrubbing; (5) cleaning glass light fixtures, blackboards, walls and ceilings, etc.; (6) operating and caring for heating and ventilating equipment, plumbing equipment, etc.; (7) and tending the lawn and other grounds.[4]

It is not the purpose of this book to describe in detail actual techniques and materials that could be used in sweeping, dusting, cleaning, and scrubbing various surfaces with particular compounds. There are special treatises of value in this area. Many are published for custodians by state education departments and others have been written by Brainard,[5] Linn *et al.,*[6] and the New England School Development Council.[7] Of primary concern in this book are the administrative problems in obtaining and developing desirable custodial services.

THE EMPLOYMENT OF CUSTODIANS

There is considerable agreement that custodial employees should be selected carefully on the basis of skill, knowledge, and personal character rather than on the basis of low wages, political favors, or sentimental considerations.[8] The employment of custodians or other school employees is the legal responsibility of the board of education, but employment should be based on the recommendations of the superintendent of schools or his assistant superintendent in charge of plant operation and maintenance. Employment made directly by the board without regard to the recommendations of administrators or supervisors who are responsible for the employee's performance is a poor procedure. In some states and city school systems, the employment of all nonteaching personnel is subject to civil service rules. In such cases, permanent employment can be made only from an eligible list established as a result of state civil service examinations. This is indeed heartening. Where

[3] N. E. Viles, *Improving School Custodial Service,* Bulletin 1949, no. 13, U.S. Office of Education, Washington, D.C.: U.S. Government Printing Office, 1949, pp. 2–3.

[4] University of the State of New York, *School Business Management Handbook,* Operation and Maintenance, no. 7, Albany, N.Y.: The State Education Department, 1955, pp. 41–46.

[5] A. D. Brainard, *Handbook for School Custodians,* Lincoln: The University of Nebraska Press, 1952.

[6] Henry H. Linn *et al., The School Custodians' Housekeeping Handbook,* New York: Teachers College, Columbia University, 1948.

[7] New England School Development Council, *Guide for School Custodial Services,* Cambridge: the Council, July, 1948.

[8] American Association of School Administrators, *American School Buildings,* 27th Yearbook, Washington, D.C.: the Association, 1949, p. 281.

the practice is followed, it removes an important position from political favoritism or the sentimental desire to help out some kindly old citizen who may be ill-suited for the responsibility of caring for a multimillion dollar structure. This is not to imply that all custodians should be selected through civil service procedures but rather to suggest the establishment of objective standards based on ability rather than political favoritism.

There have been various statements on the qualifications to be examined in the selection of a school custodian. Among these characteristics are: health, experience, abilities, character, age, intelligence, education, and appearance. An Iowa handbook for school custodians specified the following qualifications to be used in selecting a custodian. He should (1) be physically able to do his work (recommended age level at time of employment is between 21 and 45, with older persons considered only if they are physically fit); (2) be of good character; (3) be of good health (it is reasonable to require physical examinations of school custodians); (4) be mentally alert; (5) be neat and clean in appearance; (6) be dependable; (7) be able to get along with children and adults; (8) be able to grow in his job (this includes a willingness to work and assume responsibility as well as maintaining an open mind and seeking better methods and materials for plant operation and maintenance); (9) be immune to gossip (peddling gossip from teacher to teacher, exploiting confidences, or carrying school tales to the "down-town" folks can lead to many complications); (10) be orderly.[9] Where specialized skills are concerned, such as operating boilers, additional requirements beyond those stipulated could be made. The objective measurement of these qualities is a problem in custodial employment, as it is in other personnel fields. A battery of tests that may apply should be supplemented by the planned interview.

Status studies on the employment of school custodians which were completed in the 1920's and 1930's showed that most school districts used subjective and informal procedures in selection. Although more recent studies are lacking, a tendency is noted in at least the larger cities to administer civil service examinations.

Low salaries, long working hours, low prestige, and little opportunity for promotion have contributed to the high turnover among well-qualified school custodial staff members. There exists a need in all school systems to develop the kind of working conditions, salary schedule, retirement benefits, and other conditions that would enable schools to compete successfully with industry and business for custodial personnel of high caliber. A work week of 40 to 44 hours with time and one-half for overtime, 12 months' employment, and at least 2 weeks of paid (noncumulative) vacation per year would be the minimum bases for desirable working conditions. A salary schedule with annual increments large enough to be noticed on a weekly or biweekly payroll can and should be operative in every school district. The pay scale should include classification of custodial positions. Retirement benefits are a must in all avenues of our culture and there is no reason for excluding the custodial staff. Suitable storage facilities, sufficient custodial supplies and equipment, and a justifiable work load are also a part of establishing desirable working conditions for those responsible for the care of buildings.

RELATIONSHIP BETWEEN THE CUSTODIAN AND OTHERS

The school building custodian does not live in a vacuum while caring for the school plant. The social contacts are many and include pupils, teachers, principals, central office staff members, the superintendent, the board of education, and the public. His position in the educational hierarchy can be defined in a formal manner. Relationships with the public in general and the pupils in particular are more likely to be based on informal understandings than written policies.

At the building level, the custodian should look to the principal for directions. In the hierarchical organization, the principal is the immediate superior of the building custodian. The director of plant operation and maintenance at the central office bears the same relationship to building custodians as central office subject matter supervisors bear to teachers within the building.

It is not the function of teachers to spell out the responsibilities of building custodians. The custodian is not a "flunky" at the "beck and call" of all people. Any special services (other than those usually assigned by the principal) which teachers request of custodians should be referred to the principal. Confusion will result if the building custodian is expected to act on orders relayed from all teachers, the principal, and the director of plant operation and maintenance. The failure to define lines of authority can result in conflicts among teachers, principals, school plant supervisors, and building custodians.

On the other hand, the custodian has no authority

---

[9] A. B. Grimes, *Mr. Custodian, A Handbook for School Administrators and Custodians,* Des Moines, Iowa: The Iowa State Department of Public Instruction, January, 1956, pp. 8, 9.

to tell teachers what they may or may not do or use within the classroom. A custodian who has been on the job for a long time may begin to feel that he is the "power behind the throne." It would not be far wrong to say that there may be one such custodian at one time or another in every school system.

An illustration based on a real experience by one of the writers is a case in point. The kindergarten room of this school had a lovely fireplace. The teacher decided that a marshmallow roast would cap a given unit on social experiences for kindergarteners. She asked the building custodian if he would object to the use of the fireplace. He informed her that she could use the fireplace if she procured the papers and wood to start the fire and cleaned up "the mess" afterwards. The initial error must be attributed to the teacher who should have approached the building principal to obtain materials or services needed. The fireplace was designed to be used and no special permission was necessary. To finish the story, the building principal heard of the situation when the young kindergarten teacher cited it as an illustration of the fine coöperation she was receiving from the old custodian. The building principal decided that a dangerous precedent could be set and immediately informed the custodian that not only would the custodian procure for the teacher the materials to be burned in the fireplace, but he was also to clean it after the completion of the activity. There are building custodians who have a desire to recruit teachers as special assistants in cleaning the building. This should be avoided.

Teachers can complicate building housekeeping by failing to exercise the degree of disciplinary control over the youngsters that is desirable. There is little excuse to permit any youngster to throw paper on the floor. The least that can be said is that it develops undesirable habits of sloppiness in students. The teacher should help prevent needless accumulations of materials on class floors. Custodians have been known to rate teachers for certain people of the community. The sole basis of such a rating is the cleanliness of the floor of the classroom at the end of the day. It is not the function of the building custodian to rate teachers, and any tendency to do so should be strongly discouraged.

The main function of the building custodian is to keep the building in tiptop operating condition. He can attempt to stimulate the students' pride in a clean building, but there are limits to such promotions. The building custodian has no authority to discipline pupils, least of all to exercise any physical force. In his relations with pupils, it should be clearly established that the building custodian must depend upon teachers and the building principal to enforce disciplinary action against pupils who consistently deface or willfully dirty the building. It is questionable whether school systems should use the custodian as "toilet room policeman," playground "supervisor," or student disciplinarian when teachers are not in the building. These are not his responsibilities and they are better executed by other personnel employed in the school.

The custodian's relationship with the public is extremely important. He has a significant role to play in public relations. A friendly attitude toward public groups using the school building can promote harmonious relationships. A neat and clean building makes a good impression upon the public and this is perhaps one of the significant contributions the building custodian makes toward improved public relations. In his face-to-face contacts a neat appearance and a pleasant personality are the custodian's valued allies.

The director of plant operation and maintenance for the district and his staff are a source of aid to the custodian in solving technical problems related to cleaning and care of the building. They are responsible for the development of in-service programs aimed at the continual improvement of building custodians. Central office personnel supervising custodians must work with and through the principal of the building rather than around him.

In summary, it can be said that a key person in the management of custodial services is the building principal. The principal can look to the director of plant operation and maintenance for aid in solving the technical problems of housekeeping as well as in promoting the in-service growth of custodians. He bears a considerable responsibility for the development of written policies which help to establish desirable working relationships between the custodian and pupils and teachers. The building principal has many functions with instruction leadership of prime consideration. But he cannot afford to overlook the importance of a well-cared-for building in the educational program and the custodian's influence on the educational program. The building principal is often confronted with the need to evaluate the effectiveness of custodians in caring for buildings and grounds or in his relations with pupils, teachers, and the public. A formal written report by the principal on the custodian's effectiveness should be filed at least once a year and sent to the superintendent's office. This report may be filed jointly with the supervisor of custodians. It implies that specific criteria or objective standards for evaluating custodial performance are known by administrators. It is unfortunate that most administrators are unacquainted with objective standards for judging custodial performance.

WORK SCHEDULES FOR CUSTODIANS

The building custodian is confronted with a large number of varied tasks to be accomplished in keeping the building in operating condition. Sweeping, dusting, scrubbing, waxing, oiling, cleaning, tending to various service systems, etc., are a part of the daily, weekly, or monthly chores.

Custodian work schedules can be used to facilitate efficient execution of the variety of tasks. Such schedules can save work time, simplify tasks, and improve performance levels. A defensible working schedule is based on what constitutes a proper service load for each janitor. Determining a proper work load is one of the more difficult administrative problems in the operation of the school plant.

Reeves and Ganders identified 22 factors influencing the service load of custodians:

1. Pupil behavior in the school.
2. Area or number of rooms in a building.
3. Age and physical condition of the building.
4. The location of the building.
5. Climatic conditions and type of fuel burned.
6. Type of building construction.
7. The kind of school organization (elementary, junior high, senior high, etc.).
8. The social background of pupils.
9. The total enrollment.
10. The type and variety of classrooms.
11. The amount and kind of floor area.
12. The area, size, and location of windows.
13. Area, kind, and utilization of chalkboards.
14. Type and arrangements of desks and other furniture.
15. Size of site and type of playground covering.
16. Area and placement of sidewalks.
17. Type and condition of heating equipment.
18. Type and condition of ventilating equipment.
19. Amount and installation of plumbing.
20. Type and condition of service systems to facilitate custodial work.
21. Custodial shops and storerooms.
22. Cleaning equipment.[10]

Other approaches for estimating work load are based on area of floors, number of rooms, number of teachers, and students per custodian, or any combina-

[10] C. E. Reeves and H. S. Ganders, *School Building Management*, New York: Teachers College, Columbia University, 1928, pp. 28–30.

TABLE 30. Comparison of Square-Foot-per-Minute Standards for Sweeping in Syracuse and in Minneapolis

Type of Space	Minneapolis Square-Foot-per-Minute	Syracuse Square-Foot-per-Minute
Office, Nurse, Rest Rooms	80	60
Classrooms	80	70
Auditorium and Balcony	80	75
Gym, Playground, Corridor	200	180
Industrial Arts and Vocational Shops	60	70
Science Laboratories	80	80
Household Arts	80	80
Stairs, Landings, Entrances	80	40
Toilets	100	60
Dressing Rooms and Showers	100	70
Bookroom, Storerooms, Other Storage Places	80	50

SOURCE: University of the State of New York, *School Business Management Handbook*, Operation and Maintenance, no. 7, Albany, N.Y.: The State Education Department, 1955, p. 54.

tion of these. The following standards have been suggested as measures of service loads:

1. Total square feet per custodian:
   a. 16,000 square feet.
   b. 17,000 square feet.
   c. 20,000 square feet.
   (Some would differentiate and assign 16,000 square feet per day worker and 19,000 square feet per night worker.)
2. Standards for the number of rooms per custodian vary from 8 rooms plus the boiler room and grounds to 10 to 12 rooms.
3. Standards for the number of teachers per custodian vary from 5 to 14.
4. The number of pupils per custodian range from 125 to 350. The problem is to justify what are more or less rule-of-thumb designations.
5. Other estimates combine all factors and stipulate 8 teachers, 225 pupils, 15,000 square feet of floor area, and 2 acres per custodian.

The custodial requirements of a school building will vary with the type and age of the building. All rooms are not of the same area and all types of rooms are not swept or cleaned in the same period of time or with the same ease. There have been some studies made of the area in square feet swept in a given space of time. These studies have served to establish square-foot-per-minute standards for sweeping rooms of various types. All standards are based on some measure of space and time. In Table 30 a comparison is made

TABLE 31. Schedule for Room Equivalents

Routine Daily Work	Area in Square Feet	Room Equivalent[a]
Classrooms (including special rooms, teachers' rooms, library, etc.)	800	1.00
Stair and Landings (mopping floors)	1000	1.00
	400	1.00
Toilet Rooms (sweeping floors; cleaning fixtures)	1000	1.00
	17	1.00
Auditorium—Playroom (sweeping and dusting)	2400	1.00
Auditorium (with fixed seats)	1200	1.00
Gymnasium (sweeping and dusting)	2400	1.00
Locker Rooms (sweeping and dusting)	2400	1.00
Showers (mopping or hosing)	1200	1.00
Cafeteria and Dining Rooms (if mopped)	400	1.00
Cafeteria and Dining Rooms (sweeping and dusting)	800	1.00
Corridors		
Wood Floors (sweeping)	1800	1.00
Linoleum Floors (sweeping)	2400	1.00
Terrazzo Floors (sweeping,	3200	1.00
if mopped periodically)	400	1.00
Heating and Ash Removal in Season (separate force)	1 Ton	7.00
Lawns and Ground Areas in Season	5000	.333
Glass Area (windows in large single lights)	70	1.00
Glass Area (windows divided into small lights)	50	1.00

[a] A unit or room equivalent is the useful work accomplished in a 15-minute period of time.

SOURCE: Walter C. Hawkins, "Assigning Custodial Loads," *School Business Affairs*, Association of School Business Officials, February, 1953, *19*:5. See also M. M. Steen, "Formula for Estimating Custodial Work Loads," *School Business Affairs*, Association of School Business Officials, November, 1945, *11*:1–2.

of square-foot-per-minute standards developed in Syracuse, New York, and in Minneapolis, Minnesota.

The Syracuse standards seem to fortify the rule-of-thumb of 16,000 square feet per building custodian. The square-feet-per-minute standards are a simple way of determining the total time needed to care for each type of space.

In determining work load another approach is based on number of room equivalents per custodian. A schedule of room equivalents is presented in Table 31 for various types of rooms or areas in the school building. A unit or room equivalent is defined as the useful work accomplished in a 15-minute period.[11] With the

[11] Walter C. Hawkins, "Assigning Custodial Loads," *School Business Affairs*, Association of School Business Officials, February, 1953, *19*:5.

room-equivalents approach for work which can be accomplished in a 15-minute period, building custodians in an 8-hour day could handle 32 room equivalents.

Custodial man power needs can be determined on the basis of (1) the nature and number of school tasks; (2) the set-up time and total time required for each and all tasks; (3) the accepted standard for number of minutes in a man-unit; and (4) the computation of man-units by dividing (2) by (3) above.[12] The development of a custodian's schedule in a given system should follow the listing of tasks along with the estimated time past experience has shown to be necessary for the performance of each and all tasks. Various sources have described in detail the many custodial tasks and the estimated time for their completion.[13]

Describing tasks and estimations of time for completion of tasks are the backbone of schedule preparation. A schedule for the building custodian can be expressed many ways. One approach would be to list the frequency of operations, indicating the nature of operation and how often it is done (such as daily, twice daily, weekly, monthly, etc.). An illustration of this method based on the frequency of operations in the elementary schools at Terre Haute is presented in Form 20.

Work schedules can also be expressed in terms of what should be done on a daily basis. Sample schedules for a head custodian, a matron, and a part-time cleaner are presented in Table 32.

In summary, to develop a work schedule the service load and time available for its accomplishment must be known. This includes what is to be swept, dusted, cleaned, and scrubbed as well as other routine duties such as heating the building in season, baling waste paper, and caring for grounds in season.

The schedule should not be regarded as an inflexible program which must be followed without variation on a day-to-day basis. It is a plan of attack on the many duties of the day. The time sequence is founded on what can be done when school is in session and what must be deferred for other times. There is no one schedule that will fit all custodians in one school system or all systems. In other words, there is no such thing as an ideal custodial work schedule suitable for all buildings of whatever size, use, or facilities. Each district must develop a work schedule for each building in the system. Most custodians have an informal schedule which may not be reduced to writing. It is recommended that work schedules be written. Written schedules are a source of information on the extent of the building custodian's work load. They can also be used to systematize and routinize custodial ac-

[12] Linn *et al., op. cit.,* pp. 44–55.
[13] *Ibid.,* pp. 46–48.

FORM 20.

Frequency of Operations Chart for Elementary Schools, Terre Haute, Indiana

Operation	Daily	Weekly	Monthly	Longer Periods Than Monthly
Sweeping				
Classrooms	X			
Corridors and Stairs	X			
Under Radiators		X		
Gymnasium Floor	X			
Sidewalks		X		
Dusting				
Furniture	X			
Woodwork	X			
Walls and Ceilings			X	
Wall Pictures and Window Shades			X	
Radiator Tops	X			
Between Radiator Sections		X		
Ventilating Grilles		X		
Scrubbing and Mopping				
Classrooms		X		
Rest Rooms	X			
Corridors		X		
Stairs		X		
Entrances		X		
Domestic Science Rooms	X			
Shower and Locker Rooms	X			
Office and Kindergarten	X			
Waxing Floors				
Corridors and Stairs				X
Classrooms				X
Offices				X
Oiling Floors				X
Cleaning				
Furniture and Woodwork	X			
Windows (outside)				X
Windows (inside)		X		
Inside Glass Doors		X		
Cupboard Glass		X		
Toilet Room Floors	X			
Toilet Bowls	X			
Toilet Seats	X			
Urinals	X			
Blackboards	X			
Erasers		X		
Removal Sawdust and Shavings	X			
Removal Garbage	X			
Handrail and Door Knobs	X			
Drinking Fountains	X			
Light Globes			X	
Toilet and Shower Partitions		X		

SOURCE: Loring C. Halberstadt, "Frequency of Operations Chart for School Custodians," *School Business Affairs*, Association of School Business Officials, December, 1948, *14*:2.

TABLE 32.   Sample Custodial Work Schedules

I. Daily Schedule—Head Custodian

7:00–8:10	Fire boilers and care for mechanical equipment
8:10–8:20	Sweep sidewalks
8:20–8:30	Check wall clocks
8:30–8:35	Put out flag
8:35–9:00	Extra jobs
9:00–9:10	Sweep corridor, first floor
9:10–9:25	Check playground
9:25–9:35	Fire boilers
9:35–9:45	Rest period
9:45–10:32	Mop floors; clean stalls, urinals, toilet bowls and wash bowls in boys' toilet room, first floor
10:32–10:45	Fire boilers
10:45–11:35	Clean 16 entrance doors
11:35–11:45	Dust and arrange tables for lunch—gymnasium
11:45–12:00	Fire boilers
12:00–1:00	Lunch hour
1:00–1:15	Fire boilers
1:15–1:25	Sweep corridor, first floor
1:25–2:15	Extra jobs
2:15–2:40	Rest period
2:40–3:18	Extra jobs
3:18–3:33	Fire boilers
3:33–4:09	Sweep classrooms 16, 17, 18
4:09–4:24	Clean and put away tools
4:24–4:29	Take in flag
4:29–4:39	Dispose of rubbish
4:39–4:54	Bank boiler fires
4:54–5:00	Lock doors

II. Daily Schedule—Matron

7:00–7:09	Clean and dust principal's office
7:09–7:54	Dust classrooms 4, 5, 6, 7, 8, 9, 10, 11 and library
7:54–8:18	Clean gymnasium-auditorium
8:18–8:45	Mop two girls' toilets; fill soap dispensers, toilet paper and towel holders
8:45–9:20	Sweep second floor corridors and stairs
9:20–9:50	Clean corridor wainscot
9:50–10:00	Clean teachers' rest room
10:00–12:00	Lunch period—goes home
12:00–12:25	Clean and dust kindergarten department
12:25–12:37	Sweep library (not used in afternoon)
12:37–12:56	Check girls' toilet rooms
12:56–1:11	Check over tools
1:11–1:41	Sweep second floor corridors and stairs
1:41–2:14	Clean stalls, toilet bowls and wash bowls in two girls' toilets
2:14–2:24	Clean drinking fountains and slop sinks
2:24–2:44	Rest period (combines morning and afternoon rest allowances)
2:44–4:03	Clean 38 classroom doors
4:03–4:50	Sweep classrooms 1, 2, 14, and 15
4:50–5:00	Dispose of rubbish

III. Daily Schedule—Part-Time Cleaner

7:00–7:50	Dust rooms 1, 2, 3, 12, 13, 14, 15, 16, 17, and 18
7:50–8:30	Mop floors; clean stalls, urinals, toilet bowls and wash bowls in boys' toilet, second floor
3:30–5:42	Sweep classrooms, 3, 4, 5, 6, 7, 8, 9, 10, 11, 12, and 13
5:42–5:52	Dispose of rubbish
5:52–6:00	Clean and put away tools

SOURCE: New England School Development Council, *Guide for School Custodial Services*, Cambridge: the Council, July, 1948, pp. 33, 34.

tivities as an initial step toward more efficient operation. They are also an aid to substitutes for custodians.

There was a time when a single building custodian worked long hours seven days a week. This was followed by a normal working day of eight hours for six days a week. After World War II, a 44-hour week, consisting of eight hours a day for five days and a half-day on Saturday became somewhat of a standard for custodial work loads. In some communities, particularly those highly unionized, a 40-hour work week for custodians has been developed. Many authorities feel that the most effective work period should be a 44-hour work period as the half-day on Saturday when school is not in session is particularly useful for cleaning certain areas.

SUPERVISORY AND TRAINING PROGRAMS

Larger school systems with many buildings employ a director of plant maintenance and operation. Various names and conditions of employment are applied to this position. In addition to the suggested term of director of plant maintenance and operation such titles as supervisor of buildings and grounds, superintendent of buildings and grounds or associate superintendent in charge of buildings and grounds are used. Some school systems select such a person from civil service lists but most have not established it as a civil service position. The qualifications vary considerably, with most large systems requiring at least a college degree with decided preference for those who have a degree in engineering and some experience in engineering, architecture, or building construction.

In addition to other functions, the director of plant maintenance and operation has the responsibility of supervising and improving the effectiveness of building custodians. He may be responsible for a system-wide, in-service training program for custodians which may extend from a few days to several weeks. Some large cities, such as Denver, Detroit, Milwaukee, Minneapolis, and Seattle, operate their own in-service training school classes. In Milwaukee the classes are conducted in June, immediately after the closing of school, and often are located at the vocational school. The special training programs included such topics as the engineer and his job, character, responsibilities, and appearance; demonstrations on floor sanding, sealing, waxing, buffing, treating, and maintenance; and care of toilet rooms and shower rooms.[14]

Smaller school systems are not large enough to operate efficiently a special school for the improvement of custodial services. Some colleges and universities such as Iowa State, Michigan State, Ohio State, Purdue, and Teachers College, Columbia University, offer specially designed programs for school building custodians. These usually take place in June. Encouraging the building custodian to attend such special custodial clinics and paying his expenses while attending such schools will pay rich dividends to school districts. In-service training programs and special schools have done much to improve custodial services in school plants, and in a certain sense they have helped to instill pride and prestige in a profession which has not enjoyed the status commensurate with its contributions.

Viles identified the following principles for the establishment of a custodial training program:

1. It must be practical and realistic, related to the type of work the custodian has to do.
2. Instruction should be in terms the learner understands.
3. It should show the relationship of the operating and maintenance programs to the purposes and procedures of the educational program.
4. The training program should be set up in a series of attainable steps so that the learner may measure progress.
5. Instruction should be intermingled with demonstration and learner participation in discussions and in task performance. Class sizes should be limited to permit learner participation.
6. Instruction should be thorough. It should provide information on reasons and methods and the results expected. It should provide various methods of approach; complete each problem before taking up another; plan the job, practice, discuss procedures and results; and repeat to acceptable performance.
7. Training should aid the custodians in setting up work patterns and standards.

8. Each performance technique taught should become a part of a general work pattern or schedule.
9. It should point out additional sources of information and help the custodian to continue and extend his studies.
10. The custodian should be given a perspective of the whole maintenance and operation programs. The courses offered should have continuity, and the custodian should be assisted in planning his own training steps.
11. Training should aid the custodian in understanding his obligations and responsibilities and in correlating his work with that of his coworkers.
12. It should assist the custodian in evaluating his work in terms of services rendered. It should lead to a fuller understanding of the whole job, competence in performance, and a pride in craftsmanship and accomplishment.[15]

Viles went further and suggested the following units of custodial training, some or all of which could be used in local district, college, or state-wide programs.

Unit 1—The Custodial Program, Organization and Maintenance.
Unit 2—Housekeeping I—General Housekeeping Problems.
Unit 3—Housekeeping II—Floor and Special Area Cleaning.
Unit 4—Heating and Ventilation I—Systems, Fuels, and Combustion.
Unit 5—Heating and Ventilation II—Operation and Care.
Unit 6—School Plant Safety and Fire Protection.
Unit 7—Special Problems in Plant Care.
Unit 8—School Floors, Treatment, Rejuvenation.
Unit 9—Planning the Work Program.
Unit 10—Maintenance and Repairs I—Interior Repairs.
Unit 11—Maintenance and Repairs II—External Repairs, Mechanical Repairs, Shop Controls.[16]

MAINTENANCE

There is a close relation between the quality of custodial services and the need for building maintenance. Custodial care can be looked upon as a program of preventative maintenance. This is particularly obvious where the custodian has responsibility for such tasks as oiling equipment, cleaning and waxing the floors, and proper dusting of surfaces. If he fails to perform necessary responsibilities or is not given materials and equipment to accomplish certain functions, damage from neglect will be reflected in a higher appropriation for school maintenance. Custodial care in-

[14] Myron Hineline, "Plant Operation in Milwaukee," *School Business Affairs,* Association of School Business Officials, January, 1951, 17:1–3.

[15] Viles, *op. cit.,* p. 11.
[16] *Ibid.,* pp. 16–22.

fluences the functional utility of a building and its longevity. Neglect or postponement of necessary maintenance can result in more frequent needs for new school plant construction or extensive remodeling of buildings.

Systematic inspection of each school building on at least an annual basis is an important first step toward an effective maintenance program. Regular inspections can detect little difficulties for repair before they assume major proportions. Each year the school building principal and his custodial staff should tour the school building, poking into every nook and cranny to determine conditions requiring special attention. Such an inspection could be scheduled at the close of the school year in June. Annual or more frequent inspections can help the principal to gain insight into the effectiveness of custodians as well as to determine what maintenance should be done. A record of maintenance work needed should be dispatched promptly to the central office.

Periodic inspection is the basis for preparing a special summer work program for custodians in many small systems where the custodian serves as a maintenance man during the summer months. Prior to the start of school in the fall, the principal and the custodial staff can reëxamine the building, taking special care to note what was and was not accomplished during the summer months. Excellence should not be taken for granted, and a principal should be as ready with his compliments as he is with criticisms. If a written record is made of work to be accomplished during the summer months and the custodial staff is aware of the time limit imposed, there is little necessity for professional administrators to be present in the school building all summer long for the prime purpose of supervising custodians.

Specially trained personnel from the central office staff should also make periodic inspections of the building to reveal defects not readily ascertainable by untrained personnel. A technical check of the roof, exterior of the building, and service systems often requires the services of specially trained persons. A systematic examination at intervals can reveal the need for minor repairs, such as resurfacing a roof, and forestall the need for complete renewal of the roof shortly after the end of the guaranteed period.

All this points to the need for careful record keeping of needed and completed building maintenance. An official record of every time a room is painted, a roof replaced, a boiler repaired, etc., should be kept. Many schools operate on a cyclical painting schedule. This painting rotation varies from once every five years to once every ten years. With this approach the schedule is determined by the money budgeted, and a specified number of rooms and halls or other spaces is painted each year. This is in lieu of painting the entire building at one time. It is particularly effective in smaller school systems where the custodial staff serves as the maintenance staff during the summer months. In larger systems, it is often more practical to paint the entire building at one time with a special painting crew. There is no one set maintenance pattern which can be applied to all systems.

There is a need to maintain a careful record of when a room was painted, its cost, and its estimated time for repainting. Such a systematic approach or establishment of a painting cycle can insure an attractive building and prevent costly repairs to wall surfaces, as well as improve certain functional qualities of the building such as lighting. The precise time cycle for either interior or exterior painting of a building will be determined, in part, by climatic factors and location of a building. Naturally, a building located on a cramped site with loose rock or similar material for playground surfacing will require painting more often than others. Much the same can be said for those located in industrial areas as contrasted with those in residential areas. Most districts report that painting is done during the summer months and is accomplished by a special painting crew rather than through private painting contractors. Failure to paint is an example of being pennywise and pound foolish in school plant maintenance.

MAINTENANCE CREWS VERSUS CONTRACT MAINTENANCE

Is it better to have the maintenance work performed by a special maintenance staff employed by the school district or by private contractors? There has been considerable discussion with reference to the merits of each plan. The general conclusions appear to be that there is no one pattern that would apply in all cases, and each school must answer for itself the question of contract maintenance versus school maintenance by regularly employed personnel.

McEwen summarized the advantages and disadvantages in the use of a special maintenance staff employed by the school district.

A. *Advantages*
   1. Usually the hourly wage rates of full-time school maintenance personnel are slightly lower than the prevailing wages paid by private contractors;
   2. School staff maintenance workers can be dispatched

more readily to trouble spots in their order of importance;

3. The nature of many maintenance jobs defies description and often requires adjustment or redirection after work is under way. It is a lot easier to change-order a school employed staff than to wait for the next board meeting to have this accomplished where private contract workers are involved;

4. School maintenance personnel have a familiarity with the location and the difficulties experienced in various plants which enables them to proceed directly to their assignments without loss of time. Frequently trouble can be diagnosed in advance and the staff may be supplied with parts and tools which are required to restore operations with dispatch;

5. All school communities are not fortunately located in areas where competition for various maintenance services is available. Under such conditions, competitive bidding is not always possible;

6. The esprit de corps of the school-employed staff which takes pride in school operation cannot be underestimated.

B. *Disadvantages*

1. Providing staff in sufficient quantities and qualities can result in an expensive stand-by force which encourages supervisors to assign personnel to "busy" work and inconsequential tasks;

2. Widely dispersed schools, as often found in county systems, require excessive travel for centralized maintenance staff that might be obviated by the use of contractors more advantageously located;

3. It is impractical in smaller school systems to employ properly trained personnel for all the different types of maintenance work;

4. Multiple and widely dispersed breakdowns would overtax a balanced maintenance crew;

5. The work of a "jack-of-all-trades" may be inferior to the quality of specialized private contract work.[17]

As a general rule the smaller the school system, the more likely it is that maintenance work that is out of the ordinary will be done on a contract basis with outside staff employed. The nature of the maintenance job is an important factor. For more complicated maintenance work that necessitates a highly specialized staff, it is more than likely that the work will be done by contract force. Thus, major electrical repairs which will take a considerable period of time for accomplishment are usually delegated on the basis of bids to contractors with qualified personnel. In general, it can be said that it is desirable to have some

maintenance work done by the school staff and some done by outside contractors.

TYPES OF MAINTENANCE

The type of maintenance work required in the school can be classified into (1) long-range maintenance, (2) annual maintenance, and (3) emergency or unforseen maintenance.

Long-range maintenance would include rehabilitation, renovation, remodeling, or modernization of a school plant. Thus, it may be decided that the home economics room should be altered, the lighting improved, new cabinets installed, floor covering replaced, etc. In programs of long-range maintenance, a system of priorities will, in effect, determine what shall be done at a particular time. The availability of money for the project is a factor in long-range maintenance.

Annual maintenance necessitates a relatively smaller cash outlay and, of course, pertains to those tasks that can be performed on an annual basis in most schools. Much of the yearly maintenance work can be accomplished during the summer months following a spring inspection of needed corrections, repairs, etc. One illustration would be an annual boiler inspection followed by cleaning of the flues and functional parts and all other necessary repairs. Careful scheduling is necessary during the summer to satisfy the annual maintenance requirements.

Emergency or unforeseen maintenance problems are, as the term would indicate, those which occur unexpectedly and require almost immediate attention. The school maintenance staff is particularly useful in such cases.

The question arises as to what should be the size of the maintenance budget? It varies considerably among school systems. There is some agreement that the proportion should not be less than 5 percent of the total annual budget.[18] Another way of arriving at estimated expenditures for maintenance is a fixed percent of the total cost of the building or its replacement. A minimum would be 1 percent of the current replacement costs of the school plant. Some recommend a figure as high as 2 percent. A justifiable compromise would be 1½ percent of the total replacement cost of the building. It is extremely difficult to determine in advance precisely what amount of money should be devoted to maintenance. A number of factors are involved and there is no magic in a given

[17] F. W. McEwen, "Contract Versus School Maintenance Staff," *Proceedings of the Association of School Business Officials*, 43rd Convention, 1957, pp. 109–110.

[18] American Association of School Administrators, *American School Buildings, op. cit.*, pp. 278–279.

percent. Careful inspection, as well as experience of the past years with reference to emergency or unforeseen maintenance work, will determine what needs to be done. A study of past experiences and postponements can be translated into cost figures. Communities where a backlog of maintenance work has been permitted to accumulate for various reasons will require greater expenditures than others. Communities which have been able to use low maintenance cost materials in school plant construction will have lower maintenance costs than communities that were forced to be concerned with low initial building costs. Local conditions, quality of the construction, materials employed, availability of custodial supplies, quality of the custodial staff and other factors vary so greatly among schools that there is no single percent figure that all school systems should spend for maintenance. A more practical and meaningful approach is to determine by careful survey and inspection what needs to be done and translate this into cost figures.

The size and organization of the maintenance staff will depend upon such factors as the volume of work, the amount of routine maintenance schedule, and the amount of contracted maintenance hired from outside sources.[19] The size of the organization will depend upon the man-hour requirements on an annual basis by crafts and the amount of work normally accomplished. It is recommended that employees for the maintenance staff should have some training skills in the following areas: (1) general—carpentry, painting, masonry, roofing, and so on; (2) heating and ventilating; (3) pipe-fitting and plumbing; (4) electrical; (5) mechanical shops—machine, sheet metal, and so on.[20] Small school systems will have to be satisfied with a jack-of-all-trades rather than individual maintenance men who are adequately skilled in each of these areas.

Maintenance personnel should be dispatched on the basis of clearly written job descriptions and scheduled to make full utilization of the entire staff. Suffice it to say that such a staff should have similar in-service training and development as provided for the custodial staff. This training should place stress on such things as: (1) painting (types, methods, color conditioning); (2) plumbing (valves, fixtures, piping, hot water tanks, showers); (3) heating and ventilating (boilers, radiators, traps, converters, temperature control, unit heaters, dampers and regulators, stokers, smoke control, gas and oil burners); (4) electrical systems (replacement of equipment, light values,

[19] University of the State of New York, *op. cit.*, pp. 68–71.
[20] *Ibid.*

safety factors, motor maintenance).[21] Very often companies will provide special training for school personnel who purchase their equipment. It is to the advantage of the school system to send maintenance personnel to such company clinics.

SUMMARY

Age and use deteriorate buildings and equipment. It is the responsibility of professional administrators to formulate the kind of building operation and maintenance programs which will extend the useful physical life of a building and equipment.

The building custodians and matrons play an important role in executing the many and varied tasks of housekeeping. Their work can be made more effective through supervision and technical assistance from central office staff members, in-service custodial clinics, making available the equipment and supplies needed to do the job, and the preparation of written work schedules. Work schedules vary with age, constitution, and other building factors. The immediate superior of a building custodian is the building principal. A custodian does not work in a vacuum but is in a position where he makes frequent contact with pupils, teachers, and the public. He has a significant role to play in public relations.

Custodial services and building maintenance have the common objective of keeping the building in the best possible useful condition necessary to facilitate the purposes of the educational program. In a certain sense, custodial care can be regarded as preventative maintenance. Periodic inspection followed by scheduling of maintenance work is the basis for building maintenance programs. Careful record keeping of what was done at what time and what remains to be accomplished is of value. A full-time district-employed maintenance staff and private contract maintenance work each has its own advantages. The size of the maintenance budget should be determined by a survey of what needs to be done translated into cost figures. Percent of current expenditures or the total cost of the structure is a rule-of-thumb procedure to suggest minimum expenditures for maintenance rather than a formula to obtain the optimum sum.

QUESTIONS

1. What are the similarities and differences between plant operation and plant maintenance?
2. What can be done to improve the quality of work and the status of school custodians?

[21] *Ibid.*

3. What factors have a bearing on the service load of building custodians?
4. What factors should be given consideration in the development of a custodian's work schedule?

SELECTED REFERENCES

American Association of School Administrators, *School Plant Maintenance,* Washington, D.C.: the Association, 1951.

American Association of School Administrators, *American School Buildings,* 27th Yearbook, Washington, D.C.: the Association, 1949, chap. 16.

Brainard, A. D., *Handbook for School Custodians,* Lincoln: The University of Nebraska Press, 1952.

Hawkins, Walter C., "Assigning Custodial Loads," *School Business Affairs,* Association of School Business Officials, February, 1953.

Linn, Henry H., *et al., The School Custodians' Housekeeping Handbook,* New York: Teachers College, Columbia University, 1948.

McEwen, F. W., "Contract Versus School Maintenance Staff," *Proceedings of the Association of School Business Officials,* 43rd Convention, 1957.

New England School Development Council, *Guide for School Custodial Services,* Cambridge: the Council, July, 1948.

University of the State of New York, *School Business Management Handbook,* Operation and Maintenance, no. 7, Albany, N.Y.: The State Education Department, 1955.

Viles, N. E., *Improving School Custodial Service,* Bulletin 1949, no. 13, U.S. Office of Education, Washington, D.C.: U.S. Government Printing Office, 1949.

CHAPTER 14

Accounting for School Properties

IN THE PREVIOUS CHAPTER, THE GROWTH OF the total value of school properties since the end of World War II was noted. It was estimated that the total value of school property would reach the $20 billion mark in the relatively near future. This represents a tremendous investment—an investment which must be safeguarded and carefully identified through a system of accounting for property.

Public schools of America are characterized by inadequate property records. All reports presented in this book and other sources must therefore be regarded as estimates rather than as indications of precise value. Inadequate property accounting in public schools is in stark contrast with the careful procedures found in business and industry. The fact that initial worth and subsequent depreciation of property is needed for purposes of borrowing, tax computations, and estimates of profits or loss in industry can partially explain but not justify this difference. Property accounting for schools is necessary but for different reasons than those which necessitate it in the business or commercial world.

Universal standard accounts and terminology in school property accounting will (1) help to insure appropriate initial recording of property data; (2) improve the accounting for school property; (3) improve the management and utilization of school property; (4) improve school budgeting; (5) establish a sound basis for evaluating the adequacy of school property; (6) establish a sound basis for evaluating property for insurance purposes; (7) improve the accuracy of local and state and national summaries on the value of school properties; (8) facilitate comparisons of property information among communities and among states; (9) enable local and state educational authorities to obtain more suitable needed information for policy determination; (10) improve the accuracy of

educational research and (11) facilitate and improve reliable reporting to the public on the condition and progress of education.[1]

The status of school property accounting today is at least 30 years behind the status of accounting for financial transactions. The publication of the USOE *Property Accounting Handbook* eliminates whatever reasons there may have been for delaying the establishment of property accounts. A property account can be defined as a descriptive heading under which is posted specific information about land, improvements, buildings, and equipment under the jurisdiction or control of school districts.[2] The term "account" is used in this sense as a formal record rather than as a descriptive classification of a financial transaction. It serves as the basis for essential property reports prepared for various state or national agencies or the public. The very magnitude and diversity of educational property make some system of classification necessary. The system recommended in this book is based on the USOE *Property Accounting Handbook.*[3]

The amount and variety of property in school districts in the United States vary greatly, making it necessary for individual systems to adapt the specific accounts to the given situation. Few, if any, school districts will find it necessary to utilize all of the property accounts to be described herein. Those that apply should be used and the others ignored. Some districts may require special information not available from the given categories and which may not be needed for comparisons among school districts in the

---

[1] United States Office of Education, *Property Accounting Handbook,* Handbook no. 3, U.S. Office of Education, Washington, D.C.: U.S. Government Printing Office, 1958. (Based on 3rd Preliminary Draft of February 1, 1958, mimeographed.)

[2] *Ibid.*

[3] *Ibid.*

United States. The recommendations in the USOE *Property Accounting Handbook* and in this chapter are not intended as an inflexible system from which no deviations are permitted.

UNITS FOR PROPERTY ACCOUNTABILITY

Property accounts are grouped in three distinct or major categories. These are: (1) accounts for school plants used for instructional purposes, (2) accounts for noninstructional plant facilities and (3) accounts for equipment unassigned to specific facilities. A plant is defined as the site, building, and equipment used for instructional or noninstructional purposes. Accounts for instructional school plants are designed specifically for sites, buildings, and equipment used for instructional purposes. As the name implies, noninstructional plant facilities are not used for teaching-learning situations but for purposes such as administration or transportation. The site, improvements to site, building facilities, and equipment assigned which serve noninstructional purposes are accounted for in this second category. The third class is a catch-all for equipment not specifically assigned to instructional or noninstructional plant facilities but which may be used in all types of facilities.

The unit of accountability for instructional school plants is the school plant itself. This implies that a complete series of accounts be maintained for each individual instructional plant in the system to record information on its site, buildings, and equipment. Each plant becomes a complete accounting entity. A summary record for all instructional plants rounds out the instruments necessary in property accounting.

The unit of accountability for noninstructional facilities is again the school plant but in this case it is a noninstructional school plant such as the administrative plant or transportation plant. A complete series of accounts is maintained for each noninstructional facility to show the status of its site, building, and assigned equipment.

The unit of accountability for equipment unassigned to a specific facility is the piece of equipment or the equipment group. Whether the unit used is the piece or the group is dependent upon the type of control exercised. Unit control and group control will be defined later. A series of property accounts is maintained for each piece of equipment under unit control or each group under group control.

ACCOUNTING FOR SCHOOL PLANTS UTILIZED FOR INSTRUCTIONAL PURPOSES[4]

The account series for instructional school plants are assigned the numbers 100 through 599. They start with ACCOUNT SERIES 100—TYPE OF PLANT and end with ACCOUNT SERIES 500—EQUIPMENT ASSIGNED TO SCHOOL PLANTS. Keep in mind that this information is kept for each and every instructional plant in the system.

ACCOUNT SERIES 100—TYPE OF PLANT

A relatively simple entry is made at this point. A statement is inserted describing what educational level or levels are housed on a permanent basis in the plant. It could be an elementary, secondary, combined elementary-and-secondary, community college, or combined community college-and-secondary plant. To illustrate, for the Valley Elementary School which houses grade kindergarten through grade six, the entry would be simply "100—TYPE OF PLANT, *Elementary.*"

ACCOUNT SERIES 200—LAND FACILITIES FOR SCHOOL PLANTS

Posted within this series is all information necessary to describe adequately the various kinds of land which make up the school site. Playgrounds, athletic fields, walks, drives, parking areas, experimental agriculture areas, and forestry plots are some of the various types of land utilization for educational purposes.

The kinds of information required to describe accurately the land facilities for plants can be grouped under the three major categories of *Land Identification, Total Area,* and *Total Cost.*

A. *Major Category 220—Land Identification.* Identification accounts should show ownership data, date of acquisition, and date of disposal.
  1. Property Account 221—Ownership of the School Site.
    a. 221.1—Publicly Owned Land for School Sites. The various types of public ownership are:
      1) 221.11—District-Owned.
      2) 221.12—Municipally Owned.
      3) 221.13—Authority-Owned.
    b. 221.2—Nonpublicly Owned Land for School Sites.
  2. Property Account 222—Date of Acquisition of

---

[4] The account names and numbers used in this section were adapted from *ibid.*

Land for School Sites. There are frequent changes, such as additions and disposals during the use of the land for school purposes, and, therefore, the need for the following entries is apparent:

    a. 222.1—Date of Acquisition of Original Piece of Land. This is the date the transfer of the first piece of land, comprising the original school site, was consummated.

    b. 222.2—Date of Acquisition of Each Addition to the Original Piece of Land.

3. Property Account 223—Date of Disposal of Each Piece of Land in the School Site.

B. *Major Category 230—Total Area of the School Site.* The total area of the school site should be expressed in acres to the nearest tenth of an acre. This would include the developed and undeveloped acreage. If the school uses more than a single contiguous piece of land, the area should be the sum of the acres in several pieces.

C. *Major Category 240—Total Cost of Land for School Sites.* This particular category would not be applicable to nonpublicly owned land. Total cost includes purchase price, expenses for all improvements to the land existing at the time of purchase other than structures, and all expenditures related to acquiring title to the land, such as appraisal fees, search and title insurance, site surveys, and condemnation proceedings. If the purchase price includes buildings upon the land which are retained for school use, the appraised value of the buildings should be deducted from the price of the land. If the buildings are sold, the salvage value should be deducted from the price of the land. If the actual cost is unknown, an estimated figure as of time of acquisitions should be entered. If the land was obtained as a gift, the cost would be zero, plus any costs related to acquiring title. Gifts should be acknowledged in the accounts. Total costs at this point should not include improvements made after the purchase. The accounts for posting information on site costs are:

1. Property Account 240.1—Cost of the Original School Site.

2. Property Account 240.2—Cost of Additions to the Original Site.

ACCOUNT SERIES 300—IMPROVEMENTS TO SCHOOL SITE—TOTAL COSTS

Improvements add value to sites beyond the original cost and consist of initial and additional work other than buildings executed on the site or its adjacent ways following its acquisition. Some illustrations of site improvements are grading, landscaping, seeding, and planting of shrubs and trees; constructing new sidewalks, roadways, tunnels, overpasses, retaining walls, sewers, and storm drains; installing water mains, hydrants, and outdoor drinking fountains; original surfacing and soil treatment of athletic fields and tennis courts; furnishing and installing for the first time fixed playground apparatus, flagpoles, gateways, fences, and underground storage tanks which are not part of the service system; and performing any demolition work.

The kinds of information posted in this series to describe accurately the total cost of site improvements can be grouped under the five major categories of *Outdoor Service Systems, Outdoor Instruction or Play Areas, Fences and Retaining Walls, Landscaping,* and *Miscellaneous.*

A. *Major Category 310—Outdoor Service Systems on School Sites—Total Cost.* The costs of the various types of service systems are posted to the following property accounts:

1. Property Account 311—Total Cost of Parking Areas and Drives on the School Site.

2. Property Account 312—Total Cost of Pedestrian Passageways on the School Site.

3. Property Account 313—Total Cost of Water and Sewer Systems on the School Site.

4. Property Account 314—Total Cost of Outdoor Electrical Systems on the School Site.

5. Property Account 315—Total Cost of Outdoor Storage Facilities on the School Site.

6. Property Account 316—Total Cost of Other Outdoor Service Systems on the School Site.

B. *Major Category 320—Outdoor Instruction or Play Areas on the School Site—Total Cost.* The total costs of the various types of outdoor instruction or play areas are placed in the following accounts:

1. Property Account 321—Total Cost of Surfacing Outdoor Instructional or Play Areas on the School Site.

2. Property Account 322—Total Cost of Equipment Built into the Grounds.

C. *Major Category 330—Fences and Retaining Walls on the School Site—Total Cost.*

D. *Major Category 340—Landscaping the School Site —Total Cost.*

E. *Major Category 350—Miscellaneous Improvements to School Site—Total Cost.*

ACCOUNT SERIES 400—BUILDING FACILITIES FOR SCHOOL PLANTS

Buildings for instructional purposes are complex and hence the property accounts to describe a building adequately are numerous. The accounts described are maintained for each complete building or part of a building comprising a school plant. By definition a building is one continuous structure which may or may not be connected with other structures by passageways. Reported in addition to the building spaces is information about the plumbing, heating, ventilating, mechanical and electric systems and lockers, and built-in cabinets and shelves. If the individual structures are connected by breezeways, covered walks, or tunnels but each part is regarded as a separate building, the structures so connected should be accounted for as single units. The passageways enclosing the same type of construction as the building proper are considered part of the building, and two or more structures connected by such passageways would be one building.

The major categories in this account series are: *Building Identification, Costs, Size, Instruction Areas, Administration Areas, Circulation Areas, Service Areas,* and *Service Systems.*

A. *Major Category 410—Building Identification.* To identify accurately an instructional building the following property accounts are needed:

1. Property Account 411—Type of Building Program Housed. A check sheet can be used to describe the program housed.
   a. 411.01—Elementary School.
   b. 411.02—Junior High School.
   c. 411.03—Incomplete High School.
   d. 411.04—Junior-Senior High School.
   e. 411.05—Four-Year High School.
   f. 411.06—Senior High School.
   g. 411.07—Undivided High School.
   h. 411.08—Vocational or Trade High School.
   i. 411.09—Community College.
   j. 411.10—Special School for Exceptional Children.
2. Property Account 412—Type of Building Construction. The information reported would be any one of the following four construction types.
   a. 412.1—Fire-Resistive Buildings. A building of this type is defined as one constructed entirely of fire-resistive materials or with fire-resistive bearing and partitions, floors, walls, stairways, and ceilings. There may be wood finish, wood or composition floor surfaces, and wood roof construction over a fire-resistive ceiling.
   b. 412.2—Semifire-Resistive Buildings. A building of this type is defined as one with fire-resistive bearing walls, corridors, and stairways

but with combustible floors, partitions, roofs, and finish elsewhere.
   c. 412.3—Combustible Buildings. They are defined as all frame buildings or buildings with a fire-resistive veneer over a wood frame or with fire-resistive bearing walls but combustible materials in the rest of the construction.
   d. 412.4—Mixed Construction. The inevitable miscellaneous category is necessary for various combinations of constructions. This would be true of a building constructed with one or more sections or additions at various times.
3. Property Account 413—Kind of Building Facility. Very often there is more than one type of structure on the same site. Reported here are any of the following types of structures on the same site:
   a. 413.1—Instructional Building Facilities.
   b. 413.2—Central Heating Buildings.
   c. 413.3—Stadium.
   d. 413.4—Fieldhouse.
   e. 413.5—Other Buildings. This could be a storage building, a ticket booth, a tool shed, a greenhouse, a maintenance building, etc.
4. Property Account 414—Extent of Occupancy of the Building Facility. A simple statement should be inserted to show if there is:
   a. 414.1—Complete Occupancy.
   b. 414.2—Partial Occupancy. It is not unusual in old buildings to find that only the first floor is utilized and the upper floors are closed off.
5. Property Account 415—Building Mobility. Posted herein is the information to show if the building is permanent or portable.
   a. 415.1—Permanent types of buildings.
   b. 415.2—Portable types of buildings.
6. Property Account 416—Ownership of Building Facility. The information placed here is similar to that recorded in Property Account 221.
   a. 416.1—Publicly Owned Buildings. The types of public ownership are:
      1) 416.11—District-Owned.
      2) 416.12—Municipally Owned.
      3) 416.13—Authority-Owned.
   b. 416.2—Nonpublicly Owned Buildings. Sometimes buildings are rented or used but are not owned by a public body.
7. Property Account 417—Date of Acquisition.
   a. 417.1—Date of Acquisition of Original Buildings.

b. 417.2—Date of Acquisition of Each Addition to Original Building.
8. Property Account 418—Dates of Construction.
   a. 418.1—Date of Construction of Original Building.
   b. 418.2—Date of Construction of Each Addition to Original Building.
9. Property Account 419—Date of Disposal of a Building.

B. *Major Category 420—Cost of the Building.* If the actual cost of each building is not known, then the estimated cost at the time of acquisition should be used, particularly in cases of an old building whose record has been lost.
1. Property Account 421—Contract Cost of the Building. Reported here is the cost for actual erection such as expenditures for general construction contract plus extras to the contractor and less credits; heating and ventilating contracts, plumbing contracts; electrical contracts; painting contracts; built-in equipment and outdoor underground parts of building service systems; and any salaries, construction materials, rental fees for construction equipment, and similar expenses for constructions performed by school district employees.
2. Property Account 422—Costs for Architects and Engineers Services.
3. Property Account 423—Costs for Legal Services.
4. Property Account 424—Costs for Educational Consultant Services.
5. Property Account 425—Miscellaneous Costs for a Building.

C. *Major Category 430—Size of the Building.* Property account information for this category includes:
1. Property Account 431—Gross Floor Area of Building Facility. This is the sum of the areas at each floor level found within the principal outside faces of exterior walls, but excluding architectural setbacks or projections. It would include all stories with floor surfaces having clear-standing headroom of a minimum of 6 feet, 6 inches, regardless of its use. Excluded are all unroofed areas and unenclosed roofed-over areas.
   a. 431.1—Area of Basement. This is the area in square feet of any floor that is below grade level on all four sides and has clear-standing headroom of at least 6 feet, 6 inches.
   b. 431.2—Area of First Floor.
   c. 431.3—Area of Each Additional Floor.

2. Property Account 432—Pupil Capacity of a Building. The figure placed in this property account should be arrived at on the basis of an objective formula, rather than mere guesswork. There are various factors involved in measuring pupil capacity. When once established, this figure should be changed only when the standards or policies regulating the computation of capacity have definitely been changed.
3. Property Account 433—Number of Pupils Served. This is the number of different pupils assigned to a building facility for instruction or other school activity.

D. *Major Category 440—Instruction Areas in Buildings.* This is perhaps one of the more difficult and time-consuming accounting categories. There are two property accounts, one for the various types of classrooms and a second for other instructional rooms. Areas should be carefully measured or computed from blueprint dimensions that apply.
1. Property Account 441—Classrooms. The important and useful information on the numbers and areas of classrooms are recorded here. A classroom is defined as a room designed for and adapted to accommodate regularly scheduled group instruction. It includes the so-called regular classrooms and special-purpose classrooms such as laboratories and shops. Libraries, study halls, auditoriums, gymnasiums, cafeterias, and multipurpose rooms are not recorded here but under the following property account. The classrooms can be classified into:
   a. 441.1—Regular Classrooms. The records should show:
      1) 441.21—Kindergarten Rooms.
         a) 441.211—Number. b) 441.212—Area.
      2) 441.22—Laboratory Rooms.
         a) 441.221—Number. b) 441.222—Area.
      3) 441.23—Shop Rooms.
         a) 441.231—Number. b) 441.232—Area.
      4) 441.24—Home Economics Rooms.
         a) 441.241—Number. b) 441.242—Area.
      5) 441.25—Music Rooms.
         a) 441.251—Number. b) 441.252—Area.
      6) 441.26—Special Classrooms for Special Children.
         a) 441.261—Number. b) 441.262—Area.
      7) 441.27—Other Special Classrooms.
         a) 441.271—Number. b) 441.271—Area.
2. Property Account 442—Other Instruction Spaces. The various types of spaces reported in this property account are:
   a. 442.01—School Library Spaces.

1) 442.011—Number of School Library Spaces.
   2) 442.012—Area of School Library Spaces.
   b. 442.02—Study Halls.
      1) 442.021—Number. 2) 442.022—Area.
   c. 442.03—Audio-Visual Rooms.
      1) 442.031—Number. 2) 442.032—Area.
   d. 442.04—Auditoriums.
      1) 442.041—Number. 2) 442.042—Area.
   e. 442.05—Gymnasiums.
      1) 442.051—Number. 2) 442.052—Area.
   f. 442.06—Cafeterias.
      1) 442.061—Number. 2) 442.062—Area.
   g. 442.07—Gymnatoriums. A gymnatorium is a combination gymnasium-auditorium.
      1) 442.071—Number. 2) 442.072—Area.
   h. 442.08—Cafetoriums. A cafetorium is a combination lunchroom-auditorium.
      1) 442.081—Number. 2) 442.082—Area.
   i. 442.09—Multipurpose Rooms.
      1) 442.091—Number. 2) 442.092—Area.
   j. 442.10—Miscellaneous Instruction Rooms. This includes research labs, indoor swimming pools, rifle ranges, museums, etc. It can be subdivided to show the number and area of each miscellaneous instruction room.

E. *Major Category 450—School Administration Areas.* The property accounts for this category are:
   1. Property Account 451—Kinds of School Administration Spaces and Buildings. The information included in this property account should identify the following types of spaces:
      a. 451.1—Principals' Offices.
      b. 451.2—Guidance Offices.
      c. 451.3—Health Service Areas.
      d. 451.4—Miscellaneous School Administration Spaces.
   2. Property Account 452—Number of Rooms in School Administration Spaces.
   3. Property Account 453—Area of School Administration Spaces.

F. *Major Category 460—Circulation Area of a Building.*
   1. Property Account 461—Area of Enclosed Circulation Areas.
   2. Property Account 462—Area of Outside Passageways with One Side Open.

G. *Major Category 470—Service Areas in a Building.*
   1. Property Account 471—Teachers' Rooms.
      a. 471.1—Number. b. 471.2—Area.
   2. Property Account 472—Maintenance and Operation Areas. The information in this property account should reveal:

a. 472.1—Kinds of Maintenance and Operation Areas.
   1) 472.11—Mechanical Service Rooms (furnace, pump, fan, and similar mechanical service rooms).
   2) 472.12—Custodial Service Rooms.
   3) 472.13—Building, Work, or Repair Shops.
   4) 472.14—Storage Rooms.
b. 472.2—Number of Maintenance and Operation Rooms.
c. 472.3—Area of Maintenance and Operation Rooms.
   3. Property Account 473—Toilet Rooms. This property account should indicate:
      a. 473.1—Number of Separate Toilet Rooms.
      b. 473.2—Area of Separate Toilet Rooms.
      c. 473.3—Number of Toilet Rooms As Adjuncts of Another Area.
   4. Property Account 474—Shower Rooms.
      a. 474.1—Number of Separate Shower Rooms.
      b. 474.2—Area of Separate Shower Rooms.
      c. 474.3—Number of Shower Rooms As Adjuncts of Another Area.
   5. Property Account 475—Miscellaneous Service Areas in the Building.
      a. 475.1—Number of Miscellaneous Service Areas.
      b. 475.2—Area of Miscellaneous Service Areas.

H. *Major Category 480—Service Systems in the Building.* A service system is defined as a group of elements or units designed to work together to provide on a building-wide basis specific physical services of a particular type, such as heating, cooling, ventilating, water, sewage disposal, electrical communication, and fire-protection systems. Separate property accounts are kept to describe each type of service system as follows:
   1. Property Account 481—Heating Systems. The information in this property account should reveal:
      a. 481.1—Type of Heating System. A check list can be marked to indicate whether it is a central or local zone system.
         1) 481.11—Central Heating System. One of the statements below can be selected to describe the type of central heating system:
            a) 481.111—Direct Radiation.
            b) 481.112—Unit Ventilators.
            c) 481.113—Warm Air Furnaces.
            d) 481.114—Fan Blast or Forced Air.
            e) 481.115—Radiant Panel.
            f) 481.116—Heat Pump.
            g) 481.117—Split System.

2) 481.12—Local Zone Heating System. With this system heating is supplied by two or more systems which are designed and installed to function independently of other units. The same subdivisions as listed under 481.11 (above) would be used to describe the type of local zone heating system.

3) 481.13—Room-Fired Heaters.

b. 481.2—Source of Heat for a Heating System. The information reported should reveal any of the following fuels used for heating:

1) 481.21—Wood.
2) 481.22—Coal.
3) 481.23—Gas.
4) 481.24—Oil.
5) 481.25—Electricity.
6) 481.26—Heat Pump.
7) 481.27—Others.

c. 481.3—Capacity of Heating Plant. This should be expressed in BTU ratings.

2. Property Account 482—Cooling Systems. Information in this property account should indicate if the cooling system is Central, Local Zone, or Individual Units. Further data should reveal if the building is completely or partially cooled.

3. Property Account 483—Ventilating System in a Building. This property account should reveal the type of ventilation such as:

a. 483.1—Window Ventilation.
b. 483.2—Gravity Ventilation.
c. 483.3—Mechanical Exhaust Ventilation.
d. 483.4—Mechanical Supply Ventilation.

4. Property Account 484—Water Supply and Sewage Disposal Systems in a Building.

a. 484.1—Source of Water. In addition, data should reveal whether it is a municipal water system (484.11), drilled well (484.12), or dug well and other sources (484.13).

b. 484.2—Number of Heat Generators for Hot Water Supply System.

c. 484.3—Type of Sewage Disposal System. This should be elaborated upon to show whether it is a municipal sewage disposal system (484.31), septic tank (484.32), filter and sludge beds (484.33), aeration pools (484.34), or others (484.35).

5. Property Account 485—Electrical System of a Building.

a. 485.1—Building Completely Wired.
b. 485.2—Building Partially Wired.
c. 485.3—Auxiliary Lighting System.

6. Property Account 486—Communication System in the Building.

a. 486.1—Telephone System. It should be reported if it is a complete or partial system.

b. 486.2—Speaker System. It should be reported if it is a complete or partial system.

c. 486.3—Combination Speaker-Telephone System.

d. 486.4—Program System.

7. Property Account 487—Television System.

8. Property Account 488—Fire Protection System. The information in this property account should reveal:

a. 488.1—Number of Fire Alarm Boxes.
b. 488.2—Number of Automatic Sprinkler Heads.
c. 488.3—Number of Fire Hose Cabinets.
d. 488.4—Number of Fire Extinguisher Stations.

9. Property Account 489—Elevators in the Building.

a. 489.1—Number of Passenger Elevators.
b. 489.2—Number of Freight Elevators.

ACCOUNT SERIES 500—EQUIPMENT ASSIGNED TO SCHOOL PLANTS

Data on movable equipment assigned for exclusive use in an instructional building is recorded in this series of property accounts. Municipally owned equipment only temporarily loaned to the school district is not entered herein. Likewise, equipment that is stored at a school and used to service other school plants is recorded under ACCOUNT SERIES 2500 rather than in ACCOUNT SERIES 500. The major categories are simply to distinguish between unit and group control of equipment.

A. *Major Category 510—Equipment Under Unit Control.* Unit control is defined as accounting on the basis of a single unit or entity so that the equipment retains a separate identity in the records or as a line item in a ledger. The two property accounts in this major category are used to report the kinds and number of equipment under unit control.

1. Property Account 511—Kinds of Equipment Under Unit Control. If a piece of movable equipment meets one or more of the following conditions, it should be placed and described under the unit control system: (a) if the relationship of individual maintenance cost of the equipment to the original cost and other factors is

critical in determining replacement policy for the equipment; (b) if the observance of individual performance of the piece of equipment and other individual characteristics is critical in determining replacement policy for the equipment; or (c) if the piece of equipment has a serial number printed on it by the manufacturer. The kinds of equipment are reported as furniture, machinery and apparatus, or vehicles.

a. 511.1—Furniture. Described here is furniture of the movable variety used for sitting, support for writing, drawing, experimentation, work activities, and storage space for material items or decorative purposes.

b. 511.2—Machinery and Apparatus. Reported here is movable machinery equipment items, consisting of complex combinations of parts which transmit and modify a force in motion so as to perform some desired kind of work, excluding vehicles. In contrast, apparatus is defined as movable equipment items without a complex combination of parts that are used to transmit, modify, or measure energy or matter in some form. These include:

1) 511.21—Hand Tools. They are defined as instruments and machinery or apparatus which can be picked up in the hand under normal operation. Illustrations of this type of equipment would be electric power hand saws, drills, sanders, electric flat irons, and expensive sets of hand instruments such as tap and die sets, wrench sets, micrometer sets, etc.

2) 511.22—Bench and Floor Machinery and Apparatus.

c. 511.3—Vehicles. These are conveniences used to transport persons or objects and include such items as automobiles, trucks, wreckers, buses, station wagons, bookmobiles, tractors, wagons, boats, and so on.

2. Property Account 512—Accounts for Each Piece of Equipment Under Unit Control. This property account is used to identify each piece of equipment in the building. Some of the facts needed for each piece of equipment would be:

a. 512.1—Name of Equipment.

b. 512.2—Model Number of Equipment.

c. 512.3—Serial Number of Equipment.

d. 512.4—Cost of Equipment.

e. 512.5—Date of Acquisition.

f. 512.6—Date of Disposal.

g. 512.7—Description of Equipment.

h. 512.8—Ownership of Equipment. A further elaboration would show publicly owned equipment (512.81) contrasted with nonpublicly owned equipment (512.82). Publicly owned equipment should be listed as district-owned (512.811), municipally owned (512.812), or authority-owned (512.813).

i. 512.9—Purpose for Which Equipment Is Used. The records should reveal whether the equipment is used for instructional or noninstructional purposes.

B. *Major Category 520—Equipment Under Group Control.* Group control is defined as accounting for equipment on the basis of groups of single units which are somewhat similar insofar as function, material, shape, and size are concerned. The individual piece of equipment loses its identity and becomes one of a group. The property accounts in this major category are very similar to those for *Major Category 510.*

1. Property Account 521—Kinds of Equipment Under Group Control. A piece of movable equipment should be placed under group control if it meets all of the following conditions: (a) if it is a piece of equipment for which the relationship of individual maintenance cost to the original cost or other factors is not critical in determining the replacement policy; (b) if it is a piece of equipment for which the observance of individual performance and other individual characteristics is not critical in determining replacement policy; (c) if it is the same as some other pieces of school district equipment with respect to function, material, shape, and size; and (d) if it does not have a serial number printed on it by the manufacturer. The kinds of equipment are classed as furniture, machinery, or books.

a. 521.1—Furniture.

b. 521.2—Machinery and Apparatus.

1) 521.21—Hand Tools.

2) 521.22—Bench and Floor Machinery and Apparatus.

c. 521.3—Library Books.

2. Property Account 522—Accounts for Each Equipment Group Under Group Control. This property account is necessary to identify each equipment group.

a. 522.1—Name of Equipment Group.

b. 522.2—Number of Individual Items in the Group.

SCHOOL PLANT RECORD—LAND FACILITIES

Name of School *Grandin Court High School*

Location *421 Page Street, Middletown, U.S.A.* 100. Type of Plant *Secondary School Plant*

Legal Description

Original Site: Lots 2 and 3 in the John R. Jones subdivision of the N½ of Lot 9.	Addition 1: Lots 5 and 6 in the John R. Jones subdivision of the N½ of Lot 9.	Disposal 1: Lot 2 in the John R. Jones subdivision of the N½ of Lot 9.		

200—LAND	Date	Acquisitions		Disposals		Adjusted Figure		Ownership
		Cost	Area	Cost	Area	Cost	Area	
Original Site	6/10/31	$4,500	5			$4,500	5	District
Additions or Disposals Addition 1	9/12/40	8,000	5			12,500	10	District
Disposal 1	3/10/54			$900	1	11,600	9	

300—Improvements to Sites	Cost in Dollars			
	O-F	A-A	R-A	A-F
300—Total Improvements to Sites	$15,900	$1,100	$710	$16,290
310—Outdoor Service Systems—Total Cost	10,800	900	400	11,300
311—Parking Areas and Drives	4,000			4,000
312—Pedestrian Passageways	3,000	100	300	2,800
313—Water and Sewer Systems	2,000	800		2,800
314—Outdoor Electrical Systems	1,000		100	900
315—Outdoor Storage Facilities	600			600
316—Other Outdoor Service Systems	200			200
320—Outdoor Play Areas—Total Cost	1,800	200		2,000
321—Surfacing Play Areas	1,500			1,500
322—Equipment Built Into Grounds	300	200		500
330—Fences and Retaining Walls	800		100	700
340—Landscaping	2,100		210	1,890
350—Miscellaneous Improvements	400			400

(OVER)

(Since there are no serial numbers, by definition, there is no 522.3 class.)

c. 522.4—Average Unit Cost of Equipment in Group.

d. 522.5—Total Cost of Equipment Group.

e. 522.7—Description of Equipment Group.

f. 522.8—Ownership of Equipment. The description should reveal if the equipment is

FORM 21 (BACK).

DEED REFERENCES

Original Site:	Addition 2:
Reversion Clause Conditions *None*	Reversion Clause Conditions _____
Grantor *Robert S. Wright*	Grantor _____
Type of Deed *Warranty* Date *6/10/31*	Type of Deed _____ Date _____
Recorded *7/3/31* Vol. *931* Page No. *4281*	Recorded _____ Vol. _____ Page No. _____
Copy of File with *City Clerk*	Copy on File with _____
Plat Book:	Plat Book:
Page No. *132* Ward *10* Precinct *3*	Page No. _____ Ward _____ Date _____
Legislation:	Legislation:
Res'n. No. *325* Date *6/9/31* Res'n. No. ____ Date ____	Res'n. No. ____ Date ____ Res'n. No. ____ Date ____

Addition 1:	Addition 3:
Reversion Clause Conditions *None*	Reversion Clause Conditions _____
Grantor *Ralph R. Gilmore*	Grantor _____
Type of Deed *Warranty* Date *9/2/40*	Type of Deed _____ Date _____
Recorded *9/8/40* Vol. *1135* Page No. *3821*	Recorded _____ Vol. _____ Page No. _____
Copy on File with *City Clerk*	Copy on File with _____
Plat Book:	Plat Book:
Page No. *132* Ward *10* Precinct *3*	Page No. _____ Ward _____ Precinct _____
Legislation:	Legislation:
Res'n. No. *735* Date *6/11/40* Res'n. No. ____ Date ____	Res'n. No. ____ Date ____ Res'n. No. ____ Date ____

ADDITIONAL INFORMATION

Disposal 1: Sold to George R. Ramsey, Resolution No. 485, 2/10/54

NOTE: Information on this side is of local character and will vary with local needs. A school district may wish to include as part of its records: (1) a plot plan showing utility lines, roads, etc., and (2) a drawing of the building as built.

publicly owned or nonpublicly owned. If equipment is publicly owned, a further statement is necessary to show if it is district-owned, municipally owned, or authority-owned.

g. 522.9—Purpose for Which Equipment Is Used. A statement is necessary to indicate if the equipment is used for instructional or noninstructional purposes.

FORMS FOR INSTRUCTIONAL FACILITIES

The accompanying forms are taken from the USOE *Property Accounting Handbook.* The information can be placed on the forms through use of a printed check list to which an appropriate check mark is applied (see Form 22, items 481.11, 482.13, and 485.1) or by a simple statement following a given heading

such as TYPE OF PLANT (see Form 21, item 100).

Spaces are also provided for adjustment entries to property accounting forms. Changes can occur during the lifetime of a plant such as purchasing more land or disposing of equipment. Adjustment entries include: (1) Original Figure at Acquisition (abbreviated O-F); (2) Additions After Acquisition (abbreviated A-A); (3) Reductions After Acquisition (abbreviated R-A); and (4) Adjusted Figure (abbreviated A-F). The adjusted figure is the original figure at acquisition plus additions after acquisitions or minus reductions after acquisitions. Many forms provided space for adjustments, and one illustration is Form 21, items 200 and 300.

Form 21 is used for each parcel of land and improvements (ACCOUNT SERIES 100, 200, and 300) for each school plant. Form 22 applies to the same plant but is devoted to recording data on building facilities

SCHOOL PLANT RECORD—BUILDING FACILITIES

GENERAL BUILDING DATA

Name of School *Grandin Court High School*
Name of Building *Grandin Court High School*   415—Building Mobility *Permanent Type Building*
Location *421 Page Street, Middletown U.S.A.*   412—Type of Construction *Fire - Resistive*
413—Kind of Building Facility *Instructional Bldg.*   416—Ownership *District*
411—Type of Program(s) Housed *4-Year high school*   432—Pupil Capacity *400*
414—Extent of Building Facility *Complete Occupancy*   433—Number of Pupils Served _____

General Building Data	Original Building	Changes: Indicate changes in column headings, such as additions, reductions, etc.					Adjusted Figure
		Addition 1	Reduction 1				
417—Date of Acquisition	1/6/35	2/10/46					
418—Date of Construction	10/1/33	2/8/46					
419—Date of Disposal			5/3/56				
431—Gross Floor Area	28,660	1,850	510				30,000
431.1 Basement	8,000						8,000
431.2 First Floor	26,660	1,850	510				22,000
431.3 Each Floor							
420—*Cost in Dollars*	$500,000	$50,000	$17,500				$532,500
421—Contract Cost	467,000	47,900	16,650				498,250
422—Arch. and Eng. Fees	30,000	1,500	750				30,750
423—Legal Fees	800	500	25				1,275
424—Consultant's Fees	200						200
425—Miscsllaneous Costs	2,000	100	75				2,025

SERVICE SYSTEMS

481—Heating System:
  481.1—Type of Heating System:
    481.11—Central ☑ *Direct Radiation*
    481.12—Local Zone ☐ _____
  481.2—Source of Heat *Oil*
  481.3—Capacity of Heating System _____

482—Cooling System:
  482.1—Type of Cooling System:
    482.11—Central ☐ _____
    482.12—Local Zone ☐
    482.13—Individual Unit ☑ *Self-Contained*
  482.2—Extent of Cooling System:
    482.21—Building Completely Cooled ☐
    482.22—Building Partially Cooled ☑

483—Type of Ventilating System *Mechanical Supply*

484—Water Supply and Sewage Disposal System:
  484.1—Source of Water in Building *Municipal*
  484.2—Number of Heat Generators for Hot Water *2*
  484.3—Type of Sewage Disposal System *Municipal*

485—Electrical System: Yes No
  485.1—Building Completely Wired ☑ Code ☑ ☐
  485.2—Building Partially Wired ☐ Code ☐ ☐
  485.3—Auxiliary Lighting System ☑ Code ☑ ☐

487—Television System:
  487.1—Television Receiving System in Building ☑
  487.2—Program Origination Provisions ☑

FORM 22 (BACK).

486—Communication System:
486.1—Telephone System:
486.11—Complete ☐
486.12—Partial ☐
486.2—Speaker System:
486.21—Complete ☐
486.22—Partial ☐
486.3—Combination Speaker-Telephone System ☐
486.4—Program System ☑

488—Fire Protection System:
488.1—Number of Fire Alarm Boxes ___8___
488.2—Number of Automatic Sprinkler Heads ___50___
488.3—Number of Fire Hose Cabinets ___4___
488.4—Number of Fire Extinguisher Stations ___15___

489—Elevators in the Building:
489.1—Number of Passenger Elevators _____
489.2—Number of Freight Elevators _____

DETAILED BUILDING DATA

Building Facility	Number of Rooms Original Building	Number of Rooms Present Building	Area of Rooms Original Building	Area of Rooms Present Building	Building Facility	Number of Rooms Original Building	Number of Rooms Present Building	Area of Rooms Original Building	Area of Rooms Present Building
TOTAL	31	32	23,000	24,300	460—*Circulation Areas*	XX	XX	1,600	1,600
440—Instruction Areas	19	21	16,500	17,800	461—Enclosed Areas	XX	XX	1,600	1,600
441—Classrooms	15	17	10,100	11,400	462—Outside Passageways	XX	XX		
441.1—Regular	10	12	6,200	7,500	*470—Service Areas*	10	10	3,900	3,900
441.2—Special	5	5	3,900	3,900	471—Teachers' Rooms				
441.21—Kindergarten					472—Maint. & Op. Rooms	4	4	1,900	1,900
441.22—Laboratory	2	2	1,400	1,400	473—Toilet Rooms	7	7	XX	XX
441.23—Shop	1	1	1,000	1,000	473.1—Separate	4	4	1,000	1,000
441.24—Home Economics	1	1	700	700	473.3—Adjuncts	3	3	XX	XX
441.25—Music	1	1	800	800	474—Shower Rooms	2	2	XX	XX
441.26—Except. Child					474.1—Separate	2	2	1,000	1,000
441.27—Other					474.3—Adjuncts			XX	XX
442—Other Instr. Area	4	4	6,400	6,400	475—Miscellaneous				
442.01—Library	1	1	900	900	451—Kinds of School Administration Areas:				
442.02—Study Halls					451.1—Principal's Office ☑				
442.03—Audiovisual					451.2—Guidance Offices ☐				
442.04—Auditoriums					451.3—Health Service Areas ☐				
442.05—Gymnasiums					451.4—Miscellaneous School Administration Areas ☐				
442.06—Cafeterias	1	1	1,500	1,500					
442.07—Gymnatoriums	1	1	3,000	3,000	472.1—Kinds of Maintenance and Operation Areas:				
442.08—Cafetoriums					472.11—Mechanical Service Rooms ☑				
442.09—Multipurpose	1	1	1,000	1,000	472.12—Custodial Service Rooms ☑				
442.10—Other					472.13—Building Work or Repair Rooms ☑				
450—School Admin. Area	1	1	1,000	1,000	472.14—Storage Rooms ☑				

Remarks: _____

SCHOOL PLANT RECORD—EQUIPMENT-UNIT CONTROL

512.1—Name of Equipment *Typewriter*

511—Kind of Equipment *Bench and floor machinery and apparatus*

Name of School to Which Assigned
Grandin Court High School
Location of School *421 Page Street*
Middletown, U. S. A.
512.7—Description:

512.2—Model Number *B*
512.3—Serial Number *0959549*
512.8—Ownership *District*
512.9—Purpose for Which Used *Instructional*
512.6—Date of Disposal

| 512.5 Date | Description of Item | 512.4—Cost of Equipment | | | | Remarks |
		O-F	A-A	R-A	A-F	
2/8/53	Original Equipment	$525	XXX	XXX	$525	
6/5/53	Check writing attachment		$75		600	
6/10/54	Key Stroke Counter		24		624	
9/1/56	Check writing attachment			$75	549	Transferred to Lane High

rather than land. Form 23 is for equipment under unit control and assigned to the same plant noted in Forms 21 and 22. The equipment in Form 23 is a typewriter, but such a form is needed for each piece of equipment under unit control. It would probably be best to place the form on card-sized material rather than on large ledger sheets. Form 24 is necessary for equipment under group control and assigned to this particular building. Note the space for adjustment entries.

Summary records for sites and buildings assigned to instructional plants are shown as Forms 25 and 26.

ACCOUNTING FOR NONINSTRUCTIONAL PLANT FACILITIES[5]

Data concerning noninstructional facilities are reported in ACCOUNT SERIES 1200 through 1800. As defined previously, within this category are placed buildings or parts of buildings or land used for purposes other than instruction. The equipment assigned to these facilities is likewise reported in these accounts.

[5] The account names and numbers used in this section were adapted from *ibid.*

These accounts follow fundamentally the same system used in describing instructional plants. There are differences in detail. The various series of accounts are organized to record data on LAND, IMPROVEMENTS, BUILDINGS, and EQUIPMENT of noninstructional plants.

ACCOUNT SERIES 1200—LAND FOR INSTRUCTIONAL PLANT FACILITIES

The major categories in this series reveal information on *Type of Building Facilities Located on the Land, Land Identification, Total Area of Land,* and *Total Cost of Land.*

A. *Major Category 1210—Type of Building Facilities Located on Land.* Only one of the following statements would be used to identify the type of building located on the land. The entry consists of a simple statement of one of the following building types.
  1. 1210.01—Administration Building.
  2. 1210.02—Pupil Transportation Building.
  3. 1210.03—Maintenance Building.
  4. 1210.04—Warehouse.
  5. 1210.05—Services Building.
  6. 1210.06—Student Dormitory.

SCHOOL PLANT RECORD—EQUIPMENT-GROUP CONTROL

522.1—Name of Equipment Group _____ 521—Kind of Equipment *Furniture*

Storage Cabinets

Name of School to Which Assigned _____ 522.7—Purpose for Which Used _____

Grandin Court High School *Noninstructional*

Location of School *431 Page Street* 522.6—Ownership *District*

Middletown, U. S. A.

522.2—Description:

Movable metal clothing storage cabinets, 24 inches wide, 18 inches deep, 78 inches high.

Date	522.3—Number of Pieces				522.5—Cost				522.4—Average Unit Cost	Remarks
	O-F	A-A	R-A	A-F	O-F	A-A	R-A	A-F		
9/4/42	6	XXX	XXX	6	$180	XXX	XXX	$180	$30.00	
2/10/43	XXX	2		8	XXX	$76		256	32.00	
4/25/49	XXX	1		9	XXX	41		297	33.00	
6/3/57	XXX	3		12	XXX	147		444	37.00	
8/2/57	XXX		3	9	XXX		$111	333	37.00	*Salvage*
	XXX				XXX					
	XXX				XXX					
	XXX				XXX					
	XXX				XXX					
	XXX				XXX					

(OVER)

7. 1210.07—Living Quarters for Professional Personnel.
8. 1210.08—Living Quarters for Service Personnel.
9. 1210.09—Public Library Building.
10. 1210.10—Playground Building.
11. 1210.11—General Community Services Building.
12. 1210.12—Investment Buildings.
13. 1210.13—Other Buildings.

B. *Major Category 1220—Land Identification.* The property accounts in this category are used to indicate ownership, date of acquisition, and date of disposal.

1. Property Account 1221—Ownership of the Land.
   a. 1221.1—Publicly Owned Land for Noninstructional Plant Facilities.
      1) 1221.11—District-Owned.
      2) 1221.12—Municipally Owned.
      3) 1221.13—Authority-Owned.
   b. 1221.2—Nonpublicly Owned Land.

2. Property Account 1222—Date of Acquisition.
   a. 1222.1—Date of Acquisition of Original Piece of Land.
   b. 1222.2—Date of Acquisition of Each Addition to the Original Piece of Land.
3. Property Account 1223—Date of Disposal.

C. *Major Category 1230—Total Area of Land.*

D. *Major Category 1240—Total Cost of Land.* The same comments made with reference to pricing land purchased or land received as a gift in *Major Category 240* would apply here as well.

ACCOUNT SERIES 1300—IMPROVEMENTS TO SITE FOR NONINSTRUCTIONAL PLANT FACILITIES

For a description of what constitutes improvements see ACCOUNT SERIES 300. ACCOUNT SERIES 1300 is very similar to ACCOUNT SERIES 300 with the exception that it is applied to noninstructional instead of instructional facilities.

A. *Major Category 1310—Outdoor Service Systems on Site—Total Cost.* It should be noted that this fol-

FORM 25.

SITE SUMMARY

Type of School Plant: *Elementary*

Publicly Owned

Kind of Change I.e., New Site, Addition, Improvement, Disposal	Date	Number of Sites	Cost of Land	Cost of Improvements	Area	Remarks
Beginning of Year	7/1/54	23	$320,000	$55,000	160	
New Site						
Johnstown School	7/20/54	1	40,000		10	
Improvement						
Glendale School	9/20/54			10,000		Playground Area
Addition						
Cherrydale School	2/15/55		8,000		2	
Disposal						
Twin Oaks School	4/22/55	-1	-5,000	-2,000	-3	
Beginning of year	7/1/55	23	$363,000	$63,000	169	

lows pretty much the division of property accounts for *Major Category 310.*

1. Property Account 1311—Total Cost of Parking Areas and Drives on Sites.
2. Property Account 1312—Total Cost of Pedestrian Passageways on Site.
3. Property Account 1313—Total Cost of Water and Sewer Systems on Site.
4. Property Account 1314—Total Cost of Outdoor Electrical Systems on Site.
5. Property Account 1315—Total Cost of Outdoor Storage Facilities on Site.
6. Property Account 1316—Total Cost of Other Outdoor Service Systems on Site.

B. *Major Category 1320—Outdoor Play Areas on Site—Total Cost.*
   1. Property Account 1321—Total Cost of Surfacing Play Areas on Site.
   2. Property Account 1322—Total Cost of Equipment Built into Grounds or Playgrounds.

C. *Major Category 1330—Fences and Retaining Walls —Total Cost.*

D. *Major Category 1340—Landscaping the Site—Total Cost.*

E. *Major Category 1350—Miscellaneous Improvements to Site.*

ACCOUNT SERIES 1400—BUILDINGS FOR NON-INSTRUCTIONAL PLANT FACILITIES

This series of accounts parallels to some extent AC-COUNT SERIES 400. The exceptions are some of the accounts under *Major Category 430.* There are no accounts in this series which are similar to those found in *Major Category 440—Instruction Areas in a Building,* or *Major Categories 450, 460, 470, and 480.*

A. *Major Category 1410—Building Identification.*
   1. Property Account 1411—Type of Building Facilities. One of the following building types would be written into the records at this point.
      a. 1411.01—Administration Building.

FORM 26 (FRONT).

BUILDING SUMMARY

Type of School Plant: *Elementary*   *Publicly Owned*

Kind of Change I.e., New Building, Addition, Remodeling, Disposal	Date	Number of School Plants	Number of Buildings		Cost of Buildings		Pupil Capacity	Number of Instr. Bldgs. with More Than One Story[a]			
			Instr.	Other	Instr.	Other		FR	SFR	COM	MC
Beginning of Year	7/1/54	20	21	2	$10,500,000	$50,000	9,000	6		2	
New Building Johnstown School	11/30/54	1	1		500,000		400	1			
Remodeling Vernon Street School	11/30/54				200,000						
Disposal Twin Oaks School	12/4/54	-1	-2		700,000		400			-2	
Addition Glenway School	3/15/55				100,000		100	-1			1
Beginning of year	7/1/55	20	20	2	$10,600,000	$50,000	9,100	6			1

(OVER)

[a] Legend: FR = fire-resistive; SFR = semifire-resistive; COM = combustible; MC = mixed construction.

   b. 1411.02—Pupil Transportation Building.
   c. 1411.03—Maintenance Building.
   d. 1411.04—Warehouse.
   e. 1411.05—Food Services Building.
   f. 1411.06—Student Dormitory.
   g. 1411.07—Living Quarters for Professional Personnel.
   h. 1411.08—Living Quarters for Service Personnel.
   i. 1411.09—Public Library Building.
   j. 1411.10—Playground Building.
   k. 1411.11—General Community Services Building.
   l. 1411.12—Investment Building.
   m. 1411.13—Other Buildings.
2. Property Account 1412—Type of Building Construction. The definitions described in Property Account 412 would apply here. The entry to this property account is simply whichever of the following statements apply:
   a. 1412.1—Fire-Resistive Buildings.
   b. 1412.2—Semifire-Resistive Buildings.
   c. 1412.3—Combustible Buildings.
   d. 1412.4—Mixed Construction.
4. Property Account 1414—Extent of Occupancy of Building Facility.
   a. 1414.1—Complete Occupancy.
   b. 1414.2—Partial Occupancy.
5. Property Account 1415—Building Mobility.
   a. 1415.1—Permanent Type of Building.
   b. 1415.2—Portable Type of Building.
6. Property Account 1416—Ownership of Building Facilities.
   a. 1416.1—Publicly Owned Buildings. Further indication is needed to determine whether the building is district-owned (1416.11), mu-

BUILDING SUMMARY

Type of School Plant: **Elementary**

Publicly Owned

Kind of Change I.e., New Building, Addition, Re-modeling, Disposal	Date	Gross Building Area	Number of Classrooms		Number of the Following Facilities:[a]						
			Regular	Special	Libraries	Auditoriums	Gymnasiums	Cafeterias	Gymnatoriums	Cafetoriums	Multi-purpose
Beginning of Year	7/1/54	325,000	300	55	20	4	10	14	10	6	8
New Building Johnstown School	10/30/54	14,000	10	2	1	1		1			1
Disposal Twin Oaks School	12/1/54	-13,000	-20						-1		
Addition Charlestown School	3/15/55	6,000	4	1	1			1			
Beginning of Year	7/1/55	332,000	294	58	22	5	10	16	9	6	9

(OVER)

[a] A district may wish to add other captions or delete some of these.

nicipally owned (1416.12), or authority-owned (1416.13).

   b. 1416.2—Nonpublicly Owned Buildings.

7. Property Account 1417—Date of Acquisition.

   a. 1417.1—Date of Acquisition of Original Building.

   b. 1417.2—Date of Acquisition of Each Addition to the Original Building.

8. Property Account 1418—Date of Construction.

   a. 1418.1—Date of Construction of the Original Building.

   b. 1418.2—Date of Construction of Each Addition to the Original Building.

9. Property Account 1419—Date of Disposal of a Building.

B. *Major Category 1420—Cost of Building.* The same definitions reported in *Major Category 420* would apply here.

1. Property Account 1421—Contract Cost of a Building.

2. Property Account 1422—Cost for Architects' and Engineers' Services.

3. Property Account 1423—Cost for Legal Services.

4. Property Account 1424—Cost for Educational Consultant Services.

5. Property Account 1425—Miscellaneous Cost for Building.

C. *Major Category 1430—Gross Floor Area of Building Facility.* The definitions of basements and other areas noted in *Major Category 430* would apply here.

1. Property Account 1430.1—Area of Basement.

2. Property Account 1430.2—Area of Each Floor.

ACCOUNT SERIES 1500—EQUIPMENT ASSIGNED TO A NONINSTRUCTIONAL PLANT FACILITY

The various definitions for unit control and group control and what constitutes furniture, machinery, etc., reported in ACCOUNT SERIES 500 apply to this series of property accounts for noninstructional plants.

A. *Major Account 1510—Equipment Under Unit Control.*
   1. Property Account 1511—Kinds of Equipment Under Unit Control.
      a. 1511.1—Furniture.
      b. 1511.2—Machinery and Apparatus. Further elaboration is needed to describe hand tools (1511.21) and bench and floor machinery and apparatus (1511.22).
      c. 1511.3—Vehicles.
   2. Property Account 1512—Accounts for Each Piece of Equipment Under Unit Control. As in Account 512, these property accounts are needed for pieces of equipment:
      a. 1512.1—Name of Equipment.
      b. 1512.2—Model Number of Equipment.
      c. 1512.3—Serial Number of Equipment.
      d. 1512.4—Cost of Equipment.
      e. 1512.5—Date of Acquisition.
      f. 1512.6—Date of Disposal.
      g. 1512.8—Ownership of Equipment. If equipment is publicly owned (1512.81), further designation is needed to determine whether it is district-owned (1512.811), municipally owned (1512.812), or authority-owned (1512.813). In some cases it may be nonpublicly owned (1512.82).

B. *Major Category 1520—Equipment Under Group Control.*
   1. Property Account 1521—Kinds of Equipment Under Group Control. Group control was defined previously in Account 521.
      a. 1521.1—Furniture.
      b. 1521.2—Machinery and Apparatus.
      c. 1521.3—Library Books.
   2. Property Account 1522—Accounts for Each Equipment Group Under Group Control.
      a. 1522.1—Name of Equipment.
      b. 1522.2—Number of Individual Pieces of Equipment in Group.
      c. 1522.4—Average Unit Cost of Equipment in Group.
      d. 1522.5—Total Cost of Equipment Group.
      e. 1522.7—Description of Equipment Group.
      f. 1522.8—Ownership of Equipment.

FORMS FOR NONINSTRUCTIONAL FACILITIES

The forms used for individual records for noninstructional plant facilities are similar to those for in-

structional plant facilities. Form 27 is taken from the USOE *Property Accounting Handbook.* Form 27 is devoted to land and site improvement information for noninstructional plants.

ACCOUNTS FOR EQUIPMENT UNASSIGNED TO SPECIFIC FACILITIES[6]

The ACCOUNT SERIES 2500 is designed to account for each piece of equipment for each group of identical equipment items held for use throughout the school district and not assigned other than temporarily to any one plant. This category is not necessary for municipally owned equipment that is only temporarily loaned to schools for use. The explanation of unit or group control was already made elsewhere. The major categories in this series of property accounts parallel closely *Major Categories 510* and *520* and also *1510* and *1520.*

A. *Major Category 2510—Equipment Under Unit Control That Is Unassigned to a Specific Facility.*
   1. Property Account 2511—Kinds of Equipment Under Unit Control.
      a. 2511.1—Furniture.
      b. 2511.2—Machinery and Apparatus.
      c. 2511.3—Vehicles.
   2. Property Account 2512—Accounts for Each Piece of Equipment Under Unit Control.
      a. 2512.1—Name of Equipment.
      b. 2512.2—Model Number of Equipment.
      c. 2512.3—Serial Number of Equipment.
      d. 2512.4—Cost of Equipment.
      e. 2512.5—Date of Acquisition.
      f. 2512.6—Date of Disposal.
      g. 2512.7—Description of Equipment.
      h. 2512.8—Ownership of Equipment.
         1) 2512.81—Publicly Owned.
         2) 2512.82—Nonpublicly Owned.

B. *Major Category 2520—Equipment Under Group Control That Is Unassigned to a Specific Facility.*
   1. Property Account 2521—Kinds of Equipment Under Group Control.
      a. 2521.1—Furniture.
      b. 2521.2—Machines and Apparatus.
   2. Property Account 2522—Accounts for Each Group Under Group Control.
      a. 2522.1—Name of Equipment Group.
      b. 2522.2—Number of Individual Pieces of Equipment in Group.
      c. 2522.4—Average Cost of Equipment in Group.

[6] The account names and numbers used in this section were adapted from *ibid.*

FORM 27.

NONINSTRUCTIONAL PLANT FACILITIES RECORD—LAND FACILITIES

Name of Building *Randolph Building*

Location *381 Marshall Street, Middletown, U.S.A.* 1210. Type of Building Facility *Administration Bldg.*

Legal Description

Original Site: *Lots 13 and 14 in Robert Brown's subdivision of the S ½ of Lot 1.*				

1200—Land	Date	Acquisitions		Disposals		Adjusted Figure		Ownership
		Cost	Area	Cost	Area	Cost	Area	
Original Site	6/13/40	$9,000	3			$9,000	3	*District*
Additions or Disposals								

1300—Improvements to Sites	COST IN DOLLARS			
	O-F	A-A	R-A	A-F
1300—Total Improvements to Sites	$11,000	$2,000	$100	$12,900
1310—Outdoor Service Systems—Total Cost	11,000	2,000		12,900
1311—Parking Areas and Drives	6,000	1,500		7,500
1312—Pedestrian Passageways	2,000	500		2,500
1313—Water and Sewer Systems	1,500			1,500
1314—Outdoor Electrical Systems	1,000			1,000
1315—Outdoor Storage Facilities	500		100	400
1316—Other Outdoor Service Systems				
1320—Outdoor Play Areas—Total Cost				
1321—Surfacing Play Areas				
1322—Equipment Built Into Grounds				
1330—Fences and Retaining Walls				
1340—Landscaping				
1350—Miscellaneous Improvements				

d. 2522.5—Total Cost of Equipment in Group.
e. 2622.6—Description of Equipment in Group.
f. 2522.8—Ownership of Equipment.
   1) 2522.81—Publicly Owned.
   2) 2522.82—Nonpublicly Owned.

It should be obvious that what is recorded under ACCOUNT SERIES 2500 is very similar to that in AC-COUNT SERIES 500—EQUIPMENT ASSIGNED TO SCHOOL PLANTS and ACCOUNT SERIES 1500—EQUIPMENT ASSIGNED TO NONINSTRUCTIONAL PLANT FACILITIES.

FORMS FOR UNASSIGNED EQUIPMENT

Form 28 is submitted to show a record for equipment unassigned to specific facilities. This form is based on the forms shown in the USOE *Property Accounting Handbook.*

MAINTAINING PROPERTY RECORDS

The most difficult problem in property accounting is initial inventory. Once the large task of cataloguing all property is completed, the continuance of careful property accounting should not be an overly onerous burden.

SUMMARY

This chapter summary is an outline of property accounts adapted from the USOE property accounting manual.

QUESTIONS

1. Of what value are property accounts for schools?
2. Who should assume responsibility for developing and maintaining school property accounts?
3. Assume you were a superintendent where no property accounts exist. How would you go about the task of developing and maintaining property tasks?

SELECTED REFERENCES

Mort, Paul R., and Reusser, Walter C., *Public School Finance,* New York: McGraw-Hill Book Company, rev. ed., 1951, chap. 17.

United States Office of Education, *Property Accounting Handbook,* Handbook no. 3, U.S. Office of Education, Washington, D.C.: U.S. Government Printing Office.

FORM 28.

UNASSIGNED EQUIPMENT RECORD—GROUP CONTROL

2522.1—Name of Equipment Group _Files_   2521—Kind of Equipment _Furniture_

Location _Middletown School Warehouse_   2522.6—Ownership _District_

2522.2—Description:

Four-drawer metal files, 4' x 14" x 20".

Date	2522.3 Number of Pieces				2522.5 Cost				2522.4 Average Unit Cost	Remarks
	O-F	A-A	R-A	A-F	O-F	A-A	R-A	A-F		
4/10/52	10	XXX	XXX	10	$300	XXX	XXX	$300	$30.00	
7/3/52	XXX	5		15	XXX	$180		480	32.00	
7/10/52	XXX		14	1	XXX		$448	32	32.00	Salvage
	XXX				XXX					
	XXX				XXX					
	XXX				XXX					
	XXX				XXX					
	XXX				XXX					
	XXX				XXX					
	XXX				XXX					
	XXX				XXX					
	XXX				XXX					
	XXX				XXX					

(OVER)

USE: To record information about equipment under group control that is unassigned to any specific facility. See also Form 24.

Property Accounts	Adjustment Entries				W-P
	O-F	A-A	R-A	A-F	

ACCOUNTS FOR SCHOOL PLANTS
100–500 SERIES

Accounts under this heading are kept for each school plant.

100—TYPE OF PLANT

110—Elementary School Plant
120—Secondary School Plant
130—Combined Elementary and Secondary School Plant
140—Community College Plant
150—Combined Secondary and Community College Plant

200—LAND FACILITIES FOR SCHOOL PLANTS

Accounts under this heading are kept for each school plant.

220—Land Identification

221—Ownership

221.1—Publicly Owned Land (district-, municipal-, or authority-owned)
221.2—Nonpublicly Owned Land

222—Date or Acquisition (not applicable to nonpublicly owned land; includes additions)
223—Date of Disposal (not applicable to nonpublicly owned land)

	O-F	A-A	R-A	A-F
230—Total Area of the School Site	E	E	E	E
240—Total Cost of Land for the School Site (not applicable to nonpublicly owned land), 240.1 and 240.2	E	E	E	E
300—IMPROVEMENTS TO SCHOOL SITES—TOTAL COST (not applicable to nonpublicly owned land)	E	E	E	E
310—Outdoor Service Systems—Total Cost	E	E	E	E
311—Parking Areas and Drives	E	E	E	E
312—Pedestrian Passageways	E	E	E	E
313—Water and Sewer Systems	E	E	E	E
314—Outdoor Electrical Systems	E	E	E	E
315—Storage Facilities	E	E	E	E
320—Outdoor Play Areas—Total Cost	E	E	E	E
321—Surfacing Play Areas	E	E	E	E
322—Equipment Built into Grounds	E	E	E	E
330—Fences and Retaining Walls—Total Cost	E	E	E	E
340—Landscaping—Total Cost	E	E	E	E
350—Miscellaneous Improvements to the School Site—Total Cost	E	E	E	E

Property Accounts	Adjustment Entries				W-P
	O-F	A-A	R-A	A-F	

400—Building Facilities for School Plants

Accounts under this heading are kept for each individual building or facility.

410—Building Identification

411—Type of School Program Housed (elementary, secondary, etc.)   R

412—Type of Building Construction

412.1—Fire-Resistive					R
412.2—Semifire-Resistive					R
412.3—Combustible					R
412.4—Mixed Construction					R

413—Kind of Building Facility

413.1—Instruction Building					R
413.2—Central Heating Building					R
413.3—Stadium					R
413.4—Fieldhouse					R
413.5—Other Building					R

414—Extent of Facility (complete or partial occupancy)   R

415—Building Mobility (permanent or portable)   R

416—Ownership of the Building Facility (public or nonpublic)   R

417—Date of Acquisition (not applicable to non-publicly owned buildings)

418—Date of Construction (not applicable to nonpublicly owned buildings; includes original and additions)

419—Date of Disposal (not applicable to non-publicly owned buildings)

420—Cost of Building (not applicable to nonpublicly owned buildings)   E   E   E   E   R

421—Contract Cost for Building	E	E	E	E	R
422—Cost for Architects and Engineers	E	E	E	E	R
423—Cost for Legal Services	E	E	E	E	R
424—Cost for Educational Consultants	E	E	E	E	R
425—Miscellaneous Costs for the Building	E	E	E	E	R
430—Size of the Building	E	E	E	E	R

431—Gross Floor Area of the Building Facility   E   E   E   E   R

431.1—Area of the Basement	E	E	E	E	R
431.2—Area of the First Floor	E	E	E	E	R
431.3—Area of Each Additional Floor	E	E	E	E	R

432—Pupil Capacity (not applicable to non-publicly owned biildings)   E   E   E   E   R

433—Number of Pupils Served (applicable only to nonpublicly owned buildings)   E   E   E   E   R

440—Instruction Areas in Buildings

Property Accounts	Adjustment Entries				W-P
	O-F	A-A	R-A	A-F	
441—Classrooms					
441.1—Regular Classrooms (number and size)	E	E	E	E	R
441.2—Special Classrooms					
441.22—Laboratory Rooms (number and size)	E	E	E	E	R
441.23—Shop Rooms (number and size)	E	E	E	E	R
441.24—Home Economics Rooms (number and size)	E	E	E	E	R
441.25—Music Rooms (number and area)	E	E	E	E	R
441.26—Special Classrooms for Exceptional Children (number and area)	E	E	E	E	R
441.27—Other Special Classrooms	E	E	E	E	R
442—Other Instruction Areas					
442.01—School Library Areas (number and area)	E	E	E	E	R
442.02—Study Halls (number and area)	E	E	E	E	R
442.03—Audio-Visual Rooms (number and area)	E	E	E	E	R
442.04—Auditoriums (number and area)	E	E	E	E	R
442.05—Gymnasiums (number and area)	E	E	E	E	R
442.06—Cafeterias or Lunchrooms (number and area)	E	E	E	E	R
442.07—Gymnatoriums (number and area)	E	E	E	E	R
442.08—Cafetoriums (number and area)	E	E	E	E	R
442.09—Multipurpose Rooms (number and area)	E	E	E	E	R
442.10—Miscellaneous Instruction Areas (number and area)	E	E	E	E	R
450—School Administration Areas in the Building					
451—Kinds of School Administration Areas					
451.1—Principals' Offices					
451.2—Guidance Offices					
451.3—Health Service Areas					
451.4—Miscellaneous School Administration Areas					
452—Number of Rooms in the School Administration Areas	E	E	E	E	R
453—Area of School Administration Areas	E	E	E	E	R
460—Circulation Area of a Building					
461—Area of Enclosed Circulation Areas	E	E	E	E	R
462—Area of Outside Passageways with One Side Open	E	E	E	E	R
470—Service Areas in a Building					
471—Teachers' Room (number and area)	E	E	E	E	R
472—Maintenance and Operation Areas					
472.1—Kinds of Maintenance and Operation Areas					

Property Accounts	Adjustment Entries				W-P
	O-F	A-A	R-A	A-F	
472.11—Mechanical Service Rooms					
472.12—Custodial Service Rooms					
472.13—Building Work or Repair Shops					
472.14—Storage Rooms					
472.2—Number of Maintenance and Operation Areas	E	E	E	E	R
472.3—Area of Maintenance and Operation Areas	E	E	E	E	R
473—Toilet Rooms (number and area)	E	E	E	E	R
474—Shower Rooms (number and area)	E	E	E	E	R
475—Miscellaneous Service Areas (number and area)	E	E	E	E	R

480—Service Systems in the Building

481—Heating System

  481.1—Type of Heating System

    481.11—Central Heating System

      481.111—Direct Radiation
      481.112—Unit Ventilation
      481.113—Warm Air Furnace
      481.114—Fan Blast or Forced Air
      481.115—Radiant Panel
      481.116—Heat Pump
      481.117—Split System

    481.12—Local Zone Heating

      481.121—Direct Radiation
      481.122—Unit Ventilation
      481.123—Warm Air Furnace
      481.124—Fan Blast or Forced Air
      481.125—Radiant Panel
      481.126—Heat Pump
      481.127—Split System

    481.13—Room-Fired Heaters

  481.2—Source of Heat

    481.21—Wood
    481.22—Coal
    481.23—Gas
    481.24—Oil
    481.25—Electricity
    481.26—Heat Pump
    481.27—Other

	O-F	A-A	R-A	A-F	W-P
481.3—Capacity of Heating Plant(s)	E	E	E	E	R

482—Cooling System

  482.1—Type of System

    482.11—Central System
    482.12—Local Zone System
    482.13—Individual Unit

Property Accounts	Adjustment Entries				W-P
	O-F	A-A	R-A	A-F	
482.2—Extent of Cooling System					
482.21—Building Completely Cooled					
482.22—Building Partially Cooled					
483—Ventilating System					
483.1—Window Ventilation					
483.2—Gravity Ventilation					
483.3—Mechanical Exhaust Ventilation					
483.4—Mechanical Supply Ventilation					
484—Water Supply and Sewage Disposal Systems					
484.1—Source of Water					
484.11—Municipal					
484.12—Drilled Well					
484.13—Dug Well or Other Source					
484.2—Number of Heat Generators for the Hot Water Supply System	E	E	E	E	R
484.3—Type of Sewage Disposal System					
484.31—Municipal					
484.32—Septic Tank					
484.33—Filter and Sludge Beds					
484.34—Aeration Pools					
484.35—Other					
485—Electrical System					
485.1—Building Completely Wired					
485.2—Building Partially Wired					
485.3—Auxiliary Lighting					
486—Communication Systems					
486.1—Telephone System (complete and partial)					
486.2—Speaker System (complete and partial)					
486.3—Combination Speaker-Telephone System					
486.4—Program System					
487—Television System					
487.1—Television Receiving System					
487.2—Program Origination Provisions					
488—Fire Protection System					
488.1—Number of Fire Alarm Boxes	E	E	E	E	R
488.2—Number of Automatic Sprinkler Heads	E	E	E	E	R
488.3—Number of Fire Hose Cabinets	E	E	E	E	R
488.4—Number of Fire Extinguisher Stations	E	E	E	E	R
489—Elevators					
489.1—Number of Passenger Elevators	E	E	E	E	R
489.2—Number of Freight Elevators	E	E	E	E	R

500—Equipment Assigned to School Plants
The accounts under this heading are kept for each school plant

Property Accounts	Adjustment Entries				W-P
	O-F	A-A	R-A	A-F	
510—Equipment Under Unit Control					
511—Kinds of Equipment Under Unit Control					
511.1—Furniture					
511.2—Machinery and Apparatus					
511.21—Hand Tools					
511.22—Bench and Floor Machinery and Apparatus					
511.3—Vehicles					
512—Accounts for Each Piece of Equipment Under Unit Control					
512.1—Name of the Equipment					
512.2—Model Number of the Equipment					
512.3—Serial Number of the Equipment					
512.4—Cost of the Equipment (not applicable to nonpublicly owned equipment)	E	E	E	E	R
512.5—Date of Acquisition (not applicable to nonpublicly owned equipment)					
512.6—Date of Disposal (not applicable to nonpublicly owned equipment)					
512.7—Description of the Equipment					
512.8—Ownership of the Equipment (public and nonpublic)					
512.9—Purpose for Which the Equipment Is Used					
512.91—Instructional Equipment					
512.92—Noninstructional Equipment					
520—Equipment Under Group Control					
521—Kinds of Equipment Under Group Control					
521.1—Furniture					
521.2—Machinery and Apparatus					
521.21—Hand Tools					
522.22—Bench and Floor Machinery and Apparatus					
521.3—Library Books					
522—Accounts for Each Equipment Group Under Group Control					
522.1—Name of Equipment Group					
522.2—Number of Individual Items of Equipment in the Group	E	E	E	E	
522.4—Average Unit Cost (not applicable to nonpublicly owned equipment)	E			E	
522.5—Total Cost of Equipment Group (not applicable to nonpublicly owned equipment)	E	E	E	E	
522.7—Description of the Equipment Group					
522.8—Ownership of the Equipment (public and nonpublic)					

Property Accounts	Adjustment Entries				W-P
	O-F	A-A	R-A	A-F	

522.9—Purpose for Which the Equipment Is Used (instructional and noninstructional)

Accounts for Noninstructional Plant Facilities 1200–1500 Series

Accounts under this heading are kept for each facility (piece of land, building, or part of a building).

1200—Land for Noninstructional Plant Facilities

Accounts under this heading are kept for each separate piece of land.

1210—Type of Building Facilities Located on the Land

1210.01—Administration Building
1210.02—Pupil Transportation Building
1210.03—Maintenance Building
1210.04—Warehouse
1210.05—Food Services Building
1210.06—Student Dormitory
1210.07—Living Quarters for Professional Personnel
1210.08—Living Quarters for Service Personnel
1210.09—Public Library Building
1210.10—Playground Building
1210.11—General Community Services Building
1210.12—Investment Building
1210.13—Other Building

1220—Land Identification

1221—Ownership of the Land (public and nonpublic)
1222—Date of Acquisition (not applicable to nonpublicly owned land)
1223—Date of Disposal (not applicable to nonpublicly owned land)

	O-F	A-A	R-A	A-F
1230—Total Area of Land	E	E	E	E
1240—Total Cost of Land (not applicable to nonpublicly owned land)	E	E	E	E

1300—Improvements to Sites for Noninstructional Plant Facilities (not applicable to nonpublicly owned land)

Accounts under this heading are kept for each separate piece of land.

	O-F	A-A	R-A	A-F
1310—Outdoor Service Systems—Total Cost (1311 to 1316; see *310* for complete list)	E	E	E	E

Property Accounts	Adjustment Entries				W-P
	O-F	A-A	R-A	A-F	
1320—Outdoor Play Areas on Site—Total Cost (1321 to 1322)	E	E	E	E	
1330—Fences and Retaining Walls—Total Cost	E	E	E	E	
1340—Landscaping the Site—Total Cost	E	E	E	E	
1350—Miscellaneous Improvements to Site—Total Cost	E	E	E	E	

1400—BUILDINGS FOR NONINSTRUCTIONAL PLANT FACILITIES

Accounts under this heading are kept for each individual building or facility.

1410—Building Identification

1411—Type of Building Facility

1411.01—Administration Building					R
1411.02—Pupil Transportation Building					R
1411.03—Maintenance Building					R
1411.04—Warehouse Building					R
1411.05—Food Services Building					R
1411.06—Student Dormitory					R
1411.07—Living Quarters for Professional Personnel					R
1411.08—Living Quarters for Service Personnel					R
1411.09—Public Library Building					R
1411.10—Playground Building					R
1411.11—General Community Services Building					R
1411.12—Investment Building					R
1411.13—Other Building					R
1412—Type of Building Construction (see 412 for list)					R
1414—Extent of Building Facility (complete and partial)					R
1415—Building Mobility (permanent or portable)					R
1416—Ownership of the Building Facility (public or nonpublic)					
1417—Date of Acquisition (not applicable to nonpublicly owned buildings)					
1418—Date of Construction (not applicable to nonpublicly owned buildings)					
1419—Date of Disposal (not applicable to non-publicly owned buildings)					
1420—Cost of Building (not applicable to non-publicly owned buildings; see *420* for complete list)	E	E	E	E	R
1430—Gross Floor Area of Building Facility	E	E	E	E	R
1430.1—Area of the Basement	E	E	E	E	R
1430.2—Area of Each Floor	E	E	E	E	R

1500—EQUIPMENT ASSIGNED TO NONINSTRUCTIONAL PLANT FACILITIES

Accounts under this heading are kept for each building or facility.

1510—Equipment Under Unit Control (see *510* for complete list)

1511—Kinds of Equipment Under Unit Control
1512—Accounts for Each Piece of Equipment Under Unit Control (see 512 for complete list)

1520—Equipment Under Group Control

1521—Kinds of Equipment Under Group Control (see 521 for complete list)
1522—Accounts for Each Equipment Group Under Group Control (see 522 for complete list)

ACCOUNTS FOR EQUIPMENT UNASSIGNED TO SPECIFIC FACILITIES—2500 SERIES

2510—Equipment Under Unit Control That Is Unassigned to a Specific Facility

2511—Kinds of Equipment Under Unit Control

2511.1—Furniture
2511.2—Machinery and Apparatus

2511.21—Hand Tools
2511.22—Bench and Floor Machinery and Apparatus
2511.23—Construction Machinery

2511.3—Vehicles

2512—Accounts for Each Piece of Equipment (see 512 for complete list)

2520—Equipment Under Group Control That Is Unassigned to a Specific Facility

2521—Kinds of Equipment Under Group Control (see 521 for complete list)

2522—Accounts for Each Equipment Group Under Group Control (see 522 for complete list)

CHAPTER 15

School Insurance

INSURANCE AFFORDS PROTECTION AGAINST financial loss that might accrue from loss of life, crime, destruction of personal property, liability created by destruction of another person's property, or other causes. The commercial organizations which provide insurance service act as professional risk bearers. Risk can be defined simply as the chance of loss. Often the thing or person insured is called the risk.

No matter what the form of property, there always exists the chance it may be altered, destroyed, stolen, or lost. Even when carefully designed preventive measures are exercised, one cannot escape from the uncertainty of continued possession of property in its most valuable form. In return for a relatively small payment known as a premium, collected from many individuals, the company will assume the risk of the possibility of a substantial even though unknown financial loss to each party who pays the premium.

Insurance as a means of achieving financial security even though catastrophe may strike has been recognized since ancient times. One of the classic definitions of insurance is: "Insurance is a contract by which the one party, in consideration of a price paid to him adequate to the risk, becomes a security to the other that he shall not suffer loss, damage or prejudice by the happening of the peril specified to certain things which may be exposed to them."[1]

Four major classifications for insurance are property, liability, crime, and personal welfare. The fairly common varieties of property insurance give security against financial setbacks from property damage or destruction arising from perils such as fire, windstorm, and explosion. Liability insurance covers the insured if his unintentional actions result in injury or damage to another's body or property. Crime insurance provides security to the insured from financial losses incurred through the commission by others of intentional and illegal acts such as robbery, theft, and embezzle-

[1] Lucena v. Crauford, 2B. & P. N. R. 269 (H. L. 1806).

ment. Personal welfare insurance includes the various types of health, accident, and life policies. They afford protection against financial losses to companies, the individual, or beneficiaries as a result of ill health, accident, or death of the insured. There are other types such as workman's compensation insurance and surety bonds which do not fit in well with the above four classifications. It is difficult to resist the temptation to form a miscellaneous classification in which all classes of insurance other than the four listed would be placed.

SOME PRINCIPLES OF INSURANCE

The insurance business is based on the mathematical theory of probabilities and the Law of Large Numbers. The chance of loss of *some* buildings in a *large number* of *similar* buildings which are *independent* of each other can be predicted with *reasonable* certainty. This can be facilitated by comparing the number of fires in a given type of building with the total number of buildings of such a type in the country during the period in question. The analysis of fire losses for given construction types is the basis for determining the chance of loss by fire for a given type in a given location. To be more specific, assume that out of 100,000 similar school buildings throughout the country, 100 burned in a given year. The chance of loss of a single building in a large number of similar buildings during a year would be one in one thousand or 0.1 percent. Actually, this illustration is an oversimplification as fire loss experience is studied for many years rather than limited to a single year's experience. Statistics cannot predict the loss of a particular school building of a given type that is located on a certain site. But past experience points to the likelihood that one school building of a given type somewhere in the United States will suffer from fire damage or destruction during a definite period of time.

One cannot predict from the information gained

through statistical analysis of past loss experiences the precise time of the loss, the nature of the loss, and the extent of the loss. Whether the loss will be suffered by you or someone else and when it will occur is the very essence of risk. Insurance is a coöperative way of pooling many risks with financial losses paid out of a common pool of accumulated premiums and reserves. If an insurance company insured only one building of a given type in only one state, the risk assumed by the company would be entirely out of proportion to the premium. It is imperative that insurance commitments or risks be spread over a large number of similar buildings. The insurance premium is based, at least in part, on statistical experience with losses inflicted on properties of any given classification in a given location. In commercial insurance companies the premium charged must pay the expenses of business and return a profit as well as cover all the losses. Most states consider a profit of 5 percent as reasonable.

It is a practice of insurance companies to set limits upon the amount committed to a single risk or to a group of risks in a given geographical area. This practice tends to limit losses which may be occasioned by a catastrophe such as a conflagration which may hit only one area. To illustrate, an insurance organization may refuse to write $3 million of insurance upon a single school building but would without hesitation write the same $3 million worth of insurance if it were divided among 60 buildings scattered throughout the United States, each of which has an insurable value of no more than $50,000. In addition to a large number of dissimilar risks, it is desirable from the point of view of the insurer that these risks be distributed geographically to limit the chances of losses occasioned by a catastrophe.

If the number of properties at risk is not sufficient to permit the free play of the Law of Large Numbers, predictions of losses cannot be made with certainty. A limited number of risks or a concentration of risks is hazardous to the soundness of an insurance organization. The danger of a disastrous loss through conflagration always exists. To illustrate, if a fire underwriter confined its business to school buildings in one city the possibility of a widespread catastrophe such as a conflagration in that city would increase the liability of the underwriter to a point where he might not be able to meet obligations. Often insurance companies will reinsure a major portion of all the school buildings in one large city to lessen the hazard of great loss.

When a school board insures all the buildings in the district against loss due to fire, windstorm, and so on, it is shifting the burden of risk to a group willing and financially able to bear it. The risk of a substantial unknown financial loss is transferred from the school board to a professional risk bearer known as the insurance organization in return for a known charge, most commonly referred to as the premium.

SERVICES OF INSURANCE COMPANIES

The primary function of an insurance company is to assume the risk of a financial loss upon payment of a premium by those desiring such protection. The opportunity to make a profit motivated the organization of commercial underwriters. The services of insurance corporations are not limited to risk assumption alone. Insurance companies associate into a national organization for the purposes of developing programs to prevent the occurrence of losses. The National Board of Fire Underwriters is an association supported by the Stock Insurance Companies of America. It is active in recommending building construction standards, engineering standards, arson investigation, and the education of the public in fire prevention. Engineers employed by the National Board of Fire Underwriters inspect and grade the cities and towns of the United States from the standpoint of fire hazards and fire prevention. In this grading consideration is given to such things as the water supply, fire department, fire alarm system, police department, fire hazard laws, building laws, structural conditions within the municipality, and so on. The well-known Underwriters Laboratory is also maintained by Stock Fire Insurance companies of the United States through the National Board of Fire Underwriters. This organization has developed laboratories that test a great variety of products for defects that may cause fires, as well as testing fire-resistive and fire-controlling materials for their effectiveness. The Underwriters Laboratory label of approval is found on many products used today. The American Mutual Alliance is supported by the Mutual Insurance Companies and has functions similar to those of the National Board of Fire Underwriters which is supported by the Stock Insurance Companies.

STOCK COMPANIES AND MUTUAL COMPANIES

School insurance for various purposes can be purchased from either stock companies, mutual companies, a state insurance organization, or any combination of these. A stock company is a corporation organized with capital stock provided by individual investors. Capital stock is provided as a guarantee that the company will pay losses even though premiums collected are insufficient to cover them. The larger the capital stock in relation to the insurance in force (risk) or other reserves, the stronger the company. Capital stock is particularly important to the young company which has not accumulated a backlog of premiums to meet any exceptionally large loss which might occur early in the company's experience. Since the individual purchasers of capital stock in the insurance company must assume such a risk, they are in a position to demand a profit for risking their capital. When a stock company makes a profit, and premium rates are adjusted to promote such an end, the stock companies pay dividends to the holders of capital stock only on the basis of their investment in the company. The stock companies are referred to on occasion as the "old line companies."

Mutual companies are organized without the capital stock characteristic of the stock companies. These mutual insurance organizations depend primarily upon insurance premiums for the payment of losses. Mutual companies have been known to select risks carefully, refusing the more dangerous ones. This type of insurance organization looks upon policyholders as stockholders in the company. The rates charged by the mutual companies are usually less than those of stock organizations. On the other hand, the cushion necessary to meet unexpectedly large losses is made possible through the promise that mutual company policyholders are liable to additional assessment if the losses exceed the premiums paid. Although additional assessment beyond premiums paid is necessary to protect the persons suffering large losses, the chance of further insurance charges may prove to be an onerous burden upon all other mutual insurance policyholders. However, as there is no capital stock in a mutual company, any excess remaining after paying losses and expenses may be refunded to all policyholders as "dividends." The term "dividend" is inappropriate and is better called "a refund for excessive premium charge." Mutual companies in recent years have retained part of the premium payments to develop reserves or surplus to improve the position of individual policyholders. School boards in certain states cannot legally incur an indeterminate liability such as might occur with ordinary mutual companies.

Some mutual companies sell nonassessable policies. Nonassessable policies can be sold when the company has accumulated a substantial reserve. Under such conditions, the individual policyholder enjoys an improved status, as he cannot suffer from extra assessments even though losses in any year are greater than the total premiums collected in that year. Practically all of the states permit school boards to insure with mutual companies which issue nonassessable policies. Only about 10 percent of insurance premiums paid by schools to all types of commercial companies went to mutual companies as compared with 90 percent to stock companies. Many school districts continue to purchase insurance from stock companies only.

There are other types of insurance companies, such as assessment companies and reciprocal organizations, which are less frequently used by schools. An assessment insurance company is chartered by special laws to sell insurance to members of the association. The members make an initial deposit and are assessed periodically by the company to pay for losses and expenses. Often the policyholder will give notes to the assessment company which become payable when additional money over regular assessment is needed by the association. In a reciprocal organization each subscriber is an insurer as well as a policyholder. In this type of insurance organization a group of persons or corporations insures a pro rata share of the risk of each of the others. Each subscriber is liable only for his pro rata portion of each loss. These two types of special insurance organizations have some of the characteristics of mutual companies.

Insurance companies are rated as to soundness. The most frequently used authority on management, underwriting experience, adequacy of reserves, underwriting profit and loss, and investment practices of insurance companies is the Alfred M. Best Company of New York. The ratings issued by Best show the position of each insurance company in comparison with others of a similar type. An A:AA rating should be the minimum acceptable standard for companies doing business with schools. In addition to this source, state insurance departments can advise school boards on the financial standing of any company licensed to do business in that state.

STATE INSURANCE PLANS

At present Alabama, North Carolina, North Dakota, South Carolina, and Wisconsin operate state insurance programs which include protection for public elementary and secondary schools. The plans stipulate a division of the state government organized to sell insurance protection. The state insurance organization usually charges a lower premium for insurance services than do either stock or mutual types of commercial insurance corporations. The history, development, and experiences of state-operated insurance programs which involve public schools will be reviewed in greater detail in a subsequent portion of this chapter.

SELF-INSURANCE PROGRAMS

Self-insurance is practical only in very large school districts with ample financial resources and where a large number of school buildings are scattered throughout the district. In 1931, 49 cities had self-insurance on school properties.[2] The ratio of property losses to total valuation of school buildings in these 49 cities at that time was a minute fraction of 1 percent.

New York City has a long history of self-insurance. In New York City there were 585 fires during the 13-year period of 1918 to 1930. The average loss per fire was only $816.27. The average aggregate loss per year for the entire New York City system from 1918 to 1930 was only $36,732.18.[3] During 1931–1937 the average annual fire loss in New York City was less than $12,200.[4]

The Philadelphia public schools which also used self-insurance for a time had an annual fire loss to buildings during 1905 to 1933 of only $24,250. The annual income from the Philadelphia public schools' accumulated fire reserve fund of $740,445 in 1934 was $27,350 or more than $3000 more than the annual fire loss. During the late 1920's and early 1930's there was a distinct movement in city school systems toward self-insurance against fire losses. This may have been one of the factors leading to a considerable reduction in fire insurance rates on city school buildings since 1930. As late as 1941 one source estimated that the fire insurance business of city school districts only yielded stock companies upwards of $10 million per year in premiums. During 1948–1952 total school fire insurance premiums to all types of insurance companies averaged more than $29 million per year.[5]

The various systems of self-insurance for local districts may be classified as follows:

1. *The No-Insurance System.* Under this plan districts carry no insurance and set up no reserves. Financial losses are paid for out of current funds. This type of insurance plan came into being in certain cities

where it became obvious that over a number of years the annual premiums paid out of current operating funds are larger than the annual property losses suffered through fire and other causes in the district. There are certain dangers inherent in such a system, and only the few very large districts are able to use it with any degree of security. New York City, which has a credit as great as the resources of the more reputable insurance companies, has for many years carried no fire insurance on any of its public property. To date this practice has proved economical for New York City.

2. *The Insurance Reserve Plan.* Under this approach, the school district creates reserve funds from which to meet any financial losses suffered through destruction of property. This type of plan requires management on the part of the local district rather than management of funds on the part of a commercial insurance company. In 1913 the Cincinnati Board of Education embarked on this type of self-insurance and annually set aside $25,000 to be placed in a permanent fund to repair any damages caused by fire. By 1925, the reserve fund grew to $350,000 and yielded an interest of approximately $20,000 annually.

3. *Partial-Insurance Plan.* Under this system, the district insures only the most hazardous risks and carries no insurance on the select risks. Thus, the school district may insure with commercial organizations an old building constructed only partially of fire-resistive materials. On the other hand, the school district would carry no insurance on a relatively new structure made of fire-resistive materials and which was adequately protected with fire-fighting equipment.

BASES FOR SOUND SELF-INSURANCE

Before a school district adopts a plan of self-insurance of school property in preference to commercial or state insurance corporations, the following conditions should be satisfied. They are the bases upon which any sound self-insurance program should rest.

1. The number of property units to be covered should exist in sufficiently large number to make the application of averages possible.
2. The amount of coverage per risk should be reasonably small and uniform. If the value of a single risk is large enough to deplete materially or exhaust insurance reserves or overburden tax receipts necessary to replace the property unit where a loss occurs, the self-insurance plan is on a very shaky foundation.
3. Hazardous property units should be insured with other underwriters. Only the reasonably nonhazard-

[2] National Association of Public School Business Officials, *Insurance Practices and Experiences of City School Districts,* Bulletin no. 2, the Association, 1932, pp. 108–114.

[3] *Ibid.*

[4] National Association of Public School Business Officials, *Insurance,* Bulletin no. 9, the Association, 1941, p. 51.

[5] N. E. Viles, *School Property Insurance Experiences at State Level,* Bulletin 1956, no. 7, U.S. Office of Education, Washington, D.C.: U.S. Government Printing Office, 1956, p. 21.

ous property risks should be carried by the self-insurance fund.

4. The risks covered by the self-insurance fund should be independent of one another, i.e., a fire occurring in one should not be capable of spreading to another. Self-insurance is questionable if all school buildings are located on one site or adjoining sites or within areas subject possibly to a sweeping fire.

5. There should be a gradual accumulation of a self-insurance fund and a gradual transfer from commercial underwriters to assumption of financial losses by the self-insurance fund. A sudden transfer from 100 percent commercial insurance companies to 100 percent self-insurance before a sufficient reserve has been developed may wipe out the self-insurance fund if large and unexpected losses occur during the early years.

6. In considering the advisability of self-insurance, favorable loss experience during the preceding 10- or 20-year period should be cautiously and conservatively interpreted.

7. Only school districts that are in sound financial condition should plan self-insurance programs. Districts that can barely obtain sufficient funds to meet operating costs should consider other types of insurance protection.

8. The self-insurance fund should be kept inviolate. The seemingly idle insurance reserve funds needed in times of unexpected and large losses are a source of temptation. Tampering and transfers from this fund should be prohibited by school board policy if not by law.

9. There must be careful management of self-insurance reserve funds. The reserve funds should be placed in sound investments where security rather than high yields should be the keynote.[6]

REINSURANCE

Reinsurance is simply the transfer of a certain portion of the risk assumed by Insurance Company A to Insurance Companies B, C, D, etc., or to one very large underwriting firm such as Lloyd's of London. It is one way that Company A can spread risks that may be either very large or too concentrated. Most insurance organizations place a limit upon the amount of insurance they are willing to carry on a given type of risk located in a given area. When this limit is reached, the company which obtains the business re-

insures it with others. A broad distribution of risk is an aid in avoiding unusually heavy losses through concentration of risks.

THE FIRE INSURANCE POLICY

An insurance policy is a written contract between an insured and an insurer. The various conditions which apply in the written contract describe the parties of the contract, the property insured, the period the insurance is to be in force, a statement of premium or the basis and rates upon which the premium is to be computed, and the various perils to be covered on the property in question.

The 1943 New York Standard Fire Insurance Policy is practically a national standard contract since it is the basic model employed in 48 states, and the District of Columbia. The only exceptions are the two states of Minnesota and New Hampshire, which are still using versions of the New England Standard Policy. In some of these states, such as California, Georgia, Louisiana, Missouri, Nebraska, North Dakota, and Oregon, the 1943 New York Standard Policy is subject to certain minor statutory variations. It is without doubt the most liberal of the standard policies in interstate use. It specifies the ten hazards on which coverage is excluded and the seven items of uninsurable properties.

An outline of what is contained in the New York Standard Fire Insurance Policy of 1943 follows:

1. The name of the insurer and the insured.
2. The amount of insurance and the rate and premium to be paid by the insured.
3. A description of the property to be insured and its location.
4. The coverage:
   a. perils to be insured such as fire, lightning, and others.
   b. perils to be excluded, such as invasion, theft, explosion or riot, unless fire ensues.
   c. The amount of coverage, qualified in terms of actual cash value of property at the time and the qualification that loss cannot exceed cost of repair and replacement.
   d. Conditions of termination of the policy, such as expiration, cancellation, or destruction of the insured property.
   e. Conditions under which the policy is suspended.
   f. Conditions under which the policy is voided, such as willful concealment, fraud, or misrepresentation.
5. Representations and warranties.
6. Waivers.
7. Conditions relating to settlement of losses.
8. Subrogation, a right which is given the company under which it acquires a right of the district to collect from third parties who may be responsible for the loss.

[6] Adapted from S. S. Huebner, *Property Insurance,* New York: Appleton-Century-Crofts, Inc., 1938, pp. 92–95.

In addition, other clauses may be a part of the policy, such as the coinsurance clause, automatic coverage clause, extended coverage. These clauses describe special condtions not covered in the general contract. To illustrate, an extended coverage endorsement clause, if written into the fire insurance policy, extends the coverage to include such perils as explosion, riot, aircraft, smoke, and civil commotion which are usually not covered in the standard fire policy. Blanket insurance is a fire insurance contract which covers several different properties or exposures under a single policy.

INSURANCE RATES

The insurance rate actually charged a school district is influenced by factors within the community and factors related to the construction of the risk. The calculation of fire insurance rates is involved and costly. A fire insurance company often will subscribe to and use rates published by a rate-making body whose rating schedules are approved by a state insurance department.

The fire insurance rating organization engineers evaluate the water supply, fire department equipment, and alarm service in each community in the state. Community improvements result in lowered fire insurance rates. This rate is in part a reflection of the quality of fire protection in the community.

Fire-resistive buildings command a more favorable rate than nonfire-resistive buildings. A fire-resistive building is constructed of noncombustible materials which will impede or resist the spread of fire. In considering fire-resistive construction the walls, floors, and roof are of primary importance. A building is rated as fire resistive if two-thirds of its floor and roof area is made of noncombustible materials. A nonfire-resistive building cannot tolerate a burning out of contents without a collapse. Nonfire-resistive buildings are those with wood exteriors and interior wood framing, masonry walls and interior wood framing, or masonry walls and insufficiently protected interior metal framing. Wooden buildings or frame buildings represent the extreme of nonfire-resistive buildings.

Insurance can be paid with a regular flat rate for a certain amount and kind of coverage during a given period of years. In most cases, the longer the term of insurance, the lower the given rate. Usually, the three-year rate is two and one-half times the one-year rate, and the five-year rate is four times the one-year rate. The trend is toward five-year term insurance in contrast to three-year or shorter terms. It is usually wiser to purchase the insurance on the basis of an extended period of time rather than for a single year.

COINSURANCE

Insurance can also be paid for at the special coinsurance rate. The coinsurance concept was developed as a result of investigation which showed that the aggregate sum of partial losses paid by insurance organizations exceeded the aggregate sum of total losses. In other words, in the great proportion of fires and other property damage, the loss incurred is a small percent of the total value of the property. The report of the state insurance fund in Alabama for the fiscal year ending September 30, 1951, tabulated over 100 losses paid during the year, of which only 26 were total losses. If a building is underinsured and a partial loss occurs, the company suffers, for although the amount of the partial loss is but a fraction of the total value of the property, it is a proportionately larger fraction of the *insured* value of the property. Coinsurance was developed to correct such an inequity through granting credits and adjustments of base rates to those who agree to keep property insured at a stated percent of its actual value.

The coinsurance clause is an inducement to school districts to keep insurance in force at a certain percent of insurable value. It is an arrangement under which the insured receives a reduction in rate in return for purchasing insurance in quantity. It is usually available to school districts for property located in protected areas where specialized fire-fighting equipment is available to bring a blaze under control before total destruction occurs. It is usually not available on property in unprotected areas.

The principle behind it is relatively simple. The insurance company agrees to lower the rate per unit of insured value if the insured promises to carry a given amount of insurance stated as a certain percent of the full insurable value of the risk. In other words, if the insured agrees to keep in force insurance equal to no less than 90 percent of the total insurable value of the building, he will pay a lesser rate than if the amount of insurance carried is less than 90 percent of the insurable value. The higher the ratio of the insurance to insurable value of the risk, the lower the rate per $100 of insurance.

Coinsurance has helped more than any other single factor to reduce fire insurance rates. The reduction in fire insurance rates can vary from a 10 percent reduction in the standard or manual rates to a 73 percent reduction of the manual rate for 90 percent coinsur-

TABLE 33. Coinsurance Rate Adjustment Schedule

| | Percent of Actual Fire Rate Charged for | | | |
Type of Construction	70 Percent Coinsurance	80 Percent Coinsurance	90 Percent Coinsurance	100 Percent Coinsurance
1. Type 1A—Fire-Resistive Buildings	33½	30	27	27 percent less 5 percent of the adjusted rate
2. Type 3A—Semifire-Resistive Buildings	80	75	70	70 percent less 5 percent of the adjusted rate
3. Type 4A—Nonfire-Resistive Buildings	—	90	85	85 percent less 5 percent of the adjusted rate

ance clauses on certain types of buildings. Coinsurance is legal in all states.

Coinsurance rates vary with the degree of coverage required and the class of construction to which the property protected is assigned. Table 33 is an illustration of the *percent* of the actual fire rate which would be charged for three types of construction and for various percents of coinsurance coverage. It is consistent with present practices in many states.

Note that the above schedule does not give the actual fire insurance rate per $100 of property valuation. The fire rate will vary with the type of construction, the location of the property in the community, the caliber of fire protection in the community, etc. The actual rate charged is determined by the rate-setting bureaus in the state and will vary for the same type of building in different communities as the fire hazards and fire-fighting efficiency vary among communities. The schedule of adjustments for coinsurance coverage remains constant in the state even though the actual rates may vary.

An illustration is in order. In Iowa City, the stock company fire insurance rate on a Type 1A building (fire-resistive) is $0.16 per $100 of property valuation. This rate will not be the same for Type 1A buildings in other Iowa cities unless they experience the same hazards and protection as in Iowa City. The actual rate of $0.16/$100 will be charged if no coinsurance clause is in effect. If a 70 percent clause is inserted in the policy, the rate charged for this type of building would be 33½ percent (see above schedule) of the fire rate of $0.16 or $0.0536/$100. Computations for other degrees of coinsurance coverage would be as follows:

80 percent Coinsurance: 30 percent of $0.16 or $0.048/$100

90 percent Coinsurance: 27 percent of $0.16 or $0.043/$100

100 percent Coinsurance: 27 percent of $0.16 less 5 percent of the adjusted rate. The product of .27 × $0.16 is 0.043. A 5 percent reduction of 0.043 would yield $0.04-095/$100

By way of further illustration, the total annual premium on a $500,000 Type 1A building in Iowa City with various degrees of coinsurance coverage *for fire protection only* would be as shown on page 280.

The total annual premium charge for fire protection only without a coinsurance clause would vary with the amount of insurance coverage purchased. If the insurance protection desired were $400,000, the annual premium cost would be $640.00 (0.16 × 4000 units of $100) or more than three times what the same protection would cost with an 80 percent coinsurance clause. Put in another way, $400,000 worth of protection with an 80 percent coinsurance clause would cost as much as $120,000 worth of insurance protection on a $500,000 building without an 80 percent coinsurance clause.

Proportionately less savings could be affected through coinsurance on a Type 3A or semifire-resistive building than on fire-resistive structures. This is apparent from the smaller rate reductions for various degrees of coinsurance (see line 2, Table 33). To begin with the fire insurance rate on this type of structure is $.23/$100. According to the previous coinsurance

TABLE 34.   Fire Insurance Costs for Fire-Resistive Buildings with Various Degrees of Coinsurance

Degree of Coinsurance Coverage (1)	Amount of $500,000 Building Which Must Be Covered (2)	Fire Insurance Rate per $100 Property Valuation (3)	Coinsurance Adjustment Factor (4)	Total Coinsurance Fire Insurance Rate[a] (5)	Total Annual Premium Charged[b] (6)
100 Percent	$500,000	0.16	.27 Percent less 5 Percent	0.04095	$204.75
90 Percent	450,000	0.16	.27	0.043	193.50
80 Percent	400,000	0.16	.30	0.048	192.00
70 Percent	350,000	0.16	.33½	0.0536	187.60

[a] Column 3 times column 4.
[b] Column 2 times column 5.

rate adjustment schedule, the adjusted rate for 80 percent coinsurance would be 75 percent of .23 or .1725/$100. The annual premium for $400,000 worth of protection on a $500,000 building with 80 percent coinsurance is $600. This is about four times the cost for a Type 1A building. Without coinsurance the cost for the same protection would be $920.

Under the coinsurance clause, the school board is responsible for determining the insurable value of the property and for purchasing the appropriate amount of insurance in accordance with the required percent stated in the clause. Should the school board fail to purchase the minimum amount of insurance required, whether this is through error or by willful design, and a partial loss occurs, the school district will suffer a penalty. The penalty is the recovery of an amount less than the actual loss.

If total loss occurs, conditions of the coinsurance do not apply. Thus, if the school district has a building valued at $500,000 and carries $300,000 worth of insurance, the district will be paid the face of the policy, namely $300,000, if total loss occurs. The penalty clause of the coinsurance applies only in cases of partial loss.

The following formula is used to compute the amount of insurance coverage in case of partial loss.

$$\frac{\text{Amount of Insurance in Force}}{\text{Amount of Insurance Required by Coinsurance Clause}} \times \text{Loss} = \begin{array}{l}\text{Total Financial Payment but} \\ \text{Not to Exceed the Amount on} \\ \text{the Face of the Policy}\end{array}$$

Assume that the coinsurance clause demands that for the special reduced fire insurance rate, the school district will keep the property insured up to 70 percent of the value of the property. Assume further that the insurable value of the building was a half-million dollars. Seventy percent of $500,000 is $350,000. If a district is carrying $350,000 worth of insurance on the building, it is satisfying the demands of the coinsurance clause of 70 percent of the insurable value of the property. It is entitled, therefore, to full payment in case of partial loss up to $350,000, which is the face of the policy.

If the school district in the previous illustration were required by the coinsurance clause to keep in force 80 percent of the total insurable value of the building, a much different case would result. Eighty percent of a $500,000 building is $400,000 or the amount of insurance required. If the district carried only $300,000 worth of insurance on the $500,000 building, it would not satisfy the demands of an 80 percent coinsurance clause. In case of partial loss a penalty would be in order. The school district would receive only $300,000 divided by $400,000 (see above formula) or three-fourths of the partial loss. Note the computations at the top of page 281 that further illustrate the point. The district had to assume a $25,000 loss for failure to keep the amount of insurance in force required by the coinsurance clause.

Various studies indicate that practically all of the city school districts use 80 percent or 90 percent coinsurance rate reductions. Most authorities recommend a 90 percent coinsurance clause for school districts. While coinsurance clauses may be an economy enjoyed through reduced fire insurance rates, there is danger that if school property is not reappraised at various intervals to determine insurable values, the

Insurable Value of Building	Coinsurance Clause Requirements	Amount of Insurance in Force	Total Amount of Partial Loss Suffered
$500,000	80 Percent	$300,000	$100,000

Then, according to the formula quoted:

$$\frac{\$300,000 \text{ (Amount of Insurance in Force)}}{\$400,000 \text{ (Amount of Insurance Required)}} \times \$100,000 = \frac{3}{4} \times \$100,000$$

$$= \$75,000 \text{ partial loss payment to the district}$$

district may suffer losses. This is particularly true if the amount of insurance does not increase as the property appreciates in value. Prudent insurance management demands that there be careful studies of the insurable value of school properties.

INSURABLE VALUES

The determination of the insurable values of buildings is based on the knowledge of initial cost of the building. It is possible to overinsure as well as to underinsure a building. There is no advantage to overinsuring a building, for insurance companies will not pay out an amount greater than the actual loss even in cases of total loss. Land, architectural fees, and foundations are not considered in computing initial costs. The sound value of a school building is equal to its replacement cost less depreciation. Depreciation is the amount of wear and tear that every portion of a piece of property has suffered since its erection. It is evidenced by its visible existing condition rather than an arbitrary or theoretical formula. In another sense, depreciation is a reduction in value through either physical deterioration or lack of adaptability to service.

The insurable value is equal to the sound value less the value of excavations, foundations, site, and so on. In another sense the insurable value of a building is the sound value less the value of depreciation less items excluded from coverage.

The basis of property appraisal for insurance purposes is adequate record keeping. Appraisal can be defined simply as the assignment of a value to an item of property. The coinsurance clause makes it imperative that the school district have knowledge at all times of the actual value of its property. The value of property is the cost to reproduce it at the time the fire occurs at prevailing prices of labor and material less actual depreciation. Technical knowledge of the principles of valuation, depreciation, and determination of reproduction costs is necessary. Appraisals made by incompetent people unfamiliar with building costs and construction can lead to embarrassment for the board and the insurance company.

The insurance company will usually accept the value placed on property by school district officials at the time insurance is purchased. The insurance company is not obligated, however, to accept this value if loss occurs. Insurance adjusters enter the picture at the time of loss and compute values in accordance with their principles and make adjustments on their own computation of value at the time of fire. The board deceives itself at the time insurance is purchased if unqualified personnel or questionable procedures are used in arriving at the insurable value of a building.

The most effective way to appraise the risk in question is through a reliable and professional appraiser. This is a more costly procedure and there does not appear to be a standard charge among appraisers. Studies have repeatedly showed that most school boards do not know if their valuations of property for insurance purposes are reliable and acceptable in case of fire loss. Insurance salesmen are not always qualified to appraise property and their figures may or may not be accepted by adjusters.

One study of 378 school districts indicated that only 30 percent used commercial appraisal firms, 10 percent used a qualified employee of the school district, 38 percent used the engineering department of the insurance company, and 22 percent used other methods.[7]

REPLACEMENT COST INSURANCE

Considerable discussion of late has centered on the advisability of replacement cost insurance for schools. This type was at one time more commonly known as depreciation insurance. Earlier in history it was a matter of specialty underwriting but its significant development in recent years has made it a routine extension of various types of coverage offered by many insurance corporations.

Replacement cost insurance differs from the usual coverage in that settlement of losses is based on the

[7] Paul Salmon, "How Much Insurance Should You Carry?" *School Management,* November-December, 1957, *1*:28–30.

actual cost of repairing or replacing damaged property *without any deduction for depreciation* of the property. It departs sharply from a long-established principle of insurance which restricts recovery to the *actual cash value* of the property. The courts have defined *actual cash value* as replacement cost *less depreciation.*

Regular policies can be readily modified to provide replacement cost coverage by substituting the words "replacement cost" for "actual cash value" by means of an endorsement. Certain conditions must be met for the special replacement cost endorsement to apply. One is that the insured will actually repair or rebuild his property. If he does not and seeks a cash settlement instead, the coverage automatically reverts to the traditional insurance principle of payment on the basis of replacement cost less depreciation. Furthermore, restoration or repair must be undertaken with *due diligence and dispatch* to be *completed within a reasonable time* after loss. The time limitation of two years found on older forms has been dropped in most states. Most companies in recent years have dropped the requirement that the property must be rebuilt on the *same site.* This requirement of rebuilding on the same site has been dropped in most school and other governmental policies.

The *rate* for replacement cost insurance is not greater than for policies calling for loss settlement on the basis of the traditional actual cost figures. A mandatory 100 percent coinsurance clause is included in all replacement cost insurance policies. This places a burden upon school boards to appraise carefully properties so covered. It means that insurance premiums must be increased in inflationary times.

To illustrate, a Type 1A building which would cost $500,000 to replace must be insured for the full value of $500,000. Using the fire protection rates and adjustments for 100 percent of coinsurance in Iowa City, which were presented previously, the total annual premium charge would be $204.85. If this building were about 25 years old it might have depreciated to an actual or insurable value of $400,000. An 80 percent coinsurance clause would require $320,000 worth of insurance in force. The total annual fire insurance premium under such conditions would be $153.60. The charge is $51.25 more for replacement cost insurance, but greater protection is in force plus a guarantee of a replacement cost settlement.

This type of insurance would have its greatest value on older buildings which have depreciated considerably rather than on recently constructed ones. Again, there is no increase in rate, but there is a requirement that you carry insurance up to 100 percent of the replacement cost of the building. This type of insurance has been more popular to date on income-producing property than on school buildings. Usually it is a protection which applies to buildings only, but a few companies have recently extended it to apply to the replacement cost of the contents as well.

The city of Madison, Wisconsin, has an interesting insurance program which combines many features such as coinsurance, blanket coverage, replacement cost settlement, plus a degree of self-insurance expressed as a fixed amount deductible from the total damages suffered. Gaumnitz[8] reported that the insurance program in Madison, Wisconsin, included the following main features:

1. Coinsurance which enables the insured to take advantage of the favorable rates under such clauses.
2. Building and contents are covered at all locations and the board is not obligated to report value of contents periodically at any location.
3. The insurance is written on a blanket basis and, therefore, settlement is not restricted to an amount for each building.
4. Replacement cost and not actual cash value or historical value is the basis of settlement. Furthermore, reconstruction need not take place on the same site. Architect's fees are a part of replacement costs.
5. The first $250,000 loss on any one occurrence is covered by the special city fund rather than by commercial carriers. Each year the board of education pays a stipulated amount into the city fund for coverage of the first $250,000 loss. The amount of loss in excess of $250,000 is covered by regular insurance companies. If a catastrophic loss involved several buildings, it would be defined as a loss at one occurrence, with the city fund paying no more than $250,000 and commercial carriers paying the rest. This feature makes the plan a self-insurance plan up to $250,000 for any one occurrence.

PURCHASING INSURANCE

There are various ways to purchase insurance. This responsibility should be delegated by the board of education to the superintendent of schools. Often the purchase of insurance is settled on the basis of friendship or persuasiveness of a given individual. In many school districts it is advisable to employ a consultant to be sure that the insurance program is a

[8] Erwin Gaumnitz, "Co-Insurance for Fire Losses," *The Nation's Schools,* April, 1957, *59*:90–94.

defensible one. The objective should be the best possible insurance coverage at the lowest possible cost.

There are special problems of purchase in large communities where there are many different insurance agents. In some districts school insurance is apportioned to various agents within the community on the basis of school taxes paid by each agency. Another method of distributing the school's insurance business is through competitive bidding on rates. All insurance companies do not charge the same rates. Some companies have what are known as "File Deviation Agreements" on file with the state insurance departments. Such agreements permit the insurance company to discount the annual rates by a percentage authorized by the state insurance department. The mutual companies usually charge less for the same type of insurance than do stock companies. Even though this be true, in 1945 about one-half the city school districts purchased insurance only from stock companies. The relative number purchasing insurance from mutuals has been increasing of late.[9] Many communities report considerable success in awarding school insurance through bidding. Since insurance is not considered a commodity, state laws do not require that insurance be purchased on the basis of bids.

A rather common practice is for the school board to do business with the association of local insurance agents. The board purchases fire insurance through the association rather than from a given agent. The association in turn determines, according to its own formula, the proportion of the school insurance to be carried by various companies. A minority of city school districts have no planned or objective basis for awarding fire insurance to agents.

There is a difference between insurance agents and insurance brokers. The property insurance agent is usually a representative of a company or a general agency authorized to execute business for a given insurance company. In contrast to stock companies, most mutual insurance companies are direct writing organizations with paid employees in branch offices writing policies rather than working through an agency. In property insurance, the agents have the authority to bind the company on a risk. This is in contrast to life insurance, where the authority of the agent is limited to solicitation of an offer from the prospective buyer, and the company reserves the right to reject or accept the offer.

A broker, on the other hand, represents the insurance buyer rather than the company or agency. The broker does not have authority to bind an insurance company. There must be a contract between the company (or its agent) and a broker before the insurance company assumes the risk for a given loss. If the broker retains the premium, rather than placing it with the company, the insurance buyer has recourse only to the broker. In some states, special statutes have been passed to define the role of a broker as an agent of the company for the purpose of delivering policies and collecting premiums. In all cases, when a school is placing insurance, it is important that the status of the agent or broker be understood to avoid the possibility of not being covered properly.

INSURANCE PRACTICES

School districts vary considerably in the management of insurance. It is not unusual to find inadequate data upon which to base property valuations, discrepancies between the amount carried and the amount required by coinsurance clauses, policy nonconcurrency, premium rate discrepancies, overlapping of coverage, selection of insurance companies of unproved financial stability, and other inadequate procedures. The improvement of insurance procedures should be based on a careful study of the existing program as well as the recommendations of a special consultant in this field.

Most authorities recommend that: (1) one person, preferably the superintendent or the business manager, be responsible for purchasing all of the school district's insurance; (2) there be a reliable appraisal to determine insurable values based on adequate records; (3) there be an objective method of selecting companies capable of underwriting the school's insurance program and providing a desirable adjustment service in case of loss; (4) there be a careful study of the variety of clauses in insurance policies to determine which insurance form is most useful to satisfy the needs of the particular school district; (5) all possible reductions be procured through such means as adoption of at least a five-year term insurance, coinsurance, check rating sheets to obtain all possible credits, competitive bidding, and investigation of reliable mutual fire insurance companies which write nonassessable policies.[10]

There should be an insurance register which contains pertinent information relative to the status of all insurance. It should contain the number of the policy, kind of coverage, date of policy issuance and

[9] National Association of Public School Business Officials, *Insurance Committee Report on School Fire Insurance, 1938–1945,* Bulletin no. 11, the Association, 1948, p. 4.

[10] *Ibid.,* pp. 8–21.

FORM 29.

Insurance Register

SCHOOL DISTRICT

FORM No 17
APRIL '57 5M

	COMPANY	LOCAL AGENT	POLICY NUMBER	AMOUNT	KIND	RATE PER $100	PREMIUM	TERM	DATE OF EXPIRATION				CANCELLATION		EXPLANATION OF COVERAGE
									YEAR, MONTH, DAY	YEAR, MONTH, DAY	YEAR, MONTH, DAY	YEAR, MONTH, DAY	DATE	PREMIUM REFUNDED	
1															
2															
3															
4															
5															
6															
7															
8															
9															
10															
11															
12															
13															
14															
15															
16															
17															
18															
19															
20															
21															
22															
23															
24															
25															
26															
27															
28															
29															
30															
31															
32															
33															
34															
35															
36															
37															
38															
39															
40															

(Courtesy of the Missouri State Department of Education)

expiration, amounts of coverage, rate, premium, etc. Procedures should be developed to determine responsibility and course of action in case of fire loss.

SCHOOL FIRE INSURANCE LOSS EXPERIENCE

There is an overwhelming amount of evidence which emphasizes that payments for fire insurance losses to school districts in the United States are a small fraction of the total premiums paid by school districts to fire insurance companies for protection. The early studies of Melchior in New York State[11] and Lura in Iowa[12], among others, began to show how little of the school premium dollar paid to companies ever returned to schools to cover losses. The rather thorough investigations of city school systems during 1921–1930, 1931–1937, and 1938–1945 by the Association of School Business Officials gave further evidence that the financial fire loss ratio of schools over this extended period of time ranged from only 26.9 to 31.9 percent of total premiums paid.[13] These investigations which cover a period of 25 years are summarized in Table 35.

A more recent study by Viles of the school fire insurance costs, losses, and loss ratios during 1948–1952 reinforced the previous studies which proved that premiums paid by schools were far larger than loss payment to schools by commercial underwriters.[14] His report on school fire insurance costs, losses, and loss ratios for all school buildings in all locations and for all types of construction in certain states during the years 1948–1952 is summarized in Table 36. It can be seen for the nation as a whole and for all types of insurance companies that school districts received only 35.3 percent of the total premiums paid to cover fire losses during 1948–1952. It can be concluded that a downward revision of fire insurance rates for schools is in order. Extended experience has showed that school buildings must be classed as favorable and preferred risks. It was pointed out previously that school fire insurance rates have declined since 1930, but an even greater decline is in order. The trend in insurance rates for city school districts during the eight years of 1938–1945 inclusive was

downward.[15] However, the most frequent reason for the lowered rates was elimination of fire hazards rather than consideration by commercial fire insurance companies that school buildings are preferred risks.

The average fire loss during 1948–1952 for public schools totals almost $11 million a year. This is a large aggregate loss, particularly when one considers that much of it could have been prevented. The high loss ratios in some states merit careful study and attention as well as point to the need for leadership in school fire safety.

In 1931, the loss ratio on all types of insured risks for all stock fire business was 51.4 percent. The loss ratio on school properties only was 28.7 percent. On the basis of actual experience, it was reported by the Association of School Business Officials that city school districts were paying 78 percent more for their protection than are owners of all properties taken as a composite, exclusive of the loading charges. In other words, schools as a preferred risk, must assume some of the insurance costs that fall upon other more dangerous risks.[16]

STATE-OPERATED INSURANCE PROGRAMS

In 1931, seven states adopted and had in operation self-insurance plans. These states were Alabama, Florida, Michigan, North Dakota, South Carolina, Vermont, and Wisconsin.[17] At that time other states such as New Jersey, Maine, Minnesota, Mississippi, and Pennsylvania had state insurance plans under consideration but abandoned them for various reasons.

In Florida, no single risk can be carried in the fund in excess of $50,000 except with the approval of the Board of Commissions of State Institutions. Premiums charged by the State Fire Insurance Fund of Florida are comparable to the full commercial rates for state property insured in the fund.

The most recent inauguration of a state insurance fund approaching self-insurance standards was created on July 1, 1949, when the public school insurance fund of North Carolina started operations. Viles[18] reported that only the five states of Alabama, North Carolina, North Dakota, South Carolina, and

[11] William T. Melchior, *Insuring Public School Property,* Contributions to Education no. 168, New York: Teachers College, Columbia University, 1925.

[12] Casper P. Lura, *Public School Property Insurance in Iowa,* Doctoral Dissertation, Iowa City: State University of Iowa, 1932.

[13] National Association of Public School Business Officials, Bulletin no. 2, Bulletin no. 9, Bulletin no. 11, *op. cit.*

[14] Viles, *op. cit.*

[15] National Association of School Business Officials, Bulletin no. 11, *op. cit.*

[16] National Association of Public School Business Officials, Bulletin no. 2, *op. cit.,* p. 49.

[17] *Ibid.,* pp. 88–107.

[18] Viles, *op. cit.,* p. 24.

TABLE 35. Summary by States of Three Surveys of School Fire Insurance Showing Premiums Paid to Fire Loss Ratios in Selected City Systems

States	1921–1930 Survey of Fire Loss Ratio[a]	1931–1937 Survey of Fire Loss Ratio[a]	1938–1945 Survey of Fire Loss Ratio[a]
Alabama	30.45	16.61	5.86
Arizona	34.23	.00	.00
Arkansas	25.74	74.40	
California	24.81	44.79	19.55
Colorado	14.08	1.35	13.78
Connecticut	14.60	4.20	
Delaware		8.30	38.53
Florida			.72
Georgia		65.76	96.21
Idaho	.00	.00	2.83
Illinois	65.96	45.67	45.77
Indiana	7.20	18.34	31.26
Iowa	30.59	46.51	45.77
Kansas		.00	8.27
Kentucky	.00	11.03	.00
Louisiana	78.48	13.54	42.46
Maine	90.44	1.57	.53
Maryland		184.90	3.77
Massachusetts	43.56	10.38	5.44
Michigan	17.76	3.13	5.86
Minnesota	5.49	12.49	14.49
Missouri	27.78	10.95	7.24
Montana	63.59	2.35	.00
Nebraska	1.59	8.86	37.82
New Hampshire		.00	
New Jersey	4.97	1.95	14.60
New York	33.92	38.88	10.67
North Carolina	15.05	144.39	8.99
North Dakota		31.02	
Ohio	28.17	13.05	37.58
Oklahoma	2.34	24.73	.00
Oregon	170.81	120.08	106.76
Pennsylvania	20.68	5.63	76.13
Rhode Island		.00	
South Dakota	16.99	1.74	
Tennessee	7.64	2.89	
Texas	19.21	15.09	13.37
Utah		5.50	7.85
Vermont		.00	
Washington	61.67	41.74	13.47
West Virginia	.34	5.02	5.08
Wisconsin		.46	.89
Wyoming	.00	14.11	
Canada	19.08		106.79
All States and Canada	28.7	26.9	31.9

[a] Percent losses paid by school districts are of premiums paid to insurance companies by school districts.
SOURCE: Association of Public School Business Officials, *Insurance Committee Report on School Fire Insurance, 1938–1945.* Bulletin no. 11, Kalamazoo, Mich.: the Association, 1948, pp. 38–39.

TABLE 36. Summary of School Fire Insurance Costs, Losses, and Loss Ratio During 1948–1952

States	Premiums Paid to Stock and Mutual Companies	Fire Losses Paid to School Districts by Insurance Companies	Percent of Loss Ratio (Percent Losses Are of Premiums Paid)
Alabama			
Arizona	$1,287,597	$ 491,001	38.0
Arkansas	2,518,784	1,084,702	43.0
California	11,061,104	2,783,523	25.2
Colorado	1,487,087	677,484	45.6
Connecticut	2,826,983	881,305	31.2
Delaware			
Florida	3,119,726	614,976	19.7
Georgia	4,857,296	1,360,045	28.0
Idaho	1,259,466	370,259	29.5
Illinois	7,972,933	2,601,863	32.6
Indiana	4,676,444	903,801	19.3
Iowa	2,683,386	776,653	28.9
Kansas	2,568,554	1,171,498	45.6
Kentucky	2,905,763	1,322,205	45.5
Louisiana	3,271,187	1,791,047	54.7
Maine	2,090,742	383,303	13.5
Maryland	2,251,168	771,631	34.2
Massachusetts	6,899,654	2,301,968	33.4
Michigan	4,392,661	1,143,415	26.0
Minnesota	2,934,798	484,286	16.5
Mississippi	2,399,102	1,085,880	45.0
Missouri	4,461,972	1,593,007	35.7
Montana			
Nebraska	1,123,667	335,688	30.0
Nevada	282,614	55,344	19.6
New Hampshire			
New Jersey	4,739,274	1,178,134	24.8
New Mexico	1,324,650	436,464	32.9
New York	9,537,760	4,509,721	47.2
North Carolina	4,155,089	1,382,223	33.3
North Dakota			
Ohio	4,850,410	1,301,610	26.8
Oklahoma	2,587,804	1,536,234	59.4
Oregon	3,385,719	915,267	27.0
Pennsylvania	10,238,368	4,715,429	46.6
Rhode Island	860,586	371,680	43.2
South Carolina			
South Dakota	827,955	439,343	53.1
Tennessee	3,788,151	2,132,097	56.3
Texas	6,071,286	3,373,021	55.6
Utah	770,791	85,188	11.0
Vermont	999,464	124,731	12.5
Virginia	3,373,489	1,566,800	46.4
Washington	3,558,209	1,232,314	34.4
West Virginia	2,724,912	631,916	23.2
Wisconsin	1,959,406	515,668	26.3
Wyoming	503,841	38,514	7.6
United States Total	$145,589,852	$51,471,238	35.3

SOURCE: N. E. Viles, *School Property Insurance Experiences at the State Level*, Bulletin 1956, no. 7, U.S. Office of Education, Washington, D.C.: U.S. Government Printing Office, 1956, p. 21.

Wisconsin had state-operated insurance programs that included public elementary and secondary schools. These state programs varied and no consistent pattern was noted.

Alabama's state insurance fund was established in 1923. In 1952–1953 this fund insured 3493 county and 87 city elementary or secondary school buildings. Coverage in this fund is compulsory except for certain city-owned school properties, and some of these have voluntarily purchased insurance fund coverage. Premiums charged to schools are less than those that would apply to commercial corporations. It is of interest to note that about 48 percent of all county school fire coverage in 1952–1953 was reinsured with commercial corporations. The loss ratio of schools was 50.6 percent of premiums paid. At the end of its thirtieth year the Alabama insurance fund had a surplus of over $2,600,000. Most of this is invested in state and federal bonds. The fund's operating costs are low.

The North Carolina state insurance program is unique in that it was developed as a school insurance program and not as a part of another program as is true in most other states. The state developed insurance on public elementary and secondary school buildings in 1949. The state program of insurance was precipitated by the ten-year study, 1939–1948, in North Carolina which showed that the average annual premiums were about $460,000 and the fire loss was about 63 percent of the premiums paid for fire protection. The insurance program is a state-wide optional school coöperative insurance program. In 1953 it was estimated that the fund included about 40 percent of the public elementary and secondary schools in the state. A portion of this North Carolina fund is reinsured with Lloyd's of London. Insufficient data on this fund are available as it has been in force for only a few years.

The North Dakota Public School Building Insurance Fund is part of the total state insurance program, of which school buildings are only one class. This program was authorized in 1919 and some changes were made in 1953. Part of their insurance is reinsured with other corporations. The North Dakota pattern has changed from periods of free insurance, low insurance rates, and higher rates.

South Carolina's state insurance program was instituted in 1900 and is one of the oldest programs in the United States. Local school officials responsible for school property are required to insure their buildings with this fund. Failure to comply may bring penalties. In 1943, the insurance fund covered school properties valued at over $160 million. This state also reinsures parts of its responsibilities.

The Wisconsin school insurance program is a part of an overall state insurance program. It is a program which is optional with the local school districts. Most of Wisconsin's educational buildings are insured with either stock or mutual companies rather than with the state fund.

LOSS EXPERIENCES FOR OTHER TYPES OF SCHOOL INSURANCE

A limited study of school transportation insurance during 1928–1937 reported that only 13.1 percent of every premium dollar paid for liability insurance on district-owned vehicles was returned to school districts to cover losses. The ratio of losses to premiums written by all insurance companies in the United States on this type of insurance coverage for 1938 was 53.6 cents out of every dollar. School automobiles are a select risk as they are operated a fewer hours a week and are thus exposed to fewer hazards.[19] Pupil transportation contractors are a poorer risk since 40.3 cents of every premium dollar for liability insurance is used to pay losses.

About two-thirds of the states more or less definitely approve the purchase of liability insurance on buses that are publicly owned.[20] In the three states of Florida, Massachusetts, and Wisconsin it is compulsory that privately owned buses carry school bus liability insurance. School bus liability insurance on publicly owned school buses is forbidden in the six states of Alabama, Arkansas, Georgia, Illinois, Mississippi, and South Dakota. It is well established as a legal principle in most states that school districts are not liable in tort actions. Purchasing liability insurance does not waive the school district's common law immunity from damages occasioned by negligent actions such as might occur in school bus operations.

School bus property damage insurance for publicly owned buses is compulsory in the three states of Nevada, Wisconsin, and Virginia.[21] Only in Wisconsin are privately owned carriers required to have property damage insurance. Property damage insurance on publicly owned buses is prohibited in the six states of Alabama, Arkansas, Georgia, Illinois, Mississippi, and South Carolina. Property damage insurance paid for by local school boards on privately owned school buses is prohibited in the states of Alabama, Arkansas, California, Colorado, Connecticut,

[19] National Association of Public School Business Officials, Bulletin no. 9, *op. cit.*, p. 173.

[20] National Education Association, Research Division, *School Transportation Insurance*, Pamphlet no. 101, U.S. Office of Education, Washington, D.C., U.S. Government Printing Office. 1948, p. 8.

[21] *Ibid.*, p. 18.

Indiana, Georgia, Idaho, Illinois, Mississippi, New Hampshire, New Mexico, South Carolina, Vermont, and West Virginia. The principle of district immunity applies to property damage insurance as well as to liability insurance.

Fire and theft insurance carried by local school boards on privately owned school buses is compulsory in the state of Wisconsin only. Collision insurance is compulsory only in the states of Wisconsin and Nevada for publicly owned buses. Wisconsin is the only state which requires the board to carry collision insurance on privately owned buses.[22] The legal status of school bus insurance in most states is in a confused condition.

SURETY BONDS

The surety is a person or company who guarantees that another person, known as the principal, will fulfill a valid obligation to a third party. If the principal fails to fulfill his obligations and performances to the third party, then the surety is liable if any loss occurs.

There is a difference between a suretyship and a guaranty. If a suretyship prevails, then default by the employee bonded would give the district immediate recourse against the company or person guaranteeing the proper performance. Under a guaranty contract the district has no rights until all remedies against the defaulting employee have been exhausted by the district. In other words, the guarantor becomes liable if the employee cannot perform, but in the case of surety the company becomes liable if the employee does not perform.

A personal surety bond is a written obligation binding one or more individuals to guarantee the performance or faithfulness of another party known as the principal. The person or group of persons who assumed the responsibility must pay the damages or costs resulting from the failure to perform or lack of fidelity of the principal.

A corporate surety bond is a written obligation binding a corporation organized to guarantee the performance or faithfulness of the principal. The government controls surety companies through legal restrictions on organization and management, capital requirements, state insurance department supervision, legal limitation on the size of any single risk bonded by the company, and legal reserve requirements.

The corporate sureties afford greater security to school districts which must be protected against the losses accruing from the unfaithfulness or nonperformance of such important officials as the school treasurer. Corporate sureties cost more than personal bondsmen. Experience has shown that the personal surety bondsmen frequently fight the case when default occurs and seldom willingly pay. The corporate surety bond is far superior to the personal bondsman. It is regrettable that personal suretyship is permitted. Good business practices demand that the corporate surety bond be demanded whenever it is legally permissible to do so. In 1937, 83 percent of city school positions requiring a surety bond were protected by corporate bonds.[23]

There are many types of surety bonds. The fidelity bonds and contract bonds are of primary significance to schools. Fidelity bonds cover the honesty of employees. Contract bonds are designed to insure the performance of a contract previously accepted. If the contract, such as one calling for the construction of a school building, is not completed, the bondsman becomes responsible for its completion and any financial losses that befall the district.

A study of fidelity bond cost recovery during one year only in 90 cities located in 25 states revealed that the loss is only 2.98 percent of the premiums paid.[24] The premium is paid by the board in most cases. Some boards bond almost every official and employees and others board only a few. Although the study by the Association of School Business Officials gave evidence that the low recovery on fidelity bonds on school officials and employees indicated that schools are better than average risks, a later study by Nelson labeled school employees handling funds as average risks and not a select group.[25]

There is evidence that some districts are woefully underinsured in fidelity bonding and others are extravagantly overinsured. Many school districts fail to bond any of their employees who handle money and others are inadequately covered. More consistent and better business procedures are sorely needed in the area of fidelity bonding.

CRIME INSURANCE

Theft, safe burglary, and holdup insurance come under this classification. It is interesting to note that the purchase of this type of insurance increased considerably immediately following World War II.

To comprehend the coverage provided by various

[22] *Ibid.*, p. 29.

[23] National Association of Public School Business Officials, Bulletin no. 9, *op. cit.*, pp. 232–293.
[24] *Ibid.*
[25] D. Lloyd Nelson, *Public School Fidelity Bonding,* Doctoral Dissertation, Los Angeles: University of Southern California, 1942.

types of policies, it is necessary to become acquainted with the definitions of various criminal acts. Burglary refers to the loss of contents resulting from felonious entry into the premises by any person(s) when such premises are not open for business. Visible marks of forcible entrance into the premises made by tools, explosives, electricity, or chemicals must be in evidence. The distinguishing characteristics of burglary are evidence of forcible entry at a time that the premises are not open for business.

Robbery, on the other hand, is defined as felonious taking of property from a custodian. Force or placing the person in fear of safety through threats of personal force or violence must accompany the removal of property from a custodian. In other words, there can be no robbery except from a custodian of property, and then evidence of force must be present. The terms "theft" and "larceny" are synonymous. They refer to the taking of property with felonious intent with or without violence. Theft can be executed by individuals (guests or others) having access to school property and also by those who misappropriate it for their own use.

A study by Hummel of some 213 school districts and student organizations showed that the largest single loss for any of the crimes committed to either a school district or a student organization was approximately $1400.[26] In Hummel's investigation the total losses from 1934–1943 to the insured school district's and student organizations' monies and securities as a result of burglary, robbery, and theft amounted to $33,416. The amount of insurance collected for such losses during this same period totaled only $15,802. The premiums paid by the school districts and students organizations totaled $60,696. The ratio of insurance collected to premiums paid for school districts for this type of insurance was 25.5 percent and for school organizations 28 percent. In many cases, the school districts failed to collect through their failure to comply with provisions of the policy. In other words, the companies have been relieved of liability where there has been a violation of the policy terms. Likewise, failure to furnish proof of loss and to keep accurate books of account and inventory record generally prevents collection in case of loss.

It can be said that in general the ratio of losses on all types of things and activities covered by insurance paid to school districts varied from a small fraction to no more than two-fifths of premiums paid to insurance companies for protection.

[26] John E. Hummel, *A Comparative Investigation of the Public School Burglary, Robbery, and Theft Insurance Practices in the United States.* Doctoral Dissertation, Los Angeles: University of Southern California, 1944.

SUMMARY

Insurance is a means of protection against a possible financial loss. There always exists the possibility that property may be altered, destroyed, stolen, or lost even though carefully designed preventive measures be instituted. In return for a relatively small payment, known as a premium, collected from many individuals, an insurance company will assume the risk of the possibility of a substantial even though unknown financial loss to each party paying premiums.

The insurance business is based on the mathematical theory of probabilities and the Law of Large Numbers. It is imperative that insurance commitments be spread over a large number of similar buildings which are located sufficiently far apart to be independent of each other. To permit the free play of the Law of Large Numbers companies will spread their risks through reinsurance or refusal to insure beyond a certain point buildings of a certain type in a given location.

In a stock insurance company capital stock is provided by individual investors who are motivated to do so by the opportunity for profit. Premium rates are adjusted to promote a profit which is divided among investors only. Mutual companies are organized without capital stock and policyholders are the stockholders. Some mutual companies sell nonassessable policies which free the policyholder from the fear of extra assessments in case of large losses.

Self-insurance plans are only practical in very large school districts. There are many types of self-insurance plans which vary from no insurance to insurance reserve to partial insurance plans. Self-insurance plans may work if certain operating conditions are adhered to.

There are many clauses to a fire insurance policy, some of which are standard and others of which are additional or optional. Fire insurance rates depend upon the fire protection available in the community, the nature of the building structure, and other factors. The coinsurance clause is an inducement to keep insurance in force equal to at least a certain percent of the insurable value of the building. Coinsurance applies if partial loss occurs and not if total loss is experienced. Most authorities recommend that districts take advantage of 80–90 percent coinsurance rate reductions.

The insurable value of a building is equal to its sound value less depreciation less such items as excavations, foundations, sites, architect fees, etc. Records of property values form the basis of appraisal. The school board deceives itself at the time insurance is purchased if unqualified personnel or questionable procedures are used in arriving at the insurable value of a building. A rather common practice for school boards is to purchase insurance through an association of local agents. School districts vary considerably in the management of insurance programs.

A large number of careful studies and experience has shown that payments for fire insurance losses suffered by schools are a small fraction of total premiums paid by school districts. School property should be classed as a preferred risk, and insurance rates should be adjusted downward. This applies to other types of school insurance as well.

QUESTIONS

1. What is insurance? Reinsurance? Coinsurance?
2. What services are offered by insurance companies in addition to the sale of policies?
3. What are the fundamental differences between stock insurance companies and mutual companies?
4. At what stage of development can a mutual company sell a nonassessable policy?
5. When is self-insurance practical for school systems?
6. What are the various types of self-insurance plans?
7. Assume that the insurable value of a school building is $1,000,000, a 90 percent coinsurance clause is in effect, and $700,000 insurance is in force. How much can the district collect if a $810,000 partial loss is suffered? If the building is a total loss?
8. What is a defensible procedure for purchasing school insurance?
9. What arguments can be used to favor a downward revision of insurance rates on school property? What arguments can be used for keeping the rates at present levels?

SELECTED REFERENCES

Hanson, George S., *State and Municipal Self-Insurance,* New York: National Association of Insurance Agents, 1953.

Linn, Henry H., and Joyner, Schuyler E., *Insurance Practices in School Administration,* New York: The Ronald Press, 1952.

National Association of Public School Business Officials, *Insurance Practices and Experiences of City School Districts,* Bulletin no. 2, the Association, 1932.

National Association of Public School Business Officials, *Insurance,* Bulletin no. 9, the Association, 1941.

National Association of Public School Business Officials, *Insurance Committee Report on School Fire Insurance, 1938–1945,* Bulletin no. 11, the Association, 1948.

Salmon, Paul, "How Much Insurance Should You Carry?" *School Management,* November-December, 1957.

Viles, N. E., *School Property Insurance Experiences at State Level,* Bulletin 1956, no. 7, U.S. Office of Education, Washington, D.C.: U.S. Government Printing Office, 1956.

CHAPTER 16

Management of School Transportation and School Food Services

FEW OF THE VARIED PUBLIC SCHOOL OPERA-
tions are as new as the rapidly growing pupil transportation and school food services. The large number
of pupils, the special facilities, and the sizable expenditures have necessitated increasing attention to these
services by school business managers. Previously,
transportation and lunch services could be satisfactorily accounted for under what might be called the
"miscellaneous" category although it was labeled
"Auxiliary Services." The hundreds of millions spent
annually for transportation and food services now
warrant a definite account series for each as indicated
in Chapter 7 of this book.

PUPIL TRANSPORTATION

There is some evidence to support the contention that pupil transportation in American public education had its start as early as 1840. Most authorities
feel, however, that its beginning should be recorded as
of 1869 when the towns of Massachusetts were authorized to raise and appropriate money for the purpose of
conveying pupils to and from schools.

Public schools did not plunge immediately into this
service with reckless abandon. Reorganization of districts, consolidation of attendance areas, and improved
roads were necessary to spur the development of transportation systems. Transportation is the manifestation
of sparsity or residence of pupils either in terms of distance from the schools they attend or traffic conditions
which make walking to school impossible and is most
necessary in providing equality of opportunity. Either
the pupil must be transported to larger attendance
centers or the pupil-teacher ratio will be smaller. As
the small, one-room school districts began to pass
from the American educational scene, it was inevita-

ble that the magnitude of pupil transportation would
increase.

By the end of 1880, only three states—Massachusetts, Vermont, and Maine—permitted the use of
public money for pupil transportation. By 1900, 17
states had passed some sort of school transportation
law. By 1920, every state had some laws regulating
pupil transportation and 18 states provided some
transportation at public expense.

The earliest vehicles were, for the most part, horse-
drawn wagons or carriages. It was essentially a contract service, with some farmer in the neighborhood
providing the buggies and horses to transport pupils.
Contracting appeared to be more defensible than
building a barn, buying horses, and hiring someone to
look after them. Motor vehicle transportation, which is
so common today, did not come into use until the 1910
or 1920 decade. It is interesting to note that as late as
1927–1928 about 12 percent of the 48,459 school transportation vehicles used in 32 states were still "horse-
drawn" as opposed to "motor-drawn" vehicles.[1]

The growth of pupil transportation in the United
States is depicted in Table 37. By 1920, school bus
transportation had grown to the point where about
356,000 children were transported to school at a cost of
approximately $14½ million. The numbers continued
to grow. In 1925–1926, approximately 1,100,000 elementary and secondary school pupils were transported
to and from schools. The total cost of transportation at
that time was approximately $35.6 million. In 1929–
1930, the number of pupils transported reached 1.9
million and the cost had jumped to over $54.8 million.
Ten years later in 1939–1940, the number of children
transported exceeded 4 million and the cost exceeded

[1] Timon Covert, *Rural School Consolidation*, Pamphlet no. 6, U.S.
Office of Education, Washington, D.C.: U.S. Government Printing
Office, June, 1950, p. 12.

TABLE 37. Pupil Transportation Trends in the United States
(Rounded to Nearest Thousand—Percentages from Unrounded Figures)

Year	No. Pupils Transported	Percent of Total Pupils in U.S. Transported	Total Cost of Pupil Transportation	Percent of Transportation Costs Are of Total Current Receipts	Per Pupil Cost of Transportation
1919–1920	356,000	1.7	$14,538,000		$40.79
1921–1922	594,000	2.6	21,817,000		36.75
1923–1924	837,000	3.4	29,627,000		35.38
1925–1926	1,112,000	4.5	35,053,000		31.53
1927–1928	1,251,000	5.0	39,953,000		31.95
1929–1930	1,903,000	7.4	54,823,000	3.0	28.43
1931–1932	2,419,000	9.2	58,078,000	3.2	24.00
1933–1934	2,795,000	10.6	53,908,000	3.6	19.29
1935–1936	3,251,000	12.3	62,653,000	3.8	19.27
1937–1938	3,769,000	14.5	75,637,000	4.0	20.07
1939–1940	4,144,000	16.3	82,283,000	4.3	20.10
1941–1942	4,503,000	18.3	92,922,000	4.5	20.64
1943–1944	4,410,000	19.0	107,754,000	4.7	24.42
1945–1946	5,057,000	21.7	129,756,000	4.8	25.66
1947–1948	5,854,000	24.4	174,377,000	4.6	30.32
1949–1950	6,947,000	27.7	214,504,000	4.6	30.88
1951–1952	7,697,000	29.0	268,827,000	4.7	34.93
1953–1954	8,411,000	32.8	307,422,000	4.5	36.55
1954–1955	9,510,000	32.3	329,035,000	4.5	34.60
1956–1957	10,200,000	32.6	356,500,000	4.5	34.95

NOTE: Figures for 1919–1920 through 1929–1930 adapted from Walter H. Gaummitz and David T. Blose, *The One-Teacher School—Its Mid-Century Status*, Circular no. 318, U.S. Office of Education, Washington, D.C.: U.S. Government Printing Office, 1950, p. 8.

Figures for 1929–1930 through 1953–1954 adapted from Clayton D. Hutchins, Albert R. Munse, and Edna D. Booher, *Trends in Significant Facts on School Finance 1929–1930—1953–1954*, Circular no. 498, U.S. Office of Education, Washington, D.C.: U.S. Government Printing Office, 1957, pp. 44, 62–64.

Figures for 1954–1955 adapted from *Statistics on Pupil Transportation, 1954–1955*, Circular no. 484, U.S. Office of Education, Washington, D.C.: U.S. Government Printing Office, September, 1956.

Figures for 1956–1957 are estimates.

$83 million. By 1949–1950, the number of pupils had grown to almost 7 million and the cost was in excess of $214.5 million. Over 9.5 million pupils were transported in 1954–1955 at a cost of more than $329 million. Estimates for 1956 place the number transported to public schools at about 10.2 million and the total cost at $356.5 million.[2] The numbers transported represented approximately 32 percent of all pupils attending public elementary and secondary schools. Since 1941 the amount of money expended for transportation represented approximately 4.5 percent of the total current expenditures for public education. It can be seen that in 1956 the number of pupils transported each day in the United States is greater than the combined population of the cities of New York City and Philadelphia.

There is considerable variation among states in the percent of school children transported. In 1953–1954 the proportion of the number of pupils in average daily attendance who were transported ranged from 17 per-

cent in California to 53 percent in Virginia.[3] Likewise, expenditures for that year ranged from $16 per pupil in North Carolina to $87 per pupil in Montana.

Pupil transportation is fundamentally a rural or small city school district phenomenon. About 57 percent of the cities of 10,000 or more transported some children in 1949–1950.[4] However, only about 3 to 4 percent of the estimated pupil enrollment is transported in these cities. Compare this with the fact that the pupils transported in all districts in 1949–1950 were 27.7 percent of all pupils enrolled in public schools for that year. Stated another way, these large cities transported between 4 and 5 percent of all pupils transported at public expense in 1949–1950. The

[2] William McKillops, "School Bus Programs—How They Grew," *The Nation's Schools*, August, 1958, *62*:38–39.

[3] Samuel Schloss, Carol Joy Hobson, and Emery M. Foster, *Statistics of State School Systems: Organization, Staff, Pupils, and Finances, 1953–1954*. Biennial Survey of Education in the United States, 1953–1954, chap. 2, U.S. Office of Education, Washington, D.C.: U.S. Government Printing Office, 1956, p. 19.

[4] E. Glenn, Featherston, *Pupil Transportation in Cities*, Pamphlet no. 3, U.S. Office of Education, Washington, D.C.: U.S. Government Printing Office, 1951, p. 2.

amount spent by large cities in transporting pupils at public expense was less than 5 percent of the total spent for pupil transportation in 1949–1950. About 10 percent of the pupils transported in these cities were handicapped children. Approximately 30 percent to 40 percent of the cities with populations of 10,000 or more use public service vehicles to transport pupils to schools.[5] In most cases pupils who use public conveyances to reach or return from school are granted special rates. The cities studied reported that they owned 998 buses which was less than 2 percent of all publicly owned vehicles.

Transportation for instructional purposes only makes up a large part of the transportation load of the city of Los Angeles. The pupil transportation system of the Los Angeles public schools is reputed to be the largest in the nation with a significant part of it devoted to carrying pupils on "curriculum" trips or field trips with an instructional purpose. In 1958 the Los Angeles district owned 89 school buses and contracted for the use of an additional 298, making a total of 387 school buses. These buses travel 4.5 million miles a year to transport children between home and school in a district which covers 450 square miles. In addition, more than 5000 children are transported on approximately 128 "curriculum trips" daily. The district owns approximately 600 pieces of rolling stock which includes 89 passenger buses, semitrailers, refrigerator trucks, garbage trucks, automobiles, etc.[6]

PUBLIC VERSUS PRIVATE OWNERSHIP

School bus transportation started on a contract basis with the vehicles owned by private parties. Considerable research has been done in an effort to ascertain whether public ownership is better than contract arrangements. Most of the research on the subject indicates that it is less expensive to operate district-owned transportation. However, such research has been questioned in that it often failed to include the cost equivalent of the time spent by the principal, superintendent, or transportation supervisor in managing the transportation system. The advantages and disadvantages of each system can be summarized as follows:

PRIVATE CONTRACT SYSTEM

Advantages
1. Relieves school officials of part of the management responsibilities for transportation. The contractor owns the equipment and can be held responsible for its maintenance and operation.
2. Enables school officials to estimate accurately at the begin-

[5] *Ibid.,* p. 7.
[6] See McKillops, *op. cit.,* p. 45.

ning of the school year how much transportation will cost during the year.

Disadvantages
1. Generally costs more than public-ownership operation.
2. Not as readily controlled by school officials as the publicly owned system. This is largely true because of the feeling of independence on the part of drivers when they own the buses they drive.
3. High standards of service harder to maintain. Control measures are harder to enforce with independent owner-operators.
4. Maintenance of bus equipment in a safe condition more difficult.
5. Not as flexible to changing conditions as the publicly owned system. When the annual contract is signed, the contract system tends to be fixed for the year, regardless of changes in route conditions.

PUBLICLY OWNED SYSTEM

Advantages
1. Easier to control by school officials.
2. Can be integrated with the total school program and used to enrich instructional program.
3. Enables school officials to control maintenance of equipment and to train and supervise drivers.
4. More flexible to changing conditions.
5. Usually costs less than the private contract system.
6. Fits into the general pattern of public ownership of school buildings and other school facilities.

Disadvantages
1. Increases the management responsibilities of school officials in that they become responsible for maintaining and operating the buses.
2. Cost of transportation cannot be finally determined until the end of the school year.[7]

District ownership gives greater flexibility to meet changing conditions and allows for greater control over transportation problems. It would naturally eliminate any desire for profit that may lead to inferior equipment or substandard drivers. The trend is clearly toward district ownership of vehicles of transportation. In 1936, about 37 percent of the school buses were publicly owned and 63 percent privately owned. Of the 154,057 vehicles in use for pupil transportation in 1954–1955, 97,403 or 63.2 percent were publicly owned and 56,654 or 36.8 percent were privately owned.[8] In 1956, 102,194 vehicles or 64 percent used in pupil transportation were publicly owned as compared with 57,570 or 36 percent which were privately owned. These figures clearly indicate the definite trend

[7] National Education Association, Department of Rural Education, *Pupil Transportation,* 1953 Yearbook, Washington, D.C.: NEA, 1953, pp. 98–99.
[8] U.S. Office of Education, *Statistics on Pupil Transportation, 1954–1955,* Circular no. 484, Washington, D.C.: the Office, September, 1956.

toward public ownership of school transportation vehicles.

PLANNING TRANSPORTATION ROUTES

Efficient transportation routes are the product of special consideration given to planning routes at the local district level. Approval of routes is often necessary from county and state officials. Maps of the districts should be drawn to indicate district boundaries (and the transportation area if this happens to be larger than the district), kinds of road surfacing, bridges, railroad tracks, and possible hazards.

Meadows[9] suggests the following symbols to designate common hazards on transportation maps:

A	Blind curve	G	Needs gravel, slippery
B–1	Narrow bridge	H	Dangerous hill
B–2	Unguarded bridge	M	Mudhole or bog
B–3	Unsafe approach	UT	U-turn
B–4	Bridge needing repair	RT	Right-angle turn to right
C	Bad culvert	LT	Right-angle turn to left
D	Deep ditch or wash	X	Railroad crossing
F	Fill unguarded	Y	Highway crossing

Other symbols can be developed for hazards common to local roads. Pins can be used on the maps to indicate the location of children to be transported. A different colored pinhead is used to designate children going to various elementary or secondary schools or children of various grade levels. Colored string or crayons may be used to lay out routes.

"Shoestring" routes are practical in cases where the buses are stored in the rural area or starting point. The most common route is the "loop route" which starts and ends in the same general area. Alternate routes for emergency situations must likewise be designated. There is only one sure way to determine how long it takes to traverse a route with a given number of stops and that is to actually cover the route and time it with a watch. The length of time it takes to cover a route is more important than the actual miles traveled.

It is often possible to have staggered times for transportation schedules. This may permit the extended use of a single bus to cover more than one route. The length of time it takes to gather students riding on the bus depends upon such factors as whether the bus will go to the door of each home or whether children will walk to a particular point. At any rate, a time schedule should be developed for picking up pupils and returning them to homes. In some cases waiting stations are desirable so that the pupils may wait in an enclosed

area during inclement weather. In certain areas the terrain may be such that feeder routes are necessary for efficient transportation. The careful planning of school bus routes is very necessary where transportation costs are to be held at an efficient minimum. An illustration of a route schedule for school bus drivers is presented in Form 30. It serves as a report to the superintendent or the bus supervisor.

FORM 30.

BUS ROUTE SCHEDULE

Bus No. _____   Driver _____

Stop No.	Time A.M.	Pupil	Grade	Time P.M.	Dates Transported First Day	Last Day

THE SCHOOL BUS DRIVER

The school bus driver plays a vital role in safety, economy, and efficiency of the transportation program. He should be selected by the superintendent or the director of the transportation program. Local standards to supplement any existing state requirements should be developed to indicate the type of certification, age requirements, physical fitness, character, and other habits necessary. A bus driver may not be hired without the recommendation of a local school administrator in the states of Alabama, Florida, Kentucky, Maine, Maryland, New Mexico, North Carolina, and Virginia.[10] In many cases the selection of school bus drivers is regulated by special code. The data that follow on practices established in state law are based on the Featherston study in 1946.

1. *Maximum Age.* Only eight states have established a maximum age for school bus drivers—one at 55 years, three at 60 years, two at 65 years, and two at 70 years. This is accomplished by state board of education requirement rather than by law. There is little evidence of any trend in establishing maximum age limits. An acceptable alternative to setting a defensible maximum age limit for bus drivers would be to require the passing of an annual physical examination for those past a certain age level.

2. *Experience.* Twenty-two states have some sort of experience requirement for school bus drivers. Most require a limited amount of driving experience with some type of vehicle. There appears to be considerable justification for ruling out the inexperienced drivers. Even more important is the need for spe-

[9] Austin R. Meadows, *Safety and Economy in School Bus Transportation,* Montgomery, Ala.: State Department of Education, 1940, p. 167.

[10] E. Glenn Featherston, *School Bus Drivers: Current Practices in Selection and Training,* Pamphlet no. 100, U.S. Office of Education, Washington, D.C.: U.S. Government Printing Office, 1946, p. 3.

a. Gross vehicle weight.
b. Type of road surfaces in operating area.
c. Type of operation, i.e., long run versus short run, etc.
5. Type, capacity, and ratio of rear axle.
6. Transmission type.
7. Springs and shock absorbers.
8. Brakes.
9. Electrical equipment.
10. Tachometer.
11. Cooling system.
12. Bus body.[19]

SCHOOL BUS MAINTENANCE

The lack of uniformity in school cost accounting procedures makes it difficult to estimate precisely the amount of money allocated to maintaining transportation equipment. In 1948 Featherston estimated that more than 90 percent of the current cost for transporting pupils in publicly owned buses is charged against the two classifications of bus drivers' salaries and operation and maintenance.[20] The amount spent for drivers' wages in the states of the union varies from 25 to 53 percent. The amount expended for operation and maintenance ranges from 40 percent of total current transportation costs in one state to 70 percent in another. The average for all states was computed to be nearly 50 percent for salaries to drivers and 45 percent for operation and maintenance. The problem is further complicated by the fact that most states do not separate operation from maintenance costs. From the limited data available, Featherston estimated that vehicular maintenance would be roughly 15 to 25 percent of the total current cost of pupil transportation.[21]

It can be estimated on this basis that school bus maintenance costs in 1956 ranged from more than $50 million to almost $90 million. This sizable annual cost makes maintenance of buses of particular concern to school business managers. The kind and quality of maintenance programs operated in local districts vary from contract maintenance agreements at private garages (and often at regular job prices) to simple and complex district-operated maintenance garages. Service rendered by district-operated maintenance depots range from the simple tasks of keeping the buses clean, lubricating them, filling them with gas, and making minor repairs to the more complex problems of doing major motor overhauls and even major body repairs. The larger the school bus fleet, the greater the possi-

---

[19] *Ibid.*
[20] E. Glenn Featherston, *School Bus Maintenance*, Bulletin 1948, no. 2, U.S. Office of Education, Washington, D.C.: U.S. Government Printing Office, 1948, p. vi.
[21] *Ibid.*

FORM 31.

WEEKLY CHECK LIST FOR SCHOOL BUSES

Weekly check list for school buses should include inspection by competent individual of the following:
1. Doors
   Service Door Control
   Emergency Door Lock

2. Driver's Compartment
   Ammeter
   Heat Indicator
   Horn
   Lights and Signals—Stop Arm
   Oil Pressure Gauge
   Rear View Mirrors
   Windshield Wipers

3. Brakes
   Service
   Parking (hand)

4. Steering Mechanism
   Steering Play
   Tie Rod Ends

5. Cooling System
   Fan Belt
   Hose
   Radiator (antifreeze)

6. Battery—Water Level

7. Springs
   Broken Leaves—Shackle Bolts

8. Tires
   Pressure
   Cuts and Bruises
   Uneven Wear

(This check list can be printed on a card and posted within the bus.)

bility of more complex school-operated maintenance depots.

Adequate maintenance can reduce operating costs, reduce capital outlay for new equipment, and reduce emergency situations. It can also increase the safety of pupil transportation programs.

Each school must face up to the difficulties related to personnel, garage facilities, special equipment needed, and procedures to be followed in operating its own maintenance depot. Preventative maintenance begins with the purchase of the right bus to face the peculiar conditions in the district. A light chassis destined to carry a heavy load of students over rough terrain is bound to precipitate trouble in the form of many breakdowns. Another factor is the degree of uniformity in makes and models in the school bus fleet. It may be wiser to contract for maintenance if there is a high degree of heterogeneity in the fleet. The amount of money invested in spare parts is almost in direct ratio to the number of bus makes and models to be maintained.[22] This means more complex purchasing as well as a problem of storing parts. The expertness of the mechanic is spread thin when he is forced to work on a variety of bus makes. Clearly, then, it follows that purchasing practices in procuring new buses will influence school bus maintenance.

The number of mechanics required and the extent of garage facilities is dependent on the size and nature of the bus fleet. One full-time serviceman can service ten buses if he starts his work before the buses are run down.

Careful inspection and record keeping provide the foundation stones of good maintenance. Inspections should be periodic. A weekly inspection check list is shown in Form 31. The monthly or 1000 mile school bus inspection report is presented in Form 32. Another type of transportation record is shown as Form 33. This is a daily log of miles traveled, gas and oil consumed, tire repairs, etc. A summary or annual record of bus operations is shown in Form 34. It can also serve as an inventory record of individual buses. Communication between the bus driver and the supervisor of transportation or mechanics can be facilitated by a form such as the one illustrated in Form 35.

Carefully developed maintenance programs coupled with skilled drivers can do much to increase the life expectancy of school buses from 15 to 20 years.

COST ACCOUNTING FOR PUPIL TRANSPORTATION

It is significant that pupil transportation is given a separate expenditure classification in the 1957 U.S. Office of Education *Financial Accounting for Local and State School Systems.*[23] This account series is described in detail in Chapter 7. The major account classifications in pupil transportation services are:

510. *Salaries for Pupil Transportation.*
520. *Contracted Services and Public Carriers.*
530. *Replacements of Vehicles.*
540. *Pupil Transportation Insurance.*
550. *Expenditures in Lieu of Transportation.*
560. *Other Expenses for Pupil Transportation Operation, and Maintenance.*

In addition to these detailed accounts, the record forms shown as Forms 31–35 are necessary to complete the information in transportation cost analysis.

Various cost units can be used to determine the financial efficiency of bus operations. These units are cost per bus, cost per pupil, cost per mile, cost per pupil-mile. Each has its interpretation and justification. All, of course, are based on the quality of reporting used, the accounting system development, and the care in entering information into the accounting system. Again it is pointed out that cost figures in school bus transportation are not strictly comparable because conditions are not the same in all cases. The unit cost figures that are developed should be used as a challenge to explain existing differences rather than to infer immediately that one system is superior to the other. Terrain, sparsity of population, nature of road surfacing, use of student drivers, and other factors must be considered in interpreting unit costs of school bus transportation systems.

EVALUATION OF TRANSPORTATION SYSTEMS

Isenberg[24] developed a simple but meaningful guide for analyzing pupil transportation programs. This system of evaluating pupil transportation programs is based on the four quality factors of *safety, efficiency, adequacy,* and *economy.* Isenberg recommends that the following transportation records should be kept for each bus: (1) original cost and date of purchase of the bus; (2) total miles operated to date; (3) miles operated per day on an assigned route; (4) number of pupils transported on an assigned route; (5) cost of gasoline, oil, and grease; (6) cost of repairs; and (7) specific information on school bus accidents. These can all be grouped together in forming the monthly reports in operating each vehicle.

THE EDUCATIONAL USES OF SCHOOL BUSES

There are values that are derived from daily bus trips as well as from special bus trips. The daily bus trip which takes the pupils to and from school can be a social experience if the bus is well regulated and supervised. It can degenerate into a very rowdy and uncomfortable situation if permitted to do so. Discipline is needed in operating school buses.

There is a growing and continuing use of school buses for other purposes than transporting pupils to and from school. Witness the fact that the city of Los Angeles uses most of its fleet in taking pupils on spe-

[22] *Ibid.,* p. 2.
[23] Paul L. Reason and Alpheus L. White, *Financial Accounting for Local and State School Systems, Standard Receipt and Expenditure Accounts,* Bulletin 1957, no. 4, U.S. Office of Education, Washington, D.C.: U.S. Government Printing Office, 1957, pp. 57–62.
[24] Robert M. Isenberg, *Guide for Analyzing Pupil Transportation Programs,* National Education Association, Washington, D.C.: NEA, 1953.

FORM 32.

MONTHLY OR 1000-MILE SCHOOL BUS INSPECTION REPORT

School _____ Bus Number __

Make _____ Year Model _____ Speedometer Reading _____

Driver _____

To the Board of Education of _____

Item[a]	Check One O.K.	Repairs Made	To be Made	Item[a]	Check One O.K.	Repairs Made	To be Made
BODY				CHASSIS (continued)			
Driver's Compartment				*Engine (continued)*			
Instrument Panel; Gauges				Fan Belt			
Lights and Signals				Generator; Distributor			
Horn; First-Aid Kit				Starter			
Flags and Flares				Battery: Water Level; Cables; Hold-Down Clamps			
Fire Extinguisher; Axe				Cooling System			
Heater and Defroster				Governor Properly Set and Working			
Windshield Wipers				Fuel System			
Rear View Mirrors							
Body—Fenders—Grille				*Brakes*			
General Condition				Parking Brake (hand)			
Interior Cleanliness				Pedal Pressure and Clearance			
Glass: Windows; Windshield				Equalization			
Upholstery				Service Brake: Check Fluid			
Seats Tight to Floor							
Emergency Door; Release				*Clutch—Transmission—Driveline*			
Service Door; Control; Steps				Pedal Release and Clearance			
Fenders; Cowl; Bumpers; Grille				Universal Joints and D. S. Bearings			
CHASSIS							
Front End Assembly				*Rear Axle Assembly*			
King Pins and Bushings				Rear Springs: Clamps; Shackles			
Spindle and Pitman Arms				Axle Flange Nut; Lug Nuts			
Wheel Alignment							
Tie Rod Ends; Drag Links							
Front Springs: U-Bolts; Shackles							
Steering Gear Box to Frame							
Engine				*Tires*			
General Condition				Air Pressure			
Motor Supports: Front and Rear				Cuts; Bruises; Uneven Wear			
Oil and Air Filters				Worn Tread			
Manifold and Exhaust Line				Objects Between Duals			
				BUS PROPERLY LUBRICATED			

[a] If more than one item is on a line and a repair need is indicated, circle the item which has been repaired or needs repair.

Remarks: _____

This is to certify that I have this day made a careful inspection of the school bus described above.

Date _____   Signed _____

Inspecting Mechanic

FORM 33.

MONTHLY BUS OPERATING RECORD
SCHOOL DISTRICT OF SMITHVILLE, U.S.A.

Bus No. _____

For Months of _____ , 19___

Speedometer Reading First of Month_____

Day	Miles	Gasoline Gallons	Cost	Oil, Grease Quarts	Cost	Repairs Type	Cost	Tires No.	Cost	Other Expense or Comments	Total Expenses
1											
2											
3											
29											
30											
31											
Total											

Total Bus Expenses _____   Days Bus Not in Use _____
Speedometer Reading, End of Month _____   Days Bus in Use _____
Total Mileage for Month _____   Driver _____
Average Miles per Gallon _____
Average Cost per Mile _____

FORM 34.

EQUIPMENT INDEX AND COST RECORD
SCHOOL DISTRICT OF SMITHVILLE, U.S.A.

Bus No. _____   Year Model _____
Make of Chassis _____   Make of Body _____
Motor Number _____   Date Received _____
Purchase Price _____   Purchased from _____
Front Tire Size _____   Rear Tire Size _____
Depreciation Base _____   Sold to _____
                                   Sale Price _____

Annual Operating Costs

School Year	Operation and Maintenance Cost	Depreciation	Total All Costs	Miles Operated	Cost per Mile	Remarks
Totals						

FORM 35.

SCHOOL BUS DRIVERS' REPORT
SCHOOL DISTRICT OF SMITHVILLE, U.S.A.

(To be filed when necessary with mechanic, principal, transportation director, or superintendent)

Bus No. _____ School Building(s) Served _____
Date_____ Name of Driver Reporting _____

1. Mechanical Problems Experienced with Bus Operation
    a. Wheels and Steering _____
    b. Motor _____
    c. Fuel System _____
    d. Lights, Horn, Battery, or Other Electrical System _____
    e. Cooling System or Radiator _____
    f. Brakes _____
    g. Tires _____
    h. Others _____
2. Bus Route Conditions or Hazards Experienced
_____
_____
_____

3. Accident, Emergency, or Delays Experienced
_____
_____
_____

4. Changes or Problems with Pupils Transported
    a. Name of Behavior Problems   b. Nature of Behavior Problems

    c. New Pupils Riding for First Time
       Name   Residence   School Destination

    d. Pupils Discontinuing Bus Service

5. Other Matters to Report
_____
_____

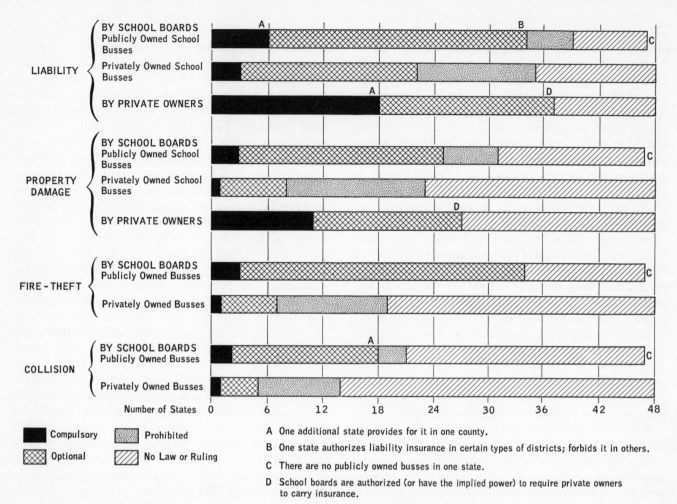

LIABILITY
- BY SCHOOL BOARDS Publicly Owned School Busses
- Privately Owned School Busses
- BY PRIVATE OWNERS

PROPERTY DAMAGE
- BY SCHOOL BOARDS Publicly Owned School Busses
- Privately Owned School Busses
- BY PRIVATE OWNERS

FIRE - THEFT
- BY SCHOOL BOARDS Publicly Owned Busses
- Privately Owned Busses

COLLISION
- BY SCHOOL BOARDS Publicly Owned Busses
- Privately Owned Busses

Number of States   0   6   12   18   24   30   36   42   48

■ Compulsory   ▨ Prohibited   ▨ Optional   ▨ No Law or Ruling

A One additional state provides for it in one county.
B One state authorizes liability insurance in certain types of districts; forbids it in others.
C There are no publicly owned busses in one state.
D School boards are authorized (or have the implied power) to require private owners to carry insurance.

FIGURE 18. Number of States Having Various Provisions for School Bus Insurance
SOURCE: National Education Association, Research Division, *School Transportation Insurance*, Pamphlet no. 101, U.S. Office of Education, Washington, D.C.: U.S. Government Printing Office, 1948, p. 32.

cial curriculum or field trips. The growing use of school buses for educational purposes during school hours as well as for transportation to and from athletic events, special picnics, special tours, etc., is something which should be encouraged. The artificial distinction between curricular and extracurricular use of school buses is rapidly dying out, as it should.

SCHOOL BUS INSURANCE

The legal status of school bus insurance remains in a confused state. Part of the difficulty lies in the application to transportation of the doctrine of nonliability of school districts for their torts. The data on various types of school bus insurance are summarized in Figure 18. Only one in three states requires school boards to carry any one kind of school bus insurance. More states forbid the carrying of each type of insurance on

school buses—especially on those privately owned—than permit it. About two-thirds of the states *permit* school boards to purchase liability or fire-theft insurance. Only about one-half look with favor on property damage insurance for publicly owned vehicles.

There is a need for clarification of school bus insurance practices in the various states. Perhaps the very fine safety record of school buses has contributed to the lack of concern for insurance practices. The traditional immunity of school districts from liability for wrongdoing must also be reëxamined in the light of the present magnitude of pupil transportation.

SCHOOL FOOD SERVICES

School food services, like pupil transportation, are of relatively recent origin. Mary de Garmo Bryan indicated that the earliest record of feeding school children was in 1853.[25] The program was carried on by the Children's Aid Society in New York City. The pressure for school lunch programs came from parents and often from charitable organizations rather than from professional educators. Bryan[26] pointed out that school lunch programs in the United States actually started in 1895, which is many years after their establishment in other countries. Thus school lunch programs were started in Germany in 1790, in France in 1849, and in Great Britain in 1866. In 1895, only one city in the United States had a school food service. The growth was slow: Only 3 cities had school lunch services in 1905; 16, in 1910; and 40, in 1920.[27] Comparable data are not available for rural areas. It can be said that school food services received an initial impetus in rural areas as a result of school consolidation and transportation. In the beginning the school merely provided a place where children too far away from home to return for lunch might eat at noon. This was subsequently followed by preparing meals at school for children who stayed during the lunch hour. The first lunch programs in public schools were acts of charity. Parent groups began to assume responsibility for sponsoring and preparing noon lunches for school pupils.

A desire to give relief to those experiencing difficulties during the Great Depression of the 1930's along with a need to provide more markets for agricultural surplus commodities eventually led to federal assistance to school lunch programs. Such assistance gave a real impetus to the development of school lunch programs in many systems. Federal assistance started with the administration of Public Law 320, Section 32, approved by the 74th Congress in 1935.[28] The Secretary of Agriculture expended a total of $240,114.00 during the 1935–1936 fiscal year for school lunch commodities. Certain agriculture products were declared to be surplus and, therefore, purchased and distributed to the schools for lunch programs. It is significant that an agricultural surplus resulted in better and less expensive lunches for school children.

The first cash reimbursements to schools from the federal government came in 1939–1940 in connection with what was then known as the "school milk program." This was combined with the so-called "indemnity plan" in 1943 whereby the Secretary of Agricul-

ture indemnified the schools in cash for the purchase of seasonally designated or overabundant agricultural products which were used in the preparation of certain defined types of school lunches. The combination of the school milk program and the indemnity plan was effected to compensate for the loss of school commodities which, because of wartime needs, could not be made available.

The National School Lunch Act of June, 1946 (enacted by the 79th Congress as Public Law 396), did even more to establish modern-day lunch programs as a regular part of the school program. This act provided for the allocation of surplus food commodities as well as funds to school lunch programs. The purpose of the act was declared to be "to safeguard the health and well being of the nation's children and to encourage the domestic consumption of nutritious agricultural commodities and other foods by assisting the states through grants and aids and other means of providing an adequate supply of foods and other facilities for the establishment, maintenance, operation and expansion of nonprofit school lunch programs." The federal funds were granted to a state educational association and the state, in turn, distributed the funds and commodities to local school systems that participated in the program. It can be seen that the school lunch program was actually stimulated by a desire to get rid of agriculture surpluses rather than primarily to safeguard the health and well-being of the nation's children. The two were, of course, inextricably entwined. On occasion, school lunch programs have been called "hot" lunch programs after the fact that a hot dish was provided. School lunch is a more appropriate term, for a few school pupils are prone to point out that some of the lunches are not so "hot."

The federal assistance to school lunch programs, which was initiated in 1935 on a rather limited basis and received new impetus in 1946, continued to grow. It is difficult, however, to obtain data on the magnitude of school food services. The only fairly accurate source of such information is based on the number of schools involved in the federally reimbursed or National School Lunch Program. There are school districts which are not involved in the federal programs, but accurate data are not available on such schools. The information on growth of school food services is based on districts in the federal lunch program administered at present by the U.S. Department of Agriculture. These are minimum figures, for the actual amounts will be in excess of the data which follow.

The number of children participating in the National School Lunch Program has more than doubled during the nine-year period of 1944 to 1952. It is in-

[25] Mary de Garmo Bryan, "The Sixty Years' Growth of School Feeding," *The Nation's Schools,* June, 1955, *55*:56–59.

[26] *Ibid.*

[27] *Ibid.*

[28] Myrtis Keels Jeffers, *State Provision for School Lunch Programs —Laws and Personnel,* Bulletin 1952, no. 4, U.S. Office of Education, Washington, D.C.: U.S. Government Printing Office, 1952, p. 2.

From 1944 to 1952...

More than twice as many children participating

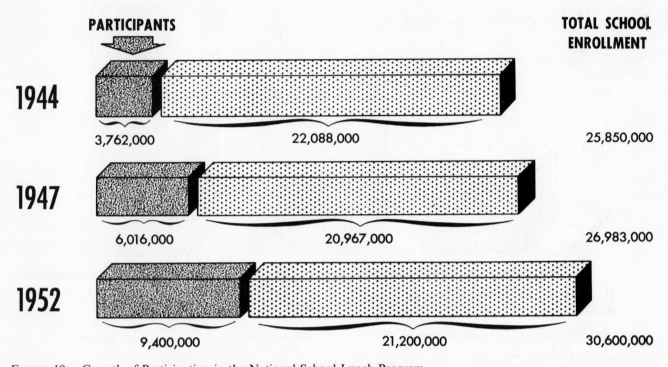

PARTICIPANTS

TOTAL SCHOOL ENROLLMENT

1944
3,762,000   22,088,000   25,850,000

1947
6,016,000   20,967,000   26,983,000

1952
9,400,000   21,200,000   30,600,000

FIGURE 19. Growth of Participation in the National School Lunch Program
SOURCE: U.S. Department of Agriculture, *The National School Lunch Program—A Progress Report*, PA–208, Washington, D.C.: U.S. Government Printing Office, June, 1952, p. 5.

creasing at a rate of 8 to 10 percent each year.[29] Federal cash assistance was first paid in 1944 and in that year over 3,762,000 children were involved in the program. By the first year of operation under the National School Lunch Act over 6 million children were participating. In 1952, 9.4 million were a part of the program and this represented about 30 percent of the children enrolled in school that year. Figure 19 is a pictorial presentation of these facts. Stated another way, three times as many meals were served in 1952 as in 1944. By 1952, 1.5 billion meals were being served. This is presented in pictorial fashion in Figure 20. As shown in Figure 21, over 2 billion pounds of food was used in school lunch programs by 1952.

The average cost of eating a complete meal in program schools was 22¢ as compared with 40¢ in non-program schools.[30] The value of food purchased locally for school lunch programs increased from $129

million in 1947 to $250 million in 1952. U.S. Department of Agriculture surplus food donations only make up about 20 percent of the value of foods used by participating schools.

Federal cash reimbursements for Type A lunches have declined considerably from the 9¢ per lunch granted in 1947. Federal, state, and local sources yielded $415 million for the operation of school food services in districts participating in the National School Lunch Program in 1952. Income from the sale of lunches totaled $235 million and this was the largest single source of income.[31] Note the growth of "Parents' Payments" as related to other sources of income depicted in Figure 22. A total of 53,600 participating schools received $153 million from the federal government in the form of cash and food commodities used in school lunch programs.[32]

The rapid development of school lunch services has led to the formation of the American School Food Service Association which is now reputed to have a

[29] U.S. Department of Agriculture, *The National School Lunch Program—A Progress Report*, PA-208, Washington, D.C.: U.S. Government Printing Office, June, 1952, p. 4.
[30] *Ibid.*, p. 10.

[31] *Ibid.*, p. 14.
[32] Schloss, *et al., op. cit.*, pp. 12–13.

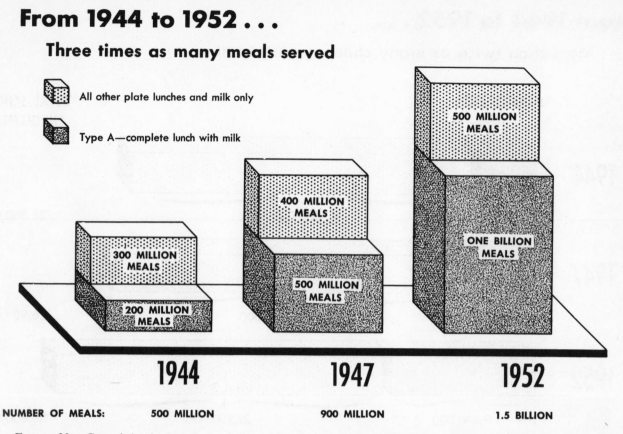

From 1944 to 1952...

Three times as many meals served

All other plate lunches and milk only

Type A—complete lunch with milk

300 MILLION MEALS

200 MILLION MEALS

1944

400 MILLION MEALS

500 MILLION MEALS

1947

500 MILLION MEALS

ONE BILLION MEALS

1952

NUMBER OF MEALS: 500 MILLION   900 MILLION   1.5 BILLION

FIGURE 20. Growth in the Numbers of School Lunches Served in the Schools Participating in the National School Lunch Program
SOURCE: U.S. Department of Agriculture, *The National School Lunch Program—A Progress Report*, PA–208, Washington, D.C.: U.S. Government Printing Office, June, 1952, p. 7.

membership of some 15,000 people, including key school lunch officials from coast to coast.[33] There is evidence that school food services at both elementary and secondary levels will continue to grow in the years ahead. It is estimated that in 1958 over 14 million children were served over 2 billion meals prepared in school lunch rooms at a total cost exceeding $500 million.

Bryan declared that although school food services have come a long way, existing programs are inadequate in scope. She pointed out that only one-third of the enrollment now eats at a public school and only 80 percent of the one-third consumes a meal that approximates one-third of the daily nutritive requirements.[34] The *School Facilities Survey*[35] reported that 84 percent of elementary school plants, 43 percent of secondary

[33] John N. Perryman, "Management Includes Food Service," *School Business Affairs,* Association of School Business Affairs, November, 1958, 24:4–6.
[34] Bryan, *op. cit.*
[35] William O. Wilson and James Woofter, *School Facilities Survey,* U.S. Office of Education, Washington, D.C.: U.S. Government Printing Office, 1953, pp. 45–49.

school plants, and 40 percent of combined elementary-secondary school plants had no cafeterias. Since more than 90 percent of these did not provide multipurpose rooms which could be used as lunchrooms, one must assume that provisions for school food services were extremely limited in 1950. Many of the new constructions since 1950 have tended to correct this existing deficiency.

SCHOOL LUNCH SYSTEMS

School food services are operated on a nonprofit basis in most districts. Approximately 30 to 35 percent of the cash income for schools is expended for labor in the preparation of food, and approximately 60–65 percent of all income is used in the purchase of food. Expenditures for utilities and other expenses account for the rather small figure of 3 to 5 percent in most school communities.

The type of school lunch preparation services influences the efficiency of operation. The traditional pattern has been to have a kitchen and a dining area for each school. Recently there has been considerable

From 1944 to 1952 . . .

Four times as much food used

1952

Milk Beverage	359,000,000	Qts
Other Dairy Products	248,000,000	Lbs
Meats, Poultry & Fish	117,000,000	Lbs
Fruits & Vegetables	570,000,000	Lbs
Eggs	25,000,000	Doz
Cereals & Bread	142,000,000	Lbs
Fats & Oils	34,000,000	Lbs
Other Foods	43,000,000	Lbs

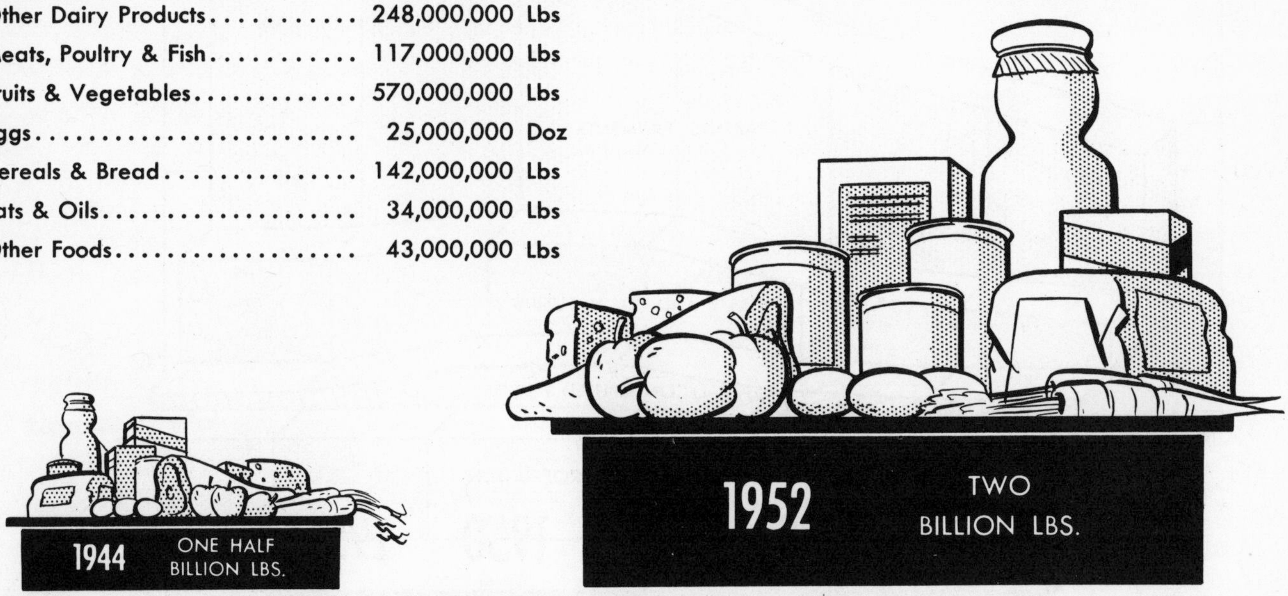

FIGURE 21. Foods Used in Schools Participating in the National School Lunch Program
SOURCE: U.S. Department of Agriculture, *The National School Lunch Program—A Progress Report*, PA–208, Washington, D.C.: U.S. Government Printing Office, June, 1952, p. 9.

interest in the development of centralized school lunch kitchens. These centralized school lunch kitchens have been made possible to a considerable degree by the development of special insulated containers and rapid delivery of foods to various dining areas within the school system. Bates reported that in the Granite City School District in Northern Salt Lake County, Utah, none of the 36 schools in the district had a kitchen to prepare school lunches yet 13,500 lunches were served in the schools of the Granite City School District every day. All lunches were prepared and distributed to the schools by the district's central kitchen.[36] In this particular case a central kitchen is housed in the 65 × 70 foot structure which was formerly a WPA cannery. The food is delivered in vacuum containers some two and one-half hours before the lunch period. Students and lunchroom attendants distribute the meals in individual schools from serving kitchens which are located in each school building. The serving kitchens in these school buildings are only about 15 × 30 feet in size

[36] L. H. Bates, "Central Kitchen Provides Lunch for 13,500," *The Nation's Schools,* December, 1958, 62:66–70.

and have a 14-foot serving counter which opens into the school's multipurpose room. Centralized food service in this particular district started in 1947 by serving lunches in only one school. Twelve years later, it serviced 36 schools, and the number of lunches served increased by 387 percent. This central kitchen is an entirely self-supporting program. Money from the lunches has purchased all the equipment used in the serving area and in the kitchen, including maintenance charges. The establishment of a central kitchen has made possible the use of high-efficiency, multiple-use equipment and machinery as well as efficient utilization of personnel in the preparation of foods.

The central kitchen can be an advantage in systems where the condition of old buildings makes it difficult to establish a school kitchen. The centralized kitchen permits the use of regular classrooms as eating spaces where this is necessary. It appears to work particularly well with younger children at the elementary school level. It must be added that there is insufficient experience with central kitchen operations to evaluate carefully its performance in comparison

From 1947 to 1952...

Total program costs have doubled

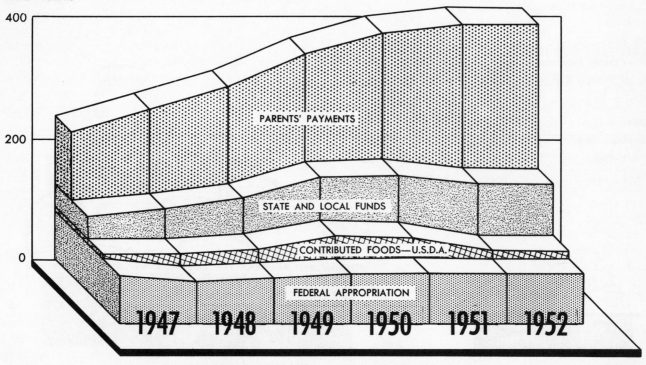

MILLION DOLLARS

PARENTS' PAYMENTS

STATE AND LOCAL FUNDS

CONTRIBUTED FOODS—U.S.D.A.

FEDERAL APPROPRIATION

1947 1948 1949 1950 1951 1952

FIGURE 22.   Trends In Financing School Lunch Programs
SOURCE: U.S. Department of Agriculture, *The National School Lunch Program—A Progress Report*, PA–208, Washington, D.C.: U.S. Government Printing Office, June, 1952, p. 15.

with food prepared in the kitchens of each building. Its efficiency is most readily apparent in districts that have many small elementary school buildings (13 rooms or less) rather than in large secondary school operations.

A variation of this central kitchen is the central kitchen and central dining area to which all pupils are transported. By means of staggered lunch periods, the elementary school pupils eat at one time and are followed by older elementary pupils and then by secondary school pupils. This system permits a greater utilization of a large cafeteria area in smaller school districts. Such a system is presently in operation at the Algona Community School District in Iowa.

The planning of new school cafeterias need not be confined to only one room. Special and separate dining facilities can be provided for teaching and nonteaching personnel. Instead of a single grouping for all pupils in one huge space, many smaller cafeteria areas which can often double for other school purposes (such as study halls) are being used in school lunch programs.

Whatever the type of space, the school lunch preparation area must be designed to provide for easy delivery of food, ease in preparation, and adequate equipment and systematic dispensing of foods to students. It also entails careful planning of the removal of used dishes and waste.

The design of the food service equipment is dictated by the functions to be performed. Among the factors to be considered are:

1. Demand for food services.
   a. How many children will be served?
   b. What type of meals are to be served?
   c. Community use of food services.
2. Time for dispensing food services.
   a. Length of lunch periods.
   b. Are lunch periods to be staggered or will entire student body eat at one time?
3. Location.
   a. Accessibility to students.
   b. Accessibility for food deliveries.
   c. Accessibility for removal of wastes.

4. Is there to be multiple utilization of dining area?
5. Safety and sanitation facilities.
6. Aesthetic atmosphere.
7. Storage facilities.
8. Equipment needs.
9. Space requirements for food preparation, dispensing, and eating.[37]

PERSONNEL FOR SCHOOL LUNCH PROGRAMS

The basic personnel policies in the school system should apply in selecting the quality and size of the school food service staff. In New York, there are four classifications for school service workers: (1) school lunch manager—a competitive position which requires a civil service examination; (2) cook-manager—a noncompetitive position with no examination; (3) cook—an exempt position with no examination, and (4) food-service helper—an exempt position with no examination.[38]

In all cases it should be established what type of work is to be performed, the type of personnel needed to do the work, the duties to be performed by each type of personnel, the breakdown in individual duties into specific tasks, the time required to perform each task, and the total time required for each type of work converted to number of personnel needed.

The school lunch manager for the system as a whole becomes increasingly important as the school lunch services become more complex. A cook-manager is in charge of school lunchroom operation and also helps to prepare foods, plan menus, purchase foods, keep records, etc. Other school lunch helpers serve under the direction of the manager of the lunch program for each school building in the system.

The salaries of directors of school food services are paid out of current expenses in most schools. Other personnel receive wages from FOOD SERVICES OPERATIONS. In addition to wages, meals and uniforms are provided to kitchen and lunchroom workers. Students are best used in operating cash registers, replenishing milk supplies, clearing lunch tables, etc. They are usually not directly involved in food preparation. Student help should be trained to do the work required. Few students are employed for more than one period per day.

The director of school lunch services cannot direct food operations in more than 40 school buildings. In districts with more buildings, the need for full-time assistants becomes apparent. There should be a com-plete operating separation between the school's home economics program and the lunch program. The programs have different objectives and requirements and hence are not compatible for close working relationships. This does not preclude employing a part-time teacher in small systems who also serves as part-time school lunch director. Home economics equipment or facilities should never be used for school lunch operations even in the smallest system.

The number of lunch employees is related to the efficiency of food services facilities such as efficiency of layout and amount of labor-saving equipment. One full-time worker is needed for every 50 to 75 students up to 300 and after that one worker is needed for every 100 students.[39] Labor time to prepare a meal ranges from 6–10 minutes. Not all workers will need to come and go at the same time. Some must come early to participate in baking and others must remain later to clean up.

ACCOUNTING FOR SCHOOL FOOD SERVICES

School lunch services are a complex operation. A large number of employes are involved in serving billions of pounds of food to millions of students. The more than $500 million spent annually for food services is enough to justify careful accounting as well as careful inventory, purchasing, and storage. As in the case of all accounting, the original documents or records play an important part. This includes such records as those for foods and supplies purchased, foods and supplies in inventory, number of patrons served, money collected for each meal, number of free meals served to food service employees, as well as expenditures for various other purposes. For the serving lines, there must be a cashier who either collects monies for deposit into a small metal box in a simple operation or into a well-constructed cash register in larger operations. In some cases, school lunch tickets are sold and punched each time a meal is sold to a student. School lunch tickets have certain conveniences. The same careful record keeping for each meal served is necessary whether a lunch ticket is punched or cash is paid. Some of the problems encountered with lunch tickets are: school lunch tickets may not have all lunches punched out, the card may be lost, or some student may sell punches on his lunch ticket to another student for cash. It is imperative that there be a policy developed as to whether the school will permit a student to have two or three lunches punched at one time from his ticket.

Money so collected must, of course, be deposited,

[37] H. H. Linn (ed.), *School Business Administration,* New York: The Ronald Press Company, 1956, pp. 468–470.
[38] University of the State of New York, *School Lunch-School Business Management Handbook,* Albany, N.Y.: The State Education Department, 1955, pp. 21, 22.

[39] Linn, *op. cit.,* p. 479.

and those in charge of depositing such funds should be bonded in the amounts appearing to be reasonable.

Most of the half-million dollars in expenditures for food services are paid for from the income derived from the sale of meals to students. Food service transactions involve the double handling of money. As indicated in Chapter 4, Clearing Accounts are necessary for such purposes. If the money received and expended were recorded in the regular Receipt and Expenditure Accounts, it would greatly distort the school's financial picture. Only the net effect of food service financial transactions is placed in the regular Receipt and Expenditure Accounts.

FOOD SERVICES OPERATIONS (ACCOUNT SERIES 1700) are described in detail in Chapter 4 and are based on the 1957 USOE financial accounting manual.[40] These accounts are used if the school food services are under the financial control of the school board and the program is financed in whole or in part by revenue produced by the activity. It is recommended that this uniform accounting classification be used in all schools. An outline of these accounts follows:

A. *Major Account 1710—Money Received.*
   1. Account 1711—Money Received from the State for Food Services.
   2. Account 1712—Money Received from Other Sources for Food Services.
B. *Major Account 1720—Money Paid Out.*
   1. Account 1720-a—Salaries for Food Services.
   2. Account 1720-b—Food.
   3. Account 1720-c—Additional Equipment for Food Services.
   4. Account 1720-d—Replacement of Equipment for Food Services.
   5. Account 1720-e—Other Expenses for Food Services.

If the school board does not have a policy of subsidizing school food services when necessary, the net receipts or net expenditures in these accounts are not recorded elsewhere. In such cases the balance or deficit is carried from year to year. If the board has a policy to assume the net balance or deficit for these services at the end of the fiscal year, the balance is recorded under the Revenue Receipt Account known as Account 14-c—Net Receipts from Revolving Funds or Clearing Accounts. The deficit is recorded under the ACCOUNT SERIES 900—FOOD SERVICES, using *Major Account 930 —Expenditure to Cover Deficit of Separate Food Services Fund or Account.*

It is recommended practice to recognize school food services as an integral part of the educational operation. If this practice is adopted, there should 'be a board policy calling for complete control of school food services operations. It would involve budgeting of food service operations for the fiscal year as well as receipt and expenditure controls. It is difficult to justify any other system of operations, particularly since the board provides the physical facilities and also permits food services to exist in school buildings.

SUMMARY

Pupil transportation and food services have grown at an unprecedented rate during the short time they have been in existence. More than 10 million pupils are transported to school each day and more than 14 million pupils are being fed daily in school food service operations. Expenditures for pupil transportation exceeded $350 million in 1958 and expenditure for food services exceeded one-half billion dollars.

Prudent business management of these services, which are somewhat indirectly but nonetheless significantly related to instruction, is almost axiomatic. There is every indication that pupil transportation and school food operations will grow in magnitude and complexity.

At present more research and more data are available on pupil transportation than on food services. Food services for public elementary and secondary schools are mentioned only casually in the 1950 edition of the *Encyclopedia of Educational Research.* The Association of School Business Officials has only recently begun its research in school food services. More and better organized data are needed in both these fields if more efficient school business management of these growing services is to be expected.

QUESTIONS

1. What relationships between the instructional program and the transportation program point to advantages and/or disadvantages of the private contract system or the publicly owned system?
2. What data would be helpful in preparing a budget for transportation? How could this information be used?
3. What are some of the desirable characteristics of school bus drivers?
4. How might a transportation system be evaluated?
5. What are the functions, as judged by its development, of the school lunch program?
6. What factors are related to making a decision on whether or not to have centralized kitchens?
7. Describe and justify the personnel required to feed 750 students at a single location.

[40] Reason and White, *op. cit.,* pp. 115–117.

SELECTED REFERENCES

Cox, Ronald W., and Davis, Randall, "Factors Which Affect and Determine the Life of a School Bus," *Proceedings of the Association of School Business Officials,* 40th Convention, 1954, pp. 217–225.

de Garmo Bryan, Mary, "The Sixty Years' Growth of School Feeding," *The Nation's Schools,* June, 1955, *55:*56–59.

Featherston, E. Glenn, *Pupil Transportation in Cities,* Pamphlet no. 3, U.S. Office of Education, Washington, D.C.: U.S. Government Printing Office, 1951.

Featherston, E. Glenn, *School Bus Drivers: Current Practices in Selection and Training,* Pamphlet no. 100, U.S. Office of Education, Washington, D.C.: U.S. Government Printing Office, 1946.

Featherston, E. Glenn, *School Bus Maintenance,* Bulletin 1948, no. 2, U.S. Office of Education, Washington, D.C.: U.S. Government Printing Office, 1948.

Linn, Henry H. (ed.), *School Business Administration,* New York: The Ronald Press Company, 1956, chaps. 15 and 16.

National Education Association, Department of Rural Education, *Pupil Transportation,* 1953 Yearbook, Washington, D.C.: NEA, 1953.

Supplies and Equipment[1]

Abrasives—S
Absorbent cotton—S
Account books—S
Accounting forms—S
Accounting machines—E
Acetylene—S
Achievement tests—S
Acids—S
Adding machine ribbons—S
Adding machine tapes—S
Adding machines—E
Addressing machine plates—S
Addressing machine ribbons—S
Addressing machine stencils—S
Addressing machines—E
Adhesive tape—S
Adzes—S
Air, compressed—S
Air compressors—E
Air conditioning units, casement—E
Air gauges, tire—S
Air hoists—E
Albums—S
Alcohol—S
Alidades, telescopic—E
Alignment gauges, camber, toe-in, etc.—E
Ammonia—S
Ampules—S
Anatomical charts—S
Anatomical models—E
Andirons—E
Anemometers—E
Anesthetics—S
Aniline dyes—S
Animal boxes—S
Anti-freeze—S
Antiseptic gauze—S
Antiseptics—S

Antitoxins—S
Anvils—E
Apparatus cabinets—E
Applicators, throat—S
Aprons—S
Aquariums—E
Arc welding apparatus—E
Arch supports—S
Archery sets—S
Architect's scales, 1 in. meas.—S
Armature growlers—E
Arrows—S
Art canvases—S
Art crayons—S
Art erasers—S
Art paints—S
Art paper—S
Asbestos—S
Ash cans—S
Asphalt—S
Asphalt roofing and siding—S
Astringents—S
Astrographs, wall—E
Athletic uniforms—S
Atlases—S
Atomizers—S
Audiometers—E
Auger bits—S
Augers—S
Autoclaves—E
Automatic regulating valves—S
Automobile accessories—S
Automobile controls for handicapped persons—S
Automobile defrosters—S
Automobile fuel tanks—S
Automobile heaters—S
Automobile lifts—E
Automobile signals—S

Automobile tires and tubes—S
Automobiles—E
Awls—S
Axes—S

Babbit metal—S
Badges—S
Badminton rackets—S
Bags, laundry—S
Baking pans—S
Baking powder—S
Baking soda—S
Balances, beam—E
Balances, small spring—S
Baling presses, compression moulding—E
Ball bearings—S
Ball peen hammers—S
Balloons—S
Ballot boxes—S
Balls—S
Band instruments—E
Band saw blades—S
Band saws—E
Bandages—S
Bands, rubber—S
Banners—S
Barber shop tools, electrical—E
Barber shop tools, hand—S
Barber type furniture—E
Barographs—E
Barometers—E
Barrels—S
Bars, horizontal, portable—E
Baseballs—S
Bases, baseball—S
Bases, electric lamp—S
Basins, portable—S
Basketball shoes—S

[1] Adapted from Paul L. Reason and Alpheus L. White, *Financial Accounting for Local and State School Systems, Standard Receipt and Expenditure Accounts,* Bulletin 1957, no. 4, U.S. Office of Education, Washington, D.C.: U.S. Government Printing Office, 1957.
E—Equipment may be capital outlay or replacement.

Basketballs—S
Baskets, container—S
Bath curtains—S
Bath mats—S
Bath robes—S
Bathtub fittings—S
Batons—S
Bats—S
Batteries, electric—S
Battery chargers—E
Battery elements—S
Batting, cotton—S
Beads, arts and crafts—S
Beakers—S
Bean bags—S
Bearings, ball—S
Bearings, roller—S
Beaters, egg, electric—E
Beaters, egg, hand—S
Beauty class furniture—E
Bed pans—S
Bed spreads—S
Bed springs—S
Bedding—S
Beds—E
Beef extract—S
Beeswax—S
Bellows, hand—S
Bellows, power—E
Bells, small hand or desk—S
Belt dressings—S
Bench stops—S
Benches—E
Benzene—S
Bevels—S
Bicycle racks, portable—E
Bicycles—E
Billheads—S
Billing machines—E
Binders, agricultural—E
Binders, looseleaf—S
Binding cloth—S
Binding cord—S
Biological charts—S
Biological models—E
Biology specimens—S
Bit braces—S
Bit tools—S
Bits—S
Blackboard pointers—S
Blackboards, portable—E
Blackboards, small slate—S
Bladders—S
Blades, saw—S
Blankets—S
Blanks, printed—S

Bleachers, portable—E
Bleaches—S
Blocks, hat—S
Blocks, kindergarten—S
Blocks, surface hardened—S
Blocks, terminal—S
Blood analysis apparatus, complete—E
Blood plasma cabinets—E
Blood pressure apparatus—E
Blotter holders—S
Blotter pads—S
Blotters—S
Blowpipes—S
Blue print machines—E
Blue print paper—S
Bluing—S
Boards, bread—S
Boards, bulletin, portable—E
Boards, carrom—S
Boards, checker—S
Boards, drawing—S
Boards, emery—S
Boards, ironing—S
Boards, lumber—S
Boards, mounting—S
Boards, sandwich—S
Boards, wash—S
Boats or canoes—E
Bobbins—S
Bodies, bus—E
Bodies, truck—E
Bodkins—S
Boiler cleaners—S
Boiler compounds—S
Boiler firing tools—S
Bolt cutters—S
Bolts—S
Bond paper—S
Book cards—S
Book ends—S
Book jackets—S
Book plates—S
Book pockets—S
Book records—S
Book stacks—E
Book trucks—E
Bookbinding machinery—E
Bookcases, sectional—E
Bookcloth—S
Bookcovers—S
Bookkeeping forms—S
Bookkeeping machines—E
Books, cash—S
Books, composition—S
Books, library—E
Books, looseleaf note—S

Books, record—S
Books, text—S
Boring machines, precision table or vertical types—E
Bottle syphons—S
Bottles—S
Bowling alley pins—S
Bowls—S
Bowls, water closet—S
Bows, archery—S
Box files, cardboard—S
Boxes, electrical—S
Boxing gloves—S
Boxing rings, complete—E
Boyle's law apparatus, complete unit—E
Brake lining—S
Brake lining machines—E
Brakes, complete replacement units—S
Brakes and folders, hand or power—E
Brass polishes—S
Brass rods—S
Brass sheet—S
Bread boards—S
Bread knives—S
Bread pans—S
Bread slicers, mechanical—E
Bread toasters, electric—E
Breakers, circuit—S
Bricks—S
Bridges, wheatstone and similar—E
Bridles—S
Briefcases—S
Broilers, electric—E
Bronze, casting—S
Bronzing liquid—S
Brooms, hand—S
Brooms, power driven—E
Brushes—S
Buck saws—S
Buckets—S
Buffers, electric—E
Bug sprays—S
Bulbs, electric light—S
Bulbs, flower—S
Bulletin boards, portable—E
Bunting—S
Burettes—S
Burlap—S
Burners, bunsen—S
Bus accessories—S
Bus repair parts—S
Bus tickets—S
Bus tires and tubes—S
Bus tokens—S
Bus wagons—E
Buses—E

E—Equipment may be capital outlay or replacement.

Bushings—S
Butter spreaders—S
Buttons—S
Buttons, push—S
Buzzers—S

Cabinets, apparatus—E
Cabinets, beverage cooling, ice or electric—E
Cabinets, filing—E
Cabinets, frozen food storage—E
Cabinets, ice cream, ice or electric—E
Cabinets, laboratory—E
Cabinets, lantern slide—E
Cabinets, print, drafting—E
Cabinets, printers, galley—E
Cabinets, printers, type—E
Cabinets, supply—E
Cable—S
Cake knives—S
Cake pans—S
Cake soaps—S
Calcimine—S
Calculating machines—E
Calendar pads—S
Calendar stands—S
Calendars—S
Calico—S
Calipers—S
Call bells—S
Calorimeters, continuous flow—E
Calorimeters, electric—E
Cameras, motion picture—E
Cameras, still—E
Can covers—S
Can openers—S
Candles—S
Candlesticks—S
Canes—S
Canners—E
Canoes—E
Cans, ash—S
Canvas—S
Caps, metal—S
Carbide—S
Carbon dioxide—S
Carbon paper—S
Carbon ribbons—S
Carborundum stones—S
Carburetors—S
Card holders—S
Card punching and sorting devices—E
Card racks—E
Card tables—E
Cardboard—S
Cardboard boxes—S

Cards—S
Carpenters' squares—S
Carpet beaters—S
Carpets—E
Carrom boards—S
Carrom cues—S
Carrom rings—S
Carving knives—S
Cases, brief—S
Cases, cardboard—S
Cases, display—E
Cases, file—E
Cases, laboratory—E
Cases, supply—E
Cases, type—E
Cash boxes—S
Cash registers—E
Casting bronze—S
Catalogue cards—S
Catches—S
Cattle—E
Caulking compounds—S
Caulking irons, all sizes—S
Caustics—S
Cellophane—S
Celluloid—S
Cement, construction—S
Cement, liquid—S
Centering machines—E
Centrifuges—E
Certificates—S
Chafing dishes—S
Chain hoists—E
Chains—S
Chains, tire—S
Chair pads—S
Chairs—E
Chairs, folding—E
Chalks—S
Chamois—S
Change holders—S
Charcoal—S
Charge slips—S
Chargers, battery—E
Chart stands—E
Charts—S
Chassis, bus—E
Chassis, truck—E
Check handling machines—E
Check writers—E
Checkbooks—S
Checker boards—S
Checkers—S
Checks, brass—S
Cheesecloth—S
Chemicals—S

Chemistry glassware—S
Chemistry rubber goods—S
Chinaware—S
Chisels, in sets—E
Chisels, not in sets—S
Choppers, food, hand-operated—S
Choppers, food, power—E
Circuit breakers—S
Clamps—S
Clay—S
Clay modeling tools—S
Cleaners, flue—S
Cleaners, steam vapor—E
Cleaners, vacuum—E
Cleaning compounds—S
Clinometers, photoelectric—E
Clippers, hair, electric—E
Clippers, hair, hand—S
Clips—S
Clocks, desk—S
Clocks, wall—E
Cloth—S
Cloth cutting machines—E
Cloth nets—S
Clothes baskets—S
Clothes brushes—S
Clothes dryers—E
Clothes hooks—S
Clotheslines—S
Clothespins—S
Clutch rebuilding apparatus—E
Coal—S
Coal bags—S
Coal hods—S
Coal screens—S
Coal scuttles—S
Coal shovels—S
Coat hangers—S
Coat hooks—S
Cocoa mats—S
Coffee cans—S
Coffee grinders—E
Coffee percolators, electric—E
Coffee pots—S
Coffee urns—E
Coin, currency, and check handling machines—E
Coke—S
Colanders—S
Collapsible tables—E
Colored pencils—S
Colorimeters—E
Coloring dyes—S
Combines—E
Combs—S
Combustion analyzers—E

E—Equipment may be capital outlay or replacement.

Comparators—E
Compasses, blackboard—S
Compasses, drawing—S
Compasses, magnetic—E
Compasses, magnetic, pocket—S
Compounds, chemical—S
Compounds, cleaning—S
Compounds, grinding—S
Compounds, patching—S
Compressed air—S
Compressors, air—E
Computing machines—E
Condensers, electronic—S
Condensers, ignition distribution—S
Condiments—S
Conduit boxes—S
Conduits and fittings—S
Connecting rod aligners—E
Connecting rod boring machines—E
Connecting rod rebabbiting jigs—E
Connectors, wire—S
Construction paper—S
Containers—S
Conveyors—E
Cookers, pressure—E
Cooking stoves—E
Cooking utensils—S
Coolers, water—E
Coping saw blades—S
Copper—S
Coppers, soldering—S
Copyholders—S
Cord—S
Cords, electric—S
Cores, valve—S
Cork—S
Corkscrews—S
Cornices, metal—S
Correction fluid, stencil—S
Corrosives—S
Corrugated paper—S
Costumers—E
Costumes, theatrical—S
Cots—E
Cotter pins—S
Cotton, absorbent—S
Cotton gauze—S
Couches—E
Counter freezers—E
Counters, revolution and stroke—S
Countersinks—S
Couplings—S
Coveralls—S
Covers—S
Crayons—S
Crockery—S

Crocks—S
Cross-section paper—S
Crucibles—S
Crude oil—S
Crushed rock—S
Crystals, watch—S
Cues, carrom—S
Cultivators—E
Culverts, sheet metal—S
Cup awards—S
Cup grease—S
Cup hooks—S
Cupboards—E
Cups—S
Curling irons—S
Curtain rods—S
Curtains, shower and window—S
Cuticle pushers—S
Cutlery—S
Cutters, glass—S
Cutters, pastry—S
Cutters, plane—S
Cylinder boring machines—E
Cylinder oils—S
Cylinders, dictating machine—S
Cylinders, gas—E
Cylinders, hydrometer jar—S
Cylinders, mailing—S

Dampers—S
Date stamps—S
Daters—S
Dating machines—E
Decorations—S
Deep fat fryers—E
Deep freezers—E
Dental abrasive points—S
Dental benches—E
Dental cabinets—E
Dental chairs—E
Dental charts—S
Dental drilling apparatus—E
Dental drills—S
Dental instruments, small—S
Deodorizers—S
Desk blotters—S
Desk lamps—S
Desk letter baskets—S
Desk pads—S
Desks—E
Developers, photographic—S
Developing tanks—S
Dextrin—S
Dextrose—S
Diaries—S
Dictating machine cylinders—S

Dictating machines—E
Dictionaries, abridged—S
Dictionaries, large unabridged—E
Dictionary stands—E
Dies, in sets—E
Dies, not in sets—S
Diesel engines, integral parts of larger units—S
Diesel engines for use in classrooms—E
Diploma covers—S
Diploma ribbons—S
Diploma seals—S
Diplomas—S
Discs, optical—E
Discs, phonograph—S
Dish brushes—S
Dish cloths—S
Dish pans—S
Dish trucks—E
Dishes—S
Dishwashing machines—E
Disinfectants—S
Display cases—E
Display mounts—S
Dissecting sets—S
Distilled water—S
Distilling apparatus—E
Distributor boxes—S
Distributors—S
Ditto machines—E
Dividers—S
Doilies—S
Dolls—S
Door mats—S
Doors—S
Dowels—S
Drafting instruments—S
Drafting machines—E
Draglines—S
Drain cleaners—S
Drain pans—S
Drain plugs—S
Drain plungers—S
Drain tile—S
Drainpipe flushers—S
Drapery cloth—S
Drapes—S
Drawing boards—S
Drawing compasses—S
Drawing instruments—S
Drawing paper—S
Drawing pens—S
Drawing tables—E
Dressers, emery wheel—S
Dressings, belt—S
Drier, ink—S

E—Equipment may be capital outlay or replacement.

Drier, paint—S
Drier, varnish—S
Drift meters—E
Drift pins, all sizes—S
Drill bits—S
Drill points—S
Drill presses, bench, floor, or radial—E
Drills, hand—S
Drills, power—E
Drinking water coolers, electric or ice —E
Drugs—S
Drums, bass, kettle, snare—E
Drums, fiber—S
Drums, metal—S
Dry cells—S
Dry measures—S
Dryers, clothes—E
Dryers, hair—E
Drygoods—S
Drying units, infra-red—E
Dumbbells—S
Duplicating machine brushes—S
Duplicating machine ink—S
Duplicating machine paper—S
Duplicating machine parts—S
Duplicating machine rolls—S
Duplicating machines—E
Dustcloths—S
Dusters—S
Dustpans—S
Dyes—S

Earthenware—S
Easels—E
Edge tools, except cutting dies—S
Educational tests—S
Eggbeaters, electric—E
Eggbeaters, hand—S
Elastic—S
Electric batteries—S
Electric clippers, sheep, horse—E
Electric cords—S
Electric dishwashers—E
Electric floor scrubbers—E
Electric fuses—S
Electric hot plates—E
Electric irons—E
Electric lamp bases—S
Electric light bulbs—S
Electric mixers—E
Electric sanding machines—E
Electric switches—S
Electric toasters—E
Electric tube testers—E
Electric vacuum cleaners—E

Electric waxing machines—E
Electric welding apparatus—E
Electric wires—S
Electrical boxes—S
Electrodes—S
Electrolysis apparatus—E
Electromagnets, laboratory—S
Electronic components—S
Electronic deviation meters—E
Electronic frequency meters—E
Electronic power supply and voltage regulators—E
Electronic recording devices, graphical and visual—E
Electronic tubes—S
Electronic volt-ohmmeters—E
Elements, battery—S
Embossers—E
Embossing fluid—S
Embossing pans—S
Emery boards—S
Emery cloth—S
Emery powder—S
Emery wheel dressers—S
Emery wheels—S
Enamel—S
Enameled ware—S
End tables—E
Engine flushing machines—E
Engineer's scales, measure—S
Engines, for use in classrooms—E
Engines, integral parts of larger units—S
Enlargers—E
Envelope sealers—E
Envelopes—S
Epsom salts—S
Eradicator, ink—S
Erasers, electric—E
Erasers, hand—S
Essences—S
Exhibit cases—E
Exposure meters, camera—E
Extensometers—E
Extinguishers, fire—E
Extractors—E
Extracts—S
Eye charts—S
Eyelets—S

Fabrics—S
Face and eye shields—S
Faces, archery—S
Falling weight rammers—E
Fans, electric, portable—E
Fasteners—S
Fasteners, apparel—S

Faucets, combination or single—S
Feldspar—S
Felt—S
Fencing foils—S
Ferrules—S
Fertilizers—S
Fiber rod—S
Fiber sheets—S
Fiber tubes—S
Fiberboard—S
Figures, geometrical, models, in sets—E
File boxes—S
File cards—S
File folders—S
Files, wood and metal working—S
Filing cabinets—E
Filing machines—E
Filings—S
Fillers, battery—S
Fillers, ink—S
Fillers, paint—S
Fillers, wood—S
Film cement—S
Films—S
Filter paper—S
Filters, small—S
Fingers, rubber—S
Fire axes—S
Fire extinguisher refills—S
Fire extinguishers—E
Fire hooks—S
Fire shovels—S
Fire tongs—S
Fireplace fixtures—E
Fittings, lubrication—S
First aid kits—S
Flags—S
Flashlights—S
Flasks—S
Flat irons, electric—E
Flavorings—S
Flaxseed—S
Flexible cord sets—S
Flexible metal hose—S
Flexible metal tubing—S
Floats, hydrometer—S
Floats, plumbing—S
Floor oil—S
Floor scrubbers, electric—E
Floor waxes—S
Flour—S
Flower bulbs—S
Flowerpots—S
Flowers—S
Flue cleaners—S
Fluorescent lamps—S

E—Equipment may be capital outlay or replacement.

Fluorescent starters—S
Fluoroscopes—E
Flush valves—S
Flushers, drainpipe—S
Flux—S
Fly sprays—S
Flypaper—S
Folders—S
Folding chairs—E
Folding tables—E
Food—S
Football dummies, tackling—S
Football shoes—S
Football uniforms—S
Footballs—S
Forceps—S
Forges—E
Forks, silverware—S
Forks, spading—S
Forks, tuning—S
Formaldehyde—S
Forms, dress—E
Forms, geometrical, model, in sets—E
Forms, printed—S
Foundry machinery—E
Frames, blueprint—E
Frames, door—S
Frames, mirror—S
Frames, ophthalmic—S
Frames, picture—S
Frames, saw—S
Frames, window—S
Freezers—E
Freezers, ice cream—E
Frequency meters—E
Friction tape—S
Fruits—S
Fuels—S
Fumigants—S
Fumigators—S
Fungicides—S
Funnels—S
Furnaces, heat treating—E
Furnaces, laboratory—E
Furnaces, remelting, type metal—E
Furniture—E
Furniture polish—S
Fuses—S

Gages, tire—S
Galvanometers—E
Galvanoscopes—E
Games—S
Garbage cans—S
Garden hose—S
Garden tools—S

Garments—S
Garnet paper—S
Gas compressors—E
Gas cylinders—E
Gas mantels—S
Gas meters, laboratory type—E
Gas plates—E
Gas stoves—E
Gases—S
Gaskets—S
Gasoline—S
Gasoline dispensing pumps, electric—E
Gasoline dispensing pumps, hand operated—S
Gauges, tire—S
Gauze—S
Gear cutting machines—E
Gears—S
Gelatin—S
Gelatin duplicators—E
Gelatin pads—S
Generators, integral parts of larger units—S
Generators, not integral parts of larger units—E
Geographic globes, large stand type—E
Geographic globes, small desk type—S
Glass—S
Glass, watch—S
Glass cutters—S
Glass wool—S
Glasses, drinking—S
Glasses, magnifying—S
Glasses, ophthalmic—S
Glassware—S
Glaze—S
Glides—S
Globes, electric light—S
Globes, geographic, large stand type—E
Globes, geographic, small desk type—S
Gloves, rubber—S
Glue—S
Glycerin—S
Goggles—S
Graduated measures—S
Graph paper—S
Graphite—S
Grass seed—S
Grass shears, hand operated—S
Grass shears, power operated—E
Grates, stove—S
Gravel—S
Grease—S
Grease guns, air, gun only—S
Grease guns, hand—S
Grinders, hand operated—S

Grinders, power operated—E
Grinding compounds—S
Grinding wheels—S
Groceries—S
Guards, arm—S
Guards, lamp—S
Guards, shin—S
Gummed cloth—S
Gummed figures—S
Gummed labels—S
Gummed seals—S
Gummed tape—S
Guns, starting—E
Gym shoes—S
Gypsum—S

Hacksaws—S
Hair clippers, electric—E
Hair clippers, hand—S
Hair dryers—E
Hairpins—S
Hall trees—E
Hammers, autobody, pneumatic, etc.—E
Hammers, ball peen—S
Hammers, electric, hand—E
Hammers, light forged—S
Hammers, sledge—S
Hampers—S
Hand bags—S
Hand saws—S
Hand stamps—S
Hand tools, in sets—E
Hand tools, not in sets—S
Hand tools, power driven, pneumatic and electric—E
Hand trucks—E
Handballs—S
Handbooks—S
Handles—S
Handscrews, wood and iron—S
Hangers, clothing—S
Hangers, hardware—S
Hardware—S
Harnesses—E
Harrows—E
Hat blocks—S
Hatchets—S
Headlights—S
Heaters, portable—E
Heating pads—S
Hectographs—E
Hemp fibre—S
Henna—S
Hinges—S
Hods, coal—S

E—Equipment may be capital outlay or replacement.

Hoes, garden—S
Hoists, electric or pneumatic—E
Holders, blotter—S
Holders, change—S
Holders, copy—S
Holders, dictionary—E
Hooks—S
Horns, motor vehicles—S
Horses—E
Horses, gym equipment—E
Horseshoes—S
Hose, apparel—S
Hose, flexible metal—S
Hose, garden—S
Hose clamps—S
Hose nozzles—S
Hot plates—E
Hot water bottles—S
Hurdles—E
Hydraulic jacks, garage type—E
Hydrometer floats—S
Hydrometers—S
Hygrometers—S
Hypodermic needles—S
Hypodermic syringes—S

Ice—S
Ice bags—S
Ice cream freezers—E
Ignition coils—S
Incandescent lamps, bulbs—S
Index cards—S
Index labels—S
Index tabs—S
Indian clubs—S
Inductance standards—E
Ink—S
Ink drier—S
Ink eradicator—S
Ink pads—S
Inkwells and parts—S
Inner tubes, auto—S
Insect nets—S
Insect screening—S
Insecticides—S
Insignia—S
Instruments, band and musical—E
Instruments, dental, small—S
Instruments, drafting—S
Instruments, drawing—S
Instruments, medical, small—S
Instruments, musical—E
Instruments, recording, electrical—E
Instruments, surgical, small—S
Insulators—S
Intelligence tests—S

Interferometers—E
Interval timers—S
Iodine—S
Iodoform—S
Iron, sheet—S
Iron filings—S
Iron gauze—S
Iron wedges—S
Ironers—E
Ironing boards—S
Irons, electric—E

Jackets, book—S
Jacks, garage type, hydraulic—E
Jacks, mechanical—S
Jars—S
Jointers—E
Joints, plumbing—S
Juice extractors, electric—E
Jump standards—E

Kerosene—S
Kettles—S
Key racks—E
Key rings—S
Keyboards, piano, paper—S
Keyhole saws—S
Keys—S
Kilns—E
Kitchen tables—E
Kitchen utensils—S
Kits, first aid—S
Knee pads—S
Knives—S

Labels—S
Laboratory balances, beam—E
Laboratory fittings, plumbing—S
Laboratory furniture—E
Laboratory glassware—S
Laboratory models—E
Laboratory mounts—S
Laboratory tools, small hand—S
Lacing—S
Lacquers—S
Lactose—S
Ladles—S
Lagscrews—S
Lamp bases—S
Lamp bulbs—S
Lamps, desk—S
Lamps, drafting table—S
Lamps, electric floor—E
Lantern slide cabinets—E
Lantern slides—S
Lanterns—S

Lathes, brake drum—E
Lathes, engine—E
Lathes, turret, or automatic screw machines—E
Lathes, wood turning—E
Laths—S
Lawn mowers—E
Lawn rollers—E
Lawn sprinklers, movable—S
Lead—S
Lead, red—S
Lead pencils—S
Lead, slug and rule casting machines, elrod—E
Leather—S
Leather brief cases—S
Leather working tools, hand—S
Lecterns—E
Ledgers—S
Lenses—S
Letter baskets—S
Letter files—S
Letter openers—S
Letter presses—E
Letter scales—S
Letterheads—S
Lettering pens—S
Levels, precision machinists'—S
Levels, small or carpenters'—S
Library books—E
Library furniture—E
Library trucks—E
Lifts, vehicle—E
Light bulbs—S
Light globes—S
Lighting units, blueprint—E
Lime—S
Line markers, large push type—E
Line markers, small—S
Linens—S
Liners, staff, music—S
Liners, type—S
Lining, brake—S
Lining, cloth—S
Linoleum—S
Linotype metals—S
Linotypes—E
Linseed oil—S
Liquid bronzing—S
Liquid polishes—S
Liquid soaps—S
Litmus paper—S
Livestock—E
Loam—S
Lockers, not built-in—E
Locknuts—S

E—Equipment may be capital outlay or replacement.

Locks, small, not built-in—S
Looms—E
Looseleaf notebooks—S
Lubricants—S
Lubricating oil—S
Lubrication fittings—S
Lugs, soldering—S
Lumber—S

Machine tools—E
Machinery, canning—E
Machinery, cement making—E
Machines, adding—E
Machines, addressing—E
Machines, billing—E
Machines, bookkeeping—E
Machines, brake lining—E
Machines, calculating—E
Machines, check handling—E
Machines, coin handling—E
Machines, coin operated—E
Machines, dating, power—E
Machines, dating, small hand—S
Machines, dictating—E
Machines, dishwashing—E
Machines, drafting—E
Machines, drycleaning—E
Machines, duplicating—E
Machines, laundry—E
Machines, mimeograph—E
Machines, mixing—E
Machines, numbering, power—E
Machines, numbering, small hand—S
Machines, polishing—E
Machines, pressing—E
Machines, sanding—E
Machines, scrubbing—E
Machines, sewing—E
Machines, stamping, power—E
Machines, stamping, small hand—S
Machines, tabulating—E
Machines, washing—E
Machines, waxing—E
Magazine covers—S
Magazine racks, large stand—E
Magnets, laboratory—S
Magnifying glasses—S
Mail boxes—S
Mallets—S
Manicuring tools—S
Manila files—S
Manila folders—S
Manila rope—S
Map tracks—S
Maps—S
Markers, line, large push type—E

Markers, line, small—S
Matches—S
Matrix, type—S
Mats, door and bath—S
Mats, gymnasium, tumbling, wrestling —S
Mattocks—S
Mattresses—S
Mauls—S
Meal—S
Meats—S
Mechanical drawing instruments—S
Mechanical pencils—S
Medals—S
Medical instruments, small—S
Medicine balls—S
Medicine cases—E
Medicines—S
Megaphones—S
Memo books—S
Mending materials—S
Mesh, steel wire—S
Metabolism apparatus—E
Metal polishes—S
Metal working machinery—E
Metal working tools, small, hand operated—S
Metals, die casting—S
Metals, laboratory—S
Metals, linotype—S
Meter sticks—S
Meters, watt, laboratory type—E
Microfilm readers and viewers for office use—E
Micrometers, in sets—E
Micrometers, not in sets—S
Microprojectors—E
Microscopes—E
Milk cans—S
Milking machines—E
Milliammeters—E
Milling machines, bench or floor—E
Millivoltmeters—E
Mimeograph machines—E
Mimeograph paper—S
Mineral wool—S
Minerals, laboratory—S
Minute books—S
Mirror frames—S
Mirrors, large wall—E
Mirrors, small—S
Mitre boxes—E
Mixers, electric—E
Modeling clay—S
Modeling tools—S
Models, shop and laboratory—E

Molding, metal—S
Mop pails—S
Mop trucks—E
Mop wringers—S
Mops—S
Mortar—S
Mortisers—E
Moss—S
Motion picture projectors—E
Motor analyzers—E
Motor generator sets—E
Motor vehicle parts—S
Motor vehicles—E
Motorcycles—E
Motors, integral parts of larger units —S
Motors, not integral parts of larger units —E
Mounting boards—S
Mouse traps—S
Mowers, lawn—E
Mucilage—S
Music, sheet—S
Music stands—E
Musical instruments—E
Muslin—S
Mustard—S

Nail polishes—S
Nails—S
Napkins—S
Napkins, sanitary—S
Neatsfoot oil—S
Needles—S
Needles, hypodermic—S
Negative racks—S
Negative tanks—S
Nets, cloth—S
Nets, steel—E
Newspapers—S
Nibbling machines—E
Nickel polishes—S
Noise and field strength meters—E
Notebook covers—S
Notebooks—S
Nozzles, hose—S
Numbering machines, power—E
Numbering machines, small hand—S
Nuts—S

Oakum—S
Oars—S
Office composing machines, varitypes, etc.—E
Office furniture—E
Ohmmeters—E

E—Equipment may be capital outlay or replacement.

Oil—S
Oil cans—S
Oilcloth—S
Ointments—S
Oleomargarine—S
Openers, letter—S
Ophthalmic frames—S
Optical discs—E
Organs—E
Oscillographs—E
Outlets, electrical—S
Outline maps—S
Output meters—E
Ovens—E
Ovenware dishes—S
Oxygen—S

Packing—S
Padding—S
Padlocks—S
Pads, chair—S
Pads, desk—S
Pads, ink—S
Pads, stamp—S
Pads, typewriter—S
Pads, writing—S
Pails—S
Paint brushes—S
Paint drier—S
Paint remover—S
Paint spraying outfits—E
Paints—S
Palettes—S
Pamphlets—S
Pans—S
Pantographs—S
Paper—S
Paper clips—S
Paper cups—S
Paper cutters—E
Paper fasteners—S
Paper napkins—S
Paper punches—S
Paper towels—S
Paraffin—S
Parts, radio, resistors, tubes, transform-
ers, etc.—S
Parts, repair—S
Paste—S
Paste brushes—S
Pasteboard—S
Pasteboard boxes—S
Pastries—S
Pastry cutters—S
Patching compounds—S
Patterns—S

Peat moss—S
Peelers, electrical—E
Peelers, hand—S
Pen points—S
Pencil sharpeners—S
Pencils—S
Pencils, mechanical—S
Penholders—S
Penknives—S
Pennants—S
Pens—S
Percolators, coffee, electric—E
Periodicals—S
Permanent waving machines—E
Pestles—S
Phonograph needles—S
Phonograph record albums—S
Phonograph records—S
Phonographs—E
Photocopying apparatus—E
Photoelectric cells—S
Photoengraving apparatus—E
Photograph mounts—S
Photographic lenses—S
Photographs—S
Photometers—E
Piano parts—S
Pianos—E
Picks—S
Picture frames—S
Picture wire—S
Pictures, large wall—E
Pigments—S
Pillows—S
Ping pong sets—S
Pinking shears—S
Pins—S
Pipe—S
Pipe, steel—S
Pipe dies, in sets—E
Pipe dies, not in sets—S
Pipe fittings—S
Pipettes—S
Piston rings—S
Pistons—S
Pitch pipes—S
Pitchers—S
Pitchforks—S
Plane cutters—S
Planers, power—E
Planes, hand—S
Planing machines, photoengravers—E
Plaques, permanent—E
Plaster—S
Plaster, adhesive—S
Plastic wood—S

Plate glass—S
Plates—S
Plates, addressing machine—S
Plates, battery—S
Plates, bench—E
Plates, book—S
Plates, hot—E
Plates, lantern slide—S
Plates, photographic—S
Platforms—E
Pliers—S
Plows, field—E
Plows, snow—E
Plugs, drain—S
Plugs, spark—S
Plumbing and heating valves—S
Plumbing fixture fittings and trim—S
Plumbs—S
Plungers, drain—S
Pockets, book—S
Pointers—S
Points, drill—S
Polarimeters—E
Polariscopes—E
Poles—S
Poles, climbing—S
Polishes—S
Portfolios, leather—S
Postal meters—E
Posters—S
Posts—S
Pot cleaners—S
Potato peelers, large, machine—E
Pots—S
Pottery—S
Powders—S
Power sprayers and dusters—E
Preservatives—S
Presses, arbor—E
Presses, book, bookbinders—E
Presses, cylinder, flat bed, printing—E
Presses, engraving—E
Presses, letter—E
Presses, lithographic or offset printing
—E
Presses, power—E
Presses, punch, foot power—E
Printed materials—S
Printing cases—E
Printing frames—E
Printing ink—S
Printing materials—S
Printing presses—E
Printing sets, rubber—S
Printing type—S
Prisms—S

E—Equipment may be capital outlay or replacement.

Projectors, motion picture—E
Projectors, still—E
Protractors—S
Pruners, hand—S
Pruners, power—E
Psychrometers—S
Public address systems, portable—E
Pulleys—S
Pumice—S
Punches—S
Push buttons—S
Push carts—E
Putty—S
Pyrometers—E

Quinine—S
Quivers, arrow—S

Rackets, badminton—S
Rackets, tennis—S
Radio receiving sets—E
Radio transmitters—E
Radio tubes—S
Raffia—S
Rags—S
Rakes, garden—S
Rakes, window—E
Ranges, cooking—E
Rasps—S
Rattan—S
Reamers—S
Receptacles—S
Record books—S
Record forms—S
Record players—E
Recorders, sound—E
Recording tape and wire—S
Records, phonograph—S
Reeds—S
Reels, hose—S
Reels, motion picture film—S
Reference books—E
Reflectors, parabolic—S
Refracting apparatus—E
Refrigerators, electric or ice, not built-in
   —E
Registers, cash—E
Registers, printed—S
Regulating valves—S
Regulators, voltage—S
Relief maps—S
Repair parts—S
Report forms—S
Resistors—S
Respirators—S
Retorts, glass laboratory—S

Ribbons, adding machine—S
Ribbons, addressing machine—S
Ribbons, cloth—S
Ribbons, typewriter—S
Ring toss, game—S
Rings, carrom—S
Rings, flying—E
Rings, key—S
Rivets—S
Rock, crushed—S
Roller bearings—S
Rollers, ink—S
Rollers, lawn—E
Roofing materials—S
Rope—S
Rosin—S
Rotten stone—S
Rouge—S
Routers, plate, photoengraving—E
Rowboats—E
Rubber goods—S
Rubbish cans—S
Rugs, room size—E
Rugs, scatter—S
Rulers—S
Rules, shrink and circumference—S

Saccharimeters—E
Safes—E
Safety glass—S
Safety pins—S
Salts—S
Sand—S
Sanding machines—E
Sandpaper—S
Sandwich boards—S
Sanitary napkins—S
Sash, combination screen and storm—S
Sash, screen—S
Sash, storm—S
Sash cords—S
Saucers—S
Saw blades—S
Saw frames—S
Sawdust—S
Saws, band—E
Saws, circular—E
Saws, hand—S
Saws, power hack—E
Scales, beam balance—E
Scales, draftsmen's—S
Scales, spring—S
Scalpels—S
Scissors—S
Scoop shovels, hand—S
Scouring powders—S

Scrapers, hand—S
Screen doors—S
Screens, projection, portable—E
Screens, window—S
Screw extractors—S
Screw eyes—S
Screw hooks—S
Screwdrivers—S
Screws—S
Scrubbing compounds—S
Scrubbing machines—E
Scythes—S
Sealers, envelope—E
Seasonings—S
Seats—E
Sectional bookcases—E
Sedatives—S
Seed, grass—S
Separators, battery—S
Serums—S
Serving trays—S
Settees—E
Sewing machines—E
Shakers, laboratory—E
Shampoo—S
Shapers, bench and floor—E
Shapers and routers—E
Sharpeners, pencil—S
Shears, hand-operated—S
Shears, power-operated—E
Sheaves—S
Sheet metal—S
Sheet music—S
Sheeting—S
Shellac—S
Shelving materials—S
Shingles—S
Shock absorbers—S
Shoes and boots—S
Shopcoats—S
Shorthand writing machines—E
Shovels, hand—S
Shower fittings—S
Shrubs—S
Shuffleboard sets—S
Shuttlecocks—S
Siding, sheet metal—S
Sifters—S
Signs—S
Silk screen printing apparatus, complete
   units—S
Silver polishes—S
Silverware—S
Sink fittings—S
Skillets—S
Skis—S

E—Equipment may be capital outlay or replacement.

Slats—S
Sledge hammers—S
Slicers, bread, mechanical—E
Slide rules—S
Slides, lantern—S
Slides, microscope—S
Slides, projector—S
Snaps—S
Sneakers—S
Snips—S
Snow shovels, hand—S
Soap dispensers—S
Soaps—S
Soccer balls—S
Soccer shoes—S
Socket wrench sets—E
Sockets, wrench—S
Socks, pairs—S
Soda, baking—S
Sodding—S
Softballs—S
Softeners, water, chemical—S
Soil—S
Soil penetrometers—E
Soil test molds—E
Soldering coppers—S
Soldering materials—S
Solvents—S
Sound recorders—E
Spades—S
Spading forks—S
Spark plug cleaning machines—E
Spark plugs—S
Spatulas—S
Specimens, laboratory—S
Spectroscopes—E
Sphygmomanometers—E
Spikes—S
Spirits—S
Spirometers—E
Splints—S
Spokes—S
Spokeshaves—S
Sponges—S
Spoons—S
Spotlights—S
Spray mixtures—S
Sprayers, hand—S
Sprayers, power—E
Spreaders, manure—E
Spreaders, tire—E
Spreads, bed—S
Springs—S
Springs, furniture—S
Sprinklers, lawn, movable—S
Sprockets—S

Squares—S
Squeegees—S
Stacks, book—E
Stadia rods—E
Stadiometers—E
Staff liners, music—S
Stain removers—S
Stains—S
Stakes—S
Stamp pads—S
Stamping machines, power—E
Stamping machines, small hand—S
Stamps, rubber—S
Standards, jump—E
Stands, calendar—S
Stands, chart—E
Stands, engine repair—E
Stands, umbrella—E
Staplers, foot or power operated—E
Staplers, small hand—S
Staples—S
Starch—S
Starters, electric—S
Stationery—S
Statuary—E
Steam packing—S
Steel, sheet—S
Steel measuring tapes—S
Steel wool—S
Stencil correction fluid—S
Stencils—S
Stenographers' notebooks—S
Stereoscopes—E
Sterile gauze—S
Sterilizers—E
Sticks, composing—S
Sticks, hockey—S
Stilts, sport—S
Stitchers—E
Stock records—S
Stockings—S
Stones, printers—E
Stools—E
Stop watches—S
Stoppers—S
Stops, bench—S
Storage batteries—S
Stoves—E
Straight edges—S
Strainers—S
Straws, drinking—S
Stretchers—S
Striking bag outfits—E
Strings—S
Stylus—S
Sunglass frames—S

Sunglasses—S
Supply cases—E
Supporters, athletic—S
Surface hardened blocks—S
Surgical instruments, small—S
Surgical powders—S
Swages—S
Switch boxes—S
Switches, electric—S
Synchronizers, camera—S
Syringes—S
Syrup—S

Table protectors—S
Table tennis balls—S
Table tennis rackets—S
Tablecloths—S
Tables—E
Tables, computing—S
Tablets, medicinal—S
Tablets, writing—S
Tabs, index—S
Tabulating machines—E
Tack hammers—S
Tacks—S
Tags—S
Talcum powder—S
Tanks, bulk storage, not integral parts of
    buildings or building services—E
Tape—S
Tape measures—S
Tapes, measuring—S
Taps—S
Tar roofing and siding—S
Targets, archery—S
Team uniforms—S
Television sets—E
Television tubes—S
Tennis balls—S
Tennis court nets, cord—S
Tennis court nets, steel—E
Tennis rackets—S
Tents, shelter—S
Tents, wall—E
Terminals, battery—S
Test tube brushes—S
Test tube racks—S
Test tubes—S
Tests, achievement—S
Textbooks—S
Theatrical costumes—S
Theodolites and tripods—E
Thermographs—E
Thermometers—S
Thermostats—S
Thimbles—S

E—Equipment may be capital outlay or replacement.

Thinners—S
Threads—S
Throat applicators—S
Thumb tacks—S
Tickets—S
Tile, drain—S
Timers—S
Tin cans—S
Tin cutters—S
Tinware—S
Tire chains—S
Tires and tubes—S
Tissues, cleansing—S
Toasters, electric—E
Toggle bolts—S
Toilet paper—S
Tokens—S
Tongs—S
Tongue depressors—S
Tool sets, hand—E
Tools, hand, not in sets—S
Topsoil—S
Tow bars—S
Towels—S
Toys—S
Tracing cloth—S
Tracing paper—S
Tractors—E
Trammels—S
Transformers, laboratory—S
Transmissions, integral parts of larger units—S
Transmissions, not integral parts of larger units—E
Triangles, drafting—S
Trimmers, hedge, hand—S
Trimmers, hedge, power—E
Tripods, camera—E
Trophies—S
Trowels—S
Trucks, hand—E
Trucks, motor—E
Tubes, inner—S
Tubes, radio—S
Tubes, television—S
Tubing materials—S
Tumblers, glass—S
Tuning forks—S
Tunnels, models, wind—E
Turpentine—S
Tweezers—S
Twine—S
Type, matrix—S
Type, printing—S
Type cases—E

Type casting machines—E
Type cleaner—S
Type liners—S
Typewriter brushes—S
Typewriter covers—S
Typewriter desks—E
Typewriter ribbons—S
Typewriters—E

Umbrella stands—E
Unguents—S
Uniforms—S
Upholstering materials—S
Urns, coffee—E
Urns, flower—S
Utensils—S

Vacuum bottles—S
Vacuum cleaners—E
Vacuum tube voltmeters—E
Valve parts—S
Valves—S
Vaporizers, electric—S
Varnish driers—S
Varnish removers—S
Varnishes—S
Vases—S
Vaulting poles—S
Vegetables—S
Vending machines—E
Vibrographs—E
Vines—S
Vises, bench—E
Vises, small hand—S
Vision charts—S
Volleyball nets—S
Volleyballs—S
Voltmeters—E

Wagons—E
Wall brushes—S
Wallboard—S
Wallpaper—S
Washbasins—S
Washcloths—S
Washers, rubber and leather—S
Washers and dryers, photographic—E
Washing machines—E
Washing powders—S
Washtubs—S
Waste, machinists, etc.—S
Wastebaskets—S
Watch crystals—S
Watches, stop—S
Watchmen's time clocks—E

Water, distilled—S
Water color brushes—S
Water coolers—E
Water glasses—S
Water meters, laboratory type—E
Water softeners—S
Watt meters, laboratory type—E
Wave meters and wave analyzers—E
Wax crayons—S
Waxes, liquid—S
Waxes, paste—S
Waxes, sealing—S
Waxing machines—E
Weaving machines—E
Weighing scales, beam—E
Weighing scales, small spring—S
Weights—S
Welding apparatus—E
Welding rods—S
Wheel straightening apparatus—E
Wheelbarrows—E
Wheels, automobile—S
Wheels, emery—S
Wheels, pottery—E
Whetstones—S
Whiskbrooms—S
Whistles—S
Window glass—S
Window screens—S
Window shades—S
Window working safety belts—S
Wipers—S
Wire—S
Wood, plastic—S
Wood fillers—S
Wood preservatives—S
Wood stains—S
Wool—S
Wool, glass—S
Wool, steel—S
Work benches—E
Work tables—E
Wrapping paper—S
Wrenches, in sets—E
Wrenches, not in sets—S
Writing paper—S

X-ray machines—E

Yard benches—E
Yard brooms—S
Yardsticks—S
Yarn—S

Zinc—S

E—Equipment may be capital outlay or replacement.

Index